THE BIGGEST FOOTBALL PUB QUIZ BOOK Ever!

THIS IS A CARLTON BOOK

10 9 8 7 6 5 4 3 2 1

ISBN 1 84222 646 0

Printed and bound in Great Britain

THE BIGGEST FOOTBALL PUB QUIZ BOOK Ever!

Contents first half

Introduction 8

EASY 10
Pot Luck 1 11
The 1950s 12
Pot Luck 2 13
Strikers 14
Pot Luck 3 15
Transfer Trail 16
Pot Luck 4 17
Three Lions 18
Pot Luck 5 19
The 1960s 20
Pot Luck 6 21
Merseysiders 22
Pot Luck 7 23
Cup Finals 24
Pot Luck 8 25
Famous Families 26
Pot Luck 9 27
Euro 96 28
Pot Luck 10 29
Keepers 30
Pot Luck 11 31
Nicknames 32
Pot Luck 12 33
The 1970s 34
Pot Luck 13 35
London Clubs 36
Pot Luck 14 37
European Cup 38
Pot Luck 15 39
Spot Kicks 40
Pot Luck 16 41
Quote Unquote 42
Pot Luck 17 43
Soccer Legends 44
Pot Luck 18 45
Scottish Internationals 46
Pot Luck 19 47
Going Up 48
Pot Luck 20 49
Going Down 50
Pot Luck 21 51
Manchester Utd 52
Pot Luck 22 53
The 1980s 54
Pot Luck 23 55
Midfield Men 56
Pot Luck 24 57
TV Pundits 58
Pot Luck 25 59
FA & SFA Cup 60
Pot Luck 26 61
Grounds 62
Pot Luck 27 63
World Cup 64
Pot Luck 28 65
Drunk & Disorderly 66
Pot Luck 29 67
Euro Cup Winners' Cup 68
Pot Luck 30 69
The 1990s 70
Pot Luck 31 71
Defenders 72
Pot Luck 32 73
The International Scene 74
Pot Luck 33 75
Derby Games 76
Pot Luck 34 77
The Midlands 78
Pot Luck 35 79
League Cup 80
Pot Luck 36 81
Managers 82
Pot Luck 37 83
The 1960s 84
Pot Luck 38 85
Red Card 86
Pot Luck 39 87
30 Somethings 88
Pot Luck 40 89
Club Colours 90
Pot Luck 41 91
Keepers 92
Pot Luck 42 93
UEFA Cup 94
Pot Luck 43 95
Scottish Sides 96
Pot Luck 44 97
The 1970s 98
Pot Luck 45 99
Golden Goals 100
Pot Luck 46 101
North-East Clubs 102
Pot Luck 47 103
Wales, NI & Eire 104
Pot Luck 48 105
The 1980s 106
Pot Luck 49 107
Super Strikers 108
Pot Luck 50 109

MEDIUM 110
Pot Luck 1 111
Keepers 112
Pot Luck 2 113
The 1950s 114
Pot Luck 3 115
Transfer Trail 116
Pot Luck 4 117
Three Lions 118
Pot Luck 5 119
Alan Shearer 120
Pot Luck 6 121
Scottish Sides 122
Pot Luck 7 123
FA & SFA Cup Finals 124
Pot Luck 8 125
Famous Families 126
Pot Luck 9 127
Euro Championship 128
Pot Luck 10 129
Strikers 130
Pot Luck 11 131
Nicknames 132
Pot Luck 12 133
The 1960s 134
Pot Luck 13 135
Midlands & The North 136
Pot Luck 14 137
European Cup 138
Pot Luck 15 139
Gary Lineker 140
Pot Luck 16 141
Quote, Unquote 142
Pot Luck 17 143
The French Connection 144
Pot Luck 18 145
Scottish Internationals 146
Pot Luck 19 147
Going Up 148
Pot Luck 20 149
Going Down 150
Pot Luck 21 151
Manchester Utd 152
Pot Luck 22 153
The 1970s 154
Pot Luck 23 155
Midfield Men 156
Pot Luck 24 157
Viva España 158
Pot Luck 25 159
FA & SFA Cup 160
Pot Luck 26 161

Gazza 162
Pot Luck 27 163
World Cup 164
Pot Luck 28 165
All Round Sportsmen 166
Pot Luck 29 167
Euro Cup Winners' Cup 168
Pot Luck 30 169
The 1980s 170
Pot Luck 31 171
Defenders 172
Pot Luck 32 173
International Scene 174
Pot Luck 33 175
Kenny Dalglish 176
Pot Luck 34 177
Merseysiders 178
Pot Luck 35 179
League Cup 180
Pot Luck 36 181
Managers 182
Pot Luck 37 183
Double Dutch 184
Pot Luck 38 185
Red Card 186
Pot Luck 39 187
Kevin Keegan 188
Pot Luck 40 189
On Song 190
Pot Luck 41 191
Germany 192
Pot Luck 42 193
UEFA Cup 194
Pot Luck 43 195
London Clubs 196
Pot Luck 44 197
The 1990s 198
Pot Luck 45 199
Golden Goals 200
Pot Luck 46 201
Hat-tricks 202
Pot Luck 47 203
Internationals 204
Pot Luck 48 205
Golden Oldies 206
Pot Luck 49 207
Italy 208
Pot Luck 50 209

HARD 210
Pot Luck 1 211
Midfield Men 212
Pot Luck 2 213
The 1950s 214
Pot Luck 3 215
Transfer Trail 216
Pot Luck 4 217
Three Lions 218
Pot Luck 5 219
Soccer Legends 220
Pot Luck 6 221
Liverpool & Everton 222
Pot Luck 7 223
FA Cup Finals 224
Pot Luck 8 225
Famous Families 226
Pot Luck 9 227
Euro Champ'ship 228
Pot Luck 10 229
Early Days 230
Pot Luck 11 231
Nicknames 232
Pot Luck 12 233
The 1960s 234
Pot Luck 13 235
Midlands & NW 236
Pot Luck 14 237
European Cup 238
Pot Luck 15 239
On The Spot 240
Pot Luck 16 241
Quote, Unquote 242
Pot Luck 17 243
Wonder Wingers 244
Pot Luck 18 245
Scotland 246
Pot Luck 19 247
Going Up 248
Pot Luck 20 249
Going Down 250
Pot Luck 21 251
Manchester Utd 252
Pot Luck 22 253
The 1970s 254
Pot Luck 23 255
Keepers 256
Pot Luck 24 257
Extra Time 258
Pot Luck 25 259
FA Cup 260
Pot Luck 26 261
Full Time 262
Pot Luck 27 263
World Cup 264
Pot Luck 28 265
Famous Firsts 266
Pot Luck 29 267
Cup Winners' Cup 268
Pot Luck 30 269
The 1980s 270
Pot Luck 31 271
Defenders 272
Pot Luck 32 273
Internationals 274
Pot Luck 33 275
Derby Games 276
Pot Luck 34 277
Arsenal & Spurs 278
Pot Luck 35 279
League Cup 280
Pot Luck 36 281
Managers 282
Pot Luck 37 283
Double Winners 284
Pot Luck 38 285
Early Bath 286
Pot Luck 39 287
England Managers 288
Pot Luck 40 289
Champions 290
Pot Luck 41 291
Hat-tricks 292
Pot Luck 42 293
UEFA Cup 294
Pot Luck 43 295
Rangers & Celtic 296
Pot Luck 44 297
The 1990s 298
Pot Luck 45 299
Golden Goals 300
Pot Luck 46 301
Englishmen Abroad 302
Pot Luck 47 303
Internationals 304
Pot Luck 48 305
Int'l Managers 306
Pot Luck 49 307
Super Subs 308
Pot Luck 50 309
Extra Time 1 310
Extra Time 2 311
Extra Time 3 312
Extra Time 4 313
Extra Time 5 314

Half time 315

Contents second half

EASY 316
Who Did What? 317
Goals Galore 318
The Premier League 319
Euro Football 320
Goalkeepers 321
Manchester United 322
Memorable Matches 323
Division One 324
Continentals in England 325
Celebrity Fans 326
Premier Stars 327
Transfers 328
The North East 329
Euro Football 2 330
Full-Backs 331
The 70s 332
Liverpool 333
European Cup 334
Who Did What? 2 335
FA Cup Finals 336
Scottish Football 337
England's World Cups 338
Midlands Clubs 339
Memorable Matches 2 340
Grounds 341
Newcastle United 342
The 80s 343
David Beckham 344
Pop and Football 345
TV and Football 346
Arsenal 347
Goals Galore 2 348
Who Did What? 3 349
England in Europe 350
South America 351
Anything But Football 352
Premier League 2 353
Great Players 354
Managers 355
The World Cup 356
The North West 357
Memorable Matches 3 358
Nicknames 359
Chelsea 360
Pot Luck 361
Centre-Forwards 362
England's World Cups 2 363
Penalties 364
Who Did What? 4 365
Old Football 366
Goals Galore 3 367
England Managers 368
Scotland 369
The 90s 370
Champions League 371
Midfielders 372
Grounds 2 373
London Teams 374
Centre-Halves 375
The North 376
Shirt Colours 377
Managers 378
Tottenham Hotspur 379
Pot Luck 2 380
Premiership Stars 2 381
Euro 2000 382
Republic of Ireland 383
Who Did What? 5 384
Nationwide League 385
Leeds United 386
Wales 387
Cup Winners 388
Paul Gascoigne 389
Everton 390
European Football 391
England Captains 392
Have Boots, Will Travel 393
Alan Shearer 394
All Around the World 395
Tony Adams 396
Commentators 397
Old Football 2 398
Eurostars 399
Pot Luck 3 400
The North West 2 401
London Teams 2 402
Midlands Clubs 2 403
Premier Stars 3 404
The 70s 2 405
The 80s 2 406
Who Are They? 407
Who Did What? 6 408
Pot Luck 4 409
City 410
United 411
Complete the Name 412
Pot Luck 5 413
Name That Team 414
Pot Luck 6 415
MEDIUM 416
Who Did What? 417
Goals Galore 418
Who Plays At...? 419
The Premier League 420
Football Italia 421
Goalkeepers 422
Manchester United 423
Memorable Matches 424
The Nationwide League 425
Pot Luck 426
Foreigners in Britain 427
Music and Football 428
Beards and Moustaches 429
Shirt Numbers 430
Leeds United 431
Euro 96 432
Liverpool 433
Nicknames 434
Scotland Internationals 435
Pot Luck 2 436
The North East 437
South American Soccer 438
Spanish Soccer 439
The 70s 440
The League Cup 441
French Football 442
Managers 443
Rangers 444
Who Plays At...? 2 445
Africa 446
Old Football 447
Pot Luck 3 448
The FA Cup 449
European Cup 450
Old Players 451
British Players Abroad 452
Red Heads 453
Arsenal 454
Wales 455
Pot Luck 4 456
Bobby Charlton 457
Scottish Domestic 458
Chelsea 459
Local Derbies 460
Hairstyles 461
Celebrity Fans 462
Bad Boys 463
Eastern Europe 464
The UEFA Cup 465
West Ham United 466
World Cup 98 467

Non-League Football 468
The 80s 469
German Football 470
Overseas Grounds 471
Hat-Tricks 472
Everton 473
Celtic 474
Transfers 475
Hard Men 476
The North 477
Italia 90 478
World Cup 94 479
The Nationwide League 2 480
Champions League 481
Name That Team 482
The 90s 483
Goals Galore 2 484
Euro 2000 485
Euro Champs Pre-1992 486
Holland and Belgium 487
African Football 488
Rest of the World 489
The Midlands 490
London 491
Manchester City 492
The North West 493
Who Did What? 2 494
Sent Off! 495
The 60s 496
Teddy Sheringham 497
England 498
Premiership Stars 599
Pot Luck 5 500
Supporters 501
Family Connections 502
Substitutes 503
Northern Ireland 504
Republic of Ireland 505
Michael Owen 506
England 2 507
Who Did What? 3 508
Short Players 509
Penalty Shootouts 510
Nicknames 2 511
Kenny Dalglish 512
Dennis Wise 513
Players' Nicknames 514
Chairmen and the Board 515

HARD 516
Referees 517
Goalkeepers 518
Bobby Moore 519
Football Awards 520
Wanderers 521
Supporters 522
Other Cups 523
Scandals 524
Continental Coaches 525
Pot Luck 526
Record Scores 527
Family Connections 528
The Boardroom 529
Who Did What? 530
Manchester United 531
Extra Time & Penalties 532
South America 533
Liverpool 534
Stranger Than Strange 535
John Gregory 536
The 90s 537
Leeds United 538
Nicknames 539
Chelsea 540
Everton 541
Gianluca Vialli 542
London 543
The Midlands 544
The North East 545
Republic of Ireland 546
Who Did What? 2 547
Tottenham Hotspur 548
Spain 549
Pot Luck 2 550
Italy 551
Terry Venables 552
Germany 553
Literary Football 554
Who Did What? 3 555
England 556
Scotland 557
Pot Luck 4 558
All Around the World 559
Memorable Matches 560
France 561
Jack Charlton 562
African Football 563
The 80s 564
Arsenal 565
Old Football 566
West Ham United 567
The Nationwide League 568
Manchester City 569
The West Country 570
East Anglia & Essex 571
Jody Morris 572
Scottish Football 573
Local Rivals 574
Bad Boys 575
Eastern Europe 576
Sol Campbell 577
Scandinavia 578
The 70s 579
Alex Ferguson 580
Premiership Stars 581
Paul Scholes 582
Full-Back/Wing-Back 583
Old Football 2 584
World Cup 98 585
Euro 2000 586
Transfers 587
Non-League 588
Who Did What? 4 589
International Legends 590
Dennis Bergkamp 591
Who Did What? 5 592
Glenn Hoddle 593
True or False? 594
Penalty! 595
Team Colours 596
Strikers 597
Politics 598
Premiership Stars 2 599
Veterans 600
Who Played For? 601
Managers 602
Rovers & Rangers 603
Men of Many Clubs 604
Glasgow Rangers 605
David Seaman 606
Town & Country 607
Who's the Slaphead? 608
Goals Galore 2 609
Hard Men 610
Losers 611
True or False? 2 612
Sackings 613
Memorable Matches 2 614
Wales 615
Kevin Keegan 616
Midfielders 617
FA Cup 618
Injuries 619
Last-gasp Goals 620

How to run a Quiz 621
Answer templates 622

Introduction

Over the past two decades snugs and lounges in pubs the length and breadth of the country have become if not seats of learning, at least seats of intellect – which makes a change from seats of worn leatherette (although these still prevail in some areas). The pub quiz has transformed the bar into an arena of knowledge where beery brethren battle to the final bell. The format is simple; some friends, acquaintances even complete strangers will do, a questioner, some paper, a collection of ragged Biros and a surfeit of beer and questions are all that is needed to create the perfect evening's entertainment. Wits are challenged, heads are huddled and patience is tested as teams attempt to outdo each other in their show of trivia retention.

At these events you will learn that no fact is too small, no soccer star too obscure and no match too insignificant to test the pub crowd's grey matter. In fact, the more obscure and wide-ranging the questions the greater the chance of involving the entire barroom – nothing will gain the pub idiot greater respect than showing that they have the team line up for every Preston North End game lodged in their head, except perhaps their switching from slip-ons to lace ups. So take heart, and a copy of *The Biggest Football Pub Quiz Book Ever!* to the boozer and have a few warm up sessions and see if you can't organise your own pub quiz. You know it makes sense; it's the only way you'll know all the answers.

The main aim of *The Biggest Football Pub Quiz Book Ever!* is to entertain, so it is important that you retain a sense of humour and good sportsmanship as you play along, whether you are testing friends at home or setting a quiz for your local hostelry. That aside you also have to ensure that you are fully in control of your questions and players; remain calm, speak in a steady voice and be constantly unflapped when challenged by any of the more heavily imbibed, as indeed you will be.

If the locals do get testy your best bet is to head for the door while throwing beer nuts in the air to confuse them, though this should happen in only the roughest pubs or on outings with the extended family – in which case you should attempt to rescue your spouse, if you can do so without spilling your drink and it isn't them causing the trouble.

The Biggest Football Pub Quiz Book Ever! is divided into Easy, Medium and Hard questions, which are all subdivided by specialist and Pot Luck rounds. The former can be chosen either to help or hinder your players. Giving Easy questions to some is bound to reveal some interesting answers, but it is possibly more challenging to tailor your questions so that the experts receive the brain-wracking Hard questions and the novices the stupefyingly simple Easy questions. Nothing hurts a fanatic more than being beaten on their specialist subject and the division of questions gives you the chance to employ a handicap system. Other handicap systems will also become apparent as you continue as quiz master, the team that wins the Sunday afternoon quiz will doubtless fail when it comes to Sunday night although if you want to set a quiz on Friday night you should check pupil dilation first, as on that evening of great relaxation you may find your teams asleep or brawling before calling the whole thing quits and joining them in a drink... or three.

In the interest of further clarification there follows a brief rundown of each section:

Easy In this primary round the main objective is to keep breathing and keep a pen in your hand. These questions are so easy that even the most docile pub idiot could gurgle his way through them in the time it takes to down a pint and still have time left to knock over the stack of pennies on the bar. If you know what shape a football is, you shouldn't have too much difficulty.

Medium On your toes people, things are getting tricky. By now the ringers on the out-of-towner's team will no longer be looking smug. These questions make for a challenge but you are bound to get the odd soccer nut who will fancy his chances, for which you should continue on to section three.

Hard Ask a full 20 of these questions and only the shrill wail of the pub cat fighting in the yard will be heard. Brows will be furrowed, glances exchanged and beer stared into.

All that is left to say is good luck with your testing and if you can't keep your spirits up at least try to keep them down.

The Easy Questions

If you don't know the difference between John Barnes and John Motson, then you will no doubt struggle through the next few questions. For the rest of us though these are the EASY questions, so called because if the quizzee falters on these they are either three sheets to the wind or far too young to be in the pub – either state rendering them toddling buffoons whose social graces will equal their breadth of knowledge.

These questions are perfect when used in the first round of an open entry quiz because they lull everyone into a false sense of security, although you must beware that contestants don't shout answers out, which creates a problematic precedent for the later, harder questions. Another way of placing these questions is to dot them about throughout your quiz, thus making sure that on every team everyone should know the answer to at least one question despite their age.

If you are running a league quiz then some of your team members may heap derision on such obvious questions but don't worry, even the cleverest quiz team member can come a cropper.

Quiz 1 **Pot Luck 1**

Answers – see page 13

1 Whose home, until May 1997, was the Baseball Ground?
2 Which city has a Wednesday and a United?
3 Rioch, Graham and Mee have all managed which club?
4 What second name is shared by Newcastle and Hartlepool?
5 Which country did diminutive striker John Spencer play for?
6 Which team are known as The Potters?
7 Which country do Ferencvaros come from?
8 With which football club did Ian Wright make his League debut?
9 Which club did Gordon Strachan join on leaving Manchester Utd?
10 What are the main colours on QPR's home shirts?
11 Which Tony was Port Vale's top League scorer in 1995–96?
12 What is Aston Villa's nickname?
13 Which overseas player was voted Footballer of the Year in 1996?
14 Bobby Robson became boss of which Spanish giants in 1996?
15 Which team does Danny Baker support?
16 Which Scotsman managed Galatasaray in 1995?
17 Which George of AC Milan was European Footballer of the Year in 1996?
18 Which country did Mikkel Beck play for?
19 What forename is shared by defenders Dodd and McAteer?
20 Which Robbie was PFA Young Player of the Year in 1995?

Answers

Pot Luck 2 (see Quiz 3)

1 Academical. **2** White. **3** The Republic of Ireland. **4** Manchester Utd. **5** Moody. **6** John. **7** McNeill. **8** Wimbledon. **9** Celtic. **10** Aston Villa. **11** The Bees. **12** Wales. **13** Leicester City. **14** Alex Ferguson. **15** Shearer. **16** Holland. **17** Bryan Robson. **18** Jack Walker. **19** Manchester Utd. **20** Mick McCarthy.

Quiz 2 The 1950s

LEVEL 1

Answers – see page 14

1 Which English team was involved in the Munich air disaster?

2 Which country did John Charles play for?

3 Which country did John Charles move to after leaving Leeds?

4 Bill Nicholson took over as manager of which London club?

5 Which country outside of Northern Ireland, the Republic of Ireland, Scotland and Wales inflicted England's first-ever Wembley defeat?

6 Stan Cullis was boss of which club side throughout the 50s?

7 In which country was Manchester City keeper Bert Trautmann born?

8 What was the nickname of Busby's young Manchester Utd team?

9 Which Walter was in charge of the England team?

10 Which club did Johnny Haynes play for?

11 Matt Busby and Andy Beattie were in charge of which international side?

12 Who did Stanley Matthews play for in the 1953 FA Cup "Matthews Final"?

13 What position did Alf Ramsey play for England?

14 Which country did Danny Blanchflower play for?

15 Who won a then-record 100th England cap in 1959?

16 Which northern team were league champions in 1952, '56 and '57?

17 Which 17-year-old played in the 1958 World Cup Final for Brazil?

18 Which country did keeper Harry Gregg play for?

19 Which Len was known as the "Clown Prince"?

20 Which club did Nat Lofthouse play for?

Answers

Strikers (see Quiz 4)

1 Blackburn Rovers. **2** Scotland. **3** Arsenal. **4** Blackburn Rovers. **5** West Ham Utd. **6** Stan Collymore. **7** Manchester Utd. **8** West Germany. **9** Dixie. **10** Aston Villa. **11** Duncan Ferguson. **12** Newcastle Utd. **13** Steve Bull. **14** England. **15** Crystal Palace. **16** Rangers. **17** Saunders. **18** Scotland. **19** Arsenal. **20** Durie.

Quiz 3 **Pot Luck 2**

LEVEL 1

Answers – see page 11

1 What is the last word in Hamilton's team name?
2 What colour are Arsenal's home shorts?
3 Which country did John Aldridge play for?
4 Who plays at home at Old Trafford?
5 Which Tom was Oxford's top league scorer in 1995–96?
6 What forename is shared by Scales and Barnes who played together at Liverpool?
7 Which Billy of Celtic was Scottish Footballer of the Year in 1965?
8 With which club did Nigel Winterburn make his league debut?
9 Which club did Charlie Nicholas leave to join Arsenal?
10 Doug Ellis has been chairman of which club?
11 What is Barnet's nickname?
12 Which country did Mark Bowen play for?
13 Garry Parker and Steve Claridge scored 1996 play-off goals for which team?
14 Which manager took Manchester Utd to the 1996 Premiership title?
15 Which Alan was PFA Player of the Year in 1995?
16 Which country does Edgar Davids play for?
17 Which 40-year old player manager was on show for Middlesbrough?
18 Who was Blackburn's 90s cash benefactor?
19 Sharp was on the shirts of which Premiership winners?
20 Who replaced Jack Charlton as manager of the Republic of Ireland?

Answers

Pot Luck 1 (see Quiz 1)

1 Derby County. **2** Sheffield. **3** Arsenal. **4** United. **5** Scotland. **6** Stoke City. **7** Hungary. **8** Crystal Palace. **9** Leeds Utd. **10** Blue and white. **11** Naylor. **12** The Villains. **13** Eric Cantona. **14** Barcelona. **15** Millwall. **16** Graeme Souness. **17** Weah. **18** Denmark. **19** Jason. **20** Fowler.

Quiz 4 **Strikers**

LEVEL 1

Answers – see page 12

---

1 Where did Alan Shearer move to on leaving Southampton?

2 Which country did John McGinlay play for?

3 Which was Dennis Bergkamp's first club in England?

4 Which club have played Sutton, Gallacher and Wilcox in the same side?

5 Tony Cottee was a favourite with which London club?

6 Who got in a tabloid tangle in 1996 about not living near enough to his club Liverpool?

7 Mark Hughes joined Chelsea from which club?

8 Which country did Gerd Müller play for?

9 What was the nickname of William Ralph Dean?

10 Milosevic and Yorke played together for which team?

11 Which Everton striker spent time in jail in 1995?

12 Malcolm Macdonald and Jackie Milburn have been famous strikers for which club?

13 Which former England striker was known as "Bully"?

14 Which country did Mick Channon play for?

15 Wright and Bright formed a strike force for which London side?

16 Which Scottish team did Mark Hateley play for?

17 Which Dean played in Turkey before joining Nottingham Forest?

18 Which country did Joe Jordan play for?

19 Which club had Kennedy and Radford as a deadly double act?

20 Which Scottish player Gordon was known as "Juke-Box"?

Answers

The 50s (see Quiz 2)

1 Manchester Utd. **2** Wales. **3** Italy. **4** Tottenham Hotspur. **5** Hungary. **6** Wolves. **7** Germany. **8** The Busby Babes. **9** Winterbottom. **10** Fulham. **11** Scotland. **12** Blackpool. **13** Fullback. **14** Northern Ireland. **15** Billy Wright. **16** Manchester Utd. **17** Pele. **18** Northern Ireland. **19** Shackleton. **20** Bolton.

Quiz 5 **Pot Luck 3**

LEVEL 1

Answers – see page 17

1 Who plays at home at Portman Road?
2 What colour are Brazil's home shorts?
3 Little, Atkinson and Taylor have all managed which club?
4 What second name is shared by Oldham and Charlton?
5 Which country does Graeme Le Saux play for?
6 Which colour goes with claret in Bradford City's home shirts?
7 Which country do Sampdoria come from?
8 With which club did Gary Flitcroft make his League debut?
9 Which club did Julian Dicks join on leaving Liverpool?
10 What colour are the stripes on Sheffield Utd's home shirts?
11 Which Daniele was QPR's top League scorer in 1995–96?
12 Which club has the nicknames Tykes, Reds and Colliers?
13 Which German player won the Footballer of the Year award in 1995?
14 Which team does John Major support?
15 Tony Parkes has been caretaker manager of which club on more than one occasion?
16 Which country did Carlos Valderrama play for?
17 Who became known as "El Tel" when he went abroad as a manager?
18 Which club did Gianfranco Zola leave to join Chelsea?
19 Which David was an ever present goalkeeper for Arsenal in 1995–96?
20 Which Kevin of Ipswich was PFA Young Player of the Year in 1974?

Answers

Pot Luck 4 (see Quiz 7)

1 Midlothian. **2** England. **3** Blue and white. **4** St James' Park. **5** Lee. **6** Manchester City. **7** Everton. **8** Leeds Utd. **9** Manchester Utd. **10** McClair. **11** The Blues. **12** Northern Ireland. **13** Southampton. **14** John Aldridge. **15** Cantona. **16** Tim. **17** Wycombe Wanderers. **18** Wolves. **19** Wimbledon. **20** Kenny Dalglish.

Quiz 6 **Transfer Trail**

Answers – see page 18

1 Which Brazilian star found his wife could not settle in Middlesbrough?
2 Which London club signed Slaven Bilic?
3 Which club did John Hartson leave to join Arsenal?
4 The first half-a-million pound deal involving a British club involved which player going from Liverpool to Hamburg?
5 Who became England's most expensive keeper when he moved to Blackburn in 1993?
6 Which club did Darren Peacock join on leaving QPR?
7 Which club did Mark Hughes join on two separate occasions?
8 Which international fullback Denis got a free from Leeds before a move to Old Trafford?
9 Which Frenchman prompted "Frog On The Tyne" headlines on his move to Newcastle?
10 Which club did Gareth Southgate leave to join Aston Villa?
11 Which Dutchman joined Arsenal for £7+ million in 1995?
12 Which fullback Warren cost Newcastle £4 million?
13 Which club did Nigel Clough join on first leaving Nottingham Forest?
14 Who moved from Argentina to Barcelona then to Napoli?
15 Which club did Duncan Ferguson leave to join Everton?
16 Which manager first brought Fabrizio Ravanelli to England?
17 Who became the world's first £15 million player?
18 Which club did Niall Quinn join on leaving Manchester City?
19 Which Spanish club signed Ronaldo for over £13 million?
20 England's first £1 million transfer involved which Trevor?

Answers

Three Lions (see Quiz 8)

1 Nottingham Forest. **2** Alan Shearer. **3** Bobby Charlton. **4** John Barnes. **5** Beardsley. **6** Ipswich Town. **7** Peter Shilton. **8** Luther. **9** Stanley Matthews. **10** Paul Gascoigne. **11** Billy Wright. **12** Trevor. **13** Blackburn Rovers. **14** West Ham Utd. **15** Jones. **16** Beckham. **17** Sansom. **18** Malcolm Macdonald. **19** Manchester Utd. **20** Steve.

Quiz 7 **Pot Luck 4**

LEVEL 1

Answers – see page 15

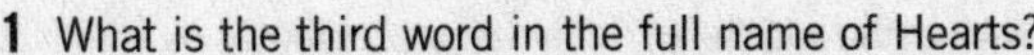

1 What is the third word in the full name of Hearts?

2 Which country has Mick Mills played for?

3 What colour are the stripes on Brighton's home shirts?

4 Which ground do Newcastle Utd play at?

5 Which Jason was Forest's joint top league scorer in 1995–96?

6 Francis Lee has been chairman of which club?

7 Which was Daniel Amokachi's first English club?

8 With which club did John Lukic make his league debut?

9 Which club did Paul McGrath leave to join Aston Villa?

10 Which Brian of Celtic was Scottish Footballer of the Year in 1987?

11 What is Birmingham's nickname?

12 Which country has Jimmy Quinn played for?

13 Dave Merrington was manager of which Premiership team for 1995–96?

14 Which veteran striker is known as "Aldo"?

15 Which Eric was PFA Player of the Year in 1994?

16 What name is shared by 1990s team-mates Flowers and Sherwood?

17 Martin O'Neill took which club into the football league?

18 The Hayward family put 90s money into which Midlands club?

19 Dean Holdsworth and Efan Ekoku played together for which team?

20 Who was Blackburn boss for the 1994–95 Premiership triumph?

Answers

Pot Luck 3 (see Quiz 5)

1 Ipswich Town. **2** Blue. **3** Aston Villa. **4** Athletic. **5** England. **6** Amber. **7** Italy. **8** Manchester City. **9** West Ham. **10** Red and white. **11** Dichio. **12** Barnsley. **13** Jürgen Klinsmann. **14** Chelsea. **15** Blackburn. **16** Colombia. **17** Terry Venables. **18** Parma. **19** Seaman. **20** Beattie.

Quiz 8 **Three Lions**

LEVEL 1

Answers – see page 16

1 Which club was Steve Stone with when he made his international debut?

2 Which player scored England's first goal in Euro 96?

3 Who is England's all-time record goalscorer?

4 Which 20-year old winger scored a wonder goal for England in Brazil in 1984?

5 Which forward Peter had an England career stretching from 1986 to 1996?

6 Terry Butcher and Paul Mariner were colleagues at which club?

7 Who was England's first choice goalkeeper in the 1990 World Cup in Italy?

8 What is the first name of 80s striker Blissett?

9 Who was known as "The Wizard of the Dribble"?

10 Who burst into tears after the World Cup semi-final defeat in 1990?

11 Which captain married one of the Beverley Sisters?

12 What forename was shared by Francis and Brooking?

13 Which club did Ronnie Clayton play for?

14 Which club was Bobby Moore with when he became England captain?

15 Which Liverpool fullback Rob made his international debut while still 20?

16 Which David made his debut against Moldova?

17 Which Kenny made 86 appearances at fullback?

18 Which striker hit five goals in one game in the 70s?

19 Which club was Steve Coppell with during his international career?

20 What forename links Bull and McManaman?

Answers

Transfer Trail (see Quiz 6)

1 Emerson. **2** West Ham Utd. **3** Luton Town. **4** Kevin Keegan. **5** Tim Flowers. **6** Newcastle Utd. **7** Manchester Utd. **8** Irwin. **9** David Ginola. **10** Crystal Palace. **11** Dennis Bergkamp. **12** Barton. **13** Liverpool. **14** Diego Maradona. **15** Rangers. **16** Bryan Robson. **17** Alan Shearer. **18** Sunderland. **19** Barcelona. **20** Francis.

Quiz 9 **Pot Luck 5**

Answers – see page 21

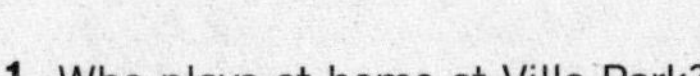

1 Who plays at home at Villa Park?
2 Which Bristol team plays in red shirts at home?
3 Dalglish and Harford have both managed which club?
4 What second name is shared by Cardiff and Bradford?
5 Which country has Andy Townsend played for?
6 Mike Newell and Chris Sutton have both played for which team?
7 Which country do Nantes come from?
8 With which club did Stuart Ripley make his League debut?
9 Which club did Vinnie Jones join on leaving Leeds?
10 What two colours are on Sheffield Wednesday's home shirts?
11 Which Jimmy was Reading's top League scorer in 1995–96?
12 What is Blackpool's nickname?
13 Which Joe became Wimbledon manager in January 1992?
14 Which country did Allan Nielsen play for?
15 Which Alan won the Footballer of the Year award in 1994?
16 Erik Thorstvedt played for which London club?
17 Which club were the first in England to have an artificial pitch?
18 What colour are the home shirts of Northern Ireland?
19 Which team does Delia Smith support?
20 Which Mervyn of West Ham was PFA Young Player of the Year in 1975?

Answers

Pot Luck 6 (see Quiz 11)

1 Thistle. **2** Blue. **3** Scotland. **4** Liverpool. **5** Agent. **6** Greig. **7** Francis. **8** Chester City. **9** Nottingham Forest. **10** The Cherries. **11** Grobbelaar. **12** The Republic of Ireland. **13** Mabbutt. **14** Joe Royle. **15** McGrath. **16** Wimbledon. **17** France. **18** Ian Wright. **19** Switzerland. **20** Eric Cantona.

Quiz 10 **The 1960s**

Answers – see page 22

LEVEL 1

1 John Sissons played in an FA Cup Final for which team?

2 Which country did Eusebio play for?

3 Which country did Jimmy Greaves move to before joining Tottenham Hotspur?

4 Alf Ramsey guided which club to the championship?

5 Who became the first active footballer to be knighted?

6 Who was manager of Liverpool throughout the 60s?

7 At which club did Jimmy Dickinson clock up his 700th league game?

8 Which team featured Auld, Gemmell and Murdoch?

9 Which team was thrashed 9–3 by England at Wembley in 1961?

10 Which team featured Kidd, Aston and Foulkes?

11 Who was Leeds' manager from 1961 onwards?

12 Which bearded former Fulham player became PFA Chairman?

13 Joe Mercer guided which club to the Championship?

14 Which country did Gary Sprake play for?

15 England's Moore, Hurst and Peters came from which club side until 1969?

16 Which Rodney scored a Wembley wonder goal for QPR?

17 In which position did Ron Springett play?

18 Which country did Mike England play for?

19 Roger Hunt was scoring goals for which club side?

20 Jock Stein was manager of which great Glasgow club side?

Answers

Merseysiders (see Quiz 12)

1 Celtic. **2** Scotland. **3** Howard Kendall. **4** Goalkeeper. **5** Michael Owen. **6** Watson. **7** Phil. **8** Gary Lineker. **9** Wales. **10** Ian Callaghan. **11** Tranmere Rovers. **12** Jan Molby. **13** Joe Royle. **14** Bill Shankly. **15** Watford. **16** McMahon. **17** *Boys From the Black Stuff.* **18** John Aldridge. **19** Kenny Dalglish. **20** Neville Southall.

Quiz 11 **Pot Luck 6**

LEVEL 1 

Answers – see page 19

1 What is the last word in Partick's name?

2 What is the main colour in Cardiff's home strip?

3 Which country did Pat Nevin play for?

4 Who plays at home at Anfield?

5 What is the job of Rune Hauge?

6 Which John of Rangers was Scottish Footballer of the Year in 1966?

7 Which Gerry became Tottenham Hotspur's manager in November 1994?

8 With which club did Ian Rush make his league debut?

9 Which club did Lars Bohinen leave to join Blackburn?

10 What is Bournemouth's nickname?

11 Which keeper Bruce was charged with match-fixing in 1995?

12 Which country did Mark Lawrenson play for?

13 Which Gary played 450 plus games in defence for Tottenham Hotspur?

14 Which manager won the 1995 FA Cup with Everton?

15 Which Paul was PFA Player of the Year in 1993?

16 Which team became known as "The Crazy Gang"?

17 Which country does Zinedine Zidane play for?

18 Who had "I Love The Lads" written on his T-shirt?

19 Artur Jorge was whose national coach during Euro 96?

20 Which player returned after an 8-month suspension in October 1995?

Answers

Pot Luck 5 (see Quiz 9)

1 Aston Villa. **2** City. **3** Blackburn Rovers. **4** City. **5** The Republic of Ireland. **6** Blackburn Rovers. **7** France. **8** Middlesbrough. **9** Sheffield Utd. **10** Blue and white. **11** Quinn. **12** The Tangerines or Seasiders. **13** Kinnear. **14** Denmark. **15** Shearer. **16** Tottenham Hotspur. **17** QPR. **18** Green. **19** Norwich. **20** Day.

Quiz 12 **Merseysiders**

LEVEL 1

Answers – see page 20

1 Which club did Kenny Dalglish leave to join Liverpool?

2 Which country did Ron Yeats come from?

3 Who was manager of Everton's 80s championship winning sides?

4 What position did Gordon West play?

5 Who was the first Liverpool player to be named European Footballer of Year in the 21st century?

6 Which Dave skippered Everton's 1995 FA Cup winning team?

7 What name was shared by Thompson and Boersma?

8 Who moved abroad from Everton after personal scoring success in the 1986 World Cup for England?

9 Which country did Kevin Ratcliffe play for?

10 Which star of the 60s and 70s set a Liverpool appearance record?

11 Which Mersey team plays at Prenton Park?

12 Which Liverpool player was referred to as "The Great Dane"?

13 Who took over as Everton manager from Mike Walker?

14 Bob Paisley took over from which manager?

15 Which club did John Barnes join Liverpool from?

16 Which midfielder Steve played for both Everton and Liverpool in the 80s?

17 Which Alan Bleasdale TV drama featured players Souness and Lee?

18 Which fellow Liverpool forward was an Ian Rush lookalike?

19 Who was player-manager in Liverpool's 1986 double-winning team?

20 Who has made most league appearances for Everton?

Answers

The 1960s (see Quiz 10)

1 West Ham Utd. **2** Portugal. **3** Italy. **4** Ipswich. **5** Stanley Matthews. **6** Bill Shankly. **7** Portsmouth. **8** Celtic. **9** Scotland. **10** Manchester Utd. **11** Don Revie. **12** Jimmy Hill. **13** Manchester City. **14** Wales. **15** West Ham. **16** Marsh. **17** Goalkeeper. **18** Wales. **19** Liverpool. **20** Celtic.

Quiz 13 **Pot Luck 7**

LEVEL 1

Answers – see page 25

1. Who plays at home at Carrow Road?
2. What is the main colour of Charlton's home shirts?
3. Kendall and Royle have both managed which club?
4. What second name is shared by Blackburn and Doncaster?
5. Which country did Ruud Gullit play for?
6. Which Lou became Stoke boss in 1994?
7. Alan Smith knocked in 23 goals when which side were champions?
8. Which British club did Oleg Salenko join in 1995?
9. Which club did Andy Thorn join on leaving Crystal Palace?
10. What colours are Southampton's home shirts?
11. Which Nathan was Sheffield Utd's top League scorer in 1995–96?
12. Which club have the nickname The Bantams?
13. Ian Branfoot was sacked in 1994 by which Premiership side?
14. Which country did Paulo Sousa play for?
15. Which team does Eddie Large support?
16. Which Chris won the Footballer of the Year award in 1993?
17. Which London club did Jan Stesjkal play for?
18. Which Mike has hit a European Cup hat-trick for Blackburn?
19. Which position did Rene Higuita play?
20. Which Peter of Manchester City was PFA Young Player of the Year in 1976?

Answers

Pot Luck 8 (see Quiz 15)

1 Rovers. **2** Crystal Palace. **3** Wales. **4** Swansea City. **5** Durie. **6** Yugoslavia. **7** Arsenal. **8** Manchester Utd. **9** Derby County. **10** McStay. **11** The Bees. **12** The Republic of Ireland. **13** Sheffield Wednesday. **14** Holland. **15** Pallister. **16** Blue. **17** Chelsea. **18** Steve Howey. **19** Arsenal. **20** Liverpool.

Quiz 14 **Cup Finals**

Answers – see page 26

LEVEL 1

1 Who scored Manchester Utd's winner in the '96 Final against Liverpool?

2 Gazza played in the 1991 Final with which London club?

3 Gordon Durie hit a hat-trick in which club's 5-1 demolition of Hearts?

4 In a 70s triumph, Jim Montgomery inspired underdogs Sunderland to victory. Which position did he play?

5 Duxbury, Albiston and McQueen played together for which Cup winning club in the 80s?

6 Which English team did manager Bobby Robson lead to Cup Final success?

7 They sound like a London team, but who were the side to win the first Scottish Cup?

8 Who was in goal for Wimbledon when they beat Liverpool in 1988?

9 What part of his anatomy did Trevor Brooking use to score West Ham's winner against Arsenal?

10 Jim Leighton played in a Final for which English club?

11 Before joining Liverpool, John Barnes was a losing finalist with which club?

12 Dave Webb scored a winning goal for which club?

13 Which club won its first ever Scottish Cup in 1994?

14 Which Norman scored a Manchester Utd winner against Everton?

15 Howard Kendall became the youngest FA Cup Finalist for which club?

16 Which star from Argentina hit a memorable goal for Tottenham Hotspur against Manchester City in a replay?

17 With which team was George Burley an FA Cup winner?

18 Sanchez hit a Wembley winner for which club?

19 Who was Manchester Utd manager when they won the 1990 Final?

20 Which Bobby scored a Final winner for Southampton?

Answers

Famous Families (see Quiz 16)

1 Jackie and Bobby Charlton. **2** Nottingham Forest. **3** Gary and Phil. **4** Manchester Utd. **5** Fashanu. **6** Leeds Utd. **7** Mike. **8** Archie. **9** No. **10** Alex Ferguson. **11** Wales. **12** Allen. **13** Coventry City. **14** Mike Summerbee. **15** Hateley. **16** Jackie Milburn. **17** Harry Redknapp. **18** Little. **19** Dean. **20** Jordi.

Quiz 15 **Pot Luck 8**

Answers – see page 23

LEVEL 1

1 What is the last word in Raith's team name?
2 Which London team wear red and blue striped shirts at home?
3 Which country has Barry Horne played for?
4 Who plays at home at the Vetch Field?
5 Which Gordon was Rangers' top league scorer in 1995–96?
6 Which national team has Savo Milosevic played for?
7 Steve Bould plays for which side?
8 With which club did Keith Gillespie make his League debut?
9 Which club did Mark Wright leave to join Liverpool?
10 Which Paul of Celtic was Scottish Footballer of the Year in 1988?
11 What is Brentford's nickname?
12 Which country has Terry Phelan played for?
13 David Pleat followed Trevor Francis as boss at which club?
14 Which country does Patrick Kluivert play for?
15 Which Gary of Manchester Utd was PFA Player of the Year in 1992?
16 What colour are Scotland's home shirts?
17 Durie and Dixon formed a striking duo at which London club?
18 Which Newcastle centre half had to pull out of England's Euro 96 squad?
19 Which club was dubbed as being "Lucky"?
20 Scales and Collymore were teammates with which losing FA Cup Finalists?

Answers

Pot Luck 7 (see Quiz 13)

1 Norwich City. **2** Red. **3** Everton. **4** Rovers. **5** Holland. **6** Macari. **7** Arsenal. **8** Rangers. **9** Wimbledon. **10** Red and white. **11** Blake. **12** Bradford City. **13** Southampton. **14** Portugal. **15** Manchester City. **16** Waddle. **17** QPR. **18** Newell. **19** Goalkeeper. **20** Barnes.

Quiz 16 **Famous Families**

LEVEL 1

Answers – see page 24

1 Which two brothers were in the England World Cup winning team?
2 At which club were father and son Clough connected?
3 What are the first names of the 90s Neville brothers?
4 With which club did they make their debuts?
5 What's the last name of strikers Justin and John?
6 Father Frank and son Andy Gray have both played for which club?
7 Who is goalkeeper Ian Walker's manager father?
8 What is the name of midfielder Scott Gemmill's father?
9 Did Bobby Charlton ever play at club level in the same side as his brother?
10 Which Manchester Utd manager sold his son Darren?
11 Which country did the Allchurch brothers play for?
12 What's the surname of Clive and Bradley both former QPR strikers?
13 Which club had Bobby Gould as boss and son Jonathan in goal?
14 What is Nicky Summerbee's father called?
15 What's the last name of dad Tony and son Mark, both tall centre forwards?
16 Which legendary striker was Bobby Charlton's uncle?
17 Which West Ham boss had a son playing for Liverpool and England?
18 Which Alan was boss at York while brother Brian was boss at Villa?
19 What's the name of David Holdsworth's striking brother?
20 Which Cruyff played for Manchester Utd?

Answers

Cup Finals (see Quiz 14)

1 Eriç Cantona. **2** Tottenham Hotspur. **3** Rangers. **4** Goalkeeper. **5** Manchester Utd. **6** Ipswich Town. **7** Queens Park. **8** Dave Beasant. **9** His head. **10** Manchester Utd. **11** Watford. **12** Chelsea. **13** Dundee Utd. **14** Whiteside. **15** Preston North End. **16** Ricky Villa. **17** Ipswich Town. **18** Wimbledon. **19** Alex Ferguson. **20** Stokes.

Quiz 17 **Pot Luck 9**

LEVEL 1

Answers – see page 29

1 Who plays at home at Goodison Park?
2 Ian Crook played over 300 games for which club?
3 Graeme Souness and Walter Smith both managed which club?
4 What is the last word in Birmingham's name?
5 Which country has Patrik Berger played for?
6 Which team does Jeremy Beadle support?
7 Which country do Cologne come from?
8 With which club did goalkeeper Bryan Gunn make his debut?
9 Which club did Ray Wilkins join on leaving Rangers?
10 What colour goes with white on Sunderland's home shirts?
11 Which Ian was Nottingham Forest's joint top League scorer in 1995–96?
12 What is Brighton's nickname?
13 Mark McGhee followed Graham Taylor as manager at which club?
14 League champions play FA Cup winners for which trophy?
15 Keeper Mark Crossley played over 200 games for which club?
16 Which country do Ajax come from?
17 Which country did Graeme Sharp play for?
18 Which Gary won the Footballer of the Year award in 1992?
19 Which country does Rui Costa play for?
20 Which Andy of Villa was PFA Young Player of the Year in 1977?

Answers

Pot Luck 10 (see Quiz 19)

1 Albion. **2** Arsenal. **3** Chelsea. **4** England. **5** Tottenham Hotspur. **6** Fleck. **7** Murdoch. **8** West Ham Utd. **9** Leeds Utd. **10** Craig Brown. **11** The Robins. **12** Scotland. **13** Orange. **14** Liverpool. **15** Hughes. **16** Southampton. **17** Argentina. **18** George Graham. **19** McNeill. **20** Croatia.

Quiz 18 **Euro 96**

LEVEL 1

Answers – see page 30

1 Who won the 1996 European Championship?

2 Which team were beaten in the Final?

3 What was the scoreline in the Final after 90 minutes?

4 Which player finished top scorer for the 96 tournament?

5 Which player was skipper of the Scottish Euro 96 squad?

6 Who was the German skipper?

7 What was the fatalistic nickname for Group C?

8 Which country was in the group with England, Holland and Scotland?

9 Who was manager of England's squad?

10 Who scored England's second goal against Scotland?

11 Which player took the last English penalty in the semi-final shoot out?

12 Did Eric Cantona play in the Euro 96 finals?

13 What was the new rule to affect games that went into extra time?

14 Who was England's first choice keeper?

15 Which Birmingham ground was a venue?

16 Did Turkey reach the Euro 96 finals?

17 What was the scoreline in England's game against Holland?

18 Who was Scotland's only goalscorer?

19 In the England v Germany semi-final which country played in their changed colours?

20 Which Premiership player manager was England's assistant coach in Euro 96?

Answers

Keepers (see Quiz 20)

1 Ogrizovic. **2** Tim Flowers. **3** Italy. **4** Tomas Ravelli. **5** Manchester Utd. **6** David James. **7** Arsenal. **8** USA. **9** David Seaman. **10** Mark Bosnich. **11** Andy. **12** Manchester City. **13** Bruce Grobbelaar. **14** West Ham Utd. **15** The Republic of Ireland. **16** Gordon Banks. **17** Newcastle Utd. **18** Manchester Utd. **19** Germany. **20** Sheffield Wednesday.

Quiz 19 **Pot Luck 10**

LEVEL 1

Answers – see page 27

1 What is the last word in Stirling's name?

2 Which London club wear red and white hooped socks?

3 With which club did Ray Wilkins make his League debut?

4 Which country did Terry Butcher play for?

5 Who plays at home at White Hart Lane?

6 Which Robert was Norwich's top league scorer in 1995–96?

7 Which Bobby of Celtic was Scottish Footballer of the Year in 1969?

8 Redknapp followed Bonds as boss at which club?

9 Which club did Eric Cantona leave to join Manchester Utd?

10 Who was the Scotland manager for Euro 96?

11 What is the nickname of Bristol City?

12 Which country did Willie Miller play for?

13 What colour are the home shirts of Holland?

14 "You'll Never Walk Alone" is the anthem of which team?

15 Which Mark was PFA Player of the Year in 1991?

16 Dave Merrington was coach for 11 years before becoming boss of which club?

17 River Plate play in which country?

18 Who was manager of Arsenal's 1990–91 championship winning side?

19 Which Billy became the first Celtic player also to manage the club?

20 Which country did Igor Stimac play for?

Answers

Pot Luck 9 (see Quiz 17)

1 Everton. **2** Norwich City. **3** Rangers. **4** City. **5** Czech Republic. **6** Arsenal. **7** Germany. **8** Aberdeen. **9.** QPR. **10** Red. **11** Woan. **12** The Seagulls. **13** Wolves. **14** FA Charity Shield. **15** Nottingham Forest. **16** Holland. **17** Scotland. **18** Lineker. **19** Portugal. **20** Gray.

Quiz 20 **Keepers**

Answers – see page 28

1 Which Steve played 400 plus times for Coventry?

2 Who was Blackburn's regular keeper when they won the Premiership in 1994–95?

3 Which country did Dino Zoff play for?

4 Who is the world's most-capped goalkeeper?

5 Jim Leighton and Les Sealey both played for which club?

6 Which Liverpool keeper modelled clothes for Giorgio Armani?

7 John Lukic won a Championship medal with Leeds and with which other club?

8 Casey Keller plays for which country?

9 Who was England's No 1 in Euro 96?

10 Who was in trouble for a Nazi-style salute made at Tottenham Hotspur in 1996?

11 Which first name was shared by keepers Dibble and Goram?

12 Joe Corrigan was a great servant for which club?

13 Which Liverpool keeper was dubbed "Jungle Man" by his teammates?

14 For which club did Ludek Miklosko play 300 plus games?

15 Which country does Shay Given play for?

16 Who was England's keeper when they won the World Cup Final?

17 Which Premiership club had keepers with Christian names of Pavel and Shaka?

18 Alex Stepney and Gary Bailey played for which club?

19 Which country did Eike Immel come from?

20 Pressman and Woods played for which club?

Answers

Euro 96 (see Quiz 18)

1 Germany. **2** Czech Republic. **3** 1–1. **4** Alan Shearer. **5** Gary McAllister. **6** Jürgen Klinsmann. **7** The Group of Death. **8** Switzerland. **9** Terry Venables. **10** Paul Gascoigne. **11** Gareth Southgate. **12** No. **13** The sudden death goal. **14** David Seaman. **15** Villa Park. **16** Yes. **17** 4–1 to England. **18** Ally McCoist. **19** England. **20** Bryan Robson.

Quiz 21 **Pot Luck 11**

LEVEL 1

Answers – see page 33

1 Who plays at home at Elland Road?

2 Which team does Sean Bean support?

3 Who did Arsenal beat in two cup finals in 1993?

4 What is the last word in Bolton's name?

5 Which country has Chris Coleman played for?

6 Which Lee was the Leeds target man when they won the Championship in 1992?

7 Which country do Grasshoppers come from?

8 With which club did Dennis Wise make his League debut?

9 Which club did Ruel Fox join on leaving Norwich?

10 What colour are Swindon's home shirts?

11 Which David was Sheffield Wednesday's top League scorer in 1995–96?

12 Which team are known as The Pirates?

13 Which Gordon of Leeds Utd won the Footballer of the Year award in 1991?

14 Hoddle followed Ardiles as manager at which club?

15 Which Premiership player rejoiced in the real name of Stig-Inge?

16 Steve Bruce played over 300 games for which team?

17 Which Liverpool legend Bob passed away in February 1996?

18 Who was Scotland's manager before Craig Brown?

19 At which stage were France knocked out of Euro 96?

20 Which Tony of Forest was PFA Young Player of the Year in 1978?

Answers

Pot Luck 12 (see Quiz 23)

1 Town. **2** The Republic of Ireland. **3** White. **4** Nottingham Forest. **5** Ferdinand. **6** West Bromwich Albion. **7** Italy. **8** Chelsea. **9** Manchester Utd. **10** Gough. **11** The Clarets. **12** Wales. **13** Graeme Souness. **14** Red. **15** Platt. **16** Middlesbrough. **17** England. **18** Merson. **19** USA. **20** Dixon.

Quiz 22 **Nicknames**

Answers – see page 34

1 Which club is known as The Gunners?
2 "Psycho" was the nickname of which fullback?
3 Which club are called The Trotters?
4 Which Midlands team have a name to be sheepish about?
5 Which London club are known as The Blues?
6 What is the animal link with Hull?
7 SLOW is an anagram of which club's nickname?
8 Which creatures could sting you at Brentford?
9 Which England player is known as Rodney?
10 At which club can you shout Cobblers to show your appreciation?
11 Management and media men Ron and Jack are usually described by what word?
12 Which Scottish team is known as The Dons?
13 And which English team is known as The Dons?
14 Who are The Blades?
15 Who is known as "Sparky"?
16 Which ground are you at if The Foxes are at home?
17 Which nickname dogs Huddersfield?
18 Who are The Toffees?
19 The Bhoys is the nickname of which team?
20 Which Liverpool player was nicknamed "Digger"?

Answers

The 1970s (see Quiz 24)

1 Arsenal. **2** Dougan. **3** Ibrox, Glasgow **4** Leeds Utd. **5** Sunday. **6** Sir Alf Ramsey. **7** Brazil. **8** Tommy Docherty. **9** Asa Hartford. **10** Malcolm Allison. **11** Holland. **12** Stoke City. **13** Brian Clough. **14** Bayern Munich. **15** Watford. **16** Manchester Utd. **17** Pele. **18** Cards. **19** Wimbledon. **20** Don Revie.

Quiz 23 **Pot Luck 12**

LEVEL 1

Answers – see page 31

1 What is the last word in Luton's name?
2 Which country did Pat Bonner play for?
3 What colour are Fulham's home shirts?
4 Who plays at home at the City Ground?
5 Which Les was Newcastle's top league scorer in 1995–96?
6 Alan Buckley followed Keith Burkinshaw as boss at which club?
7 Gianfranco Zola plays for which country?
8 With which club did Graeme Le Saux make his League debut?
9 Which club did Dion Dublin leave to join Coventry?
10 Which Richard of Rangers was Scottish Footballer of the Year in 1989?
11 What is Burnley's nickname?
12 Which country did John Toshack play for?
13 Which manager took Liverpool to FA Cup Final triumph over Sunderland?
14 What colour are the home shirts of Switzerland?
15 Which David was PFA Player of the Year in 1990?
16 Which club brought Juninho to play in England?
17 Which national team decided to accept "collective responsibility" for damage done on a plane in 1996?
18 Which Paul said his manager gave him "unbelievable belief"?
19 Which country did Roy Wegerle play for?
20 Which England fullback Lee has made more than 400 appearances for Arsenal?

Answers

Pot Luck 11 (see Quiz 21)

1 Leeds Utd. **2** Sheffield Utd. **3** Sheffield Wednesday. **4** Wanderers. **5** Wales. **6** Chapman. **7** Switzerland. **8** Wimbledon. **9** Newcastle. **10** Red. **11** Hirst. **12** Bristol Rovers. **13** Strachan. **14** Swindon Town. **15** Bjornebye. **16** Manchester Utd. **17** Paisley. **18** Andy Roxburgh. **19** Semi-finals. **20** Woodcock.

Quiz 24 **The 1970s**

LEVEL 1

Answers – see page 32

1 Charlie George helped which side to the double?

2 Which Derek was elected chairman of the PFA?

3 More than 60 people died at which Scottish ground in 1971?

4 Giles, Lorimer and Clarke were stars of which club side?

5 League soccer was played on which day for the first time?

6 The 11-year reign of which England boss ended in 1974?

7 Which country won the 1970 World Cup?

8 Which Manchester Utd boss was sacked for an affair?

9 Which West Brom player was suspected of having a hole in the heart?

10 Which manager was known as "Big Mal"?

11 Which country was credited with developing total football?

12 Gordon Banks and George Eastham played together for which club?

13 Which manager led both Derby and Forest to the championship?

14 Which German club won the European Cup three years in a row?

15 Elton John was elected chairman of which club?

16 McGuinness and O'Farrell were managers at which club?

17 Which Brazilian player scored his 1,000th goal?

18 Which red and yellow items were introduced in the Football League in 1976?

19 Which London team were elected into the league?

20 Which England boss was banned for 10 years for bringing the game into disrepute?

Answers

Nickname*s* (see Quiz 22)

1 Arsenal. **2** Stuart Pearce. **3** Bolton. **4** Derby County (The Rams). **5** Chelsea. **6** Tigers. **7** Sheffield Wednesday (Owls). **8** Bees. **9** Tony Adams. **10** Northampton. **11** Big. **12** Aberdeen. **13** Wimbledon. **14** Sheffield Utd. **15** Mark Hughes. **16** Filbert Street. **17** Terriers. **18** Everton. **19** Celtic. **20** John Barnes.

Quiz 25 **Pot Luck 13**

LEVEL 1

Answers – see page 37

1 Who plays at home at Bloomfield Road?
2 Grobbelaar and Beasant were together at which club?
3 Brian Clough and Frank Clark both managed which club?
4 What is the last word in Bradford's name?
5 Which country has Iain Dowie played for?
6 Who resigned as Newcastle manager in January 1997?
7 Which country do Fenerbahce come from?
8 With which club did Alan Stubbs make his league debut?
9 Which club did Colin Hendry join on leaving Manchester City?
10 What colour are Tottenham Hotspur's home shirts?
11 Which player was Southampton's top league scorer in 1995–96?
12 What is Bury's nickname?
13 What kind of creature found the stolen World Cup in 1966?
14 Which team does Elton John support?
15 Which John of Liverpool won the Footballer of the Year award in 1990?
16 Venables followed Pleat as manager at which club?
17 Which country has Danny Blind played for?
18 Which Cyrille of West Brom was PFA Young Player of the Year in 1979?
19 What colour are the Republic of Ireland's home shorts?
20 Which keeper Tony had spells for both Manchester Utd and City in the 90s?

Answers

Pot Luck 14 (see Quiz 27)

1 Town. **2** England. **3** Blue and white. **4** Chelsea. **5** Barmby. **6** Jason Lee. **7** Jardine. **8** Crystal Palace. **9** Manchester Utd. **10** The U's. **11** Swindon Town. **12** Northern Ireland. **13** Martin O'Neill. **14** Southampton. **15** Barnes. **16** Ian Wright. **17** Noades. **18** Croatia. **19** Leeds Utd. **20** Black.

Quiz 26 **London Clubs**

LEVEL 1

Answers – see page 38

1 Who plays at home at Griffin Park?

2 Which London club did Anders Limpar play for?

3 Who beat Fulham to win the 70s all London FA Cup Final?

4 John Spencer left which London club to join QPR?

5 Graham Roberts played for Chelsea and which other London club?

6 Barry Hearn became chairman of which East London club?

7 At which Park do Wimbledon play their home games?

8 Which London club did Stan Bowles play for?

9 Have Charlton ever won an FA Cup Final?

10 Which club plays nearest to the River Thames?

11 Which London club did Peter Osgood play for?

12 Which Billy has made a record number of league appearances for West Ham?

13 George Graham and John Docherty have both managed which London club?

14 Which side did manager Steve Coppell take to an FA Cup Final?

15 Jimmy Hill has been chairman of which London team?

16 Who won 108 England caps playing for one club?

17 For which London side did Peter Shilton make his 1,000th League appearance?

18 Who are nicknamed the Hornets?

19 Which London club did Gary Lineker play for?

20 Which London side finished highest in the Premiership in season 1995–96?

Answers

European Cup (see Quiz 28)

1 Blackburn **2** Rangers. **3** Juventus. **4** Celtic. **5** Rapid Vienna. **6** Juventus. **7** Nottingham Forest. **8** Matt Busby. **9** The 70s. **10** Four. **11** Real Madrid. **12** Alfredo di Stefano. **13** Celtic. **14** Benfica. **15** Bob Paisley. **16** Barcelona. **17** Juventus. **18** Fabrizio Ravanelli (Juventus and Middlesbrough). **19** Ajax. **20** Peter Shilton.

Quiz 27 **Pot Luck 14**

LEVEL 1

Answers – see page 35

1 What is the last word in Mansfield's name?

2 Which country did defender Mark Wright play for?

3 What colour are the stripes on Huddersfield's home shirts?

4 Who plays at home at Stamford Bridge?

5 Which Nick was Middlesbrough's top league scorer in 1995–96?

6 Which Nottingham Forest player was ribbed for his "pineapple" hair cut?

7 Which Sandy of Rangers was Scottish Footballer of the Year in 1975?

8 With which club did John Salako make his league debut?

9 Which club did Andrei Kanchelskis leave to join Everton?

10 What is Cambridge United's nickname?

11 Steve McMahon followed John Gorman as manager at which club?

12 Which country did Pat Rice play for?

13 Which manager was with Wycombe Wanderers when they came into the Football League?

14 Mick Channon is the leading all-time scorer for which club?

15 Which John of Liverpool was PFA Player of the Year in 1988?

16 Who was top scorer for Arsenal for five consecutive seasons in the 90s?

17 Which Ron has been chairman of Crystal Palace?

18 Which country has Davor Suker played for?

19 Howard Wilkinson managed which side to the league title?

20 What is the colour of Germany's home shorts?

Answers

Pot Luck 13 (see Quiz 25)

1 Blackpool. **2** Southampton. **3** Nottingham Forest. **4** City. **5** Northern Ireland. **6** Kevin Keegan. **7** Turkey. **8** Bolton Wanderers. **9** Blackburn Rovers. **10** White. **11** Matthew Le Tissier. **12** The Shakers. **13** A dog. **14** Watford. **15** Barnes. **16** Tottenham Hotspur. **17** Holland. **18** Regis. **19** White. **20** Coton.

Quiz 28 **European Cup**

LEVEL 1

Answers – see page 36

1 Alan Shearer first played in the competition with which club?
2 Which Scottish side represented its country in the 1996–97 tournament?
3 Which Italian side won the European Cup in 1996?
4 Which team were the first British side to win the trophy?
5 Which Austrian team did Manchester Utd beat in their final group game of 96–97?
6 Which Italian side topped Manchester Utd's group in the same season?
7 Trevor Francis scored a Final goal for which club?
8 Who was Manchester Utd's manager when they won the trophy in the 60s?
9 In which decade did Liverpool first win the competition?
10 How many times did Liverpool win the European Cup in the 20th century?
11 Which Spanish side won the first five Finals?
12 And which striker scored in all five of those Finals?
13 Which side became known as "The Lions of Lisbon"?
14 Which were the first team from Portugal to win the tournament?
15 Who was Liverpool's manager when they first won the trophy?
16 A Ronald Koeman Final goal gave which side the trophy?
17 Who were Liverpool playing in the 1985 Final overshadowed by crowd trouble?
18 Who scored for a foreign club in the '96 Final and started 1996–97 in English soccer?
19 Which Dutch team won the title three times in succession in the 70s?
20 Who was Nottingham Forest's goalkeeper when they first won the trophy?

Answers

London Clubs (see Quiz 26)

1 Brentford. **2** Arsenal. **3** West Ham. **4** Chelsea. **5** Tottenham Hotspur. **6** Leyton Orient. **7** Selhurst. **8** QPR. **9** Yes (1947). **10** Fulham. **11** Chelsea. **12** Bonds. **13** Millwall. **14** Crystal Palace. **15** Fulham. **16** Bobby Moore. **17** Leyton Orient. **18** Watford. **19** Tottenham Hotspur. **20** Arsenal.

Quiz 29 **Pot Luck 15**

LEVEL 1

Answers – see page 41

1. Who plays at home at Upton Park?
2. What is the main colour of Watford's home shirts?
3. Jack Charlton and Kevin Keegan both managed which club?
4. What is the last word in Brighton & Hove's name?
5. Which country did Phil Babb play for?
6. Which Glenn of Tottenham Hotspur was PFA Young Player of the Year in 1980?
7. Which country do Atletico Madrid come from?
8. With which club did Andy Hinchcliffe make his league debut?
9. Which club did Tony Dorigo join on leaving Chelsea?
10. Which John was Hearts' top League scorer in 1995-96?
11. What colour are Aston Villa's home shorts?
12. What is Cardiff's nickname?
13. Which team does David Mellor support?
14. Denis Smith followed Lawrie McMenemy as boss at which club?
15. What is the main colour of Spain's home shirts?
16. Which Steve of Liverpool won the Footballer of the Year award in 1989?
17. Which country did Gerson play for?
18. With which club did Chris Sutton make his League debut?
19. Who hit 34 league goals in Newcastle's first season in the Premier League?
20. Defenders Parker and Pallister were teammates with which club?

Answers

Pot Luck 16 (see Quiz 31)

1 Town. **2** Wales. **3** Amber. **4** QPR. **5** Eric Cantona. **6** Liverpool. **7** Dozzell. **8** Ipswich Town. **9** Coventry City. **10** McLeish. **11** Carlisle Utd. **12** The Republic of Ireland. **13** A lion. **14** Sheffield Utd. **15** Allen. **16** Red and white. **17** David James. **18** Neill. **19** Arsenal. **20** Knox.

Quiz 30 **Spot Kicks**

LEVEL 1

Answers – see page 42

1 Who missed a spot kick and put a bag on his head in a pizza place?
2 Beardsley and Shearer have been on the spot for which club?
3 Andy Brehme scored a World Cup Final winning penalty for which country?
4 Where should a goalkeeper stand for a penalty?
5 Who made the first Wembley save from an FA Cup Final spot kick?
6 Ron Flowers was on the spot for which country?
7 Which England player missed in a shoot out in Italy in 1990 but scored in Euro 96?
8 Which Julian became a 90s penalty expert for West Ham?
9 Yorke and Townsend were on the spot for which club?
10 Robbie Rensenbrink scored four penalties in the '78 World Cup finals for which team?
11 Which London team won the UEFA Cup Final of 1984 after a shoot out?
12 Who missed from the spot for Scotland against England in Euro 96?
13 Which country did The Republic of Ireland beat in a 1990 World Cup shootout?
14 Who scored two spot kicks in an FA Cup Final for Manchester Utd in the 90s?
15 Dennis Wise and Mark Hughes have been on the spot for which club?
16 Which country was awarded a penalty in the Euro 96 Final?
17 In 1994 the Final of which major tournament was decided on a penalty shootout for the first time?
18 Which Tottenham Hotspur player failed to score from the spot in the 1991 FA Cup Final?
19 In a league game can a taker score from a rebound off the keeper?
20 Which Francis was a spot kick king for Manchester City in the 70s?

Answers

Quote, Unquote (see Quiz 32)

1 Alan Ball. **2** Sardines. **3** Mabbutt. **4** Paul Gascoigne. **5** Stan Collymore. **6** Nike. **7** George Graham. **8** Graham Taylor. **9** Pele. **10** Neal. **11** Beardsley. **12** George Best. **13** Paul Gascoigne. **14** Jürgen Klinsmann. **15** Tomatoes. **16** Before the Euro 96 semi-final. **17** Argentina (in 1966). **18** Glenn Hoddle. **19** Gareth Southgate. **20** Paul Gascoigne.

Quiz 31 **Pot Luck 16**

LEVEL 1

Answers – see page 39

1 What is the last word in Northampton's name?
2 Which country did Vinnie Jones play for?
3 What is the main colour of Hull's home shirts?
4 Which team has its stadium in South Africa Road, London?
5 Which player was Manchester Utd's top league scorer in 1995–96?
6 Which club traditionally selected its managers from the Boot Room?
7 Which midfielder Jason went from Ipswich to Tottenham Hotspur in the 90s?
8 With which club did John Wark make his league debut?
9 Which club did Kevin Gallacher leave to join Blackburn?
10 Which Alex of Aberdeen was Scottish Footballer of the Year in 1990?
11 Who are The Cumbrians?
12 Which country has Roy Keane played for?
13 What kind of animal was World Cup Willie?
14 Howard Kendall followed Dave Bassett as manager at which club?
15 Which Clive was PFA Player of the Year in 1987?
16 What colour are Croatia's home shirts?
17 Who was in goal when Liverpool won the 1995 Coca Cola Cup?
18 Which Terry managed both Arsenal and Tottenham Hotspur?
19 England striker Alan Smith won a championship medal at which club?
20 Which Archie has been assistant manager to Walter Smith?

Answers

Pot Luck 15 (see Quiz 29)

1 West Ham Utd. **2** Yellow. **3** Newcastle Utd. **4** Albion. **5** The Republic of Ireland. **6** Hoddle. **7** Spain. **8** Manchester City. **9** Leeds Utd. **10** Robertson. **11** White. **12** The Bluebirds. 13 Chelsea. **14** Sunderland. **15** Red. **16** Nicol. **17** Brazil. **18** Norwich City. **19** Andy Cole. **20** Manchester Utd.

Quiz 32 **Quote, Unquote**

LEVEL 1

Answers – see page 40

1 Which Manchester City manager said, "We've got one point from 27 but it's not as bad as that"?

2 According to Eric Cantona what would be thrown off the trawler?

3 Which Gary said, "This is not a normal injury. Fashanu was playing without due care and attention"?

4 Whose departure from Lazio caused the president to remark, "He will only return to Rome as a tourist"?

5 Which Liverpool player was supposedly, "happier at Southend"?

6 Which company decided that, "1966 was a great year for English football. Eric was born"?

7 Which ex-Arsenal boss said, "I am as weak as the next man when it comes to temptation"?

8 Which manager suffered from the Sun's turnip jibes?

9 Which Brazilian great talked of "the beautiful game"?

10 Which short-stay boss Phil said, "Watching Manchester City is probably the best laxative you can take"?

11 Which England international Peter said, "I often get called Quasimodo"?

12 Which modest 60s player said in the 90s, "I'd be worth around £14 to £15 million by today's prices"?

13 Who claimed in 1996 that he had "given up beer and guzzling"?

14 Which German said in 1994, "Me dive? Never!"?

15 What did Arrigo Sacchi say might be thrown at him after Euro 96?

16 When did Terry Venables say, "It's a football match, not a war"?

17 Which team did Alf Ramsey liken to "Animals"?

18 Who in 1996 took "the only job I would have left Chelsea for"?

19 Who said, "I've only taken one penalty before, for Crystal Palace"?

20 "As daft as a brush" – who was Bobby Robson talking about?

Answers

Spot Kicks (see Quiz 30)

1 Gareth Southgate. **2** Newcastle Utd. **3** West Germany. **4** On the goalline and between the posts. **5** Dave Beasant. **6** England. **7** Stuart Pearce. **8** Dicks. **9** Aston Villa. **10** Holland. **11** Tottenham Hotspur. **12** Gary McAllister. **13** Romania. **14** Eric Cantona. **15** Chelsea. **16** Czech Republic. **17** The World Cup. **18** Gary Lineker. **19** Yes. **20** Lee.

Quiz 33 **Pot Luck 17**

LEVEL 1

Answers – see page 45

1 Who plays at home at Easter Road?

2 Which Ian of Liverpool was PFA Young Player of the Year in 1983?

3 Gerry Francis and David Pleat both managed which club?

4 What is the second word in Cambridge's name?

5 Which country has Peter Schmeichel played for?

6 Which team did Eric Morecambe support?

7 Which country do Sturm Graz come from?

8 With which club did keeper David James make his league debut?

9 Which club did Pat Jennings join on leaving Tottenham Hotspur?

10 What pattern is on West Bromwich Albion's home shirts?

11 Which Mike was Stoke's top League scorer in 1995-96?

12 Who are The Addicks?

13 Which Terry of Liverpool won the Footballer of the Year award in 1980?

14 What is the main colour of the Romanian home strip?

15 What forename links players Parlour and Houghton?

16 Which Lou got the Celtic sack in 1994?

17 Which club was banned from the 1994–95 FA Cup then allowed back in?

18 Which country did Stefan Effenberg play for?

19 Ruel Fox and Andy Cole were teammates at which club?

20 Which energy-giving drink did John Barnes advertise?

Answers

Pot Luck 18 (see Quiz 35)

1 City. **2** The Republic of Ireland. **3** Blue. **4** Crystal Palace. **5** Uwe Rosler. **6** Leeds Utd. 7 McGrain. **8** Nottingham Forest. **9** Crystal Palace. **10** The Blues. **11** White. **12** Northern Ireland. **13** Saunders. **14** Mills. **15** Lineker. **16** Brian Kidd. **17** Southampton. **18** Notts County. **19** Arsenal. **20** Bolton Wanderers.

Quiz 34 **Soccer Legends**

LEVEL 1

Answers – see page 46

---

1 What position did Stanley Matthews play?

2 Which legend married a 23-year-old air hostess on his 49th birthday?

3 Which Dutch international player went on to managerial success at Barcelona in the 1990s?

4 With which London club did Jimmy Greaves begin his career?

5 Who was the first England captain of a World Cup winning team?

6 Which country did Zbigniew Boniek play for?

7 Which League club did Billy Wright play for?

8 Who was "Wor Jackie"?

9 In which country was Ferenc Puskas born?

10 At which club did Denis Law finish his career?

11 Who was "Kaiser Franz"?

12 How many clubs did Tom Finney play for?

13 Who was known as "The Black Panther"?

14 Who was England's keeper in the 1966 World Cup winning side?

15 How did Edson Arantes do Nascimento become better known?

16 Which goalkeeper with Christian names Patrick Anthony played over 100 times for his country?

17 Which French midfielder of the 70s and 80s became France's top scorer?

18 In which city did Billy Meredith play much of his soccer?

19 Which player turned out in a then record 21 World Cup finals matches for Argentina?

20 At which club did Stanley Matthews begin and end his career?

Answers

Scottish Internationals (see Quiz 36)

1 Coventry City. **2** Goalkeeper. **3** Celtic. **4** Denis Law. **5** John. **6** Celtic. **7** John Greig. **8** Jim Baxter. **9** Liverpool. **10** Johnston. **11** Aberdeen. **12** Jim Holton. **13** Alan Hansen. **14** Willie Johnston. **15** His front teeth. **16** Bob Wilson. **17** Willie. **18** Tottenham Hotspur. **19** John Collins. **20** McStay.

Quiz 35 **Pot Luck 18**

LEVEL 1

Answers – see page 43

---

1 What is the second word in Norwich's name?

2 Which country did Jason McAteer play for?

3 What is the main colour in Ipswich's home shirts?

4 Which London club did Wimbledon ground-share with in the 90s?

5 Which German player was Manchester City's top scorer in 1995–96?

6 Rod Wallace and Gary Speed were teammates at which club?

7 Which Danny of Celtic was Scottish Footballer of the Year in 1977?

8 With which club did Roy Keane make his league debut?

9 Which club did Chris Armstrong leave to join Tottenham Hotspur?

10 What is Chelsea's nickname?

11 What colour are Denmark's home shirts?

12 Which country did Norman Whiteside play for?

13 Which Dean was Aston Villa's top scorer in 1994–95?

14 Which Mick played a record number of games for Ipswich?

15 Which Gary was PFA Player of the Year in 1986?

16 Who was manager Alex Ferguson's assistant for Manchester Utd for the 1995–96 double season?

17 Jeff Kenna and Ken Monkou were teammates at which club?

18 Howard Kendall got the boot as boss of which Division 1 club in 1995?

19 Graham Rix played over 350 games with which club?

20 Alan Stubbs was a losing Coca-Cola Cup Finalist with which club?

Answers

Pot Luck 17 (see Quiz 33)

1 Hibernian. **2** Rush. **3** Tottenham Hotspur. **4** United. **5** Denmark. **6** Luton Town. **7** Austria. **8** Watford. **9** Arsenal. **10** Stripes. **11** Sheron. **12** Charlton Athletic. **13** McDermott. **14** Yellow. **15** Ray. **16** Macari. **17** Tottenham Hotspur. **18** Germany. **19** Newcastle Utd. **20** Lucozade Sport.

Quiz 36 **Scottish Internationals**

LEVEL 1

Answers – see page 44

1 Where did Eoin Jess move to on leaving Aberdeen?
2 In what position did Frank Haffey play?
3 Which club was Kenny Dalglish with when he was first capped?
4 Which striker played for Manchester Utd and Torino in the 60s?
5 What forename is shared by strikers Collins and Spencer?
6 With which club did fullback Tommy Gemmell spend most of his career?
7 Which defender or midfielder clocked up a record 496 league games for Rangers?
8 Who was "Slim" Jim?
9 Which club did Billy Liddell play for in the 40s and 50s?
10 Which Glasgow born striker Mo notched 14 goals for his country?
11 Which club did Alex McLeish play for?
12 The chant, 'Six foot two, Eyes of Blue' was about which defender?
13 Which classy Liverpool defender of the 70s and 80s landed only 26 caps?
14 Which player failed a dope test and was sent home from the 1978 World Cup in Argentina?
15 What did a certain lager claim to restore for Joe Jordan?
16 Which Arsenal goalkeeper of the 70s played for Scotland?
17 What forename was shared by defenders Donachie and Miller?
18 Which London club did Alan Gilzean play for?
19 Who moved to Monaco as a free agent in the summer of 1996?
20 Which Paul of Celtic was injured and missed Euro 96?

Answers

Soccer Legends (see Quiz 34)

1 Outside right. **2** George Best. **3** Johan Cruyff. **4** Chelsea. **5** Bobby Moore. **6** Poland. **7** Wolves. **8** Jackie Milburn. **9** Hungary. **10** Manchester City. **11** Franz Beckenbauer. **12** One. **13** Lev Yashin. **14** Gordon Banks. **15** Pele. **16** Jennings. **17** Michel Platini. **18** Manchester. **19** Diego Maradona. **20** Stoke City.

Quiz 37 **Pot Luck 19**

LEVEL 1

Answers – see page 49

1 Who plays at home at The Hawthorns?
2 Gavin Peacock and Dennis Wise were teammates at which club?
3 Stewart Houston and Ray Wilkins have both managed which club?
4 What is the second word in Carlisle's name?
5 Which country has Georgiou Kinkladze played for?
6 Which Mark of Manchester Utd was PFA Young Player of the Year in 1985?
7 Which country do Standard Liege come from?
8 With which club did Gary Speed make his league debut?
9 Which club did Peter Beardsley join on leaving Everton?
10 What is the main colour of West Ham's home shirts?
11 Which Craig was Sunderland's top League scorer in 1995–96?
12 What is Crewe's nickname?
13 Stan Flashman was connected with which club?
14 Which player is a great admirer of the 19th century poet Rimbaud?
15 Which team does Jim Bowen support?
16 What is the main colour of France's home shirts?
17 Which Frans of Ipswich won the Footballer of the Year award in 1981?
18 Which club plays at the Nou Camp Stadium?
19 Which Scottish team are known as The Honest Men?
20 Which Paul was Everton's top scorer in 1994–95?

Answers

Pot Luck 20 (see Quiz 39)

1 United. **2** England. **3** White. **4** Charlton Athletic. **5** Roberts. **6** Malpas. **7** Yeboah. **8** John Spencer. **9** Celtic. **10** The Eagles. **11** Bolton Wanderers. **12** Wales. **13** Green. **14** Spink. **15** Wimbledon. **16** Platt. **17** Reid. **18** Endsleigh. **19** Palmer. **20** Manchester City.

Quiz 38 **Going Up**

LEVEL 1

Answers – see page 50

1 Which team did Kenny Dalglish lead into the Premiership?

2 Which team went up to the Premiership in 1994 and again in 1996?

3 Who was manager of Newcastle when they were promoted to the Premiership in 1993?

4 Which club made it to the First Division for the first time ever in 1985?

5 Ludek Miklosko has been in two promotion campaigns with which club?

6 Steve McMahon took which team to the First Division at the first attempt?

7 Which team did Frank Clark lead back to the Premiership in the 1990s?

8 Who gained promotion for Middlesbrough in his first season as a player/manager in 1995?

9 Which club were in Division 4 in 1982 and Division 1 in 1986?

10 John McGinlay was with which club in promotions from the Second division to the Premiership?

11 Which Wanderers entered the League in 1993?

12 Steve Bruce was ever-present when which East Anglian side were Second Division champions?

13 Who was manager of Sunderland when they were promoted in 1996?

14 Which Chris took Bradford to Division 1 in 1996?

15 Which London team joined the League in 1991?

16 Which Stan was Nottingham Forest's top marksman in their '94 promotion?

17 Joachim and Walsh played in a play-off Final for which team?

18 Goals by Deane and Agana took which United to the top flight?

19 Batty and Strachan helped which club to promotion?

20 Who was the boss who took Swansea to their 1980s promotions?

Answers

Going Down (see Quiz 40)

1 Ipswich Town. **2** Ray Wilkins. **3** Four. **4** The Canaries. **5** Newport County. **6** Manchester City. **7** Sunderland. **8** Arsenal. **9** Saunders. **10** Nottingham Forest. **11** Swindon Town. **12** Lawrence. **13** Oldham Athletic. **14** Sheffield Utd. **15** 1970s. **16** Brighton. **17** No. **18** Crystal Palace. **19** The 1970s. **20** Norwich City.

Quiz 39 **Pot Luck 20**

Answers – see page 47

1 What is the second word in Oxford's name?
2 Which country did Des Walker play for?
3 What is the main colour of Leeds' home shirts?
4 Who plays home games at The Valley?
5 Which Iwan was Leicester City's top scorer in 1995–96?
6 Which Maurice of Dundee Utd was Scottish Footballer of the Year in 1991?
7 Which Tony was Leeds' top scorer in 1994–95?
8 Who was Chelsea's leading League goalscorer in the 1995–96 season?
9 Which club did Brian McClair leave to join Manchester Utd?
10 What is Crystal Palace's nickname?
11 Jason McAteer and John McGinlay were teammates at which club?
12 Which country did Ian Rush play for?
13 What colour are Portugal's home shorts?
14 Which goalkeeper Nigel made over 300 appearances with Aston Villa?
15 Sam Hammam was connected with which club in the 1990s?
16 Which David was made England's new captain in March 1994?
17 Which Peter of Everton was PFA Player of the Year in 1985?
18 Which Gloucester-based insurance company agreed to sponsor the Football League in 1993?
19 Which Carlton has played for Sheffield Wednesday and Leeds Utd?
20 Peter Swales was chairman of which club?

Answers

Pot Luck 19 (see Quiz 37)

1 West Bromwich Albion. **2** Chelsea. **3** QPR. **4** United. **5** Georgia. **6** Hughes. **7** Belgium. **8** Leeds Utd. 9. Newcastle Utd. **10** Claret. **11** Russell. **12** The Railwaymen. **13** Barnet. **14** Eric Cantona. **15** Blackburn Rovers. **16** Blue. **17** Thijssen. **18** Barcelona. **19** Ayr. **20** Rideout.

Quiz 40 **Going Down**

LEVEL 1

Answers – see page 48

1 Five-goal Claus Thomsen was which relegated team's top scorer?

2 Which player/manager took QPR down in 1995–96?

3 Three teams went out of the Premiership in 1994. What did that number change to the following season?

4 When the Eagles flew out of the Premiership in 1995 what other feathered friends joined them?

5 Which Welsh side went out of the League in 1988?

6 Which team went out of the Premiership on goal difference in 1996?

7 Marco Gabbiadini was top scorer as which side went down in 1991?

8 Which club has been in the top flight without relegation since 1913?

9 Which Dean was top scorer as Derby went down in 1991?

10 Stuart Pearce and Mark Crossley were in which relegated side?

11 Fjortoft went up with Middlesbrough the season that he left which team to go down?

12 Which Lennie did an annual escape act to keep Charlton in the top flight in the 80s?

13 Veteran striker Graeme Sharp was top scorer for which side leaving the Premiership?

14 A last-minute goal put which Dave Bassett team down in 1994?

15 In which decade were Manchester Utd last relegated from the top flight?

16 Which side rock bottom in the League in the 1996–97 season were in the top flight in 1983?

17 Have Celtic ever been relegated?

18 Which London team went out of the Premiership in 1993 and 1995?

19 In which decade were Carlisle last in the top division in England?

20 Which team were seventh in the Premiership at the start of January, yet were relegated at the end of the season in 1995?

Answers

Going Up (see Quiz 38)

1 Blackburn Rovers. **2** Leicester City. **3** Kevin Keegan. **4** Oxford Utd. **5** West Ham Utd. **6** Swindon Town. **7** Nottingham Forest. **8** Bryan Robson. **9** Wimbledon. **10** Bolton Wanderers. **11** Wycombe. **12** Norwich City. **13** Peter Reid. **14** Kamara. **15** Barnet. **16** Collymore. **17** Leicester City. **18** Sheffield. **19** Leeds Utd. **20** John Toshack.

Quiz 41 **Pot Luck 21**

LEVEL 1

Answers – see page 53

1 Who plays at home at The Dell?

2 Which flying winger was Manchester Utd's top League scorer in 1994–95?

3 Glenn Hoddle and Ruud Gullit have both managed which club?

4 What is the second word in Chester's name?

5 Which country did Keith Gillespie play for?

6 Which Tony of West Ham was PFA Young Player of the Year in 1986?

7 Which country do Slavia Sofia come from?

8 With which club did Michael Thomas make his League debut?

9 Which club did Tony Mowbray join on leaving Middlesbrough?

10 Wimbledon's home shirts are a dark shade of which colour?

11 Which Wayne was Swindon's top League scorer in 1995–96?

12 What is Darlington's nickname?

13 John Salako and Ray Houghton were teammates at which club?

14 Which country did Michael Laudrup play for?

15 Which team does Jo Brand support?

16 Which Steve of Tottenham Hotspur won the Footballer of the Year award in 1982?

17 What is the colour of Bulgaria's home shorts?

18 Which London club briefly had a "famous five" lineup of attackers in the 90s?

19 Which country did Dmitri Kharine, formerly of Chelsea, come from?

20 Which Steve scored most League goals in a career for Wolves?

Answers

Pot Luck 22 (see Quiz 43)

1 United. **2** The Republic of Ireland. **3** Blue. **4** Barnsley. **5** Fowler. **6** Johnstone. **7** Tottenham Hotspur. **8** Crystal Palace. **9** Rangers. **10** Ince. **11** Paine. **12** England. **13** Beardsley. **14** Yes. **15** Plymouth Argyle. **16** Rivera. **17** Rush. **18** Romania. **19** Rangers. **20** Karel Poborsky.

Quiz 42 **Manchester Utd**

LEVEL 1

Answers – see page 54

1 Which United manager signed Eric Cantona?

2 How old was Ryan Giggs when he made his first-team debut?

3 Who wrote the autobiography *The Good, The Bad And The Bubbly*?

4 Which player went to Newcastle as part of the deal that brought Andy Cole to Old Trafford?

5 In which country was Sir Matt Busby born?

6 Which club was Paul Ince bought from?

7 Mark Hughes has moved from Manchester Utd twice. Which clubs did he join?

8 Which team were the opponents in the Cantona Kung-Fu spectator attack in January 1995?

9 Alex Ferguson sold his son Darren to which club?

10 Who is the elder of the Neville brothers?

11 What was Denis Law's usual shirt number?

12 What infamous first went to Kevin Moran in the 1985 FA Cup Final?

13 What is the surname of 1970s brothers Brian and Jimmy?

14 Which United manager signed Bryan Robson?

15 Who was the scoring skipper in the 1996 FA Cup Final?

16 Paddy Roche was an international keeper for which country?

17 Who was dubbed "El Beatle" after a 60s European triumph?

18 Which forename links Beckham, May and Sadler?

19 Which two United players were members of England's World Cup winning team?

20 Who was the first Manchester Utd player to hit five goals in a Premier League match?

Answers

The 1980s (see Quiz 44)

1 Manchester City. **2** Points for a win. **3** Crystal Palace. **4** Robert Maxwell. **5** Swansea City. **6** Italy. **7** The Milk Cup. **8** Bob Paisley. **9** Tottenham Hotspur. **10** Kevin Keegan. **11** Gary Lineker. **12** Liverpool. **13** Jock Stein. **14** France. **15** England. **16** France. **17** Terry Venables. **18** Arsenal. **19** Chelsea. **20** Play-offs.

Quiz 43 **Pot Luck 22**

LEVEL 1

Answers – see page 51

1 What is the second word in Peterborough's name?
2 Which country did Frank Stapleton play for?
3 What is the main colour of Leicester's home shirts?
4 Who plays home games at Oakwell?
5 Which Robbie was Liverpool's top scorer in 1995–96?
6 Which Derek of Rangers was Scottish Footballer of the Year in 1978?
7 Campbell and Calderwood were teammates at which club?
8 With which club did Stan Collymore make his League debut?
9 Which club did Gary Stevens join on leaving Everton?
10 Which Paul first captained England in June 1993?
11 Which Terry played 800 plus league games, mostly for Southampton?
12 What country did Paul Mariner play for?
13 Which Peter was Newcastle's top league scorer in 1994–95?
14 Has there ever been an England international with the surname Bastard?
15 Which team did politician Michael Foot support?
16 Which Gianni was known as Italy's "Golden Boy"?
17 Which Ian of Liverpool was PFA Player of the Year in 1995?
18 Which country did Gica Popescu play for?
19 Which was the first Scottish side that Stuart McCall played for?
20 Who scored an amazing chip goal in Euro 96 for the Czech Republic against Portugal?

Answers

Pot Luck 21 (see Quiz 41)

1 Southampton. **2** Andrei Kanchelskis. **3** Chelsea. **4** City. **5** Northern Ireland. **6** Cottee. **7** Bulgaria. **8** Arsenal. **9** Celtic. **10** Blue. **11** Allison. **12** The Quakers. **13** Crystal Palace. **14** Denmark. **15** Crystal Palace. **16** Perryman. **17** Green. **18** Tottenham Hotspur. **19** Russia. **20** Bull.

Quiz 44 **The 1980s**

LEVEL 1

Answers – see page 52

1 Which club did both Malcolm Allison and John Bond manage?

2 What changed from two to three in all games at the start of the 1981–82 campaign?

3 Which London team were hailed as "The Team of the Eighties"?

4 Which tycoon became Oxford chairman?

5 Which team was top of the First Division during 1981 but back in the Fourth Division by 1986?

6 Who won the 1982 World Cup?

7 What was the League Cup known as after a deal with the National Dairy Board?

8 Who retired as Liverpool boss after a season in which both the Championship and League Cup were won?

9 Garth Crooks and Steve Archibald played together at which club?

10 Which former England captain ended his playing days at Newcastle Utd?

11 Which Englishman was the top scorer in the 1986 World Cup finals?

12 Who did Wimbledon beat in their 80s FA Cup Final victory?

13 Which manager collapsed and died seconds before the end of a Wales v Scotland World Cup qualifying game?

14 On leaving Tottenham Hotspur, Chris Waddle moved to which country?

15 UEFA banned the clubs of which country from participation in European competitions?

16 Which host nation won the 1984 European Championship?

17 Which English manager took over at Barcelona?

18 Which team won the 1988–89 championship in the last minute of the season?

19 Kerry Dixon was Division 1 top scorer in 1984–85 with which team?

20 Which extra games were introduced to decide promotion?

Answers

Manchester Utd (see Quiz 42)

1 Alex Ferguson. **2** 17. **3** George Best. **4** Keith Gillespie. **5** Scotland. **6** West Ham. **7** Barcelona and Chelsea. **8** Crystal Palace. **9** Wolves. **10** Gary. **11** 10. **12** First sending off in a Final. **13** Greenhoff. **14** Ron Atkinson. **15** Eric Cantona. **16** The Republic of Ireland. **17** George Best. **18** David. **19** Bobby Charlton and Nobby Stiles. **20** Andy Cole.

Quiz 45 **Pot Luck 23**

LEVEL 1

Answers – see page 57

1. Who plays at home at Fratton Park?
2. Which country won the 1992 European Championship?
3. Dave Bassett and Joe Kinnear have both managed which club?
4. What is the second word in Coventry's name?
5. Which country does Fabrizio Ravanelli come from?
6. Limpar and Rideout were teammates at which club?
7. Which country do Brondby come from?
8. With which club did Nigel Clough make his League debut?
9. Which club did Dan Petrescu join on leaving Sheffield Wednesday?
10. What colour are Wolves' home shirts?
11. Which Teddy was Tottenham Hotspur's top League scorer in 1995–96?
12. Who are The Cottagers?
13. Which Kenny of Liverpool won the Footballer of the Year award in 1983?
14. Which Mark was Sheffield Wednesday's top League scorer in 1994–95?
15. Which team does Jasper Carrott support?
16. Fullback Gary Stevens played three FA Cup Finals for which club?
17. Which country staged the World Cup finals when "Nessun Dorma" became an anthem?
18. What is Scotland's national football stadium called?
19. What make of crisps has Gary Lineker advertised?
20. Which Tony of Arsenal was PFA Young Player of the Year in 1987?

Answers

Pot Luck 24 (see Quiz 47)

1 Argyle. **2** Northern Ireland. **3** Red. **4** Leicester City. **5** Ghana. **6** McCoist. **7** Sweden. **8** Arsenal. **9** Arsenal. **10** Gillingham. **11** Sheffield Wednesday. **12** Scotland. **13** Benfica. **14** Red. **15** *Viz.* **16** Wimbledon. **17** Gigg Lane. **18** Norway. **19** Cottee. **20** Wallace.

Quiz 46 **Midfield Men**

LEVEL 1

Answers – see page 58

1 Tim Sherwood led which club to the Premiership?

2 David Platt, Ray Parlour and Liam Brady have all played for which club?

3 Which French superstar was European Player of the Year three times in the 80s?

4 According to song, who was dreaming of Wembley with Tottenham Hotspur?

5 Which Billy was at the heart of Leeds' success in the 1960s and '70s?

6 Which English club did Kazimierz Denya join in the 70s?

7 Which former Liverpool skipper moved to Sampdoria?

8 Which midfield dynamo captained the West Germans in Italia 90?

9 Which Gary played for Luton, Forest, Villa and Leicester?

10 Which London team did Stefan Schwartz play for?

11 What name is shared by Minto and Sellars?

12 Enzo Scifo played for which country?

13 Which was Johnny Haynes' only English club?

14 Which-long serving Celtic and Scotland skipper first played back in 1982?

15 Michael Thomas scored an FA Cup Final goal for which team?

16 What is the first name of West German 60s and 70s stalwart Overath?

17 Who was England's "Captain Marvel"?

18 Which club had the dream midfield of Ball, Harvey and Kendall?

19 Paul Ince was at which club when he made his England debut?

20 Has Robert Lee ever played for England?

Answers

TV Pundits (see Quiz 48)

1 Ian St John. **2** Scotland. **3** Brian Clough. **4** 1964 (1960–68 is OK). **5** Brighton. **6** Arsenal. **7** Kenneth Wolstenholme. **8** Alan Hansen. **9** True. **10** Gillingham. **11** John Motson. **12** Garth Crooks. **13** Rory Bremner. **14** Icke. **15** Gabby Yorath. **16** John Motson. **17** Alan Hansen. **18** Ian St John. **19** David O'Leary. **20** Jimmy Hill.

Quiz 47 **Pot Luck 24**

Answers – see page 55

1 What is the last word in Plymouth's name?
2 Which country has Alan McDonald played for?
3 What colour are Liverpool's home shorts?
4 Who plays home games at Filbert Street?
5 Where did Tony Yeboah of Leeds United come from?
6 Which Ally was Scottish Footballer of the Year in 1992?
7 Which country hosted the 1992 European Championship?
8 With which London club did Niall Quinn make his league debut?
9 Which club did Anders Limpar leave to join Everton?
10 Which team is known as The Gills?
11 Chris Waddle and Des Walker were teammates at which club?
12 Which country did Andy Goram play for?
13 Which club plays at the Stadium of Light?
14 What colour are Belgium's home shirts?
15 Football character "Billy the Fish" appeared in which magazine?
16 Which London club did Hans Segers play for?
17 Where do Bury play?
18 What country did Liverpool's Bjornebye play for?
19 Which Tony was West Ham's top league scorer in 1994–95?
20 Which Rodney won a championship medal with Leeds in the 1990s?

Answers

Pot Luck 23 (see Quiz 45)

1 Portsmouth. **2** Denmark. **3** Wimbledon. **4** City. **5** Italy. **6** Everton. **7** Denmark. **8** Nottingham Forest. **9** Chelsea. **10** Old Gold. **11** Sheringham. **12** Fulham. **13** Dalglish. **14** Bright. **15** Birmingham City. **16** Everton. **17** Italy. **18** Hampden Park. **19** Walkers. **20** Adams.

Quiz 48 **TV Pundits**

LEVEL 1

Answers – see page 56

1 Who formed a double act with Jimmy Greaves?

2 Which country did Sky man Andy Gray play for?

3 Who famously called a Polish keeper a "clown" on the box in 1973?

4 To four years either way, when did BBC TV first show *Match of the Day* on Saturday evening?

5 Which team does Des Lynam support?

6 Which club did Bob Wilson mainly play for?

7 Which commentator said, "They think it's all over... it is now!"?

8 Who, in the season Manchester Utd won their first double, said about them, "You don't win anything with kids"?

9 True or false – Jimmy Hill is a qualified referee?

10 Which club did the late Brian Moore support and was a director?

11 Who commentated at a Wembley Final presentation, "How apt that a man named Buchan should climb the 39 steps"?

12 Which former Tottenham Hotspur and Stoke striker has reported for the BBC?

13 Which impersonator features Des Lynam and Motty in his TV shows?

14 Which former presenter David went politically green?

15 Which TV pundit married rugby union star Kenny Logan in 2001?

16 Who in 1977 became the youngest commentator on an FA Cup Final?

17 Who was a regular golfing partner of Kenny Dalglish?

18 Which 1980s and 90s pundit was manager of Portsmouth in the 70s?

19 Which former *Match of the Day* expert succeeded George Graham as manager of Leeds?

20 Who declared Cantona was "nothing more than a brat" after a stamping incident against Norwich?

Answers

Midfield Men (see Quiz 46)

1 Blackburn Rovers. **2** Arsenal. **3** Michel Platini. **4** Osvaldo Ardiles. **5** Bremner. **6** Manchester City. **7** Graeme Souness. **8** Lothar Matthäus. **9** Parker. **10** Arsenal. **11** Scott. **12** Belgium. **13** Fulham. **14** Paul McStay. **15** Liverpool. **16** Wolfgang. **17** Bryan Robson. **18** Everton. **19** Manchester Utd. **20** Yes.

Quiz 49 **Pot Luck 25**

LEVEL 1

Answers – see page 61

1. Who plays at home at Ewood Park?
2. Which Paul of Tottenham Hotspur was PFA Young Player of the Year in 1988?
3. Ron Atkinson and Gordon Strachan both managed which club?
4. What is the second word in Crewe's name?
5. Which country has Frank Leboeuf played for?
6. Who was Aberdeen manager from 1978 to '86?
7. Which country do Panathinaikos come from?
8. With which club did David Batty make his League debut?
9. Which club did Lee Dixon join on leaving Stoke?
10. What colour are Wrexham's home shirts?
11. Which John was Tranmere's top League scorer in 1995–96?
12. What is Grimsby's nickname?
13. What is the colour of Italy's home shirts?
14. Which team does June Whitfield support?
15. Which Ian of Liverpool won the Footballer of the Year award in 1984?
16. Jeremy Goss and Ruel Fox were teammates at which club?
17. In which decade did Blackburn first play European soccer?
18. Which Scottish United does Lorraine Kelly support?
19. Which country did Branco play for?
20. Who brought a libel case against a paper involving his ex-wife Danielle?

Answers

Pot Luck 26 (see Quiz 51)

1 North. **2** The Republic of Ireland. **3** White. **4** Selhurst Park. **5** Marshall. **6** Strachan. **7** Chelsea. **8** QPR. **9** Nottingham Forest. **10** Leicester City. **11** White. **12** Wales. **13** Tottenham Hotspur. **14** Leeds Utd. **15** Yes. **16** Mark Hateley. **17** Keegan. **18** Red. **19** Aston Villa. **20** Liverpool.

Quiz 50 FA & SFA Cup

LEVEL 1

Answers – see page 62

1 Which non-league team beat Newcastle in February 1972?

2 Which Paul scored a 90s FA Cup winning goal for Everton?

3 Which London club won the FA Cup in 1981 and 1982?

4 Who was Des Walker playing for when he scored a Final own goal?

5 Dickie Guy was a goalkeeping hero with which 1970s non-league side?

6 Which United won the Scottish FA Cup for the first time in the 80s?

7 In which decade was the first Wembley Final?

8 Which Harry Redknapp team did a giant killing act by knocking out Manchester Utd in 1984?

9 Andy Linighan scored a last-minute Final winner for which team?

10 Who beat Chelsea in the 1996 semi-finals?

11 Brian Flynn was boss as which club shocked Arsenal in 1992?

12 Cornishman Mike Trebilcock hit Final goals for which team in the 60s?

13 Ray Walker hit a screamer as which Midland team dumped Tottenham Hotspur in the 80s?

14 Arnold Muhren hit a Final goal for which club?

15 In 1989 Sutton United beat which First Division team 2–1?

16 Who was the first Frenchman to captain an FA Cup winning side?

17 Ray Crawford inspired which team to the ultimate giant killing by beating Leeds 3-2 in 1971?

18 In the 1980s, which South coast side were losing finalists the year they were relegated from the First Division?

19 What accounted for the 1990 Scottish Final score of Aberdeen 9 Celtic 8?

20 Geoff Thomas captained which London side in a 1990s Final?

Answers

Grounds (see Quiz 52)

1 Birmingham City. **2** Reebok. **3** The Goldstone Ground. **4** Heysel. **5** Arsenal. **6** Bristol City. **7** Chelsea. **8** Deepdale. **9** Huddersfield Town. **10** Aberdeen. **11** Old Trafford. **12** Oldham Athletic. **13** Blackburn Rovers. **14** Selhurst Park. **15** Sunderland. **16** Wembley. **17** Bradford City. **18** Watford. **19** Hillsborough. **20** Brazil.

Quiz 51 **Pot Luck 26**

LEVEL 1

Answers – see page 59

1 What does the N stand for in PNE?
2 Which country did Liam Brady play for?
3 What is the main colour of Luton's home shirts?
4 Where do Crystal Palace play home games?
5 Which Ian was Ipswich's top scorer in 1995–96?
6 Which Gordon of Aberdeen was Scottish Footballer of the Year in 1980?
7 Ken Bates has been chairman of which London club?
8 With which club did Les Ferdinand make his league debut?
9 Which club did Stan Collymore leave to join Liverpool?
10 Which team is known as The Foxes?
11 What is the main colour of German home shirts?
12 Which country has Gary Speed played for?
13 Barmby and Anderton played together at which club?
14 Phil Masinga started in England with which club?
15 Can a goal be scored directly from a corner kick?
16 Which veteran striker moved from Rangers in Scotland to Rangers in London for £1.5 million at the end of 1995?
17 Which Kevin of Southampton was PFA Player of the Year in 1982?
18 What colour are Wales's home shirts?
19 Andy Townsend and John Fashanu were teammates at which club?
20 Ronnie Whelan made over 350 appearances for which club?

Answers

Pot Luck 25 (see Quiz 49)

1 Blackburn Rovers. **2** Gascoigne. **3** Coventry City. **4** Alexandra. **5** France. **6** Alex Ferguson. **7** Greece. **8** Leeds Utd. **9** Arsenal. **10** Red. **11** Aldridge. **12** The Mariners. **13** Blue. **14** Wimbledon. **15** Rush. **16** Norwich City. **17** 1990s. **18** Dundee. **19** Brazil. **20** Graeme Souness.

Quiz 52 **Grounds**

LEVEL 1

Answers – see page 60

1 Which team's ground is called St Andrews?

2 At which stadium do Bolton play?

3 In the 90s Brighton were dogged by the attempted sale of which ground?

4 At which Stadium was there crowd trouble at the Liverpool v Juventus European Cup Final of 1985?

5 Which club plays at Highbury?

6 Which side is at home if the venue is Ashton Gate?

7 Which London team ground is in Fulham Road?

8 What is Preston's ground called?

9 Who play at home at the Alfred McAlpine Stadium?

10 Which Scottish side were the first with an all-seater stadium?

11 Which stadium is situated in Sir Matt Busby Way?

12 Who plays at home at Boundary Park?

13 Which club has the Walker Steel stand on its ground?

14 Crystal Palace have extended ground-share to Wimbledon at which stadium?

15 Roker Park was home for most of the 20th century to which team?

16 Which stadium had the Twin Towers?

17 At which Yorkshire club was there a fire tragedy in 1985?

18 Who plays at Vicarage Road?

19 The 1991 Liverpool and Nottingham Forest FA Cup semi-final was at which ground?

20 The Maracana Stadium is in which country?

Answers

FA & SFA Cup (see Quiz 50)

1 Hereford Utd. **2** Rideout. **3** Tottenham Hotspur. **4** Nottingham Forest. **5** Wimbledon. **6** Dundee Utd. **7** 1920s. **8** Bournemouth. **9** Arsenal. **10** Manchester Utd. **11** Wrexham. **12** Everton. **13** Port Vale. **14** Manchester Utd. **15** Coventry City. **16** Eric Cantona. **17** Colchester Utd. **18** Brighton. **19** Game decided on penalties. **20** Crystal Palace.

Quiz 53 **Pot Luck 27**

LEVEL 1

Answers – see page 65

1 Who plays at home at Craven Cottage?
2 Can a player be offside in his team's own half of the pitch when the ball is played?
3 Howard Wilkinson and George Graham have both managed which club?
4 What is the second word in Derby's name?
5 Which country has Tomas Brolin played for?
6 Which Paul of Arsenal was PFA Young Player of the Year in 1989?
7 Which country do Metz come from?
8 With which club did Nick Barmby make his league debut?
9 Which club did Kevin Richardson join on leaving Aston Villa?
10 Which Bob was WBA's top league scorer in 1995–96?
11 What colour are Barnsley's home shirts?
12 Which team is known as the Os?
13 Which England cricketer played league football for Scunthorpe?
14 Which hymn has been traditionally sung before the FA Cup Final?
15 Which team does Nick Hancock support?
16 What colour are the home shirts of Brazil?
17 Which Neville won the Footballer of the Year award in 1985?
18 Bobby Tambling is the career record scorer for which club?
19 Dave Bassett was manager for eight years at which Yorkshire club?
20 Darren Huckerby left which club to join Coventry City?

Answers

Pot Luck 28 (see Quiz 55)

1 Park. **2** The Republic of Ireland. **3** Sky blue. **4** Hearts. **5** Booth.
6 West Ham Utd. **7** Boris Becker. **8** Crewe Alexandra. **9** QPR. **10** The Red Imps.
11 Goram. **12** Wales. **13** Norwich City. **14** Edinburgh. **15** John Barnes.
16 Pale blue and white stripes. **17** Wark. **18** Eric Cantona. **19** Nottingham Forest.
20 Liverpool.

Quiz 54 **World Cup**

LEVEL 1

Answers – see page 66

1 Dunga was captain of which World Cup-winning country?
2 Which team knocked England out of the 1990 semi-finals?
3 Which ex president of FIFA gave his name to the original trophy?
4 Who was the manager of the 1990 West German trophy-winning team?
5 Goycochea played in a Final as goalkeeper for which country?
6 Which Central American side shocked Scotland with a 1–0 win in 1990?
7 Prior to 1998 had the final stages ever been held in France?
8 Who was the Scottish manager for the trip to Argentina in 1978?
9 Which country knocked the Republic of Ireland out of the quarter-finals in 1990?
10 Which country was the only one beaten by the Republic of Ireland in the final stages of the 1994 tournament?
11 Which country did Lato play for?
12 When was the first ever Final played?
13 In which country was the first Final held?
14 Which Norman became the youngest scorer in final stages, in 1982?
15 For which country did Oleg Salenko score the individual record of five goals in a game?
16 Which team reached the Final in 1982, 1986 and 1990?
17 Which team were beaten finalists in 1994?
18 Which England goalkeeper retired from internationals after Italia 90?
19 In which decade were Sweden the host country?
20 For which country did Alexi Lalas play?

Answers

Drunk and Disorderly (see Quiz 56)

1 Dennis Wise. **2** Eric Cantona. **3** Match fixing for an illegal betting ring. **4** Vinnie Jones. **5** Tottenham Hotspur. **6** George Best. **7** China. **8** Marseille. **9** Diego Maradona. **10** Paul Merson. **11** Liverpool. **12** Nose. **13** FA Charity Shield. **14** Blackburn Rovers. **15** Tony Adams. **16** George Graham. **17** For dropping his shorts in front of spectators. **18** Duncan Ferguson. **19** Paul Gascoigne. **20** Wimbledon.

Quiz 55 **Pot Luck 28**

LEVEL 1 

Answers – see page 63

1 What does the letter P stand for in QPR?
2 Which country did Tony Cascarino play for?
3 What is the colour of Manchester City's home shirts?
4 Who plays at home at Tynecastle Park?
5 Which Andy was HuddersfieldTown's top scorer in 1995–96?
6 Which team are "forever blowing bubbles"?
7 Who had trials with Bayern Munich before becoming a tennis champion?
8 With which club did fullback Rob Jones make his league debut?
9 Which club did Roy Wegerle leave to join Blackburn?
10 What is Lincoln City's nickname?
11 Which Andy of Rangers was Scottish Footballer of the Year in 1993?
12 Which country has Dave Phillips played for?
13 Which East Anglian side did John Bond manage?
14 Which former Tottenham Hotspur defender shared his surname with a Scottish city?
15 Which England player was the son of a Jamaican international?
16 What colour are Argentina's home shirts?
17 Which John of Ipswich was PFA Player of the Year in 1981?
18 Who was the first player to win the league championship with different teams in consecutive seasons?
19 Des Walker and Roy Keane were teammates at which club?
20 Which club did Ray Clemence leave to join Tottenham Hotspur?

Answers

Pot Luck 27 (see Quiz 53)

1 Fulham. **2** No. **3** Leeds Utd. **4** County. **5** Sweden. **6** Merson. **7** France. **8** Tottenham Hotspur. **9** Coventry City. **10** Taylor. **11** Red. **12** Leyton Orient. **13** Ian Botham. **14** "Abide With Me". **15** Stoke City. **16** Yellow. **17** Southall. **18** Chelsea. **19** Sheffield Utd. **20** Newcastle Utd.

Quiz 56 **Drunk and Disorderly**

Answers – see page 64

1 Which 90s Chelsea skipper was unwise in his dealing with a London cabbie?

2 Who was made to serve 120 hours community service in 1995?

3 Why was Italian superstar Paolo Rossi banned in 1980?

4 Who got in trouble with the FA for narrating the video "Soccer Hard Men"?

5 The Sugar v Venables High Court rumpus concerned which club?

6 Which player appeared drunk on Terry Wogan's TV chat show?

7 In 1996, which country had the England squad played in prior to the reports of mid-air vandalism?

8 A 90s scandal forced Bernard Tapie out as President of which club?

9 Which star was tested positive for taking cocaine before a game for Napoli?

10 In 1995, who said, "I'm going to Gamblers' Anonymous, that's my night out now"?

11 Jan Molby was at which club when he was jailed for driving offences?

12 What part of a reporter's anatomy did Vinnie Jones bite in a Dublin bar?

13 At which Wembley event were Keegan and Bremner sent off for fighting?

14 Teammates Batty and Le Saux had a punch up at which club?

15 Which player went back to drink after England's Euro 96 defeat?

16 In 1995, who was banned for 12 months after a 'bung' inquiry?

17 Why was Arsenal's Sammy Nelson banned and fined in 1979?

18 Which Scottish player was nicknamed "Duncan Disorderly"?

19 Whose move to Lazio was delayed by a nightclub fracas?

20 Alan Cork reputedly had a hangover while playing in an FA Cup Final for which team?

Answers

World Cup (see Quiz 54)

1 Brazil. **2** West Germany. **3** Jules Rimet. **4** Franz Beckenbauer. **5** Argentina. **6** Costa Rica. **7** Yes, in1934 **8** Ally MacLeod. **9** Italy. **10** Italy. **11** Poland. **12** 1930. **13** Uruguay. **14** Whiteside. **15** Russia. **16** West Germany. **17** Italy. **18** Peter Shilton. **19** 1950s. **20** USA.

Quiz 57 **Pot Luck 29**

LEVEL 1

Answers – see page 69

1 Who plays at home at Highfield Road?
2 At which club did Kevin Keegan make his first League appearance?
3 Ron Atkinson and Alex Ferguson have both managed which club?
4 What is the second word in Exeter's name?
5 Which country has John Collins played for?
6 Which Matt was PFA Young Player of the Year in 1990?
7 Which country do Werder Bremen come from?
8 With which club did Chris Waddle make his League debut?
9 Which club did Paul Warhurst join on leaving Sheffield Wednesday?
10 Which Tony was West Ham's joint top League scorer in 1995–96?
11 What colour are Bolton's home shorts?
12 Which team is known as the Reds or the Pool?
13 Which Clive of Tottenham Hotspur won the Footballer of the Year award in 1987?
14 Which team lost both the 1994 and 1995 Charity Shield games?
15 Which team does Bruce Forsyth support?
16 Which country does George Weah play for?
17 Which Scottish team won the Championship nine times in a row starting in 1966?
18 Who was Chief Executive of Manchester United before Peter Kenyon?
19 Which London club had a long-time sponsorship with JVC?
20 What is the Neville brothers' father called?

Answers

Pot Luck 30 (see Quiz 59)

1 United. **2** England. **3** White. **4** Port Vale. **5** Kanchelskis. **6** Italy. **7** Rough. **8** Ipswich Town. **9** Cambridge Utd. **10** Arsenal and Tottenham Hotspur. **11** The Hatters. **12** Scotland. **13** Arsenal. **14** Armfield. **15** Manchester Utd. **16** Sweden. **17** McDermott. **18** Tottenham Hotspur. **19** Quinn. **20** Switzerland.

Quiz 58 **Euro Cup Winners' Cup**

LEVEL 1

Answers – see page 70

1 Who were the first British side to win the competition?

2 An Alan Smith goal won the trophy for which club?

3 Which English side won the 1990–91 trophy?

4 Which came first, the European Cup or the Cup Winners' Cup?

5 Which French team won the competition in 1996?

6 Sandy Jardine got a winners' medal with which club?

7 With which team did Alex Ferguson first win the trophy as a manager?

8 What colour home shirts did Manchester Utd wear when they beat Barcelona in a 1990s Final?

9 Who skippered West Ham's victorious team in the 1960s?

10 Which team did Peter Reid win the competition with?

11 Which west London team won the trophy in 1971?

12 Eoin Jess scored four goals in the 1993–94 competition for which club?

13 To qualify, what is the trophy a team has to win in its domestic competition of the previous season?

14 Which home country have Crusaders represented in this tournament?

15 Did Celtic win the tournament in the 1970s and 1980s?

16 Who represented England in the 1996–97 tournament?

17 Which England international striker helped Barcelona in the 1989 Final?

18 Which Premier League team represented England in the 1995–96 tournament?

19 Which Welsh team hit a cricket score, 12–0, in the early 1980s?

20 Have Ajax ever won the competition?

Answers

The 1990s (see Quiz 60)

1 Japan. **2** Bobby Moore. **3** Mick McCarthy. **4** Bosman. **5** Bobby Robson. **6** Faustino Asprilla. **7** Brighton. **8** Yugoslavia. **9** Shearer and Sutton **10** Sunderland. **11** Arsenal. **12** Manchester Utd. **13** Graeme Souness. **14** Leeds Utd. **15** Graham Taylor. **16** Birmingham City. **17** Gary Lineker. **18** Barclays. **19** Rangers. **20** Maidstone Utd.

Quiz 59 **Pot Luck 30**

LEVEL 1

Answers – see page 67

1. What is the second word in Rotherham's name?
2. Which country did Mark Hateley play?
3. What colour are Manchester Utd's home shorts?
4. Who plays home games at Vale Park?
5. Which Andrei was Everton's top scorer in 1995–96?
6. Serie A takes place in which country?
7. Which Alan of Partick was Scottish Footballer of the Year in 1981?
8. With which club did Alan Brazil make his league debut?
9. Which club did Dion Dublin leave to join Manchester Utd?
10. Which teams played in the 1991 all-London Charity Shield game?
11. What is Luton's nickname?
12. Which country did the late Jim Baxter play for?
13. The late David Rocastle played over 200 games for which London club?
14. Which Jimmy helped the FA to find a new England coach in 1996?
15. Which team does Mick Hucknall support?
16. What country did Thomas Ravelli play for?
17. Which Terry of Liverpool was PFA Player of the Year in 1980?
18. Irving Scholar was chairman of which London club?
19. Which Mick knocked in over 30 league goals for Newcastle in 1989–90?
20. Which country does Marc Hottiger play for?

Answers

Pot Luck 29 (see Quiz 57)

1 Coventry City. **2** Scunthorpe. **3** Manchester Utd. **4** City. **5** Scotland. **6** Le Tissier. **7** Germany. **8** Newcastle Utd. **9** Blackburn Rovers. **10** Cottee. **11** Navy blue. **12** Liverpool. **13** Allen. **14** Blackburn Rovers. **15** Tottenham Hotspur. **16** Liberia. **17** Celtic. **18** Martin Edwards. **19** Arsenal. **20** Neville Neville.

Quiz 60 **The 1990s**

LEVEL 1

Answers – see page 68

1 In which country did Gary Lineker finish his playing career?
2 Which former England skipper died of cancer in February 1993?
3 Who took over from Jack Charlton as manager of the Republic of Ireland?
4 Which Jean-Marc went to the European Court of Justice with a contractual dispute?
5 Which former England manager went to Barcelona?
6 Who moved from Parma to Newcastle for £7 million?
7 Which seaside club's last game of 1995–96 was abandoned after a crowd invasion?
8 Which war-torn country qualified for, but were excluded from, the 1992 European Championship?
9 Who were Blackburn's "SAS" strikeforce?
10 Which Second Division side played Liverpool in the 1992 FA Cup Final?
11 A Steve Morrow goal gave which club League Cup success?
12 Which English club achieved three FA Cup and Premier League doubles in the 90s?
13 Which Liverpool manager had a triple heart bypass operation in 1992?
14 Which Yorkshire club was taken over by London-based group Caspian?
15 Which former England coach got the sack as manager of Wolves?
16 Where did Steve Bruce go to when he left Manchester Utd?
17 Which striker's son was diagnosed as having a rare form of leukaemia?
18 Which bank did not renew their sponsorship of the league?
19 Which team in 1991–92 won the Scottish League by 9 points?
20 Which club resigned from the league in August 1992?

Answers

European Cup Winners' Cup (see Quiz 58)

1 Tottenham Hotspur. **2** Arsenal. **3** Manchester Utd. **4** The European Cup. **5** Paris St Germain. **6** Rangers. **7** Aberdeen. **8** White. **9** Bobby Moore. **10** Everton. **11** Chelsea. **12** Aberdeen. **13** A national cup played on a knockout basis. **14** Northern Ireland. **15** No. **16** Liverpool. **17** Gary Lineker. **18** Everton. **19** Swansea City. **20** Yes, in 1987.

Quiz 61 **Pot Luck 31**

Answers – see page 73

1. Who plays at home at The New Den?
2. Marc Reiper first played in England for which club?
3. Dave Bassett and Howard Kendall have both managed which club?
4. What is the second word in Grimsby's name?
5. Which country has Martin Keown played for?
6. Which Lee of Manchester Utd was PFA Young Player of the Year in 1991?
7. Which country do Feyenoord come from?
8. With which club did Frank Stapleton make his League debut?
9. Which club did Pat Nevin join on leaving Everton?
10. Which Bryan was Forest's joint top League scorer in 1995–96?
11. What colour are Blackburn's home shorts?
12. Which team is known as The Citizens?
13. Tim Flowers and Neil Ruddock were in the same team at which club?
14. Dr Josef Venglos was manager of which English team?
15. Which team does Hugh Grant support?
16. Which country did Hristo Stoichkov play for?
17. Which Kenny of Forest won the Footballer of the Year award in 1978?
18. Who was West Ham manager from 1974–1989?
19. Dwight Yorke plays international soccer for which team?
20. Ray Wilkins and Andy Sinton were at which club together?

Answers

Pot Luck 32 (see Quiz 63)

1 United. **2** Northern Ireland. **3** Red. **4** Southend Utd. **5** Sturridge. **6** Denmark. **7** Aston Villa. **8** Wimbledon. **9** Newcastle Utd. **10** Manchester Utd. **11** Hateley. **12** England. **13** Oldham Athletic. **14** Barry Fry. **15** Crystal Palace. **16** Coventry City. **17** Brady. **18** Liverpool. **19** Brazil. **20** Coppell.

Quiz 62 **Defenders**

LEVEL 1

Answers – see page 74

1 Which international stopper played for Manchester Utd, Villa and Derby?

2 Ratcliffe and Mountfield were a partnership at which club?

3 Manuel Amaros played for which country?

4 Which Leeds defender was known as "The Giraffe"?

5 Which club did England fullback Eddie Hapgood play for?

6 Which fullback became Bryan Robson's assistant at Middlesbrough?

7 Which defender was supposed to "Bite Yer Legs"?

8 Which AC Milan sweeper is known as "Franco"?

9 At which club was the Butcher and Osman partnership?

10 Which John made a record number of appearance for Rangers before becoming manager?

11 Mike Duxbury won 10 England caps while at which League club?

12 Which country did Ronald Koeman play for?

13 Which club did Jimmy Armfield play for?

14 What forename links Leeds greats Madeley and Reaney?

15 What nickname did Chelsea's Ron Harris earn?

16 Djalma and Nilton Santos were fullbacks for which country?

17 Which country did Kevin Beattie play for?

18 Which defensive hardman is known as "Razor"?

19 Which Keith was involved in the 1996 televised bust up with Asprilla?

20 Frank Lampard was a great servant of which club?

Answers

The International Scene (see Quiz 64)

1 Sweden. **2** Brazil. **3** Holland. **4** 'Toto". **5** Argentina. **6** USA. **7** Leighton. **8** Belgium. **9** Portugal. **10** Czech Republic. **11** Italy. **12** Robson. **13** France. **14** England. **15** Argentina. **16** England. **17** Aston Villa. **18** He wasn't picked to play. **19** Uwe Seeler. **20** Tony Adams.

Quiz 63 **Pot Luck 32**

LEVEL 1

Answers – see page 71

1 What is the second word in Scunthorpe's name?

2 Which country has Nigel Worthington played for?

3 What colour are Middlesbrough's home shirts?

4 Who plays at home at Roots Hall?

5 Which Dean was Derby County's top scorer in 1995–96?

6 Which country has Kim Vilfort played for?

7 Curcic and Milosevic played together at which English club?

8 With which club did Vinnie Jones make his league debut?

9 Which club did Ruel Fox leave to join Tottenham Hotspur?

10 Which team is known as The Red Devils?

11 Which Mark of Rangers was Scottish Footballer of the Year in 1994?

12 Which country did Phil Neal play for?

13 Gunnar Halle first played in England for which club?

14 Who put his money into Peterborough in 1996?

15 Jim Cannon made a record number of appearances for which club?

16 Kevin Richardson and John Salako were together at which club?

17 Which Liam was PFA Player of the Year in 1979?

18 Which club did Mark Walters leave to join Southampton?

19 Which country did Socrates play for?

20 Which Steve has been Technical Director at Crystal Palace?

Answers

Pot Luck 31 (see Quiz 61)

1 Millwall. **2** West Ham Utd. **3** Sheffield Utd. **4** Town. **5** England. **6** Sharpe. **7** Holland. **8** Arsenal. **9** Tranmere Rovers. **10** Roy. **11** White. **12** Manchester City. **13** Southampton. **14** Aston Villa. **15** Fulham. **16** Bulgaria. **17** Burns. **18** John Lyall. **19** Trinidad & Tobago. **20** QPR.

Quiz 64 The International Scene

LEVEL 1

Answers – see page 72

1 Which country finished third in the 1994 World Cup?

2 Which country does Bebeto play for?

3 Which country knocked the Republic of Ireland out of the 1994 World Cup finals?

4 What was the nickname of Italy's Schillaci?

5 The British-sounding Brown scored a World Cup Final goal for which country?

6 The NASL was founded in which country?

7 Which Jim was in goal for Scotland in the heroic draw in Russia in 1995?

8 Which country does Degryse play for?

9 Who beat North Korea 5–3 in an epic 1966 World Cup quarter-final?

10 Nemec, Nedved and Nemeck played in a European Championship Final for which country?

11 Which country finished second in the 1994 World Cup?

12 Which Bryan was in England's World Cup final squads in 1982, 86 and 90?

13 Which country did Laurent Blanc play for?

14 Who were the Republic of Ireland's opponents in the abandoned 1995 game?

15 Cesar Luis Menotti was manager of which World Cup winning country?

16 Turkyilmaz scored a penalty for Switzerland against which country in Euro 96?

17 Which club was David Platt with when he first played for England?

18 Why did Roberto Baggio not impress in Euro 96?

19 Who was the captain of the West German side that lost the World Cup Final in 1966?

20 Which English defender spent part of the 1990–91 season in prison?

Answers

Defenders (see Quiz 62)

1 Paul McGrath. **2** Everton. **3** France. **4** Jack Charlton. **5** Arsenal. **6** Viv Anderson. **7** Norman Hunter. **8** Baresi. **9** Ipswich Town. **10** Greig. **11** Manchester Utd. **12** Holland. **13** Blackpool. **14** Paul. **15** "Chopper". **16** Brazil. **17** England. **18** Neil Ruddock. **19** Curle. **20** West Ham Utd.

Quiz 65 **Pot Luck 33**

Answers – see page 77

1 Who plays at home at Pittodrie?

2 Which team does violinist Nigel Kennedy support?

3 Peter Reid and Alan Ball have both managed which club?

4 What is the second word in Hartlepool's name?

5 In which year did Dean Saunders first play for Wales?

6 Which Ryan was PFA Young Player of the Year in 1992?

7 Which country do Maccabi Tel Aviv come from?

8 With which club did Teddy Sheringham make his League debut?

9 Which club did keeper Chris Woods join on leaving Norwich?

10 Which Robbie was Wimbledon's top League scorer in 1995–96?

11 What colour are Burnley's home shorts?

12 What is Mansfield's nickname?

13 Which city does David Beckham come from?

14 Which country has midfielder Luis Figo played for?

15 Which Emlyn of Liverpool won the Footballer of the Year award in 1977?

16 What colour are Holland's home shorts?

17 Glenn Helder first played in England for which club?

18 Which Manchester Utd star appeared as a model on the catwalks of Paris in 1992?

19 In which city was Steve Coppell born?

20 Gary Megson has had two spells in charge of which East Anglian team?

Answers

Pot Luck 34 (see Quiz 67)

1 Burnley. **2** Wimbledon. **3** Celtic. **4** United. **5** The Republic of Ireland. **6** Cole. **7** Italy. **8** Blackburn Rovers. **9** Leeds Utd. **10** Goodman. **11** White. **12** The Lions. **13** Keegan. **14** White. **15** Manchester City. **16** Crystal Palace. **17** Italy. **18** Celtic. **19** Norwich City. **20** Zimbabwe.

Quiz 66 **Derby Games**

LEVEL 1

Answers – see page 78

1 Which Denis played for both sides in the Manchester derby?
2 Which England forward star Peter played for both Liverpool and Everton?
3 Who are the opponents if Sheringham and Adams have scored in a north London derby?
4 Erik Bo Andersen scored twice for which Scottish team in a derby game?
5 Which teams have played in the derby by the River Trent?
6 Who managed rivals Leicester City and Aston Villa in the 1990s?
7 Which overseas player has taken part in Manchester and Merseyside derby games?
8 Alex Miller has been boss of which team in a Scottish derby?
9 What flower is linked to games between teams from different sides of the Pennines?
10 Which side won both Merseyside FA Cup Finals of the 1980s?
11 Lou Macari has played for and managed which team with a great derby tradition?
12 Keith Curle has played for which blue-shirted team in a northern derby?
13 Which team were relegated after a 1974 Manchester derby?
14 Which two Scottish clubs have their grounds closest together?
15 Which Robbie scored in both Mersey League meetings in 1995–96?
16 Alan Oakes is a veteran of many clashes in which city?
17 Which Paul has played in Glasgow, London, Tyne-Tees-Wear and Liverpool derby games?
18 Which Brian played for both Manchester Utd and Manchester City before joining the United management team?
19 Who are Norwich's traditional derby rivals?
20 Which derby traditionally takes place at the beginning of the year?

Answers

The Midlands (see Quiz 68)

1 WBA. **2** Red and white. **3** Gareth Southgate. **4** Nottingham Forest. **5** Peter Shilton. **6** Meadow. 7 Birmingham's Karen Brady. **8** Wolves. **9** Coventry City. **10** Mark McGhee. **11** Walsall. **12** "Bomber". **13** 1950s. **14** WBA. **15** Derby, Nottingham Forest. **16** Graham. **17** Birmingham City. **18** Notts County. **19** Webb. **20** Peter Taylor.

Quiz 67 **Pot Luck 34**

LEVEL 1

Answers – see page 75

1 Who plays at home at Turf Moor?

2 Oyvind Leonhardsen first played in England for which club?

3 Brady and Burns have both managed which club?

4 What is the second word in Hereford's name?

5 Which country did Eddie McGoldrick play for?

6 Which Andy of Newcastle was PFA Young Player of the Year in 1994?

7 Which country do Cagliari come from?

8 With which club did David May make his league debut?

9 Which club did David O'Leary join on leaving Arsenal?

10 Which Don was Wolves' top league scorer in 1995–96?

11 What colour are Bury's home shirts?

12 What is Millwall's nickname?

13 Which Kevin of Liverpool won the Footballer of the Year award in 1976?

14 What is the main colour of Bulgaria's home shirts?

15 Which team do the Gallagher brothers of Oasis support?

16 Matthew Simmons is the most famous – or infamous - fan of which club?

17 Which country did Luigi Riva play for?

18 Which Scottish side signed Paulo Di Canio from AC Milan?

19 Which club had Deehan, O'Neill and Megson as managers in 1995?

20 Peter Ndlovu played for which country?

Answers

Pot Luck 33 (see Quiz 65)

1 Aberdeen. **2** Aston Villa. **3** Manchester City. **4** United. **5** 1986. **6** Giggs. **7** Israel. **8** Millwall. **9** Rangers. **10** Earle. **11** White. **12** The Stags. **13** London. **14** Portugal. **15** Hughes. **16** White. **17** Arsenal. **18** Eric Cantona. **19** Liverpool. **20** Norwich City.

Quiz 68 **The Midlands**

Answers – see page 76

LEVEL 1

1 Which team does comedian and chat show host Frank Skinner support?

2 What colour are the stripes on Stoke's home shirts?

3 Which Aston Villa player was in England's Euro 96 squad?

4 Which Midland club has a tree on its badge?

5 Which goalkeeper played for Leicester City, Stoke City, Nottingham Forest and Derby County, among others?

6 At which Lane do Notts County play?

7 Which club director said that she was, "More male than most men"?

8 Wagstaffe, Dougan and Richards have played for which team?

9 John Sillett led which team to FA Cup success?

10 In the 90s which manager walked out on Leicester City to go to Wolves?

11 Which team plays at the Bescot Stadium?

12 What was the nickname of WBA's long serving, high scoring, Tony Brown?

13 Aston Villa set a record with a seventh FA Cup win, but in which decade was this win?

14 Which club has had Bobby Gould and Ossie Ardiles as manager?

15 Which two Midland clubs did Brian Clough take to the championship?

16 What name is shared by former Wolves managers Taylor and Turner?

17 With which club did Trevor Francis begin his playing career?

18 of which club was Jimmy Sirrel manager for three separate spells between 1969 and 1987?

19 Which England midfielder Neil had two spells with Nottingham Forest?

20 Who was Clough's assistant in his early trophy-winning years?

Answers

Derby Games (see Quiz 66)

1 Law. **2** Beardsley. **3** Arsenal and Tottenham Hotspur. **4** Rangers. **5** Nottingham Forest and Notts County. **6** Brian Little. **7** Andrei Kanchelskis. **8** Hibs. **9** Rose. **10** Liverpool. **11** Celtic. **12** Manchester City. **13** Manchester Utd. **14** Dundee and Dundee Utd. **15** Fowler. **16** Manchester. **17** Gascoigne. **18** Kidd. **19** Ipswich Town. **20** Celtic v Rangers.

Quiz 69 **Pot Luck 35**

LEVEL 1

Answers – see page 81

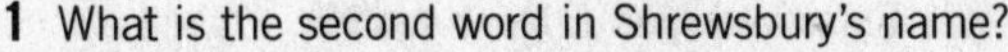

1 What is the second word in Shrewsbury's name?
2 Which country did Chris Woods play for?
3 What colour are Norwich's home shorts?
4 Where do Birmingham play home games?
5 Which Dougie was Crystal Palace's top scorer in 1995–96?
6 Which Paul of Dundee Utd was Scottish Footballer of the Year in 1982?
7 Which country did Robert Rivelino play for?
8 With which club did Jason McAteer make his League debut?
9 Which club did Gary McAllister leave to join Leeds?
10 Which club was Matthew Harding connected with?
11 What is Newcastle United's nickname?
12 Which country did Ronnie Whelan play for?
13 The Chimes were traditionally heard at which club?
14 Which team has Michael Parkinson supported since he was a boy?
15 Adidas awarded what type of Boot to Europe's leading scorer?
16 Which team does John Parrott support?
17 Which Peter of Nottingham Forest was PFA Player of the Year in 1978?
18 Which country did Craig Forrest play for?
19 Gazza recorded "Fog On The Tyne" with which group?
20 Which John was Wimbledon's top league scorer in 1989–90?

Answers

Pot Luck 36 (see Quiz 71)

1 Wolves. **2** Australia. **3** Norwich City. **4** City. **5** The Republic of Ireland. **6** Baggio. **7** Norway. **8** Arsenal. **9** Newcastle Utd. **10** Booth. **11** Red. **12** The Canaries. **13** Rod Stewart. **14** Manchester Utd. **15** Jennings. **16** Tottenham Hotspur. **17** Argentina. **18** Sheffield Wednesday. **19** Manchester City. **20** Aberdeen.

Quiz 70 **League Cup**

LEVEL 1

Answers – see page 82

1 Charlie Nicholas scored two goals in a Final for which English team?

2 Which was established first, The Football League Cup or the Scottish League Cup?

3 Which Kenny played in six finals between 1978 and 1987 in England?

4 Which manager took Sheffield Wednesday to 1991 success against his former club Manchester Utd?

5 Which pools firm sponsored the Cup from 1986–90?

6 Clive Allen netted 12 times in the 1986–87 competition, for which club?

7 Atkinson and Saunders were on target in a Final for which club?

8 Third Division Swindon caused a 60s shock by beating which team in the Final?

9 Jason McAteer was a losing finalist in 1995 with which team?

10 Dodds and Shearer were on target for which Scottish team?

11 Which drink's name was added to the trophy's name in the 1990s?

12 Howard Wilkinson was manager of which 1990s beaten finalists?

13 Marsh, Morgan and Lazarus were in which winning Third Division team?

14 Which Rovers had their first ever triumph in Scotland in 1995?

15 Which venue was used for English Finals in the 1980s?

16 Which team played in three out of four finals from 1989 to 1992?

17 York sensationally knocked out which giants in 1995–96?

18 Which club has won the Scottish League Cup most times?

19 John Sheridan got a winners' medal with which Yorkshire club?

20 Who was Nottingham Forest boss for the triumphs in the 1980s?

Answers

Managers (see Quiz 72)

1 Ray Harford. **2** Graham Taylor. **3** Leeds Utd. **4** Birmingham City. **5** Dave Bassett. **6** Jim Smith. **7** Everton. **8** Alan Ball. **9** Tottenham Hotspur. **10** Walker. **11** Aston Villa. **12** Celtic. **13** Graeme Souness. **14** Coventry City. **15** Bruce Rioch. **16** Frank Clark. **17** Sir Matt Busby. **18** Arsenal. **19** Chapman. **20** Coventry City.

Quiz 71 **Pot Luck 36**

LEVEL 1

Answers – see page 79

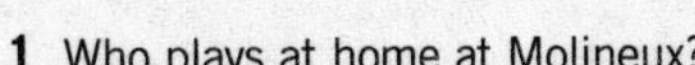

1. Who plays at home at Molineux?
2. Which country does Mark Bosnich come from?
3. Walker and O'Neill have both managed which club?
4. What is the second word in Hull's name?
5. Which country has Steve Staunton played for?
6. Which Roberto was European Footballer of the Year in 1993?
7. Which country do Rosenborg come from?
8. With which club did David O'Leary make his league debut?
9. Which club did Dave Beasant join on leaving Wimbledon?
10. Which Scott was Aberdeen's joint top League scorer in 1995–96?
11. What colour are Manchester Utd's home shirts?
12. What is Norwich's nickname?
13. Who sang with the Scottish squad in the Euro 96 record?
14. Which team does Terry Christian support?
15. Which Pat of Tottenham Hotspur won the Footballer of the Year award in 1973?
16. Sedgley and Howells were teammates at which club?
17. Which country did Daniel Passarella play for?
18. Regi Blinker first played in England for which club?
19. In 1996 Phil Neal resigned as caretaker manager of which club?
20. Which club sold Steve Archibald to Tottenham Hotspur?

Answers

Pot Luck 35 (see Quiz 69)

1 Town. **2** England. **3** Green. **4** St Andrew's. **5** Freedman. **6** Sturrock. **7** Brazil. **8** Bolton. **9** Leicester City. **10** Chelsea. **11** The Magpies. **12** The Republic of Ireland. **13** Portsmouth. **14** Barnsley. **15** Golden. **16** Everton. **17** Shilton. **18** Canada. **19** Lindisfarne. **20** Fashanu.

Quiz 72 **Managers**

LEVEL 1

Answers – see page 80

1 Who followed Dalglish as Blackburn manager?

2 Who has managed Watford and England?

3 Which club side did Don Revie manage in the 60s and early 70s?

4 In 1996 Trevor Francis became manager of which Midlands club?

5 Which manager's CV reads Wimbledon, Watford, Sheffield Utd and Crystal Palace?

6 Who is known as "The Bald Eagle"?

7 Which club did Joe Royle steer to an FA Cup Final victory over Manchester Utd?

8 Who was in charge of Manchester City when they were relegated in 1996?

9 Which club did Terry Venables manage before taking over the England team?

10 Which Mike has twice become manager of Norwich?

11 Brian Little followed Ron Atkinson at which club?

12 Which Scottish side was managed by Liam Brady?

13 Who returned from Turkey to become manager of Southampton?

14 Which club links Bobby Gould, Phil Neal and Ron Atkinson as managers?

15 Who took Bolton to the Premiership then left for Arsenal?

16 Who took over from Brian Clough at Nottingham Forest?

17 The 50s and 60s at Old Trafford were the years of which manager?

18 Which club made a statement saying that, "Mr Graham did not act in the best interests of the club"?

19 Which Herbert steered Arsenal to two Championships in the 1930s?

20 Terry Butcher took over at which Midlands team in 1990?

Answers

League Cup (see Quiz 70)

1 Arsenal. **2** Scottish League Cup. **3** Dalglish. **4** Ron Atkinson. **5** Littlewoods. **6** Tottenham Hotspur. **7** Aston Villa. **8** Arsenal. **9** Bolton. **10** Aberdeen. **11** Coca-Cola. **12** Leeds Utd. **13** QPR. **14** Raith. **15** Wembley. **16** Nottingham Forest. **17** Manchester Utd. **18** Rangers. **19** Sheffield Wednesday. **20** Brian Clough.

Quiz 73 **Pot Luck 37**

LEVEL 1

Answers – see page 85

1 What is the second word in Southend's name?
2 Which country has Gordon Durie played for?
3 What is the main colour of Nottingham Forest's home shirts?
4 Who plays home games at Blundell Park?
5 Which tall striker was Coventry's top scorer in 1995–96?
6 Karel Poborsky plays for which national team?
7 Campbell and Keown were together at which club?
8 With which club did Gary Pallister make his League debut?
9 Which club did Eddie McGoldrick leave to join Arsenal?
10 Which Brian of Rangers was Scottish Footballer of the Year in 1995?
11 What is Notts County's nickname?
12 Which country did Kevin Moran play for?
13 Which team did Alf Garnett support?
14 Which striker Frank played over 200 games for both Arsenal and Manchester Utd?
15 Chris Waddle scored an FA Cup Final goal for which club in the 1990s?
16 Sasa Curcic first played in England for which club?
17 Which Andy of Villa was PFA Player of the Year in 1977?
18 What is the first name of Matteo who first played for Liverpool?
19 Which striker Chris became Tottenham Hotspur's record signing in June 1995?
20 Eric Gates played for which East Anglian club?

Answers

Pot Luck 38 (see Quiz 75)

1 Sheffield Wednesday. **2** Van Basten. **3** West Ham Utd. **4** Town. **5** Norway. **6** Lineker. **7** Portugal. **8** Nottingham Forest. **9** Sheffield Wednesday. **10** Dicks. **11** White. **12** The Latics. **13** Whittingham. **14** France. **15** Liverpool. **16** Woods. **17** Aston Villa. **18** Red. **19** Nottingham Forest. **20** None.

Quiz 74 **The 1960s**

LEVEL 1

Answers – see page 86

1 Which country did Joe Baker move from to play in Italy?

2 What was abolished on January 9th 1960 to affect all players?

3 Who scored a record six goals in an FA Cup tie only for the game to be abandoned?

4 Which Sir Stanley was elected president of FIFA?

5 Bobby Collins moved from Everton to start a revival of which club?

6 Who was the skipper of Tottenham Hotspur's double-winning team?

7 Ray Crawford was on target for which championship winning team?

8 Which founder members of the League resigned in 1962?

9 Which Brian moved after scoring 197 goals in 213 games for Middlesbrough?

10 Chile were the host nation for the World Cup in which year?

11 Ralph Brand and Jimmy Millar were scoring goals for which Scottish side in the early 1960s?

12 Jon Sammels was starring for which London club?

13 How did John White of Tottenham Hotspur tragically die?

14 Wishing to avoid the first £100,000 player tag, who did Tottenham Hotspur buy for £99,999?

15 Who were Scottish First Division champions for five years in a row?

16 Which country were hosts for the 1966 World Cup tournament?

17 Early 60s stars Ronnie Clayton and Bryan Douglas were with which Lancashire club?

18 England internationals from which club were revealed to have made money by betting on their club to lose?

19 Roger Hunt was scoring goals for which club?

20 Bell, Lee and Summerbee were sparkling for which team?

Answers

Red Card (see Quiz 76)

1 Graeme Souness. **2** Argentina. **3** Flitcroft. **4** Liverpool. **5** Never. **6** Roy Keane. **7** Hartson. **8** Two. 9 Russia. **10** Newcastle Utd. **11** Arsenal. **12** Holland. **13** Mullery. **14** Peter Shilton. **15** 1960s. **16** Eric Cantona. **17** Wimbledon. **18** Paul Ince. **19** Babb. **20** Bergkamp.

Quiz 75 **Pot Luck 38**

Answers – see page 83

1. Which club play at home at Hillsborough?
2. Which Marco was European Footballer of the Year in 1992?
3. Bonds and Redknapp have both managed which club?
4. What is the second word in Ipswich's name?
5. Which country has Henning Berg played for?
6. Which Gary of Everton won the Footballer of the Year award in 1986?
7. Which country do Benfica come from?
8. With which club did Des Walker make his league debut?
9. Which club did Steve Nicol join on leaving Notts County?
10. Which Julian was West Ham's joint top League scorer in 1995–96?
11. What colour are Manchester City's home shorts?
12. What is Oldham's nickname?
13. Which Guy has hit goals for Portsmouth, Aston Villa and Sheffield Wednesday?
14. Which country does Marcel Desailly play for?
15. Which team does veteran DJ John Peel support?
16. Which Chris was in goal as Sheffield Wednesday lost the 1993 FA Cup Final?
17. Teale and Townsend were together at which club?
18. What is the colour of Hungary's home shirts?
19. Alf Inge Haaland first played in England for which club?
20. How many games did Germany lose in Euro 96?

Answers

Pot Luck 37 (see Quiz 73)

1 United. **2** Scotland. **3** Red. **4** Grimsby Town. **5** Dion Dublin. **6** Czech Republic. **7** Arsenal. **8** Middlesbrough. **9** Crystal Palace. **10** Laudrup. **11** The Magpies. **12** The Republic of Ireland. **13** West Ham Utd. **14** Stapleton. **15** Sheffield Wednesday. **16** Bolton Wanderers. **17** Gray. **18** Dominic. **19** Armstrong. **20** Ipswich Town.

Quiz 76 **Red Card**

LEVEL 1

Answers – see page 84

1 Which Rangers player/manager was sent off on his 1986 club debut?

2 In 1966, who was Rattin playing for when sent off at Wembley?

3 In 1996, which Gary was sent off in the third minute of his home Blackburn debut?

4 Kevin Keegan was sent off in the Charity Shield playing for which team?

5 How many times was Gary Lineker sent off in his career?

6 Which Manchester Utd player was dismissed in the 1995 FA Cup semi-final against Crystal Palace?

7 Which Arsenal striker John celebrated New Year by getting sent off on Jan 1, 1997 after appearing as a substitute?

8 How many of the Argentinian side were sent off in the 1990 World Cup Final?

9 In which country was Colin Hendry sent off in a European Cup game?

10 With which league club was David Batty first sent off?

11 Lee Dixon was with which club when ordered off in an FA Cup semi-final against Tottenham Hotspur?

12 In the 1990 World Cup final stages who were Germany's opponents when a man from each side was sent off in a notorious spitting incident?

13 Which Alan became the first England player to be sent off?

14 Which goalkeeper was sent off for the first time in his career in his 971st league game?

15 In which decade was the violent Chile v Italy World Cup "battle"?

16 Which Manchester Utd player was sent off twice in four days in 1994?

17 Vinnie Jones was first sent off while playing for which league club?

18 Which Englishman was sent off four times with Internazionale in 1996?

19 Which Phil was Liverpool's only player sent off in the 1994–95 season?

20 Which Dennis got his first red card in England in January 1997?

Answers

The 1960s (see Quiz 74)

1 Scotland. **2** Maximum wage. **3** Denis Law. **4** Rous. **5** Leeds Utd. **6** Danny Blanchflower. **7** Ipswich Town. **8** Accrington Stanley. **9** Clough. **10** 1962. **11** Rangers. **12** Arsenal. **13** Struck by lightning. **14** Jimmy Greaves. **15** Celtic. **16** England. **17** Blackburn Rovers. **18** Sheffield Wednesday. **19** Liverpool. **20** Manchester City.

Quiz 77 **Pot Luck 39**

LEVEL 1

Answers – see page 89

1 What is the second word in Stockport's name?
2 Which country has Florin Raducioiu played for?
3 What colour goes with blue on Oldham's home shirts?
4 Who plays home games at Vicarage Road?
5 Who won the FA Cup in 1970?
6 Which Charlie of Celtic was Scottish Footballer of the Year in 1983?
7 Paul Parker won the championship with which club?
8 With which club did Nigel Spink make his League debut?
9 Which club did Alan Smith leave to join Arsenal?
10 Ille Dumitrescu first played in England for which club?
11 Which team is known as "The Posh"?
12 Which country has Pat Bonner played for?
13 Which Franz was European Footballer of the Year in 1976?
14 Martin Edwards succeeded his father at which club?
15 Cascarino and Wise were together at which club?
16 Which country has Paulo Maldini played for?
17 Which Pat of Tottenham Hotspur was PFA Player of the Year in 1976?
18 Van Hooijdonk and Cadete were together at which Scottish club?
19 Jan Molby first became a player/manager at which club?
20 At which club did Stone and Woan play in the same side?

Answers

Pot Luck 40 (see Quiz 79)

1 Middlesbrough. **2** Australia. **3** Liverpool. **4** Orient. **5** Scotland. **6** Bremner. **7** Spain. **8** Blackpool. **9** Everton. **10** Payton. **11** Blue. **12** The Pilgrims. **13** Papin. **14** Everton. **15** Chelsea. **16** Red. **17** Brazil. **18** Aston Villa. **19** Belfast. **20** Keith Gillespie.

Quiz 78 **30 Somethings**

LEVEL 1

Answers – see page 90

1 Which Colin starred in defence for Scotland in Euro 96?

2 Which veteran goalkeeper played his 1,000th League game in December 1996?

3 Which Arsenal striker notched League goal number 200 in 1997?

4 Which Ray was player/manager of QPR in his thirties?

5 Which 34-year old fullback played for England in Euro 96?

6 Which Liverpool scoring legend moved to Leeds in 1996?

7 Which Peter returned to Newcastle to complete a century of goals for the club?

8 Which Italian moved to Chelsea in May 1996?

9 Which veteran Liverpool defender was recalled to the England side in 1996, four years after his last international selection?

10 Which Bryan was Middlesbrough player/manager in his thirties?

11 Which veteran Everton goalkeeper won a 1995 FA Cup winner's medal?

12 Who started a new career with Derby at the age of 36?

13 Which 40-plus goalkeeper John turned out for Manchester City in 1994?

14 Which Brian was in Premiership-winning Manchester Utd sides in his thirties?

15 Who was Tottenham Hotspur's 38-year old keeper in the 1987 FA Cup Final?

16 Leslie Compton became the oldest player to make an international debut for which country?

17 Which Israeli international Ronny moved to Tottenham Hotspur after his thirtieth birthday?

18 Which midfielder Paul began his third spell at Sunderland in his 30s?

19 Who did veteran Tommy Hutchison play for in an FA Cup Final?

20 Who was the 30-plus goalkeeper for Northern Ireland during the 1986 World Cup final games?

Answers

Club Colours (see Quiz 80)

1 Royal Blue. **2** Arsenal. **3** Claret. **4** Blue. **5** White. **6** Red and blue. **7** Manchester Utd. **8** Liverpool, Manchester Utd. **9** White. **10** Blackpool. **11** White. **12** White. **13** White. **14** Leeds Utd. **15** Black. **16** Red. **17** Black and white. **18** White. **19** Internazionale. **20** Orange.

Quiz 79 **Pot Luck 40**

Answers – see page 87

1 Who plays at home at the Riverside Stadium?
2 Which country does Robbie Slater come from?
3 Dalglish, Souness and Evans have all managed which club?
4 What is the second word in Leyton's name?
5 Which country has Kevin Gallacher played for?
6 Which Billy of Leeds won the Footballer of the Year award in 1970?
7 Which country do Valencia come from?
8 With which seaside club did Alan Ball make his league debut?
9 Which club did Nick Barmby join on leaving Middlesbrough?
10 Which Andy was Barnsley's top league scorer in 1995–96?
11 What colour are Chelsea's home shirts?
12 What is Plymouth's nickname?
13 Which Jean-Pierre was European Footballer of the Year 1991?
14 Ablett and Hinchcliffe were together at which FA Cup-winning club?
15 Which team does Sebastian Coe support?
16 What colour are Wales's home shorts?
17 Which country did Jairzinho play for?
18 Charles and Wright were full-backs together at which club?
19 In which city are Glentoran based?
20 Which Newcastle winger was in the tabloids in 1996 for running up gambling debts of around £60,000?

Answers

Pot Luck 39 (see Quiz 77)

1 County. **2** Romania. **3** Red. **4** Watford. **5** Chelsea. **6** Nicholas. **7** Manchester Utd. **8** Aston Villa. **9** Leicester City. **10** Tottenham Hotspur. **11** Peterborough Utd. **12** The Republic of Ireland. **13** Beckenbauer. **14** Manchester Utd. **15** Chelsea. **16** Italy. **17** Jennings. **18** Celtic. **19** Swansea City. **20** Nottingham Forest.

Quiz 80 **Club Colours**

LEVEL 1 

Answers – see page 88

1 What colour are Everton's home shirts?

2 Which London club wear red home shirts with white sleeves?

3 What is the main colour of Aston Villa's home shirts?

4 What colour are Birmingham City's home shirts?

5 What colour along with blue is a major part of Blackburn's strip?

6 What colours are Barcelona's home shirts?

7 In the 1990s, which team changed their home shirts at half time in an away game at Southampton?

8 Which two teams who normally play in red met in the 1996 FA Cup Final?

9 What is the main colour of Ajax's home shirts?

10 Which north-west club wears tangerine home shirts?

11 What colour are Bolton's home shirts?

12 What colour are Real Madrid's home shirts?

13 What colour are Celtic's home shorts?

14 At which English club did Eric Cantona wear white as first choice kit?

15 What colour goes with red on AC Milan's home shirts?

16 What colour are Aberdeen's home shirts?

17 What colour are the stripes on Juventus's home shirts?

18 What colour are Rangers' home shorts?

19 Paul Ince wore a blue and black striped shirt with which club?

20 What colour are the home shirts of Dundee Utd?

Answers

Thirty Somethings (see Quiz 78)

1 Hendry. **2** Peter Shilton. **3** Ian Wright. **4** Wilkins. **5** Stuart Pearce. **6** Ian Rush. **7** Beardsley. **8** Gianluca Vialli. **9** Mark Wright. **10** Robson. **11** Neville Southall. **12** Paul McGrath. **13** Burridge. **14** McClair. **15** Ray Clemence. **16** England. **17** Rosenthal. **18** Bracewell. **19** Manchester City. **20** Pat Jennings.

Quiz 81 **Pot Luck 41**

Answers – see page 93

1 What is the second word in Stoke's name?
2 Which country did Emlyn Hughes play for?
3 What is the colour along with white and black on Plymouth's home shirts?
4 Who plays home games at Tannadice Park?
5 Which Carl was Charlton's top scorer in 1995–96?
6 Zeljko Kalac first played in England for which club?
7 Which Paul of Rangers was Scottish Footballer of the Year in 1996?
8 With which club did Dave Beasant make his League debut?
9 Which club did Robert Lee leave to join Newcastle?
10 Batty and McAllister were together at which club?
11 What is Portsmouth's nickname?
12 Which country has Colin Hendry played for?
13 Which Gerd of Bayern was European Footballer of the Year in 1970?
14 Darren Anderton played in an FA Cup semi-final for which Second Division club?
15 How many times did Arsenal win the championship with George Graham as boss?
16 What colour are Sweden's home shirts?
17 Which Colin was PFA Player of the Year in 1975?
18 Steven and Stevens were together at which Scottish club?
19 Which Gary played in every game when Leeds Utd were champions in 1992?
20 Which country did John Harkes play for?

Answers

Pot Luck 42 (see Quiz 83)

1 Manchester City. **2** Best. **3** Tottenham Hotspur. **4** City. **5** England. **6** Red. **7** Switzerland. **8** Tottenham Hotspur. **9** Chelsea. **10** Nogan. **11** White. **12** The Valiants. **13** Nottingham Forest. **14** Fleck. **15** Ruud Gullit. **16** Sheffield Wednesday. **17** Jürgen Klinsmann. **18** Port Vale. **19** Shaka Hislop. **20** Sunderland.

Quiz 82 **Keepers**

LEVEL 1

Answers – see page 94

1 Which country did Rene Higuita play for?

2 Who was Manchester Utd's goalkeeper when they won the title in 1993 and 1994?

3 Which Coventry goalkeeper played in the 1987 FA Cup Final?

4 With which London club did Bob Wilson make his name?

5 Kevin Pressman and Chris Woods have both played for which club?

6 Which Dave has played for Wimbledon, Newcastle, Chelsea and Southampton?

7 Who played in his 1,000th game while with Leyton Orient in 1996?

8 Which Bobby was in goal when Blackburn went up to the top flight in the 1990s?

9 Who was Scotland's No 1 in Euro 96?

10 With which London club did Ian Walker make his League debut?

11 Which country did Frank Swift play for?

12 Peter Bonetti was a great servant for which London club?

13 Who played at international level with club colleague Tony Adams in his defence?

14 For which club did Bryan Gunn play 350 plus games?

15 Which country did Bruce Grobbelaar play for?

16 Which Tottenham Hotspur goalkeeper scored a freak goal in a Charity Shield game against Manchester Utd?

17 Which goalkeeper Andoni holds a record number of caps for Spain?

18 Branagan and Ward kept goal as which team went out of the Premiership in 1996?

19 Which country did Tony Waiters play for?

20 Which 1970s Partick goalkeeper Alan landed over 50 caps for his country?

Answers

UEFA Cup (see Quiz 84)

1 Bayern Munich. **2** 1960s. **3** Leeds Utd. **4** Yes. **5** Two legs. **6** London. **7** Arsenal. **8** False. **9** Wolves. **10** Jack Charlton. **11** John Wark. **12** Bobby Robson. **13** Bayern Munich. **14** Norwich City. **15** David Fairclough. **16** Dundee United. **17** Derby County. **18** Wales. **19** True. **20** Juventus.

Quiz 83 **Pot Luck 42**

Answers – see page 91

1 Who plays at home at Maine Road?

2 Which George of Manchester Utd won the Footballer of the Year award in 1968?

3 Venables and Ardiles have both managed which club?

4 What is the second word in Lincoln's name?

5 Which country has John Salako played for?

6 What colour are Norway's home shirts?

7 Which country do Grasshopper Zurich come from?

8 With which club did Glenn Hoddle make his league debut?

9 Which club did Gianluca Vialli join on leaving Juventus?

10 Which Kurt was Burnley's top League scorer in 1995–96?

11 What colour are Nottingham Forest's home shorts?

12 What is Port Vale's nickname?

13 Chettle and Phillips were together at which club?

14 Which striker Robert returned to Norwich City in 1995 after an unhappy spell with Chelsea?

15 Which Dutch player with AC Milan was European Footballer of the Year in 1987?

16 Which team does politician Roy Hattersley support?

17 Which player said in 1995, "I would not have wanted to leave 'Spurs if Sugar had shown more ambition"?

18 John Rudge had 15 years as manager of which club?

19 Which goalkeeper cost Newcastle £1.5 million in August 1995?

20 Ord and Bracewell were together at which club?

Answers

Pot Luck 41 (see Quiz 81)

1 City. **2** England. **3** Green. **4** Dundee Utd. **5** Leaburn. **6** Leicester City. **7** Gascoigne. **8** Wimbledon. **9** Charlton Athletic. **10** Leeds Utd. **11** Pompey. **12** Scotland. **13** Müller. **14** Portsmouth. **15** Twice. **16** Yellow. **17** Todd. **18** Rangers. **19** McAllister. **20** USA.

Quiz 84 **UEFA Cup**

LEVEL 1

Answers – see page 92

1 Which German side won the UEFA Cup in 1996?

2 In which decade did the competition become an annual event?

3 Which Yorkshire side were in the Final in 1967, 1968 and 1971?

4 Have Watford ever taken part in the competition?

5 In the 1990s, is the Final one game or played over two legs?

6 In the first Final, England were represented not by a club but by which city?

7 Frank McLintock played for which London winners?

8 True or false – Manchester Utd have never taken part in the tournament?

9 When Tottenham Hotspur won the Cup in 1972, which English club did they play in the Final?

10 Which player later to manage the Republic of Ireland won a winners' medal in 1971?

11 Which Ipswich player created a record by scoring 14 goals in the tournament in 1980–81?

12 Who was the Ipswich manager at the time?

13 Which team knocked out Nottingham Forest in the 1996 quarter-finals?

14 Jeremy Goss was on target in 1993–94 for which club?

15 Who was Liverpool's scoring "Supersub" in the 1976 Final v Bruges?

16 Name the first Scottish team to have contested a Final.

17 Which club was Kevin Hector playing for when he scored five goals in a 12–0 defeat of Finn Harps?

18 Which country did Borough United represent in the tournament?

19 True or false – Birmingham City were the first English League club to reach a Final of the competition?

20 Vialli was on the mark in the 1995 Final for which club?

Answers

Keepers (see Quiz 82)

1 Colombia. **2** Peter Schmeichel. **3** Ogrizovic. **4** Arsenal. **5** Sheffield Wednesday. **6** Beasant. **7** Peter Shilton. **8** Mimms. **9** Andy Goram. **10** Tottenham Hotspur. **11** England. **12** Chelsea. **13** David Seaman. 14 Norwich City. **15** Zimbabwe. **16** Pat Jennings. **17** Zubizarreta. **18** Bolton Wanderers. **19** England. **20** Rough.

Quiz 85 **Pot Luck 43**

LEVEL 1

Answers – see page 97

1 Shipperley and Magilton were together at which club?
2 Which country did Garrincha play for?
3 What is the main colour of Portsmouth's home shirts?
4 The Manor Ground has been the home of which club?
5 Which John was Bolton's top scorer in 1995–96?
6 Striker Andy Booth moved from Huddersfield to which club in 1996?
7 Which Willie of Aberdeen was Scottish Footballer of the Year in 1984?
8 With which club did Viv Anderson make his League debut?
9 Which club did Kerry Dixon leave to join Chelsea?
10 Which northern team was nicknamed "The Lillywhites"?
11 Which Lothar was European Footballer of the Year in 1990?
12 Which country has Gary Kelly played for?
13 What colour are Northern Ireland's home shorts?
14 Fox and Calderwood were together at which club?
15 In 1996, which Ian had an on/off transfer from Norwich to Ipswich?
16 Which seaside club finished bottom of Division Three in 1996 but stayed in the League?
17 Which Norman of Leeds was PFA Player of the Year in 1974?
18 Which Ron was the oldest Premiership boss in 1996?
19 Which north London team does Tom "Lofty" Watt follow?
20 Who were the first side to hit nine goals in a Premier League game?

Answers

Pot Luck 44 (see Quiz 87)

1 Luton Town. **2** True (in 1990–91). **3** Manchester City. **4** United. **5** Scotland. **6** Law. **7** Greece. **8** West Ham Utd. **9** Rangers. **10** White. **11** Yellow. **12** The Royals/Biscuitmen. **13** Blanchflower. **14** Colombia. **15** Wolves. **16** Blackburn Rovers. **17** West Ham Utd. **18** Aberdeen. **19** Green. **20** Liverpool.

Quiz 86 **Scottish Sides**

Answers – see page 98

1 Willie Miller played over 550 games for which club?

2 Which United did Ally MacLeod manage before taking over the national team?

3 Which are the only Scottish team to win the European Cup?

4 Which side as known as "The Bairns"?

5 Which League sides have the word East in their name?

6 Which goalkeeper moved from Hibernian to Rangers for £1 million in 1991?

7 What is the colour of Hearts' home shirts?

8 Who were runners-up five times in six League seasons starting in 88–89?

9 At which ground do Queens Park play?

10 Which London club sold Richard Gough to Rangers?

11 'The Terrors" is the nickname of which club?

12 Which team did Alex McLeish take to runners-up spot in 1994–95?

13 Which club did Paul Elliott play for?

14 Which Rovers are known as "The Wee Rovers"?

15 Which side won the treble in 1992–93?

16 Which club plays at Dens Park?

17 With which club did Jim Leighton begin his career?

18 David Narey played over 600 games for which club?

19 Which team is known as "The Buddies"?

20 Kilmarnock play at which Park?

Answers

The 1970s (see Quiz 88)

1 QPR. **2** USA. **3** Arsenal. **4** Nottingham Forest. **5** Liverpool. **6** Swansea City. **7** Leeds Utd. **8** Rangers. **9** Tottenham Hotspur. **10** Manchester Utd. **11** Lawrie McMenemy. **12** Aston Villa. **13** Diego Maradona. **14** West Ham Utd. **15** Bill Shankly. 16 Scotland. **17** Gray. **18** Greenwood. **19** Fulham. **20** Scotland.

Quiz 87 **Pot Luck 44**

LEVEL 1

Answers – see page 95

1 Who plays at home at Kenilworth Road?

2 Steve Bruce was once Manchester Utd's joint top League scorer. True or false?

3 Horton and Coppell have both managed which club?

4 What is the second word in Ayr's name?

5 Which country has Gordon Strachan played for?

6 Which Denis was European Footballer of the Year in 1964?

7 Which country do AEK Athens come from?

8 With which club did Paul Ince make his league debut?

9 Which club did Paul Gascoigne join on leaving Lazio?

10 Which veteran striker Steve was Hereford's top league scorer in 1995–96?

11 What colour are Norwich's home shirts?

12 What is Reading's nickname?

13 Which Danny of Tottenham Hotspur won the Footballer of the Year award in 1961?

14 Which country's fullback was shot dead after scoring an own goal in the 1994 World Cup tournament?

15 Which team does veteran rock singer Robert Plant support?

16 Warhurst and Wilcox were together at which club?

17 Alvin Martin made 450 plus appearances for which club?

18 Which was the first Scottish side that Dean Windass played for?

19 What colour is the Nigerian national kit?

20 The names Crown and Carlsberg have appeared on the red home shirts of which club?

Answers

Pot Luck 43 (see Quiz 85)

1 Southampton. **2** Brazil. **3** Blue. **4** Oxford Utd. **5** McGinlay. **6** Sheffield Wednesday. **7** Miller. **8** Nottingham Forest. **9** Reading. **10** Preston North End. **11** Matthäus. **12** The Republic of Ireland. **13** White. **14** Tottenham Hotspur. **15** Crook. **16** Torquay Utd. **17** Hunter. **18** Atkinson. **19** Arsenal. **20** Manchester Utd.

Quiz 88 **The 1970s**

Answers – see page 96

1 Stan Bowles was a star at which London club?

2 Which country attracted Pele and Bobby Moore to end their careers?

3 Who did Ipswich Town beat to win the FA Cup for the first time?

4 Dave Needham and Kenny Burns were together at which club?

5 Which club did Steve Heighway play for?

6 Which Welsh club did John Toshack join as player/manager?

7 Jack Charlton played his 600th game for which club?

8 In Barcelona the first European trophy triumph of which Scottish club was marred by crowd disturbances?

9 Which team signed Villa and Ardiles?

10 Lou Macari and George Graham joined which club?

11 Who was the boss who led Southampton to FA Cup glory?

12 Brian Little made his name playing for which club?

13 Which Argentinian was dubbed "the new Pele"?

14 Paul Allen became the youngest FA Cup Final player with which club?

15 Which manager bowed out after Liverpool's 1974 FA Cup Final triumph?

16 Who were you supporting if you were part of Ally's Army?

17 Which striker Andy went from Aston Villa to Wolves in a £1.5 million transfer?

18 Which Ron took over as England boss in the late 70s?

19 Bobby Moore played for which team against West Ham Utd in an FA Cup Final?

20 Which country did Don Masson play for?

Answers

Scottish Sides (see Quiz 86)

1 Aberdeen. **2** Ayr. **3** Celtic. **4** Falkirk. **5** Fife, Stirling. **6** Andy Goram. **7** Maroon. **8** Aberdeen. **9** Hampden Park. **10** Tottenham Hotspur. **11** Dundee Utd. **12** Motherwell. **13** Celtic. **14** Albion. **15** Rangers. **16** Dundee. **17** Aberdeen. **18** Dundee Utd. **19** St Mirren. **20** Rugby.

Quiz 89 **Pot Luck 45**

LEVEL 1

Answers – see page 101

1 What is the second word in Swindon's name?
2 Which country did Kenny Sansom play for?
3 What is the main colour of Port Vale's home shirts?
4 Who plays at home at Valley Parade?
5 Which Alan was Blackburn's top scorer in 1995–96?
6 Which Republic of Ireland player was known as "Chippy"?
7 Which Sandy of Hearts was Scottish Footballer of the Year in 1986?
8 With which club did Alan Shearer make his League debut?
9 Which club did Denis Irwin leave to join Manchester Utd?
10 What is Rochdale's nickname?
11 What colour are Italy's home shorts?
12 Which country has Tommy Coyne played for?
13 Sellars and Ferdinand were together at which club?
14 In which country is the club Penarol?
15 Who resigned as Liverpool boss on February 22nd 1991?
16 Which Dutchman was European Footballer of the Year three times in the 1970s?
17 Which Alan became Fotball League secretary in the late 1950s?
18 Defenders Taggart and Bergsson were together at which club?
19 Who wrote the book titled *It's A Funny Old Life*?
20 At which club were Flitcroft and Lomas in the same side?

Answers

Pot Luck 46 (see Quiz 91)

1 Swansea City. **2** Red. **3** Leicester City. **4** Rangers. **5** The Republic of Ireland. **6** Charlton. **7** Germany. **8** Leicester City. **9** Middlesbrough. **10** Navy blue. **11** Rotherham. **12** Charlton. **13** Leeds Utd. **14** Italy. **15** Leeds Utd. **16** Derby County. **17** Bobby Robson. **18** Reading. **19** Brazil. **20** Port Vale.

Quiz 90 **Golden Goals**

LEVEL 1

Answers – see page 102

1 Who scored for England in the 1990 World Cup semi-final?

2 A rare John Jensen goal in the 1992 European Championship Final helped beat which team?

3 Who is Rangers' all-time leading goal grabber?

4 In 1992–93 which Guy hit a record 42 goals for Portsmouth?

5 Who scored a goal for the "They think it's all over" commentary?

6 Mark Hughes scored twice in a European Cup Winners' Cup Final for which team?

7 Which two England players bagged a brace against Holland in Euro 96?

8 Basil Boli hit a European Cup Final winner for which French club?

9 Which Andy was the first man to hit five goals in a Premier League game?

10 Ian Porterfield scored an FA Cup winner for which club?

11 Which Ian set a post-war scoring record of FA Cup goals?

12 Nayim scored a last-minute European Cup Winners' Cup Final goal aginst which Arsenal goalkeeper?

13 Who was the first player to score 100 Premiership goals?

14 Ronnie Radford hit a much-televised screamer for which then non-league side as they beat Newcastle in the FA Cup?

15 Who scored an incredible 60 League goals in season 1927–28?

16 Who scored the extra time winner in the Euro 96 Final?

17 Who is Manchester Utd's all-time leading scorer?

18 Which Tony scored a screamer for Leeds v Liverpool in 1995?

19 Against which team did Gazza hit a Euro 96 Wembley wonder goal?

20 Who is Newcastle's all-time leading scorer with 178 goals?

Answers

North East Clubs (see Quiz 92)

1 Black. **2** Ayresome Park. **3** Stokoe. **4** Darlington. **5** David Batty. **6** Lawrence. **7** Hartlepool. **8** Paul Gascoigne. **9** Newcastle Utd and Liverpool. **10** McMenemy. **11** Jack Charlton. **12** Bracewell. **13** Peter Beardsley. **14** Jim Montgomery. **15** QPR. **16** Newcastle Utd. **17** Bristol City. **18** Middlesbrough. **19** Blackburn Rovers. **20** Middlesbrough.

Quiz 91 **Pot Luck 46**

LEVEL 1

Answers – see page 99

1 Who plays at home at the Vetch Field?

2 What colour are Portugal's home shirts?

3 Little, McGhee and O'Neill have all managed which club?

4 What is the second word in Berwick's name?

5 Which country has Ray Houghton played for?

6 Which Jack of Leeds won the Footballer of the Year award in 1967?

7 Which country do Fortuna Dusseldorf come from?

8 With which club did Gary Lineker make his league debut?

9 Which club did Fabrizio Ravanelli join on leaving Juventus?

10 What colour are Tottenham Hotspur's home shorts?

11 What club's nickname is The Merry Millers?

12 Which Bobby was European Footballer of the Year in 1966?

13 Palmer and Wetherall were together at which club?

14 Which country does Alessandro Del Piero play for?

15 Which team does Jeremy Paxman support?

16 Lionel Pickering pumped money into which club?

17 Which former England boss won a league title for PSV Eindhoven?

18 Quinn and Gooding were joint player/managers with which club?

19 Which country did Carlos Alberto play for?

20 Which team does ex-Take That member Robbie Williams support?

Answers

Pot Luck 45 (see Quiz 89)

1 Town. **2** England. **3** White. **4** Bradford City. **5** Shearer. **6** Liam Brady. **7** Jardine. **8** Southampton. **9** Oldham Athletic. **10** The Dale. **11** White. **12** The Republic of Ireland. **13** Newcastle Utd. **14** Uruguay. **15** Kenny Dalglish. **16** Johan Cruyff. **17** Hardaker. **18** Bolton Wanderers. **19** Jimmy Greaves. **20** Manchester City.

Quiz 92 North-East Clubs

LEVEL 1

Answers – see page 100

1 What colour are Newcastle's home shorts?

2 Which was Middlesbrough's home ground from 1903 to 1995?

3 Sunderland won the FA Cup in the 70s under which boss Bob?

4 Which club are nicknamed the Quakers?

5 When Alan Shearer moved to Newcastle he was reunited with which former teammate?

6 Which Lennie was in charge at Middlesbrough before Bryan Robson?

7 Coventry's FA Cup Final scorer Keith Houchen was manager at which North Eastern club?

8 Who left Newcastle for Tottenham Hotspur for £2 million in July 1988?

9 Keegan and McDermott were teammates at which two clubs?

10 Which Lawrie went back to manage Sunderland after success with Southampton?

11 Who managed Middlesbrough and Newcastle Utd before becoming a national manager in the 1980s?

12 Which England midfielder Paul signed three times for Sunderland?

13 Which Newcastle-born folk-hero was made an MBE in 1995?

14 Which goalkeeper holds Sunderland's league appearance record?

15 Peacock and Ferdinand both joined Newcastle from which club?

16 Which club had a ground with the Gallowgate End?

17 Which club did Newcastle sign Andy Cole from?

18 In 1995–96, which club managed only two league victories in the second half of the season?

19 An away defeat at which club is supposed to have prompted Keegan's decision to leave Newcastle in January 1997?

20 Which North-East team did the great Wilf Mannion play for?

Answers

Golden Goals (see Quiz 90)

1 Gary Lineker. **2** Germany. **3** Ally McCoist. **4** Whittingham. **5** Geoff Hurst. **6** Manchester Utd. **7** Shearer and Sheringham. **8** Marseille. **9** Cole. **10** Sunderland. **11** Rush. **12** David Seaman. **13** Alan Shearer. **14** Hereford. **15** Dixie Dean. **16** Oliver Bierhoff. **17** Bobby Charlton. **18** Yeboah. **19** Scotland. **20** Jackie Milburn.

Quiz 93 **Pot Luck 47**

LEVEL 1

Answers – see page 105

1 What is the second word in Wycombe's name?

2 Which country did Yordan Lechkov play for?

3 Along with navy blue what is the colour of Preston's home shirts?

4 Who plays at home at Gresty Road?

5 Which Dwight was Aston Villa's top scorer in 1995–96?

6 Which George was European Footballer of the Year in 1968?

7 Borrows and Burrows were fullbacks together at which club?

8 With which club did Tony Adams make his League debut?

9 Which club did David Speedie leave to join Blackburn?

10 What is Southampton's nickname?

11 Which Hamish of Dundee Utd was Scottish Footballer of the Year in 1985?

12 What colour are the Republic of Ireland's home shorts?

13 What country has Daniel Amokachi played for?

14 What was remarkable about the unfortunate collision that ended goalkeeper Chic Brodie's career?

15 Who has had "More clubs than Jack Nicklaus"?

16 Who was banned after video evidence showing a stamping incident involving John Spencer in 1995?

17 Fairclough and Stubbs were together at which club?

18 Paulo Futre joined West Ham from which club?

19 Which position did Dai Davies play?

20 Who was in charge of Bolton when they were relegated in 1996?

Answers

Pot Luck 48 (see Quiz 95)

1 Rangers. **2** Black. **3** Crystal Palace. **4** City. **5** The Republic of Ireland. **6** Howard Wilkinson. **7** Italy. **8** Newcastle Utd. **9** England. **10** Black. **11** Southend Utd. **12** Moore. **13** Holland. **14** Birmingham City. **15** Leyton Orient. **16** Manchester Utd. **17** Terry Venables. **18** West Ham Utd. **19** Keegan. **20** Arsenal.

Quiz 94 **Internationals**

Answers – see page 102

1 Republic of Ireland defender David O'Leary made a record number of appearances for which London club?

2 Which Welsh Mark has played for Norwich City and West Ham?

3 Which goalkeeper is Northern Ireland's most capped player?

4 Who, in October 1991, became the youngest ever Welsh international?

5 Did George Best ever play in the finals of the World Cup?

6 Which English club was Roy Keane with when he made his Republic of Ireland debut?

7 Which Welsh goalkeeper holds most caps for his country?

8 Which club links internationals Staunton, Rush and Babb?

9 What surname is shared by Northern Ireland's former midfielders Jimmy and Sammy?

10 Which country has Eric Young played for?

11 Who became the Republic of Ireland's all-time leading goalscorer in 2001?

12 Which Steve became the Republic of Ireland's most-capped player?

13 In which position did Welshman Jack Kelsey play?

14 Which John ended his career with the Republic of Ireland to concentrate on his job as Tranmere's player/manager?

15 Which great Northern Ireland player Danny became national manager between 1976 and 1979?

16 Which club was Gary Speed with when he made his international debut?

17 Which country did Gerry Armstrong represent?

18 Which Frank has headed the Republic of Ireland's all-time scoring list?

19 Who was Welsh skipper for the 7–1 hammering by Holland in 1996?

20 Which Hughes has the most cap: England's Emlyn, Scotland's John, Northern Ireland's Michael or Wales's Mark?

Answers

The 1980s (see Quiz 96)

1 Everton. **2** Diego Maradona. **3** Tottenham Hotspur. **4** It was made of artificial turf. **5** Aston Villa. **6** Alex Ferguson. **7** Rangers. **8** Manchester Utd. **9** Pat Jennings. **10** Liverpool. **11** Chris Waddle. **12** Charlton Athletic. **13** Kenny Dalglish. **14** The FA Cup. **15** Jack Charlton. **16** Hillsborough. **17** Taylor. **18** Tottenham Hotspur. **19** Woodcock. **20** Watford.

Quiz 95 **Pot Luck 48**

LEVEL 1

Answers – see page 103

1 Who plays at home at Ibrox Stadium?

2 What colour are Germany's home shorts?

3 Steve Coppell and Dave Bassett have both managed which club?

4 What is the second word in Brechin's name?

5 Which country has Niall Quinn played for?

6 Who took over as manager of Leeds Utd in 1988?

7 Which country do Napoli come from?

8 With which club did Paul Gascoigne make his League debut?

9 In The Sun headline "Yanks 2 Planks 0" who were the Planks?

10 What colour are Sunderland's home shorts?

11 Which club has the nicknames "The Shrimpers" and "The Blues"?

12 Which Bobby of West Ham Utd won the Footballer of the Year award in 1964?

13 Which country has Frank de Boer played for?

14 Millionaire David Sullivan was connected with which club?

15 Which London team does musician Julian Lloyd Webber support?

16 With which English club did Norman Whiteside begin his career?

17 Who was manager when Tottenham Hotspur won the FA Cup in 1991?

18 Moncur and Bishop were in the same team at which club?

19 Which Kevin was European Footballer of the Year in 1978?

20 Kevin Campbell first played in an FA Cup Final for which club?

Answers

Pot Luck 47 (see Quiz 93)

1 Wanderers. **2** Bulgaria. **3** White. **4** Crewe Alexandra. **5** Yorke. **6** Best. **7** Coventry City. **8** Arsenal. **9** Liverpool. **10** The Saints. **11** McAlpine. **12** White. **13** Nigeria. **14** It was with a stray dog on the pitch. **15** Tommy Docherty. **16** Julian Dicks. **17** Bolton Wanderers. **18** AC Milan. **19** Goalkeeper. **20** Colin Todd.

Quiz 96 **The 1980s**

LEVEL 1

Answers – see page 104

1 Peter Reid won the Championship as a player with which club?

2 Who reckoned the "hand of God" had come to his aid?

3 Which First Division club was directly affected by the Falklands War?

4 What was different about the new pitch laid at QPR in 1981?

5 Allan Evans and Gordon Cowans played together with which club?

6 Which manager took Aberdeen to European Cup Winners' Cup glory?

7 Which club caused a storm by signing a Catholic?

8 Gidman and Albiston were together at which club?

9 Which great goalkeeper became the first player to appear in 1,000 senior matches in England?

10 Sammy Lee won the Championship with which club?

11 Who went to Marseille for a British record fee?

12 Former European Footballer of the Year Allan Simonsen signed for which English club?

13 Who won his 100th cap for Scotland?

14 What did Coventry City win for the only time in their history?

15 Which manager took the Republic of Ireland to the European Championship in 1988?

16 An inquiry under Lord Justice Taylor was set up after the disaster at which ground?

17 Which Gordon was secretary of the PFA?

18 Micky Hazard played in an FA Cup Final for which team?

19 Which striker Tony with a bird-surname played for England?

20 Luther Blissett was at which club when he was 1983–84 First Division top scorer?

Answers

Internationals (see Quiz 94)

1 Arsenal. **2** Bowen. **3** Pat Jennings. **4** Ryan Giggs. **5** No. **6** Nottingham Forest. **7** Neville Southall. **8** Liverpool. **9** McIlroy. **10** Wales. **11** Niall Quinn. **12** Staunton. **13** Goalkeeper. **14** Aldridge. **15** Blanchflower. **16** Leeds Utd. **17** Northern Ireland. **18** Stapleton. **19** Vinnie Jones. **20** Mark.

Quiz 97 **Pot Luck 49**

Answers – see page 109

1 What is the second word in York's name?

2 Which country has Youri Djorkaeff played for?

3 What shapes are the colours on QPR's home shirts?

4 Who plays at home at Deepdale?

5 Which Ian was Arsenal's top scorer in the 1995–96 season?

6 Which Ronnie of Celtic was Scottish Footballer of the Year in 1967?

7 What is the nickname of Airdrieonians?

8 Uwe Rosler first played in England with which club?

9 Which club did Ray Wilkins join on leaving Paris St Germain?

10 In which city was George Best born?

11 What is Stockport's nickname?

12 Who plays at home at Ochilview Park?

13 Which Karl-Heinz was European Footballer of the Year in 1980?

14 What is the main colour of Denmark's home shirts?

15 Simon Barker has played 250 plus games for which club?

16 At which ground is the Holte End?

17 Which country did Faustino Asprilla play for?

18 Who was in charge of Northern Ireland from 1980 to 1993?

19 Which Frank was Manchester Utd's top League scorer in the early 1980s?

20 Ben Thatcher became the record signing for which London club?

Answers

Super Strikers (see Quiz 98)

1 Seeler. **2** Tottenham Hotspur. **3** Hungary. **4** Ajax. **5** Blokhin. **6** Jimmy Greaves. **7** Ruud Gullit. **8** Argentina. **9** Juventus. **10** France. **11** Rummenigge. **12** Barcelona. **13** Graham Taylor. **14** Roger Milla (accept Miller). **15** Austria. **16** Müller. **17** England. **18** AC Milan. **19** Geoff Hurst. **20** Kenny Dalgleish.

Quiz 98 Super Strikers

LEVEL 1

Answers – see page 107

1 Which Uwe scored 43 goals for West Germany in the 1950s, 60s and 70s?
2 Which London club did Jürgen Klinsmann play for in 1994–95?
3 Which country did Florian Albert play for?
4 With which club did Dennis Bergkamp begin his career?
5 Which Oleg was the first Russian to gain 100 caps?
6 Which London-born striker scored 44 goals in 57 games for England?
7 Who skippered Holland to the 1988 European Championship?
8 Which country did Marco Kempes play for?
9 Roberto Baggio moved from Fiorentina to which club in 1990?
10 Just Fontaine hit a record number of goals in a World Cup Finals tournament for which country?
11 Which Karl-Heinz was twice European Player of the Year?
12 Hristo Stoichkov moved to Spain in 1990 – to which club?
13 Who was England manager when Gary Lineker played his last international game?
14 Which Cameroon striker played in the 1994 World Cup at the age of 42?
15 For which country did Hans Krankl score over 30 goals?
16 Which Gerd hit the 1974 World Cup winner for West Germany?
17 Which country did Steve Bloomer play for?
18 In 1995 George Weah moved to which Italian club?
19 Who is the only player to score a World Cup Final hat-trick?
20 Which star striker took over as manager of Newcastle Utd in January 1997?

Answers

Pot Luck 50 (see Quiz 99)

1 Sheffield Utd. **2** York City. **3** Arsenal. **4** Athletic. **5** Holland. **6** Luther Blissett. **7** Portugal. **8** Brighton. **9** Wolves. **10** Blue. **11** The Swans. **12** Derby County. **13** Tottenham Hotspur. **14** Romania. **15** Oxford Utd. **16** Ajax. **17** Check. **18** Jimmy Hill. **19** Adidas. **20** Newcastle Utd.

Quiz 99 **Pot Luck 50**

LEVEL 1

Answers – see page 108

1 Who plays at home at Bramall Lane?
2 "The Minstermen" is the nickname of which club?
3 Howe and Wenger have both managed which club?
4 What is the second word in Dunfermline's name?
5 Which country did Brian Roy play for?
6 Which former Watford striker was transferred to AC Milan?
7 Which country do FC Porto come from?
8 Which team did Jimmy Case play for and later manage?
9 Which club did Mark Atkins join on leaving Blackburn?
10 What are Southend's colours?
11 What is Swansea's nickname?
12 Igor Stimac first played in England for which team?
13 At which club did Gascoigne and Lineker play together?
14 Which country did Georghe Hagi play for?
15 Which team does Desmond Morris support?
16 Which team play at the Amsterdam Arena?
17 What pattern is on the Croatian home shirts?
18 Which TV pundit is known as "The Chin"?
19 Which football boots did David Beckham endorse?
20 Which team does Cardinal Basil Hulme support?

Answers

Pot Luck 49 (see Quiz 97)

1 City. **2** France. **3** Hoops. **4** Preston North End. **5** Wright. **6** Simpson. **7** The Diamonds. **8** Manchester City. **9** Rangers. **10** Belfast. **11** County, or The Hatters. **12** Steinhousemuir. **13** Rummenigge. **14** Red. **15** QPR. **16** Villa Park. **17** Colombia. **18** Billy Bingham. **19** Stapleton. **20** Wimbledon.

The Medium Questions

This next selection of questions is getting a little more like it. For an open entry quiz then you should have a high percentage of medium level questions – don't try to break people's spirits with the hard ones, just make sure that people play to their ability.

Like all questions this level of question can be classed as either easy or impossible depending on whether you know the answer or not, and although common knowledge is used as the basis for these questions there is a sting in the tail of quite a few. Also, if you have a squad who are just there for laughs, they can more or less say goodbye to the winners' medals, but that isn't to say they will feel any worse about it.

Specialists are the people to watch out for, as those with a good knowledge of a particular subject will doubtless do well in these rounds, so a liberal sprinkling of pot-luck questions is needed to flummox them.

Quiz 1 **Pot Luck 1**

LEVEL 2

Answers – see page 113

1. In which decade did Charlton Athletic first win the FA Cup?
2. What colour are Barnsley's home socks?
3. Which was Iain Dowie's first league club?
4. Which club was Teddy Sheringham with when he was Premier League leading scorer in 1992–93?
5. What is Wrexham's ground called?
6. Which England player was born on Guernsey in 1968?
7. Cyrille Regis and Kevin Richardson were in the same team at which club?
8. Which club did Peter Shilton join on leaving Stoke City?
9. Which club's nickname is The Saddlers?
10. Julio Iglesias was reserve team goalkeeper with which club?
11. In which decade was Ron Atkinson born?
12. Who was the regular keeper in QPR's 1995–96 relegation season?
13. Which country did Terry Mancini play for?
14. Which £13 million player was involved in a 1993 car crash?
15. Bob McKinlay set a league appearance record at which club?
16. Which team were beaten 2–1 by Arsenal in the 1993 FA Cup Final?
17. Which Colin became Middlesbrough manager in 1991?
18. Craig Short joined Everton from which club?
19. What is Chris Armstrong's middle name?
20. Chairman Francis Lee flew to Marbella to sign which holidaymaker as manager for his club, Manchester City?

Answers

Pot Luck 2 (see Quiz 3)

1 Crystal Palace. **2** Red and black. **3** Middlesbrough. **4** Ruud Gullit and Mark Hughes. **5** Springfield Park. **6** Blackburn Rovers. **7** Chesterfield. **8** Sampdoria. **9** Bristol. **10** McNeill. **11** Eike Immel. **12** 1920s. **13** Manchester City. **14** Clive Allen. **15** Wolves. **16** Wales. **17** Nigel Martyn. **18** David Pleat. **19** Paul. **20** 1950s.

Quiz 2 **Keepers**

LEVEL 2

Answers – see page 114

1 Which keeper Paul played 400+ times for Ipswich?
2 Who was Arsenal's regular keeper when they won the Premiership in 1988–89?
3 What was the nickname of Peru's Ramon Quiroga?
4 With which club did Neville Southall make his League debut?
5 Kevin Carr and Martin Thomas have both played for which club?
6 Bulgarian Boris (Bobby) Mikhailov first played in England for which club?
7 Which club did Jack Kelsey play for?
8 Who did David Seaman play for before his move to QPR?
9 Bernard Lama played for which country in Euro 96?
10 Which two clubs did Gordon Banks play for?
11 Which forename is shared by ex-keepers Grew and Wallington?
12 Which keeper along with Grobbelaar was involved in the alleged 1990s match fixing charges?
13 Who left Hibernian in 1991 to become Scotland's most expensive keeper?
14 Which ex-England keeper, working as a journalist, lost his life in the Munich air disaster?
15 Hans Van Breukelen first played for which English club?
16 Which keeper Steve of the 70s, 80s and 90s shares his name with a fruit?
17 Schmeichel played all but two games for Manchester Utd in 1993–94. Who played in those two games?
18 Who was in goal for Tottenham Hotspur in the 1991 FA Cup Final?
19 Who was the first keeper to skipper a World Cup winning side?
20 Terry Gennoe and Jim Arnold played for which club?

Answers

The 1950s (see Quiz 4)

1 1950. **2** Switzerland. **3** Hungary. **4** Brian Clough. **5** Manchester Utd. **6** Juventus. **7** Derek Dooley. **8** 1959. **9** 1954–55. **10** February 1958. **11** Charles Buchan. **12** Norwich City. **13** Wolves. **14** Ferenc Puskas. **15** Manchester Utd. **16** Stanley Matthews. **17** Argentina. **18** Bert Trautmann. **19** Nat Lofthouse. **20** Polio.

Quiz 3 **Pot Luck 2**

LEVEL 2

Answers – see page 111

1 Which team were beaten 1–0 by Manchester Utd in the replayed 1990 FA Cup Final?
2 What are the two main colours on Bournemouth's home shirts?
3 What was Colin Cooper's first league club?
4 The gate for a Paul Elliott benefit game in July 1995 was boosted by which two new Chelsea signings?
5 What is Wigan Athletic's ground called?
6 Kevin Moran and Colin Hendry were in the same team at which club?
7 Who are nicknamed The Spireites?
8 Which club did David Platt leave to join Arsenal?
9 In which city was Gary Mabbutt born?
10 Which Billy became Aston Villa manager in 1986?
11 Who played every game in goal in Manchester City's 1995–96 relegation season?
12 In which decade did Cardiff win the FA Cup?
13 Eddie Large was a trainee at which club?
14 Which Tottenham Hotspur player was the First Division's leading scorer in 1986–87?
15 Derek Parkin set a league appearance record at which club?
16 Which country did Tony Norman play for?
17 Who was the regular goalkeeper in Crystal Palace's 1994–95 relegation season?
18 Luton Town chairman David Kohler demanded £300,000 compensation after which manager moved?
19 What is Teddy Sheringham's middle name?
20 In which decade was Dave Beasant born?

Answers

Pot Luck 1 (see Quiz 1)

1 1940s. **2** Red. **3** Luton Town. **4** Tottenham Hotspur. **5** Racecourse Ground. **6** Matt Le Tissier. **7** Aston Villa. **8** Nottingham Forest. **9** Walsall. **10** Real Madrid. **11** 1930s. **12** Jurgen Sommer. **13** The Republic of Ireland. **14** Gianluigi Lentini. **15** Nottingham Forest. **16** Sheffield Wednesday. **17** Todd. **18** Derby County. **19** Peter. **20** Alan Ball.

Quiz 4 **The 1950s**

Answers – see page 112

LEVEL 2

1 In what year did Portsmouth last win the Championship?

2 In which country was the 1954 World Cup Final played?

3 Which great national side included Grosics, Bozsik and Kocsis?

4 Who was the young Middlesbrough striker who made his England debut against Wales in 1959?

5 Who were the first English team to play in the European Cup?

6 Which Italian club did John Charles play for?

7 Who was the Sheffield Wednesday striker who had a leg amputated?

8 Tom Finney last played for England in which year?

9 What was the season when Chelsea won the Championship?

10 In which month was the Munich air disaster?

11 Who started the magazine Football Monthly?

12 Which Third Division giant-killers reached the 1959 FA Cup semi-final?

13 Which team did Slater and Clamp play for?

14 Which Hungarian player was nicknamed "The Galloping Major"?

15 Roger Byrne and Johnny Berry played for which team?

16 Which Blackpool and England player won the 1956 Footballer of the Year award?

17 In which country was Alfredo di Stefano born?

18 Who broke his neck in the 1956 FA Cup Final?

19 Who was nicknamed "The Lion Of Vienna"?

20 Which disease claimed the life of England defender Jeff Hall?

Answers

Keepers (see Quiz 2)

1 Cooper. **2** John Lukic. **3** El Loco. **4** Bury. **5** Newcastle Utd. **6** Reading. **7** Arsenal. **8** Birmingham City. **9** France. **10** Leicester City and Stoke City. **11** Mark. **12** Hans Segers. **13** Andy Goram. **14** Frank Swift. **15** Nottingham Forest. **16** Cherry. **17** Gary Walsh. **18** Erik Thorstvedt. **19** Gianpietro Combi (1934, Italy). **20** Blackburn Rovers.

Quiz 5 **Pot Luck 3**

Answers – see page 117

1 Which player with 430 games set a Wimbledon appearance record?
2 What colours are Brentford's home shirts?
3 What was Tony Daley's first league club?
4 To five years each way, when did Burnley first win the FA Cup?
5 Who plays at home at Plainmoor?
6 Which Phil became Bolton manager in 1985?
7 Which team are known as the Accies?
8 Which club did Richard Jobson join on leaving Oldham?
9 In which town was Nat Lofthouse born?
10 In which decade was Tommy Docherty born?
11 Which defender played in all Aston Villa's 1995–96 League games?
12 Dave Beasant and Andy Townsend were in the same team at which club?
13 Which club was Bob Latchford with when he was First Divison leading scorer in 1977–78?
14 Comedian Stan Boardman was once on the books of which club?
15 Which team were beaten 3–2 by Arsenal in the 1979 FA Cup Final?
16 Which Newcastle player was sent off in a 1996 Coca Cola quarter-final after clashing with Arsenal's Lee Dixon?
17 Francis Benali has played 200+ games for which club?
18 Which Tottenham Hotspur manager signed Jürgen Klinsmann?
19 Who was the regular goalkeeper for Ipswich in their 1994–95 relegation season?
20 Which country has Fredi Bobic played for?

Answers

Pot Luck 4 (see Quiz 7)

1 Porterfield. **2** White. **3** Crewe Alexandra. **4** 1960s. **5** Stockport County. **6** Newcastle Utd. **7** The Grecians. **8** Eintracht Frankfurt. **9** 1911. **10** Little. **11** Billy Bonds. **12** Coventry City. **13** Australia. **14** David Seaman. **15** Manchester Utd. **16** WBA. **17** Doncaster Rovers. **18** Bryan Gunn. **19** England. **20** Malcolm.

Quiz 6 **Transfer Trail**

LEVEL 2 

Answers – see page 118

1 Which striker was involved in Britain's first £300,000 transfer?

2 Who moved from Charlton in 1996 to become Britain's most expensive teenager?

3 Which club did Karel Poborsky leave to join Manchester Utd?

4 Who made 34 separate transfer requests to leave QPR?

5 Who became England's most expensive goalkeeper when he moved to Crystal Palace in 1989?

6 Which club did Alan Ball join on leaving Blackpool in 1966?

7 Which Scottish player has joined Ipswich Town on three occasions?

8 How much did Gianluca Vialli cost in a transfer fee when he joined Chelsea?

9 Which club did John Moncur leave to join West Ham United?

10 Who was the first British player to move for £1,000?

11 A £2.5 million fee set a record purchase for Notts County in 1992, when they bought which player?

12 Roberto Di Matteo joined Chelsea from which club?

13 A club record fee stood for ten years after which player left Everton for Tottenham Hotspur in the mid 80s?

14 Which club did Ray Houghton leave to join Liverpool?

15 Roberto Baggio cost £10 million when he moved to AC Milan from where?

16 Which German international joined Celtic in July 1995?

17 Fernando Nelson moved from Sporting Lisbon to which club in 1996?

18 Stefan Schwarz left Arsenal for which club?

19 Which club did Emerson leave to join Middlesbrough?

20 Which club did Mark Draper leave to join Aston Villa?

Answers

Three Lions (see Quiz 8)

1 QPR. **2** Stanley Matthews. **3** Once. **4** Gary Stevens. **5** They all scored. **6** Sweden. **7** Two. **8** Dixie Dean. **9** Viv Anderson. **10** Bobby Moore. **11** Nigeria. **12** Rangers. **13** Neil Webb. **14** Ian Wright. **15** Tom Finney. **16** David Platt. **17** Ray Wilson. **18** Emlyn. **19** 84. **20** Stuart Pearce.

Quiz 7 **Pot Luck 4**

Answers – see page 115

LEVEL 2

1 Which Ian became Chelsea manager in 1991?

2 What colour are the home shorts of both Bristol clubs?

3 What was Bruce Grobbelaar's first league club?

4 In which decade was Tony Adams born?

5 Who plays at home at Edgeley Park?

6 Which club was Malcolm Macdonald with when he was First Divison leading scorer in 1974–75?

7 What is the nickname of Exeter City?

8 Which club did Tony Yeboah leave to join Leeds?

9 To five years either way, when did Bradford City first win the FA Cup?

10 Which player and manager Brian was born in Peterlee in November 1953?

11 Who played 663 times to set West Ham Utd's League appearance record?

12 Kevin Gallacher and Paul Furlong were in the same team at which club?

13 Ned Zelic has captained which country?

14 Who was the only ever-present league player for Arsenal in 1995–96?

15 Which team was beaten 2–0 by Bolton in the 1958 FA Cup Final?

16 Bryan Robson was at which League club when he made his England debut?

17 Which club did comedian Charlie Williams play for in the 1950s?

18 Who was the regular keeper for Norwich City in their 1994–95 relegation season?

19 San Marino hit a goal in nine seconds in 1993 against which team?

20 What is Jason Wilcox's middle name?

Answers

Pot Luck 3 (see Quiz 5)

1 Alan Cork. **2** Red and white. **3** Aston Villa. **4** 1914. **5** Torquay Utd. **6** Neal. **7** Hamilton Academical. **8** Leeds Utd. **9** Bolton. **10** 1920s. **11** Alan Wright. **12** Chelsea. **13** Everton. **14** Liverpool. **15** Manchester Utd. **16** David Ginola. **17** Southampton. **18** Ossie Ardiles. **19** Craig Forrest. **20** Germany.

Quiz 8 **Three Lions**

Answers – see page 116

LEVEL 2

1 David Seaman was at which club when he made his international debut?

2 Who played his first England game in 1935 and his last in 1957?

3 How many times did Brian Little play for England?

4 In the 1986 World Cup which two England players in the squad had the same name?

5 What links the debuts of Alan Shearer, Robert Lee and Dennis Wise?

6 Gary Lineker played his last game against which country?

7 How many hat-tricks did Geoff Hurst score for England?

8 Who began his international career by scoring 2, 3, 2, 2, 3?

9 Who was the first black player to represent England in a full international?

10 Who was voted best defender in the world by journalists after the 1970 World Cup?

11 Steve McManaman first came on as a sub in November 1994, against which country?

12 Which club was Mark Walters with when he made his one and only England appearance?

13 In September 1987 who became the 1,000th England player?

14 Who hit his first England hat-trick in the 7–1 San Marino romp?

15 Who played left wing, right wing and centre forward and hit 30 goals?

16 In season 1992–93 who scored 9 goals in 10 England appearances?

17 Who was left back in the 1966 World Cup winning side?

18 Who is the most capped Hughes to play for England?

19 To five each way, how many times did Ray Wilkins play for England?

20 Which fullback has listed 'Anarchy in The UK' by the Sex Pistols as his favourite musical track?

Answers

Transfer Trail (see Quiz 6)

1 Bob Latchford. **2** Lee Bowyer. **3** Slavia Prague. **4** Stan Bowles. **5** Nigel Martyn. **6** Everton. **7** John Wark. **8** Nothing (he was out of contract). **9** Swindon Town. **10** Alf Common. **11** Craig Short. **12** Lazio. **13** Gary Lineker. **14** Oxford Utd. **15** Juventus. **16** Andreas Thom. **17** Aston Villa. **18** Fiorentina. **19** F.C. Porto. **20** Leicester City.

Quiz 9 **Pot Luck 5**

LEVEL 2

Answers – see page 121

1 In which decade did Bolton Wanderers first win the FA Cup?
2 What colour goes with amber on Cambridge United's home shirts?
3 Which was Trevor Steven's first League club?
4 Which Scottish captain was born in Motherwell in 1964?
5 Where do Shrewbury Town play at home?
6 Geoff Thomas and Eddie McGoldrick were team-mates at which club?
7 Which Brian became Leicester City manager in 1991?
8 Which club did Vinnie Jones join on leaving Chelsea?
9 What is Hereford United's nickname?
10 Which Brian of Celtic was Scottish Premier Divison leading scorer in 1983–84?
11 As a teenager Rod Stewart had trials with which club?
12 In which decade was Alan Ball born?
13 Who was the only League ever-present for Blackburn Rovers in the 1995–96 season?
14 Who holds the WBA League appearance record?
15 Which team were beaten 3–1 by Newcastle United in the 1955 FA Cup Final?
16 Which country did Alfred Strange play for?
17 Which English club did Jock Stein manage?
18 Which Scottish captain was born in Stockholm?
19 What is Ray Wilkins' middle name?
20 Who was the regular keeper for Sheffield Utd in their 1993–94 relegation season?

Answers

Pot Luck 6 (see Quiz 11)

1 1930s. **2** Blue. **3** Sunderland. **4** Neville Southall. **5** Scunthorpe Utd. **6** Southampton. **7** Shrewbury Town. **8** Brondby. **9** 1950s. **10** Manchester Utd. **11** Francis. **12** Steve Pears. **13** Phelan. **14** Luther Blissett. **15** Leeds United. **16** McDermott. **17** Vinnie Jones. **18** Mirandinha. **19** Iceland. **20** Robert.

Quiz 10 **Alan Shearer**

LEVEL 2

Answers – see page 122

1 Shearer hit the quickest goal of a game in Euro 96 against which side?
2 Against which country did Alan make his full international debut?
3 In which city was Shearer born?
4 Who was the Southampton boss when Alan made his League debut?
5 At Blackburn Rovers, Shearer said before a match he always ate chicken and what?
6 To five goals, how many League goals did Shearer score in his years at Southampton?
7 In what month was Shearer born?
8 Who was the last player before Alan to hit 30+ League goals in three consecutive seasons?
9 Which manager said that Alan was "so good it's frightening"?
10 Who were the regular numbers 7 and 11 who supplied Shearer in Blackburn Rovers's championship-winning season?
11 Who were the opponents when Shearer was first England skipper?
12 Which Southampton boss sold Shearer to Blackburn Rovers?
13 How many goals did Alan score in the season after he made his debut?
14 His last Blackburn Rovers goal was against which team?
15 Shearer's first Wembley game for Newcastle United was against who?
16 Who held the British transfer record before Shearer's '96 move?
17 How many games had he not scored in for England before Euro 96?
18 Which other England regular was controversially sent off for a foul on Shearer in December 1996?
19 Discounting shoot-outs, how many goals did Alan score in Euro 96?
20 How many Blackburn Rovers hat-tricks did he hit in 1995–96?

Answers

Scottish Sides (see Quiz 12)

1 Jimmy McGrory. **2** Dunfermline. **3** Rangers. **4** Dumbarton. **5** Hibernian. **6** Stenhousemuir. **7** Aberdeen. **8** Rangers. **9** St Johnstone. **10** Third Lanark. **11** Livingston. **12** Airdrie. **13** Ross County. **14** Motherwell. **15** No. **16** The Gable Endies. **17** Arbroath. **18** Norrie McCathie. **19** Aberdeen. **20** Stirling Albion.

Quiz 11 **Pot Luck 6**

Answers – see page 119

LEVEL 2

1. In which decade did Arsenal first win the FA Cup?
2. What is the main colour of Carlisle Utd's home shirts?
3. What was Barry Venison's first league club?
4. Who was the only league ever-present for Everton in 1995–96?
5. Who plays at home at Glanford Park?
6. Which club was Kevin Keegan with when he was First Division leading scorer in 1981–82?
7. Which team are known as The Shrews?
8. Which club did Peter Schmeichael leave to join Manchester Utd?
9. In which decade was John Aldridge born?
10. Paul Parker and Clayton Blackmore were in the same team at which club?
11. Which Trevor became QPR manager in 1988?
12. Who was the regular keeper for Middlesbrough in their 1992–93 relegation season?
13. Which Mike of Manchester Utd won his only England cap in 1989?
14. With 415 games, who holds Watford's league appearance record?
15. Which team was beaten 1–0 by Sunderland in the 1973 FA Cup Final?
16. Which midfielder Terry was born in Kirby in December 1951?
17. Who was booked within five seconds of the start of the Chelsea v Sheffield Utd 1992 FA Cup tie?
18. Which Brazilian player joined Newcastle United in 1987?
19. Which country has Gudni Berggson played for?
20. What is Darren Anderton's middle name?

Answers

Pot Luck 5 (see Quiz 9)

1 1920s. **2** Black. **3** Burnley. **4** Gary McAllister. **5** Gay Meadow. **6** Crystal Palace. **7** Little. **8** Wimbledon. **9** United. **10** McClair. **11** Brentford. **12** 1940s. **13** Henning Berg. **14** Tony Brown. **15** Manchester City. **16** England. **17** Leeds Utd. **18** Richard Gough. **19** Colin. **20** Alan Kelly.

Quiz 12 **Scottish Sides**

LEVEL 2

Answers – see page 120

1 Who has scored most League goals for Celtic?

2 Which side is known as The Pars?

3 Alex Ferguson appeared in a Scottish Cup Final for which team?

4 Which team plays at Boghead Park?

5 Beating Dunfermline in the 1991 League Cup Final gave which club its first major trophy for 19 years?

6 Which side provided a great Scottish Cup shock by knocking Aberdeen out in 1995?

7 Which club broke their own transfer record to buy Paul Bernard from Oldham Athletic in 1995?

8 Which club got a 0–4 home drubbing from Juventus in the 90s?

9 Which League team comes from Perth?

10 Which club left the League in 1967?

11 What did Meadowbank Thistle change its name to?

12 Which team made their European debut in 1992?

13 Who joined the League in 1994 along with Caledonian Thistle?

14 Tommy Coyne joined which club when he left Tranmere Rovers?

15 Were Hibs founder members of the Scottish League?

16 What is the nickname of Montrose?

17 Which team holds the British record for a League victory?

18 Which Dunfermline player tragically died in the 1995–96 season?

19 Who beat Real Madrid in the 1983 European Cup Winners' Cup Final?

20 Who were the first Scottish club to play home games on artificial turf?

Answers

Alan Shearer (see Quiz 10)

1 Germany. **2** France. **3** Newcastle. **4** Chris Nicholl. **5** Beans. **6** 23. **7** August. **8** Jimmy Greaves. **9** Terry Venables. **10** 7 Stuart Ripley, **11** Jason Wilcox. **11** Moldova. **12** Ian Branfoot. **13** None. **14** Wimbledon. **15** Manchester Utd. **16** Stan Collymore. **17** 12. **18** Tony Adams. **19** Five. **20** Five.

Quiz 13 **Pot Luck 7**

LEVEL 2

Answers – see page 125

1 In which decade was Danny Blanchflower born?

2 What colour are Charlton's home shorts?

3 Which was Scott Sellars' first League club?

4 Steve Perryman set a League appearance record at which club?

5 Who plays at home at Nene Park?

6 David White and Keith Curle were in the same team at which club?

7 Martin Peters had a short stay as manager of which club in 1981?

8 Which club did Pat Rice join on leaving Arsenal?

9 What is Swindon Town's nickname?

10 In which decade did Aston Villa first win the FA Cup?

11 In which Scottish city was Dave Mackay born?

12 Which club was John Charles with when he was First Divison leading scorer in 1956–57?

13 Chamberlain and Sutton shared the goalkeeping duties in the 1991–92 relegation season for which club?

14 Who said "That's life" when asked why a new England kit was launched soon after Christmas 1996?

15 Which Bill of Manchester Utd won his only England cap in 1954?

16 Who started his second spell as Stoke City boss in September 1994?

17 Which team were beaten 3–2 by Liverpool in the 1989 FA Cup Final?

18 Who was the only League ever-present for Nottingham Forest in 1995–96?

19 Which country did Zvonimir Boban play for in Euro 96?

20 The French player Prunier played twice in 1995–96 season for which Premiership side?

Answers

Pot Luck 8 (see Quiz 15)

1 1950s. **2** Blue and white. **3** Leicester City. **4** Brown. **5** Steve Cherry. **6** Rotherham Utd. **7** Steve McManaman. **8** Wimbledon. **9** The Gulls. **10** Oldham Athletic. **11** David James. **12** 1930s. **13** Watford. **14** Swindon Town. **15** Branfoot. **16** Gidman. **17** Leeds Utd. **18** Howard. **19** England. **20** Mark Lawrenson.

Quiz 14 **FA & SFA Cup Finals**

LEVEL 2

Answers – see page 126

1 Who scored for Nottingham Forest in the 1991 Final?

2 Paul Miller, Graham Roberts and Paul Price played for which 1980s finalists?

3 Who came off the bench to hit two goals in a Final for Crystal Palace?

4 To ten years either way, when did Manchester Utd first win the FA Cup?

5 Which club won the Scottish FA Cup three times in a row in the 1980s?

6 Who were the teams when there was a Rush on both sides in a Final?

7 Who were the first Welsh team to win the trophy?

8 At which ground was the first FA Cup Final played?

9 Who was Andy Gray playing for when he scored in an FA Cup Final?

10 Which player appeared in FA Cup Finals in the 1970s, '80s and '90s?

11 Brian Kilcline was skipper of which trophy-winning club?

12 Who was the first player to fail to score from an FA Cup Final penalty at Wembley?

13 Who was in goal for Manchester Utd in the Final replay against Crystal Palace in 1990?

14 In which decade did Liverpool first win the trophy?

15 To 5,000 either way what was the attendance of the first Scottish FA Cup Final between Queens Park and Clydesdale?

16 Who was Southampton skipper in their 1970s triumph?

17 Who were the first team to win the FA Cup three years in succession?

18 Who won the first Scottish Final decided on penalties?

19 Who hit a hat-trick in the Matthews' Final?

20 Who scored Ipswich Town's 1978 winner against Arsenal?

Answers

Famous Families (see Quiz 16)

1 Eddie and Frank. **2** Wolves. **3** Ronald and Erwin. **4** Ian and Roger. **5** 1970. **6** Bob. **7** Frank. **8** Wilkins. **9** Southampton. **10** Gary and Phil Neville. **11** Paul and Ron. **12** Roy Dwight. **13** Michael. **14** Hereford United. **15** Les. **16** Bond. **17** Kenny. **18** Charles. **19** Clarke. **20** Stockport County.

Quiz 15 **Pot Luck 8**

Answers – see page 123

LEVEL 2

1 In which decade did Blackpool first win the FA Cup?

2 What colour are the stripes on Chester's home shirts?

3 What was Peter Shilton's first League club?

4 Which Tony of WBA was First Divison leading scorer in 1970–71?

5 Who was the regular keeper for Notts County in their 1991–92 relegation season?

6 Who plays at home at the Millmoor Ground?

7 Which England attacking midfielder was born in Bootle in February 1972?

8 Which club did Andy Thorn leave to join Newcastle United?

9 What is Torquay's nickname?

10 Ian Marshall and Graeme Sharpe were in the same team at which club?

11 Steve McManaman and which other player were league ever-presents for Liverpool in 1995–96?

12 In which decade was Sir John Hall born?

13 Which team were beaten 2–0 by Everton in the 1984 FA Cup Final?

14 John Trollope set a league appearance record at which club?

15 Which Ian became Southampton manager in 1991?

16 Which John of Villa won his only England cap in 1977?

17 David Harvey played over 300 games for which club?

18 What is Nigel Clough's middle name?

19 Which country did Harry Daft play for?

20 Which ex-Liverpool star was manager at Oxford Utd for a short time in 1988?

Answers

Pot Luck 7 (see Quiz 13)

1 1920s. **2** White. **3** Leeds Utd. **4** Tottenham Hotspur. **5** Rushden and Diamonds. **6** Manchester City. **7** Sheffield Utd. **8** Watford. **9** The Robins. **10** 1880s. **11** Edinburgh. **12** Leeds Utd. **13** Luton Town. **14** Alan Shearer. **15** Foulkes. **16** Lou Macari. **17** Everton. **18** Mark Crossley. **19** Croatia. **20** Manchester Utd.

Quiz 16 **Famous Families**

Answers – see page 124

LEVEL 2

1 Which Gray brothers were in the Leeds Utd team of the 1970s?

2 Striker Gary came back to League soccer with Barnet in the 1990s while brother Steve was scoring goals for which club?

3 What were the forenames of the Dutch Koeman brothers?

4 What were the names of QPR's Morgan twins of the 60s?

5 In which year did both Charlton brothers play their last international?

6 What was the name of Bill Shankly's brother who was also a soccer manager?

7 Who is Chris Casper's footballing father?

8 Which brothers Graham and Ray played at Chelsea in the 1970s?

9 Brothers Danny, Rodney and Ray Wallace were together at which club?

10 Who were the first brothers to be at an English double winning club?

11 What were the names of the Futcher twins?

12 What is the name of Elton John's footballing uncle?

13 Which of the Laudrup brothers did not play when Denmark won the European Championship?

14 Player/manager Ian Bowyer was in the same side as son Gary at which club?

15 What is the name of Clive Allen's dad who was also a Tottenham Hotspur player?

16 If dad John is the manager and son Kevin is a defender, what is the surname?

17 What was the name of Terry Hibbitt's soccer-playing brother?

18 Which brothers Mel and John played together for Wales in the 1950s?

19 What is the surname of strikers Allan, Frank and Wayne?

20 At which club did Eric Cantona's brother Joel make his English League debut?

Answers

FA & SFA Cup Finals (see Quiz 14)

1 Stuart Pearce. **2** Tottenham Hotspur. **3** Ian Wright. **4** 1909. **5** Aberdeen. **6** Liverpool and Sunderland. **7** Cardiff City. **8** Kennington Oval. **9** Everton. **10** David O'Leary. **11** Coventry City. **12** John Aldridge. **13** Les Sealey. **14** 1960s. **15** 3,500. **16** Peter Rodrigues. **17** Blackburn Rovers. **18** Aberdeen. **19** Stanley Mortensen. **20** Roger Osborne.

Quiz 17 **Pot Luck 9**

LEVEL 2 

Answers – see page 129

1 Which Alan became Stoke City manager in 1989?
2 What colour are Chesterfield's home shirts?
3 Which was David Platt's first league club?
4 Which Scotland captain was born in Finnieston in 1950?
5 What is the name of York City's ground?
6 Which Roger was First Divison leading scorer in 1965–66?
7 Which country did Bob McNab play for?
8 Which club did Gordon Strachan join on leaving Aberdeen?
9 Which club are nicknamed The Chairboys?
10 In which decade did Blackburn Rovers first win the FA Cup?
11 Andy Sinton and Roy Wegerle were in the same team at which club?
12 Jim Montgomery set a League appearance record at which club?
13 Who was the only League ever present for Rangers in 1995–96?
14 In which city was Mark Hateley born?
15 Which Andy of Palace won his only England cap in 1991?
16 In which decade was Trevor Francis born?
17 Which team were beaten 3–2 by Coventry in the 1987 FA Cup Final?
18 Who was the regular keeper for Derby in their 1990–91 relegation season?
19 Which Glenn left as Watford manager in February 1996?
20 Which defender played 240 games for Wimbledon before going to Liverpool?

Answers

Pot Luck 10 (see Quiz 19)

1 Sheffield Wednesday. **2** Black. **3** Bristol Rovers. **4** 1970s. **5** Wycombe Wanderers. **6** Shreeves. **7** Liverpool. **8** Paris St Germain. **9** Queens Park. **10** 1912. **11** Graham le Saux. **12** Stoke City. **13** Bolton Wanderers. **14** Tony Coton. **15** Gordon Marshall. **16** Marwood. **17** Tony Norman. **18** Preston North End. **19** Maurice. **20** Les Ferdinand.

Quiz 18 **Euro Championship**

LEVEL 2

Answers – see page 130

1 Who scored the Republic of Ireland's goal against England in the 1988 Championship?
2 Who were England's scorers v Scotland in Euro 96?
3 Which country were the first ever winners of the competition?
4 In the qualifying tournament for Euro 96, which country finished top in the group that included the Republic of Ireland and N. Ireland?
5 Who beat Italy in Euro 96 to stop them from reaching the quarter-finals?
6 Which country played in the distinctive red and white chequered shirts in Euro 96?
7 Who was Scotland's number two keeper for Euro 96?
8 Which penalty did Stuart Pearce take in the semi-final shootout?
9 Who was the first outfield player in a tournament-winning side to have played English League soccer?
10 Which England player missed the Euro 96 quarter-final after collecting two yellow cards in the tournament?
11 What was the scoreline in the Scotland v Switzerland Euro 96 game?
12 How many groups were in the Finals for the 1988 tournament?
13 Which country won the 1988 tournament?
14 Who was skipper of the victorious side in 1988?
15 Which country won the Fair Play Award in Euro 96?
16 Who was England's captain for the 1992 European Championship?
17 In which group did Germany play in Euro 96?
18 Which German player became the first to score in consecutive Finals?
19 Who was the Russian keeper in the first ever Championship?
20 Who was manager of England's first team ever to enter the tournament?

Answers

Strikers (see Quiz 20)

1 Tranmere Rovers. **2** George Best. **3** Derby County. **4** Arthur Rowley. **5** Ipswich Town. **6** Ted MacDougall. **7** Jimmy Greaves. **8** Oldham Athletic. **9** Southampton. **10** Matt Le Tissier. **11** Simon Garner. **12** Jimmy Greaves. **13** Bristol City. **14** Middlesbrough. **15** 10. **16** Bolton Wanderers. **17** Jackie Milburn. **18** Hector. **19** Peterborough. **20** Faustino Asprilla.

Quiz 19 **Pot Luck 10**

Answers – see page 127

LEVEL 2

1 Carlton Palmer and Paul Warhurst were in the same team at which club?
2 What colour are Port Vale's home shorts?
3 What was John Scales' first league club?
4 In which decade was Juninho born?
5 Who plays at home at Adams Park?
6 Which Peter became Tottenham Hotspur manager in 1991?
7 Burrows, Thomas and Wright appeared in an FA Cup Final team for which club?
8 Which club did Ray Wilkins leave to join Rangers?
9 Which Scottish club is nicknamed the Spiders?
10 To five either way, in which year did Barnsley first win the FA Cup?
11 Which England player was born on Jersey in 1968?
12 Eric Skeels set a League appearance record at which club?
13 Which club was Frank Worthington with when he was First Division leading scorer in 1978–79?
14 Which keeper can list Birmingham, Watford and Sunderland among his clubs?
15 Who was the only league ever-present for Celtic in 1995–96?
16 Which Brian of Arsenal won his only England cap in 1988?
17 Who was the regular keeper for Sunderland in their 1990–91 relegation season?
18 Which team were beaten 3–2 by West Ham Utd in the 1964 FA Cup Final?
19 What is Roy Keane's middle name?
20 Which striker – who has since played for England – was loaned to Istanbul side Besiktas in 1989?

Answers

Pot Luck 9 (see Quiz 17)

1 Ball. **2** Blue. **3** Crewe Alexandra. **4** Danny McGrain. **5** Bootham Crescent. **6** Hunt. **7** England. **8** Manchester Utd. **9** Wycombe Wanderers. **10** 1880s. **11** QPR. **12** Sunderland. **13** Alan McLaren. **14** Liverpool. **15** Gray. **16** 1950s. **17** Tottenham Hotspur. **18** Peter Shilton. **19** Roeder. **20** John Scales.

Quiz 20 **Strikers**

LEVEL 2

Answers – see page 128

1 At which club did John Aldridge score his highest number of goals?

2 Which player, recognised as a winger, hit 147 goals in 411 league games for Manchester Utd?

3 Where did Dean Saunders move to when he left Oxford Utd?

4 Who holds the career record for League goals, with 434?

5 Chris Kiwomya was leading scorer with which club?

6 Who scored nine goals in a 1970s FA Cup match against Margate?

7 Who scored debut goals for Chelsea, Tottenham Hotspur, West Ham Utd and England?

8 Who was Frankie Bunn playing for when he hit a record six in a League Cup game?

9 Phil Boyer was Division One top scorer in the 1980s when he was at which club?

10 Who won the *Match Of The Day* Goal of the Season in 1995 for a 35-yard chip shot against Blackburn Rovers?

11 Who has scored most goals in a career for Blackburn Rovers?

12 Who holds Chelsea's record of 41 goals in a season?

13 Which club did John Atyeo score 314 League goals for?

14 George Camsell hit 59 goals in a season for which club?

15 Luton's Joe Payne still holds the record for goals in Football League game. How many?

16 Which club was Frank Worthington with when he was the First Divison's top scorer?

17 Who has scored most goals in a career for Newcastle Utd?

18 Which Kevin was a scoring machine for Derby County in the 1970s?

19 Who was Terry Bly playing for when he hit 52 goals in 1960–61?

20 Who was the first Colombian striker to play in English soccer?

Answers

Euro Championship (see Quiz 18)

1 Ray Houghton. **2** Shearer and Gascoigne. **3** USSR. **4** Portugal. **5** Czech Republic. **6** Croatia. **7** Jim Leighton. **8** Third. **9** Arnold Muhrén. **10** Paul Ince. **11** 1–0 to Scotland. **12** Two. **13** Holland. **14** Ruud Gullit. **15** England. **16** Gary Lineker. **17** Group C. **18** Gerd Müller. **19** Lev Yashin. **20** Alf Ramsey.

Quiz 21 **Pot Luck 11**

Answers – see page 133

LEVEL 2

1 Tony Barton followed Ron Saunders as manager of which club?

2 Which country did Tony Galvin play for?

3 Which was Steve Bould's first League club?

4 In which decade was Duncan Edwards born?

5 Who plays at home at East End Park?

6 The resignation of director Richard Thompson in May 1996 meant that which club was up for sale?

7 Charlie Aitken set a League appearance record at which club?

8 Which club did Dave Beasant join on leaving Chelsea?

9 Which team were beaten 4–1 in the first post-World War Two FA Cup Final?

10 Tommy Coyne was at which club when he made his international debut?

11 Which 38-year old goalkeeper was released by Southampton in May 1996?

12 Who moved from Barnsley to Nottingham Forest in 1991 to set a club record for transfer fee received?

13 What colour are Aberdeen's home shorts?

14 In which decade did Chelsea first win the FA Cup?

15 Which Republic of Ireland defender was born in Lambeth, London in 1970?

16 Which Adrian became manager of Burnley in March 1996?

17 Which club did Mervyn Day leave to join Aston Villa?

18 Who was stripped of the captaincy of the Republic of Ireland in 1996 for holidaying without informing his boss?

19 Which Ted became secretary of the FA in September 1973?

20 Mel Sterland and Tony Dorigo were in the same team at which club?

Answers

Pot Luck 12 (see Quiz 23)

1 Swansea City. **2** 1940s. **3** Tottenham Hotspur. **4** Manager of Wales. **5** David Batty. **6** Creaney. **7** Gold. **8** Birmingham City. **9** Leyton Orient. **10** David O'Leary. **11** Wales. **12** 1980s. **13** Arsenal. **14** Bristol City. **15** Everton. **16** Fry. **17** Liverpool. **18** Leeds United. **19** Ipswich Town. **20** Rune Hauge.

Quiz 22 **Nicknames**

LEVEL 2

Answers – see page 134

1 Which two Athletics have the same nickname?

2 The Bankies is the nickname of which club?

3 Who was known in France as "El Magnifico"?

4 Which club supposedly got their nickname in 1934 as fans responded to the smart and stylish new kit worn by the players?

5 Which England player was known as "Crazy Horse"?

6 The Ironsides is an old nickname of which club?

7 Which club are known as The Loons?

8 Who was the striker known as "Supermac"?

9 Which team have a nickname linked with fictional litter collecting creatures on a real common?

10 Oxford and Cambridge share which nickname?

11 Who was dubbed "Mighty Mouse"?

12 What is Dumbarton's nickname?

13 Who are the Doonhammers?

14 Which player was known as "Glenda"?

15 Which international star was known as "The Little Bird"?

16 Who is "The Divine Ponytail"?

17 The Glaziers is a long-standing nickname for which team?

18 Which Sheffield Wednesday striker was nicknamed "Bronco"?

19 Who was nicknamed "The Black Panther" after the 1966 World Cup?

20 Who liked to be called Bill Dean and hated his nickname?

Answers

The 1960s (see Quiz 24)

1 Stanley Matthews. **2** Chile. **3** Brazil and Czechoslovakia. **4** Alf Ramsey. **5** David Webb. **6** George Best. **7** Pat Jennings. **8** John White. **9** Burnley. **10** Bobby Charlton. **11** Real Madrid. **12** Johnny Haynes. **13** Gordon Banks. **14** Bill Nicholson. **15** Dave Mackay. **16** Pickles. **17** European Cup. **18** Allan Clarke. **19** Alf Ramsey. **20** Jimmy Greaves.

Quiz 23 **Pot Luck 12**

LEVEL 2

Answers – see page 131

1 Who was keeper Roger Freestone playing for when he scored two penalty goals in 1995–96?
2 In which decade was commentator Barry Davies born?
3 Which was Mark Bowen's first League club?
4 Atkinson, Kendall and Walker were in contention for which management job in August 1995?
5 Who moved from Blackburn Rovers in 1996 for £3,750,000, to set a club record for transfer fee received?
6 Which Gerry went from Portsmouth to Manchester City in 1995?
7 What colour are Dumbarton's home shirts?
8 Which club did David Seaman leave to join QPR?
9 Who plays at home at Brisbane Road?
10 Who holds the Arsenal league appearance record?
11 Which country did George Berry play for?
12 In which decade did Coventry City first win the FA Cup?
13 Don Howe followed Terry Neill as boss of which club?
14 Which club did Rob Newman leave to join Norwich City?
15 Which team were beaten 1–0 by Manchester Utd in the 1985 FA Cup Final?
16 Which Barry became manager of Birmingham City in 1993?
17 In which city was John Aldridge born?
18 Terry Yorath was at which club when he made his international debut?
19 Frank Yallop and Neil Thompson were fullbacks at which club?
20 Who was the Norwegian agent in the George Graham 'bung' case?

Answers

Pot Luck 11 (see Quiz 21)

1 Aston Villa. **2** The Republic of Ireland. **3** Stoke City. **4** 1930s. **5** Dunfermline Athletic. **6** QPR. **7** Aston Villa. **8** Southampton. **9** Charlton Athletic. **10** Celtic. **11** Bruce Grobbelaar. **12** Carl Tiler. **13** Red. **14** 1970s. **15** Phil Babb. **16** Heath. **17** Leyton Orient. **18** Roy Keane. **19** Croker. **20** Leeds Utd.

Quiz 24 **The 1960s**

LEVEL 2

Answers – see page 132

1. Who retired from football, aged 50, in April 1965?
2. Which country was the venue for the 1962 World Cup?
3. Which teams played in the 1962 World Cup Final?
4. Who was manager of Ipswich Town's championship winning team?
5. Who scored Chelsea's winner against Leeds Utd in the replayed FA Cup Final of 1969–70?
6. Which Manchester Utd star was named European Footballer of the Year in 1968?
7. Which goalkeeper scored a goal in the 1967 Charity Shield match?
8. Which famous player was killed by lightning on a golf course in 1965?
9. Which Lancashire side won the championship in 1960?
10. Who became England's leading scorer when he netted against Sweden in 1968?
11. Which club won the first World Club Championship in 1960?
12. Who became Britain's first £100-a-week footballer?
13. Who was keeper for the losing Leicester City side in the 1961 FA Cup Final?
14. Which manager bought Jimmy Greaves back from Italy?
15. Returning from a broken leg, which Scottish star broke his leg in his comeback game in 1964?
16. What was the name of the dog who found the stolen World Cup in 1966?
17. What trophy was won with Celtic's 200th goal of the season in 1967?
18. Which Leeds Utd player was nicknamed "Sniffer"?
19. Which manager was knighted in the 1967 New Year's Honours List?
20. In the 1966 World Cup quarter-finals, which injured player did Geoff Hurst replace?

Answers

Nicknames (see Quiz 22)

1 Oldham and Wigan, the Latics. **2** Clydebank. **3** David Ginola. **4** Peterborough, the Posh. **5** Emlyn Hughes. **6** Middlesbrough. **7** Forfar. **8** Malcolm Macdonald. **9** The Wombles, Wimbledon. **10** The Us. **11** Kevin Keegan. **12** The Sons. **13** Queen of the South. **14** Glenn Hoddle. **15** Garrincha. **16** Roberto Baggio. **17** Crystal Palace. **18** David Layne. **19** Eusebio. **20** "Dixie" Dean.

Quiz 25 **Pot Luck 13**

Answers – see page 137

LEVEL 2

1 Who was Jimmy Case playing for when he knocked his old club Liverpool out of the FA Cup in a 1980s shock result?
2 In which decade did Derby County first win the FA Cup?
3 Which was Mark Draper's first League club?
4 Who plays at home at Somerset Park?
5 John Aldridge was at which club when he made his international debut?
6 In which city was the draw for the qualifying rounds of the 1998 World Cup made?
7 Who moved from Birmingham City in February 1996 for £1,100,000 to set a club record for transfer fee received?
8 Which club did Ray Wilkins join on leaving Manchester Utd?
9 Which team were beaten 2–1 by Manchester Utd in the 1977 FA Cup Final?
10 Which country did Ashley Grimes play for?
11 What colour goes with black on Barnet's home shirts?
12 In which decade was Faustino Asprilla born?
13 Derek Fazackerley set a League appearance record at which club?
14 Shearer and Ferdinand first formed a strike-force for which team?
15 Gareth Southgate and Chris Coleman were in the same team at which club?
16 Which Roy became manager of Bolton Wanderers in 1995?
17 Where was Tony Adams born?
18 Terry Cooper followed Lou Macari as boss of which club?
19 Which club did Mike Phelan leave to join Manchester Utd?
20 Which Blackburn Rovers and England defender suffered a long-term injury against Middlesbrough in December 1995?

Answers

Pot Luck 14 (see Quiz 27)

1 Paul Gascoigne. **2** 60. **3** Carlisle United. **4** 1906. **5** Swansea. **6** Blackburn Rovers. **7** Jimmy Armfield. **8** Crystal Palace. **9** Alloa. **10** Kevin Richardson. **11** Arsenal. **12** Case. **13** Scotland. **14** White. **15** 1940s. **16** Chelsea. **17** Manchester City. **18** Nottm Forest. **19** Chester. **20** Trevor Sinclair.

Quiz 26 **Midlands & The North**

LEVEL 2

Answers – see page 138

1 Which famous comedian and TV personality is a supporter of WBA?

2 Which team were originally known as Small Heath Alliance?

3 Who did Blackburn Rovers play in the 1994 Charity Shield match?

4 Which club did Danny Blanchflower play before he joined Tottenham Hotspur?

5 Name the two goalkeepers in the 1983 Manchester Utd v Liverpool League Cup Final?

6 Which international star moved to Bari in August 1992?

7 Gordon Banks won the League Cup with which different clubs?

8 Alan Hudson and Geoff Hurst both played for which Midlands team?

9 Which Midlands' star made a goalscoring England debut against Scotland in 1989?

10 Who was manager of Stockport at the start of the 1996–97 season?

11 Who scored a hat-trick for Blackpool in the 1953 FA Cup Final?

12 Which club dropped from First to Fourth Divisions between 1984–86?

13 What was the nickname of Aston Villa's 1930s player Thomas Waring?

14 In 1960 the Blackpool v Bolton game achieved a first. What was it?

15 Which player did Real Madrid sign from WBA for £1 million in 1979?

16 Who created the first £10,000 transfer fee joining Arsenal from Bolton?

17 Which Aston Villa forward won the Young Player of the Year award in 1977?

18 Who played for Arsenal and Everton and managed Aston Villa, Manchester City and England?

19 What happened to Manchester City in 1938 after being champions in 1937?

20 Which club did Bobby Charlton manage between 1973 and 75?

Answers

European Cup (see Quiz 28)

1 AC Milan. **2** Trevor Francis. **3** Manchester Utd. **4** Wembley. **5** Bobby Charlton. **6** Aston Villa. **7** Marseille. **8** Tommy Gemmell. **9** Leeds United. **10** 1956. **11** Terry McDermott. **12** Yes, in 1992. **13** It was the first Final to be replayed. **14** Eintracht Frankfurt. **15** Rome. **16** Panathinaikos. **17** Kenny Dalglish. **18** Wembley. **19** Brian Clough. **20** Steaua Bucharest.

Quiz 27 **Pot Luck 14**

LEVEL 2

Answers – see page 135

1 Who in December 1995 got booked for "showing" the referee a yellow card after it fell from his pocket?

2 To one year each way, how old was Jack Charlton when he stood down as manager of the Republic of Ireland?

3 With which club did Peter Beardsley make his League debut?

4 To five years each way, when did Everton first win the FA Cup?

5 In which city was Ivor Allchurch born?

6 Kenny Dalglish followed Don Mackay as manager of which club?

7 Who holds the league appearance record for Blackpool?

8 Which club did Iain Dowie leave to join Southampton?

9 Which Scottish side plays at home at Recreation Park?

10 Who, in December 1995, got sent off playing for Coventry City on his return to his former club Aston Villa?

11 Paul Davis and Anders Limpar were in the same team at which club?

12 Which Jimmy became manager of Brighton in November 1995?

13 Which country did Adam Blacklaw play for?

14 What colour are Blackpool's home shorts?

15 In which decade was Roy Evans born?

16 Which team were beaten 2–1 by Tottenham Hotspur in the 1967 FA Cup Final?

17 Colin Bell was at which club when he made his international debut?

18 Which club did Lee Chapman leave to join Leeds Utd the first time?

19 Which Sir Norman produced the 1980s report "The State of Football"?

20 Who moved from Blackpool in August 1993 for £750,000 to set a club record for transfer fee received?

Answers

Pot Luck 13 (see Quiz 25)

1 Brighton. **2** 1940s. **3** Notts County. **4** Ayr Utd. **5** Oxford Utd. **6** Paris. **7** Liam Daish. **8** AC Milan. **9** Liverpool. **10** The Republic of Ireland. **11** Amber. **12** 1960s. **13** Blackburn Rovers. **14** England. **15** Crystal Palace. **16** McFarland. **17** Romford. **18** Birmingham City. **19** Norwich City. **20** Graeme Le Saux.

Quiz 28 **European Cup**

Answers – see page 136

LEVEL 2

1 Who in 1963 became the first Italian team to win the trophy?

2 Who scored the Nottingham Forest match winner in the 1979 Final?

3 Which side represented England for the first time in 1956–57?

4 What was the venue for the Manchester Utd v Benfica 1968 Final?

5 Which English player scored twice in the 1968 Final?

6 Which Midlands team won the 1982 Final?

7 Which French team had the trophy subsequently taken away after winning the Final in 1993?

8 Who scored Celtic's first goal in the 1967 Final triumph?

9 In 1975 which team became the second English side to reach a Final?

10 In which year was the first ever European Cup Final played?

11 Who scored Liverpool's first goal in a European Cup Final?

12 Have Barcelona ever won the trophy?

13 When Bayern Munich won the trophy in 1974, what was special about the Final?

14 Who did Real Madrid beat in their famous 7–3 victory in 1960?

15 Which city hosted the 1968 European Championship Final?

16 Which Greek side reached the semi-finals in 1996?

17 Who scored Liverpool's match-winning goal of the 1978 Final?

18 At which stadium did that match take place?

19 Who was manager of the Nottingham Forest team when they first won the trophy?

20 Who were the first Romanian team to win the European Cup?

Answers

Midlands & The North (see Quiz 26)

1 Frank Skinner. **2** Birmingham City. **3** Manchester Utd. **4** Aston Villa. **5** Bailey and Grobbelaar. **6** David Platt. **7** Leicester City, Stoke City. **8** Stoke City. **9** Steve Bull. **10** Dave Jones. **11** Stan Mortensen. **12** Wolves. **13** Pongo. **14** First live TV match. **15** Laurie Cunningham. **16** David Jack. **17** Andy Gray. **18** Joe Mercer. **19** They were relegated. **20** Preston North End.

Quiz 29 **Pot Luck 15**

LEVEL 2

Answers – see page 141

1. Kevin Sheedy was at which club when he made his international debut?
2. Where was John Barnes born?
3. Which was Colin Hendry's first League club?
4. In which decade was Garrincha born?
5. Which team were beaten 4–2 by Manchester Utd in the 1948 FA Cup Final?
6. Which Joe became manager of Bristol City in November 1994?
7. Which 46-year-old physiotherapist became Arsenal manager?
8. Which club did Peter Beardsley join on leaving Liverpool?
9. Airdrieonians and Clyde have shared which ground?
10. Who moved from Bolton to Celtic in 1994 to set a club record for transfer fee received?
11. Which country did Ralph Coates play for?
12. In which decade did Huddersfield Town first win the FA Cup?
13. What colour are Barcelona's home shorts?
14. Howard Wilkinson followed Billy Bremner as boss of which club?
15. In 1985 which Harry died while watching Everton, a club he had once managed?
16. Eddie Hopkinson set a League appearance record at which club?
17. Regis and Atkinson were the strike force at which club?
18. Who won his 100th Scottish cap in March 1986?
19. Which club did Mike Milligan leave to join Everton?
20. At which club did former England boss Bobby Robson begin his playing career?

Answers

Pot Luck 16 (see Quiz 31)

1 Liverpool. **2** Chris Woods. **3** Nottm Forest. **4** Red. **5** 1900. **6** Nigel Martyn. **7** Hull City. **8** Wrexham. **9** Leeds. **10** Oldham Athletic. **11** Allan Harris. **12** Arsenal. **13** 1940s. **14** Blackburn Rovers. **15** Millwall. **16** Billy McNeill. **17** Hollins. **18** The Republic of Ireland. **19** Manchester Utd. **20** Leicester City.

Quiz 30 **Gary Lineker**

LEVEL 2

Answers – see page 142

1 How many international goals did Gary Lineker score?

2 Who was the boss who took him to Everton in 1985?

3 Who were the opponents for the World Cup hat-trick in Mexico?

4 What is Gary's starsign?

5 At which club did he hit his best League goals total of 30 in a season?

6 Who was in charge of Barcelona when Lineker went there?

7 How many goals did Gary score in the World Cup in Italy in 1990?

8 What is Gary Lineker's middle name?

9 What was the only major European club trophy that Lineker won?

10 Which Gordon was his regular strike partner in his last League season in England?

11 Gary scored all four of England's goals in games against Malaysia and which other country?

12 How many red cards did he receive in his career?

13 Who went on when Gary was substituted in his last international?

14 Who saved his penalty in an FA Cup Final?

15 Who was in charge of Tottenham Hotspur when Lineker went there?

16 Gary was top scorer in the 1986 World Cup final stages – with how many goals?

17 Who is Gary's long-standing pal in the snooker world?

18 Which Frank was Leicester manager at the time of Gary's 1979 League debut?

19 Which university awarded Lineker an honorary Master of Arts degree in 1991?

20 At which club was Gary playing when he retired from soccer?

Answers

Quote, Unquote (see Quiz 32)

1 The Hillsborough tragedy 1989. **2** Gary Lineker. **3** Barry Fry. **4** Jack Charlton. **5** Hall. **6** Tommy Docherty. **7** Ian Rush. **8** Rod Stewart. **9** Brian Clough. **10** Alex Ferguson. **11** Dave Bassett. **12** Beat them. **13** USA. **14** Kenny Dalglish. **15** Altrincham. **16** Stan Flashman. **17** Brian Clough. **18** Karen Brady. **19** Graeme Souness. **20** Graham Taylor.

Quiz 31 **Pot Luck 16**

LEVEL 2

Answers – see page 139

1 Craig Johnston scored an FA Cup Final goal for which club?
2 Who in July 1986 moved to Rangers for £600,000, a new record fee for a keeper?
3 What was Steve Hodge's first League club?
4 What colour are Benfica's home shirts?
5 To ten years either way, when did Bury first win the FA Cup?
6 Who moved from Bristol Rovers in November 1989 to set a club record for transfer fee received?
7 Which club plays at home at Boothferry Park?
8 Which club did Joey Jones leave to join Liverpool?
9 In which city was David Batty born?
10 Andy Goram was at which club when he made his international debut?
11 Who was Terry Venables's assistant at Barcelona?
12 Which team were beaten 1–0 by Ipswich in the 1978 FA Cup Final?
13 In which decade was Sir Geoff Hurst born?
14 Alan Wright and Scott Sellars were in the same team at which club?
15 Which club did Wimbledon buy John Fashanu from?
16 Who holds the League appearance record at Celtic?
17 Which John became manager of Chelsea in March 1985?
18 Which country did Mick Robinson play for?
19 Ron Atkinson followed Dave Sexton as boss of which club?
20 Which club did Gary McAllister leave to join Leeds Utd?

Answers

Pot Luck 15 (see Quiz 29)

1 Everton. **2** Kingston, Jamaica. **3** Dundee. **4** 1930s. **5** Blackpool. **6** Jordan. **7** Bertie Mee. **8** Everton. **9** Broadwood Stadium. **10** Andy Walker. **11** England. **12** 1920s. **13** Blue. **14** Leeds Utd. **15** Catterick. **16** Bolton Wanderers. **17** Aston Villa. **18** Kenny Dalglish. **19** Oldham Athletic. **20** Fulham.

Quiz 32 **Quote, Unquote**

Answers – see page 140

LEVEL 2

1 After what event did Kenny Dalglish say, "Football is irrelevant now"?

2 Who said, "I'm not as nice as all that. In fact I swore last week"?

3 Who said, "If ...Liverpool is a danger to your health, try managing Barnet"?

4 After a check up and brain scan, who said, "It proves that I do have a brain"?

5 Which Stuart on Radio 5 said, "Lee Sharpe has got dynamite in his shorts"?

6 "Barnes' problem is that he gets injured on *A Question of Sport*!" Who said this?

7 "His goals do the talking, but so far he hasn't spoken very much"? Who was the Juventus president talking about?

8 Which soccer-mad pop singer said after the birth of his daughter, "It's like seeing Scotland score a goal. You never got used to it"?

9 Which manager, when he heard about Souness having heart surgery, said, "My heart goes out to Graeme Souness"?

10 Who said, "The Old Trafford job was one I simply could not turn down"?

11 Who said on promotion to the top flight, "Contrary to popular opinion I don't tell my players to kick the opposition in the nuts"?

12 Complete the quote from the Danish Foreign Minister after Denmark opted out of the Maastricht Treaty and won Euro 92, "If you can't join them ..."?

13 "Played them on the wrong day," – Graham Taylor's said after loss to who?

14 Who said in 1997, "The temptation of a job like this was too much"?

15 Which club was called "the Manchester Utd of non League football"?

16 Who was Barry Fry talking about: "If you didn't know him, you'd think he was an ignorant pig"?

17 Who said, "The Trent is lovely, too. I've walked on it for 18 years"?

18 Which lady said,"everyone thinks I earned this job between the sheets"?

19 "The best players will be signed, no matter what they are," was the response of which manager to Catholic/Protestant controversy?

20 Who said, "This is a bloody awful job"?

Answers

Gary Lineker (see Quiz 30)

1 48. **2** Howard Kendall. **3** Poland. **4** Sagittarius. **5** Everton. **6** Terry Venables. **7** Four. **8** Winston. **9** European Cup Winners' Cup. **10** Durie. **11** Spain. **12** None. **13** Alan Smith. **14** Mark Crossley. **15** Terry Venables. **16** Six. **17** Willie Thorne. **18** McLintock. **19** Leicester. **20** Nagoya Grampus 8.

Quiz 33 **Pot Luck 17**

LEVEL 2

Answers – see page 145

1 Jock Stein followed Jimmy Armfield as boss of which club?

2 In which decade did Leeds United first win the FA Cup?

3 Which was Tony Dorigo's first League club?

4 Which country did Paul Bodin play for?

5 Who said on revealing his new haircut in 1994 at the World Cup Finals, "I asked for a Valderrama and they gave me a Val Doonican"?

6 Kevin Wilson and Clive Allen were in the same team at which club?

7 In which decade was Des Lynam born?

8 Which club did Gary Taggart join on leaving Barnsley?

9 Which club plays at home at The Memorial Ground?

10 Peter Barnes was at which club when he made his international debut?

11 Which Terry became manager of Coventry City in 1990?

12 What was the score in the drawn Manchester Utd v Brighton FA Cup Final of 1983?

13 What colour are Hearts' home shirts?

14 Brondby knocked which English team out of the UEFA Cup in 1995?

15 Tony Blair is a fan of which team?

16 Which club did Stephen Pears leave to join Middlesbrough?

17 Willie Miller set a League appearance record at which club?

18 Where was Raich Carter born?

19 Who moved from Bradford to Wolves in 1995 to set a club record for transfer fee received?

20 Kevin Campbell and Chris Bart-Williams both moved on the same day to which club?

Answers

Pot Luck 18 (see Quiz 35)

1 Charlton Athletic. **2** Recreation Ground. **3** West Ham Utd. **4** 1950s. **5** Scotland. **6** Millwall. **7** Michel Platini. **8** Crewe Alexandra. **9** Green. **10** Mark Lawrenson. **11** Blackburn Rovers. **12** Fulham. **13** Dublin. **14** Wimbledon. **15** Everton. **16** Smith. **17** Never. **18** Crystal Palace. **19** South Africa. **20** Alan Shearer.

Quiz 34 **French Connection**

LEVEL 2

Answers – see page 146

1 Which French club did Mo Johnston play for?
2 How much, to the nearest million pounds, did Marseille pay for Trevor Steven?
3 What is the main stadium used for French home internationals?
4 David Ginola and George Weah have played for which French club?
5 Which team lost in the Final of the 1992 European Cup Winners' Cup?
6 At what stage did France get knocked out of the 1994 World Cup?
7 Which French keeper joined Sunderland in 1996?
8 How many different clubs in France did Eric Cantona play for before coming to England?
9 At which Italian club did Michel Platini end his career?
10 At which ground do Marseille play?
11 Which team are known as The Greens – Les Verts?
12 Which Arsenal and England player moved to Le Havre in the early 1990s?
13 With 82, which Manuel held the appearance record for France?
14 Which club won the 1996 European Cup Winners' Cup?
15 Which French club did Chris Waddle play for?
16 Which team scored within 27 seconds against France in the 1982 World Cup?
17 Which two English internationals helped Monaco to the Championship in 1988?
18 In which country did France first win the European Championship?
19 Which French Player of the Year in 1994 moved to England in 1995?
20 For which club did Eric Cantona make most appearances?

Answers

Scottish Internationals (see Quiz 36)

1 Andy Roxburgh. **2** 1990. **3** Denis Law & Kenny Dalglish. **4** Archie Gemmill. **5** 1958. **6** Hughie Gallacher. **7** 3–2 to Scotland. **8** Ally McCoist. **9** Denis Law. **10** Leeds (Gary McAllister was involved). **11** Pat Nevin. **12** Fullback. **13** Dundee Utd. **14** Alex Ferguson. **15** Aberdeen. **16** 8. **17** 1984. **18** Celtic & Albion Rovers. **19** First goalless draw. **20** Leeds.

Quiz 35 **Pot Luck 18**

Answers – see page 143

LEVEL 2

1 Sam Bartram set a League appearance record at which club?
2 Which ground do Chesterfield play at?
3 What was Ray Houghton's first League club?
4 In which decade was Sam Hamman born?
5 Which country did Jimmy Crapnell play for?
6 Mick McCarthy followed Bruce Rioch as boss of which club?
7 Who resigned as coach of France in July 1992?
8 Which club did David Platt leave to join Aston Villa?
9 What is the main colour of Hibernians' home shirts?
10 Who moved from Brighton to Liverpool in 1981 to set a club record for transfer fee received?
11 Which club withdrew from a £3 million bid for Geoff Thomas in 1992?
12 Which team were beaten 2–0 by West Ham Utd in the 1975 FA Cup Final?
13 In which city was Liam Brady born?
14 Terry Phelan was at which club when he made his international debut?
15 Tony Cottee and Peter Beardsley were in the same team at which club?
16 Which Alan became manager of Crystal Palace in March 1993?
17 In which decade did Leicester City win the FA Cup before the 1990s?
18 Which club did Kenny Sansom leave to join Arsenal?
19 In July 1992, which country was re-elected to FIFA after an absence of 18 years?
20 On July 26, 1992 the move of which player to Blackburn Rovers broke the British transfer record?

Answers

Pot Luck 17 (see Quiz 33)

1 Leeds Utd. **2** 1970s. **3** Aston Villa. **4** Wales. **5** Andy Townsend. **6** Chelsea. **7** 1940s. **8** Bolton Wanderers. **9** Bristol Rovers. **10** Manchester City. **11** Butcher. **12** 2–2. **13** Maroon. **14** Liverpool. **15** Newcastle Utd. **16** Manchester Utd. **17** Aberdeen. **18** Sunderland. **19** Dean Richards. **20** Nottingham Forest.

Quiz 36 **Scottish Internationals**

LEVEL 2

Answers – see page 144

1 Who did Craig Brown replace in charge of the Scottish team?

2 In which year did Scotland last play Brazil in a World Cup tournament?

3 Which two players are joint top scorers for Scotland?

4 Which Scottish player scored a brilliant solo goal against Holland in a 1978 World Cup match?

5 When did Scotland first qualify for the World Cup finals?

6 Who scored 23 goals in only 20 games for Scotland?

7 What was the score of Wembley's England v Scotland game in 1967?

8 Which Scottish international won Europe's Golden Boot award in 1992?

9 Who retired from international soccer after the 1974 World Cup game against Zaire?

10 In 1995 which English club were incensed when their player was injured playing for Scotland against Sweden?

11 Which Scottish Pat was on Tranmere's books at the start of 1996–97?

12 In which position did Ray Stewart play?

13 Duncan Ferguson was with which club when he made his international debut?

14 Who was Scotland's caretaker manager in the mid 80s?

15 In which city was Denis Law born?

16 To five each way, how many times did Alex James play for Scotland?

17 To one either way, in which year was Paul McStay first capped?

18 Which two Scottish clubs did Jock Stein play for?

19 What was notable about the draw between England and Scotland in the 1970s Home International Championship?

20 Which club links McQueen, McAllister and Lorimer?

Answers

French Connection (see Quiz 34)

1 Nantes. **2** Five. **3** Stade de France. **4** Paris St Germain. **5** Monaco. **6** They failed to qualify. **7** Lionel Perez. **8** Five. **9** Juventus. **10** Stade Velodrome. **11** St Etienne. **12** Graham Rix. **13** Amaros. **14** Paris St Germain. **15** Marseille. **16** England. **17** Mark Hateley and Glenn Hoddle. **18** France. **19** David Ginola. **20** Manchester Utd.

Quiz 37 **Pot Luck 19**

LEVEL 2

Answers – see page 149

1 How many home League games did Manchester United lose in 1995–96?
2 Where does the Alexandra come from in Crewe's name?
3 Which was Denis Irwin's first League club?
4 In which decade did Ipswich Town first win the FA Cup?
5 Ossie Ardiles followed Jim Smith as manager of which club?
6 Which country did Gary Waddock play for?
7 Whose home ground was briefly renamed the Pulse Stadium?
8 Which club did Ian Rush join on leaving Liverpool for the first time?
9 Which club was Roger Stanislaus with when he failed a random drug test?
10 Who moved from Bristol City in March 1993 to set a club record for transfer fee received?
11 What is the main colour of Walsall's home shirts?
12 Which team were beaten 4–3 by Blackpool in the 1953 FA Cup Final?
13 In which decade was Ron Greenwood born?
14 Jim Cannon set a League appearance record at which club?
15 Which Bolton Wanderers boss got the sack on 2nd January 1996?
16 Which club did David Phillips leave to join Nottingham Forest?
17 Which Colin became manager of Everton in 1987?
18 In which city was Les Ferdinand born?
19 Kevin Moran was at which club when he made his international debut?
20 Eric Cantona and Steve Hodge were in the same team at which club?

Answers

Pot Luck 20 (see Quiz 39)

1 Arsenal. **2** Aberdeen. **3** Bradford City. **4** Blackburn Rovers. **5** Plymouth. **6** Colchester United. **7** Manchester City. **8** Barnsley. **9** San Marino. **10** Celtic. **11** White. **12** 1960s. **13** Manchester Utd. **14** Bolton Wanderers and Sheffield United. **15** QPR. **16** Wales. **17** Adams. **18** 1920s. **19** Norwich City. **20** Dion Dublin.

Quiz 38 **Going Up**

LEVEL 2

Answers – see page 150

1 Which former Liverpool player was Blackburn Rovers's top scorer in their 1992 promotion season?

2 Kernaghan and Slaven played for which promoted team?

3 Who did Bolton beat 3–2 in the thrilling 1995 play-off Final, having trailed 2–0 at one stage?

4 Which manager John took Ipswich Town up as Second Division Champions?

5 Ian Marshall's goals helped which club to the top flight in 1991?

6 To two years each way, when did Liverpool last gain promotion?

7 Which team lost a play-off Final yet still went up in 1990?

8 Vinnie Jones and Mel Sterland were part of which promoted team?

9 Which 1960s team won the Championship directly after promotion?

10 Which 1970s team won the Championship directly after promotion?

11 Which boss who took Newcastle United into the Premier League?

12 Which team got promotion via the play-offs in their first season in the League in 1993–94?

13 A Mike Newell play-off Final goal took which club into the Premier League?

14 Which City were Second Division Champions in 1971 and 1980?

15 Chris Waddle was an ever-present in which promoted 1980s side?

16 Which United were Third Division Champions in 1984 and Second Division Champions the following season?

17 Who was the Sheffield Wednesday boss in the 1990–91 season?

18 Maurice Malpass was assistant manager and a player for which team on the up in 1996?

19 Neil Warnock took which side up to the top flight in 1991?

20 Marco Gabbiadini was top scorer for which team on the up in 1990?

Answers

Going Down (see Quiz 40)

1 Sheffield Weds. **2** Manchester Utd. **3** Lincoln City. **4** 1960s. **5** Mark McGhee. **6** Charlton. **7** Falkirk. **8** West Ham United. **9** Newport County. **10** John Gorman. **11** Luton Town. **12** Dave Bassett. **13** 1960s. **14** Sheffield Weds. **15** Halifax Town. **16** Ipswich Town. **17** Southport. **18** Never. **19** Norwich City. **20** Alan Ball.

Quiz 39 **Pot Luck 20**

Answers – see page 147

LEVEL 2

1 Which London club has a fanzine called *The Gooner*?

2 Alphabetically, which is the first Scottish League team?

3 What was Phil Babb's first League club?

4 Which team were beaten 3–0 by Wolves in the 1960 FA Cup Final?

5 In which city was Trevor Francis born?

6 Who plays at home at Layer Road?

7 Alan Oakes set a League appearance record at which club?

8 Which club did Gary Taggart join on leaving Manchester City?

9 Which team did Wales beat 5–0 in their first game in the 1998 World Cup campaign?

10 Chris Morris was at which club when he made his international debut?

11 What colour goes with black stripes on Swansea's home shirts?

12 In which decade did Liverpool first win the FA Cup?

13 Mal Donaghy and Denis Irwin were in the same team at which club?

14 Nathan Blake and Mark Patterson swapped over between which clubs?

15 Which club did Paul Parker leave to join Fulham?

16 Which country did Kenny Jackett play for?

17 Which Micky became manager of Fulham in February 1996?

18 In which decade was Jimmy Hill born?

19 Dave Stringer followed Ken Brown as boss of which club?

20 Who moved from Cambridge in 1992 to Manchester Utd to set a club record for transfer fee received?

Answers

Pot Luck 19 (see Quiz 37)

1 None. **2** Princess Alexandra. **3** Leeds Utd. **4** 1970s. **5** Newcastle Utd. **6** The Republic of Ireland. **7** Bradford City. **8** Juventus. **9** Leyton Orient. **10** Andy Cole. **11** Red. **12** Bolton Wanderers. **13** 1920s. **14** Crystal Palace. **15** Roy McFarland. **16** Norwich City. **17** Harvey. **18** London. **19** Manchester Utd. **20** Leeds Utd.

Quiz 40 **Going Down**

Answers – see page 148

LEVEL 2

1 Pressman and Turner were the keepers as which club went down?

2 Who went down in 1974 after 37 years in the top flight?

3 In the 1980s, which club was the first to be automatically demoted from the League?

4 In which decade were Fulham last in the top flight in England?

5 Who was manager when Leicester City went down in 1994–95?

6 Robert Lee missed just one League game as which side went down?

7 Which team were relegated from the Scottish Premier League in 1993 and again in 1996?

8 Parris and Potts played for which relegated side?

9 Which Welsh club was finally wound up in February 1989?

10 Who was boss when Swindon Town went down in 1994–95?

11 Mark Pembridge played every 1992 game as which team went down?

12 In 1994, after going down, which boss said, "If you continually play Russian roulette eventually you're going to get the bullet"?

13 In which decade did Blackpool last play in the top division?

14 In 1990 which Sheffield team went down while the other went up?

15 Which Yorkshire team went out of the League in 1993?

16 Which team went down two seasons after winning the championship in the 60s?

17 Which seaside club went out of the League in 1978?

18 How many times were Aberdeen relegated in the 50 years following the Second World War?

19 Robins and Ekoku started the season as strikers, but left before which club went out of the Premiership?

20 Who was Portsmouth's manager when they went down from the top flight in 1988?

Answers

Going Up (see Quiz 38)

1 David Speedie. **2** Middlesbrough. **3** Reading. **4** Lyall. **5** Oldham Athletic. **6** 1962. **7** Sunderland. **8** Leeds Utd. **9** Ipswich Town. **10** Nottingham Forest. **11** Kevin Keegan. **12** Wycombe Wanderers. **13** Blackburn Rovers. **14** Leicester. **15** Newcastle Utd. **16** Oxford. **17** Ron Atkinson. **18** Dundee Utd. **19** Notts County. **20** Sunderland.

Quiz 41 **Pot Luck 21**

Answers – see page 153

LEVEL 2

1 Who won the last FA Cup Final before the Second World War?

2 Bobby Saxton followed Howard Kendall as manager of which club?

3 Which was Stuart Pearce's first League club?

4 Which country did David Langan play for?

5 Which team plays at home in front of the Kippax Stand?

6 In which decade was Daniel Amokachi born?

7 Gordon Davies set a most League goals in total record at which club?

8 Which club did Niall Quinn join on leaving Manchester City?

9 Which Bobby became Wimbledon manager in 1987?

10 Ashley Ward joined Derby County from which club?

11 What is Ian Rush's middle name?

12 Which club has a fanzine called *Gulls Eye*?

13 Which keeper Peter was with Stoke City throughout the entire 1980s?

14 In what decade did Manchester Utd first win the FA Cup?

15 Which club did Mel Sterland leave to join Rangers?

16 Peter Cormack was an FA Cup winner with which club?

17 In which city was Andy Hinchcliffe born?

18 Which club plays at home at Sincil Bank?

19 Which England player set a League appearance record for Ipswich Town?

20 Which Colin was Minister for Sport in the 1980s?

Answers

Pot Luck 22 (see Quiz 43)

1 Leicester City. **2** 1940s. **3** Wimbledon. **4** Watford. **5** Coventry City. **6** Ipswich Town. **7** Jimmy Case. **8** Birmingham City. **9** 1900s. **10** Norwich City. **11** White. **12** Liverpool. **13** Leeds United. **14** The club flag. **15** Mills. **16** Birmingham City. **17** Andrew. **18** Scotland. **19** King. **20** Hereford United.

Quiz 42 **Manchester Utd**

LEVEL 2

Answers – see page 154

1 Which sport was played professionally by Ryan Giggs' father?

2 Which Scottish club bought Lee Martin?

3 Which Manchester Utd manager signed Gordon Strachan?

4 Which ex-United player became Jack Charlton's assistant with the Republic of Ireland?

5 A win in the final game of the 1994–95 season would have made United Premiership winners. Which team held them to a draw?

6 Who was the 1970s favourite "Pancho"?

7 How many times did Bryan Robson win the FA Cup as United skipper?

8 Which Dutch master joined United from Ipswich Town?

9 To one year either way, when did Bobby Charlton first play for United?

10 In which country was Gary Bailey born?

11 How many Championships did Sir Matt Busby win for United?

12 Which club did Graeme Hogg move to from United?

13 Who beat Manchester United at Old Trafford in their first European defeat of the 1990s?

14 Pat Crerand became assistant to which United manager?

15 In the 1960s David Herd left which club to join United?

16 1970s international centres Ron and Wyn share what surname?

17 Which player moved to Vancouver Whitecaps in the early 1980s and then came back to collect over 50 England caps?

18 Who followed Sir Matt as United boss?

19 Which keeper did Alec Ferguson sign from his former club Aberdeen?

20 What was Robson's shirt number for most of his United career?

Answers

The 1970s (see Quiz 44)

1 Brian Clough. **2** Alberto Tarantini. **3** Billy Bremner and Kevin Keegan. **4** Don Revie. **5** Bobby Moore. **6** Aberdeen. **7** Hereford United. **8** Frank McLintock. **9** Ipswich Town. **10** Kevin Keegan. **11** Carlos Alberto. **12** Ibrox Park. **13** Ally MacLeod. **14** Nottingham Forest. **15** Billy Bremner. **16** Cyprus. **17** Gordon Banks. **18** Bobby Charlton. **19** West Ham Utd. **20** David Fairclough.

Quiz 43 **Pot Luck 22**

LEVEL 2

Answers – see page 151

1 Which team were beaten 1–0 by Man City in the 1969 FA Cup Final?
2 In which decade was Pat Jennings born?
3 What was Alan Cork's first League club?
4 Graham Taylor followed Glenn Roeder as manager of which club?
5 Swan Lane and Thackhall Street lead to which club's ground?
6 Which club was Kevin Beattie with when he first played international soccer?
7 Which 41-year-old hung up his boots in November 1995 after a serious neck injury in a reserve team game?
8 Which club did Paul Furlong join on leaving Chelsea?
9 In what decade did Manchester City first win the FA Cup?
10 Which club has a fanzine called *I Can Drive A Tractor*?
11 What is the main colour of Stockport County's home shirts?
12 In which city was Michael Branch born?
13 Which club did Mervyn Day leave to join Aston Villa?
14 What did Graeme Souness place in the centre of the pitch after his team won the Turkish Cup Final?
15 Which Mick became Stoke City manager in 1985?
16 Steve Claridge joined Leicester City from which club?
17 What is Peter Beardsley's middle name?
18 Which country did Arthur Albiston play for?
19 Which John 'went upstairs' at Tranmere Rovers when John Aldridge took over team affairs?
20 Which former club plays at home at Edgar Street?

Answers

Pot Luck 21 (see Quiz 41)

1 Portsmouth. **2** Blackburn Rovers. **3** Coventry City. **4** The Republic of Ireland. **5** Manchester City. **6** 1970s. **7** Fulham. **8** Sunderland. **9** Gould. **10** Norwich City. **11** James. **12** Brighton. **13** Fox. **14** 1900s. **15** Leeds Utd. **16** Liverpool. **17** Manchester. **18** Lincoln City. **19** Mick Mills. **20** Moynihan.

Quiz 44 **The 1970s**

LEVEL 2

Answers – see page 152

1 Who was John McGovern referring to when he said, "I can only say he makes you want to play for him"?

2 Which Argentinian player joined Birmingham City in October 1978?

3 Which two players were sent off in the 1975 Charity Shield?

4 Who succeeded Alf Ramsey as England boss?

5 Which England player made his 100th appearance against Scotland in 1973?

6 Rangers and Celtic won the Scottish FA Cup each season in the 70s apart from 1970, when which team triumphed?

7 Which non-League side defeated Newcastle Utd in a third round 1971–72 FA Cup replay?

8 Who was Footballer of the Year in his club's double-winning season?

9 Geddis and Talbot played for which 1970s FA Cup winners?

10 Which player returned from Hamburg to play for Southampton?

11 Who was skipper of Brazil's 1970 World Cup team?

12 At which Scottish ground did 66 people die in a New Year's Day tragedy in 1971?

13 Which manager took Scotland to the 1978 World Cup finals?

14 Which English club ended Liverpool's European Cup reign in 1978?

15 Who was the Leeds Utd player banned by the Scottish FA from playing for his country in 1975?

16 Against which country did Malcolm Macdonald score 5 goals?

17 Which international keeper lost an eye in a car crash in 1972?

18 Who resigned as Preston North End's manager in 1975 after transfer disputes?

19 Mervyn Day played in goal for which 1970s FA Cup-winning team?

20 Which Liverpool player was nicknamed "Supersub" by the media?

Answers

Manchester Utd (see Quiz 42)

1 Rugby League. **2** Lee Martin. **3** Ron Atkinson. **4** Maurice Setters. **5** West Ham Utd. **6** Stuart Pearson. **7** Three. **8** Arnold Muhren. **9** 1956. **10** England (in Ipswich). **11** Five. **12** Portsmouth. **13** Juventus. **14** Tommy Docherty. **15** Arsenal. **16** Davies. **17** Peter Beardsley. **18** Wilf McGuinness. **19** Jim Leighton. **20** 7.

Quiz 45 **Pot Luck 23**

Answers – see page 157

LEVEL 2

1 With 700+ games, which player set a League appearance record for Southampton?

2 Liam Brady followed Barry Lloyd as manager of which club?

3 Which was Alan Wright's first League club?

4 Which club play at home at the Abbey Stadium?

5 Which club has a fanzine called *United We Stand*?

6 Pat Nevin and Kevin Sheedy were in the same side at which club?

7 In which decade did Nottingham Forest first win the FA Cup?

8 Which club did David Platt join on leaving Aston Villa?

9 Which country did Chris Hughton play for?

10 Which manager said, "Newcastle supporters have, in the last few years, been through thick and thin"?

11 What colour are Brighton's home shorts?

12 Which team were beaten 1–0 by Celtic in the 1995 Scottish FA Cup Final?

13 Which club did Paul Rideout leave to join Everton?

14 In which decade was Tom Finney born?

15 Which Danny became boss of Barnsley in June 1994?

16 Who moved from Portsmouth for £2 million in May 1992 to set a club record for a transfer fee received?

17 Viv Anderson was with which club when he made his international debut?

18 How much did the transfer of Ruud Gullit cost Chelsea?

19 Which Danish midfielder was loaned from Liverpool to Barnsley in 1995?

20 Which Canadian side did Peter Beardsley play for?

Answers

Pot Luck 24 (see Quiz 47)

1 Alf Ramsey. **2** Manchester City. **3** Middlesbrough. **4** Joe Shaw. 5 West Ham United. **6** 1910. **7** Rob Jones. **8** Kevin Keegan. **9** Barlinnie. **10** Glasgow. **11** Plymouth Argyle. **12** Clemence. **13** Sheffield Weds. **14** 1960s. **15** Blackburn Rovers. **16** Robert. **17** Arsenal. **18** Leicester City. **19** White. **20** England.

Quiz 46 **Midfield Men**

LEVEL 2

Answers – see page 158

1 At which club did Peter Reid start his playing career?

2 Which midfielder Gordon was awarded an OBE in 1993?

3 At QPR in 1994, which ex-England midfielder followed another ex-England midfielder as manager?

4 Tim Sherwood moved to Norwich City from which club?

5 How old was Duncan Edwards when he made his League debut?

6 Which WBA and Manchester Utd player was forced to retire through injury in 1988?

7 Which country did Gerry Daly play for?

8 Which England midfielder scored the only goal in the World Cup quarter-final against Belgium in Bologna in 1990?

9 Which team did Robert Lee support as a boy?

10 To 10 each way how many League games did Glenn Hoddle play for Chelsea?

11 At which club did Bobby Charlton end his playing career?

12 Which midfielder did Ron Atkinson call "The Crab" because he was always moving sideways?

13 In what year did Paul McStay make his international debut?

14 Which country did Barry Hole play for?

15 Which club honours did Johnny Haynes gain in his 18 years at Fulham?

16 Which midfielder did Glenn Hoddle make skipper of Chelsea?

17 Which club did Roy Keane turn down when he joined Manchester Utd?

18 Which injury forced Bryan Robson out of the 1986 World Cup?

19 Which English midfielder scored in a World Cup Final?

20 Which England midfielder's autobiography was called *Rock Bottom*?

Answers

Viva España (see Quiz 48)

1 Estadio Santiago Bernabeu. **2** Real Sociedad. **3** 0–0. **4** Barcelona. **5** The Vulture. **6** Seville. **7** Miguel Angel Nadal. **8** Suarez. **9** Archibald. **10** White. **11** Espanol. **12** Clemente. **13** Valencia. **14** John Toshack. **15** Laurie Cunningham. **16** Mexico. **17** Barcelona. Gary Lineker & Mark Hughes. **18** Julio Salinas. **19** Real Madrid. **20** Pope John Paul II.

Quiz 47 **Pot Luck 24**

LEVEL 2

Answers – see page 155

1 Which future England manager won a championship medal with Tottenham Hotspur in 1951?

2 Howard Kendall followed Mel Machin as manager of which club?

3 With which club did Graeme Souness make his League debut?

4 Playing from the 1940s to the 1960s, who set a League appearance record for Sheffield Utd?

5 Alan Devonshire made his international debut while at which club?

6 To five years, when did Newcastle Utd first win the FA Cup?

7 Who moved from Crewe Alexandra for £600,000 in October 1991, to set a club record for a transfer fee received?

8 Who teamed up with Henry Cooper to advertise Brut?

9 In which prison did Duncan Ferguson do time?

10 In which city was Tommy Docherty born?

11 Who plays at home at Home Park?

12 Which Ray became boss of Barnet in January 1994

13 Which club did Nigel Worthington leave to join Leeds Utd?

14 In which decade was Robert Lee born?

15 Which club has a fanzine called *Loadsamoney*?

16 What is Keith Gillespie's middle name?

17 Brian Marwood and Martin Hayes were in the same side at which club?

18 Which team were beaten 3–1 by Wolves in the 1949 FA Cup Final?

19 What colour are Portsmouth's home shorts?

20 Which country did Mike Bailey play for?

Answers

Pot Luck 23 (see Quiz 45)

1 Terry Paine. **2** Brighton. **3** Blackpool. **4** Cambridge Utd. **5** Manchester Utd. **6** Everton. **7** 1890s. **8** Bari. **9** The Republic of Ireland. **10** Kevin Keegan. **11** Blue. **12** Airdrie. **13** Rangers. **14** 1920s. **15** Wilson. **16** Darren Anderton. **17** Nottingham Forest. **18** Nothing. He came on a free transfer. **19** Jan Molby. **20** Vancouver Whitecaps.

Quiz 48 **Viva España**

LEVEL 2

Answers – see page 156

1 Real Madrid play at which stadium?

2 Which Spanish club did John Aldridge play for?

3 What was the half-time score in the England v Spain Euro 96 game?

4 Which team won the Spanish league in 1991, '92, '93 and '94?

5 What was the nickname of 1980s striker Emil Butragueno?

6 Real Betis come from which city?

7 In Euro 96, David Seaman produced a penalty shoot-out save to deny which Spanish player?

8 Which Luis was the last Spanish European Footballer of the Year before the 1990s?

9 Which Scottish Steve played for Barcelona in the 80s?

10 What colour are Real Madrid's home socks?

11 At which club did Alfredo di Stefano end his playing career?

12 Which coach Javier was in charge of Spain for Euro 96?

13 Which club did Zubizarreta move to from Barcelona?

14 Which Welshman managed Real Madrid and Real Sociedad?

15 Which former England player died in a car crash in Madrid in July 1989?

16 Which country did Real Madrid's scoring star Hugo Sanchez play for?

17 At which club did an English and a Welsh international link up?

18 Who had a goal disallowed for offside against England in Euro 96?

19 Castilla are the nursery side of which club?

20 Which special person was enrolled as member No. 108,000 at Barcelona?

Answers

Midfield Men (see Quiz 46)

1 Bolton Wanderers. **2** Strachan. **3** Ray Wilkins followed Gerry Francis. **4** Watford. **5** 16. **6** Remi Moses. **7** The Republic of Ireland. **8** David Platt. **9** West Ham Utd. **10** 31. **11** Preston North End. **12** Ray Wilkins. **13** 1983. **14** Wales. **15** None. **16** Dennis Wise. **17** Blackburn Rovers. **18** Dislocated shoulder. **19** Martin Peters. **20** Paul Merson.

Quiz 49 **Pot Luck 25**

Answers – see page 161

LEVEL 2

1 Martin Dobson made his international debut while at which club?

2 Which Gary became manager of Blackpool in July 1996?

3 Which was Neil Webb's first League club?

4 Paul Groves was an ever-present for which team in 1995–96?

5 Ossie Ardiles followed Jim Smith as manager of which club?

6 Barry Kitchener set a League appearance record for which club?

7 Which club signed a reputed £60 million kit deal with Umbro in February 1996?

8 Which club did Derek Mountfield join on leaving Everton?

9 Which country did Noel Brotherston play for?

10 Who was fined in 1996 for a newspaper article criticising Ruud Gullit?

11 Who plays at home at the Field Mill Ground?

12 Which team were beaten 1–0 by Dundee Utd in the 1994 Scottish FA Cup Final?

13 Which club did Dean Yates leave to join Derby County?

14 In which decade was Bobby Gould born?

15 Which former league club has a fanzine called *Talking Bull* and a bull mascot?

16 What is Andy Cole's middle name?

17 Geraint Williams and Dean Saunders were in the same side at which club?

18 Who moved from Oldham Athletic for £1,700,000 in February 1992, to set a club record for a transfer fee received?

19 What colour are Brentford's home shorts?

20 At which ground do Linfield play?

Answers

Pot Luck 26 (see Quiz 51)

1 Reading. **2** £60 million. **3** Blackburn Rovers. **4** Norwich City. **5** Dennis Bergkamp. **6** 1940s. **7** Chris Armstrong. **8** Plymouth Argyle. **9** Manchester Utd. **10** Martin Peters. **11** Carlisle United. **12** Machin. **13** Manchester Utd. **14** 1940s. **15** Bolton Wanderers. **16** Peter. **17** Aston Villa. **18** Arsenal. **19** Blue. **20** Northern Ireland.

Quiz 50 **FA and SFA Cup**

LEVEL 2

Answers – see page 162

1 Danny Wilson played in an FA Cup Final for which side?
2 How many times did Arsenal win the FA Cup in the 1980s?
3 Chris Waddle scored a wonder goal for which underdogs to knock out Everton in the 4th round in 1997?
4 For which team did Steve Archibald play in an FA Cup Final?
5 Which Chelsea player has scored in every round, including the Final?
6 In the 1980s, who scored for both sides in an FA Cup Final?
7 Webb and Wallace lined up together for which trophy-winning team?
8 Who were the winners in the Scottish FA Cup record score of 36–0?
9 And which team was on the receiving end of that thrashing?
10 Which club was Peter Beardsley with when he first won the FA Cup?
11 Which non-League side hit a last minute goal to draw at Coventry in 1997?
12 Which player has scored most FA Cup goals in total since 1945?
13 How many 1980s FA Cup Finals did Graeme Sharp take part in?
14 Which team won the Scottish FA Cup ten times, but never in the 20th century?
15 Who was the player-manager of the beaten 1994 London finalists?
16 Hednesford Town took the lead against which Premiership side in a 1997 4th Round tie?
17 Before the 1990s, who were the last team not in the top division to win the FA Cup?
18 Mark Bright played in FA Cup Finals for which two clubs?
19 Darren Anderton first played in a semi-final for which club?
20 Who was Wimbledon manager when they won in the 1980s?

Answers

Gazza (see Quiz 52)

1 1967. **2** £2 million. **3** Arsenal. **4** Roeder. **5** Gemini. **6** Denmark. **7** FA Cup Final. **8** Colin Hendry. **9** Terry Venables. **10** 14. **11** 8. **12** A leg. **13** Gary Charles. **14** Ipswich Town. **15** *Hello*. **16** Jack Charlton. **17** Third. **18** Sky Blue. **19** Fog (on the Tyne). **20** George Reilly.

Quiz 51 **Pot Luck 26**

LEVEL 2

Answers – see page 159

1. Martin Hicks set a League appearance record at which club?
2. How much to the nearest million did Kevin Keegan spend in transfer fees at Newcastle Utd?
3. For which club did Graeme Le Saux leave Chelsea?
4. Gary Megson followed Martin O'Neill as manager of which club?
5. Which player did manager Bruce Rioch buy in 1995 to set a new English club record?
6. In which decade did Aberdeen first win the Scottish FA Cup?
7. Who moved from Crystal Palace for £4.5 million in June 1995 to set a club record for a transfer fee received?
8. Which is the most southerly English League club?
9. Andy Cole was at which club when he made his international debut?
10. Which World Cup winner was born in Plaistow in 1943?
11. Who plays at home at Brunton Park?
12. Which Mel became boss of Bournemouth in August 1994
13. Which club did Mark Robins leave to join Norwich City?
14. In which decade was Brian Kidd born?
15. Which club has a fanzine called *Tripe'N'Trotters*?
16. What is Vinnie Jones' middle name?
17. Chris Price and Nigel Callaghan were in the same side at which club?
18. Which team were beaten 1–0 by Leeds Utd in the 1972 FA Cup Final?
19. What is the main colour of Rochdale's home shirts?
20. Which country did Billy Hamilton play for?

Answers

Pot Luck 25 (see Quiz 49)

1 Burnley. **2** Megson. **3** Reading. **4** Grimsby Town. **5** Newcastle Utd. **6** Millwall. **7** Manchester Utd. **8** Aston Villa. **9** Northern Ireland. **10** Vinnie Jones. **11** Mansfield. **12** Rangers. **13** Notts County. **14** 1940s. **15** Hereford Utd. **16** Alexander. **17** Derby County. **18** Earle Barrett. **19** Black. **20** Windsor Park.

Quiz 52 **Gazza**

LEVEL 2

Answers – see page 160

1 In what year was Paul Gascoigne born?

2 How much did he cost when he moved from Newcastle Utd to Tottenham Hotspur?

3 In 1991 Gazza scored a fantastic FA Cup semi-final goal against which team?

4 Which Glenn was Newcastle Utd skipper when Gazza started out?

5 What is his star sign?

6 Gazza made his international debut against which country?

7 What was his last competitive match of 1991?

8 Which Scottish player's challenge did Gazza ride before scoring for England in Euro 96?

9 Who was the boss at Tottenham Hotspur when Gazza arrived?

10 To one each way, how many league goals did Gazza score in his 28 games for Rangers in 1995–96?

11 What shirt number did Gazza wear at Tottenham Hotspur?

12 What did Gazza manage to break in a training match at Lazio?

13 Who was on the receiving end of the wild FA Cup Final tackle in which Gazza hurt himself?

14 At which club was he rejected after a trial in 1982?

15 Which magazine bought exclusive photos of his 1996 wedding?

16 Who was Newcastle Utd manager when Gazza made his debut?

17 What was the highest position Tottenham Hotspur finished in the League in Gazza's time?

18 What colour are Lazio's home shirts?

19 What weather conditions in his native north-east did he sing about?

20 Which Newcastle Utd centre forward went off as Gazza went on as sub for his debut?

Answers

FA and SFA Cup (see Quiz 50)

1 Sheffield Wednesday. **2** Never. **3** Bradford City. **4** Tottenham Hotspur. **5** Peter Osgood. **6** Gary Mabbutt. **7** Manchester Utd. **8** Arbroath. **9** Bon Accord. **10** Liverpool. **11** Woking. **12** Ian Rush. **13** Four. **14** Queen's Park. **15** Glenn Hoddle. **16** Middlesbrough. **17** West Ham Utd – 1980. **18** Crystal Palace and Sheffield Weds. **19** Portsmouth. **20** Bobby Gould.

Quiz 53 **Pot Luck 27**

LEVEL 2

Answers – see page 165

1 Which Ian became boss of Bristol Rovers in May 1996?

2 The minimum size of a pitch is 50 yards by how many yards?

3 Which was Steve Bruce's first League club?

4 Glenn Roeder left as boss of which club in February 1996?

5 How many Premiership games did Bolton win in the first half of the 1995–96 season?

6 Albert Ironmonger set a League appearance record for which club?

7 Brian Little followed David Pleat as manager of which club?

8 Which club did Peter Withe join on leaving Nottingham Forest?

9 Which country did George Wood play for?

10 Which England boss was born in Dagenham in 1920?

11 Who former League club in Yorkshire plays at home at the Belle Vue Ground?

12 Which team were beaten 2–1 by Rangers in the 1993 Scottish FA Cup Final?

13 Which club did Clive Wilson leave to join Tottenham Hotspur?

14 In which decade was Gerson born?

15 Which club has a fanzine called *Sing When We're Fishing*?

16 Which top manager has a son called Jason who has been part of the Sky Sports' production teams?

17 David Speedie and Cyrille Regis were in the same side at which club?

18 Who moved from Leeds United for £3.5 million in June 1996, to set a club record for a transfer fee received?

19 What colour are Bradford City's home shorts?

20 Stuart McCall made his international debut while at which club?

Answers

Pot Luck 28 (see Quiz 55)

1 David May. **2** 1974. **3** QPR. **4** Webb. **5** Alan Kelly. **6** 1920s. **7** Dean Saunders. **8** 0–2. **9** Southampton. **10** 1966. **11** Barnet. **12** Leeds Utd. **13** Rangers. **14** 1930s. **15** Chelsea. **16** Raymond. **17** Blackburn Rovers. **18** Blackpool. **19** Red. **20** The Republic of Ireland.

Quiz 54 **World Cup**

LEVEL 2

Answers – see page 164

---

1 In which city was the 1990 England v West Germany semi-final?

2 Who was the Italian skipper in the 1994 World Cup Final?

3 Which country knocked Germany out of the 1994 tournament?

4 Who was the goalkeeper in the controversial "Hand Of God" goal?

5 Who were England's first choice fullbacks for Italia 90?

6 Which three teams were in the Republic of Ireland's group in USA in 1994?

7 Which country hosted the World Cup in the wake of a tragic earthquake?

8 Which 1994 World Cup winner later played for Middlesbrough?

9 England and the Republic of Ireland were in which Group in Italia 90?

10 Who became the first person to captain and manage World Cup winning sides?

11 Which country did Scotland beat in the 1990 finals?

12 Which Trevor went on as an English sub in the 1990 semi-final?

13 What was the score after 90 minutes in the 1994 Final?

14 Who was English boss in Spain in 1982?

15 Before the 90s when did Brazil last win the trophy?

16 Illgner was in goal for which World Cup winning country?

17 McGrath, McCarthy, Morris – who was the fourth defender with an initial M in the Republic of Ireland's great 1990 campaign?

18 Who did England beat in the 1990 quarter-final?

19 Bertoni scored a Final goal for which country?

20 In which year was the Final held at the Rose Bowl?

Answers

All Round Sportsmen (see Quiz 56)

1 Andy Goram. **2** Viv Richards. **3** Gary Lineker. **4** Geoff Hurst. **5** Denis Compton. **6** Scunthorpe. **7** Hampshire. **8** Morris. **9** Bradford. **10** Gaelic football. **11** Neale. **12** Manchester Utd. **13** Charlton Athletic. **14** Balderstone. **15** Mick Channon. **16** West Ham Utd. **17** Goalkeeper. **18** Aston Villa. **19** Bayern Munich. **20** Bairstow.

Quiz 55 **Pot Luck 28**

Answers – see page 163

LEVEL 2

1 Who was the only Premiership player in 1996 to share his name with a calendar month?

2 In which year did George Best last play for Manchester Utd?

3 What was Clive Allen's first League club?

4 Which David was boss of Chelsea in 1993?

5 Which keeper set a League appearance record for Preston North End?

6 In which decade did Airdrieonians first win the Scottish FA Cup?

7 Who moved from Derby County to Liverpool in July 1991 to set a club record for a transfer fee received?

8 What was the half-time score in the Chelsea v Liverpool 1997 4th Round FA Cup game, which the home side won 4-2?

9 Tim Flowers was at which club when he made his international debut?

10 In which year was Eric Cantona born?

11 Who former league club plays at home at the Underhill Stadium?

12 Howard Wilkinson followed Billy Bremner as manager of which club?

13 Which club did John Spencer leave to join Chelsea?

14 In which decade was Ken Bates born?

15 Which club has a fanzine called *The Red Card*?

16 What is Martin Keown's middle name?

17 Simon Garner and Mark Atkins were in the same side at which club?

18 Which team were beaten 2–0 by Newcastle Utd in the 1951 FA Cup Final?

19 What is the main colour of Rotherham's home shirts?

20 Which country did Joe Kinnear play for?

Answers

Pot Luck 27 (see Quiz 53)

1 Holloway. **2** 100 yards. **3** Gillingham. **4** Watford. **5** Two. **6** Notts County. **7** Leicester City. **8** Newcastle Utd. **9** Scotland. **10** Alf Ramsey. **11** Doncaster Rovers. **12** Aberdeen. **13** QPR. **14** 1940s. **15** Grimsby. **16** Alex Ferguson. **17** Coventry City. **18** Gary Speed. **19** Black. **20** Everton.

Quiz 56 **All Round Sportsmen**

LEVEL 2

Answers – see page 164

1 Which 1990s goalkeeper has played soccer and cricket for Scotland?

2 Which West Indian batsman played soccer for Antigua in the 1978 World Cup qualifying games?

3 Which soccer striker played for the MCC against the Germans, scored a run and said, "It's always nice to score one against the Germans"?

4 Which member of England's 1966 World Cup winning side played first-class cricket with Essex?

5 Which England batsman played in the 1950 FA Cup Final for Arsenal?

6 Which Football League club did Ian Botham play for?

7 Which county did England centre forward Ted Drake play cricket for?

8 Which Republic of Ireland defender Chris won cricket honours for Cornish schools?

9 England's cricket captain Brian Close played soccer for which team?

10 Apart from soccer, Kevin Moran was a star in which sport?

11 Which Phil skippered both Lincoln and Worcester CCC in the 1980s?

12 Which club did cricketer Arnold Sidebottom play for in the mid 1970s?

13 England's Mickey Stewart played for which Football League club?

14 Which Chris played for Leicestershire at cricket in the day and for Doncaster Rovers in an evening match on the same date?

15 Which Southampton and England striker turned to breeding and training racehorses?

16 In the 1960s, cricketer Jim Standen played soccer for which London club?

17 Worcestershire CCC's Jimmy Cumbes played which position in soccer?

18 Which 1970s League Cup-winning side was Jimmy Cumbes in?

19 Boris Becker had soccer trials for which club?

20 Which David was a Yorkshire wicket keeper and Bradford City player?

Answers

World Cup (see Quiz 54)

1 Turin. **2** Franco Baresi. **3** Bulgaria. **4** Peter Shilton. **5** Paul Parker, Stuart Pearce. **6** Italy, Mexico, Norway. **7** Mexico. **8** Branco. **9** Group F. **10** Franz Beckenbauer. **11** Sweden. **12** Steven. **13** 0–0. **14** Ron Greenwood. **15** 1970. **16** West Germany. **17** Moran. **18** Cameroon. **19** Argentina. **20** 1994.

Quiz 57 **Pot Luck 29**

LEVEL 2

Answers – see page 169

1 What was Matt Busby's occupation before he became a footballer?
2 Which Brian became boss of Manchester City in 1993?
3 Which was Jamie Redknapp's first League club?
4 George Burley was player-manager of which Scottish side?
5 Ian Wood set a League appearance record for which club?
6 Steve Coppell followed Alan Ball as manager of which club?
7 How many times did Norwich win the FA Cup in the 20th century?
8 Which team does Angus Deayton support?
9 Which country did Eric Gates play for?
10 In which city was Andy Cole born?
11 Who plays at home at Sixfields Stadium?
12 Which team were beaten 2–1 by Rangers in the 1992 Scottish FA Cup Final?
13 Which club did Russell Hoult leave to join Derby County?
14 In which decade was Roy Keane born?
15 Which club has a fanzine called *Speke From The Harbour*?
16 Mark Robins was leading scorer for which Premiership side when they finished third?
17 Steve Clarke and Clive Wilson were in the same side at which club?
18 Who moved from Ipswich Town to Tottenham Hotspur in 1993 to set a club record for a transfer fee received?
19 What colour are Barnsley's home shorts?
20 Steve Hodge was at which club when he made his international debut?

Answers

Pot Luck 30 (see Quiz 59)

1 By shouting at his teammates. **2** Charlton Athletic. **3** Burnley. **4** Sharp. **5** Port Vale. **6** 1890s. **7** Gary Croft. **8** Wimbledon. **9** Portsmouth. **10** Don Revie. **11** Wigan Athletic. **12** Grimsby Town. **13** Manchester City. **14** 1930s. **15** Crystal Palace. **16** Matthew. **17** Charlton Athletic. **18** Manchester Utd. **19** Red. **20** Northern Ireland.

Quiz 58 **Euro Cup Winners' Cup**

LEVEL 2

Answers – see page 170

1 Alex Ferguson managed which two Cup Winners' Cup winners?

2 Which Borussia Dortmund player scored a record 14 goals in 1965–66?

3 Who were the first English team to win the trophy in the 1990s?

4 Kevin Sheedy played in a trophy-winning team with which club?

5 Who were the first Soviet side to win the competition?

6 Which team beat Liverpool in a 1960s Final?

7 Rangers' victory in 1972 was marred by hooligan trouble. What was the Scottish team's penalty for this trouble?

8 Which Italian side were the first winners of the competition?

9 In what year was the first Final played?

10 Who was coach of the Spanish team that won the 1989 Final?

11 Who was in goal for that Final?

12 What was strange about the West Ham Utd v Castilla 1980 game?

13 Who lost a Final to Valencia in 1980 in a penalty shoot out?

14 Paul Furlong scored three times in the 1994–95 competition for which club?

15 But for UEFA's ban, which two sides would have represented England in 1985–86?

16 And why would there have been two English clubs in the 1985–86 season?

17 Which Welsh player, rejected by Barcelona, scored the winning goal against the Spanish side in the 1991 Final?

18 1860 Munich and Anderlecht have both played which English team in Finals?

19 West Ham Utd played their first Final in which stadium?

20 Which Russian side did Rangers beat in the 1972 Final?

Answers

The 1980s (see Quiz 60)

1 Trevor Brooking. **2** Hearts. **3** Ron Atkinson. **4** None. **5** Glenn Hoddle. **6** Michel Platini. **7** Kenny Dalglish. **8** Alan Shearer. **9** 24. **10** Bill Shankly. **11** Porto. **12** Tottenham Hotspur. **13** WBA. **14** Brian Clough. **15** Danny, Rodney and Ray. **16** Bayern Munich. **17** Laurie Sanchez. **18** Today. **19** Hans Van Breukelen. **20** Arsenal.

Quiz 59 **Pot Luck 30**

LEVEL 2

Answers – see page 167

1 How did keeper Alex Stepney dislocate his jaw in August 1975?

2 Kenny Dalglish's first home game as Newcastle Utd boss was against which team in the FA Cup?

3 What was Leighton James' first league club?

4 Which Graeme became boss of Oldham Athletic in November 1994?

5 Roy Sproson set a League appearance record for which club?

6 In which decade did Celtic first win the Scottish FA Cup?

7 Who moved from Grimsby Town to Blackburn Rovers for £1 million to set a club record for a transfer fee received?

8 ME I'D BLOWN conceals which team?

9 Mark Hateley was at which club when he made his international debut?

10 Which international manager was born in Middlesbrough in 1927?

11 Who used to be at home at Springfield Park?

12 Brian Laws followed Alan Buckley as manager of which club?

13 Which club did Ian Bishop leave to join West Ham Utd?

14 In which decade was Brian Clough born?

15 Which club has a fanzine called *Eastern Eagle*?

16 What is Ian Wright's middle name?

17 Carl Leaburn and John Humphries were in the same side at which club?

18 Which team were beaten 2–1 by Aston Villa in the 1957 FA Cup Final?

19 What colour goes with white on Scarborough's home shirts?

20 Which country did Allan Hunter play for?

Answers

Pot Luck 29 (see Quiz 57)

1 Miner. **2** Horton. **3** Bournemouth. **4** Ayr. **5** Oldham Athletic. **6** Manchester City. **7** Never. **8** Manchester Utd. **9** England. **10** Nottingham. **11** Northampton Town. **12** Airdrieonians. **13** Leicester City. **14** 1970s. **15** Everton. **16** Norwich City. **17** Chelsea. **18** Jason Dozzell. **19** White. **20** Aston Villa.

Quiz 60 **The 1980s**

LEVEL 2

Answers – see page 168

1 Whose two goals against Hungary clinched England's place in the 1982 World Cup?

2 Which club lost out in both the Scottish League and FA Cup in 1986?

3 Who was sacked to be replaced by Alex Ferguson at Manchester Utd?

4 How many games did England lose in the 1982 World Cup finals?

5 Who scored Tottenham Hotspur's penalty to beat QPR in an FA Cup Final replay?

6 Which Frenchman won the European Footballer of the Year award three consecutive times?

7 Which manager brought Ian Rush back to Liverpool from Juventus?

8 Which Southampton player became the youngest to score a First Division hat-trick v Arsenal on April 9, 1988?

9 How many teams competed in the 1982 World Cup in Spain?

10 Which famous former Liverpool manager died in 1981?

11 Which Portuguese side won the World Club Championship in 1987?

12 Which club paid £2 million to sign Paul Gascoigne?

13 Which club did Bryan Robson play for before joining Manchester Utd?

14 Which manager clashed with fans invading the pitch during a League Cup-tie?

15 Give the first names of the three Wallace brothers who played in the same Southampton team?

16 Which German club did Karl-Heinz Rummenigge play for?

17 Who scored the goal when Wimbledon won the FA Cup in 1988?

18 Which newspaper sponsored the Football League in the 1980s?

19 Who saved a penalty in the 1988 European Championship Final?

20 Anderson and Sansom were in the same team at which club?

Answers

Euro Cup Winners' Cup (see Quiz 58)

1 Manchester Utd and Aberdeen. **2** Lothar Emmerich. **3** Manchester Utd. **4** Everton. **5** Dynamo Kiev. **6** Borussia Dortmund. **7** A one-year ban from European games. **8** Fiorentina. **9** 1961. **10** Johan Cruyff. **11** Les Sealey. **12** Played behind closed doors. **13** Arsenal. **14** Chelsea. **15** Everton and Manchester Utd. **16** Everton won the Cup in 1985. **17** Mark Hughes. **18** West Ham Utd. **19** Wembley. **20** Moscow Dynamo.

Quiz 61 **Pot Luck 31**

LEVEL 2

Answers – see page 173

1 Which Russell became manager of Bristol City in 1993?

2 How old was Steve Coppell when he retired from playing?

3 Which was Julian Dicks' first League club?

4 The book Macca Can was about which player?

5 Who wanted a "loyalty" payment from Tottenham Hotspur after spending season 1992–93 with them before moving to Liverpool?

6 How is Jimmy Gardner better known?

7 Steve Coppell followed Alan Mullery as manager at which club?

8 Terry Phelan played in an FA Cup Final for which team?

9 Which country did Dave Clements play for?

10 Which future England player was born in Rotherham in 1963?

11 Who plays at home at Love Street?

12 Which team were beaten 4–3 by Motherwell in the 1991 Scottish FA Cup Final?

13 Which club did Paul Rideout leave to join Everton?

14 In which decade was Darren Anderton born?

15 Which club has a fanzine called *Bert Trautmann's Helmet*?

16 What is Dean Holdsworth's middle name?

17 Steve Vickers and Neil Cox were in the same side at which club?

18 Who moved from Southend for £2 million in June 1993 to set a club record for a transfer fee received?

19 What colour are Southampton's home shorts?

20 Terry Fenwick was at which club when he made his international debut?

Answers

Pot Luck 32 (see Quiz 63)

1 Manchester Utd. **2** Terry Venables. **3** West Ham Utd. **4** Leeds Utd. **5** Everton. **6** 1890s. **7** Kevin Francis. **8** Sam Bartram. **9** Ipswich Town. **10** Paul Rideout. **11** PSV Eindhoven. **12** Kamara. **13** Crewe Alexandra. **14** 1930s. **15** Nottingham Forest. **16** Ron Greenwood. **17** Manchester Utd. **18** Luton Town. **19** Blue and white. **20** Scotland.

Quiz 62 **Defenders**

LEVEL 2

Answers – see page 174

1 Miller and Roberts formed a partnership at which London club?

2 Which fullback captained England in the World Cup in Spain?

3 Shaun Teale went to which club after leaving Villa?

4 Which 17-year-old made his debut at left-back for AC Milan in 1985 and was holding the position ten years later?

5 Which club did England's Bob Crompton play for?

6 In a 1994 England game the goalkeeper and two centre halves all came from which club?

7 Whose clubs read: Leeds Utd, Wimbledon, Manchester City, Chelsea, Everton?

8 Which club did Phil Neal play for before he joined Liverpool?

9 To a year each way, when did Stuart Pearce first play for England?

10 Did iron man Tommy Smith ever play for England?

11 Butterworth and Culverhouse were in the same team at which club?

12 Which Scottish side did Neil Pointon move to?

13 Gary Pallister went on loan to which other north-east club in his Middlesbrough days?

14 Which left-back was displaced by Graeme Le Saux at Blackburn Rovers?

15 George Cohen was with which club when he played for England?

16 Which club did Booth and Caton play for?

17 Which England full-back Roger died in the Munich air disaster?

18 Which ex-Blackburn Rovers defender faced his old team in the 1994 Charity Shield?

19 Which country did Paul Breitner play for?

20 Which Kevin played for Norwich, Manchester City and Southampton?

Answers

International Scene (see Quiz 64)

1 Bulgaria. **2** Belgium. **3** David Platt. **4** Sweden. **5** The Azteca in Mexico City. **6** Marco Van Basten. **7** Jan Ceulemans. **8** 40. **9** Roger Milla. **10** Argentina. **11** Mo Johnston. **12** Lev Yashin. **13** Arnold Muhren. **14** Zico. **15** Terry Venables. **16** Basil Boli. **17** 16. **18** Igor Stimac. **19** Strachan. **20** Thomas Ravelli.

Quiz 63 **Pot Luck 32**

Answers – see page 171

LEVEL 2

1 Ray Wilkins first played in an FA Cup Final for which team?
2 Which Barcelona manager bought Mark Hughes?
3 What was Mervyn Day's first League club?
4 Eddie Gray followed Allan Clarke as manager at which club?
5 What is the middle name of ex-Liverpool player Mark Walters?
6 In which decade did Notts County first win the FA Cup?
7 Who moved from Stockport County to Birmingham City for £800,000 in January 1995 to set a club record for a transfer fee received?
8 With 583 games, which goalkeeper established Charlton's League appearance record?
9 In the 1970s, David Johnson was at which club when he made his international debut?
10 In the 1994–95 FA Cup winning season, who was Everton's top League scorer?
11 Which former European Cup-winners play at home at the Philips Stadium?
12 Which Chris became manager of Bradford City in November 1995?
13 Which club did Ashley Ward leave to join Norwich City?
14 In which decade was Gordon Banks born?
15 Which club has a fanzine called *The Tricky Tree*?
16 Which England manager gave Bryan Robson his first cap?
17 Paul Parker and Lee Sharpe were in the same side at which club?
18 Which team was beaten 2–1 by Nottingham Forest in the 1959 FA Cup Final?
19 What are the two colours of Reading's home shirts?
20 In the 1930s, which country did HM Wales play for?

Answers

Pot Luck 31 (see Quiz 61)

1 Osman. **2** 28. **3** Birmingham City. **4** Steve McMahon. **5** Neil Ruddock. **6** "Five Bellies". **7** Crystal Palace. **8** Wimbledon. **9** Northern Ireland. **10** David Seaman. **11** St Mirren. **12** Dundee Utd. **13** Rangers. **14** 1970s. **15** Manchester City. **16** Christopher. **17** Middlesbrough. **18** Stan Collymore. **19** Black. **20** QPR.

Quiz 64 **International Scene**

LEVEL 2

Answers – see page 172

1 Which country finished fourth in the 1994 World Cup?

2 Which country did Nico Claesen play for?

3 Who scored England's only goal in Euro 92?

4 In which country was Richard Gough born?

5 In which stadium was the 1986 World Cup Final played?

6 Which Dutchman hit a Euro 88 hat-trick against England?

7 Who set a record by playing 96 times for Belgium?

8 How old was Dino Zoff when he was in Italy's World Cup-winning side?

9 Whose World Cup corner flag dance started the craze for dance routine celebrations?

10 Which country did Oscar Ruggeri play for?

11 Which Scot scored in five successive World Cup qualifiers between 1988 and 1989?

12 Which player, who died in 1990, was awarded the Order of Lenin?

13 Which Dutch outfield player was 37 when Holland won Euro 88?

14 Who, with 54 goals, was second only to Pele as a Brazilan scorer?

15 Which Australian manager got off to a winning start in January 1997?

16 Which French player went head to head with Stuart Pearce in Euro 92?

17 How old was Diego Maradona when he first played for Argentina?

18 Who was the first Croatian international to play in the English League?

19 Which Gordon scored Scotland's only World Cup goal in Mexico?

20 Which goalkeeper is Sweden's most capped player?

Answers

Defenders (see Quiz 62)

1 Tottenham Hotspur. **2** Mick Mills. **3** Tranmere Rovers. **4** Paolo Maldini. **5** Blackburn Rovers. **6** Arsenal (Seaman, Adams, Bould) **7** Terry Phelan. **8** Northampton. **9** 1987. **10** Yes (Once in 1971). **11** Norwich City. **12** Hearts. **13** Darlington. **14** Alan Wright. **15** Fulham. **16** Manchester City. **17** Byrne. **18** David May. **19** West Germany. **20** Bond.

Quiz 65 **Pot Luck 33**

Answers – see page 177

LEVEL 2

1 Gary Gillespie played in an FA Cup Final for which team?

2 Which forename links Hibbitt and Swain, both sacked as managers on the same day in 1994?

3 Which was Paul Bracewell's first League club?

4 Which Dave became boss of Brentford in May 1993?

5 Which team were once known as Eastville Rovers?

6 Which player's book *A Double Life* appeared in 1990?

7 George Curtis followed Don Mackay as manager at which club?

8 Which club did Steve Sedgley join on leaving Tottenham Hotspur?

9 Which country did Mark Chamberlain play for?

10 Which England skipper was born in Chester-le-Street in 1957?

11 Which Scottish side plays at home at the Almondvale Stadium?

12 Which team were beaten 1–0 by Celtic in the 1989 Scottish FA Cup Final?

13 Which club did Kevin Richardson leave to join Arsenal?

14 In which decade was Emlyn Hughes born?

15 Which club has a fanzine called *Beyond The Boundary*?

16 A 1994 League Cup defeat by Notts County was the sign for which Tottenham Hotspur boss that his days were numbered?

17 Which club had Venison and Fox on the same team?

18 Who moved from Sheffield Wednesday to Blackburn Rovers in 1993 to set a club record for a transfer fee received?

19 What colour are Sheffield Utd's home shorts?

20 Trevor Francis was at which club when he made his international debut?

Answers

Pot Luck 34 (see Quiz 67)

1 Wolves. **2** Nigeria. **3** Wolves. **4** Fourth. **5** Graeme Le Saux. **6** 1930s. **7** Marco Gabbiadini. **8** Carlisle United. **9** Everton. **10** Lou Macari. **11** Everton. **12** Rioch. **13** Derby County. **14** 1930s. **15** Plymouth Argyle. **16** York City. **17** Manchester City. **18** Liverpool. **19** Blue. **20** The Republic of Ireland.

Quiz 66 **Kenny Dalglish**

LEVEL 2 

Answers – see page 178

1 Which team did Kenny support as a boy?

2 How many Scottish caps did Dalglish win?

3 What is the first name of Mrs Dalglish?

4 In which year did Kenny win his first Scottish Championship medal?

5 Which Liverpool manager signed Kenny?

6 How many times did Kenny win the championship for Liverpool when he was the boss?

7 Which manager gave Kenny his first Scottish cap?

8 What is Kenny's starsign?

9 Who were the opponents on the day that Dalglish's Blackburn Rovers won the Premiership?

10 Kenny replaced Kevin Keegan at Liverpool. Which transfer cost most?

11 Who did Kenny replace as skipper of Celtic?

12 Kenny scored the only goal in the 1978 European Cup Final against which side?

13 Which managers picked Kenny's teams in his 1986 testimonial?

14 Who was Kenny's Liverpool skipper for the 1986 double-winning side?

15 How many World Cup final tournaments did Kenny play in?

16 Who advised Kenny, "If you are going to get kicked, get kicked in the box, it's worth it in there"?

17 How old was Kenny when he first played for Celtic?

18 Who was acting manager at Blackburn Rovers when Kenny arrived?

19 What decoration was Kenny awarded in February 1985?

20 Which former Liverpool teammate was assistant manager at Newcastle Utd when Kenny arrived?

Answers

Merseysiders (see Quiz 68)

1 Howard Kendall (during his second spell). **2** 60. **3** Real Sociedad. **4** Phil Neal. **5** Brian Labone. **6** Andrei Kanchelskis. **7** Gary Lineker. **8** Bell. **9** Kenny Dalglish. **10** Bournemouth. **11** Bobby Mimms. **12** 1991. **13** Everton in 1890–91, before Liverpool were formed. **14** Blackburn Rovers. **15** Harry Catterick. **16** Joe Fagan. **17** Kenny Dalglish. **18** Oldham Athletic. **19** European Cup. **20** John Wark.

Quiz 67 **Pot Luck 34**

LEVEL 2

Answers – see page 175

1. Graham Turner followed Brian Little as manager at which club in October 1986?
2. Which country did John Chiedozie play for?
3. Which was Tim Flowers' first League club?
4. From 1965 to 1974 what was the lowest position that Leeds Utd finished in the First Division?
5. Which future England international was born in October 1968 in Jersey?
6. In which decade did Portsmouth first win the FA Cup?
7. Who moved from Sunderland to Crystal Palace for £1.5 million in 1991 to set a club record for a transfer fee received?
8. Alan Ross set a league record for appearances at which club?
9. Paul Bracewell was at which club when he made his international debut?
10. Which manager, still living in England, was dismissed by Celtic in June 1994?
11. Pat Van Den Hauwe first played in an FA Cup Final for which team?
12. Which Bruce became boss of Millwall in 1992?
13. Which club did Paul Kitson leave to join Newcastle Utd?
14. In which decade was Johnny Haynes born?
15. Which club has a fanzine called *Rub of the Greens*?
16. Alphabetically, which is the last English League team?
17. Paul Walsh and Keith Curle were in the same side at which club?
18. Which team were beaten 2–1 by Arsenal in the 1971 FA Cup Final?
19. What is the main colour of Shrewsbury's home shirts?
20. Which country did Mark Lawrenson play for?

Answers

Pot Luck 33 (see Quiz 65)

1 Liverpool. **2** Kenny. **3** Stoke City. **4** Webb. **5** Bristol Rovers. **6** Phil Neal. **7** Coventry City. **8** Ipswich Town. **9** England. **10** Bryan Robson. **11** Livingston. **12** Rangers. **13** Watford. **14** 1940s. **15** Oldham Athletic. **16** Ossie Ardiles. **17** Newcastle Utd. **18** Paul Warhurst. **19** Black. **20** Birmingham City.

Quiz 68 **Merseysiders**

LEVEL 2

Answers – see page 176

---

1 Who was manager of Everton before Mike Walker?

2 How many League goals did Dixie Dean score in his record-breaking 1927–28 season?

3 From which club did John Aldridge join Tranmere Rovers?

4 Who was Bob Paisley's first buy for Liverpool?

5 Which Everton centre-back played in the 1970 World Cup in Mexico?

6 Which player created Everton's record transfer fee paid in 1995?

7 Which Everton player won the Footballer of the Year award in 1986?

8 Which 'Bunny' scored most goals in a season for Tranmere Rovers?

9 Which ex-Liverpool player holds Scotland's most-capped record?

10 From which club did Liverpool sign Jamie Redknapp?

11 Who was in goal for Everton in the 1986 FA Cup Final?

12 Which year did Tranmere Rovers win the play-off final to gain promotion to Division Two?

13 Who won the League championship first – Liverpool or Everton?

14 Before joining Everton, where was Howard Kendall player/manager?

15 Which Everton manager captured the League championship in 1963?

16 Who took over at Liverpool when Bob Paisley retired in 1983?

17 Who hit Liverpool's last League goal in the 1985–86 double season?

18 Which club was Mike Milligan bought from and sold back to?

19 Kevin Keegan's last game for Liverpool was in which competition?

20 Which Scottish midfielder was Liverpool's top league scorer in 1984–85?

Answers

Kenny Dalglish (see Quiz 66)

1 Rangers. **2** 102. **3** Marina. **4** 1972. **5** Bob Paisley. **6** Three. **7** Tommy Docherty. **8** Aquarius. **9** Liverpool. **10** Keegan's. **11** Billy McNeill. **12** Bruges. **13** Tommy Docherty and Alex Ferguson. **14** Alan Hansen. **15** Three. **16** Bob Paisley. **17** 20. **18** Tony Parkes. **19** MBE. **20** Terry McDermott.

Quiz 69 **Pot Luck 35**

Answers – see page 181

LEVEL 2

1 Whose book was called Man On The Run?

2 Hales, Flanagan and Peacock all scored goals for which club?

3 Which was David Kelly's first League club?

4 Which Howard became manager of Notts County in 1995?

5 How many goals did Peter Osgood score for England?

6 Which player describing his upbringing said, "There's only one word to describe Raploch, and that's hard"?

7 Ian Porterfield followed Bobby Campbell as manager at which club?

8 Steve Spriggs set an appearance record at which club?

9 Which country did Colin Viljoen play for?

10 Veteran Graham Rix appeared as a substitute in the Premiership for which club in 1995?

11 Scotsman Andy Gray played in an FA Cup Final for which team?

12 Which team were beaten 3–0 by Aberdeen in the 1986 Scottish FA Cup Final?

13 Which club did David Rocastle leave to join Manchester City?

14 In which decade was Gary Mabbutt born?

15 Which club has a fanzine called *Beat About The Bush*?

16 In what position did Swindon Town's Fraser Digby play?

17 Which club had Lyttle and Chettle in the same side?

18 Who moved from Sheffield Utd to Leeds Utd for £2,700,000 in 1993 to set a club record for a transfer fee received?

19 What colour goes with navy on Torquay's home shirts?

20 Alan Hudson was at which club when he made his international debut?

Answers

Pot Luck 36 (see Quiz 71)

1 Wimbledon. **2** David Platt. **3** Blackburn Rovers. **4** Deehan. **5** Chris Sutton. **6** 1960s. **7** Jan-Aage Fjortoft. **8** Cardiff City. **9** West Ham Utd. **10** Crewe Alexandra. **11** Cowdenbeath. **12** Tottenham Hotspur. **13** Rangers. **14** 1940s. **15** Sheffield United. **16** Uruguay. **17** Arsenal. **18** Preston North End. **19** Black. **20** Wales.

Quiz 70 **League Cup**

Answers – see page 182

LEVEL 2

1 Which England international scored in both the FA and Coca-Cola Cup Finals of 1993?
2 To two years each way, when did the first Final go to extra time?
3 Which TV expert scored a Final winner for Wolves?
4 Which manager dealt with four fans who invaded the pitch in a League Cup match at the City Ground in 1989?
5 Which Charlie scored the winner against Liverpool in the 1987 Final?
6 Which team finally landed the trophy in 1985 in their third Wembley Final?
7 What was the added bonus for Stoke City in the 1972 success?
8 In 1983, who became the youngest ever player to score a League Cup Final goal at Wembley?
9 Which player scored his 100th Manchester Utd goal in the 1992 Final?
10 Which London side became the first club to win the trophy twice?
11 Who scored two of Swindon Town's goals to defeat Arsenal in 1969?
12 Which relegated London team reached the semi-finals in 1993?
13 Steve Bruce first played in a Final for which club?
14 Which year was the first-ever all Merseyside Final?
15 Name the grounds of the first two winners of the League Cup?
16 Which club won the trophy four times during the 1980s?
17 Who was injured by his own skipper after the Final in 1993?
18 Which manager was the first to win the trophy as the Coca-Cola Cup?
19 In which year was the Final first played at Wembley?
20 Who beat West Ham Utd 6–1 on their plastic pitch in a League Cup semi-final match in 1990?

Answers

Managers (see Quiz 72)

1 Osman. **2** Arsenal. **3** Coventry City. **4** Crystal Palace. **5** Chelsea. **6** Wilf McGuinness. **7** David Pleat. **8** 62. **9** Huddersfield & Arsenal. **10** Peter Withe. **11** Kenny Dalglish. **12** Port Vale. **13** Crystal Palace. **14** Haslam. **15** Bill Nicholson. **16** Ray Wilkins. **17** Derby County. **18** Bob Paisley. **19** Colchester United. **20** Billy McNeill.

Quiz 71 **Pot Luck 36**

LEVEL 2

Answers – see page 179

1 Andy Thorn first played in an FA Cup Final for which team?
2 Which player born in Oldham in 1966 set a world record in transfer fees?
3 What was Simon Barker's first League club?
4 Which John became manager of Norwich City in 1994?
5 In 1994 which player was transferred to Blackburn for £5.5 million?
6 In which decade did Dunfermline first win the Scottish FA Cup?
7 Who moved from Swindon Town for £1,300,000 in March 1995 to set a club record for a transfer fee received?
8 Phil Dwyer set a League appearance record at which club?
9 Paul Goddard was at which club when he made his international debut?
10 Dario Gradi became manager for which club in 1983?
11 Which Scottish team plays at home at Central Park?
12 Keith Burkinshaw followed Ossie Ardiles as manager at which club?
13 Which club did Nigel Spackman leave to join Chelsea for the second time?
14 In which decade was Eusebio born?
15 Which club has a fanzine called *The Flashing Blade*?
16 Which country do the club Penarol come from?
17 Alan Smith and Kevin Campbell were in the same side at which club?
18 Which team were beaten 3–2 by WBA in the 1954 FA Cup Final?
19 What colour are Wolves' home shorts?
20 Which country did Roy Vernon play for?

Answers

Pot Luck 35 (see Quiz 69)

1 Mick Channon. **2** Charlton Athletic. **3** Walsall. **4** Kendall. **5** None. **6** Billy Bremner. **7** Chelsea. **8** Cambridge Utd. **9** England. **10** Chelsea. **11** Everton. **12** Hearts. **13** Leeds Utd. **14** 1960s. **15** QPR. **16** Goalkeeper. **17** Nottingham Forest. **18** Brian Deane. **19** Yellow. **20** Stoke City.

Quiz 72 **Managers**

Answers – see page 180

LEVEL 2

1 Which Russell has been manager of Bristol City and Cardiff City?

2 Don Howe was manager of which team in 1984?

3 Bobby Gould has twice been manager of which club?

4 At which club could fans shout in 1980, "There's only one Ernie Walley"?

5 Which London club did Geoff Hurst manage?

6 Who followed Matt Busby at Manchester Utd?

7 Who was Luton's boss when they went out of the top flight in 1992?

8 How old was Joe Fagan when he became Liverpool manager?

9 With which two sides did Herbert Chapman win the Championship?

10 Who was Wimbledon boss before Joe Kinnear?

11 Who was the first player/manager to win the championship?

12 John Rudge has spent more than ten years as boss of which club?

13 In 1984 Dave Bassett left Wimbledon, but returned after only a few days spent at which club?

14 Which Harry was Luton manager from 1972–78?

15 Who won the Championship as a player and a manager with Tottenham Hotspur?

16 When he became Watford manager at the start of the 2001–02 season who did Gianluca Vialli take to Vicarage Road as his number two?

17 Brian Clough won his first championship as a manager at which club?

18 Who was manager of the year in 1976, 1977, 1979, 1980, 1982 and 1983?

19 Which was Mike Walker's first club as a manager?

20 Who followed David Hay as Celtic manager?

Answers

League Cup (see Quiz 70)

1 Chris Waddle. **2** 1961. **3** Andy Gray. **4** Brian Clough. **5** Charlie Nicholas. **6** Norwich City. **7** Qualification for Europe. **8** Norman Whiteside. **9** Brian McClair. **10** Tottenham Hotspur. **11** Don Rogers. **12** Crystal Palace. **13** Norwich City. **14** 1984. **15** Villa Park and Carrow Road. **16** Liverpool. **17** Steve Morrow. **18** George Graham in 1993. **19** 1967 **20** Oldham Athletic.

Quiz 73 **Pot Luck 37**

LEVEL 2

Answers – see page 185

1 Tony Barton followed Ron Saunders as manager of which club?
2 In which Northumberland village was Bobby Charlton born?
3 Which was Ray Clemence's first League club?
4 Which 1980's and 1990's striker hit 111 Everton League goals?
5 Ian Pearce first played in an FA Charity Shield for which club?
6 Which George became manager of Ipswich Town in December 1994?
7 Jesper Olsen won an FA Cup winners' medal with which club?
8 Which club did Mark Kennedy join on leaving Millwall?
9 Which country did Gerry Peyton play for?
10 Which team play at home in front of the Cobbold Stand?
11 Which ex-England skipper died in September 1994?
12 Which team were beaten 2–0 by Tottenham Hotspur in the 1961 FA Cup Final?
13 In 1996, Kevin Keegan was incensed by Alex Ferguson's comments concerning which opposing team?
14 In which decade was Kenny Dalglish born?
15 Which club has a fanzine called *Red Stripe*?
16 What was the first name of Bolton's De Freitas?
17 Cowan and Bullock were in the same side at which club?
18 Who moved from Leicester City to Aston Villa in July 1995 to set a club record for a transfer fee received?
19 What colour are Watford's home shorts?
20 Andy Townsend was at which club when he made his international debut?

Answers

Pot Luck 38 (see Quiz 75)

1 1–1. **2** Oldham Athletic. **3** Swindon Town. **4** 1930. **5** Julian. **6** 1890s. **7** Alan Shearer. **8** Bradford City. **9** Rangers. **10** Terry Venables. **11** Hull City. **12** Harford. **13** Poland. **14** 1950s. **15** Stoke City. **16** Nigel Clough. **17** Sheffield Wednesday. **18** Everton. **19** White. **20** Northern Ireland.

Quiz 74 **Double Dutch**

LEVEL 2

Answers – see page 186

---

1 Which Dutch team were the first to win a major European trophy?

2 As a player which club did Johan Cruyff move to when he left Ajax?

3 With 83 games who set an appearance record for Holland?

4 In which city was Ruud Gullit born?

5 Who was the top scorer in Euro 88?

6 Who were Dutch champions in 1994, 1995 and 1996?

7 Who was the Dutch coach for Euro 88?

8 Which English club did Dennis Bergkamp support as a child?

9 Which Dutch player scored against England in Euro 96?

10 Ruud Gullit became the world's most expensive player when he moved from which club to AC Milan in 1987?

11 Which English manager won two consecutive titles with PSV Eindhoven in the 1990s?

12 Who was top scorer for the Dutch in both 1974 and 1978 World Cups?

13 What are the colours of Ajax?

14 At which club did Ronald Koeman start his League career?

15 Who was the first Dutch skipper to lift a major international trophy for his country?

16 Which team knocked Holland out of the 1994 World Cup?

17 Which Dutch club did the Brazilian Romario play for?

18 In which city is the club Feyenoord?

19 Which was the first World Cup tournament that Holland qualified for after the Second World War?

20 Gullit, Van Basten and Rijkaard lined up at which Italian club?

Answers

Red Card (see Quiz 76)

1 Gianfranco Zola. **2** Chelsea. **3** Johnston. **4** Peter Reid. **5** Trevor Hockey. **6** Andrei Kanchelskis. **7** Stefan Schwartz. **8** Rangers. **9** Dion Dublin. **10** Stimac. **11** Peter Schmeichel. **12** Blackburn Rovers. **13** Sweden. **14** Kidd. **15** Paul Gascoigne. **16** Hristo Stoichkov. **17** Vinnie Jones. **18** Lee Chapman. **19** Frank McAvennie. **20** Eric Cantona.

Quiz 75 **Pot Luck 38**

LEVEL 2

Answers – see page 183

---

1 What was the 90-minute score in the 1993 Manchester Utd v Liverpool Charity Shield game?

2 Joe Royle followed Jimmy Frizzell as boss of which club?

3 Which was Jimmy Quinn's first League club?

4 When did the USA first take part in the World Cup?

5 What is the first name of Joachim of Leicester City and Aston Villa?

6 In which decade did Hearts first win the Scottish FA Cup?

7 Who moved from Southampton for £3,300,000 to set a club record for a transfer fee received?

8 Cec Podd set an appearance record at which club?

9 Jim Baxter was at which club when he made his international debut?

10 Which England manager was born in London on 6th January, 1943?

11 Which club has a ground situated in Boothferry Road?

12 Which Ray became manager of Wimbledon in 1990?

13 Which country does Dariusz Kubicki come from?

14 In which decade was Liam Brady born?

15 Which club has a fanzine called *The Victoria Voice*?

16 Who was signed by Manchester City from Liverpool in January 1996?

17 Petrescu and Pembridge were in the same side at which club?

18 Which team was beaten 3–1 by Liverpool in the 1986 FA Cup Final?

19 What is the main colour of Tranmere Rovers' home shirts?

20 Which country did Lawrie Sanchez play for?

Answers

Pot Luck 37 (see Quiz 73)

1 Aston Villa. **2** Ashington. **3** Scunthorpe. **4** Graeme Sharp. **5** Blackburn Rovers. **6** Burley. **7** Manchester Utd. **8** Liverpool. **9** The Republic of Ireland. **10** Ipswich Town. **11** Billy Wright. **12** Leicester City. **13** Leeds Utd. **14** 1950s. **15** Southampton. **16** Fabian. **17** Huddersfield Town. **18** Mark Draper. **19** Black. **20** Norwich City.

Quiz 76 **Red Card**

Answers – see page 184

LEVEL 2

1 Which Italian got an early bath against Nigeria in the 1994 World Cup?

2 Darren Peacock was sent off as which London club knocked Newcastle Utd out of the 1995–96 FA Cup?

3 Which Scottish winger Willie of the 1960s to the 1980s was sent off 15 times?

4 Which Everton player was fouled when Kevin Moran got his 1985 FA Cup Final marching orders?

5 Who was the first Welsh player to be sent off in an international?

6 Which Manchester Utd player was sent off in the 1994 League Cup Final?

7 Who, ex-Arsenal, saw red in a Sweden v Romania World Cup quarter-final?

8 Woods and Butcher were at which club when they were off in the same game?

9 In 1996–97 which Coventry City player was dismissed in successive League games?

10 Which Igor was the only Croatian to see red in Euro 96?

11 Which keeper was sent off in the quarter-finals of the 1994 FA Cup?

12 At which club was Paul Warhurst sent off in a European Cup game?

13 Jonas Thern was playing for which country when he got sent off in a 1994 World Cup semi-final?

14 Which Brian of Everton got an early bath in a 1980 FA Cup semi-final?

15 Which Rangers player saw red in the 1996 European Cup game against Borussia Dortmund in Germany?

16 Which Bulgarian striker was banned for life after a brawl in 1985, only to be reinstated six months later?

17 Which Wimbledon player walked in 1995 after tangling with Ruud Gullit?

18 Which striker was sent off on his on-loan return to Leeds Utd in 1996?

19 Which ex-West Ham player at Celtic was sent off with Butcher and Woods?

20 Which Manchester Utd player got a red card after the final whistle in 1993?

Answers

Double Dutch (see Quiz 74)

1 Feyenoord. **2** Barcelona. **3** Ruud Krol. **4** Amsterdam. **5** Marco Van Basten. **6** Ajax. **7** Rinus Michels. **8** Tottenham Hotspur. **9** Patrik Kluivert. **10** PSV Eindhoven. **11** Bobby Robson. **12** Johan Neeskens. **13** Red and white. **14** Groningen. **15** Ruud Gullit (Euro 88). **16** Brazil. **17** PSV Eindhoven. **18** Rotterdam. **19** 1974. **20** AC Milan.

Quiz 77 **Pot Luck 39**

LEVEL 2

Answers – see page 189

1 Which team does Alison Moyet support?

2 Which Brian became boss of Wrexham in November 1989?

3 Which was Gary Mabbutt's first League club?

4 Which club play at the Steaua Stadium?

5 What job did Neville Southall do before becoming a footballer?

6 John Bond followed Malcolm Allison as boss of which club?

7 In which decade did Wolves first win the FA Cup?

8 Earl Barrett first played in an FA Charity Shield for which club?

9 Which country did Tony Grealish play for?

10 Which great Scottish manager was born in Burnbank in October, 1923?

11 Which club have a ground with the Bob Lord stand?

12 Which team was beaten 4–1 after extra time by Aberdeen in the 1982 Scottish FA Cup Final?

13 Which club did Gary Croft leave to join Blackburn Rovers?

14 In which decade was Ivor Allchurch born?

15 Which club has a fanzine called *A Love Supreme*?

16 What is the first name name of striker De Souza, a Wycombe goal grabber in 1996?

17 Wallace and Whelan were in the same attack at which club?

18 Who moved from WBA for £1,500,000 in 1981 to set an English record for a transfer fee received?

19 What colour are West Ham Utd's home shorts?

20 Phil Babb was at which club when he made his international debut?

Answers

Pot Luck 40 (see Quiz 79)

1 Walter Smith. **2** Arsenal. **3** Portsmouth. **4** 0–0 (after extra time). **5** Leeds Utd. **6** 1880s. **7** Mark Stein. **8** Plymouth Argyle. **9** Birmingham City. **10** Socrates. **11** Carlisle United. **12** Nicholl. **13** South Africa. **14** 1940s. **15** Tottenham Hotspur. **16** Edinburgh. **17** Stoke City. **18** Arsenal. **19** White. **20** Wales.

Quiz 78 **Kevin Keegan**

LEVEL 2

Answers – see page 190

1 Where was Kevin born?

2 Which manager took Keegan to Liverpool?

3 Which was Keegan's first club?

4 What is Kevin Keegan's first name?

5 As Newcastle United manager, which former team-mate did Keegan sign as a player?

6 Which Welshman was Kevin's main Liverpool strike partner?

7 Kevin's first three internationals were all against which country?

8 Which manager brought him to England after playing in Germany?

9 To one each way, in which year did Kevin first skipper England?

10 Against which team did Kevin hit two goals in an FA Cup Final?

11 In which country did Keegan briefly take part in a World Cup tournament?

12 At which club did Kevin have Manfred Kaltz as a team-mate?

13 To three each way, how many times did Kevin play for England?

14 Which German player had the task of trying to mark Kevin in Liverpool's epic triumph in the 1977 European Cup Final?

15 Which ex-Liverpool defender did Kevin get to advise Newcastle United about their defence?

16 What was the name of his chart single of the 1970s?

17 To three each way, how many goals did Kevin get for England?

18 At which club did Kevin have Imre Varadi as a strike partner?

19 Which English club did Kevin play against in a European Cup Final?

20 Keegan's last game as Newcastle United manager was an FA Cup tie against which London club?

Answers

On Song (see Quiz 80)

1 Manchester Utd. **2** 30. **3** Gazza ('Fog On the Tyne'). **4** 'Back Home'. **5** Rod Stewart. **6** 1972. **7** 'You'll Never Walk Alone'. **8** Scotland. **9** 'This Time (We'll Get It Right)'. **10** Hillsborough 1989. **11** The Crowd. **12** Gerry and The Pacemakers. **13** Cyril Knowles. **14** 'Anfield Rap'. **15** 'We've Got The Whole World At Our Feet'. **16** Stock, Aitken and Waterman. **17** Nottingham Forest. **18** Lightning Seeds. **19** England World Cup Squad. **20** Status Quo.

Quiz 79 **Pot Luck 40**

LEVEL 2

Answers – see page 187

---

1 Which manager won his first Scottish Championship after being in charge of the team for only four games?

2 Dreamcast replaced JVC on the shirts of which English club?

3 What was Darren Anderton's first League club?

4 What was the score in the 1991 Arsenal v Tottenham Hotspur FA Charity Shield?

5 Howard Wilkinson followed Billy Bremner as boss of which club?

6 In which decade did Preston North End first win the FA Cup?

7 Who moved from Stoke City for £1,500,000 to Chelsea to set a club record for a transfer fee received?

8 Which club did Peter Shilton join as player/manager in 1992?

9 Trevor Francis was at which club when he made his international debut?

10 Who was captain of Brazil for the 1982 and 1986 World Cups?

11 Which club's ground has the Warwick Road End?

12 Which Chris became manager of Walsall in September 1994?

13 Which country does Phil Masinga come from?

14 In which decade was George Best born?

15 Which club has a fanzine called *Cock A Doodle Do*?

16 In which city was Graeme Souness born?

17 Sheron and Cranson were in the same side at which club?

18 Which team was beaten 1–0 by West Ham United in the 1980 FA Cup Final?

19 What colour goes with blue on Wigan's shirts?

20 Which country did Mark Aizlewood play for?

Answers

Pot Luck 39 (see Quiz 77)

1 Southend Utd. **2** Flynn. **3** Bristol Rovers. **4** Steaua Bucharest. **5** Dustman. **6** Manchester City. **7** 1890s. **8** Everton. **9** The Republic of Ireland. **10** Jock Stein. **11** Burnley. **12** Rangers. **13** Grimsby Town. **14** 1920s. **15** Sunderland. **16** Manuel. **17** Leeds Utd. **18** Bryan Robson. **19** White. **20** Coventry City.

Quiz 80 **On Song**

Answers – see page 188

LEVEL 2

1 Which team won the FA Cup and then found their single at No. 1?

2 How many years of hurt were there in "Three Lions"?

3 Which footballer was "sitting in a sleazy snack bar, sucking sickly sausage rolls"?

4 Which football song was No. 1 for three weeks in May 1970?

5 Who sang with the Scotland squad on "Ole, Ola (Mulher Brasileira)"?

6 In which year did the originally titled "Leeds United" by Leeds United hit the charts?

7 Which Rodgers and Hammerstein song became the Anfield anthem?

8 Which squad charted in 1982 with "We Have A Dream"?

9 What was the England squad's song for Spain in 1982 called?

10 "Ferry Across The Mersey" was a charity song following which soccer disaster?

11 The Bradford City fire disaster led to a June 1985 No. 1 for various performers under which name?

12 Who had the original 1960s hit with the song?

13 Who was Cyril, the subject of "Nice One Cyril"?

14 Which Liverpool record reached No. 3 in the charts in 1988?

15 What was the England squad's song for the 1986 World Cup?

16 Which production team handled the charity version of "Ferry Across The Mersey"?

17 Which team recorded with Paper Lace?

18 "Pure" was the first hit for which soccer-connected group?

19 Who recorded the song that topped the charts for three weeks in May 1970?

20 Which group helped Manchester Utd for their 1994 chart success?

Answers

Kevin Keegan (see Quiz 78)

1 Doncaster. **2** Bill Shankly. **3** Scunthorpe. **4** Joseph. **5** Peter Beardsley. **6** John Toshack. **7** Wales. **8** Lawrie McMenemy. **9** 1976. **10** Newcastle Utd. **11** Spain. **12** Hamburg. **13** 63. **14** Berti Vogts. **15** Mark Lawrenson. **16** "Head Over Heels In Love". **17** 21. **18** Newcastle Utd. **19** Nottingham Forest. **20** Charlton Athletic.

Quiz 81 **Pot Luck 41**

Answers – see page 193

LEVEL 2

1. In which decade did Wimbledon first win the FA Cup?
2. Which Jan became boss of Swansea in February 1996?
3. With which club did Neil Ruddock make his League debut?
4. Which club's ground is by the River Darwen?
5. What was the Gazza rap record called?
6. Eddie McGoldrick first played in an FA Charity Shield for which club?
7. Arthur Cox followed Roy McFarland as boss of which club in 1984?
8. Which club did Tony Mowbray join on leaving Celtic?
9. Which country did Peter Nicholas play for?
10. Which Southampton keeper came back late from international duty in December 1995?
11. Which club's ground includes the Doug Ellis Stand?
12. Which team were beaten 2–1 by Chelsea in the 1970 FA Cup Final replay?
13. Dani came from Sporting Lisbon on loan to which London club?
14. In which decade was Jim Baxter born?
15. Which club has a fanzine called *Blazing Saddlers*?
16. At which club did Colin Griffin set a League appearance record?
17. In 1995–96 Ball and Hall were in the same side at which club?
18. Who moved from Leyton Orient to Notts County for £600,00 in 1981 to set a club record for a transfer fee received?
19. What colour are Charlton's home socks?
20. Ricky Hill was at which club when he made his international debut?

Answers

Pot Luck 42 (see Quiz 83)

1 Shamrock Rovers. **2** Peter Reid. **3** Port Vale. **4** QPR. **5** Blackburn Rovers. **6** 1890s. **7** Tranmere Rovers. **8** 1981. **9** Leeds Utd. **10** Coventry City. **11** Newcastle Utd. **12** Jackett. **13** Canada. **14** 1930s. **15** Cardiff City. **16** Michael. **17** Leicester City. **18** Sheffield Wednesday. **19** Black. **20** Wales.

Quiz 82 **Germany**

LEVEL 2

Answers – see page 194

1 Who is the most capped German player?

2 What colour are the socks of the German team?

3 Who was in charge of the Euro 96 team?

4 Where in Germany was Jürgen Klinsmann born?

5 Which Hamburg player was European Footballer of the Year in 1978 and 1979?

6 Who was West German manager from 1963–78?

7 In which decade did the Germans first win the World Cup?

8 In 1996 how many teams were there in the German Bundesliga?

9 Which club did Uwe Seeler play for?

10 Who was Germany's top scorer in Euro 96 and with how many goals?

11 Who was skipper of the 1990 World Cup-winning team?

12 Which club were German champions in 1995–96?

13 What two colours are in Hamburg's strip?

14 Who was the Tottenham Hotspur boss when Klinsmann left the club?

15 Which group were the Germans in at the start of Euro 96?

16 Which city do the club with 1860 in their name come from?

17 To three either way, how many goals did Gerd Müller score for Germany?

18 Which striker had played for Magdeburg, Dynamo Dresden and Nuremberg before coming to play in England?

19 Who took the final spot kick in the England v Germany Euro 96 game?

20 Which German club did England striker Tony Woodcock play for?

Answers

UEFA Cup (see Quiz 84)

1 Parma and Juventus. **2** Newcastle Utd. **3** Anderlecht. **4** Ipswich Town. **5** Ajax. **6** Tottenham Hotspur. **7** Watford. **8** Espanol. **9** Bordeaux. **10** Hungary. **11** 1970s. **12** Napoli. **13** 1980s. **14** Manchester Utd. **15** Newcastle Utd. **16** Luxembourg. **17** IFK Gothenburg. **18** England. **19** AZ (Alkmaar). **20** Dundee Utd.

Quiz 83 **Pot Luck 42**

LEVEL 2

Answers – see page 191

1 Which club plays home games at the Royal Dublin Society Showground?

2 Who wrote *Everton Winter Mexican Summer: A Football Diary*?

3 What was Robbie Earle's first League club?

4 Terry Venables followed Tommy Docherty's second term as boss of which club?

5 Which team lost 2–0 to Manchester Utd in the 1994 FA Charity Shield?

6 In which decade did Sheffield Utd first win the FA Cup?

7 Ian Nolan's move to Sheffield Wednesday in August 1994 set a club record for a transfer fee received at which club?

8 To a year each way, when did Neville Southall make his Everton League debut?

9 David Batty was at which club when he made his international debut?

10 At which club did George Curtis set a League appearance record that stood until the mid-90s?

11 Which club have a ground that contains The Milburn Stand?

12 Which Kenny became manager of Watford in May 1994

13 Which country does Frank Yallop come from?

14 In which decade was Billy Bingham born?

15 Which club has a fanzine called *Watch The Bluebirds Fly*?

16 What is the first name of Reading's long-serving Gilkes?

17 Marshall and Claridge were in the same side at which club?

18 Which team were beaten 3–2 by Everton in the 1966 FA Cup Final?

19 What colour are Fulham's home shorts?

20 Which country did Clayton Blackmore play for?

Answers

Pot Luck 41 (see Quiz 81)

1 1980s. **2** Molby. **3** Tottenham Hotspur. **4** Blackburn Rovers. **5** "Geordie Boys". **6** Arsenal. **7** Derby County. **8** Ipswich Town. **9** Wales. **10** Bruce Grobbelaar. **11** Aston Villa. **12** Leeds Utd. **13** West Ham Utd. **14** 1930s. **15** Walsall. **16** Shrewsbury Town. **17** Sunderland. **18** John Chiedozie. **19** Red. **20** Luton Town.

Quiz 84 **Fairs/UEFA Cup**

LEVEL 2

Answers – see page 192

1. Which two Italian sides contested the Final in 1995?
2. To which English team did Ujpest Dosza lose to in the Final?
3. Which Belgian side lost to a London club in the 1970 Final?
4. Trevor Whymark scored four goals in a Euro game for which club?
5. Which Dutch team beat Red Boys a record 14–0 in 1984?
6. Who won the trophy the first time it was decided on penalties?
7. Wilf Rostron scored in the competition for which club?
8. Which Spanish side lost the 1988 Final after winning the first leg 3–0?
9. In 1996, which team became the second from France to reach a Final?
10. Which country did Ujpest Dozsa represent?
11. In which decade did Liverpool win the trophy for the first time?
12. Which winners did Diego Maradona play for?
13. In which decade did Real Madrid win the trophy in successive seasons?
14. Alan Brazil scored UEFA Cup goals for Ipswich Town and which other club?
15. Bobby Moncur led which team to win the trophy?
16. Which country did Red Boys represent?
17. Which Swedish side have won the competition twice?
18. Which country has provided most winners?
19. The club beaten by Ipswich Town in a Final was prefixed by which two letters?
20. Which Scottish side did Paul Hegarty play for in a Final?

Answers

Germany (see Quiz 82)

1 Lothar Matthäus. **2** White. **3** Berti Vogts. **4** Stuttgart. **5** Kevin Keegan. **6** Helmut Schön. **7** 1950s. **8** 18. **9** Hamburg. **10** Jürgen Klinsmann, three. **11** Lothar Matthäus. **12** Borussia Dortmund. **13** White and red. **14** Gerry Francis. **15** Group C. **16** Munich. **17** 68. **18** Uwe Rosler. **19** Andy Möller. **20** Cologne (Köln).

Quiz 85 **Pot Luck 43**

Answers – see page 197

LEVEL 2

1 Which club's ground is by the River Wensum?

2 What was Ian Wright's job before he became a footballer?

3 Which was Steve Coppell's first League club?

4 Which Malcolm became manager of Sunderland in 1992 after being caretaker in their run to the FA Cup Final?

5 Kevin Campbell first played in an FA Charity Shield for which club?

6 In which decade did West Ham Utd first win the FA Cup?

7 David Pleat followed Bryan Hamilton as manager of which club?

8 In 1985, which Cup finalists recorded "Here We Go"?

9 Which country did Peter Rodrigues play for?

10 Bobby Gould was born in which city where he went on to manage the football team?

11 Which club has its ground next to Gillespie Road?

12 Which team were beaten 1–0 by WBA in the 1968 FA Cup Final?

13 Which country does Andrea Silenzi come from?

14 In which decade was Bryan Hamilton born?

15 Which club has a fanzine called *Yidaho*?

16 What is the first name of Ipswich's Ulhenbeek?

17 Batty and Barton were in the same side at which club?

18 Who moved from Norwich City for £5.5 million in July 1994, to set a club record for a transfer fee received?

19 What colours are Colchester United's striped shirts?

20 Gary Charles was at which club when he made his international debut?

Answers

Pot Luck 44 (see Quiz 87)

1 Liverpool. **2** WBA. **3** Leeds Utd. **4** Tommy Smith. **5** The Fourth Division. **6** 1880s. **7** Paul Furlong. **8** Yes (Once). **9** Sheffield Utd. **10** 1990. **11** Norwich City. **12** Whelan. **13** Bulgaria. **14** 1920s. **15** Cambridge United. **16** Nigel. **17** QPR. **18** Newcastle Utd. **19** Blue. **20** England.

Quiz 86 **London Clubs**

Answers – see page 198

LEVEL 2

1 Who became the first goalkeeper to save a penalty in a Wembley FA Cup Final?

2 Which Northern Ireland star is QPR's most capped player?

3 What nationality was West Ham United's Slaven Bilic?

4 If you were walking down South Africa Road, which London club's ground would you be nearest?

5 Have Millwall ever won the FA Cup?

6 Which London side did Johnny Haynes play for?

7 Who holds Chelsea's record for the most League appearances?

8 Goalkeeper Pat Jennings played for which three London area sides?

9 Which London side defeated Wales in a friendly in May 1996?

10 Who play in red and white vertical striped shirts?

11 Dennis Wise was transferred to Chelsea from which other London club?

12 Who was Trevor Brooking's 'minder' on the pitch at West Ham?

13 Who scored the final goal to win Arsenal the title in 1989?

14 Who moved from West Ham United to Celtic for £1.5 million in 1992?

15 At which club did John Barnes make his League debut?

16 Who became the chairman of Leyton Orient in 1996?

17 Which Wimbledon player joined them from Brentford in 1992?

18 Name the London team whose address is 748 High Road?

19 Who did Crystal Palace beat in the 1990 FA Cup semi-final?

20 Frank Clark managed which London side?

Answers

The 1990s (see Quiz 88)

1 Wimbledon. **2** Rene Higuita. **3** Nottingham Forest. **4** York City. **5** Plymouth Argyle. **6** Swindon Town. **7** Portsmouth. **8** David Platt. **9** Jason McAteer. **10** Franz Beckenbauer. **11** Diego Maradona. **12** Cameroon. **13** Frank Clark. **14** Marco van Basten. **15** Chris Waddle & Stuart Pearce. **16** Brian Clough. **17** Newcastle's Sir John Hall. **18** China & Hong Kong. **19** Roy Keane. **20** Barnet.

Quiz 87 **Pot Luck 44**

LEVEL 2

Answers – see page 195

1 Which team lost 4–3 to Leeds Utd in the 1992 FA Charity Shield?

2 Brian Talbot followed Ron Atkinson's second spell as boss of which club?

3 What was John Sheridan's first League club?

4 Who had a 1980 book titled *I Did It The Hard Way*?

5 What was formed in 1958 to change the English League?

6 In which decade did Hibernian first win the Scottish FA Cup?

7 Who moved from Watford to Chelsea in May 1994 to set a club record for a transfer fee received?

8 Did Nobby Stiles ever score for England?

9 Noel Blake was at which club when he made his international debut?

10 In what year did the Scotland World Cup squad release "Say It With Pride"?

11 Which club have a River End Stand and City Stand at their ground?

12 Which Ronnie became manager of Southend United in July 1995?

13 Which country does Bontcho Guentchev come from?

14 In which decade was Nat Lofthouse born?

15 Which club has a fanzine called *The Abbey Rabbit*?

16 What is much-travelled Gleghorn's first name?

17 Impey and Barker were in the same side at which club?

18 Which team were beaten 3–0 by Liverpool in the 1974 FA Cup Final?

19 What is the main colour of Gillingham's home shirts?

20 Which country did Eddie Hopkinson play for?

Answers

Pot Luck 43 (see Quiz 85)

1 Norwich City. **2** Plasterer. **3** Tranmere Rovers. **4** Crosby. **5** Arsenal. **6** 1960s. **7** Leicester City. **8** Everton. **9** Wales. **10** Coventry. **11** Arsenal. **12** Everton. **13** Italy. **14** 1940s. **15** Wimbledon. **16** Gus. **17** Newcastle Utd. **18** Chris Sutton. **19** Blue and white. **20** Nottingham Forest.

Quiz 88 **The 1990s**

LEVEL 2

Answers – see page 196

1 Which club announced in November 1995 they were thinking of moving to Dublin?
2 Who performed the "scorpion kick" at Wembley?
3 Who were Britain's last club in Europe in the 1995–96 season?
4 Which lowly side knocked Manchester Utd out of the 1995–96 Coca-Cola Cup?
5 Who was Peter Shilton playing for when he was sent off for the first time in his career?
6 Which side won promotion but were not allowed to take their place in the top flight?
7 Which team knocked Leeds Utd out of the FA Cup in 1996-97?
8 Dario Gradi said that which ex-Crewe Alexandra player "can go on to become a truly great player"?
9 Who did Liverpool sign from Bolton in September 1995?
10 Who did Berti Vogts succeed as Germany's national team chief?
11 Who tested positive for cocaine following a Serie A game?
12 Which African side reached the 1990 World Cup quarter-finals?
13 Which manager sparked the Manchester City revival in 1997?
14 Which Dutch player was the 1992 European Footballer of the Year?
15 Which two England players missed penalties in Italia 90?
16 Who retired, aged 58, after his club were relegated in 1993?
17 Which chairman said in 1991, "Let's kill off once and for all that Ossie's job is on the line"?
18 In their pre-Euro 96 tour, which countries did England visit?
19 Who only lasted less than a week as captain of the Republic of Ireland?
20 Which club's first ever League Cup tie, in August 1991, ended in a 5–5 first leg draw?

Answers

London Clubs (see Quiz 86)

1 Dave Beasant. **2** Alan McDonald. **3** Croatian. **4** QPR. **5** No. **6** Fulham. **7** Ron Harris. **8** Watford, Arsenal and Tottenham Hotspur. **9** Leyton Orient. **10** Brentford. **11** Wimbledon. **12** Billy Bonds. **13** Michael Thomas. **14** Frank McAvennie. **15** Watford. **16** Barry Hearn. **17** Dean Holdsworth. **18** Tottenham Hotspur. **19** Liverpool. **20** Leyton Orient.

Quiz 89 **Pot Luck 45**

Answers – see page 201

LEVEL 2

1 Which international Chris used to work adding seasoning to sausages?

2 Which John became boss of Shrewsbury in 1991?

3 Which was Alan Hansen's first Scottish League club?

4 Which Cambridgeshire club's ground is by the River Nene?

5 In which decade did WBA first win the FA Cup?

6 Andrei Kanchelskis first played in an FA Charity Shield for which club?

7 Howard Wilkinson followed Jack Charlton as boss of which club?

8 Which TV presenter did Ryan Giggs go out with?

9 Which country did Phil Woosnam play for?

10 Chris Turner kept goal for Sheffield Wednesday in a League Cup Final when they beat which former club of his?

11 Which club has the Revie Stand in their ground?

12 Which team were beaten a record 6–1 by Celtic in the 1972 Scottish FA Cup Final?

13 Which country does Mixu Paatelainen come from?

14 In which decade was Andrei Kanchelskis born?

15 Which club has a fanzine called *A Load Of Bull*?

16 Which Manchester Utd great made a trademark of pulling his cuffs over his hands?

17 Pollock and Stamp were in the same side at which club?

18 Who moved from QPR for £6 million in June 1995 to set a club record for a transfer fee received?

19 What is the main colour of Crewe Alexandra's shirts?

20 Tony Currie was at which club when he made his international debut?

Answers

Pot Luck 46 (see Quiz 91)

1 Aberdeen. **2** Liverpool. **3** Tottenham Hotspur. **4** Smith. **5** Morris. **6** 1950s. **7** Steve Daley. **8** Wimbledon. **9** Arsenal. **10** Bill Shankly. **11** Nottingham Forest. **12** Oxford United. **13** Norway. **14** 1950s. **15** Aston Villa. **16** Francis. **17** Sheffield Wednesday. **18** Manchester City. **19** Black and white. **20** Northern Ireland.

Quiz 90 **Golden Goals**

Answers – see page 202

LEVEL 2

1 Which Cliff set a career goals record at Arsenal?

2 Dennis Bergkamp's goals led which team to Euro success in 1992?

3 Who is credited – or blamed – for bringing the shirt-over-the-head- after-scoring routine to English soccer?

4 Which player of the 1950s and 60s set up Chelsea's record for most league goals for the club?

5 Whose amazing Euro 96 lob knocked out Portugal?

6 Neil Shipperley's goals kept which side in the Premiership in 1995–96?

7 Which German striker was known as "Der Bomber"?

8 Steve Bloomer notched 292 League goals for which club?

9 Who dived full length on the pitch after his first goal for Tottenham Hotspur in the Premiership?

10 To 20 each way, what was Dixie Dean's Everton League goals total?

11 Which two clubs has Ian Wright scored for in FA Cup Finals?

12 A Brett Angell goal took which team to the Coca-Cola Cup semi-final in 1997?

13 A Charlie George goal won the FA Cup for which team?

14 A fine Davor Suker shot bamboozled which Danish keeper in Euro 96?

15 Who scored a last-gasp equaliser for Manchester Utd v Oldham in a 1990s semi-final?

16 Who was the Brazilian top scorer in the 1994 World Cup tournament?

17 Andy Linighan scored a last-minute FA Cup Final winner for which team?

18 Craig Brewster scored the only goal to win the Scottish League Cup for which club in 1993–94?

19 Which Scot was Europe's top league scorer in 1991–92?

20 Who scored England's first in the 1966 World Cup Final?

Answers

Hat-tricks (see Quiz 92)

1 Alan Shearer. **2** Matt Le Tissier. **3** Gary McAllister. **4** Mortensen. **5** West Germany. **6** Everton. **7** John Wark. **8** Ian Wright. **9** Coventry City. **10** Rangers. **11** Alan Shearer. **12** Turkey. **13** Mike Newell. **14** Andy Cole. **15** Gary Lineker. **16** Manchester City. **17** Gordon Durie. **18** Les Ferdinand. **19** Jimmy Greaves. **20** Eric Cantona.

Quiz 91 **Pot Luck 46**

Answers – see page 199

LEVEL 2

1 Alphabetically, which is Scotland's first League side?

2 In 1977 which club released 'We Can Do It'?

3 What was Vinny Samways' first League club?

4 Which Jim became boss of Portsmouth in 1991?

5 Which Desmond's 1981 book was *The Soccer Tribe*?

6 In which decade did Motherwell first win the Scottish FA Cup?

7 Who moved from Wolves to Manchester City for over £1 million in 1979 to set a club record for a transfer fee received?

8 Which team lost 2–1 to Liverpool in the 1988 FA Charity Shield?

9 George Eastham was at which club when he made his international debut?

10 Which great Scottish boss was born in Glenbuck in 1913?

11 The Bridgford Stand is part of the ground of which club?

12 Denis Smith followed Brian Horton as boss of which club?

13 Which country does Jostein Flo come from?

14 In which decade was Kevin Keegan born?

15 Which club has a fanzine called *Heroes And Villains*?

16 What is the first name of long-serving Southampton defender Benali?

17 Walker and Waddle were in the same side at which club?

18 Which team were beaten 3–2 by Tottenham Hotspur in the replayed 1981 FA Cup Final?

19 What colour are Grimsby Town's striped home shirts?

20 Which country did Alex Elder play for?

Answers

Pot Luck 45 (see Quiz 89)

1 Waddle. **2** Bond. **3** Partick Thistle. **4** Peterborough Utd. **5** 1880s. **6** Everton. **7** Sheffield Wednesday. **8** Dani Behr. **9** Wales. **10** Manchester Utd. **11** Leeds Utd. **12** Hibernian. **13** Finland. **14** 1960s. **15** Wolves. **16** Denis Law. **17** Middlesbrough. **18** Les Ferdinand. **19** Red. **20** Sheffield Utd.

Quiz 92 **Hat-tricks**

LEVEL 2

Answers – see page 200

1 Who scored five Premiership hat-tricks in 1995–96?

2 Who finished Southampton's joint top scorer in 1995–96 with seven goals, having hit a hat-trick in the first game?

3 Which Leeds Utd midfielder hit a 1995 hat-trick against Coventry City?

4 Which Stan hit an FA Cup Final hat-trick in the 1950s?

5 Geoff Hurst hit his first England hat-trick against which team?

6 Who was Andy Gray playing for when he hit a mid-1980s European Cup Winners' Cup treble?

7 Which Ipswich player hit two hat-tricks in 1980–81 UEFA Cup games?

8 Which England player got four against San Marino in November 1993?

9 Who was Dion Dublin playing for when he hit three against Sheffield Wednesday in 1995 and still ended up on the losing side?

10 Robert Fleck hit three in a Euro game for which club?

11 Whose 1997 hat-trick for Newcastle Utd, who were losing 3–1, turned into a 4–3 victory over Leicester City?

12 Bryan Robson got his only England hat-trick in an 8–0 rout of which country in 1984?

13 Who hit Blackburn Rovers's hat-trick in the 1995–96 European Cup?

14 Who hit three-plus as Manchester Utd beat Ipswich Town 9–0 in 1995?

15 Which England player hit hat-tricks against Turkey in 1985 and 1987?

16 Adcock, Stewart and White each hit three for which team in the same game in 1987?

17 Who hit a Scottish FA Cup Final hat-trick in 1996?

18 Which player hit his first Newcastle Utd hat-trick, against Wimbledon in October 1995?

19 Which player hit six England hat-tricks from 1960 to 1966?

20 Who hit a Charity Shield hat-trick for Leeds Utd in 1992?

Answers

Golden Goals (see Quiz 90)

1 Bastin. **2** Ajax. **3** Fabrizio Ravanelli. **4** Bobby Tambling. **5** Karel Poborsky. **6** Southampton. **7** Gerd Müller. **8** Derby County. **9** Jürgen Klinsmann. **10** 349. **11** Crystal Palace and Arsenal. **12** Stockport County. **13** Arsenal. **14** Peter Schmeichel. **15** Mark Hughes. **16** Romario. **17** Arsenal. **18** Dundee Utd. **19** Ally McCoist. **20** Geoff Hurst.

Quiz 93 **Pot Luck 47**

LEVEL 2

Answers – see page 205

1 John Docherty followed George Graham as manager of which club?
2 Barry Horne first played in an FA Charity Shield for which club?
3 Which was John Aldridge's first League club?
4 To five each way, in what year did Tottenham Hotspur first win the FA Cup?
5 Joint managers Archie Gemmill and John McGovern took over which club in September 1994?
6 Who was the first Danish goalkeeper to play in the English League?
7 Which club's ground is by the River Severn?
8 David Beckham has spent time on loan at which Lancashire club?
9 Which country did Jim Magilton play for?
10 In January 1996, which manager announced he would be standing down six months later because of impending litigation?
11 The Kemlyn Road goes past the ground of which club?
12 Which team were beaten 3–1 by Man Utd in the 1963 FA Cup Final?
13 Which country does Jan-Aage Fjortoft come from?
14 In which decade was Jimmy Greaves born?
15 Which club has a fanzine called *The Voice of the Valley*?
16 Who plays at The Stadium Of Light?
17 Clough and Harkness were in the same side at which club?
18 Who moved from Reading to Newcastle United in August 1995, to set a club record for a transfer fee received?
19 What colours are Kidderminter's home shirts?
20 Tony Dorigo was at which club when he made his international debut?

Answers

Pot Luck 48 (see Quiz 95)

1 Billy Bremner. **2** Watford. **3** Nottingham Forest. **4** Arsenal. **5** "It's more important than that." **6** 1890s. **7** Warren Barton. **8** Bayern Munich. **9** Leeds United. **10** Jairzinho. **11** Sheffield Wednesday. **12** McGhee. **13** Canada. **14** 1920s. **15** Notts County. **16** Dean. **17** Derby County. **18** Manchester Utd. **19** Blue and white. **20** Wales.

Quiz 94 **Internationals**

Answers – see page 206

LEVEL 2

1 Who is the oldest player to turn out for Wales?

2 In which decade did Wales first beat England at Wembley?

3 Who became manager of Northern Ireland in 1994?

4 Which ex-Liverpool player has managed Wales?

5 At which ground do the Republic of Ireland play home matches?

6 Which Peter scored twice for Northern Ireland in their magnificent draw with West Germany in the 1958 World Cup?

7 Who was Tony Cascarino playing for when he won his first cap?

8 When did the Republic of Ireland first qualify for the World Cup finals?

9 Which country has Vinnie Jones played for?

10 Which Welsh player was the most capped before Neville Southall?

11 Which Christian name links Northern Ireland's McIlroy and Quinn?

12 Which Northern Ireland skipper said, "Our tactics are to equalize before the other side scores"?

13 Which Republic of Ireland player was nicknamed "Chippy"?

14 In 1992 Michael Hughes made his debut for which country?

15 Which Republic of Ireland player appeared in five FA Cup Finals between 1963 and 1973?

16 In which year did Jack Charlton become manager of the Republic of Ireland?

17 Which home international countries were present in the 1982 World Cup Finals?

18 Which Arsenal and Tottenham Hotspur manager was also team boss of Northern Ireland?

19 Which London-based striker captained Northern Ireland in 1996?

20 When did Wales last qualify for the World Cup?

Answers

Golden Oldies (see Quiz 96)

1 Stanley Matthews. **2** Preston North End. **3** Leicester City. **4** West Ham Utd. **5** Billy Wright. **6** Dixie Dean. **7** Huddersfield Town. **8** Ted Drake. **9** Joe Mercer. **10** Nat Lofthouse. **11** 33 years. **12** Alex James. **13** Mackay. **14** Newcastle Utd. **15** Middlesbrough. **16** Manchester Utd. **17** Scotland. **18** Hungary. **19** Pat Jennings. **20** Yes. (He played once for Scotland).

Quiz 95 **Pot Luck 48**

LEVEL 2

Answers – see page 203

1 You Get Nowt For Being Second was the 1969 book of which player?
2 Steve Harrison followed Dave Bassett as boss of which club?
3 What was Hans Segers' first English League club?
4 Which team lost 1–0 to Liverpool in the 1989 FA Charity Shield?
5 How did Bill Shankly end the observation that, "Football isn't a matter of life and death: ..."?
6 In which decade did Sheffield Wednesday first win the FA Cup?
7 Who moved from Wimbledon for £4 million in June 1995 to set a club record for a transfer fee received?
8 Which club did Jürgen Klinsmann join on leaving Tottenham Hotspur?
9 Allan Clarke was at which club when he made his international debut?
10 How is Brazil's Jair Ventura Filho better known?
11 Leppings Lane runs by which club's ground?
12 Which Mark was Reading manager from 1991 to 1994?
13 Which country does Paul Peschisolido come from?
14 In which decade was Alfredo Di Stefano born?
15 Which club has a fanzine called *The Pie*?
16 What is Mr Windass' first name?
17 Willems and Van Der Laan were in the same side at which club?
18 Which team were beaten 1–0 by Southampton in the 1976 FA Cup Final?
19 What two colours are on Hartlepool's home shirts?
20 Which country did Paul Price play for?

Answers

Pot Luck 47 (see Quiz 93)

1 Millwall. **2** Everton. **3** Newport County. **4** 1901. **5** Rotherham. **6** Peter Schmeichel. **7** Shrewsbury Town. **8** Preston North End. **9** Northern Ireland. **10** Terry Venables. **11** Liverpool. **12** Leicester City. **13** Norway. **14** 1940s. **15** Charlton Athletic. **16** Benfica. **17** Liverpool. **18** Shaka Hislop. **19** Red and white. **20** Chelsea.

Quiz 96 **Golden Oldies**

LEVEL 2

Answers – see page 204

1. Who was born on February 1, 1915, in Hanley, Stoke on Trent?
2. Bobby Charlton came out of retirement to play for which League club?
3. Which club had goalkeepers Banks and Shilton on their books in the 1960s?
4. What was the third London side that Jimmy Greaves played for?
5. Who was travelling on a bus when he learnt that he had been made England skipper?
6. Who fractured his skull in a motorbike accident in the 1920s?
7. With which League club did Denis Law make his debut?
8. Who hit 42 goals in a season for Arsenal in the 1930s?
9. Who was aged 60 when he became England's caretaker manager?
10. Who bagged 255 league goals for Bolton in the 1940s and 1950s?
11. To two each way, how many years did Stanley Matthews play League soccer in England?
12. Who became Britain's most expensive player when he moved from Preston North End to Arsenal in 1929?
13. Which Dave of Tottenham Hotspur broke his left leg twice in a year in the 1960s?
14. Hughie Gallacher hit 36 league goals in a season for which club?
15. Where was Wilf Mannion born?
16. At which club did Brian Kidd begin his career?
17. Liverpool's legendary striker Billy Liddell came from which country?
18. Which country developed the deep-lying centre forward role just after World War II?
19. Which great goalkeeper was born in Newry on June 12, 1945?
20. Did Matt Busby ever play international soccer?

Answers

Internationals (see Quiz 94)

1 Billy Meredith. **2** 1970s. **3** Bryan Hamilton. **4** John Toshack. **5** Lansdowne Road. **6** McParland. **7** Gillingham. **8** 1990. **9** Wales. **10** Ivor Allchurch. **11** Jimmy. **12** Danny Blanchflower. **13** Liam Brady. **14** Northern Ireland. **15** Johnny Giles. **16** 1986. **17** Northern Ireland, England and Scotland. **18** Terry Neill. **19** Iain Dowie. **20** 1958.

Quiz 97 **Pot Luck 49**

LEVEL 2

Answers – see page 208

1 In which decade did Sunderland first win the FA Cup?

2 Which Scot played for Torino in 1961–62?

3 With which club did Trevor Sinclair make his League debut?

4 Which Ian became manager of Northampton Town in January 1995?

5 Stuart Ripley first played in an FA Charity Shield for which club?

6 Which club's ground is near the River Don?

7 Ken Brown followed John Bond as boss of which club?

8 In 1996–97, Port Vale were 4–0 up at home yet had to settle for a 4–4 draw against which London team?

9 Which country did John McClelland play for?

10 Which lifelong soccer fan was born in May 1929, in Blackburn?

11 Which club is situated in Moss Side?

12 Which team was beaten 3–1 by Tottenham Hotspur in the 1962 FA Cup Final?

13 Which country does Lucas Radebe come from?

14 In which decade was Johan Cruyff born?

15 Which club has a fanzine called *The Cumberland Sausage*?

16 How many full England caps did Steve Bruce win?

17 Lennon and Parker were in the same side at which club?

18 Who moved from Torquay for £600,000 in May 1988, to set a club record for a transfer fee received?

19 What colour are Exeter City's striped shirts?

20 Gordon Cowans was at which club when he made his international debut?

Answers

Pot Luck 50 (see Quiz 99)

1 Liverpool & Tottenham Hotspur. **2** Everton. **3** Arsenal. **4** Lawrence. **5** John Lyall. **6** 1970s. **7** Tony Cottee. **8** Blackburn Rovers. **9** Stoke City. **10** QPR. **11** Tottenham Hotspur. **12** Nottingham Forest. **13** Denmark. **14** 1919. **15** Gillingham. **16** Craig. **17** Stan Collymore. **18** QPR. **19** Black and white. **20** Wales.

Quiz 98 **Italy**

Answers – see page 209

LEVEL 2

1 What was Paolo Maldini's first club?

2 Which club have won the League most times?

3 Who was Italy's top scorer in the 1994 World Cup in the USA?

4 How old was Paolo Rossi when he retired from playing?

5 Which club did Graeme Souness join in Italy?

6 German imports Klinsmann and Matthäus helped to bring which club the league title in 1989?

7 Which team are known as the Zebras?

8 Dino Zoff became coach and later president of which club?

9 Which team knocked Italy out of Italia 90?

10 The import of what was banned in 1964, only to be lifted in the 1980s?

11 Who were the opponents for Cesare Maldini's first match as coach?

12 Who was Italy's top scorer in the 1982 World Cup tournament?

13 Michel Platini inspired Juventus to European Cup Final victory over which English side?

14 Gianfranco Zola took over the number 10 shirt at Napoli from which superstar?

15 In which decade did the Italians first win the World Cup?

16 Who were champions of Serie A in 1995–96?

17 Thomas Brolin joined Leeds United from which Italian club?

18 Who missed the final penalty for Italy in the 1994 World Cup Final?

19 Lazio play in which Italian city?

20 Who was in charge of Italy for Euro 96?

Answers

Pot Luck 49 (see Quiz 97)

1 1930s. **2** Denis Law. **3** Blackpool. **4** Atkins. **5** Blackburn Rovers. **6** Sheffield Wednesday. **7** Norwich City. **8** QPR. **9** Northern Ireland. **10** Jack Walker. **11** Manchester City. **12** Burnley. **13** South Africa. **14** 1940s. **15** Carlisle United. **16** None. **17** Leicester City. **18** Lee Sharpe. **19** Red and white. **20** Aston Villa.

Quiz 99 **Pot Luck 50**

Answers – see page 207

LEVEL 2

1 Ray Clemence was an FA Cup winner with which two clubs?

2 Which team took part in the Charity Shield from 1984 to 1987?

3 What was Martin Keown's first League club?

4 Which Lennie became manager of Luton Town in December 1995?

5 *Just Like My Dreams:* was part of the title of which manager's book?

6 In which decade did Southampton first win the FA Cup?

7 Who moved from West Ham Utd to Everton in July 1988 to set a club record for a transfer fee received?

8 Bill Fox was chairman of which club?

9 Mark Chamberlain was at which club when he made his international debut?

10 Bardsley and Brevett were in the same side at which club?

11 Paxton Road goes by the ground of which club?

12 Brian Clough followed Allan Brown as boss of which club?

13 Which country did Claus Thomsen come from?

14 To five years each way, when was Tommy Lawton born?

15 Which club has a fanzine called *Brian Moore's Head* (Looks Uncannily Like The London Planetarium)?

16 What is the first name of the footballing Mr Shakespeare?

17 In January 1996, who lost his appeal for a pay-off from his old club Nottingham Forest?

18 Which team were beaten 3–2 by Tottenham Hotspur in the replayed 1982 FA Cup Final?

19 What two colours are on Hereford United's home shirts?

20 Which country did Malcolm Page play for?

Answers

Italy (see Quiz 98)

1 AC Milan. **2** Juventus. **3** Roberto Baggio. **4** 29. **5** Sampdoria. **6** Internazionale. **7** Juventus. **8** Lazio. **9** Argentina. **10** Foreign players. **11** Northern Ireland. **12** Paolo Rossi. **13** Liverpool. **14** Diego Maradona. **15** 1930s. **16** AC Milan. **17** Parma. **18** Roberto Baggio. **19** Rome. **20** Arrigo Saachi.

The Hard Questions

If you thought that this section of this book would prove to be little or no problem, or that the majority of the questions could be answered and a scant few would test you, then you are sorely mistaken. These questions are the *hardest* questions *ever*! So difficult are they that any attempt to answer them all in one sitting will addle your mind and mess with your senses. You'll end up leaving the quiz via the window while ringing your best mate, who happens to be standing next to you. Don't do it!

For a kick-off there are 2,080 questions in both sections, so at 20 seconds per question it will take you over 23 hours, and that's just the time it will take to read them. What you should do instead is set them for others – addle your friends' minds.

Note the dangerous nature of these questions, though. These are your secret weapons – use them accordingly unless, of course, someone or some team is getting your back up. In which case you should hit them hard and only let up when you have them cowering under the table or in the corner, whimpering "offside".

These questions work best against league teams; they are genuinely tough and should be used against those people who take their pub quizzes seriously. NEVER use these questions against your in-laws.

Quiz 1 **Pot Luck 1**

Answers – see page 213

LEVEL 3

1 Who played for Croydon, Carshalton Athletic and Sutton and became a Premier League manager?

2 Who was in goal when Leeds Utd won the FA Cup in the 1970s?

3 What is Jimmy Greaves' middle name?

4 At which club did Lee Dixon make his League debut?

5 In what decade did Arsenal first win the Championship?

6 Who scored for the Czech Republic in the Final of Euro 96?

7 Alan Mullery followed Steve Kember as manager of which club?

8 Who moved from Bournemouth to Everton in 1994 to set a club record for a transfer fee received?

9 Which club was once known as Dial Square?

10 To one each way, how many international goals did Viv Anderson score?

11 Kevin Gage and Steve Sims were in the same team at which club?

12 Which Colin became boss of Hull City in 1989?

13 John Bailey first played in an FA Cup Final for which team?

14 What is the historic link between Harrow Chequers, Hitchin Town and Reigate Priory?

15 On the day of the 1995 FA Cup Final which Premiership club announced that their manager was leaving?

16 Which European team did World Cup newcomers Saudi Arabia beat in the first round of USA 94?

17 Which club used to play at Fullfordgate?

18 Kevin Langley set a League appearance record at which club?

19 Which country did Mike O'Grady play for?

20 How many years was Bruce Grobbelaar at Liverpool?

Answers

Pot Luck 2 (see Quiz 3)

1 West Ham Utd. **2** Everton. **3** Wycombe Wanderers. **4** Wallace. **5** Luton Town. **6** Hereford Utd. **7** Chewing Gum (Dentyne). **8** Tow Law Town. **9** Partick Thistle. **10** Ambrose. **11** Manchester Utd. **12** Westley. **13** Manchester City. **14** Leeds Utd. **15** 1950s. **16** Everton. **17** Nottingham Forest. **18** Steve Sedgley. **19** Bristol City. **20** 10.

Quiz 2 **Midfield Men**

Answers – see page 214

LEVEL 3

1. Liam Brady finished his playing career at which club?
2. Steve Williams and Brian Talbot were together at which club?
3. To two each way, how many caps did Alan Ball win?
4. Which Manchester Utd player scored on his English League debut v Watford in August, 1984?
5. Who was born on September 29, 1939 at Hill o'Beath, Fife?
6. Which club did Billy Bremner move to after his glory days at Leeds?
7. Nick Holmes was a long-serving player with which club?
8. Which English team did Roy Keane support as a boy?
9. What was Johan Cruyff's first family links with Ajax?
10. Which heavy-smoking midfielder scored Brazil's second goal in the 1970 World Cup Final?
11. Who was skipper of England from 1960 until involved in a serious car accident in 1962?
12. Johnny Metgod came from Real Madrid to which English side?
13. Micky Horswill played for which team in an FA Cup Final?
14. How old was Ray Wilkins when he was made captain at Chelsea?
15. Graeme Souness was at which club for three years without playing in the first team?
16. Bryan Robson's last England game was against which country?
17. Mills, Wigley and Walsh featured for which top-flight 80s team?
18. Cockerill and Case formed a formidable partnership at which club?
19. What number did Johan Cruyff wear for most of his Ajax career?
20. Bobby Robson was with which club when he first played for England?

Answers

The 1950s (see Quiz 4)

1 Hearts. **2** Red Star Belgrade. **3** Joe Harvey. **4** Portsmouth. **5** Jimmy Greaves. **6** Harold Bell. **7** Arsenal. **8** Alec and David Herd. **9** USA. **10** Leslie Compton. **11** Just Fontaine. **12** Sunderland. **13** Hearts. **14** Ian St John. **15** Ronnie Clayton. **16** Charlton Athletic. **17** Ted Fenton. **18** Bolton Wanderers. **19** Manchester Utd. **20** It finished as a four-way tie.

Quiz 3 **Pot Luck 2**

Answers – see page 211

LEVEL 3

1 At which club did Jimmy Greaves finish his League career?

2 In June 1994 Swedish player Martin Dahlin turned down a transfer to which English club?

3 Which club used to play at Loakes Park?

4 Which Danny played his only England game in 1986 against Egypt?

5 Before meeting up at West Ham Utd, where had Tim Breaker and Les Sealey been in the same side?

6 What was the first club that John Sillett managed?

7 What type of product was advertised on Southampton's open top bus as it paraded the FA Cup in the 70s?

8 Which non-League side did Chris Waddle play for before he became a full international?

9 Alan Rough set a League appearance record at which club?

10 What was Billy Wright's middle name?

11 Mal Donaghy and Mark Robins were in the same team at which club?

12 Which Terry was in charge at Luton Town during 1995?

13 Ray Ranson first played in an FA Cup Final for which team?

14 At which club did Terry Phelan make his League debut?

15 In what decade did Aberdeen first win the championship?

16 Which club had a fanzine called *When Skies Are Grey*?

17 Dave Mackay followed Matt Gillies as manager of which club?

18 Who was bought by Ipswich Town in 1994 at a club record fee?

19 Which club was once known as Bristol South End?

20 To two each way, how many international goals did Billy Bingham score?

Answers

Pot Luck 1 (see Quiz 1)

1 Lennie Lawrence. **2** David Harvey. **3** Peter. **4** Burnley. **5** 1930s. **6** Patrick Berger. **7** Crystal Palace. **8** Joe Parkinson. **9** Arsenal. **10** 2. **11** Aston Villa. **12** Appleton. **13** Everton. **14** Entered the first FA Cup competition. **15** Sheffield Wednesday. **16** Belgium. **17** York City. **18** Wigan Athletic. **19** England. **20** 13.

Quiz 4 **The 1950s**

Answers – see page 212

LEVEL 3

1 Which Scottish side hit a record 132 Division One goals in 1957–58?

2 Which team had Manchester United played before the Munich crash?

3 After the 1952 FA Cup Final which Newcastle Utd skipper said, "Joe Mercer is the greatest player I have ever met"?

4 On February 22, 1956, Newcastle Utd visited which club for the first English League game to be played under floodlights?

5 Which Chelsea star finished as the League's top scorer in 1959?

6 Which Tranmere Rovers centre-half made a record 401 consecutive League appearances in the 1950s?

7 Which side narrowly failed to win the double in the 1951–52 season?

8 Which father and son duo played in the same Stockport County side?

9 Who beat England in a Group Two 1950 World Cup match in Belo Horizonte?

10 Who was affectionately known as "Big 'Ead" by the Arsenal fans?

11 Which French player finished as top scorer in the 1958 World Cup?

12 In 1958 which team were relegated for the first time in 68 years?

13 Who won their first trophy in 50 years when they beat Celtic 3–1 to claim the 1950 Scottish FA Cup?

14 Which Motherwell forward hit three goals in three minutes in 1959?

15 Who took over as England skipper from Billy Wright?

16 Which Division Two side were losing 5–1 to Huddersfield, but fought back to win 7–6 in 1957?

17 Who was manager of West Ham Utd's promotion-winning side of 1958?

18 Bill Ridding was boss of which team from 1951?

19 Which team was the Anderlecht captain referring to when he said,"Why don't they pick the whole side for England"?

20 What was remarkable about the Home International Championship of 1955–56?

Answers

Midfield Men (see Quiz 2)

1 West Ham Utd. **2** Arsenal. **3** 72. **4** Gordon Strachan. **5** Jim Baxter. **6** Hull City. **7** Southampton. **8** Tottenham Hotspur. **9** His mother was a cleaner in the offices. **10** Gerson. **11** Johnny Haynes. **12** Nottingham Forest. **13** Sunderland (1973). **14** 18. **15** Tottenham Hotspur. **16** Turkey. **17** Nottingham Forest. **18** Southampton. **19** 14. **20** WBA.

Quiz 5 **Pot Luck 3**

Answers – see page 217

LEVEL 3

1 In 1966, which Leeds Utd defender won his only Scottish cap?

2 What is Tony Adams' middle name?

3 Which Welsh club used to play at Acton Park?

4 Which England keeper was featured in *Hello* magazine in February 1997?

5 In what decade did Liverpool first win the championship?

6 Which club had a fanzine called *Not The 8502*?

7 Dario Gradi followed Malcolm Allison as manager of which club?

8 Who moved from Brentford to Wimbledon in 1992 to set a club record for a transfer fee received?

9 Which London former League club once had Alston as part of its name?

10 To one each way, how many international goals did Alan Ball score?

11 Perry Groves and Brian Marwood were in the same team at which club?

12 Which Billy became manager of Leeds Utd in 1985?

13 Ray Wilkins played in an FA Cup Final for which team?

14 To three each way, how many goals did Phil Neal score in his 20-year League career?

15 What was the first club that Alan Ball managed?

16 Which Millwall defender scored over 40 goals during the 1960s and early 70s?

17 What are the main colours of IFK Gothenburg's home shirts?

18 Who was keeper Ray Cashley playing for when he scored against Hull City in 1973?

19 Tony Fitzpatrick set a Scottish League appearance record at which club?

20 Who was in goal when WBA won the FA Cup in the 1960s?

Answers

Pot Luck 4 (see Quiz 7)

1 Hearts. **2** Ron Greenwood. **3** Wolves. **4** Bournemouth. **5** 2 (Steve Daley and Andy Gray). **6** Smith. **7** Elland Road. **8** Cambridge Utd. **9** Harvey. **10** William. **11** Middlesbrough. **12** Machin. **13** Brighton. **14** Chesterfield. **15** 1890s. **16** Huddersfield Town. **17** Burnley. **18** Gordon Durie. **19** Cambridge Utd. **20** 19.

Quiz 6 **Transfer Trail**

Answers – see page 218

LEVEL 3

1 Allan Clarke became the first £150,000 man when he moved to Leicester City from which club?

2 Which player was involved the only time that the British transfer ceiling has been doubled in one move?

3 In the first £5,000 transfer Syd Puddefoot moved to which Scottish club?

4 Alberto Tarantini came from Argentina to which British club?

5 Kevin Moran left Manchester Utd in 1988 for which club?

6 Who was the first player to move for £20,000?

7 Who were Nottingham Forest's main rivals for the signature of Birmingham City's Trevor Francis?

8 Trevor Francis was Britain's most expensive player until who moved?

9 How old was Charles Buchan when he went to Arsenal?

10 Who was the first £1 million player to leave Norwich City?

11 Ayr's record fee received was £300,000 in 1981 when which player moved to Liverpool?

12 Hughie Gallacher joined Newcastle Utd from which club?

13 Who became the first British player to move in a £500,000 transfer?

14 Who played for Leeds Utd in the first leg of a Fairs Cup Final but was transferred before the second?

15 Where did Charlie George go when he left Arsenal?

16 Partick Thistle's record fee received was £200,000 in 1981 when which player moved to Watford?

17 Arriving in 1972 from Nottingham Forest, who was Manchester Utd's first £200,000 signing?

18 Who was Norwich City manager when Chris Sutton left for £5 million?

19 What was the last French club that Eric Cantona played for?

20 Where did Danny Wallace go when he left Manchester Utd?

Answers

Three Lions (see Quiz 8)

1 11. **2** Scotland. **3** Alan Mullery. **4** Peter Ward. **5** Three. **6** Tom Finney. **7** Brazil. **8** 53. **9** 90. **10** QPR & Manchester City. **11** Tony Adams. **12** Three. **13** Dave Watson. **14** European Championship 1988. **15** Jimmy Greaves. **16** 18 minutes. **17** 73. **18** Tommy Lawton. **19** 1970. **20** Tony Cottee.

Quiz 7 **Pot Luck 4**

LEVEL 3

Answers – see page 215

1 Comedian Ronnie Corbett had a trial at which Scottish club?

2 Which England manager was born in Burnley in 1921?

3 Which side from the Midlands used to play at Goldthorn Hill?

4 Sean O'Driscoll set a League appearance record at which club?

5 The first £1 million British move was in February 1979. How many more players moved for a million in the same year?

6 Which Alan went on from non-League Alvechurch to play for England?

7 The first home England international since 1966 to be played away from Wembley was in 1995 v Sweden. Where was it played?

8 What was the first League club that Ron Atkinson managed?

9 Which Colin played his only England game in 1971 against Malta?

10 What is John Aldridge's middle name?

11 Peter Davenport and Gary Pallister were in the same team at which club?

12 Which Mel became boss of Manchester City in 1987?

13 Mick Robinson first played in an FA Cup Final for which team?

14 At which club did Steve Ogrizovic make his League debut?

15 In what decade did Hearts first win the Championship?

16 Which club had a fanzine called *A Slice of Kilner Pie*?

17 Jimmy Mullen followed Frank Casper as manager of which club?

18 Who moved from Chelsea to Tottenham Hotspur for £2,200,000 in 1991 to set a club record for a transfer fee received?

19 Which club was once known as Abbey United?

20 To one each way, how many international goals did Tony Cascarino score?

Answers

Pot Luck 3 (see Quiz 5)

1 Willie Bell. **2** Alexander. **3** Wrexham. **4** David Seaman. **5** 1900s. **6** Bournemouth. **7** Crystal Palace. **8** Dean Holdsworth. **9** Barnet. **10** 9. **11** Arsenal. **12** Bremner. **13** Manchester United. **14** 73. **15** Portsmouth. **16** Harry Cripps. **17** White and blue. **18** Bristol City. **19** St Mirren. **20** John Osborne.

Quiz 8 **Three Lions**

LEVEL 3

Answers – see page 216

1 How many goals did Stanley Matthews score for England?

2 Bobby Charlton's first international goal was against which country?

3 Which player was outjumped by Pele before Banks made his save in Mexico 1970?

4 Which Brighton forward went on as a substitute for eight minutes in his only England appearance?

5 How many internationals did Jimmy Greaves play after the 1966 World Cup?

6 Who was the first player to score 30 goals for England?

7 Gary Lineker missed a penalty against which team in 1992?

8 To two each way, how many caps did Glenn Hoddle win?

9 In how many games was Bobby Moore skipper of England?

10 Rodney Marsh was capped while playing for which two clubs?

11 Who scored for both sides in the friendly v Holland in 1988?

12 How many games did Billy Wright miss between his first and last appearance for England?

13 Who was capped for England while playing for Werder Bremen in 1980?

14 Kenny Sansom played his last England game in which tournament?

15 Who, in a 1962 World Cup game, picked up a dog which urinated on him?

16 To five each way, how many minutes was Kevin Hector on the field for his two England appearances?

17 How many caps did Gordon Banks win?

18 Timed at 17 seconds in 1947, who scored England's fastest goal?

19 In what year did Peter Shilton first play for England?

20 Who is the first striker whose career lasted at least six games but never scored for England?

Answers

Transfer Trail (see Quiz 6)

1 Fulham. **2** Trevor Francis. **3** Falkirk. **4** Birmingham City. **5** Sporting Gijon. **6** Tommy Lawton. **7** Coventry City. **8** Steve Daley. **9** 33. **10** Kevin Reeves. **11** Steve Nicol. **12** Airdrie. **13** David Mills. **14** Jimmy Greenhoff. **15** Derby County. **16** Mo Johnston. **17** Ian Storey Moore. **18** John Deehan. **19** Nîmes. **20** Birmingham City.

Quiz 9 **Pot Luck 5**

Answers – see page 221

LEVEL 3

1 Which England player went to the same school as Gazza?

2 In Scotland, which club has its ground nearest to the sea?

3 Who was in goal when Sheffield Wednesday lost the FA Cup Final in 1993?

4 At which club did Andy Townsend make his League debut?

5 In what decade did Manchester Utd first win the Championship?

6 Which club had a fanzine called *City Gent*?

7 Bobby Gould followed Dave Sexton as manager of which club?

8 Steve Davis' move to Luton in August 1995 set a club record for a transfer fee received at which club?

9 Which club, formed in 1881, were originally known as Stanley?

10 To one each way, how many international goals did John Barnes score?

11 Neil McDonald and Adrian Heath were in the same team at which club?

12 Which Bobby was Ipswich Town manager from 1982 to 1987?

13 Paul Power played in an FA Cup Final for which team?

14 Who, at Lincoln in 1972 aged 28, became the youngest ever League manager?

15 Who spent a night in a police cell two days before breaking the British transfer record?

16 What is Clive Allen's middle name?

17 Which present day club used to play at the Memorial Recreation Ground, Canning Town?

18 What was the first club that Ian Branfoot managed?

19 Stuart Taylor set a League appearance record at which club?

20 Bill Shankly played for which FA Cup-winning side?

Answers

Pot Luck 6 (see Quiz 11)

1 John Aldridge. **2** Newcastle Utd. **3** Walsall. **4** Nigel. **5** Bournemouth. **6** Bolton Wanderers. **7** 16. **8** Greenwich Borough. **9** Colchester Utd. **10** Steve Perryman. **11** Norwich City. **12** King. **13** Crystal Palace. **14** Wolves. **15** 1940s. **16** Ipswich Town. **17** Hull City. **18** Ian Rush. **19** Cardiff City. **20** 19.

Quiz 10 **Soccer Legends**

LEVEL 3

Answers – see page 222

1 With which club did Gordon Banks make his League debut?

2 Who was the first Scottish player to be European Footballer of the Year?

3 Who said that he was "supremely grateful" to have played against the great Hungarian side of the 1950s?

4 Who was Footballer of the Year in 1948 and 1963?

5 Against which country did Jimmy Greaves make his scoring debut?

6 How many championships did Bobby Charlton win with Manchester Utd?

7 At which club did Wilf Mannion end his career?

8 In the season he set a new scoring record, how many goals did Dixie Dean get in his last three games?

9 At which Italian club did Dino Zoff begin his career?

10 To two each way, how many caps did Alex James get for Scotland?

11 In which country was Alfredo Di Stefano born?

12 Which county did Raich Carter play cricket for?

13 Which NASL team did George Best play for?

14 What was the job of Stanley Matthews' father?

15 Which club name was one of Bobby Moore's names?

16 Who hit a record 59 goals in a season for Middlesbrough?

17 To three each way, how many goals did Ferenc Puskas score for Hungary?

18 Which free-scoring England forward moved to Germany in 1914 and was interned during the War?

19 Danny Blanchflower started out with which Irish club?

20 How many Scottish League clubs did Denis Law play for?

Answers

Liverpool/Everton (see Quiz 12)

1 Kevin Ratcliffe. **2** Ian Callaghan. **3** Kenny Dalglish. **4** Huddersfield Town. **5** Bill Kenwright. **6** 1930. **7** Brian Hall. **8** Home Farm. **9** Telford United. **10** Dixie Dean. **11** 68 points. **12** Tottenham Hotspur. **13** Dean Saunders & Mark Wright. **14** Kevin Keegan. **15** Brian Labone. **16** Crystal Palace. **17** John Barnes. **18** Crystal Palace. **19** Billy Liddell. **20** 1981.

Quiz 11 **Pot Luck 6**

Answers – see page 219

LEVEL 3

1. Which player was involved in the substitute row in the Mexico v the Republic of Ireland 1994 World Cup game?
2. Which club had the fullback pairing of Ranson and Sansom?
3. Until 1990 which team used to play at Fellows Park?
4. What is Mark Atkins' middle name?
5. What was the first club that John Bond managed?
6. Brian Kidd finished his playing career in England with which club?
7. How many goals did Liverpool's mean machine defence concede in the 42 League games of 1978–79?
8. Which non-League side did Ian Wright play for?
9. Micky Cook set a League appearance record at which club?
10. Which Tottenham Hotspur star played his only England game in 1982, against Iceland?
11. Andy Linighan and Mike Phelan were in the same team at which club?
12. Which Andy became manager of Mansfield in 1993?
13. Phil Barber played in an FA Cup Final for which team?
14. At which club did Tim Flowers make his League debut?
15. In which decade did Portsmouth first win the First Division Championship?
16. Which club had a fanzine called *A Load of Cobbolds*?
17. Eddie Gray followed Brian Horton as manager of which club?
18. Who moved from Chester for £300,000 in 1980 to set a club record for a transfer fee received?
19. Which club was once known as Riverside Albion?
20. To two each way, how many international goals did Don Givens net?

Answers

Pot Luck 5 (see Quiz 9)

1 Steve Stone. **2** Arbroath. **3** Chris Woods. **4** Southampton. **5** 1900s. **6** Bradford City. **7** Coventry City. **8** Burnley. **9** Newcastle Utd. **10** 11. **11** Everton. **12** Ferguson. **13** Manchester City. **14** Graham Taylor. **15** Chris Sutton. **16** Darren. **17** West Ham Utd. **18** Reading. **19** Bristol Rovers. **20** Preston North End.

Quiz 12 **Liverpool/Everton**

Answers – see page 220

LEVEL 3

1 Who was Everton's skipper in the 1985 European Cup Winners' Cup?

2 Who holds Liverpool's record for most League appearances?

3 Which Liverpool player appeared three times at Wembley in 1977–78, his first season in England?

4 Which Yorkshire team did Bill Shankly manage between 1956 and 1959?

5 Which theatre impresario is listed as one of Everton's directors?

6 To two each way, in what year were Everton first relegated?

7 Which Liverpool outfield player was the only one not to score in the 11–0 rout of Stromsgodset in 1974?

8 Which Irish club did Ronnie Whelan come from?

9 Which non-League side did Everton beat in 1985 in the FA Cup?

10 Which famous player died at Goodison at the 1980 Merseyside derby?

11 Under the 2 points for a win system how many points did Liverpool gain to create a record in 1979?

12 Which side inflicted a 10–4 thrashing on Everton in season 1958–59?

13 Which two internationals – one Welsh, one English – did Graeme Souness sign in July 1992?

14 Which ex Liverpool star played only 27 minutes in the final stages of a World Cup to earn the last of his 63 caps?

15 Who was skipper of Everton's 1966 FA Cup winning side?

16 In 1990, Liverpool beat which club 9–0 in the League and lost to them in an FA Cup semi-final?

17 Which Liverpool player scored his first international goal in Rio?

18 At which ground did Everton first win the FA Cup in 1906?

19 Who retired in 1961 to become a lay preacher and a JP?

20 Which year in the 1980s did neither club contest the Charity Shield?

Answers

Soccer Legends (see Quiz 10)

1 Chesterfield. **2** Denis Law. **3** Billy Wright. **4** Stanley Matthews. **5** Peru. **6** 4. **7** Hull City. **8** 9. **9** Udinese. **10** 8. **11** Argentina. **12** Derbyshire. **13** Los Angeles Aztecs. **14** Barber. **15** Chelsea. **16** George Camsell. **17** 83. **18** Steve Bloomer. **19** Glentoran. **20** None.

Quiz 13 **Pot Luck 7**

Answers – see page 225

LEVEL 3

1 Who was 18 years and 14 days old when he played in the Brighton v Manchester Utd FA Cup Final?

2 Sir Stanley Matthews was manager of which English club?

3 Who got into bother for calling referee Robbie Hart a "Muppet"?

4 At which club did Tim Sherwood make his League debut?

5 In which decade did Ipswich Town first win the Championship?

6 Which club had a fanzine called *Voice of the Beehive*?

7 John Neal followed Geoff Hurst as manager of which club?

8 Who moved from Bury to Southampton for £375,000, in October 1991, to set a club record for a transfer fee received?

9 Which club was once known as Christ Church FC?

10 To one each way, how many international goals did Kevin Beattie score?

11 Mike Newell and Gary McAllister were in the same team at which club?

12 Which Pat became manager of Leyton Orient in 1995?

13 Jim Beglin first played in an FA Cup Final for which team?

14 What was the first name of ex-WBA and Ipswich Town player Zondervan?

15 Which defender was making his Leeds Utd debut in the same game as Gordon Strachan's first appearance?

16 Who was in goal when Tottenham Hotspur won the FA Cup Final in 1987?

17 What was the first club that Billy Bremner managed?

18 Who created a record for Derby County by playing 486 League games?

19 What is Phil Babb's middle name?

20 Which club used to play at Steeles Field and Ravenshaws Field?

Answers

Pot Luck 8 (see Quiz 15)

1 Southampton. **2** Peterborough. **3** Graham Taylor. **4** Sterland. **5** Jonathan. **6** Tottenham Hotspur. **7** Grimsby Town. **8** Wealdstone. **9** Blackburn Rovers. **10** Hartlepool Utd. **11** Oldham Athletic. **12** Todd. **13** Tottenham Hotspur. **14** Norwich City. **15** 1890s. **16** Hull City. **17** Southend Utd. **18** Phil Babb. **19** Carlisle Utd. **20** 10.

Quiz 14 **FA Cup Finals**

Answers – see page 226

1 Who were the first team to beat Tottenham Hotspur in an FA Cup Final?

2 Which 1990s Final had opposing players with the same surname?

3 In which decade was the trophy won by a team not from England?

4 Which team were the first to arrive at Wembley by helicopter?

5 Kevin Reeves hit a Final goal for which club?

6 Bramall Lane, Goodison Park and Villa Park – which of these grounds has not staged an FA Cup Final replay?

7 In the 1980s and 1990s, which player appeared in four Finals and was on the losing team each time?

8 What was the first FA Cup Final to be drawn at Wembley?

9 Which Arsenal defender brought Paul Allen down from behind in 1980 when he was clear on goal?

10 In which decade could the crowd at a Final correctly name the referee by shouting, "The referee's a Bastard!"?

11 What is the biggest victory in a Final, and who were the teams?

12 Who was in goal for Spurs when they won the trophy in 1981?

13 Where were Finals played immediately before the opening of Wembley?

14 Which club captain played in the Brighton v Manchester Utd replay but not in the first game?

15 In 1978, which spectator said, "I thought the No 10 Whymark played exceptionally well", when in fact he hadn't played at all?

16 Who were the first side to lose a Wembley FA Cup Final?

17 Which brothers played together in a 1970s Final?

18 In which decade was extra time first played?

19 Which Blackburn player scored an own goal – for Wolves – in 1960?

20 Andy Lochhead played in a Final for which club?

Answers

Famous Families (see Quiz 16)

1 Chester, Luton, Manchester City. **2** Erwin and Ronald Koeman. **3** Brondby. **4** Allan and Ron Harris. **5** Atkinson. **6** Busby. **7** Millwall. **8** Robledo. **9** Fulham. **10** Brighton. **11** Arthur and Jack Rowley. **12** Neil. **13** Hartlepool Utd. **14** Moss Brothers. **15** The Springetts (Ron and Peter). **16** Barnes. **17** Clive and Paul Allen. **18** Brian Laudrup. **19** John Bond. **20** George.

Quiz 15 **Pot Luck 8**

Answers – see page 223

LEVEL 3

1 Dennis Wise joined Wimbledon after which club released him?

2 Which club had 19 points deducted in 1968 for making illegal payments to players?

3 Which manager brought Dwight Yorke to Villa Park?

4 Which Mel was with Sheffield Wednesday when he made his only England appearance in 1988 against Saudi Arabia?

5 What is Nick Barmby's middle name?

6 Which London team used to play at Northumberland Park?

7 With 448 League games in the 1950s and 1960s, Keith Jobling set an appearance record at which club?

8 Which non League club did Stuart Pearce leave to go into the League?

9 Which club in the north of England did Ossie Ardiles play for?

10 What was the first club that Brian Clough managed?

11 Paul Warhurst and Earl Barrett were in the same team at which club?

12 Which Colin became boss of Middlesbrough in 1990?

13 Steve Hodge first played in an FA Cup Final for which team?

14 At which club did Robert Fleck make his English League debut?

15 In what decade did Dumbarton first win the championship?

16 Which club had a fanzine called *Tiger Rag*?

17 Peter Taylor followed Barry Fry as manager of which club?

18 Who moved from Coventry City for £3,750,000 in September 1994 to set a club record for a transfer fee received?

19 Which club was once known as Shaddongate United?

20 To two each way, how many international goals did Leighton James score?

Answers

Pot Luck 7 (see Quiz 13)

1 Norman Whiteside. **2** Port Vale. **3** Ian Wright. **4** Watford. **5** 1960s. **6** Brentford. **7** Chelsea. **8** David Lee. **9** Bolton Wanderers. **10** One. **11** Leicester City. **12** Holland. **13** Liverpool. **14** Romeo. **15** Chris Fairclough. **16** Ray Clemence. **17** Doncaster Rovers. **18** Kevin Hector. **19** Andrew. **20** Tranmere Rovers.

Quiz 16 **Famous Families**

LEVEL 3

Answers – see page 224

1 At which three clubs did the Futcher twins play together?

2 Who were the first brothers to win European Championship medals?

3 At which club did the Laudrup brothers begin their careers?

4 Who were the only brothers to play on the same side in a 60s FA Cup Final?

5 Which brothers Graham and Ron were at Oxford Utd in the 1960s?

6 In the 1980 Luton v QPR game, which brothers Martyn and Viv were opponents after going on as subs?

7 Liam Brady's elder brothers Ray and Pat were together at which club?

8 What was the surname of 1950s Newcastle Utd brothers Ted and George?

9 Jimmy and John Conway were at which club together in the 1970s?

10 Mike Gatting's brother Steve played in an FA Cup Final for which team?

11 In the 50s which brothers each reached 200 League goals on the same day?

12 Which brother was at Aston Villa with Bruce Rioch?

13 The Linighan boys – Andy and David – started out at which club?

14 Which brothers were together at Villa for 18 years from the late 1930s?

15 Who were the goalkeeping brothers who exchanged clubs in the 60s?

16 What was the surname of dad Ken and son Peter both of Manchester City?

17 Which cousins played together in an FA Cup losing team in the 1980s?

18 Which member of a footballing family became the first non-British Scottish PFA Footballer of the Year?

19 Which Manchester City manager bought his own son Kevin?

20 What was the first name of George Eastham's father, who played for England in 1935?

Answers

FA Cup Finals (see Quiz 14)

1 Coventry City. **2** 1992, Liverpool, Rush (Ian) v Sunderland, Rush (David). **3** 1920s (Cardiff). **4** Brighton. **5** Manchester City. **6** Villa Park. **7** Paul Bracewell. **8** Chelsea v Leeds (1970). **9** Willie Young. **10** 1870s (S.R. Bastard). **11** Bury 6 v Derby County 0. **12** Milija Aleksic. **13** Stamford Bridge. **14** Steve Foster. **15** Margaret Thatcher. **16** West Ham. **17** Brian and Jimmy Greenhoff. **18** 1870s. **19** Mick McGrath. **20** Leicester City (1969).

Quiz 17 **Pot Luck 9**

Answers – see page 229

LEVEL 3

1. What colour are FC Porto's shirts?
2. Mel Pejic set a League appearance record at which club?
3. Who was in goal when West Ham Utd won the FA Cup in 1980?
4. At which club did John McGinlay make his League debut?
5. In what decade did Derby County first win the Championship?
6. Which club had a fanzine called *Trumpton Times*?
7. Jim Smith replaced Gordon Lee as manager of which club?
8. Who moved from Cardiff to Sheffield Utd for £300,000 in 1994, to set a club record for a transfer fee received?
9. Which club was once known as Boscombe St Johns?
10. To one each way, how many international goals did Peter Beardsley score?
11. Haddock and Swan were in the same team at which club?
12. Which John became manager of Lincoln City in 1995?
13. Greg Downs played in an FA Cup Final for which team?
14. Who used to play at Abbs Field, Fulwell?
15. What is Warren Barton's middle name?
16. What was the first club that Bobby Gould managed?
17. Where did Portugal finish in the 1994 World Cup?
18. Which manager was dismissed by Manchester City 12 days into the 1993–94 season?
19. Ferenc Puskas played international soccer for which two countries?
20. John Arlott, the voice of cricket, was a fan of which soccer club?

Answers

Pot Luck 10 (see Quiz 19)

1 1980s. **2** Martyn. **3** 27. **4** Sydney. **5** Southampton. **6** Miller. **7** Chesterfield. **8** Leyton Orient. **9** Brighton. **10** 12. **11** QPR. **12** Docherty. **13** Wimbledon. **14** Oxford Utd. **15** 1960s. **16** Leeds Utd. **17** Sheffield Utd. **18** Doncaster Rovers. **19** Coventry City. **20** 13.

Quiz 18 **Euro Champ'ship**

LEVEL 3

Answers – see page 230

1 Who were the only team not to score in Euro 96?

2 Which country was the first to appear in three consecutive Finals?

3 In what year was the first European Championship Final played?

4 Which country hosted the 1992 competition?

5 In which year did Spain win the trophy?

6 The home countries, except Scotland, entered the second tournament. When was this?

7 Name the first two cities to have hosted Finals twice.

8 When did Italy win the trophy?

9 Which country won the Championship on penalties in 1976?

10 Who were the Dutch scorers in their Final victory over Russia?

11 Who scored the two goals to win Euro 96?

12 How many games were there in Euro 96?

13 When Andy Sinton went off, who was the last player to go on as a substitute for England in Euro 92?

14 Which French player finished as the top scorer in 1984?

15 At which two grounds were the Euro 96 semi-finals held?

16 Which English headmaster was a referee in Euro 96?

17 Who scored England's first ever European Championship goal?

18 Who inspired the starting of the Championship?

19 Who contested the first ever Championship final?

20 Who were the first host country to win the European Championship?

Answers

Early Days (see Quiz 20)

1 Royal Engineers. **2** Aston Villa. **3** Sunderland. **4** Wanderers. **5** Crystal Palace. **6** Leeds City. **7** Shinguards. **8** Blackburn Rovers. **9** George V was the first monarch at a Final. **10** Lord Arthur Kinnaird. **11** Hyde United. **12** Albert Ironmonger. **13** Liverpool. **14** FIFA. **15** Ibrox. **16** James Forrest. **17** Bradford. **18** Professional player. (A Scot paid to play in England). **19** None. **20** Clydesdale.

Quiz 19 **Pot Luck 10**

Answers – see page 229

LEVEL 3

1 In which decade did Chester add City to their name?

2 Which Nigel went on from non League St Blazey to play for England?

3 How many points did Newcastle Utd take from their first 10 games of the 1995–96 League season?

4 What is Peter Beagrie's middle name?

5 Which club used to play at the Antelope Ground?

6 Which Brian of Burnley made his only England appearance in 1961?

7 What was the first club that Arthur Cox managed?

8 Peter Allen set a League appearance record at which London club?

9 Gerry Ryan took temporary charge of which club in November 1991?

10 Manchester City in 1995 and Blackburn in 1996 both played how many League games before a win?

11 David Seaman and Peter Reid were in the same team at which club?

12 Which John first became manager of Millwall in 1986?

13 Clive Goodyear played in an FA Cup Final for which team?

14 At which club did England's Mark Wright make his League debut?

15 In what decade did Dundee first win the championship?

16 Which club had a fanzine called *Marching Altogether*?

17 Dave Bassett followed Billy McEwan as manager of which club?

18 Rufus Brevett moved for £250,000 to QPR in 1991, to set a record for a transfer fee received at which club?

19 Which club was once known as Singers FC?

20 To two each way, how many international goals did John Toshack score?

Answers

Pot Luck 9 (see Quiz 17)

1 Blue and white. **2** Hereford Utd. **3** Phil Parkes. **4** Shrewsbury Town. **5** 1970s. **6** Bristol Rovers. **7** Blackburn Rovers. **8** Nathan Blake. **9** Bournemouth. **10** 9. **11** Leeds Utd. **12** Beck. **13** Coventry City. **14** Sunderland. **15** Dean. **16** Bristol Rovers. **17** Failed to qualify. **18** Peter Reid. **19** Hungary, Spain. **20** Reading.

Quiz 20 **Early Days**

Answers – see page 228

LEVEL 3

1. Who were the first team to lose an FA Cup Final?
2. William McGregor, who pushed for the formation of a League, was a director of which club?
3. Which club did Alf Common move from in the first £1,000 transfer?
4. Who were the first team to win the FA Cup three times in a row?
5. From 1895 to the First World War where were FA Cup Finals played?
6. Leeds United were formed following the demise of which team?
7. Samuel Widdowson of Nottingham Forest is credited with which innovation?
8. Who were the first team to score six goals in an FA Cup Final?
9. Which important spectator created a first at the Burnley v Liverpool 1914 FA Cup Final?
10. Which player turned out in nine of the first 12 FA Cup Finals?
11. Preston North End's 26 goals in an FA Cup game was against which team?
12. In 1904, which giant keeper made the first of 564 Notts County appearances?
13. Which club was the first to win promotion and the First Division in successive seasons?
14. What was formed in Paris on May 21, 1904?
15. At which ground did terracing collapse in 1902 killing 25 people?
16. Who was the first professional to play for England against Scotland?
17. In 1911 a new FA Cup was made in – and then won by the team from – which place?
18. In footballing terms what was a "Scottish professor"?
19. How many games did Preston North End lose in the first League season?
20. Who were the first team to lose a Scottish FA Cup Final?

Answers

Euro Champ'ship (see Quiz 18)

1 Turkey. **2** West Germany. (1972, 1976, 1980). **3** 1960. **4** Sweden. **5** 1964. **6** 1964. **7** Paris and Rome. **8** 1968. **9** Czechoslovakia. **10** Gullit and Van Basten. **11** Oliver Bierhoff. **12** 31. **13** Paul Merson. **14** Michel Platini. **15** Old Trafford and Wembley. **16** David Elleray. **17** Ron Flowers. **18** Henri Delaunay. **19** Soviet Union and Yugoslavia. **20** Spain (In 1964).

Quiz 21 **Pot Luck 11**

Answers – see page 233

LEVEL 3

1 Who were the opponents when Ian Rush hit his record breaking 24th goal for Wales?

2 Which brothers played in the 1976 European Cup Final?

3 Gary Bull established a record for most League goals in a season at which former League club?

4 At which club did Keith Curle make his League debut?

5 In what decade did Tottenham Hotspur first win the Championship?

6 Which club had a fanzine called *The Fox*?

7 Vic Crowe followed Tommy Docherty as manager of which club?

8 Who moved from Manchester City to Tottenham Hotspur for £1.7 million in 1988, to set a club record for a transfer fee received?

9 Which club was once known as St Domingo FC?

10 To two each way, how many international goals did Mike Channon score?

11 Goddard and Hebberd were in the same team at which club?

12 Which Sammy became boss of Doncaster in July 1994?

13 Tony Grealish played in an FA Cup Final for which team?

14 What is Dave Beasant's middle name?

15 With 467 League games from 1964 to 1982, Colin Harrison set an appearance record at which club?

16 Stuart Williams won 33 of his Welsh caps while at which club?

17 Owlerton was the original name of which ground?

18 Which is the only country to have qualified for every World Cup finals since 1982 without being exempt as hosts or defending champions?

19 Aged 29 Frank Sibley became the youngest League manager when he was at which club?

20 In which decade did Wales first win at Wembley?

Answers

Pot Luck 12 (see Quiz 23)

1 Scunthorpe Utd. **2** William. **3** Birmingham City. **4** Billy Bremner. **5** Leeds Utd. **6** Norwich City. **7** Hibernian. **8** Wales. **9** Notts County. **10** Torquay Utd. **11** West Ham Utd. **12** Buxton. **13** Fulham. **14** QPR. **15** 1980s. **16** Newcastle Utd. **17** Plymouth Argyle. **18** Richard Money. **19** Clapton Orient. **20** 4.

Quiz 22 **Nicknames**

LEVEL 3

Answers – see page 234

1 Which Scottish team are known as "The Loons"?

2 What was the nickname of Brazil's Garrincha?

3 Who was known as "Pele" in his Ipswich Town days?

4 Which great international forward became known as "The Little Canon"?

5 How was Austria's goal machine of the 1930s, Franz Binder, known?

6 Which Scottish team are known as Wee Jays?

7 United isn't the most original nickname, but how many teams could that apply to in the Premiership and English League sides in 2001–02?

8 What was Alan Kennedy's nickname at Liverpool?

9 Bauld, Conn and Wardhaugh formed "The Terrible Trio" at which club in the 1950s?

10 What is the nickname shared by clubs situated in McDiarmid Park, Perth, Scotland, and Friends Provident St Mary's Stadium, England?

11 Which Scottish team are known as The Ton?

12 What was the nickname of early 20th century keeper Bill Foulke?

13 Which Scotland and Arsenal player was "The Wee Wizard"?

14 Which Manchester Utd player was known as "The Black Prince"?

15 If the Foxes faced the Terriers at The New Den who would have the shorter journey?

16 Which Scottish team are known as The Sons?

17 "The Famous Five" helped which Scottish club to the Championship just after the Second World War?

18 Which Liverpool player was "The Flying Pig"?

19 Who is nicknamed "Choccy"?

20 What was the nickname of Manchester Utd's early 20th century player Enoch West?

Answers

The 1960s (see Quiz 24)

1 Tony Kay, David Layne, Peter Swan. **2** Accrington Stanley. **3** Billy Wright. **4** Terry Bly. **5** Denis Law. **6** Tommy Docherty. **7** First League substitute. **8** George Best. **9** Rangers & Hibs. **10** Northampton Town. **11** Malcolm Allison. **12** Wolves. **13** Rest of the World XI. **14** Jimmy Dickinson. **15** Eusebio. **16** Don Revie. **17** Bobby Moncur. **18** WBA. **19** Swiss. **20** George Eastham.

Quiz 23 **Pot Luck 12**

Answers – see page 231

LEVEL 3

1 Up to the late 1980s which club played at The Old Showground?

2 What is Ian Bishop's middle name?

3 Joe Bradford set a record for most League goals in a season at which club?

4 Which Scottish captain was banned for life from playing for his country?

5 Hankin and Hart scored in the same European game for which club?

6 At which club did Dion Dublin make his League debut?

7 Keeper Andy Goram was at which club when he scored v Morton?

8 Which country did John Mahoney play for?

9 Who were the first English club to play 3,000 matches in the League?

10 Playing from 1947 to 1959, Dennis Lewis set a League appearance record at which seaside club?

11 Dicks and Dickens were in the same team at which club?

12 Which Mick became manager of Scunthorpe in March 1996?

13 Peter Mellor played in an FA Cup Final for which team?

14 At which club did Chris Woods make his League debut?

15 In what decade did Dundee Utd first win the Championship?

16 Which club had a fanzine called *The Number Nine*?

17 Steve McCall followed Peter Shilton as manager of which club?

18 Who moved from Fulham to Liverpool for £333,333 in 1980 to set a club record for a transfer fee received?

19 What was Leyton Orient's name between entering the League in 1905 and the end of World War Two in 1946?

20 How many international goals did Steve Archibald score?

Answers

Pot Luck 11 (see Quiz 21)

1 Belgium. **2** Eddie and Frank Gray. **3** Barnet. **4** Bristol Rovers. **5** 1950s. **6** Leicester City. **7** Aston Villa. **8** Paul Stewart. **9** Everton. **10** 21. **11** Derby County. **12** Chung. **13** Brighton. **14** John. **15** Walsall. **16** WBA. **17** Hillsborough. **18** Belgium. **19** QPR. **20** 1970s.

Quiz 24 **The 1960s**

Answers – see page 232

LEVEL 3

1 Which three Sheffield Wednesday players were involved in the 1962 match-fixing scandal?

2 Which club resigned from the League in 1962?

3 Who followed George Swindin as manager of Arsenal?

4 Which Peterborough forward hit 52 goals in a season?

5 Who scored six for Manchester City in an abandoned FA Cup game?

6 Who managed Rotherham, QPR and Aston Villa in just six weeks?

7 What record did Keith Peacock set on the first day of the 1965–66 season?

8 Which player was labelled "El Beatle" by the Portuguese press?

9 Which two Scottish clubs were involved in Colin Stein's £100,000 transfer?

10 In the 1960s, which club went from Division 4 to Division 1 and back again?

11 Who was Joe Mercer's assistant when Manchester City won the Championship?

12 In 1960, which club hit 100 goals for a third successive season?

13 Who did England play to celebrate the centenary of the Football Association?

14 Which Portsmouth and England wing-half retired in 1965?

15 Who was leading scorer in the 1966 World Cup tournament?

16 Who took over as manager of Leeds Utd in 1961?

17 Which Newcastle Utd player hit his first goals for seven years in the 1969 Inter-Cities Fairs Cup Final?

18 Alan Ashman was manager of which FA Cup winners?

19 What was the nationality of the referee in the 1966 World Cup Final?

20 Which player took Newcastle Utd to court?

Answers

Nicknames (see Quiz 22)

1 Forfar. **2** "The Little Bird". **3** Alan Brazil. **4** Ferenc Puskas. **5** "Bimbo". **6** Livingston. **7** 15. **8** "Barney". **9** Hearts. **10** Saints (St Johnstone, Southampton). **11** Greenock Morton. **12** "Fatty". **13** Alex James. **14** Alex Dawson. **15** Leicester City (v Huddersfield Town at Millwall). **16** Dumbarton. **17** Hibernian. **18** Tommy Lawrence. **19** Brian McClair. **20** "Knocker".

Quiz 25 **Pot Luck 13**

Answers – see page 237

LEVEL 3

1 In 1984, who at Derby County became the League's youngest club chairman?

2 Where did Thomas Hässler go when he left Juventus in July 1991?

3 Dick Krzywicki played for which country in the 1970s?

4 At which club did Brian McClair make his League debut?

5 In what decade did Chelsea first win the Championship?

6 Which club has a fanzine called *Into The O Zone*?

7 Willie Maddren followed Malcolm Allison as manager of which club?

8 Who moved from Middlesbrough in August 1989 to set a club record for a transfer fee received?

9 Which club was once known as New Brompton?

10 To one each way, how many international goals did Terry Butcher score?

11 Speedie and Regis were in the same team at which club?

12 Which Peter became manager of Exeter in June 1995?

13 Cyrille Regis played in an FA Cup Final for which team?

14 Ted Harper established a record for most League goals in a season at which two clubs?

15 What is Clayton Blackmore's middle name?

16 Which club played at the White City in the 1930s and in the 1960s?

17 Mary Brown was involved in an affair with which soccer manager?

18 What was the first London club that Chris Armstrong played for?

19 Who was the Derby County chairman when Brian Clough resigned?

20 Which club claimed to have signed Gordon Strachan before he moved to Manchester Utd?

Answers

Pot Luck 14 (see Quiz 27)

1 Stranraer. **2** Gillingham & Ipswich Town. **3** John Toshack. **4** Port Vale. **5** Lloyd George. **6** Liverpool. **7** David May. **8** Juventus. **9** John Motson. **10** Blackpool. **11** WBA. **12** Smith. **13** Ipswich Town. **14** Port Vale. **15** 1960s. **16** Norwich City. **17** Notts County. **18** Hartlepool Utd. **19** Manchester City. **20** Three.

Quiz 26 **Midlands & NW**

LEVEL 3

Answers – see page 238

1 Who scored all the goals in Aston Villa's 2–2 draw with Leicester City in 1976?

2 Where are you going if you walk down Bescot Crescent?

3 Who did Stoke sell to Chelsea in October 1993 for a club record fee?

4 Who is Burnley's most capped player?

5 Which Midlands side was founded by cricketing enthusiasts of the Wesleyan Chapel?

6 When did Manchester City last win the FA Cup?

7 Which club in the north west was the first outside London to install floodlights?

8 Which Wolves player moved for a £1 million to Manchester City in 1979?

9 Which side beat Hyde by a massive 26 goals to nil?

10 Who played for Blackpool, Coventry City, Manchester City, Burnley and Swansea, while clocking up 795 League appearances?

11 Which club did Martin Dobson manage between 1984 and 1989?

12 Blackburn's Colin Hendry began his career with which Scottish club?

13 Who is Blackpool's most capped player?

14 Name the trophy won by Birmingham City in 1991?

15 Who beat Stoke in the First Division play-offs in 1996?

16 Which manager took Coventry City into the First Division in the 1960s?

17 Which club's score in two FA Cup Finals is 10 for and none against?

18 How many times did Wolves' Billy Wright play for England?

19 Who was Birmingham City boss between 1965 and 1970?

20 Who was Aston Villa's two-goal hero in the 1957 FA Cup Final?

Answers

European Cup (see Quiz 28)

1 Ferenc Puskas. **2** Reims. **3** Hibernian. **4** AC Milan. **5** Peter Withe. **6** Rome. **7** Phil Thompson. **8** Burnley. **9** Liverpool & Nottingham Forest. **10** Linfield. **11** Barcelona. **12** 1963. **13** Ronnie Simpson. **14** Real Madrid in 1957. **15** Ray Crawford. **16** Eusebio. **17** Feyenoord in 1970. **18** Manchester (League champions City and holders United, in 1968–69). **19** Chelsea. **20** Bobby Charlton.

Quiz 27 **Pot Luck 14**

Answers – see page 235

LEVEL 3

1 Alphabetically, which is the last Scottish League club?

2 Which two English clubs have a badge with a horse on it?

3 Who was manager of Wales for 47 days?

4 In the 1920s, 1930s and 1940s which club used to play at the Recreation Ground, Hanley?

5 What are the two middle names of Noel Blake?

6 Wark and Walsh scored in the same European game for which club?

7 Who scored for Manchester Utd in the Cantona Kung-Fu game?

8 Jürgen Kohler moved for £4 million plus from Bayern Munich to which club?

9 Who commentated, "Stuart Pearce has got the taste of Wembley in his nostrils"?

10 Jimmy Hampson established a record for most League goals in a season at which club?

11 Talbot and Ford were in the same team at which club?

12 Which Alan became boss of Wycombe Wanderers in June 1995?

13 Clive Woods first played in an FA Cup Final for which team?

14 At which club did Mark Bright make his League debut?

15 In what decade did Kilmarnock first win the championship?

16 Which club has a fanzine called *Ferry Cross The Wensum*?

17 Neil Warnock followed John Barnwell as manager of which club?

18 Joe Allon moved to Chelsea in 1991 to set a record for a transfer fee received at which club?

19 Which club was once known as Ardwick FC?

20 To one each way, how many international goals did Chris Nichol score?

Answers

Pot Luck 13 (see Quiz 25)

1 Ian Maxwell. **2** Roma. **3** Wales. **4** Motherwell. **5** 1950s. **6** Leyton Orient. **7** Middlesbrough. **8** Gary Pallister. **9** Gillingham. **10** Three. **11** Coventry City. **12** Fox. **13** Coventry City. **14** Blackburn Rovers and Preston North End. **15** Graham. **16** QPR. **17** Tommy Docherty. **18** Millwall. **19** Sam Longson. **20** Cologne.

Quiz 28 **European Cup**

Answers – see page 236

LEVEL 3

1 Who was the first player to score a hat-trick in a European Cup Final?

2 Which French team became the first to lose two Finals?

3 Who were the first British team to compete in the European Cup?

4 Which team appeared in the Final in 1993, 1994 and 1995?

5 Who scored the only goal to win the trophy for Aston Villa?

6 Which city hosted the Final when Liverpool first won?

7 Who was Liverpool skipper for the 1981 triumph?

8 Which Lancashire town team represented England in 1960–61?

9 Who met in the first all-English tie in 1978–79?

10 Which team has represented Northern Ireland most times?

11 Who were the first club to eliminate Real Madrid from the competition?

12 To two years each way, when was the first Final played at Wembley?

13 Who was in goal for the first British European Cup winners?

14 Which was the first club to play a European Cup Final on their own ground?

15 Which Ipswich Town player scored five goals in the European Cup?

16 Who scored an amazing 46 goals in the European Cup for Benfica?

17 Which were the first team from Holland to win the trophy?

18 Which was the first British city to have two teams entering the same season's competition?

19 Which London club pulled out of the first competition?

20 Who scored first for Manchester Utd in the 1968 Final v Benfica?

Answers

Midlands & NW (see Quiz 26)

1 Chris Nicholl of Aston Villa. **2** Walsall. **3** Mark Stein. **4** Jimmy McIlroy. **5** Aston Villa. **6** 1969. **7** Carlisle Utd. **8** Steve Daley. **9** Preston North End. **10** Tommy Hutchison. **11** Bury. **12** Dundee. **13** Jimmy Armfield. **14** Auto Windscreens Shield. **15** Leicester City. **16** Jimmy Hill. **17** Bury. **18** 105. **19** Stan Cullis. **20** Peter McParland.

Quiz 29 **Pot Luck 15**

Answers – see page 241

LEVEL 3

1. At which club did Terry Paine finish his playing career?
2. Who was the first black player to be named in an England under-21 squad?
3. Frank O'Farrell became manager of which country?
4. At which club did Paul Parker make his League debut?
5. In which decade did Leeds Utd first win the Championship?
6. Which club had a fanzine called *Deranged Ferret*?
7. Frank Worthington followed Bryan Hamilton as manager of which club?
8. Who moved from Oxford Utd to Derby County in 1988, to set a club record for a transfer fee received?
9. What was Grimsby Town once known as?
10. To one each way, how many international goals did Steve Coppell score?
11. Peter Nicholas and Clive Wilson were together at which club?
12. Which Steve became boss of Colchester Utd in January 1995?
13. Chris Waddle first played in an FA Cup Final for which team?
14. Who is Bolton Wanderers' all-time leading goalscorer?
15. Who scored 11 goals in QPR's first European season?
16. Who was manager of Millwall between 1982 and 1986?
17. Which club started out playing at Headington Quarry?
18. What is Reggie Blinker's middle name?
19. Who resigned as Tottenham Hotspur manager on June 23rd 1976?
20. Who retired, as a player in 1975 following the Celtic v Airdrie Scottish Cup Final?

Answers

Pot Luck 16 (see Quiz 31)

1 Manchester Utd (They never scored together at Ipswich Town). **2** Bournemouth. **3** Oldham Athletic. **4** Mike Bamber. **5** Marseille. **6** Glasgow. **7** Stamford Bridge. **8** Derby County. **9** Manchester Utd. **10** John. **11** Southampton. **12** York City. **13** Sunderland. **14** Stoke City. **15** 1930s. **16** Nottingham Forest. **17** Chelsea. **18** Darren Peacock. **19** Manchester Utd. **20** Three.

Quiz 30 **On The Spot**

Answers – see page 242

LEVEL 3

1 Who scored an 1980s FA Cup Final replay penalty for Manchester Utd?

2 To three each way, it what year was the penalty kick introduced?

3 Blanchflower scored against which keeper in the 1962 FA Cup Final?

4 In 1991 who became the first club to win an FA Cup penalty shootout?

5 To one each way, how many penalty goals did Francis Lee get in 1971–72?

6 Which Birmingham City keeper saved a penalty with his first touch in his first match?

7 John Wark hit a penalty hat-trick against which European team?

8 Who was on the spot for Aston Villa v Manchester Utd in the 1994 League Cup Final?

9 Who missed Italy's final penalty in the 1994 World Cup?

10 Which international keeper scored three penalties in 1988 and 1989?

11 Who were the first nation to win a World Cup shootout, in 1982?

12 Who saved eight out of ten penalties faced in 1979–80?

13 Who was beaten by Nigel Clough's 1989 League Cup Final penalty?

14 How many penalties were there in the Palace 2 v Brighton 1 game in 1989?

15 Ronnie Allen hit an FA Cup Final penalty in 1954 for which club?

16 Who were winners in 1992 in the first game where a top flight team went out of the FA Cup competition in a shoot out?

17 Which Nottingham Forest player was fouled in the incident leading to the penalty in the 1970s League Cup Final replay v Liverpool?

18 Which Manchester Utd keeper was club joint top scorer in mid-season 1974–75, because of his spot-kick success?

19 Which nation won in the first major tournament decided on penalties?

20 Eddie Shimwell hit an FA Cup Final penalty for Blackpool in 1948 against which club?

Answers

Quote, Unquote (see Quiz 32)

1 Jasper Carrott. **2** John Motson. **3** Alex Ferguson. **4** Ron Atkinson. **5** Tommy Docherty. **6** Elton John. **7** Bill Nicholson. **8** Roy Hodgson. **9** Barry Fry. **10** Charlie Nicholas. **11** Trevor Phillips. **12** Vinnie Jones. **13** Graeme Souness. **14** Graham Kelly. **15** Ken Bates. **16** Kevin Keegan. **17** Paul Gascoigne. **18** The Chancellor. **19** Bob Paisley. **20** An artist.

Quiz 31 **Pot Luck 16**

Answers – see page 239

LEVEL 3

1 At which club did Brazil and Muhren score in the same European game?

2 In 1970–71 Ted MacDougall set a record for most League goals in a season at which club?

3 Which club used to play at Sheepfoot Lane?

4 Who was chairman of Brighton when Brian Clough was manager?

5 Dragan Stoijkovic moved from Red Star to which club in July 1990?

6 Which university did Brian McClair attend?

7 Which ground shares its names with a battle in England against the Norman invaders?

8 What was the first English club that Ted McMinn played for?

9 Colin McKee's only Manchester Utd appearance, in the last game of 1993–94, came when which club were champions?

10 What is Mark Bosnich's middle name?

11 Osman and Ruddock were in the same team at which club?

12 John Ward was manager of which club from 1991 to 1993?

13 Vic Halom played in an FA Cup Final for which team?

14 At which club did Lee Chapman make his League debut?

15 In what decade did Motherwell first win the Championship?

16 Which club has a fanzine called *Garibaldi*?

17 Danny Blanchflower followed Ken Shellito as manager of which club?

18 Who moved from Hereford Utd to QPR in 1990, to set a club record for a transfer fee received?

19 Which club was once known as Newton Heath?

20 To two each way, how many international goals did Jim Baxter score?

Answers

Pot Luck 15 (see Quiz 29)

1 Hereford Utd. **2** Laurie Cunningham. **3** Iran. **4** Fulham. **5** 1960s. **6** Lincoln City. **7** Tranmere Rovers. **8** Dean Saunders. **9** Grimsby Pelham. **10** 7. **11** Chelsea. **12** Wignall. **13** Tottenham Hotspur. **14** Nat Lofthouse. **15** Stan Bowles. **16** George Graham. **17** Oxford Utd. **18** Waldie. **19** Terry Neill. **20** Billy McNeill.

Quiz 32 **Quote, Unquote**

LEVEL 3

Answers – see page 240

1 Who said, of Birmingham City, "You lose some, you draw some"?

2 Who said, "For those watching in black & white, Spurs are in yellow shirts"?

3 Which manager declared, "Goalkeepers are a more protected species than the Golden Eagle"?

4 Who in 1991 would be "bananas" to leave Sheffield Wednesday?

5 Who said in 1977, "I have been punished for falling in love"?

6 Which new chairman said, "I hope people will not treat it as a gimmick"?

7 Who resigned from 'Spurs saying, "Players have become impossible"?

8 "Even the Pope would have second thoughts about the England job," was the response of which international manager?

9 Who was David Sullivan talking about when he said, "...after three years and 61 players, we think it is time someone else is entitled to a go"?

10 Which player's leaving caused Jimmy Greaves to say, "Stringfellows will miss him"?

11 Which FA commercial director had "Not necessarily" resigned in 1996?

12 Who said his pigs did not squeal as much as Ruud Gullit?

13 In 1990 which Scot said, "You cannot guarantee a thing in this game"?

14 Which football executive said, "People ... think I'm a short, fat bloke, whereas I'm really a tall fat bloke"?

15 Who said, "John Hollins ... has a very strong wife, maybe I should have made her manager"?

16 Which manager said, "I don't want to talk about Andy Cole"?

17 Who said, "They say injuries come in threes. In my case it seems to be 33s"?

18 Ossie Ardiles thought the England manager to be the most hated person in the country apart from who?

19 Which boss said, "Nobody has the right to win anything they haven't earned"?

20 According to Eric Cantona, who is "someone who can lighten up a dark room"?

Answers

On the Spot (see Quiz 30)

1 Arnold Muhren. **2** 1891. **3** Adam Blacklaw. **4** Rotherham Utd. **5** 13. **6** Tony Coton. **7** Aris Salonika. **8** Dean Saunders. **9** Roberto Baggio. **10** Rene Higuita. **11** West Germany. **12** Paul Cooper. **13** Les Sealey. **14** Five (Palace had four and scored just one). **15** WBA. **16** Southampton. **17** John O'Hare. **18** Alec Stepney. **19** Czechoslovakia (1976 European Championship). **20** Manchester Utd.

Quiz 33 **Pot Luck 17**

Answers – see page 245

LEVEL 3

1 What was the most notable feature of David Platt's debut for Bari?

2 What did Leeds Utd's shirts have written on them when they won the 1992 Championship?

3 Howard Kendall moved to Birmingham City as part of the deal that took which player to Everton in the 1970s?

4 At which extinct club did Darren Peacock make his League debut?

5 In which decade did Wolves first win the Championship?

6 Which club had a fanzine called *When Sunday Comes*?

7 Steve Perryman followed Frank McLintock as manager of which club?

8 Who moved from Port Vale to Sheffield Wednesday for £1 million in 1994, to set a club record for a transfer fee received?

9 What was dropped by Hartlepool United in 1968?

10 To two each way, how many England goals did Geoff Hurst score?

11 Eric Gates and Colin Pascoe were in the same team at which club?

12 Which Brian became manager of Huddersfield Town in June 1995?

13 Nigel Worthington played in an FA Cup Final for which team?

14 In 1976–77 Peter Ward established a record for most League goals in a season at which club?

15 Gary Pierce was in goal as which club won the League Cup?

16 Part of whose CV would read – manager of Grimsby in 1951, moved to Workington in 1953?

17 Which club used to play at the Beeston Cricket Ground?

18 Which country did John Devine play for?

19 Samesh Kumar was first chairman at which club?

20 What is Steve Bould's middle name?

Answers

Pot Luck 18 (see Quiz 35)

1 John Toshack. **2** Abraham. **3** Arsenal. **4** Smallest League pitches. **5** Nottingham Forest. **6** Burnley. **7** Birmingham City. **8** Lazio. **9** Tottenham Hotspur. **10** Chris Balderstone. **11** Sheffield Wednesday. **12** Deehan. **13** Tottenham Hotspur. **14** Everton. **15** 1890s. **16** Notts County. **17** Coventry City. **18** Andy Payton. **19** Wesleyans. **20** Two.

Quiz 34 **Wonder Wingers**

Answers – see page 246

LEVEL 3

1 Who played on the left wing when Manchester Utd beat Benfica in the European Cup Final of 1968?

2 Who was Aston Villa's flying winger when they won the 1981 title?

3 Who hit the winning goal in the 1953 Matthews Final?

4 How was Manoel Francisco dos Santos better known?

5 Who was the first player to be Footballer of the Year twice?

6 Keith Gillespie made his League debut while on loan at which club?

7 At which club did Cliff Jones finish his playing career?

8 "This is the best amateur footballer I've seen," was Bob Paisley's assessment of which winger?

9 Which future England left winger was born in Bolton in July, 1971?

10 In which town was Ruel Fox born?

11 Left-winger Alan Hinton won the Championship with which team?

12 Which England winger had the middle names Charles Bryan?

13 A injury to which knee ended Steve Coppell's career?

14 Ryan Giggs scored in his first international against which country?

15 According to Bobby Charlton who "still had his magic" when nearing 50?

16 Which winger John was in England's 1966 World Cup squad?

17 Peter Barnes won England caps while at which three clubs?

18 George Best played for which Scottish club?

19 Which Scottish winger was nicknamed "The Flea"?

20 Which English club did Scotsman Willie Henderson play for?

Answers

Scotland (see Quiz 36)

1 Billy Steele. **2** John Hewie. **3** John Lambie. **4** 1870s. **5** Rangers. **6** Wembley Wizards. **7** Danny McGrain. **8** Five. **9** Preston North End. **10** Jim Baxter. **11** Hearts. **12** Five. **13** Billy Liddell. **14** Hughie Gallacher. **15** 1–1. **16** Cannonball. **17** Jimmy McMullan. **18** Don Masson. **19** 1990. **20** Tommy Docherty.

Quiz 35 **Pot Luck 18**

Answers – see page 243

LEVEL 3

1 Which Welshman signed a three-year contract as coach to Sporting Lisbon in July 1984?

2 What is Mark Bright's middle name?

3 Joe Mercer was nearly 38 when he played in an FA Cup Final for which club?

4 In 1995–96, Arsenal, Colchester Utd and Preston North End shared what in common?

5 Which club used to play at the Town Ground?

6 George Beel established a record for most League goals in a season at which club?

7 Which club did Gary Sprake join when he left Leeds Utd?

8 Thomas Doll went from Hamburg to which club in June 1991?

9 At which club did Miller and Hazard score in the same Euro game?

10 Who was stripped of the Carlisle captaincy for playing cricket until the end of the county season?

11 Nigel Pearson and Alan Harper were in the same team at which club?

12 Which John became manager of Wigan in November 1995?

13 Terry Venables played in an FA Cup Final for which team?

14 At which club did Steve McMahon make his League debut?

15 In what decade did Rangers first win the Championship?

16 Which club had a fanzine called *No More Pie In The Sky*?

17 Gordon Milne followed Joe Mercer as manager of which club?

18 Who moved from Hull to Middlesbrough for £750,000 in 1991, to set a club record for a transfer fee received?

19 What was Mansfield's last name before Town was added?

20 To one each way, how many international goals did Danny Blanchflower score?

Answers

Pot Luck 17 (see Quiz 33)

1 Missed a penalty. **2** Top Man. **3** Bob Latchford. **4** Newport County. **5** 1950s. **6** Liverpool. **7** Brentford. **8** Ian Taylor. **9** The letter s from the name Hartlepools. **10** 24. **11** Sunderland. **12** Horton. **13** Sheffield Wednesday. **14** Brighton. **15** Wolves. **16** Bill Shankly. **17** Notts County. **18** Republic of Ireland. **19** Birmingham City. **20** Andrew.

Quiz 36 **Scotland**

Answers – see page 244

LEVEL 3

1 Who was the first Scottish player to be sent off in an international?
2 Which Scottish player became Charlton Athletic's most capped player?
3 Who is Scotland's youngest player to win a full international cap?
4 In what decade was the first official Scotland v England game?
5 Which club did George Young play for?
6 When Scotland hammered England 5–1 at Wembley in 1928, what nickname were they given?
7 Which Celtic star was diagnosed diabetic after playing in the 1974 World Cup squad?
8 From 1974, how many consecutive World Cup tournaments did Scotland reach?
9 What was the first English club that Alex James played for?
10 Who scored twice for Scotland at Wembley in 1963, in the 2–1 victory?
11 At which Scottish club did Dave Mackay start his career?
12 How many caps did Bill Shankly win?
13 Which Liverpool and Scottish international star played twice for Great Britain against the Rest of Europe?
14 Which Scottish international took Newcastle Utd to the title in 1927?
15 What was the result of Scotland's Group 4 game against Iran in the 1978 World Cup?
16 What nickname was given to striker Charlie Fleming?
17 Who captained the great 1920s, 5–1-winning Scottish side?
18 Whose last game for Scotland was the 1978 World Cup defeat by Peru, in which he missed a penalty?
19 In which year did Scotland pull out of the Rous Cup?
20 Which Scottish manager suffered only three defeats in his 12 games?

Answers

Wonder Wingers (see Quiz 34)

1 John Aston. **2** Tony Morley. **3** Bill Perry. **4** Garrincha. **5** Tom Finney. **6** Wigan. **7** Fulham. **8** Steve Heighway. **9** Jason Wilcox. **10** Ipswich. **11** Derby County. **12** John Barnes. **13** Left. **14** Belgium. **15** Stanley Matthews. **16** Connelly. **17** Manchester City, WBA, Leeds Utd. **18** Hibernian. **19** Jimmy Johnstone. **20** Sheffield Wednesday.

Quiz 37 **Pot Luck 19**

Answers – see page 249

LEVEL 3

1 Signed in the 1990s, who was the first Bolivian to play English football?

2 Which Liverpool manager sold Peter Beardsley?

3 What is Tim Breaker's middle name?

4 At which club did Warren Barton make his League debut?

5 In which decade did Aston Villa first win the Championship?

6 Which club had a fanzine called *No One Likes Us*?

7 Terry Cooper followed Roy Hodgson as manager of which club?

8 Who moved from Dundee Utd to Rangers for £4 million in 1993, to set a club record for a transfer fee received?

9 Which club once had Fosse at the end of its name?

10 To one each way, how many international goals did Bob Latchford score?

11 Curle and Scales were in the same team at which club?

12 Which Dave became manager of Stockport County in March 1995?

13 Terry McDermott first played in an FA Cup Final for which team?

14 In 1981–82 Craig Madden established a record for most League goals in a season at which club?

15 Which club used to play at the The Nest?

16 On Good Friday, 1936, Swansea travelled to Plymouth. In what may be the worst-ever example of holiday travel planning, where did they play the following day?

17 Who went from Real Madrid to Torino in June 1990?

18 Who was top scorer when Manchester Utd were Champions in 1993–94?

19 Which Italian team did Luther Blissett play for?

20 Which former Boston player/manager became England Technical Director?

Answers

Pot Luck 20 (see Quiz 39)

1 Dave Watson. **2** Lou Macari. **3** Bobby Gould. **4** Albert Quixall. **5** Jim McCalliog. **6** County Ground. **7** Roger. **8** Cambridge Utd. **9** Had advertising on shirts in a match. **10** West Ham Utd. **11** QPR. **12** May. **13** Everton. **14** Coventry City. **15** 1900s. **16** Portsmouth. **17** Crystal Palace. **18** Darren Huckerby. **19** Millwall. **20** 10.

Quiz 38 **Going Up**

Answers – see page 250

LEVEL 3

1 Who took Swindon Town to successive promotions in 1986 and 1987?

2 Keith Edwards hit 35 goals in a season to take which club out of the old Fourth Division?

3 Who were the last Fourth Division Champions?

4 Micky Stockwell was ever present as which club made the top flight?

5 Which club went up to Division One for the first time in 2000?

6 Who was boss when Manchester Utd were last promoted?

7 Which London club were twice Second Division champions in the 1980s?

8 Houston and Holton played in which team on the up?

9 How many points did Newcastle Utd get from the first 10 games of the 1992–93 promotion season?

10 Who was manager when Oxford Utd reached the top flight for the first time ever?

11 Howard Kendall took which team out of the Third Division?

12 Who was top scorer when Swansea hit the First Division in 1981?

13 Peter Hucker was in goal as which club reached the First Division?

14 Who was boss when Norwich City were 1986 Second Division Champions?

15 Noel Blake and Kenny Swain played in which 1980s promoted team?

16 Who was Manchester City's keeper in the 1989 promotion to the top flight?

17 Who was Newcastle Utd's top scorer in the 1992–93 promotion season?

18 Who were the first club to gain promotion and win the First Division in consecutive seasons?

19 Who was boss when Chelsea were Division 2 champions in 1988–89?

20 Price and Sellars played in which team on the up?

Answers

Going Down (see Quiz 40)

1 Frank Worthington. **2** Tommy Docherty. **3** 31. **4** Luton Town. **5** Wolves. **6** West Ham Utd & Ipswich Town. **7** Three. **8** Hammond. **9** 18. **10** Notts County. **11** Billy McNeill. **12** Sunderland. **13** Workington. **14** Ipswich Town. **15** Gateshead. **16** Bottom (22nd). **17** Sunderland. **18** Four. **19** Manchester Utd. **20** Bristol City.

Quiz 39 **Pot Luck 20**

Answers – see page 247

LEVEL 3

1. Which defender was the only ever present for England after eight games with Don Revie in charge?
2. Which manager has spent the shortest time as boss of West Ham Utd?
3. Who signed Stuart Pearce for Coventry City?
4. Alf Quantrill was the first English international whose surname began with a Q. Who is the only other one?
5. Which ex Manchester Utd player's pass set up the Bobby Stokes FA Cup winning goal in 1976?
6. Which ground used to be home to Northampton?
7. What is Steve Bruce's middle name?
8. In 1985–86 David Crown set a record for most League goals in a season at which club?
9. What did Kettering do in the mid-1970s that made the FA tell them not to do it again, but everybody does now?
10. Pike and Goddard scored in the same European game for which club?
11. Dave Thomas and John Hollins were in the same team at which club?
12. Which Eddie became boss of Torquay Utd in 1995?
13. Jimmy Gabriel played in an FA Cup Final for which team?
14. At which club did Mark Hateley make his League debut?
15. In what decade did Newcastle Utd first win the Championship?
16. Which club has a fanzine called *January 3rd 88*?
17. Terry Venables followed Malcolm Allison as manager of which club?
18. Who moved from Lincoln City to Newcastle Utd in 1995, to set a club record for a transfer fee received?
19. Which London club were Rovers, then Athletic, then went to a single name?
20. To two each way, how many international goals did Colin Stein grab?

Answers

Pot Luck 19 (see Quiz 37)

1 Jaime Moreno (Middlesbrough). **2** Graeme Souness. **3** Sean. **4** Maidstone Utd. **5** 1890s. **6** Millwall. **7** Bristol City. **8** Duncan Ferguson. **9** Leicester City. **10** 5. **11** Wimbledon. **12** Jones. **13** Newcastle Utd. **14** Bury. **15** Norwich City. **16** Newcastle. **17** Martin Vasquez. **18** Eric Cantona. **19** AC Milan. **20** Howard Wilkinson.

Quiz 40 **Going Down**

Answers – see page 248

LEVEL 3

1 Who was joint top scorer with Arthur Graham as Leeds Utd went down in 1982?
2 Who was boss when Manchester Utd were last relegated?
3 Cambridge Utd in 1983–84 set a record for the longest sequence without a win. How many games did this last?
4 Kamara and Dreyer played in which team leaving the top flight?
5 Paul Bradshaw was ever present in goal as which team went down in 1982?
6 In the 1990s John Lyall was at which two clubs in relegation seasons?
7 To two each way, how many Division 1 games did Stoke City win in 1984–85?
8 Digby, Sheffield and which other keeper shared the 100 goals Swindon Town let in on leaving the Premier League in 1994?
9 On their way out of the League for ever, Darwen chalked up how many consecutive defeats in 1898–99?
10 Craig and Chris Short played in which team leaving the top flight?
11 Who was Aston Villa boss in their 1986–87 relegation season?
12 Clive Walker was top scorer in which side's relegation season?
13 Which team left the League after being bottom of the Fourth Division in 1976 and 1977?
14 Guentchev and Paz played in which team leaving the top flight?
15 Which team, third from the bottom of the League in 1960, applied for re-election for the first time in over twenty years, yet still got voted out?
16 What was the highest position that WBA reached in 1985–86?
17 Who were in the First Division from 1890 until relegation in 1958?
18 How many keepers did Oldham Athletic use in 1993–94?
19 McCalliog and Macari played in which team leaving the top flight?
20 Which team was relegated in 1980, 1981 and 1982?

Answers

Going Up (see Quiz 38)

1 Lou Macari. **2** Sheffield Utd. **3** Burnley. **4** Ipswich Town. **5** Gillingham. **6** Tommy Docherty. **7** Chelsea. **8** Manchester Utd. **9** 30. **10** Jim Smith. **11** Blackburn Rovers. **12** Leighton James. **13** QPR. **14** Ken Brown. **15** Portsmouth. **16** Andy Dibble. **17** David Kelly. **18** Liverpool (1905–06). **19** Bobby Campbell. **20** Blackburn Rovers.

Quiz 41 **Pot Luck 21**

Answers – see page 253

LEVEL 3

1 Which manager was sacked six weeks after winning the FA Cup in the 1970s?

2 What is Robbie Fowler's middle name?

3 Gary O'Reilly scored in an FA Cup Final for which club?

4 At which club did Andy Sinton make his League debut?

5 In which decade did Nottingham Forest first win the Championship?

6 Which club has a fanzine called *The Holy Trinity*?

7 Dixie McNeil followed Bobby Roberts as manager of which club?

8 Who set the most League goals in a season record at Manchester Utd with 32 in 1959–60?

9 Which club was once known as Thames Ironworks FC?

10 To two each way, how many England goals did Steve Bloomer score?

11 Ossie Ardiles and Trevor Francis were in the same team at which club?

12 Kevin Cullis was briefly boss of which League club in 1996?

13 Alec Lindsay played in two FA Cup Finals for which team?

14 Which club beat Arsenal to win the European Super Cup in 1995?

15 Who was Gordon Chisholm playing for when he scored a League Cup Final own goal?

16 Kindon and Munro hit Euro goals in the same game for which club?

17 Who beat England in the quarter-finals of the 1962 World Cup?

18 Who in 1979 became the first person to play 100 League games for each of four different clubs?

19 Who was the manager when Bolton Wanderers went down to the Fourth Division for the first time ever?

20 Who lost to Parma in the 1995 UEFA Cup Final?

Answers

Pot Luck 22 (see Quiz 43)

1 Brian Kidd. **2** Bradford Park Avenue. **3** Adrian. **4** Southampton. **5** Malmo. **6** Glenn Cockerill. **7** Eamon Dunphy. **8** Nottingham Forest. **9** Mo Johnston. **10** Manchester City. **11** Leicester City. **12** Eustace. **13** Sunderland. **14** Bournemouth. **15** Notts County. **16** Carlisle Utd. **17** Middlesbrough. **18** Italy. **19** Strollers. **20** 10.

Quiz 42 **Manchester Utd**

LEVEL 3

Answers – see page 254

1 Who played in both Manchester Utd's 1985 and 1995 FA Cup Final sides?

2 Which two Munich crash survivors played in the 1968 European Cup Final?

3 Who was United's first-ever League substitute?

4 What was the name of Martin Buchan's brother, who also had a spell with United?

5 What was the offence for which Andrew Kanchelskis was sent off in the 1994 League Cup Final?

6 In which country was Jimmy Nicholl born?

7 Against which side did Ryan Giggs score his first League goal?

8 In the club's founding days, what did the letters LYR stand for?

9 Which other player joined United as part of the Bryan Robson deal?

10 Who took over as an emergency keeper in the 1957 FA Cup Final?

11 To two either way, how many international caps did George Best win?

12 Who was the only ever present in the title-winnning team of 1993–94?

13 In what year did Sir Matt first become United manager?

14 Against which team did Bryan Robson score his last goal in a competitive match?

15 David Beckham hit his first Euro goal against which team?

16 Who was sent off in the 1990s European Champions League 3–1 defeat in Gothenburg?

17 What shirt number did Mark Hughes usually wear in his first three years at Manchester Utd?

18 Which team did Lee Sharpe support as a boy?

19 Tommy Docherty's first signing was which Scottish fullback?

20 Bobby Charlton's last United League appearance was at which ground?

Answers

The 1970s (see Quiz 44)

1 Peter Bonetti. **2** Czechoslovakia. **3** Sammy Nelson. **4** Allan Simonsen. **5** 44. **6** Total football. **7** Denis Law. **8** Jack Charlton. **9** Jan Tomaszewski. **10** Ted MacDougall. **11** Terry Paine. **12** George Best. **13** Pele. **14** Ron Saunders. **15** David Nish. **16** Greaves and Armfield. **17** Colchester Utd. **18** Nottingham Forest. **19** Tottenham Hotspur. **20** Jack Taylor.

Quiz 43 **Pot Luck 22**

Answers – see page 251

LEVEL 3

1 Which British player played in a European Cup Final on his 19th birthday?

2 Which former league club had a pavilion called the Dolls House?

3 What is Ruel Fox's middle name?

4 Blyth, Gilchrist and Steele played for which 1970s FA Cup Finalists?

5 Who lost 1–0 to Nottingham Forest in the Final of the 1979 European Cup?

6 In 1988, TV film evidence showed that Paul Davis of Arsenal had broken which Southampton player's jaw?

7 Which Republic of Ireland international of the 1960s wrote the book *Only A Game* in the 1970s?

8 Lee Chapman first played in a League Cup Final for which club?

9 Which Catholic international was signed by Graeme Souness at Rangers?

10 Kidd and Power scored Euro goals in the same game for which club?

11 Mike Newell and Gary McAllister were in the same team at which club?

12 Which Peter was Leyton Orient boss from 1991 to 1994?

13 Anton Rogan first played in an FA Cup Final for which team?

14 At which club did Efan Ekoku make his League debut?

15 With 124 goals Les Bradd is all-time top League scorer at which club?

16 Which club had a fanzine called *So, Jack Ashurst, Where's My Shirt*?

17 Malcolm Allison followed Bobby Murdoch as manager of which club?

18 Which team first beat England at Wembley in a World Cup game?

19 What followed West Bromwich before the name Albion was introduced?

20 To one each way, how many international goals did Northern Ireland's Johnny Crossan score in the 1960s?

Answers

Pot Luck 21 (see Quiz 41)

1 Tommy Docherty. **2** Bernard. **3** Crystal Palace. **4** Cambridge Utd. **5** 1970s. **6** Aston Villa. **7** Wrexham. **8** Dennis Viollet. **9** West Ham Utd. **10** 28. **11** QPR. **12** Swansea City. **13** Liverpool. **14** AC Milan. **15** Sunderland. **16** Wolves. **17** Brazil. **18** Alan Ball. **19** Phil Neal. **20** Juventus.

Quiz 44 **The 1970s**

Answers – see page 252

LEVEL 3

1 Who was in goal as England lost to West Germany in the 1970 World Cup?

2 Who were the opponents when Viv Anderson became England's first black international footballer?

3 Which Arsenal player dropped his shorts to the crowd in a 1979 game against Coventry City?

4 Which Dane was named as European Footballer in the Year in 1977?

5 How many days did Brian Clough reign as boss of Leeds Utd in 1974?

6 What was the term used to describe Holland's fluid soccer?

7 Which ex-Manchester Utd star scored the goal that condemned his old club to relegation?

8 Which manager took Middlesbrough into the top flight?

9 Who kept goal for Poland at Wembley in the 1974 World Cup qualifier?

10 Which Bournemouth striker hit nine goals in an FA Cup tie?

11 Which ex-England player made 824 League appearances?

12 Who scored within 71 seconds of his Fulham debut in 1977?

13 Which international made his final appearance for his current team New York Cosmos against former team from the same continent in front of 77,000 at Giants Stadium?

14 Which manager was in four out of five consecutive League Cup Finals?

15 Which fullback moved for a record fee from Leicester City to Derby County in 1972?

16 Which two ex-England players – both Jimmy – retired in 1971?

17 Which giant-killers knocked Leeds Utd out of the 1970–71 FA Cup?

18 Which team went 42 consecutive League games without defeat?

19 Who did Arsenal beat in the final league game of the double season?

20 Which English referee controlled the 1974 World Cup Final?

Answers

Manchester Utd (see Quiz 42)

1 Mark Hughes. **2** Bobby Charlton & Bill Foulkes. **3** John Fitzpatrick. **4** George. **5** Deliberate handball. **6** Canada. **7** Manchester City. **8** Lancashire and Yorkshire Railway. **9** Remi Moses. **10** Jackie Blanchflower. **11** 37 **12** Denis Irwin. **13** 1945. **14** Oldham Athletic. **15** Galatasaray. **16** Paul Ince. **17** No 9. **18** Aston Villa. **19** Alex Forsyth. **20** Stamford Bridge.

Quiz 45 **Pot Luck 23**

Answers – see page 257

LEVEL 3

1 Nigel Jemson scored in a League Cup Final for which club?

2 How many days was Jock Stein in charge of Leeds Utd?

3 Who lost to Arsenal in the 1970 UEFA Cup Final?

4 At which club did Pat Nevin make his Scottish League debut?

5 In what decade did Sunderland first win the Championship?

6 Which club had a fanzine called *Beesotted*?

7 Danny Bergara followed Asa Hartford as manager of which club?

8 Which Celtic player fractured his skull against Falkirk in 1972?

9 Which club was once known as West Herts?

10 To two each way, how many international goals did Martin Chivers score?

11 The Harris brothers were in the same team at which London club in the 1960s?

12 Which Alan became manager of York City in 1983?

13 Barry Venison first played in an FA Cup Final for which team?

14 What is Marcus Gayle's middle name?

15 Holland and Jennings scored Euro goals in the same game for which club?

16 With 39 scored, Derek Reeves set the most League goals in a season record at which club?

17 Which was the first country to stage the World Cup in Europe?

18 Stuart McCall scored twice in an FA Cup Final for which club?

19 Which club beat Rangers to win the European Super Cup in 1972?

20 Colin Irwin played in a League Cup Final for which club?

Answers

Pot Luck 24 (see Quiz 47)

1 David. **2** QPR. **3** Coventry City. **4** Liverpool. **5** Hull City. **6** David & Ian. **7** Oldham Athletic. **8** John Bond & Ken Brown. **9** Leeds Utd. **10** Real Madrid. **11** Liverpool. **12** Docherty. **13** Sheffield Wednesday. **14** Morton. **15** Bayern Munich. **16** Chester City. **17** Newcastle Utd. **18** Coventry City. **19** Walsall. **20** 12.

Quiz 46 **Keepers**

Answers – see page 258

LEVEL 3

1 Who was in goal for Nottingham Forest in the 1992 League Cup Final?

2 Who was in goal for England in the 1997 World Cup qualifier v Italy at Wembley?

3 Who was in goal for Leeds Utd in the 1972 and 1973 FA Cup Finals?

4 John Burridge made his League debut for which club, who are now no longer in the League?

5 Who, in the 1990s, saved five penalties in three days – three against Tranmere in a League Cup semi-final and two v Tottenham Hotspur?

6 At which League club did Chris Turner make his debut?

7 Which club did Coventry sign Steve Ogrizovic from?

8 Harry Dowd was in an FA Cup winning 1960s team at which club?

9 Phil Parkes made his League debut at which club?

10 Which club did Jim Leighton join when he finally left Manchester Utd?

11 Who was in goal for Oldham Athletic in the 1990 League Cup Final?

12 Who went down from the top flight with Millwall in 1990 and Bolton in '96?

13 Which veteran keeper became player/manager of Exeter in 1995?

14 Which League Cup Final winning side did Alan Judge play for?

15 Which keeper spent 20 years with Portsmouth?

16 Which keeper was injured in the 1957 FA Cup Final?

17 Northern Ireland's Harry Gregg was first capped while at which League club?

18 Who was in goal for Brighton in the 1980s FA Cup Final?

19 At which club did Bobby Mimms make his League debut?

20 Dave Gaskell was in an FA Cup winning 1960s team at which club?

Answers

Extra Time (see Quiz 48)

1 David O'Leary. **2** Belgium. **3** Italy. **4** Charlton Athletic. **5** 1875. **6** Argentina. **7** Mexico. **8** 0–0. **9** 3–3. **10** Aberdeen. **11** Leeds Utd. **12** Sweden v Romania. **13** Three. **14** Gordon West. **15** 2–2. **16** Liverpool. **17** Derby (1946). **18** Belgium. **19** Stefan Kuntz. **20** Five.

Quiz 47 **Pot Luck 24**

LEVEL 3

Answers – see page 255

1 What is Bruce Grobbelaar's middle name?

2 Gillard, Hazell and Waddock played for which 1980s FA Cup Finalists?

3 With 171 goals Clarrie Bourton became all-time top League scorer at which club?

4 Hodgson and Neal scored Euro goals in the same game for which club?

5 Which club did Raich Carter and Don Revie play for in the 1950s?

6 What were the first names of the soccer playing Brightwell brothers?

7 Barlow, Barrett and Bunn played for which League Cup finalists?

8 Which two ex-West Ham Utd players have managed Norwich City in the post-war period?

9 With which team did John Lukic make his League debut?

10 Who lost 5–3 to Benfica in the Final of the 1962 European Cup?

11 Mike Hooper and John Barnes were in the same team at which club?

12 Which Tommy became manager of Wolves in 1984?

13 John Harkes played in an FA Cup Final for which team?

14 At which Scottish club did John Spencer make his League debut?

15 Which German team is the most successful in domestic competitions?

16 Which club has a fanzine called *Hello Albert*?

17 Jim Smith followed Willie McFaul as manager of which club?

18 Liverpool sold Larry Lloyd to which club?

19 Which club once had Town Swifts added to its name?

20 To one each way, how many international goals did Gerry Armstrong score?

Answers

Pot Luck 23 (see Quiz 45)

1 Nottingham Forest. **2** 44. **3** RSC Anderlecht. **4** Clyde. **5** 1890s. **6** Brentford. **7** Stockport. **8** Danny McGrain. **9** Watford. **10** 13. **11** Chelsea. **12** Little. **13** Liverpool. **14** Anthony. **15** West Ham Utd. **16** Southampton. **17** Italy. **18** Everton. **19** Ajax. **20** Liverpool.

Quiz 48 **Extra Time**

Answers – see page 256

LEVEL 3

1 Who went on in extra time for the Republic of Ireland in the Italia 90 World Cup game against Romania?
2 Preud'homme was in goal for which team sent out of Italia 90 in extra time?
3 An extra time goal by which country sent Nigeria out of the 1994 World Cup?
4 A 1940s extra time FA Cup goal by Duffy won the cup for which club?
5 To three years each way, when did the first FA Cup Final go to extra time?
6 In Italia 90 which country played extra time in both the quarter-finals and semi-finals?
7 English-based Bontcho Guentchev went on in extra time in USA 1994, against which side?
8 What was the 90-minute score in the Arsenal v Liverpool 1971 FA Cup Final?
9 What was the a.e.t. score in the France v West Germany 1982 World Cup semi-final?
10 Which team won three Scottish FA Cup Finals in a row – all after extra time?
11 An extra-time goal by Ian St John beat which team in an FA Cup Final?
12 Andersson and Raducioiu hit 1994 World Cup ET goals in which game?
13 How many quarter-finals went to extra time in the 1986 World Cup?
14 Which keeper was beaten by Jeff Astle's 1968 FA Cup-winner?
15 What was the 90-minute score in England v Cameroon in Italia 90?
16 Which club beat Tottenham Hotspur after extra time in a League Cup Final?
17 After World War II, which team first won an FA Cup Final a.e.t.?
18 In Mexico 1986 who beat the USSR 4–3 after an extra-time gripper?
19 Which German had a 'goal' disallowed v England in extra time of Euro 96?
20 How many minutes of extra-time were needed in the Euro 96 Final?

Answers

Keepers (see Quiz 46)

1 Andy Marriott. **2** Ian Walker. **3** David Harvey. **4** Workington. **5** Mark Bosnich. **6** Sheffield Wednesday. **7** Shrewsbury Town. **8** Manchester City. **9** Walsall. **10** Dundee. **11** Andy Rhodes. **12** Keith Branagan. **13** Peter Fox. **14** Oxford Utd. **15** Alan Knight. **16** Ray Wood. **17** Doncaster Rovers. **18** Graham Moseley. 19 Rotherham Utd. **20** Manchester Utd.

Quiz 49 **Pot Luck 25**

Answers – see page 261

LEVEL 3

1 Which American has played in England for Derby County, Sheffield Wednesday and West Ham Utd?
2 Which player of the 1990s with Forest has the middle name Rasdal?
3 Rostron and Gilligan scored Euro goals in the same game for which club?
4 At which club did Les Sealey make his League debut?
5 In what decade did WBA first win the Championship?
6 Which club has a fanzine called *On the 2nd May*?
7 Dave Sexton followed Gordon Jago's first spell as manager of which club?
8 Which ground is in Floyd Road?
9 Which club was once known as Belmont AFC?
10 To one each way, how many international goals did Colin Bell score?
11 The severe weather in 1963 caused which event to be put back three weeks?
12 Which Terry became boss of Birmingham City in 1991?
13 Danny Wallace played in an FA Cup Final for which team?
14 Which club beat AC Milan to win the European Super Cup in 1994?
15 Williams, Walker and Wassall played in a League Cup Final for which club?
16 What was the name of the ITV theme for the 1986 World Cup Finals?
17 Freddie Steele is all-time top League scorer at which club?
18 Alan Taylor scored twice in an FA Cup Final for which club?
19 Who lost to Leeds Utd on the away goals rule in the 1971 UEFA Cup Final?
20 33 spectators died in 1946 after crash barriers gave way at which ground?

Answers

Pot Luck 26 (see Quiz 51)

1 Sheffield Wednesday. **2** Newcastle Utd. **3** Nottingham Forest. **4** Helmut Haller. **5** Southampton. **6** Aston Villa. **7** Leeds Utd. **8** John Barnes. **9** Hamburg. **10** Wayne. **11** Alan Ashman. **12** Everton. **13** Sunderland. **14** Bolton Wanderers. **15** Howard Kendall. **16** Arsenal. **17** Luton Town. **18** Barnsley. **19** Torquay Town. **20** Three.

Quiz 50 **FA Cup**

Answers – see page 262

LEVEL 3

1 Brooke and Henry were subs for which two Final opponents?
2 Which player in recent times took the actual FA Cup out of England?
3 Who were the first team outside the First Division to win the FA Cup in the 20th century?
4 What was the cost of the original FA Cup trophy?
5 Barrie Williams was boss of which 1989 giant-killers?
6 Who were the first club from the top flight to go out of the trophy on penalties?
7 Who scored an FA Cup Final winner against Everton in the 1980s and later moved to Goodison Park?
8 David Nish became youngest FA Cup Final skipper with which team?
9 What links the teams of Leicester City in 1961, Sunderland in 1973 and Crystal Palace in 1990?
10 Who was 17 years 256 days old when he played for a London side in a Final?
11 Who were the first team from outside the First Division to win the FA Cup after the Second World War?
12 In 1958, 83-year-old Harry Burge claimed what link with the FA Cup?
13 Ian Callaghan played in 88 FA Cup games, mostly with Liverpool, but with which other two clubs?
14 How many teams entered the first FA Cup tournament?
15 Up to the end of the 20th century, which side has appeared in most semi-finals?
16 Where was the Chelsea v Leeds Utd replayed FA Cup Final held?
17 Who was the first post-war player to score in every round of the FA Cup?
18 In the pre shoot-out days, how many hours of play did the 1979 tie between Arsenal and Sheffield Wednesday last for?
19 Who scored within 120 seconds of the 1987 Tottenham Hotspur v Coventry City Final?
20 Who did Billy Hampson, aged 41 years, 257 days, play for in a 1920s Final?

Answers

Full Time (see Quiz 52)

1 Germany. **2** Real Zaragoza. **3** Luton Town. **4** Leicester City. **5** Barrow. **6** W Germany. **7** Hewitt. **8** Alan Sunderland. **9** McQueen & McIlroy. **10** Sweden. **11** Michael Thomas. **12** Wigan Athletic. **13** Bobby Moore. **14** Roberto Baggio. **15** Crystal Palace (v Leicester City). **16** Making illegal payments. **17** Bradford Park Avenue. **18** Paul Gascoigne. **19** Sammy McIlroy, Gordon McQueen. **20** Maidstone.

Quiz 51 **Pot Luck 26**

Answers – see page 259

LEVEL 3

1 Which club did Alan Harper join when he left Everton for the first time?

2 Richard Dinnis was manager of which club in 1977?

3 Charles, Chettle and Glover played for which 1980s FA Cup Finalists?

4 Who scored first for West Germany in the 1966 World Cup Final?

5 Fullback David Peach scored for which club in a League Cup Final?

6 With 215 goals Harry Hampton is all-time top League scorer at which club?

7 Strachan and Shutt scored Euro goals in the same game for which club?

8 Which England player once played for Sudbury Court?

9 Who lost 1–0 to Nottingham Forest in the Final of the 1980 European Cup?

10 What is Mark Hateley's middle name?

11 Who was Carlisle Utd's manager when they won promotion to the First Division in 1974?

12 Ted Sager played 465 League games for which club from 1929 to 1953?

13 Kevin Ball first played in an FA Cup Final for which team?

14 At which club did Jimmy Phillips make his league debut?

15 In the 1980s, which League-Championship winning manager was labelled "A young pup" by Brian Clough?

16 Which club has a fanzine called *One Nil Down... Two One Up*?

17 Jim Ryan followed Ray Harford as manager of which club?

18 Barry Murphy set an appearance record at which Yorkshire club?

19 What were Torquay once known as before they took on the name United?

20 To one each way, how many international goals did Ronnie Whelan score?

Answers

Pot Luck 25 (see Quiz 49)

1 John Harkes. **2** Alf-Inge Haaland. **3** Watford. **4** Coventry City. **5** 1920s. **6** Bristol Rovers. **7** QPR. **8** Charlton Athletic. **9** Tranmere Rovers. **10** Nine. **11** FA Cup Final. **12** Cooper. **13** Manchester Utd. **14** Parma. **15** Nottingham Forest. **16** "Aztec Gold". **17** Stoke City. **18** West Ham Utd. **19** Juventus. **20** Burnden Park.

Quiz 52 **Full Time**

Answers – see page 260

LEVEL 3

1 Philippe Albert's 90th minute goal did not save Belgium being knocked out of the 1994 World Cup by which team?

2 Nayim scored a last-minute Cup Winners' Cup Final goal for which club?

3 Brian Stein hit a late League Cup Final winner for which club?

4 In 1997 which team led 3–1 at Newcastle Utd in the Premiership but lost 4–3 to a Shearer hat-trick completed in the last minute?

5 Who did Hereford Utd replaced in the League in 1972?

6 Who was Weber playing for when he hit a late World Cup Final equalizer?

7 Who scored Aberdeen's winner in the 1983 Cup Winners' Cup Final?

8 Who scored Arsenal's last-minute winner v Man Utd in the '79 FA Cup Final?

9 Who pegged two late goals back for Manchester Utd in the same game?

10 In the 1994 World Cup quarter-finals, Romania equalised at the death against which country?

11 Who beat Liverpool with the last kick of the 1988–89 season?

12 Which club replaced Southport in the league in 1978?

13 Who sent the ball forward for Geoff Hurst's final goal in the 1966 World Cup Final?

14 In 1994, who equalised for Italy three minutes from time v Nigeria and in the next round hit the winner v Spain two minutes from time?

15 A last-gasp Steve Claridge goal beat which team in a Wembley play-off?

16 It was all over for Leeds City when they were expelled from the League in 1919 – but for what?

17 Cambridge Utd joined the league in 1970 at whose expense?

18 Who provided the free-kick from which David Platt hit the late goal v Belgium in Italia 90?

19 George Mutch won an FA Cup Final with a penalty in the 1930s for which club?

20 It was all over at Watling Street when which league club left the league in the 1900s?

Answers

FA Cup (see Quiz 50)

1 Spurs v Man City. **2** Craig Johnston. (Took it to show family in Australia). **3** Spurs (1901). **4** £20. **5** Sutton Utd. **6** Manchester Utd. **7** Norman Whiteside. **8** Leicester City. **9** No internationals. **10** Paul Allen. **11** Sunderland. **12** Claimed to have stolen it in the 1890s **13** Swansea City and Crewe Alexandra. **14** 15. **15** Everton. **16** Old Trafford. **17** Jeff Astle. **18** Nine. **19** Clive Allen. **20** Newcastle.

Quiz 53 **Pot Luck 27**

Answers – see page 265

LEVEL 3

1 Viv Anderson played for which three clubs in League Cup Finals?

2 Which club beat Hamburg to win the European Super Cup in 1977?

3 Which Adrian moved to Espanol from Everton in the 1980s?

4 At which club did Mick Harford make his League debut?

5 In what decade did Sheffield Utd first win the Championship?

6 Which club has a fanzine called *Forever and a Day*?

7 Brian Horton followed Mark Lawrenson as manager of which club?

8 Who moved to Sunderland from Millwall in 1996, to set a club record for a transfer fee paid?

9 To five years each way, when did Swansea Town become Swansea City?

10 To two each way, how many international goals did Trevor Brooking score?

11 Chris Whyte and George Wood were in the same team at which club?

12 Which Peter became manager of Southend Utd in 1993?

13 Neil Webb first played in an FA Cup Final for which team?

14 Which Leicester-born striker of the 1990s has the middle names William Ivanhoe?

15 Tuttle and Durie scored Euro goals in the same game for which club?

16 Who said "The years of patching up grounds... must be over"?

17 Who lost to Leeds Utd in the 1968 Fairs Cup Final?

18 Neil Young scored in an FA Cup Final for which club?

19 Who was Graham Taylor's assistant when Watford reached the FA Cup Final in 1984?

20 Alan Irvine played in the 1984 League Cup Final for which club?

Answers

Pot Luck 28 (see Quiz 55)

1 Leeds Utd. **2** George. **3** Case. **4** Leicester City. **5** Reims. **6** QPR. **7** Bradford City. **8** FIFA. **9** Kevin Keegan. **10** Arthur Rowe. **11** Third Lanark. **12** Crewe Alexandra, Exeter, Halifax and Oxford. **13** West Ham Utd. **14** QPR. **15** Stanley Rous. **16** Derby County. **17** Nottingham Forest. **18** Florence. **19** Sunderland. **20** Five.

Quiz 54 **World Cup**

Answers – see page 266

LEVEL 3

1 Oman Biyik played in the World Cup for which country?

2 In 1994, Leonardo of Brazil was sent off against which country?

3 Which French player was victim of Schumacher's appalling challenge in 1984?

4 Which country took the first penalty in the 1994 Final shoot out?

5 20 of the Republic of Ireland's 22-man USA 94 squad played in the English league – which two didn't?

6 Which country, other than the Republic of Ireland, included a high proportion of English League players in USA in 1994?

7 Which Czechoslovakian player was second-top scorer in Italia 90?

8 In USA 94 which country scored most goals in the group games yet still went out?

9 How many games did England lose in Spain in 1982?

10 Who were the first host country to win the World Cup?

11 What was the half-time score in the 1994 third place match?

12 Olguin, Gallego and Ortiz played for which World Cup-winning team?

13 In 1982, what was the nickname of England's mascot?

14 Felix was in goal for which World Cup winners?

15 Who were Scotland's joint top scorers in Italia 90?

16 Whose last international goal was a World Cup Final winner?

17 Which country were top of the Republic of Ireland's Group in USA 1994?

18 Who were the only team to beat West Germany in the 1974 finals?

19 In Italia 90 who scored England's winner against Egypt?

20 Which country failed to score in the USA in 1994?

Answers

Famous Firsts (see Quiz 56)

1 1870s. **2** 1981. **3** Denis Law. **4** Tottenham Hotspur v Wolves (UEFA Cup 1972). **5** 1965. **6** Steve Bull. **7** Hungary. **8** Ronnie Simpson. **9** Queens Park (1876). **10** Referee's whistle. **11** Blackburn Rovers. **12** Dennis Clarke (WBA 1968). **13** Peter Taylor. **14** Tottenham Hotspur. **15** FA Cup was stolen. **16** Ted Drake. **17** 1940s (Rangers 1949). **18** Newcastle Utd. **19** First own goal in a Final. **20** Jimmy Dickinson.

Quiz 55 **Pot Luck 28**

Answers – see page 263

LEVEL 3

1 Rod Belfitt scored in a Euro game for which club?

2 What is Andy Hinchcliffe's middle name?

3 Which Jimmy played in 1970s and 1980s FA Cup Finals for different teams and lost both times?

4 McIlmoyle, Keyworth and Cheesebrough played for which 1960s FA Cup Finalists?

5 Who lost 4–3 to Real Madrid in the Final of the 1956 European Cup?

6 Michael Robinson played in 1980s League Cup Finals for Liverpool and which other club?

7 121-goal Bobby Campbell is all-time top League scorer at which club?

8 Which organization is based at Hitzigweg 11, CH–8032 Zurich?

9 Which former Scunthorpe footballer sang solo on *Top Of The Pops* in 1979?

10 Alf Ramsey was the only player bought by which Tottenham Hotspur boss?

11 Which club dropped out of the Scottish League in 1967?

12 In 2001–02 which were the four league teams in England with an x in their names?

13 David Cross first played in an FA Cup Final for which team?

14 At which club did Gavin Peacock make his League debut?

15 Who was referee at the 1934 FA Cup Final and later became a world figure in soccer administration?

16 Which club has a fanzine called *Hey Big Spender*?

17 Matt Gillies followed Johnny Carey as manager of which club?

18 Which city is home to Fiorentina?

19 Which club once had "and District Teachers' AFC" added to their name?

20 To two each way, how many international goals did Lou Macari score?

Answers

Pot Luck 27 (see Quiz 53)

1 Nottingham Forest, Arsenal and Sheffield Wednesday. **2** Liverpool. **3** Heath. **4** Lincoln City. **5** 1890s. **6** Burnley. **7** Oxford Utd. **8** Alex Rae. **9** 1970. **10** Five. **11** Arsenal. **12** Taylor. **13** Manchester Utd. **14** Emile Heskey. **15** Tottenham Hotspur. **16** Lord Justice Taylor. **17** Ferencvaros. **18** Manchester City. **19** Bertie Mee. **20** Everton.

Quiz 56 **Famous Firsts**

Answers – see page 264

LEVEL 3

1 In what decade was the corner-kick first taken?

2 When did the English League adopt three points for a win?

3 Who, during the 1974 World Cup Finals, was the first player to make 55 appearances for Scotland?

4 Which teams were in the first all-British European Final?

5 When – to a year each way – did Stanley Matthews become the first man to be knighted for services to Football?

6 Who was the first Third Division player in the 1980s to be capped by England?

7 Which was the first country to lose two World Cup Finals?

8 Which European Cup-winner was the first player over 35 to make his Scottish debut?

9 Who were the first team to win a replayed Scottish FA Cup Final?

10 What was introduced in 1878 to help control a game?

11 The first FA Cup Final hat-trick was scored by William Townley in 1890 for which northern club?

12 Who was the first substitute to go on in an FA Cup Final?

13 Who was the first Division 3 player in the 1970s to be capped by England?

14 Which club did the first English double of the 20th century?

15 In 1895, what famous first happened in a Birmingham shop?

16 Who was the first person in England to win the Championship as a player and as a manager?

17 In what decade was the first treble won in Scotland?

18 Which club were the first in the 20th century to retain the FA Cup?

19 What (in)famous first went to Lord Kinnaird in the 1877 FA Cup Final?

20 Who was the first player to make 700 Football League appearances?

Answers

World Cup (see Quiz 54)

1 Cameroon. **2** USA. **3** Patrick Battiston. **4** Italy. **5** Bonner and Coyne. **6** Norway. **7** Tomas Skuhravy. **8** Russia. **9** None. **10** Italy (1934). **11** Sweden 4 v Bulgaria 0. **12** Argentina. **13** Bulldog Bobby. **14** Brazil (1970). **15** McCall and Johnston (1 each). **16** Gerd Müller. **17** Mexico. **18** East Germany. **19** Mark Wright. **20** Greece.

Quiz 57 **Pot Luck 29**

Answers – see page 269

LEVEL 3

1 Which British team lost to Feyenoord in the 1974 UEFA Cup Final?

2 Which father and son strikers played a total of 16 games for England without managing to score a goal?

3 Which country lost just once in 48 matches between 1950 and 1956?

4 At which club did Phil Neal make his League debut?

5 In which decade did Huddersfield Town first win the Championship?

6 Which club has a fanzine called *The Thin Blue Line*?

7 Dave Stringer followed Ken Brown as manager of which club?

8 Blackburn Rovers established a record of going how many FA Cup games without defeat?

9 Which club was once known as Heaton Norris Rovers?

10 To two each way, how many international goals did Trevor Francis score?

11 Andy Ritchie and Michael Robinson were in the same team at which club?

12 Jimmy Frizzell was manager of which club from 1970 to 1982?

13 Steve Sedgley played in an FA Cup Final for which team?

14 What is David Hirst's middle name?

15 Which club beat Werder Bremen to win the European Super Cup in 1992?

16 Melville and James scored Euro goals in the same game for which club in their only UEFA Cup run?

17 Haylock and Van Wyck played for which 1980s League Cup winners?

18 Mick Jones scored in an FA Cup Final for which club?

19 With 209 goals Charlie Buchan is all-time top League scorer at which club?

20 Which defender won 77 caps for Scotland between 1980 and 1991?

Answers

Pot Luck 30 (see Quiz 59)

1 Brian. **2** Liverpool. **3** Argentina. **4** Ron Yeats. **5** Oldham Athletic. **6** Ipswich Town. **7** Luton Town. **8** 1987–88. **9** Hull City. **10** Real Madrid. **11** Oxford Utd. **12** Manchester Utd. **13** Everton. **14** Mansfield Town. **15** Hearts. **16** Exeter City. **17** Leeds Utd. **18** Nottingham Forest. **19** Southampton. **20** 15.

Quiz 58 **Cup Winners' Cup**

Answers – see page 270

LEVEL 3

1 Who were the first English club to play in the competition?

2 Who were the first team to appear in three consecutive Finals?

3 When did AC Milan first win the trophy?

4 What was the scoreline in the 1963 Final, the first English success?

5 Who managed the 1963 winners?

6 In which city did Arsenal first win the tournament?

7 Who were the first English clubs to meet in the competition?

8 What is the furthest stage Cardiff City have reached?

9 When did Sunderland appear in the competition?

10 Who won the first Final played at Wembley?

11 Which club was ordered to transfer a home game 250 miles and went to Plymouth?

12 Which British side won the Cup Winners' Cup and their national cup in the same season?

13 Who were the first Eastern European side to win the trophy?

14 In the 1960s Sporting Lisbon set a record by scoring how many goals in a game?

15 Which English side knocked out Manchester City in 1971?

16 What happened to the referee after Leeds Utd's defeat in the 1973 Final?

17 Who beat Leeds Utd in that Final?

18 Heslop and Towers played for which trophy-winning team?

19 Who was Manchester Utd's victorious skipper in 1991?

20 Keith Weller played for which trophy-winning team?

Answers

The 1980s (see Quiz 60)

1 Ipswich Town. **2** Northern Ireland. **3** Luton Town. **4** Lawrie McMenemy. **5** Scarborough. **6** Eight. **7** Michael Knighton. **8** Spain. **9** Lincoln City. **10** (Rep of Ireland international) Mark Lawrenson. **11** The Rous Cup. **12** AC Milan. **13** Alan Brazil. **14** Brazil. **15** Fulham & QPR. **16** Trevor Francis. **17** Diego Maradona. **18** Huddersfield Town. **19** Oxford Utd. **20** Six.

Quiz 59 **Pot Luck 30**

Answers – see page 267

LEVEL 3

1 What is Steve Hodge's middle name that links him to his first boss?

2 Byrne, Lawler and Strong played for which 1960s FA Cup Finalists?

3 Who did Cameroon beat in the 1990 World Cup opener?

4 Which Liverpool skipper said of compatriot Bill Shankly, "His motivation could move mountains"?

5 Which Second Division side reached the Final of the League Cup and the semis of the FA Cup in the same season?

6 Gates and McCall scored Euro goals in the same game for which club?

7 Ashley Grimes played in 1980s League Cup Finals for which team?

8 When was the Football League's Centenary Season?

9 With 195 goals scored in the 1960s and 1970s, Chris Chilton became all-time top League scorer at which east coast club?

10 Who lost 1–0 to Liverpool in the Final of the 1981 European Cup?

11 Trevor Hebberd and Kevin Brock were in the same team at which club?

12 Francis Burns was at which club when he won his only Scottish cap?

13 Gary Lineker first played in an FA Cup Final for which team?

14 At which club did Kevin Hitchcock make his League debut?

15 With 44 goals, Barney Battles set a League season scoring record at which Scottish club?

16 Which club had a fanzine called *In Exile*?

17 Allan Clarke followed Jimmy Adamson as manager of which club?

18 Grenville Morris is all-time top League scorer at which Midlands club?

19 Which coastal club once had St Mary's added to its current name?

20 To one each way, John Charles got how many international goals?

Answers

Pot Luck 29 (see Quiz 57)

1 Tottenham Hotspur. **2** Brian and Nigel Clough. **3** Hungary. **4** Northampton Town. **5** 1920s. **6** Cardiff City. **7** Norwich City. **8** 24. **9** Stockport County. **10** 12. **11** Brighton. **12** Oldham Athletic. **13** Tottenham Hotspur. **14** Eric. **15** Barcelona. **16** Swansea City. **17** Norwich City. **18** Leeds Utd. **19** Sunderland. **20** Alex McLeish.

Quiz 60 **The 1980s**

Answers – see page 268

LEVEL 3

1 Which team's players gained a 1–2–3 in the PFA Player of the Year awards in 1981?

2 Who won the 1986 – and final – Home International Championship?

3 Which club banned away fans in April 1986?

4 Who resigned as Sunderland manager in 1987 as they dropped into Division Three?

5 Which GM Vauxhall Conference club were first to gain automatic promotion to the League?

6 How many goals did England rattle in v Turkey in 1984?

7 Which property dealer abandoned his hopes of owning Manchester Utd?

8 Which country beat Malta 12–1 to pip Holland to a place in the 1984 European Championship?

9 Who were Bradford City's opponents in the fire disaster game?

10 Who was Liverpool's only English-born player in the 1986 FA Cup Final?

11 Which tournament had only Brazil, England and Scotland competing?

12 After a bribery scandal which Italian side were demoted to Division 2?

13 Who hit five goals for Ipswich Town v Southampton in 1981–82?

14 Pat Jennings played his last international against which team?

15 Which two London clubs were denied a merger by the Football League Management Committee?

16 Rangers signed which player from Atalanta in the late 1980s?

17 Who joined Napoli from Barcelona for a record £6.9 million fee?

18 Malcolm Macdonald briefly took over as manager of which club in 1987?

19 John Aldridge was in which side promoted to the top flight?

20 How many goals did Gary Lineker score in the 1986 World Cup?

Answers

Cup Winners' Cup (see Quiz 58)

1 Wolves. **2** Anderlecht. **3** 1968. **4** 5–1. **5** Bill Nicholson. **6** Paris. **7** Spurs & Man Utd (1963–64). **8** Semi-final. **9** 1973–74. **10** West Ham Utd (1965). **11** Manchester Utd. **12** Aberdeen. **13** Slovan Bratislava. **14** 16. **15** Chelsea. **16** He was suspended by UEFA. **17** AC Milan. **18** Manchester City. **19** Steve Bruce. **20** Chelsea.

Quiz 61 **Pot Luck 31**

Answers – see page 273

LEVEL 3

1 Mick Lyons scored in a League Cup Final for which club?

2 Former Prime Minister Harold Wilson supported which club?

3 Who lost to Gothenburg in the 1987 UEFA Cup Final?

4 At which club did Garry Parker make his League debut?

5 In which decade did Sheffield Wednesday first win the Championship?

6 Which club has a fanzine called *The Ugly Inside*?

7 Alan Durban followed Alan A'Court as manager of which club?

8 Which defender went from Scunthorpe to Aston Villa in 1991, to set a club record for a transfer fee received?

9 Which club dropped Lindsey from its name in the 1950s?

10 To one each way, how many international goals did Chris Waddle score?

11 Andy King and Steve McMahon were in the same team at which club?

12 Which Maurice became manager of Oxford Utd in 1985?

13 John Barnes first played in an FA Cup Final for which team?

14 Who is Steve Howey's soccer-playing elder brother?

15 Hughes and Tueart scored Euro goals in the same 1970s game for which club?

16 With 297 goals Andy Jardine became all-time top League scorer at which Scottish club?

17 To three years, when did Fulham install floodlights?

18 Frank Saul scored in an FA Cup Final for which club?

19 Who beat Nottingham Forest to win the European Super Cup in 1980?

20 Who in 1987 became the first team to be automatically relegated from the Fotball League?

Answers

Pot Luck 32 (see Quiz 63)

1 Hibernian. **2** Newcastle Utd. **3** Chelsea. **4** Carl. **5** Bert Trautmann. **6** Barcelona. **7** Tommy Lawton. **8** Alan Smith. **9** Barnsley. **10** Aston Villa. **11** West Ham Utd. **12** Holder. **13** Sunderland. **14** Dumbarton. **15** Scottish League founder members now out of the League. **16** Huddersfield Town. **17** Burnley. **18** Hartlepool Utd. **19** Rotherham Utd. **20** He didn't score any.

Quiz 62 **Defenders**

Answers – see page 274

LEVEL 3

1 To two each way, how many caps did Phil Thompson win?

2 At which German club did Franz Beckenbauer end his playing days?

3 Which English club did Celtic fullback Tommy Gemmell play for?

4 Which England defender tried to tackle Gianfranco Zola as he scored in the 1997 World Cup qualifier at Wembley?

5 Which defender was the last skipper to lift the Jules Rimet Trophy after a World Cup Final?

6 Which club did West Ham Utd sign Slaven Bilic from?

7 To two each way, how many League goals did Jack Charlton score?

8 Branagan, Keeley and Rathbone each played over 200 League games in which club's defence in the 1980s?

9 In Steve Bruce's first season with Manchester Utd, who played most times as his central defensive partner?

10 Which defender scored the only golden goal of the 1998 World Cup?

11 At which club did Mick Lyons finish his playing career?

12 Which Jeff of Arsenal won his only England cap against Yugoslavia in 1972?

13 To 20 each way, how many Chelsea League games did Ron Harris play?

14 At which club did Julian Dicks make his League debut?

15 Which defender was born in Alloa on 13th June, 1955?

16 Which England defender scored a screamer against Brazil in June 1995?

17 Angus and Elder formed a fullback pairing at which club?

18 Who became the first player to skipper both English and Scottish FA Cup winning sides?

19 Which club did Russell Osman go to when he left Ipswich Town?

20 Which player wrote *Soccer The Hard Way*?

Answers

Internationals (see Quiz 64)

1 Paolo Maldini. **2** W Germany (1954). **3** Ajax. **4** Trevor Steven. **5** Brazil & England. **6** Mick McCarthy. **7** Zico. **8** Karl-Heinz Schnellinger. **9** Dino Zoff. **10** Four. **11** Bank clerk. **12** Rudi Voller. **13** Jan Jongbloed. **14** Switzerland. **15** Morocco. **16** Rene Van der Kerkhof. **17** John Barnes. **18** Germany & Holland. **19** Fritz Walter. **20** 1954.

Quiz 63 **Pot Luck 32**

Answers – see page 271

LEVEL 3

---

1. Blackley and Brownlie scored Euro goals in the same 1970s game for which British club?
2. Bob Stokoe won an FA Cup Winner's medal with which club?
3. Hinton and Houseman played for which 1970s FA Cup winners?
4. What is Darren Huckerby's middle name?
5. Which ex-Manchester City keeper recommended Eike Immel to his old club?
6. Who lost on penalties to Steaua Bucharest in the Final of the 1986 European Cup?
7. Who holds the record for the fastest-ever England goal?
8. Which Arsenal player was booked, for the first time in his career, in the 1993 FA Cup Final replay?
9. Viv Anderson was player/manager of which club in 1993–94?
10. Ray Graydon scored a League Cup Final winner for which club?
11. Slater and Small were in the same team at which London club?
12. Which Phil became manager of Brentford in 1990?
13. Republic of Ireland international John Byrne played in an FA Cup Final for which team?
14. At which Scottish club did Graham Sharp make his League debut?
15. What links Abercorn, Cowlairs and Cambuslang?
16. Which club has a fanzine called *Hanging on the Telephone*?
17. Jimmy Mullen followed Frank Casper as manager of which club?
18. In 1993 which club set a record by going 13 games without a goal?
19. Which club was once known as Thornhill United?
20. How many international goals did Terry Venables score?

Answers

Pot Luck 31 (see Quiz 61)

1 Everton. **2** Huddersfield Town. **3** Dundee Utd. **4** Luton Town. **5** 1900s. **6** Southampton. **7** Stoke City. **8** Neil Cox. **9** Scunthorpe Utd. **10** 6. **11** Everton. **12** Evans. **13** Watford. **14** Lee Howey. **15** Sunderland. **16** Dumbarton. **17** 1962. **18** Tottenham Hotspur. **19** Valencia. **20** Lincoln City.

Quiz 64 **Internationals**

Answers – see page 272

LEVEL 3

1 Who was Italy's captain in the 1997 World Cup qualifier at Wembley?

2 Turek was in goal for which World Cup-winners?

3 At the time of the 1974 World Cup, Dutch players Rep, Haan and Krol were all with which club?

4 Which England substitute went on in the 1990 World Cup semi-final?

5 Which two countries played, in the first 0–0 draw in a World Cup finals match, in 1958?

6 Which Republic of Ireland player committed most fouls in Italia 90?

7 How is Artur Antunes Coimbra more widely known?

8 Which defender hit West Germany's last-minute equaliser in the 1970 World Cup semi-final?

9 In the 1970s, which keeper went 1,143 minutes in international soccer without conceding a goal?

10 Gary Lineker was on the spot twice against Cameroon in Italia 90, but how many years had gone by without an English penalty award?

11 What job did Karl-Heinz Rummenigge once do?

12 Who was the German skipper who broke an arm in his first game in the 1992 European Championship in Sweden?

13 Who was in goal for Holland in the 1974 World Cup Final?

14 Heinz Hermann is the highest-capped player for which country?

15 Against which country was England's Ray Wilkins sent off?

16 In the 1978 World Cup Final, which Dutchman wore a cast on one arm?

17 Which Englishman had a 'goal' disallowed in the Belgium game in Italia 90?

18 Which two countries in Euro 92 did not contain any English based players?

19 Who was the first German captain to claim the World Cup?

20 When did Scotland first appear in a World Cup?

Answers

Defenders (see Quiz 62)

1 42. **2** Hamburg. **3** Nottingham Forest. **4** Sol Campbell. **5** Carlos Alberto (Brazil won their third World Cup in 1970 and kept the Jules Rimet Trophy forever). **6** Karlsruhe. **7** 70. **8** Blackburn Rovers. **9** Mal Donaghy. **10** Laurent Blanc. **11** Grimsby Town. **12** Blockley. **13** 655. **14** Birmingham City. **15** Alan Hansen. **16** Graeme Le Saux. **17** Burnley. **18** Martin Buchan. **19** Leicester City. **20** Ron Harris.

Quiz 65 **Pot Luck 33**

Answers – see page 277

LEVEL 3

1 Roger Smee was a former centre-forward, then chairman of which club, where he helped repel Robert Maxwell?
2 Terry Conroy scored in a League Cup Final for which club?
3 Who lost on penalties to Bayer Leverkusen in the 1988 UEFA Cup Final?
4 At which club did Geoff Thomas make his League debut?
5 In which decade did Burnley first win the Championship?
6 Which club had a fanzine called *The Greasy Chip Buttie*?
7 Bill Dodgin Jnr followed Alec Stock as manager of which club?
8 Who moved from Celtic to Chelsea in 1991 to set a club record for a transfer fee received?
9 Which club was once known as St Jude's?
10 To one each way, how many international goals did Bobby Moore score?
11 Alan Shearer and Iain Dowie were in the same team at which club?
12 Which Steve became manager of Plymouth Argyle in 1995?
13 Gary Bailey played in FA Cup Finals for which club?
14 Which QPR winger of the 1990s has the middle name of Rodney?
15 Who beat Hamburg to win the European Super Cup in 1983?
16 Which clubs were involved in Justin Fashanu's £1 million move?
17 What was the title of Crystal Palace's 1990 Cup Final song?
18 Jim McCalliog scored in an FA Cup Final for which club?
19 Conroy and Ritchie scored Euro goals in the same 1970s game for which club?
20 What links Maidenhead, Donington School (Spalding) and the Civil Service?

Answers

Pot Luck 34 (see Quiz 67)

1 Joseph. **2** Sheffield Wednesday. **3** Blackburn Rovers & Bolton Wanderers. **4** QPR. **5** Colin Garwood. **6** WBA, Manchester City & Norwich City. **7** Bobby Charlton. **8** United States Soccer Federation. **9** Hearts. **10** Steaua Bucharest. **11** Manchester City. **12** Beck. **13** Everton. **14** Stoke City. **15** *Turandot*. **16** Leeds Utd. **17** Peterborough. **18** Grimsby Town. **19** Burslem. **20** Eight.

Quiz 66 **Derby Games**

LEVEL 3

Answers – see page 278

1 Which player hit a hat-trick in the November 1994 Manchester derby?

2 Which is the most isolated British club?

3 Who scored the winner in the all Sheffield FA Cup semi-final of 1993?

4 Who is the only Manchester Utd boss never to have lost to Manchester City?

5 Which match was the first shown live on English TV on Sept 9, 1960?

6 Irving Natrass played for which two rival sides?

7 Which Scottish clubs with grounds half a mile apart are alphabetically next to each other?

8 Where was the replayed Mersey League Cup Final of the 1980s held?

9 To three years either way, when was the first Manchester derby in the FA Charity Shield?

10 Which player scored the only goal in the Celtic v Rangers 1980 Scottish FA Cup Final?

11 Which player opened the scoring in the 1986 Mersey FA Cup Final?

12 In what decade was the first Hearts v Hibs Scottish FA Cup Final?

13 To five miles, what is the distance between Norwich City and Ipswich Town?

14 Whose 1970 testimonial was a Manchester derby?

15 Which Nigel has played in Mersey, Glasgow and London derby games?

16 The 4–4 Mersey 5th round FA Cup replay was whose last match at Liverpool?

17 What was the 90-minute score in the 1989 Mersey FA Cup Final?

18 Geographically, which is the nearest club to Aberdeen?

19 Who managed the teams in the first all-London FA Cup Final in the 20th century?

20 Who won a Scottish FA Cup medal for Rangers against Celtic and then for Celtic against Rangers?

Answers

Arsenal & Spurs (see Quiz 68)

1 1913. **2** Arthur Rowe. **3** Alan Ball. **4** Liverpool, 7–0. **5** Five. **6** Ted Ditchburn. **7** A broken nose. **8** Jimmy Greaves. **9** Juventus. **10** 31. **11** Tom Parker. **12** MBE. **13** Ted Drake. **14** Dundee. **15** Frank Stapleton. **16** Graeme Souness. **17** Frank McLintock. **18** 70 points. **19** 1930. **20** 1901.

Quiz 67 **Pot Luck 34**

Answers – see page 275

LEVEL 3

1 What is Denis Irwin's first name – and it isn't Denis?

2 Pugh, Fantham and Quinn played for which 1960s FA Cup Finalists?

3 Which two teams beginning with B were relegated to the Third Division for the first time in 1971?

4 Which London side won 6–2 at home in the first leg of a UEFA Cup game in the 1980s and were beaten 4–0 away?

5 Who was top scorer for both Portsmouth and Aldershot in 1979–80?

6 Which three teams did Asa Hartford play for in League Cup Finals?

7 Who scored for England in his 100th international?

8 What do the initials USSF stand for?

9 Baird and Levein scored Euro goals in the same 1990s game for which Scottish club?

10 Who lost 4–0 to AC Milan in the Final of the 1989 European Cup?

11 Matt Busby was in an FA Cup-winning team at which club?

12 Which John became manager of Preston in 1992?

13 Kevin Richardson first played in an FA Cup Final for which team?

14 At which club did Garth Crooks make his League debut?

15 The adopted Italia 90 anthem "Nessun Dorma" comes from which opera?

16 Which club has a fanzine called *The Square Ball*?

17 Chris Turner followed Mark Lawrenson as manager of which club?

18 Kevin Drinkell, Matt Tees and Ron Rafferty were all big scorers for which club?

19 Port Vale used to have which word at the front of their name?

20 To one either way, Tony Grealish scored how many international goals?

Answers

Pot Luck 33 (see Quiz 65)

1 Reading. **2** Stoke City. **3** Espanol. **4** Rochdale. **5** 1920s. **6** Sheffield Utd. **7** Fulham. **8** Paul Elliott. **9** QPR. **10** Two. **11** Southampton. **12** McCall. **13** Manchester Utd. **14** Andrew Impey. **15** Aberdeen. **16** Norwich City and Nottingham Forest. **17** "Glad All Over". **18** Sheffield Wednesday. **19** Stoke City. **20** All original FA Cup entrants.

Quiz 68 **Arsenal & Spurs**

Answers – see page 276

LEVEL 3

1 In what year were Arsenal relegated for the first time in their history?

2 Which manager developed the "push and run" style of soccer?

3 Who joined Arsenal for a record British fee in December 1971?

4 Which side inflicted Tottenham Hotspur's record League defeat?

5 How many times did Arsenal win the championship in the 1930s?

6 Which Gillingham-born Tottenham keeper of the 1940s and 1950s played over 450 times for them and made six England appearances?

7 Which injury was Andy Linighan carrying when he scored in the 1993 FA Cup Final replay?

8 When Martin Peters joined Tottenham Hotspur, who moved to his old club?

9 Which foreign team did Liam Brady join in 1980?

10 How many League games did Tottenham Hotspur win in 1960–61, when the team created a record for most wins in a season?

11 Who was skipper of Arsenal's FA Cup-winning side of 1930?

12 Which honour did Ray Clemence of Tottenham Hotspur receive in the Queen's Birthday Honours' List in 1987?

13 Who scored seven times for Arsenal against Aston Villa in 1935?

14 Which club was keeper Bill Brown with before he went to Spurs?

15 Which ex-Arsenal player played for both Ajax and Le Havre?

16 Who made just one appearance for Tottenham Hotspur as a substitute in a UEFA Cup game before joining Middlesbrough?

17 Which Arsenal player was Footballer of the Year in 1971?

18 In 1919–20 Tottenham Hotspur established a record for points in the Second Division under the two-point system. How many did they get?

19 What year did Arsenal first win the FA Cup?

20 What year did Tottenham Hotspur first win the FA Cup?

Answers

Derby Games (see Quiz 66)

1 Andrei Kanchelskis. **2** Carlisle Utd. **3** Mark Bright. **4** Ron Atkinson. **5** Blackpool v Bolton Wanderers. **6** Newcastle Utd & Middlesbrough. **7** East Stirlingshire & Falkirk. **8** Maine Road. **9** 1956. **10** George McCluskey. **11** Gary Lineker. **12** 1890s. **13** 42. **14** Bill Foulkes. **15** Spackman. **16** Manager Kenny Dalglish. **17** 1–1. **18** Peterhead. **19** Bill Nicholson (Spurs), Tommy Docherty (Chelsea). **20** Alfie Conn.

Quiz 69 **Pot Luck 35**

LEVEL 3

Answers – see page 281

1 Which great player made a presentation to Kenny Dalglish on his 100th international appearance?

2 Ray Houghton scored in a League Cup Final for which club?

3 Which Arsenal midfielder of the 1990s has the middle name Faxe?

4 At which club did Eric Young make his League debut?

5 In which decade did Manchester City first win the Championship?

6 Which club has a fanzine called *The Seadog Bites Back*?

7 Who followed Alf Ramsey as manager of Ipswich Town?

8 Charnley, Mudie and Perry all hit 100 plus goals for which club?

9 Which club was once known as Argyle Athletic Club?

10 To one each way, how many international goals did Ray Kennedy score?

11 In the 1990s Abel Resino went 1,275 minutes without conceding a goal at which Spanish club?

12 Howard Wilkinson was player/manager of which non-League side?

13 John Scales first played in an FA Cup Final for which team?

14 Who lost to Napoli in the 1989 UEFA Cup Final?

15 Armstrong and Moran scored Euro goals in the same game for which club?

16 Major Frank Buckley and Raich Carter both managed which club in the 1940s and 1950s?

17 Chris Waddle scored in an FA Cup Final for which club?

18 Which club beat Liverpool to win the European Super Cup in 1984?

19 Italian politician and media magnate Silvio Berlusconi has invested heavily in which club?

20 Which club play at Bayview Park?

Answers

Pot Luck 36 (see Quiz 71)

1 Luton Town. **2** Torquay Utd. **3** Paul. **4** WBA. **5** Tommy Lawton. **6** Swiss League. **7** Everton. **8** Losers climbed the steps first. **9** Jimmy Quinn. **10** Benfica. **11** Rangers. **12** McCreadie. **13** Manchester Utd. **14** Clyde. **15** Bill Fox. **16** Leicester City. **17** Fulham. **18** Hibernian. **19** Oxford Utd. **20** 11.

Quiz 70 **League Cup**

Answers – see page 282

LEVEL 3

1 Les Sealey played in League Cup Finals for which two clubs?
2 Who were the first club to retain the League Cup?
3 It was third time lucky for who when he took Aston Villa to success in 1975?
4 In which Final were both teams relegation-bound from the top flight?
5 Who were the first team to win the Scottish League Cup in the 1990s on a penalty shoot out?
6 Which year did the League Cup become the Milk Cup?
7 Which two teams appeared in it?
8 In which season did it become compulsory for all 92 League clubs to enter the English trophy?
9 Who made his twelfth and last visit to Wembley as a manager for the 1983 Final?
10 Who were the first team to retain the Scottish League Cup?
11 Which Fourth Division side competed in the 1962 Final?
12 Who were the first London side to win the trophy?
13 Which three English clubs did Chris Woods play for in Finals?
14 Which club first won the League Cup three years in a row?
15 When did Manchester Utd first win the League Cup?
16 Mick Channon first played for which club in a Final?
17 After winning the Scottish League Cup five years in a row from 1966–70, how many times did Celtic win the trophy in the following 25 years?
18 Which WBA forward became the first player to score in every round of the competition?
19 Who were Villa's opponents in the first Final needing a second replay?
20 Who was the first player to appear in three League Cup Finals with different clubs?

Answers

Managers (see Quiz 72)

1 Scunthorpe Utd. **2** Eddie May. **3** QPR. **4** Johnny Giles. **5** Peter Reid. **6** Doug Ellis. **7** 46 years. **8** Carlisle Utd. **9** Cardiff City. **10** Graham Taylor. **11** West Ham & Manchester Utd. **12** Charlton Athletic. **13** Lou Macari. **14** John Toshack. **15** Barry Fry. **16** Five days. **17** Ipswich Town. **18** Howard Kendall. **19** Eight. **20** Terry Venables (Spurs).

Quiz 71 **Pot Luck 36**

LEVEL 3

Answers – see page 279

1 Roy Wegerle played in a League Cup Final for which club?

2 Who were the first club to win promotion on a penalty shootout?

3 What is Matt Le Tissier's middle name?

4 Lovett, Collard and Hope played for which 1960s FA Cup Finalists?

5 Which England player hit 22 goals in only 23 games?

6 Which League do FC Sion play in?

7 Grant and Rideout scored Euro goals in the same 1990s game for which club?

8 What FA Cup Final tradition was altered in 1992?

9 Which turn-of-the-century Celtic striker was known as "The Iron Man"?

10 Who lost 1–0 to AC Milan in the Final of the 1990 European Cup?

11 Paul Rideout and Dale Gordon were in the same team at which club?

12 Which Eddie became boss of Chelsea in 1975?

13 Gordon Hill played in two FA Cup Finals, for which team?

14 At which Scottish club did Steve Archibald make his League debut?

15 Who was Blackburn Rovers' chairman when Kenny Dalglish went to Rovers?

16 Which club had a fanzine called *Where's The Money Gone*?

17 Ray Harford followed Malcolm Macdonald as manager of which club?

18 Joe Baker set a most goals in a season record at which British club?

19 Which club was once known as Headington?

20 To one each way, how many international goals did Joe Jordan score?

Answers

Pot Luck 35 (see Quiz 69)

1 Franz Beckenbauer. **2** Oxford Utd. **3** John Jensen. **4** Brighton. **5** 1930s. **6** Scarborough. **7** Jackie Milburn. **8** Blackpool. **9** Plymouth Argyle. **10** Three. **11** Atletico Madrid. **12** Boston Utd. **13** Wimbledon. **14** Stuttgart. **15** Southampton. **16** Leeds Utd. **17** Sheffield Wednesday. **18** Juventus. **19** AC Milan. **20** East Fife.

Quiz 72 **Managers**

Answers – see page 280

LEVEL 3

1 In 1959 Neil Lambton managed only three days as boss of which club?

2 Who was sacked in November 1994 by Cardiff City, then reappointed in March 1995?

3 Tommy Docherty managed only 29 days at which club in 1968?

4 Which ex-WBA manager said, "The only certainty about management is the sack"?

5 Who was sacked at Manchester City 12 days into the 1993–94 season?

6 Who in 1994 said, "I believe Ron to be one of the top three managers in the country" – and then sacked him three weeks later?

7 Fred Everiss was doing something right at WBA: he holds the record of longest reign as a boss – how long?

8 Which club did Bob Stokoe manage on three separate occasions?

9 Which club did Phil Neal leave to join Steve Coppell at Manchester City?

10 Which manager said, "Napoleon wanted his generals to be lucky. I don't think he would have wanted me"?

11 Which two English League clubs went 50 years after the Second World War with only seven managers?

12 From 1933 to 1956 Jimmy Seed was boss of which club?

13 Who was the first Celtic manager sacked by Fergus McCann?

14 In 1983–84, who resigned as Swansea City boss, returned and even played, then was sacked in the same season?

15 Who had an ansaphone message in 1996 that went, "Kristine's out shopping as usual. I'm down the Job Centre looking for employment"?

16 In 1980 Steve Murray was manager of Forfar for how long?

17 Brian Clough's last League game as Forest boss was against who?

18 Who said, "If I made a mistake at Notts County it was probably to mention publicly that I'd never been sacked in my life" just after he was fired?

19 How many times was Stan Flashman supposed to have sacked Barry Fry at Barnet?

20 Which sacked boss said, "I feel like Robin Hood – feared by the bad, loved by the good"?

Answers

League Cup (see Quiz 70)

1 Luton Town and Manchester Utd. **2** Nottingham Forest. **3** Ron Saunders. **4** Norwich City v Sunderland 1985. **5** Raith Rovers. **6** 1982. **7** Liverpool v Spurs. **8** 1967–68. **9** Bob Paisley. **10** Dundee. **11** Rochdale. **12** Chelsea. **13** Nottingham Forest, Norwich City, Sheffield Wednesday. **14** Liverpool. **15** 1992. **16** Norwich City. **17** Twice. **18** Tony Brown. **19** Everton. **20** George Graham.

Quiz 73 **Pot Luck 37**

LEVEL 3 

Answers – see page 285

1 Martin Hayes scored in a League Cup Final for which club?

2 Which film featured Bobby Moore and Pele?

3 Who lost to Tottenham Hotspur in the 1984 UEFA Cup Final?

4 At which club, no longer in the League, did Peter Withe make his League debut?

5 In which decade did Blackburn Rovers first win the Championship?

6 Which club had a fanzine called *Windy and Dusty*?

7 Alex Smith followed Ian Porterfield as manager of which club?

8 What is the name of Glenn Hoddle's brother, once with Barnet?

9 Which club was once known as Pine Villa?

10 To one each way, how many international goals did Francis Lee score?

11 Who said, "As much as I love women and music, my first love will always be football"?

12 Peter Schmeichel scored in a UEFA game against which club?

13 Nigel Spackman first played in an FA Cup Final for which team?

14 What England player has the middle name Pierre?

15 Who beat Red Star Belgrade to win the European Super Cup in 1991?

16 Which is the oldest Scottish team?

17 Paul Stewart scored in an FA Cup Final for which club?

18 Bart-Williams and Warhurst scored Euro goals in the same game for which club?

19 What work did Pat Jennings do before he become a footballer?

20 What is the inscription above the Bill Shankly gates at Anfield?

Answers

Pot Luck 38 (see Quiz 75)

1 Dundee Utd. **2** Glenn Hoddle. **3** Slovenia. **4** AS Roma. **5** Manchester City. **6** Alan Ball. **7** 1951. **8** Athletic Bilbao. **9** Kingsley Black. **10** Francis. **11** Manchester Utd. **12** Buxton. **13** Nottingham Forest. **14** Swansea City. **15** Boca Juniors. **16** Leyton Orient. **17** Portsmouth. **18** Plymouth Argyle. **19** 1913. **20** Seven.

Quiz 74 **Double Winners**

Answers – see page 286

LEVEL 3

1 Eric Cantona scored for Manchester Utd in his 1995 October comeback game against which team?

2 In 1970–71 Arsenal were 2–0 down to which team in an FA Cup semi-final?

3 George Ramsay guided which team to the double?

4 Who in a double season beat Bootle, Grimsby Town and Wolves in the FA Cup?

5 Which midfielder sent a glorious pass to set up Ian Rush for his first goal in the 1986 FA Cup Final?

6 Who beat Manchester Utd 3–1 on the opening day of the 1995–96 season?

7 Who were Tottenham Hotspur's wing duo in their double season?

8 What was the 90-minute score in the 1971 Arsenal v Liverpool FA Cup Final?

9 Which is the only team to go through a League season without losing?

10 Which subsequent double-winners, in the 1950s, won the Championship but missed the double by losing the FA Cup Final?

11 Who was Liverpool's only League ever-present in the 85–86 double season?

12 In 1960–61 Tottenham Hotspur started by winning how many League games in a row?

13 Who was in goal for Manchester Utd in 1995–96 for the League games that Schmeichel missed?

14 Who replaced Alan Kennedy for Liverpool in 1985–86?

15 Who went on as a substitute for Arsenal in the 1971 FA Cup Final?

16 Which player opened the scoring for Spurs in the 1961 FA Cup Final?

17 Which player started most League games for Manchester Utd in 1995–96?

18 John and James Cowan played for which double winners?

19 Which Kevin played for Liverpool in the 1985–86 double season?

20 Which team did not concede a goal in winning the FA Cup in their double season?

Answers

Early Bath (see Quiz 76)

1 Leeds Utd. **2** Crewe Alexandra. **3** Paul Gascoigne. **4** Billy Ferguson. **5** Doug Rougvie. **6** First player sent off at Wembley. **7** Ray Wilkins. **8** Sent off on his debut. **9** Luxembourg. **10** Russia. **11** Peter Willis. **12** Alvin Martin. **13** Poland. **14** Five. **15** Peruvian. **16** 32. **17** He was a sub on the bench. **18** Uruguay. **19** Stoke City. **20** Four.

Quiz 75 **Pot Luck 38**

Answers – see page 283

LEVEL 3

1. Kirkwood and Milne scored Euro goals in the same 1980s game for which club?
2. Who in 1979 scored on his England debut, v Bulgaria?
3. Which country's leading teams are SCT Olimpija and Maribor?
4. Who lost on penalties to Liverpool in the 1984 European Cup Final?
5. Gow, Power and McDonald played for which 1980s FA Cup Finalists?
6. Which England midfielder played in white boots for Everton?
7. To five years each way, when did Arsenal install floodlights?
8. Which Spanish side did Howard Kendall manage?
9. Who played in League Cup Finals for Luton Town and Nottingham Forest?
10. What is Neil Lennon's middle name?
11. Colin Gibson and Terry Gibson were in the same team at which club?
12. Which Mick became boss of Sunderland in 1993?
13. Gary Crosby first played in an FA Cup Final for which team?
14. At which club did Dean Saunders make his League debut?
15. Diego Maradona made his name playing for which Argentine team?
16. Which club had a fanzine called *Frankly Speaking*?
17. Frank Burrows followed John Gregory as manager of which club?
18. Kevin Hodges set up a League appearance record at which club?
19. In which year did keepers first have to wear different-coloured shirts from their team mates?
20. To one each way, how many international goals did Andy Gray score for Scotland?

Answers

Pot Luck 37 (see Quiz 73)

1 Arsenal. **2** *Escape To Victory*. **3** RSC Anderlecht. **4** Southport. **5** 1910s. **6** Rotherham. **7** Aberdeen. **8** Carl. **9** Oldham Athletic. **10** 10. **11** Rod Stewart. **12** Roto Volgograd. **13** Liverpool. **14** Graeme Le Saux. **15** Manchester Utd. **16** Queen's Park. **17** Tottenham Hotspur. **18** Sheffield Wednesday. **19** Milkman. **20** "You'll Never Walk Alone".

Quiz 76 **Early Bath**

Answers – see page 284

LEVEL 3

1 Duncan McKenzie was sent off in a European game playing for which club?
2 Who was keeper Mark Smith playing for when he was sent off after 19 seconds in a 1993–94 match against Darlington?
3 Who in January 1991 became the first player to be sent off in a live TV League match?
4 In 1966, which Northern Ireland player became the first to be sent off in a British Home International match?
5 Which Aberdeen player saw red in the 1978–79 Scottish League Cup Final?
6 What famous first goes to Boris Stankovic?
7 Which England player was sent off in the Mexico 1986 World Cup?
8 What unwanted first did John Burns of Rochdale achieve in 1923?
9 Gilbert Dresch was sent off at Wembley in 1977 playing for which country?
10 Republic of Ireland skipper Roy Keane was red carded in 1996 against which country?
11 Which referee sent off Manchester Utd's Kevin Moran in an FA Cup Final?
12 Which West Ham Utd player had his red card reduced to a yellow one after TV evidence showed he was wrongly dismissed v Sheffield Wednesday?
13 England's Alan Ball was sent off in 1973 against which country?
14 How many players were sent off in the 1967 World Club Championship between Celtic and Racing Club?
15 What nationality was De Las Casas, the first player sent off in the final stages of a World Cup tournament?
16 In 1971, Sammy Chapman became the first Nottingham Forest player to be sent off for how many years?
17 What was unusual about the dismissal of Ian Banks in December 1989?
18 Jose Battista was sent off in 55 seconds playing for which country against in the World Cup?
19 In 1972, John Ritchie was sent off within 30 seconds as appearing in a Euro game for which club?
20 How many Hereford players were sent off against Northampton in September 1992?

Answers

Double Winners (see Quiz 74)

1 Liverpool. **2** Stoke City. **3** Aston Villa. **4** Preston North End. **5** Jan Molby. **6** Aston Villa. **7** Cliff Jones & Terry Dyson. **8** 0–0. **9** Preston North End. **10** Manchester Utd (1957). **11** Bruce Grobbelaar. **12** 11. **13** Keith Pilkington. **14** Jim Beglin. **15** Eddie Kelly. **16** Bobby Smith. **17** Andy Cole. **18** Aston Villa. **19** MacDonald. **20** Preston North End.

Quiz 77 **Pot Luck 39**

Answers – see page 289

LEVEL 3

1 Mick Harford scored in a League Cup Final for which club?
2 Who lost to Liverpool in the 1976 UEFA Cup Final?
3 What is Gary Mabbutt's middle name?
4 At which club did Paul Mariner make his League debut?
5 In what decade did Portsmouth first win the Championship?
6 Which club had a fanzine called *Exceedingly Good Pies*?
7 John Barnwell followed Sammy Chung as manager of which club?
8 In which decade did Ipswich Town enter the League?
9 Who was Keith Edwards playing for when he was the League's leading scorer in 1981–82?
10 To one each way, how many international goals did Frank Worthington score?
11 Jim Lawrence set an appearance record at which club?
12 Bryan Hamilton was boss of which club twice in the 1980s?
13 Vinny Samways played in an FA Cup Final for which team?
14 McAnespie and Rougier scored Euro goals in the same 1990s game for which club?
15 Bobby Charlton scored in a 1956 Youth Cup Final against which Chesterfield keeper?
16 In the 50 years following the Second World War which clubs had the fewest managers?
17 Which club beat Sampdoria to win the European Super Cup in 1990?
18 Norman Deeley scored twice in an FA Cup Final for which club?
19 At which non-League club did Jimmy Greaves play out his career?
20 In which year did the FA Cup Final become an all-ticket game?

Answers

Pot Luck 40 (see Quiz 79)

1 Sunderland. **2** Real Madrid. **3** *United.* **4** Tottenham Hotspur & Norwich City. **5** Joe Jordan. **6** Derby County. **7** Chelsea. **8** Hughie Gallacher. **9** Marseille. **10** Chris Morris. **11** Jimmy Rimmer. **12** Liverpool. **13** Sheffield Wednesday. **14** Huddersfield Town. **15** Jack Charlton. **16** Liverpool. **17** Manchester City. **18** Exeter City. **19** Norwich City. **20** Six.

Quiz 78 **England Managers**

LEVEL 3

Answers – see page 290

1 Which England manager was born in Worksop?
2 How many games did Joe Mercer serve as caretaker manager?
3 Which was Alf Ramsey's first club as a player?
4 Who were the opponents in Terry Venables' first game as boss?
5 How many of his 29 games as England manager did Don Revie lose?
6 Which manager accused his players of "running round like headless chickens"?
7 Walter Winterbottom led England into how many World Cups?
8 How many England caps did Bobby Robson win as a player?
9 For how many games was Alf Ramsey in charge of England?
10 Which manager had his biggest victory in his last game?
11 Who formed a management partnership with Joe Mercer at Coventry in the 1970s?
12 Who was made skipper in Terry Venables' first game in charge?
13 Ron Greenwood's 1982 World Cup campaign was marred by injuries to which two key players?
14 Who scored for England in the Swedes 2 v Turnips 1 game?
15 Which England manager has won most World Cup games?
16 Where was Walter Winterbottom born?
17 Including penalty shoot-outs, who scored the last England goal under Terry Venables?
18 Which club did Ron Greenwood become a director of in 1983?
19 Who scored the last England goal for Graham Taylor?
20 How many England managers did Kevin Keegan play for?

Answers

Champions (see Quiz 80)

1 Dave Mackay (Derby). **2** Bill Nicholson (Spurs). **3** Alan Shearer. **4** Bryan Robson. **5** Jimmy Rimmer. **6** 1947. **7** John McClelland. **8** Derby County. **9** Hearts & Kilmarnock. **10** Liverpool. **11** O'Hare & McGovern. **12** Chelsea. **13** David Seaman. **14** John Barnes. **15** 14. **16** Blackburn Rovers. **17** Aberdeen & Rangers. **18** Chelsea. **19** Joe Mercer. **20** Eight.

Quiz 79 **Pot Luck 40**

LEVEL 3

Answers – see page 287

1 Owers, Atkinson and Armstrong played for which 1990s FA Cup Finalists?

2 Who knocked Dundee out of the semis of the 1962–63 European Cup?

3 Which soccer soap was shown on BBC in the mid 1960s?

4 Jimmy Neighbour played for which two clubs in League Cup Finals?

5 Which striker at Leeds Utd was known as "The Shark"?

6 Rioch and George scored Euro goals in the same 70s match for which club?

7 What was Tommy Docherty's first League club as a manager?

8 Which great ex-Newcastle Utd player committed suicide on a railway track?

9 Who lost 5–3 on penalties to Red Star Belgrade in the Final of the 1991 European Cup?

10 Which Republic of Ireland defender of the 1990s has the middle name Barry?

11 Which English keeper was on the bench in a 1960s European Cup Final and started a 1980s Final?

12 Don Welsh and Phil Taylor managed which club?

13 Carlton Palmer first played in an FA Cup Final for which team?

14 At which club did Frank Worthington make his League debut?

15 Which Middlesbrough manager said – days before resigning – "We are on the crest of a slump"?

16 Which club had a fanzine called *Our Days Are Numbered*?

17 Billy McNeill followed John Benson as manager of which club?

18 Who was Fred Binney playing for when he was the League's leading scorer in 1972–73?

19 Ron Ashman set an appearance record at which club?

20 How many international goals did Kevin Moran score?

Answers

Pot Luck 39 (see Quiz 77)

1 Luton Town. **2** Bruges. **3** Vincent. **4** Plymouth Argyle. **5** 1940s. **6** Rochdale. **7** Wolves. **8** 1930s. **9** Sheffield Utd. **10** Two. **11** Newcastle Utd. **12** Wigan. **13** Tottenham Hotspur. **14** Raith Rovers. **15** Gordon Banks. **16** West Ham Utd & Manchester Utd. **17** AC Milan. **18** Wolves. **19** Barnet. **20** 1924.

Quiz 80 **Champions**

LEVEL 3

Answers – see page 288

---

1 Which member of the Tottenham Hotspur double side went on to manage a Championship team?
2 Who was the first person to play in and manage League Championship sides at the same club?
3 Who was Blackburn Rovers's only League ever present in 1994–95?
4 Who scored his first and Manchester Utd's last goal of the 1992–93 season?
5 Who played every game in goal for Aston Villa in the 1981 side?
6 When did Bob Paisley play in a Championship-winning side at Liverpool?
7 Which Rangers and Watford defender featured in Leeds Utd's 1992 triumph?
8 Which club in the 70s won the Championship while on holiday in Majorca?
9 Which two Scottish teams met in the final game of the 1964–65 season to decide which of them were champions?
10 David Burrows won a Championship medal with which club?
11 Which two Johns were with Clough's champions at Derby County and Nottingham Forest?
12 Who were the first post-war English champions to have won fewer than half their fixtures?
13 Who played every League game in his first season with the club as Arsenal won the 1990–91 title?
14 Who was top scorer in Liverpool's 1989–90 Championship team?
15 How many players did Villa use in their 1980s Championship success?
16 Tony Gale won a Championship medal at which club?
17 Which two Scottish teams met in the final game of the 1990–91 season to decide which of them were champions?
18 In 1993–94, Manchester Utd lost only four League games but which team beat them home and away?
19 Who was the first man to play for two different English League Champions sides and then become manager of champions?
20 How many Championship medals did Phil Neal win?

Answers

England Managers (see Quiz 78)

1 Graham Taylor. **2** Seven. **3** Southampton. **4** Denmark. **5** 7. **6** Graham Taylor. **7** Four. **8** 20. **9** 113. **10** Graham Taylor v San Marino 7–1. **11** Gordon Milne. **12** David Platt. **13** Keegan and Brooking. **14** David Platt. **15** Bobby Robson. **16** Oldham. **17** Teddy Sheringham. **18** Brighton. **19** Ian Wright. **20** Four.

Quiz 81 **Pot Luck 41**

LEVEL 3

Answers – see page 293

1 Who lost to Juventus in the 1990 UEFA Cup Final?
2 Stuart Pearson scored in an FA Cup Final for which club?
3 Who is the soccer-playing son of former Everton winger Johnny Morrissey?
4 At which club did Alex Matthie make his League debut?
5 Which club used to be the 'third' Edinburgh side?
6 Which club had a fanzine called *In The Loft*?
7 Nobby Stiles followed Harry Catterick as manager of which club?
8 To three years each way, when did Gillingham install floodlights?
9 Whose 1985 autobiography was called *No Half Measures*?
10 To one each way, how many international goals did Johnny Haynes score?
11 Scotsman Andy Gray and Simon Stainrod were in the same team at which club?
12 Which Peter became boss of Derby County in 1982?
13 Cyrille Regis played in an FA Cup Final for which team?
14 Which Scottish winger has the middle names Kevin Francis Michael?
15 Which club beat Barcelona to win the European Super Cup in 1989?
16 Bannister and Stainrod scored Euro goals in the same 1980s game for which club?
17 John Harkes scored in a League Cup Final for which club?
18 Who did Graham Kelly succeed as secretary of the Football Association?
19 Which famous Brazilian player died of alcohol poisoning in 1983?
20 Who left Charlton Athletic for Sampdoria in July 1955?

Answers

Pot Luck 42 (see Quiz 83)

1 Celtic. **2** QPR. **3** John. **4** Coventry City. **5** Neville. **6** Bobby Charlton. **7** Portsmouth. **8** Peterborough. **9** Coventry City. **10** Oldham Athletic. **11** Newcastle Utd. **12** Mackay. **13** Arsenal. **14** Barnsley. **15** Manchester City. **16** Luton Town. **17** Chelsea. **18** Steve Archibald. **19** Jim Baxter. **20** Six.

Quiz 82 **Hat-tricks**

LEVEL 3

Answers – see page 294

1 Alan Shearer's first Newcastle Utd hat-trick was against which side?
2 Who scored a 1991 UEFA Cup hat-trick for Liverpool v Swarovski Tirol?
3 Who scored England's first ever hat-trick in a World Cup match?
4 Who scored the last England hat-trick before Michael Owen against Germany in 2001?
5 Which Colin marked his Southampton debut in 1986 with a hat-trick?
6 Who hit a hat-trick when Chelsea beat Manchester City 5–4 in the Full Members Cup?
7 Harold Bell scored the first League triple hat-trick but for which club?
8 David Platt's first England hat-trick was against which country?
9 Who is the youngest scorer of a hat-trick in top-flight English soccer?
10 Before hitting his Final hat-trick, how many goals had Geoff Hurst scored in the 1966 World Cup?
11 Who was Joe Harper playing for when he hit a Scottish League Cup hat-trick and still ended up a loser?
12 Who scored England's first hat-trick in the 1990s – against which country?
13 Roger Hunt and Fred Pickering both scored hat-tricks in a 10–0 thrashing of which country in 1964?
14 Who hit the first post-World War II FA Cup Final hat-trick?
15 Which Celtic player hit three in the 1972 Scottish FA Cup Final?
16 Four of Alan Shearer's five Blackburn Rovers hat-tricks in 1995–96 were scored at home, but where was the away hat-trick scored?
17 How many times did Jimmy Greaves score three or more for England?
18 Who scored a double hat-trick on his Newcastle Utd debut in the 1940s?
19 Who was the first British player to score a hat-trick of penalties in a Euro game?
20 Which Jimmy of Celtic hit the first hat-trick in a Scottish FA Cup Final?

Answers

UEFA Cup (see Quiz 84)

1 Ferencvaros. **2** John Wark. **3** London XI. **4** Valencia. **5** Bayer Leverkusen. **6** Jeremy Goss. **7** Thomas Helmer & Mehmet Scholl. **8** Galatasaray. **9** PSV Eindhoven. **10** Wolves. **11** The toss of a coin. **12** Juventus (lost on away goals rule). **13** Bertie Mee. **14** Lothar Matthäus. **15** All blue. **16** Tony Parks. **17** Newcastle Utd. **18** Stan Bowles. **19** Ipswich Town. **20** Billy Thompson.

Quiz 83 **Pot Luck 42**

LEVEL 3

Answers – see page 291

1 Who lost 2–1 to Feyenoord in the Final of the 1970 European Cup?
2 John Byrne played in a League Cup Final for which club?
3 What is Niall Quinn's middle name?
4 McGrath, Peake and Gynn played for which 1980s FA Cup Finalists?
5 What was England winger Mark Chamberlain's soccer playing brother called?
6 Who captained the Manchester Utd team to lift the European Cup in 1968?
7 Which was the first team since the Second World War to win the Championship two seasons in a row?
8 With 482 League games Tommy Robson set an appearance record at which club?
9 Martin and O'Rourke scored Euro goals in the same 1970s game for which club?
10 Which ground has the Lookers Stand and the George Hill Stand?
11 Goddard and Gascoigne were in the same team at which club?
12 Which Dave became manager of Birmingham City in 1989?
13 Steve Walford first played in an FA Cup Final for which team?
14 At which club did David Speedie make his League debut?
15 With 158 goals in the 1920s Tommy Johnson set up a scoring record for which club?
16 Which club has a fanzine called *Mad As A Hatter*?
17 Danny Blanchflower followed Ken Shellito as manager of which club?
18 Mark Hughes had his registration at Barcelona cancelled to make way for which player?
19 Which soccer player told his story in the book *The Party's Over*?
20 To one each way, how many international goals did Andy McEvoy score?

Answers

Pot Luck 41 (see Quiz 81)

1 Fiorentina. **2** Manchester Utd. **3** John. **4** Celtic. **5** Meadowbank. **6** QPR. **7** Preston North End. **8** 1963. **9** Graeme Souness. **10** 18. **11** Aston Villa. **12** Taylor. **13** Coventry City. **14** Pat Nevin. **15** AC Milan. **16** QPR. **17** Sheffield Wednesday. **18** Ted Croker. **19** Garrincha. **20** Eddie Firmani.

Quiz 84 **UEFA Cup**

LEVEL 3

Answers – see page 292

1 Who were the first Eastern European trophy winners?

2 Which Scot scored 14 goals in the 1980–81 competition?

3 What was the generic title of the first ever team to represent England in the competition?

4 Which Spanish side were first to reach three consecutive Finals?

5 South Korea's Cha Bum-Kun played for which trophy winners in the late 1980s?

6 Who was top scorer in Norwich City's UEFA games in 1993–94?

7 Who were the two scorers in the 1996 Final?

8 Which team did Dean Saunders play for in the 1995–96 competition?

9 Who knocked Leeds Utd out of the 1995–96 tournament?

10 Jim McCalliog scored a Final goal for which team?

11 After three drawn games, the Racing Strasbourg v Barcelona game of 1964–65 was decided which way?

12 In 1970–71 which team played 12 games without defeat yet failed to win the trophy?

13 Who was manager of the English side that won the trophy in 1970?

14 Which German captain won the trophy with Internazionale in 1991?

15 When Juventus were beaten in the 1971 final what unfamiliar colour did they play in?

16 Who was in goal for Tottenham Hotspur for the 1984 triumph, achieved after a shoot out?

17 Which English team knocked Southampton out of the 1970 competition?

18 Which QPR player scored 11 goals in 1976–77?

19 Kevin Steggles was a Euro scorer for which English team?

20 Who was in goal for both legs of Dundee Utd's 1987 Final?

Answers

Hat-tricks (see Quiz 82)

1 Leicester City. **2** Dean Saunders. **3** Jackie Milburn. **4** Paul Scholes. **5** Clarke. **6** David Speedie (Chelsea). **7** Tranmere Rovers. **8** San Marino. **9** Alan Shearer. **10** One. **11** Hibernian. **12** Gary Lineker v Malaysia. **13** USA. **14** Stan Mortensen. **15** Dixie Deans. **16** White Hart Lane. **17** Six. **18** Len Shackleton. **19** John Wark. **20** Quinn.

Quiz 85 **Pot Luck 43**

Answers – see page 297

LEVEL 3

1 Who scored an own goal in the Aston Villa v Everton replayed League Cup Final in the 1970s?

2 Who is the record transfer signing for Bristol City?

3 Who is Peter Reid's soccer playing brother?

4 At which club did Brian Talbot make his League debut?

5 Who handed out Fulham's record 10–0 defeat in a League Cup game in 1986?

6 Which club has a fanzine called *Blue and White*?

7 What was the lowest position Manchester Utd finished in the League under Ron Atkinson?

8 John Gavin is the all-time top scorer at which club?

9 Which manager had the backroom staff of Owen, Lindley and Cocker?

10 To one each way, how many international goals did Tony Woodcock score?

11 Paul Ince and Liam Brady were in the same team at which club?

12 Which Martin was manager of Bury from 1984 to 1989?

13 Ian Wilson played in an FA Cup Final for which team?

14 What is Jamie Redknapp's middle name?

15 Who lost to Internazionale in the 1991 UEFA Cup Final?

16 Under what name did Rod Argent record music used by ITV for the Mexico World Cup finals in 1986?

17 In what year was the World Cup first transmitted in colour in the UK?

18 Which club beat Barcelona to win the European Super Cup in 1982?

19 Alan Sunderland scored in an FA Cup Final for which club?

20 Ace scorer Arthur Rowley was player-manager of which club when he hung up his boots?

Answers

Pot Luck 44 (see Quiz 87)

1 Rocastle. **2** Arsenal. **3** Manchester City. **4** Joe Payne. **5** Liam Brady. **6** Chelsea. **7** Exeter City. **8** John Chiedozie. **9** Arsenal. **10** Sampdoria. **11** QPR. **12** Herbert Chapman (Arsenal). **13** QPR. **14** Bury. **15** Oldham Athletic. **16** Manchester Utd. **17** Coventry City. **18** Steve Sherwood. **19** Rotherham Utd. **20** Nine.

Quiz 86 Rangers & Celtic

LEVEL 3

Answers – see page 298

1 What did Celtic's Chalmers and Rangers' Wilson achieve when they went out for the 1966–67 Scottish League Cup Final?

2 In what year was the first Old Firm Cup Final played?

3 What year was the Scottish FA Cup withheld after two draws between Rangers and Celtic?

4 Who won the first game between the sides back in 1888?

5 Which team with a ground in England knocked Rangers out of the 1967 Scottish FA Cup?

6 Who said, "For a while I did unite Rangers and Celtic fans. There were people in both camps that hated me"?

7 How many players were red carded in the March 1991 League game?

8 Which Celtic keeper let nine goals in in an international match?

9 When Rangers won the Scottish Southern Cup in 1946 it was the forerunner of which tournament?

10 Who is Celtic's all time top goalscorer?

11 What did Rangers achieve in season 1898–99?

12 Who was Rangers manager for 37 years from 1920 to 1957?

13 In 1977 who became the first player to win Scottish FA Cup medals with both clubs?

14 Jim Baxter joined Rangers from which club?

15 What season did Celtic achieve Scotland's first double?

16 Which two players called Woods did Graeme Souness bring in from England to Rangers?

17 Who scored Celtic's 1967 European Cup Final winner?

18 Who has won most Scottish caps during his time with Rangers?

19 When did Rangers first achieve the treble?

20 What season did Aberdeen beat Rangers and Celtic in major Cup Finals?

Answers

The 1990s (see Quiz 88)

1 Sao Paulo. **2** John Toshack. **3** First British club to have four players sent off in a game. **4** Jack Petchey. **5** Vinnie Jones. **6** Five. **7** PSV Eindhoven. **8** Sweden. **9** Norwich City. **10** Trevor Morley. **11** 1992–93. **12** Sweden. **13** Franz Beckenbauer. **14** English. **15** Dino & Roberto. **16** Ten. **17** Neville Southall. **18** Monaco. **19** Peter Reid. **20** Chelsea & Aston Villa.

Quiz 87 **Pot Luck 44**

Answers – see page 295

LEVEL 3

1 Which Lewisham-born midfield England player has the first names David Carlyle?

2 McNab, Storey and Simpson played for which 1970s FA Cup Finalists?

3 In the 1995–96 season, which was the first English club to field four overseas players?

4 Which player of the 1930s has scored most goals in a season for Luton Town?

5 Which player wrote *So Far So Good*?

6 Birchenall and Boyle scored Euro goals in the same 1960s game for which club?

7 Which ground had the Cowshed covered terrace?

8 Which Nigerian became Leyton Orient's most capped player?

9 Perry Groves played in a League Cup Final for which club?

10 Who lost 1–0 to Barcelona in the Final of the 1992 European Cup?

11 Alan Brazil and David Seaman were in the same team at which club?

12 Manager George Allison followed which legend in 1934?

13 Tony Currie first played in an FA Cup Final for which team?

14 At which club did Terry McDermott make his League debut?

15 Roger Palmer became all time top scorer at which club?

16 Which club had a fanzine called *Red Issue*?

17 Bobby Gould followed Dave Sexton as manager of which club?

18 Which 40-something keeper turned out for Northampton in 1993–94?

19 Which club originally played at the Red House ground?

20 To one each way, how many international goals did Liam Brady score?

Answers

Pot Luck 43 (see Quiz 85)

1 Roger Kenyon (Everton). **2** Ade Akinbiyi. **3** Shaun. **4** Ipswich Town. **5** Liverpool. **6** Portsmouth. **7** Fourth. **8** Norwich City. **9** Don Revie. **10** 16. **11** West Ham Utd. **12** Dobson. **13** Everton. **14** Frank. **15** AS Roma. **16** Silsoe. **17** 1970. **18** Aston Villa. **19** Arsenal. **20** Shrewsbury Town.

Quiz 88 **The 1990s**

LEVEL 3

Answers – see page 296

1 Which club did Juninho play for before joining Middlesbrough?

2 Which British manager was sacked by Real Madrid in 1990?

3 When Millwall's Malcolm Allen was sent off in 1992–93 what unwelcome first did he achieve?

4 Who did Elton John sell Watford to for £6 million in 1991?

5 Who received a £20,000 fine from the FA for voicing a video nasty?

6 How many players were sent off in the 1997 Chesterfield v Plymouth Argyle Division Two League game?

7 Which Dutch side did Bobby Robson manage after leaving England?

8 Which country did Scotland beat in the 1990 World Cup tournament?

9 Which club finished third in 1993 in the Premier League, with a 61–65 goal difference?

10 Which London-based player was stabbed in a domestic row?

11 What season was the new back-pass law seen for the first time?

12 Gary Lineker played his last international against which country?

13 Who became the first man to captain and manage World Cup winning teams?

14 A FIFA ruling stated that all international referees must be able to speak what language?

15 What are the first names of Juventus' 1993 UEFA Cup-winning Baggios?

16 What championship win number was it for Arsenal in 1991?

17 Which keeper did a goalmouth sit-in at half time in 1990?

18 In 1992 Jürgen Klinsmann left Inter Milan to join which club?

19 Simply Red's cover of "Daydream Believer" was for which manager?

20 Who were the beaten semi-finalists in the 1995–96 FA Cup?

Answers

Rangers & Celtic (see Quiz 86)

1 First subs to be used in a Final. **2** 1894. **3** 1909. **4** Celtic. **5** Berwick Rangers. **6** Mo Johnston. **7** Four. **8** Frank Haffey. **9** Scottish League Cup. **10** Jimmy McGrory. **11** Won all their League games. **12** Bill Struth. **13** Alfie Conn. **14** Raith Rovers. **15** 1906–07. **16** Chris and Neil. **17** Steve Chalmers. **18** George Young. **19** 1948–49. **20** 1989–90.

Quiz 89 **Pot Luck 45**

LEVEL 3

Answers – see page 301

1 Who lost to Ajax on away goals in the 1992 UEFA Cup Final?

2 Bobby Gould scored a League Cup Final goal for which club?

3 In which country was John Salako born?

4 At which club did Emlyn Hughes make his League debut?

5 When did Chelsea hit the charts with "Blue Is The Colour"?

6 Which club has a fanzine called *No More Pie In The Sky*?

7 John Docherty followed Ron Atkinson as manager of which club?

8 Which non-League side does John Motson follow?

9 Where was Welsh international Mark Crossley born?

10 To one each way, how many international goals did Neil Webb score?

11 Wayne Clarke and Alan Harper were in the same team at which club?

12 Which Dennis has been boss at Bristol City, Oxford, Sunderland and York?

13 Mark Bright first played in an FA Cup Final for which team?

14 What is David Seaman's middle name?

15 Which club beat Liverpool to win the European Super Cup in 1978?

16 Which former Northern Ireland manager took charge of the Greek national side in 1971?

17 Bowen and Goss scored Euro goals in the same game for which club?

18 Which Scottish player scored for the Italian League in 1961?

19 Who is Dundee's all-time top League scorer?

20 Fullback Chris Lawler scored goals for Liverpool, Stockport and which other club?

Answers

Pot Luck 46 (see Quiz 91)

1 South Africa. **2** AC Milan. **3** Wolves. **4** Everton. **5** Arsenal. **6** Celtic. **7** The Sandpipers. **8** Runcorn. **9** Manchester Utd. **10** David. **11** Sheffield Wednesday. **12** Newcastle Utd. **13** Wimbledon. **14** Ayr. **15** Jason Dozzell. **16** Mansfield Town. **17** Notts County. **18** Middlesbrough. **19** Ipswich Town. **20** 12.

Quiz 90 **Golden Goals**

LEVEL 3

Answers – see page 302

1 Who failed to stop a shot from the halfway line on the opening day of the 1996–97 Premier League season?

2 Who scored a great Final Euro 92 goal and then moved to play in London?

3 Which Liverpool player scored from a free-kick to beat Blackburn Rovers in the last game of the 1994–95 season?

4 How many goals did Gary Lineker score for England?

5 Who scored Manchester Utd's goals v Barcelona in the 1991 European Cup Winners' Cup Final?

6 Which German player scored the only goal of the 1990 World Cup Final?

7 Who was the first winner of the Golden Boot award?

8 Which Wimbledon player scored the only goal of the 1988 FA Cup Final?

9 Which Italian player scored six goals in Italia 90?

10 Who scored Liverpool's extra time winner v Leeds Utd in 1965?

11 On Manchester Utd's 1968 Euro trail, who was the unlikely scorer of the last goal v Real Madrid?

12 Who scored twice for Colchester Utd in the 1970s as they toppled Leeds Utd in the FA Cup?

13 Who scored Forest's European Cup Final goal to beat Hamburg?

14 Who scored Arsenal's first goal in the title decider at Anfield in 1989?

15 Brian Talbot scored in an FA Cup Final for which club?

16 Who scored in the 1970 England v Brazil World Cup game?

17 Which Scottish player scored a goal v Holland in the 1978 World Cup?

18 Which Northern Ireland player scored to defeat W Germany in a European Championship qualifier in 1983?

19 Which defender Roy of Blackpool and Manchester City managed 415 League games without ever scoring?

20 Which Polish international hit 4 goals for Celtic v Partizan Belgrade in 1989?

Answers

Englishmen Abroad (see Quiz 92)

1 42. **2** Barcelona & Grampus Eight. **3** Gerry Hitchens. **4** Glenn Hoddle & Mark Hateley. **5** AC Milan. **6** Jack Taylor. **7** Marseille. **8** Vancouver Whitecaps. **9** AC Milan. **10** Standard Liege. **11** Johan Cruyff. **12** Des Walker. **13** Hamburg. **14** Mark Hateley. **15** Steaua Bucharest. **16** Nick Barmby. **17** France. **18** Bob Houghton. **19** 44. **20** Kevin Richardson.

Quiz 91 **Pot Luck 46**

LEVEL 3

Answers – see page 299

1 In which country was Mark Stein born?

2 Who lost 1–0 to Marseille in the Final of the 1993 European Cup?

3 Hancocks, Pye and Shorthouse played for which 1940s FA Cup Finalists?

4 Paul Power was a Championship winner at which club?

5 Gus Caesar played in a League Cup Final for which club?

6 Donnelly and Walker scored Euro goals in the same 1990s game for which club?

7 "Guantanamera" – the tune of thousands of terrace chants – was a 1960s hit for which group?

8 Ian Woan joined Nottingham Forest from which non-League team?

9 Gordon McQueen scored in an FA Cup Final for which club?

10 What is Gordon Strachan's middle name?

11 Lee Chapman and Mark Chamberlain were in the same team at which club?

12 Stan Seymour won the FA Cup once as a player and twice as a manager with which club?

13 Laurie Cunningham first played in an FA Cup Final for which team?

14 At which Scottish club did Steve Nicol make his League debut?

15 Which 16-year-old became the First Division's youngest scorer with a goal for Ipswich Town in 1984?

16 Which club had a fanzine called *Follow The Yellow Brick Road*?

17 Neil Warnock followed John Barnwell as manager of which club?

18 Graeme Souness was first capped while at which club?

19 Roger Osborne scored in an FA Cup Final for which club?

20 To one each way, how many international goals did Alan Gilzean score?

Answers

Pot Luck 45 (see Quiz 89)

1 Torino. **2** Arsenal. **3** Nigeria. **4** Blackpool. **5** 1972. **6** Notts County. **7** Cambridge Utd. **8** Boston Utd. **9** Barnsley. **10** Four. **11** Everton. **12** Smith. **13** Crystal Palace. **14** Andrew. **15** RSC Anderlecht. **16** Billy Bingham. **17** Norwich City. **18** Denis Law. **19** Alan Gilzean. **20** Portsmouth.

Quiz 92 **Englishmen Abroad**

Answers – see page 300

LEVEL 3

1 How many League games did Gazza play in three years at Lazio?

2 Which two foreign teams did Gary Lineker play for?

3 Who was the first player to be capped for England while on the books of a foreign team?

4 In 1988 which Englishmen played for the French Champions?

5 Which foreign club did Ray Wilkins play for?

6 Which English referee officiated in the 1974 World Cup Final?

7 Chris Waddle was at which club when he played in Italia 90?

8 Which foreign team did Peter Beardsley play for?

9 Luther Blissett joined which Italian club in the mid 1980s?

10 Which club in Belgium did Mike Small play for?

11 Which manager sold Gary Lineker to Tottenham Hotspur?

12 Which defender took a detour to Sampdoria on his way from Nottingham to Sheffield?

13 Southampton manager Lawrie McMenemy brought Kevin Keegan back to England from which club?

14 Who in the 1980s went from Portsmouth to AC Milan?

15 Which team did "El Tel" lose to in the 1986 European Cup Final?

16 Which English player scored two goals against China in 1996?

17 Which country did Graham Rix go to play his football in?

18 Who was Malmo's English manager when they met Nottingham Forest in the European Cup Final?

19 How many goals did Gary Lineker score in his 99 League games for Barcelona?

20 Which English midfielder joined John Aldridge at Real Sociedad in 1990?

Answers

Golden Goals (see Quiz 90)

1 Neil Sullivan. **2** John Jensen. **3** Jamie Redknapp. **4** 48. **5** Mark Hughes. **6** Andy Brehme. **7** Eusebio. **8** Lawrie Sanchez. **9** Schillachi. **10** Ian St John. **11** Billy Foulkes. **12** Ray Crawford. **13** John Robertson. **14** Alan Smith. **15** Arsenal. **16** Jairzinho. **17** Archie Gemmill. **18** Norman Whiteside. **19** Gratrix. **20** Dariusz Dziekanowski.

Quiz 93 **Pot Luck 47**

LEVEL 3

Answers – see page 305

1 Mike Doyle scored a League Cup Final goal for which club?

2 Who lost to Juventus in the 1993 UEFA Cup Final?

3 Which former Bolton centre-half Alan was born in Liverpool in 1971?

4 At which club did Joe Jordan make his League debut?

5 Martin Allan with 343 league games broke the appearance record at which Scottish club?

6 Which club had a fanzine called *The Almighty Brian*?

7 Who was manager of Brighton for the 1980s FA Cup Final?

8 Who moved from Walsall to West Ham Utd in 1988, to set a club record for a transfer fee received?

9 Which players, with the same surname, scored in consecutive European Championship Finals?

10 To one each way, how many international goals did Mike Summerbee score?

11 Steve Hodge and Chris Waddle were team mates in which club side?

12 Which Jim was manager of Birmingham from 1978–82?

13 Justin Edinburgh first played in an FA Cup Final for which team?

14 What is Chris Sutton's middle name?

15 Coyne and Kirk scored Euro goals in the same 1990s game for which club?

16 Which Derek scored most goals in a season for Sheffield Wednesday?

17 Which two clubs have the same name as terminus stations on London Underground?

18 Which club beat Barcelona to win the European Super Cup in 1979?

19 Keith Houchen scored in an FA Cup Final for which club?

20 Who – after being made boss of Arsenal – said,"I hadn't planned to be a football manager"?

Answers

Pot Luck 48 (see Quiz 95)

1 Andy Townsend. **2** West Ham Utd. **3** Barcelona. **4** Original Scottish FA Cup entrants. **5** Hereford Utd. **6** Charlie George. **7** Aston Villa. **8** Dundee Utd. **9** Oldham Athletic. **10** Tanner. **11** Leeds Utd. **12** Porterfield. **13** Manchester City. **14** Everton. **15** Kevin Richardson. **16** Middlesbrough. **17** Jimmy Dickinson. **18** WBA. **19** QPR. **20** Three.

Quiz 94 **International Players**

Answers – see page 306

LEVEL 3

1 Who is the Luton Town and Everton forward who went on to manage Northern Ireland?

2 When was the last time Wales qualified for the World Cup tournament?

3 In what year did the Republic of Ireland become the first team outside the UK to defeat England in England?

4 Which was the Republic of Ireland's keeper in the penalty shoot out v Romania in the 1990 World Cup?

5 When was Neville Southall voted Footballer of the Year?

6 Which Manchester Utd and Republic of Ireland player was known as "Gentlemen John"?

7 Which Welsh player capped over 50 times, won the double with Spurs?

8 Who made his debut for Wales aged 18 years 71 days?

9 At which ground did the last Home International match take place in 1984, between Wales and England?

10 Against which of the home countries did Ian Rush make his debut?

11 A late goal by which team meant that the Republic of Ireland failed to reach the semi-finals of the 88 Euro Championship?

12 Who kept goal for Northern Ireland in the 1958 World Cup?

13 Who beat Ivor Allchurch's appearance record – 20 years after it was set?

14 World champions West Germany were beaten 2–1 by which home international team in 1991?

15 Who did Wales beat 3–2 to celebrate their FA's centenary in 1951?

16 Don Givens was at which club when he was first capped?

17 Which Welsh player was 45 years and 229 days old when he won a cap against England in 1920?

18 While at Crystal Palace, who was the first Fourth Division player to be picked for Wales?

19 How many international goals did Trevor Ford score?

20 Northern Ireland beat Italy at which English ground to qualify for the 1958 World Cup?

Answers

International Managers (see Quiz 96)

1 Johnny Giles. **2** Six. **3** Matt Busby. **4** Craig Brown. **5** Austria. **6** Argentina. **7** Mike Smith. **8** Eoin Hand. **9** Josef Herberger. **10** Bristol City. **11** Gusztav Sebes. **12** Brazil. **13** Helmut Schön. **14** Wales. **15** Bayer Leverkusen. **16** Vittorio Pozzo. **17** Franz Beckenbauer. **18** Cesare Maldini. **19** Decorate his kitchen. **20** Open University.

Quiz 95 **Pot Luck 48**

LEVEL 3

Answers – see page 303

1 Which Republic of Ireland international was born in Maidstone in July 1963?

2 Bond, Brown and Bovington played for which 1960s FA Cup Finalists?

3 Who lost 4–0 to AC Milan in the Final of the 1994 European Cup?

4 What links Blytheswood, Renton, Southern and Western?

5 Who was Dixie McNeil playing for when he was the League's leading scorer in 1974–75 and 1975–76?

6 Which English League-and-Cup double winner lost a finger in an accident with a lawnmower?

7 Gibson and Ormsby scored Euro goals in the same 1980s game for which club?

8 Eamonn Bannon's goal in April 1983 clinched the Scottish Championship for which team?

9 Rick Holden played in a League Cup Final for which club?

10 Which Ipswich player Adam was banned after a drug test?

11 Mervyn Day and Vince Hilaire were in the same team at which club?

12 Which Ian became boss of Sheffield Utd in 1981?

13 Steve MacKenzie played in an FA Cup Final for which team?

14 At which club did Ian Bishop make his League debut?

15 Who played in League Cup Finals for Everton, Arsenal and Aston Villa?

16 Which club had a fanzine called *Fly Me To The Moon*?

17 Who followed Ian St John as manager of Portsmouth?

18 Who was Colin Suggett playing for in a 1970s League Cup Final?

19 Tony Ingham set up a League appearance record at which club?

20 To one each way, how many international goals did Billy Bremner score?

Answers

Pot Luck 47 (see Quiz 93)

1 Manchester City. **2** Borussia Dortmund. **3** Stubbs. **4** Morton. **5** Montrose. **6** Nottingham Forest. **7** Jimmy Melia. **8** David Kelly. **9** Müller (Gerd in 1972, Dieter in 1976). **10** One. **11** Tottenham Hotspur. **12** Smith. **13** Tottenham Hotspur. **14** Roy. **15** Motherwell. **16** Dooley. **17** Watford and Wimbledon. **18** Nottingham Forest. **19** Coventry City. **20** Bertie Mee.

Quiz 96 International Managers

Answers – see page 304

1 Who resigned as the Republic of Ireland's manager in April 1980?
2 How many different Scotland managers did Kenny Dalglish play for?
3 Who managed the Great Britain team in the 1948 Olympic Games?
4 Which future national manager was born in Lanarkshire on July 1, 1940?
5 Hugo Meisl was manager and general secretary of which country from 1906 to 1937?
6 In which country was Helenio Herrera born?
7 Who was Welsh boss for the vital 1977 World Cup qualifier v Scotland?
8 Who was manager of the Republic of Ireland directly before Jack Charlton?
9 Who was manager of the West German World Cup winners in 1954?
10 Before Switzerland, Roy Hodgson managed which English League club?
11 Which coach created the "Magic Magyars" of the 1950s?
12 Which country did Tele Santana manage?
13 Who managed West Germany in the 1966 World Cup Final?
14 Norwich City coach David Williams took charge of which country for one game?
15 Dutch master Rinus Michels coached which German League side?
16 Who took Italy to two World Cup triumphs in the 1930s?
17 Who was the first person to captain and coach World Cup winners?
18 Which international manager captained AC Milan to their first European Cup success as a player?
19 What had Denmark's manager Richard Moller Nielsen reputedly planned to do during Euro 92, before his team's surprise late call up?
20 Where is Craig Brown's university degree from?

Answers

International Players (see Quiz 94)

1 Billy Bingham. **2** 1958. **3** 1949. **4** Pat Bonner. **5** 1985. **6** Johnny Carey. **7** Cliff Jones. **8** John Charles. **9** Wrexham. **10** Scotland. **11** Holland. **12** Harry Gregg. **13** Joey Jones. **14** Wales. **15** Rest of UK XI. **16** Manchester Utd. **17** Billy Meredith. **18** Vic Rouse. **19** 23. **20** Wembley Stadium.

Quiz 97 **Pot Luck 49**

LEVEL 3

Answers – see page 309

1 Ralph Coates scored a League Cup Final goal for which club?

2 Who lost to Internazionale in the 1994 UEFA Cup Final?

3 Which Derby player of the 1990s has the middle name Petrus?

4 Blackmore and Webb scored Euro goals in which same club team?

5 Which member of the crowd was on the receiving end of Cantona's infamous Kung Fu kick?

6 Which club has a fanzine called *What A Load of Cobblers*?

7 Gordon Jago followed Benny Fenton as manager of which club?

8 Who was FIFA World Footballer of the Year in 1993?

9 In which year did all four British teams qualify for the World Cup?

10 How many international goals did Paul Mariner score?

11 Trevor Morley and David White were in the same team at which club?

12 Which Tony became boss of Bournemouth in 1992?

13 John Pemberton played in an FA Cup Final for which team?

14 At which club did Stan Bowles make his League debut?

15 Which Peter was Manchester Utd top scorer in the season Alex Ferguson arrived?

16 Who won the FA Cup once as a player in 1920 with Aston Villa and as a manager in the 1930s and the 1950s?

17 Who was Bill Pirie playing for when he was the Scottish League's leading scorer in 1976–77 and 1977–78?

18 Which club beat Ajax to win the European Super Cup in 1987?

19 Terry Fenwick scored in an FA Cup Final for which club?

20 Ian Allinson had made over 300 appearances for which club before joining Arsenal in the 1980s?

Answers

Pot Luck 50 (see Quiz 99)

1 Grimsby Town. **2** 1970s. **3** Brighton. **4** Watford. **5** Arsenal. **6** Sheffield Wednesday. **7** 1981. **8** Nottingham Forest. **9** AC Milan. **10** Roland. **11** West Ham Utd. **12** Rudge. **13** Wimbledon. **14** Stoke City. **15** Teacher. **16** Millwall. **17** QPR. **18** Howard Wilkinson. **19** Wolves. **20** Nine.

Quiz 98 **Super Subs**

Answers – see page 310

LEVEL 3 

1 Who replaced Gary Lineker when he went off in his last international?
2 Which Motherwell sub hit the extra time winner v Dundee in the 1991 Scottish FA Cup Final?
3 Who went on when Gazza injured himself in the 1991 FA Cup Final?
4 Which Republic of Ireland sub scored in a penalty shoot-out in Italia 90?
5 In which year were substitutes first used in the Scottish FA Cup Final?
6 Which Wolves player became the first England scoring substitute?
7 What position did Alf Pugh play for Wales in the 1890 when he became the first substitute?
8 In 1971 who scored the first goal by a substitute in a Scottish FA Cup Final?
9 In Mexico 1970, which players replaced Bobby Charlton and Martin Peters?
10 Who went on against Poland in 1993 and scored his first England goal?
11 Who was the first substitute to score in a World Cup Final?
12 Which Tottenham Hotspur player in 1992 became the first Premier League substitute?
13 Which substitute beat Jim Leighton twice in an FA Cup Final?
14 Who was the first scoring substitute in an FA Cup Final?
15 Who was the first substitute to score in a League Cup Final?
16 Who were the scoring substitutes in the 1986 Mersey FA Cup Final?
17 Which was the last of the then 92 English League clubs to make a substitution in a League game?
18 Who began Euro 88 as a substitute, but finished as a Final goalscorer?
19 What career milestone did Norman Hunter achieve when he went on as an England substitute v Spain in 1965?
20 What did Bobby Knox achieve on August 21, 1965?

Answers

Extra Time 1 (see Quiz 100)

1 Graham Roberts. **2** Chris Woods. **3** Paul Goddard. **4** Steve Daley. **5** Dave Watson. **6** Four. **7** Crewe Alexandra. **8** Cyrille Regis. **9** George Best. **10** Torquay Utd. **11** Four. **12** Semi-final (1930). **13** Swindon Town. **14** QPR. **15** Arconada. **16** Andy Brehme. **17** Chester City. **18** Norwich City. **19** Deportivo la Coruña. **20** Watford & Aston Villa.

Quiz 99 **Pot Luck 50**

Answers – see page 307

LEVEL 3

1 Which English club has its ground nearest to the sea?

2 In what decade was the first Women's FA Cup Final?

3 Gordon Smith scored in an FA Cup Final for which club?

4 Who was Ross Jenkins playing for when he was the League's leading scorer in 1978–79?

5 McDermott and Meade scored Euro goals in the same 1980s game, for which club?

6 Which top-flight club once managed only two goals in ten games, both scored by Atkinson?

7 To three years each way, when did Stranraer install floodlights?

8 Teddy Sheringham first played in a League Cup Final for which club?

9 Who lost 1–0 to Ajax in the Final of the 1995 European Cup?

10 What is Chris Waddle's middle name?

11 Mark Ward and Frank McAvennie were in the same team at which club?

12 Which John became manager of Port Vale in 1984?

13 Dennis Wise first played in an FA Cup Final for which team?

14 At which club did Garth Crooks make his League debut?

15 What had Bob Wilson qualified to be before taking up soccer?

16 Which club had a fanzine called *The Lion Roars*?

17 Venables, Jago, Mullery and Sibley all managed which club in 1984?

18 Who had pictures of the Revie era removed from the foyer at Elland Road?

19 Which club's record win is a 14–0 thrashing of Cresswell's Brewery in 1886?

20 To one each way, how many international goals did Norman Whiteside score?

Answers

Pot Luck 49 (see Quiz 97)

1 Tottenham Hotspur. **2** Salzburg. **3** Robbie Van Der Laan. **4** Manchester Utd. **5** Matthew Simmons. **6** Northampton Town. **7** Millwall. **8** Roberto Baggio. **9** 1958. **10** 13. **11** Manchester City. **12** Pulis. **13** Crystal Palace. **14** Manchester City. **15** Davenport. **16** Billy Walker. **17** Dundee. **18** Porto. **19** QPR. **20** Colchester Utd.

Quiz 100 **Extra Time 1**

LEVEL 3

Answers – see page 308

1 Who was David Pleat talking about when he said, "He kicked people in England and now I suppose he'll go up and kick people in Scotland"?

2 Which England keeper had the middle names Charles Eric?

3 Which West Ham Utd player scored on his first England apearance in 1982?

4 Who was the first uncapped player to move for £1 million?

5 Who was capped while playing for Sunderland, Manchester City, Werder Bremen, Southampton and Stoke?

6 How many League games did Steve Ogrizovic play in his four years at Liverpool?

7 Playing in the 1960s and 1970s, Tommy Lowry set a League appearance record at which club?

8 Dalian Atkinson and Steve Staunton scored on their Aston Villa debuts in 1991–92, as did which third player in the same match?

9 Whose 1982 book was called *Where Do I Go From Here*?

10 Which club's ground is situated by Marnham Road and Ellacombe Road?

11 To one each way, Kerry Dixon scored how many international goals?

12 What is the furthest stage USA have reached in the World Cup?

13 Welshman Rod Thomas won 30 of his 50 caps while at which club?

14 In 1976 who would have won the Championship if Liverpool had lost their last game at Wolves?

15 Who was the Spanish keeper in the 1984 European Championship Final?

16 In his England career Peter Shilton saved one penalty – taken by who?

17 Stuart Rimmer is the all-time top League scorer at which club?

18 Who was Phil Boyer playing for when he won his only England cap?

19 In early 1997 John Toshack parted company with which Spanish side?

20 Which teams did Graham Taylor take to runner-up spot in the old First Division?

Answers

Super Subs (see Quiz 98)

1 Alan Smith. **2** Steve Kirk. **3** Nayim. **4** David O'Leary. **5** 1968. **6** Jimmy Mullen. **7** Goalkeeper. **8** Derek Johnstone. **9** Norman Hunter & Colin Bell. **10** Ian Wright. **11** Dirk Nanniga (Holland 1978). **12** Erik Thorstvedt. **13** Ian Wright. **14** Eddie Kelly. **15** Ralph Coates. **16** Ian Rush & Stuart McCall. **17** Notts County. **18** Marco van Basten. **19** First England player whose debut was as a substitute. **20** First substitute to score a League goal.

Quiz 101 **Extra Time 2**

Answers – see page 313

LEVEL 3

1 A tackle by Josef Toth for Hungary in November 1981 led to the end of whose playing career?

2 What is Dennis Wise's middle name?

3 What is the famous first held by Cuthbert Ottaway?

4 Whose 1993 autobiography was called *Top Mark!*?

5 Graham Taylor's first match as England boss was against which country?

6 In which city was Howard Wilkinson born?

7 Playing in the 1960s and 70s, Paul Jonquin set a League appearance record at which club?

8 Whose ground is by Madoc Street and William Street?

9 Liverpool's Kop first taunted which keeper by singing "Careless Hands"?

10 Who was Jimmy Rimmer playing for when he won his only England cap?

11 Ernest Hine is the all-time top League scorer at which club?

12 Which is the only club to have played in all the old six divisions in England as well as the Premiership?

13 Which coach wrote *The Winning Formula*?

14 Which two Chelsea players played their 700th games, including cup-ties, for the club on the same day in March 1978?

15 Queen of the South come from which town?

16 Which London ground other than Wembley staged a match in the 1966 World Cup?

17 Which Arsenal manager was born in Aldershot in 1947?

18 To two each way, how many internationals did Martin O'Neill play?

19 Which Polish player has made 21 World Cup tournament appearances?

20 Jimmy Hill and Ron Greenwood were both players at which club?

Answers

Extra Time 4 (see Quiz 103)

1 Monaco. **2** Gerald. **3** Portsmouth. **4** Howard Kendall. **5** Derby County. **6** Gordon Taylor. **7** Oxford Utd. **8** West Ham Utd. **9** A bomb scare. **10** QPR. **11** Derby County. **12** Tranmere Rovers. **13** Six. **14** Algeria. **15** Barry Venison. **16** Wales. **17** 84. **18** Reading. **19** Gordon Lee & Jim Smith. **20** Neville Southall.

Quiz 102 **Extra Time 3**

Answers – see page 314

1 Who was involved in the incident that ended Paul Elliott's career?

2 What is Rod Wallace's middle name?

3 Who was the first goalkeeper to captain England?

4 Whose 1987 autobiography was called *Both Sides Of The Border*?

5 Nick Hancock is a fan of which club?

6 How old was Barry Venison when he first skippered a League Cup Final side?

7 Playing in the 1980s and 90s, Gary Mackay set a League appearance record at which Scottish club?

8 Where was Bob Wilson born?

9 In 1995, who described agents as "Dogs, worms, vermin"?

10 Suffolk Road and Norfolk Road go by whose ground?

11 Nick Pickering was at which club when he won his only England cap?

12 With 205 goals, Harry Johnson is the all-time top League scorer at which club?

13 To one each way, Mo Johnston scored how many international goals?

14 Who were the first Scottish club to play on artificial turf?

15 John White joined Tottenham Hotspur from which club?

16 Terry Fenwick was first capped playing for which club?

17 To two each way, how many internationals did Danny McGrain play?

18 Which player has scored most goals in World Cup final stages?

19 Who was the first person to play for and then manage Arsenal in FA Cup-winning teams?

20 Which team began their League career in the 1970s with a 3–3 home draw to Halifax?

Answers

Extra Time 5 (see Quiz 104)

1 Tom Dooley & Alexi Lalas. **2** Lauriston. **3** Jimmy Greaves. **4** Billy Walker. **5** Paul & Willie McStay. **6** Ipswich Town. **7** Middlesbrough. **8** Birmingham City. **9** Hibernian. **10** Luton Town. **11** Chelsea. **12** Ipswich Town. **13** 13. **14** Southampton. **15** Terry Venables. **16** Neil Webb & Chris Waddle. **17** Aston Villa. **18** Third. **19** Ten. **20** 66.

Quiz 103 **Extra Time 4**

LEVEL 3

Answers – see page 311

1. George Weah moved to Paris St Germain from which club?
2. What is David Unsworth's middle name?
3. Mark Hateley was first capped playing for which club?
4. Whose story appeared in the book *Only The Best Is Good Enough*?
5. David Nish was first capped playing for which club?
6. Who said, "I've no doubt that Alan Shearer's salary would make an ideal minimum for everyone"?
7. Playing in the 1960s and 1970s, John Shuker set a League appearance record at which club?
8. Vic Watson is all-time leading League scorer at which club?
9. What delayed the kick off in the 1992 League Cup semi between Tottenham Hotspur and Nottingham Forest?
10. Bloemfontein Road is by the ground of which club?
11. Who was Charlie George playing for when he won his only England cap?
12. In the 1980s and 90s, Ian Muir became the all-time top League scorer at which club?
13. To one each way, Jack Charlton scored how many international goals?
14. While with Notts County, Rachid Harkouk appeared for which country?
15. Which player made his England debut three weeks after his 30th birthday in September 1994?
16. Which country was Jock Stein playing in before he went to Celtic as a player?
17. To two each way, how many internationals did Ray Wilkins play?
18. Who was keeper Steve D'eath playing for when he set an English record of 1,103 minutes without letting a goal in?
19. As well as Kenny Dalglish, which other two managers have been at Blackburn Rovers and Newcastle Utd?
20. Which FA Cup Final man of the match drove straight home rather than attend the celebrations?

Answers

Extra Time 2 (see Quiz 101)

1 Steve Coppell. **2** Frank. **3** First England captain. **4** Mark Hateley. **5** Hungary. **6** Sheffield. **7** Airdrieonians. **8** Swansea City. **9** Gary Sprake. **10** Arsenal. **11** Barnsley. **12** Coventry City. **13** Charles Hughes. **14** Ron Harris & Peter Bonetti. **15** Dumfries. **16** White City. **17** Bruce Rioch. **18** 64. **19** Wladislaw Zmuda. **20** Brentford.

Quiz 104 **Extra Time 5**

LEVEL 3

Answers – see page 312

1 Who scored for America in the "Yanks 2 Planks 0" match of 1993?

2 What is Michael Thomas' middle name?

3 Which footballer's 1971 book was titled *Let's Be Honest*?

4 Who was manager of Nottingham Forest from 1939 to 1960?

5 Which pair of brothers played for the 1985 Scottish FA Cup winners?

6 Who came back with three goals in the last six minutes to draw 3–3 in a 1996 away game at Barnsley?

7 Playing in the early 20th century, Tim Williamson set a League appearance record at which club?

8 With which English club was Bertie Auld a League Cup winner?

9 Who were the first Scottish club to wear a company logo on their shirts?

10 Oak Road and Maple Road go past which club's ground?

11 Who was John Hollins playing for when he won his only England cap?

12 Ray Crawford is the all-time top League scorer at which club?

13 To one each way, Gerry Daly scored how many international goals?

14 Peter Shilton earned 49 of his international caps while at which club?

15 Who was the first player to represent England at all levels?

16 Who were the last two substitutes that Bobby Robson sent on for England?

17 Steve Hodge was first capped playing for which club?

18 In his World Cup Final hat-trick, which of his goals did Geoff Hurst score with his left foot?

19 How many World Cup goals did Teofilio Cubillas score for Peru?

20 To two each way, how many internationals did Brian Flynn play?

Answers

Extra Time 3 (see Quiz 102)

1 Dean Saunders. **2** Seymour. **3** Frank Swift. **4** Terry Butcher. **5** Stoke City. **6** 20. **7** Hearts. **8** Chesterfield. **9** Joe Kinnear. **10** Reading. **11** Sunderland. **12** Sheffield Utd. **13** 14. **14** Stirling Albion. **15** Falkirk. **16** QPR. **17** 62. **18** Gerd Müller. **19** George Graham. **20** Wimbledon.

Half-Time

If this was a football match, you'd all be trotting off to the touchline or dressing room for a cup of tea, oranges or some juice. But this is a quiz so your choice of lubrication can be more varied. Unless you want to flag late in the proceedings and blow any chance of victory, keep the alcohol level within reasonable proportions.

It is a time for you and your team to consider how things have gone, where you are strong, your weaknesses, how stupid table so-and-so is, etc. Unlike football matches, there is no tricky winger to stop, no centre forward to keep quiet, a well-disciplined offside trap to beat. There is always one very simple tactic in all quizzes, and it is one that never fails: get every question right.

You didn't think of that one. Oh, well, if you take that piece of information on board, at least the team-talk doesn't have to take too long.

It looks like the quiz-master is getting ready for the start of the second half, time to start concentrating again. Now who did score the opening goal in the 1874 FA Cup Final (no that isn't a question here)?

Second Half

Hope it was a good break. The second half will be easier in only one way and that is because you have an idea of what to expect – OK it may be the unexpected.

The format for the second half is the same as the first, but the questions are different; many of the topics will be similar, but as a famous question-master likes to say, "A question is only easy if you know the answer."

On balance, this first round of the second half should be easy, but if you don't know that Liverpool wear red shirts at home then working out their nickname might be a really tough question.

Serious football puzzlers might be offended at the simplicity of these questions, but very few people don't have some holes in their knowledge.

Quiz 1 **Who Did What?**

LEVEL 1

Answers – see page 31

1 Which team won the Premiership in 1999–2000?
2 Which team won the World Cup in 1998?
3 Which team won the FA Cup in 1999?
4 Which team won the European Super Cup in 1998?
5 Which team won the Worthington Cup in 2000?
6 Who was Footballer of the Year in 1999 in England?
7 Which team won Division One in 1999–2000?
8 Which team won Euro 96?
9 Which team finished bottom of the Premiership in 1999–2000?
10 Which team won the European Cup in 1999?
11 Which team won the World Cup in 1994?
12 Who scored the Premier League Goal of the Season for 1999–2000?
13 Who wrote *Fever Pitch*?
14 Which country hosted the World Cup in 1998?
15 Which countries staged Euro 2000?
16 Who scored the winning goal in the Euro 2000 final?
17 Which team won the Premiership in 1997–98?
18 Which team won the Scottish Premier League in 1997–98?
19 Who joined Real Madrid from Barcelona in summer 2000?
20 Which team won the UEFA Cup in 1999?

Answers

The Premier League (see Quiz 3)

1 Robbie Fowler. **2** Three. **3** Ipswich Town. **4** West Ham United. **5** Tottenham Hotspur. **6** Manchester United. **7** Newcastle United. **8** Leicester City. **9** Kevin Phillips **10** Charlton Athletic. **11** Arsenal. **12** Sunderland. **13** Everton. **14** The referee. **15** Dennis Bergkamp. **16** Aston Villa. **17** West Ham and Aston Villa. **18** Chelsea. **19** Coventry City. **20** Chelsea and Leeds.

Quiz 2 **Goals Galore 1**

LEVEL 1

Answers – see page 320

1. What is the record score in English football?
2. What is the record home win in a Premier League game?
3. Who beat Bury 10–0 in a League Cup game in 1983?
4. What was the score in the quarter-final between Holland and Yugoslavia in Euro 2000?
5. What is Chelsea's record win?
6. What is the record score in British football?
7. Who holds the record for England goals?
8. How many goals did he score for England?
9. Who holds the record for most international goals?
10. How many goals did he score?
11. Who beat Sheffield Wednesday 7–1 in March 1995?
12. Who holds the record for goals scored in FA Cup finals?
13. Who holds the record for hat-tricks scored in one season?
14. Who beat Fulham 10–0 in a League Cup game in 1986?
15. Who scored 306 goals in 559 appearances for Wolves?
16. Who scored 27 goals for Glasgow Rangers during season 1998–99?
17. Who scored a hat-trick for Italy in a World Cup game against Brazil in 1982?
18. Which team has scored most goals in a Premier League season?
19. How many goals did they score?
20. Who scored four times in an international match for West Germany v Switzerland?

Answers

Euro Football (see Quiz 4)

1 Belgium. **2** Coruna. **3** Real and Atletico Madrid. **4** Juventus. **5** Real Madrid. **6** Frankfurt. **7** Roma and Lazio. **8** Germany. **9** Inter Milan. **10** Valencia. **11** Barcelona. **12** Baggio. **13** Vigo. **14** Internazionale and AC Milan. **15** Eindhoven. **16** Lazio. **17** Yugoslavia. **18** Northern Ireland. **19** Channel 4. **20** Zinedine Zidane.

LEVEL 1

Quiz 3 The Premier League

Answers – see page 317

1 Which Liverpool player was fined after an alleged "cocaine-sniffing" goal celebration?

2 How many teams are relegated from the Premier League each season?

3 Which East Anglian team gained promotion to the Premier League in 1999–2000?

4 Which team had Steve Potts, Trevor Sinclair and Rio Ferdinand in their squad?

5 Whose 1999–2000 leading scorer was Steffen Iversen?

... won the Premier League the most times?

... team is managed by Bobby Robson?

... Izzett and Steve Guppy?

... scorer in 99–2000?

10 Which Premier League team plays at The Valley?

11 Euro 2000 winners Robert Pires, Thierry Henry and Patrick Vieira play for which Premier League team?

12 Which team had Niall Quinn, Alex Rea and Steve Bould in their squad?

13 Whose 1999–2000 leading scorer was Kevin Campbell?

14 Who did Paulo Di Canio push over to earn a suspension in 1999?

15 Which Arsenal striker is frightened of flying?

16 Which Premier League team is managed by John Gregory?

17 Which two Premier League teams play in claret and blue?

18 Ken Bates is the chairman of which Premier League team?

19 Which Premier League team have Hadji and Chippo in their squad?

20 For which two Premier League teams has Jimmy Floyd Hasselbaink played?

Answers

Who Did What? (see Quiz 1)

1 Manchester United. **2** France. **3** Manchester United. **4** Chelsea. **5** Leicester City. **6** David Ginola. **7** Charlton Athletic. **8** Germany. **9** Watford. **10** Manchester United. **11** Brazil. **12** Paolo Di Canio. **13** Nick Hornby. **14** France. **15** Holland and Belgium. **16** David Trezeguet. **17** Arsenal. **18** Celtic. **19** Luis Figo. **20** Parma.

Quiz 4 Euro Football

Answers – see page 318

LEVEL 1

1 Anderlecht have dominated which country's national league for the past 30 years?

2 Complete the Spanish League team name: Deportivo La... ?

3 Which two teams share Madrid's Bernabeu stadium?

4 Which Italian team played Liverpool in the tragic European Cup Final at H[illegible] Stadium?

5 For which Spanish team does England's Steve McM[illegible]

6 Complete the German league team name: [illegible]

7 What are the nam[illegible] two R[illegible]

8 The Bundesliga is the n[illegible] country's highest league?

9 Which Italian club did Robbie Keane sign for in summer 2000?

10 Which Spanish club played Real Madrid in the 2000 Champions League final: Valencia, Atletico Madrid or Barcelona?

11 Which Spanish club have Terry Venables and Bobby Robson both managed?

12 Which Roberto is known in Italy as "the divine ponytail"?

13 Complete the Spanish league team name: Celta... ?

14 What are the names of the two Milan teams?

15 Complete the Dutch league team name: PSV... ?

16 Which Italian team did Paul Gascoigne play for?

17 Partizan and Red Star are from which Eastern European country?

18 Glentoran and Crusaders play in which country's league?

19 Which English television channel broadcasts live Italian football?

20 Which Frenchman playing for Juventus was the 1998 European and World Footballer of the Year?

Answers

Goals Galore (see Quiz 2)

1 Preston North End 26 Hyde United 0. **2** Manchester United 9 Ipswich Town 0. **3** West Ham. **4** 6–1 to Holland. **5** 13–0 v Jeunesse Hautcharage, 1971. **6** Arbroath 36 Bon Accord 0. **7** Bobby Charlton. **8** 49. **9** Ferenc Puskas. **10** 83, for Hungary. **11** Blackburn Rovers. **12** Ian Rush (5). **13** Jimmy Greaves. **14** Liverpool. **15** Steve Bull. **16** Rod Wallace. **17** Paolo Rossi. **18** Manchester United. **19** 97. **20** Gerd Müller.

Quiz 5 Goalkeepers

Answers – see page 323

1 Who kept goal for England in the 1998 World Cup Finals?

2 Which French keeper did Manchester United buy in May 2000?

3 From which club did they buy him?

4 What nationality is Chelsea's Ed de Goey?

5 Who is the only English keeper with a World Cup winner's medal?

6 Which English keeper was beaten by Maradona's "Hand of God" goal?

7 What number do keepers traditionally wear?

8 Who saved John Aldridge's penalty in the 1988 FA Cup final?

9 Which keeper was sent off after 12 seconds of his first match of a season?

10 Which Russian goalkeeper was known as the "Black Panther"?

11 Which keeper was transferred from Wimbledon to Tottenham in 2000?

12 Who was Arsenal's Austrian keeper in 2000?

13 Who kept goal for England against Romania in Euro 2000?

14 Which club side does he play for?

15 Who did he play for before joining his present club?

16 Who does David James keep goal for?

17 Which keeper joined Manchester United from Villa in June 1999?

18 Which Dutch international keeper kept goal for Liverpool in the 2001 UEFA Cup Final?

19 Who keeps goal for Manchester City?

20 Which former keeper managed Italy in Euro 2000?

Answers

Memorable Matches (see Quiz 7)

1 Manchester United. **2** Arsenal. **3** 7–3 to Real. **4** West Germany. **5** Socrates and Julio Cesar. **6** Zinedine Zidane. **7** Iran. **8** France. **9** Germany. **10** Wimbledon. **11** Manchester United and Barcelona. **12** Nayim. **13** 1979. **14** 3–2 to Argentina. **15** Roma. **16** Carlisle United. **17** Cameroon. **18** 5–0. **19** Crystal Palace. **20** Argentina.

Quiz 6 **Manchester United**

LEVEL 1

Answers – see page 324

1 Where do Manchester United play home games?

2 What is Manchester United's nickname?

3 Who is Manchester United's most successful manager?

4 Who was Manchester United's regular captain at the end of the 90s?

5 Who was their top scorer in the 1999–2000 season?

6 How many goals did he score in total?

7 Who made the most appearances for United in that season?

8 Against whom was the biggest league crowd at Old Trafford of the 1999- 2000 season?

9 Who kept goal in the championship-clinching match of the 1999–2000 season?

10 Against whom was that match played?

11 Who knocked Manchester United out of the Champions League in the 1999–2000 season?

12 In what round were they knocked out?

13 Who did Manchester United beat in the Toyota Inter-Continental Cup?

14 Where do they come from?

15 Who scored the winning goal in that match?

16 Who did Manchester United play in the UEFA Super Cup?

17 Where was that match played?

18 What was the final score?

19 By how many points did Manchester United win the Premiership in the 1999–2000 season?

20 Who were the runners-up?

Answers

Division One (see Quiz 8)

1 Charlton Athletic. **2** Manchester City. **3** Ipswich Town. **4** Bolton Wanderers. **5** 5. **6** Jean Tigana. **7** Kent. **8** Prenton Park. **9** Sheffield. **10** Burnley. **11** Preston North End. **12** Graeme Souness. **13** The Canaries. **14** Bolton Wanderers. **15** Walsall, Port Vale and Swindon Town. **16** 1995. **17** The Endsleigh League. **18** Barnsley. **19** West Bromwich Albion. **20** 24.

Quiz 7 **Memorable Matches**

LEVEL 1

Answers – see page 321

1 Who beat Arsenal 2–1 in an FA Cup semi-final replay in April 1999?
2 Who won the First Division title in 1988–89 by beating Liverpool 2–0?
3 What was the score when Real Madrid met Eintracht Frankfurt in the European Cup final in 1960?
4 Who did Italy beat 4–3 after extra time in the 1970 World Cup semi-final?
5 Name the two Brazilians who both missed a penalty in their shootout against France in a 1986 World Cup quarter-final.
6 A golden goal penalty settled the Euro 2000 semi-final between France and Portugal. Who scored it?
7 Who beat the USA 2–1 in a politically-charged World Cup match in France in 1998?
8 Which team equalised in the 90th minute of the Euro 2000 final?
9 Who did England beat for the first time in 34 years during Euro 2000?
10 Who beat West Ham 4–3 at Upton Park in 1998 having been 3–0 down?
11 Which two teams drew 3–3 twice during the 1998–99 European Cup?
12 Whose goal sunk Arsenal in the 1995 European Cup Winners' Cup final?
13 In which year did Trevor Francis score the winner for Nottingham Forest in the European Cup final against Malmo?
14 What was the score in the 1986 World Cup final?
15 Who did Liverpool beat on penalties in the 1984 European Cup final?
16 Whose on-loan goalkeeper scored a last-minute winner to keep his temporary team in the football league in 1998–99?
17 Which team did England beat in the quarter-finals of the 1990 World Cup?
18 Chelsea thrashed Manchester United in October 1999 by what score?
19 After a 9–0 league loss, who beat Liverpool in the 1990 FA Cup semi-final?
20 Who beat England in Saint Etienne during the 1998 World Cup?

Answers

Goalkeepers (see Quiz 5)

1 David Seaman. **2** Fabien Barthez. **3** AS Monaco. **4** Dutch. **5** Gordon Banks. **6** Peter Shilton. **7** One. **8** Dave Beasant. **9** Sheffield Wednesday's Kevin Pressman. **10** Lev Yashin. **11** Neil Sullivan. **12** Alex Manninger. **13** Nigel Martyn. **14** Leeds United. **15** Bristol Rovers and Crystal Palace. **16** Aston Villa. **17** Mark Bosnich. **18** Sander Vesterveld. **19** Nicky Weaver. **20** Dino Zoff.

Quiz 8 **Division One**

Answers – see page 322

1 Who won the Division One title in 1999–2000?

2 Who were the runners-up?

3 Who were also promoted to the Premiership that season, via the play- offs?

4 Who did they beat in the play-off final?

5 How many London teams were there in Division One in 2000–01?

6 Which Fulham manager came from France?

7 In which county do Gillingham play their home games?

8 What is the name of Tranmere Rovers' ground?

9 Which city in Yorkshire had two teams in Division One in 2000–01?

10 Who plays at Turf Moor?

11 Who were promoted to Division One in 1999–2000 as champions of Division Two?

12 Who was the manager of Blackburn Rovers in 2000?

13 What is Norwich City's nickname?

14 Which Nationwide League team reached the semi-finals of the FA Cup in 1999–2000?

15 Which three clubs were relegated from Division One in 1999–2000?

16 When did the Nationwide League become the Nationwide League?

17 What was it previously called?

18 Who finished fourth in the league in 1999–2000?

19 Who escaped relegation by one place during 1999–2000?

20 How many teams are there in Division One?

Answers

Manchester United (see Quiz 6)

1 Old Trafford. **2** The Red Devils. **3** Sir Alex Ferguson. **4** Roy Keane. **5** Dwight Yorke. **6** 23. **7** Jaap Stam. **8** Tottenham Hotspur. **9** Raimond van der Gouw. **10** Southampton. **11** Real Madrid. **12** Quarter-finals. **13** SE Palmeiras. **14** Brazil. **15** Roy Keane. **16** SS Lazio. **17** Monaco. **18** Manchester United 0 SS Lazio 1. **19** 18 points. **20** Arsenal.

Quiz 9 **Continentals in England**

LEVEL 1

Answers – see page 327

1 Which temperamental Frenchman won the league with Leeds United and Manchester United?

2 Which former Chelsea player captained France to World Cup 98 and Euro 2000 glory?

3 Which West Ham United Italian pushed a referee to the ground when playing for Sheffield Wednesday?

4 Manchester United's Ole Gunnar Solskjaer hails from which country?

5 For which team does former Dynamo Kiev striker Sergei Rebrov play?

6 Tottenham's Gustavo Poyet is from which South American country?

7 American goalkeeper Kasey Keller played for which Premier League club?

8 Which former Premier League team fielded Moroccans Hadji and Chippo?

9 Which Georgian has played for Manchester City and Derby County?

10 From which country does Leeds United's Harry Kewell come?

11 Germans Dietmar Hamann and Markus Babbel appear for which Reds?

12 Middlesbrough's former star Christian Karembeu is from New Caledonia but plays international football for which country?

13 Peruvian Nolberto Solano appears in which team's striped shirts?

14 What is the surname of Southampton's Latvian Marian?

15 For which country does Chelsea's Jimmy Floyd Hasselbaink play?

16 French teammates Vieira and Pires play for which London club?

17 Which Romanian Dan went from Chelsea to Bradford City in the summer of 2000?

18 Which French exile went from Tottenham to Aston Villa in summer 2000?

19 What is the nationality of managers Arsene Wenger and Gerard Houllier?

20 For which country did Manchester United and Aston Villa goalkeeper Peter Schmeichel play?

Answers

Premier Stars (see Quiz 11)

1 Neville. **2** Redknapp. **3** Speed. **4** Scholes. **5** Coventry City, Leeds and Liverpool. **6** Kelly. **7** Heskey. **8** Sutton. **9** Bergkamp. **10** Wise. **11** Barmby. **12** Irwin. **13** Seaman. **14** Dalglish. **15** Sheringham. **16** Desailly. **17** Merson. **18** Le Tissier. **19** Owen. **20** Harte.

Quiz 10 Celebrity Fans

LEVEL 1

Answers – see page 328

1 Which absolutely fabulous celebrity is a Wimbledon fan?

2 Actress Catherine Zeta Jones shows a high fidelity to her home-town Swans. Who are they?

3 Who would have a south bank show at Arsenal?

4 Des Lynam rarely sees his south coast favourites live on TV. Name them.

5 Which East Anglian team cooks up a treat for TV's Delia Smith?

6 Former Prime Minister John Major supported the blues – which ones?

7 For which team does Nick Berry's heart beat like a hammer?

8 It's not difficult to guess professional Geordies Ant and Dec's team?

9 Who would athlete Steve Cram run to the North East to see?

10 Which club brought sunshine to the late great comedian Eric Morecambe?

11 It's nice to see Bruce Forsyth at White Hart Lane, watching which team?

12 Which comedian takes his "Funky Moped" to Birmingham City?

13 GMTV presenter Lorraine Kelly supports which orange-shirted Scottish side?

14 Foreign Secretary Jack Straw shares his first name with his team's steel magnate former chairman – which team?

15 Who has been framed watching the Gunners?

16 Boris Becker and Steffi Graf kick up a racket for which European side?

17 Of which team has disc jockey John Peel has been a long-time supporter?

18 Notting Hill isn't a million miles from Hugh Grant's favourite cottage.

19 Which London club do Jo Brand, Sean Hughes and Eddie Izzard go to for a laugh?

20 *A Question of Sport*'s John Parrott is true blue... but which club?

Answers

Transfers (see Quiz 12)

1 Luis Figo. **2** Real Madrid. **3** Jimmy Floyd Hasselbaink. **4** £15m. **5** Fabien Barthez. **6** Paulo Wanchope. **7** Christian Karembeu. **8** Paul Gascoigne. **9** Gary McAllister. **10** The Bosman Ruling. **11** Trevor Francis. **12** Johan Cruyff. **13** Ruud van Nistelrooy. **14** PSV Eindhoven. **15** Marseille. **16** Lyons. **17** Fiorentina. **18** Real Madrid. **19** Juventus. **20** Emile Heskey.

Quiz 11 **Premier Stars**

Answers – see page 325

1 Which Gary is a Manchester United and England defender?
2 Which Jamie's father used to manage West Ham?
3 Which Gary is a Newcastle and Wales midfielder?
4 Which Paul scored England's first goal in Euro 2000?
5 What are Gary McAllister's last three Premiership clubs?
6 Which Leeds Gary is a Republic of Ireland full-back?
7 Which Emile used to play for Leicester City?
8 Which Chris joined Celtic after disappointing at Chelsea?
9 Which Dennis is an Arsenal and Holland marksman?
10 Which Dennis left Chelsea for Leicester?
11 Which Nicky swapped Everton Blue for Liverpool Red?
12 Which Dennis has been Manchester United and the Republic of Ireland's Mr Reliable?
13 Which David has been England's No 1 for years?
14 Which Kenny managed Blackburn's Premiership winning team?
15 Which Teddy helped Manchester United to European Cup glory?
16 Which Marcel was one of France's Euro 2000 stars?
17 Which Paul has played for Arsenal, Middlesbrough, Aston Villa and England?
18 Which Matthew is affectionately called "Le God" at Southampton?
19 Which Michael is England's youngest ever goalscorer?
20 Which Ian is Leeds United's tough-tackling full-back?

Answers

Continentals in England (see Quiz 9)

1 Eric Cantona. **2** Didier Deschamps. **3** Paulo Di Canio. **4** Norway. **5** Tottenham Hotspur. **6** Uruguay. **7** Leicester City. **8** Coventry City. **9** Kinkladze. **10** Australia. **11** Liverpool. **12** France. **13** Newcastle United. **14** Pahars. **15** Holland. **16** Arsenal. **17** Petrescu. **18** David Ginola. **19** French. **20** Denmark.

Quiz 12 **Transfers**

LEVEL 1

Answers – see page 326

1 Who was the most expensive player in the world by the end of 2000?

2 Which club has paid the world's two biggest transfer fees?

3 Who is Chelsea's record signing?

4 How much did Chelsea pay Atletico Madrid for their star striker in June 2000?

5 Who joined Manchester United from Monaco in May 2000?

6 Which striker joined West Ham in 1999 and left for Manchester City in 2000?

7 Which World Cup winner joined Middlesbrough from Real Madrid in 2000?

8 Who left Middlesbrough for Everton in 2000?

9 Which veteran midfielder joined Liverpool from Coventry in 2000?

10 What is the name of the ruling that allows players to change clubs for free when out of contract?

11 Who was Britain's first million-pound transfer?

12 Who was the world's first million-pound transfer?

13 Whose injury in training delayed a proposed move to Manchester United by 12 months?

14 Which club was going to sell their star striker to Manchester United in 2000 and eventually did so in 2001?

15 From whom did Robert Pires join Arsenal?

16 Mark Vivien-Foe left West Ham for which club in 2000?

17 Gabriel Batistuta joined Roma from which club in 2000?

18 Which European club broke the world transfer record in summer 2001?

19 Which club received a world record transfer fee in 2001?

20 Who left Leicester for Liverpool in 1999–2000?

Answers

Celebrity Fans (see Quiz 10)

1 June Whitfield. **2** Swansea City. **3** Melvyn Bragg. **4** Brighton and Hove Albion. **5** Norwich City. **6** Chelsea. **7** West Ham. **8** Newcastle United. **9** Sunderland. **10** Luton Town. **11** Spurs. **12** Jasper Carrott. **13** Dundee United. **14** Blackburn Rovers. **15** Jeremy Beadle. **16** Bayern Munich. **17** Liverpool. **18** Fulham. **19** Crystal Palace. **20** Everton.

Quiz 13 **North East**

LEVEL 1

Answers – see page 331

1. What stadium does the Sunderland team illuminate?
2. In what colour shirts do Middlesbrough play?
3. Which former England captain was Middlesbrough's manager for seven years until July 2001?
4. "H'way the lads" is the rallying cry of which team?
5. With which North East lower league club did Brian Clough begin his managerial career?
6. Which club used to be spurred on by the "Roker roar"?
7. Who did Sunderland beat to win the FA Cup in 1973?
8. Which north-east club was managed by Argentinian Osvaldo Ardiles?
9. Which Republic of Ireland manager had spells in charge of Newcastle and Middlesbrough?
10. What did Hartlepools lose in 1968?
11. Whose supporters are known as "the Toon Army"?
12. Who are the Mackems?
13. Which North East lower league side are known as the Quakers?
14. Peter Reid is the manager of which club?
15. Which diminutive Brazilian starred for Middlesbrough?
16. Whose chairman resigned after making disparaging comments about the local womenfolk?
17. What colour shirts do Darlington and Newcastle United have in common?
18. Which Geordie left home to play for Spurs, Lazio, Rangers, Middlesbrough and Everton?
19. Who played for Liverpool, Hamburg, Southampton and Newcastle?
20. Which Geordie ex-sausage stuffer played for Newcastle, Tottenham, Marseille and Sheffield Wednesday?

Answers

Full-backs (see Quiz 15)

1 France. **2** Dixon. **3** Aston Villa. **4** Chelsea. **5** Republic of Ireland. **6** Phillip Neville. **7** Germany. **8** Missed a penalty in the shoot-out. **9** Brazil. **10** Ben Thatcher. **11** Stuart Pearce. **12** Liverpool. **13** Italy. **14** West Ham. **15** French. **16** George Burley. **17** Wing-backs. **18** Sir Alf Ramsey. **19** Graeme Le Saux. **20** Silvinho.

Quiz 14 **Euro Football 2**

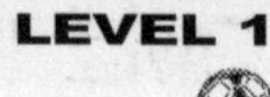

Answers – see page 332

1 Torino and which other Italian club are based in Turin?
2 Which Dutch team plays in white shirts with a wide red stripe?
3 Which Argentinian Gabriel was transferred from Fiorentina to Roma in May 2000?
4 Sparta and which other Dutch team are based in Rotterdam?
5 Which German team did Manchester United beat in the 1999 Champions League final?
6 In which country is the San Siro stadium?
7 Complete the German league team name: Hertha...?
8 Saint-Etienne and Lens play in which country's league?
9 In what colour shirts do Fiorentina play?
10 Which southern Italian team did Maradona inspire to the league and cup double in 1987?
11 In which city are French club PSG based?
12 2000 EUFA Cup winners Galatasaray are from which county?
13 Which European city completes the names of Spartak, Lokomotiv and CSKA?
14 Olympiakos and Panathinaikos hail from which European country?
15 Benfica and Porto are two of the biggest teams in which country?
16 What is the name of the top Italian league?
17 Bayern and 1860 are based in which European city?
18 Bohemians and Finn Harps play in which country's league?
19 Who was transferred from Dynamo Kiev to AC Milan for £15.7m in 1999?
20 Which Brazilian playing for Barcelona was the 1999 European and World Footballer of the Year?

Answers

The 70s (see Quiz 16)

1 Brazil. **2** George Best. **3** Bill Shankly. **4** Billy Bremner. **5** Sunderland. **6** Argentina. **7** Atkinson. **8** Arsenal. **9** Manchester City. **10** Johan Cruyff. **11** Bobby Moore. **12** Alan Ball. **13** Kenny Dalglish. **14** Chelsea. **15** West Germany. **16** Germany. **17** Brady. **18** Goalkeeper. **19** Poland. **20** Andy Gray.

Quiz 15 **Full-backs**

LEVEL 1

Answers – see page 329

1 Lillian Thuram scored two goals in a 1998 World Cup semi-final, for which country?
2 Which Lee is Arsenal's long-serving full-back?
3 England's Gareth Barry plays for which Premier League team?
4 Spanish international Albert Ferrer defended for which Blues?
5 For which country do Leeds United's Ian Harte and Gary Kelly play?
6 Which Manchester United full-back gave away the penalty to send England home from Euro 2000?
7 Tottenham's Christian Ziege played for which Euro 2000 team?
8 What was Michael Gray of Sunderland's fatal error in the 1998 play-offs?
9 Carlos Alberto was captain of which World Cup winning team?
10 Which full-back signed for Tottenham from Wimbledon in the summer of 2000?
11 Which England international full-back missed a penalty against Germany in the 1990 World Cup semi-final shoot-out, but made amends in 1996?
12 Norwegian Vegard Heggem plays for which Premier League team?
13 Paolo Maldini has been a regular full-back for which country?
14 Frank Lampard's father (also Frank Lampard) played for which team?
15 What nationality is Manchester United's Mikael Silvestre?
16 Which Ipswich manager and former player was a Scottish international?
17 What name is given to attacking full-backs in a five-man midfield?
18 Which 50s Tottenham full-back went on to become England's greatest manager?
19 Which Chelsea and England full-back has had run-ins with David Batty and Robbie Fowler?
20 Who is Brazil's former Arsenal full-back now at Celta Vigo?

Answers

The North East (see Quiz 13)

1 The Stadium of Light. **2** Red. **3** Bryan Robson. **4** Newcastle United. **5** Hartlepool. **6** Sunderland. **7** Leeds. **8** Newcastle United. **9** Jack Charlton. **10** An "s" (they became Hartlepool) **11** Newcastle United's. **12** Sunderland. **13** Darlington. **14** Sunderland. **15** Juninho. **16** Newcastle United. **17** Black and white. **18** Paul Gascoigne. **19** Kevin Keegan. **20** Chris Waddle.

Quiz 16 **The 70s**

LEVEL 1

Answers – see page 328

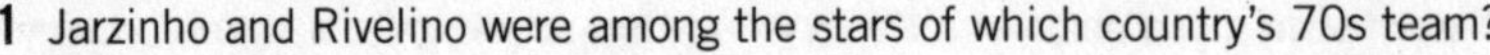

1 Jarzinho and Rivelino were among the stars of which country's 70s team?

2 Which Belfast boy left Manchester United in 1975 for a life of champagne, girls and some football in Fulham and the USA?

3 Which Liverpool manager retired in 1974 having taken his team to the top?

4 Which fiery Scotsman captained Leeds to FA Cup and League Championship success in the 70s?

5 Who sensationally beat Leeds in the 1973 FA Cup Final?

6 Ossie Ardiles and Ricardo Villa came from which country to Spurs?

7 Which Big Ron managed West Bromwich in the 70s?

8 For which club did Leeds manager David O'Leary play?

9 Lee, Bell and Summerbee were the stars of which top 70s English team?

10 Which great Dutch player helped Ajax win three European cups in the 70s before joining Barcelona?

11 Which legendary England captain joined Fulham in 1974 after nearly 20 years at West Ham?

12 Which England World Cup winner took his white boots to Arsenal in 1971?

13 Which King Kenny did Liverpool sign from Celtic in 1977?

14 Charlie Cooke and Peter Osgood were stars of which cup-winning team?

15 Gerd Müller scored the winner for which country in the 1974 World Cup Final?

16 In which foreign country did Kevin Keegan play during the 70s?

17 Which Liam was Arsenal and Ireland's creative force in the 70s?

18 In which position did Peter Shilton play for England during the 70s?

19 Which Eastern European country earned a draw at Wembley and prevented England from qualifying for the 1974 World Cup?

20 Which Sky-TV pundit played for Dundee United, Aston Villa, Wolves and Everton?

Answers

Euro Football 2 (see Quiz 14)

1 Juventus. **2** Ajax. **3** Batistuta. **4** Feyenoord. **5** Bayern Munich. **6** Italy. **7** Berlin. **8** France. **9** Purple. **10** Naples. **11** Paris. **12** Turkey. **13** Moscow. **14** Greece. **15** Portugal. **16** Serie A. **17** Munich. **18** Republic of Ireland. **19** Andriy Shevchenko. **20** Rivaldo.

Quiz 17 **Liverpool**

LEVEL 1

Answers – see page 335

1 What is the name of Liverpool's ground?

2 Which lager is advertised on the team's shirts?

3 Who did Liverpool sign for £11m from Leicester City in February 2000?

4 Liverpool's Patrick Berger plays for which national team?

5 Who was Liverpool's manager at the start of the 2000–01 season?

6 Which Liverpool striker scored a memorable goal for England against Argentina in the 1998 World Cup?

7 Which Scottish former Liverpool player was manager from 1985–91?

8 Which 80s Liverpool striker is Wales' record goalscorer?

9 Which Liverpool manager won six championships and three European Cups between 1974 and 1983?

10 Which player captained Liverpool, England and *A Question of Sport* teams?

11 Which Liverpool midfielder has missed three of England's major tournaments through injury?

12 What is written on the Liverpool club crest?

13 For which team did former keeper Sander Westerveld play in Euro 2000?

14 Which Red was named Footballer of the Year in 1988 and 1990?

15 Steve McManaman supported which team as a boy?

16 Which England midfielder joined Liverpool from Inter Milan in 1997?

17 Which former Liverpool player has been a manager of Newcastle United, Fulham and England?

18 Which team did Liverpool beat to win their third UEFA Cup?

19 Which former Liverpool striker was fined for displaying a T-shirt supporting sacked Liverpool dockers?

20 What is the first name of former Liverpool African star Camara?

Answers

Who Did What 2? (see Quiz 19)

1 Manchester United. **2** Lee Martin. **3** Lazio. **4** Chelsea. **5** Real Madrid. **6** Rangers. **7** Tottenham Hotspur. **8** Chelsea. **9** Nottingham Forest. **10** Dwight Yorke. **11** Peter Shilton. **12** Inter Milan. **13** Andy Cole. **14** Coventry City. **15** Ryan Giggs. **16** Denmark. **17** Bobby Moore. **18** Roberto Di Matteo. **19** Nantes **20** Wimbledon.

Quiz 18 European Cup

LEVEL 1

Answers – see page 336

1 Who won the Champions League in 2000?
2 Who did they beat in the final?
3 Which other Spanish club reached the semi-final stage?
4 Who were the last English club to win the Champions League?
5 The game was decided on a penalty shoot-out. True or false?
6 In which city did they win the final?
7 In what year did the European Cup start?
8 Who won the first competition?
9 Which English club has won the European Cup the most times?
10 How many times have they won it?
11 When did Manchester United win the European Cup for the first time?
12 Who did they beat in the final?
13 Where was the match played?
14 Which club have won the European Cup the most times?
15 How many times have they won it?
16 Who were the losing finalists in 1997 and 1998?
17 In which city do they play their home games?
18 Who were the last Dutch club to win the tournament?
19 When did they last win it?
20 Who were the last Eastern European team to win the tournament?

Answers

FA Cup Finals (see Quiz 20)

1 Chelsea. **2** Aston Villa. **3** Manchester United. **4** Ten times. **5** Arsenal. **6** Newcastle United. **7** Eric Cantona. **8** Roberto Di Matteo in 1997 after 43 seconds. **9** Sunderland. **10** Kevin Moran, Manchester Utd. **11** 1998. **12** Everton. **13** 1993 Arsenal v Sheffield Wednesday. **14** Manchester United 4, Chelsea 0. **15** 1994. **16** 1923. **17** Bolton Wanderers & West Ham United. **18** 2000. **19** 1872. **20** 1970.

Quiz 19 **Who Did What 2?**

LEVEL 1

Answers – see page 333

1 Who won the FA Cup in 1990?

2 Who scored the winning goal in that match?

3 Who won Serie A in 1999–2000?

4 Who won the European Cup Winners' Cup in 1998?

5 Who won the European Cup in 1998?

6 Who won the Tennent's Scottish Cup in 1999?

7 Who won the Worthington Cup in 1999?

8 Who won the Charity Shield in 2000?

9 Who finished bottom of the Premiership in 1998–99?

10 Who was the Premiership's leading scorer in 1998–99?

11 Who is the most capped England international?

12 Who won the UEFA Cup in 1998?

13 Who holds the record for number of goals scored in a Premiership match?

14 Who won the FA Cup in 1987?

15 Who scored a "wonder goal" to defeat Arsenal in the 1999 FA Cup semi-final replay?

16 Who won the European Championships in 1992?

17 Who captained England to World Cup glory in 1966?

18 Who scored the winning goal in the 2000 FA Cup final?

19 Which club won the French League in 2000–01?

20 Who were relegated from the Premiership in 1999–2000 along with Watford and Sheffield Wednesday?

Answers

Liverpool (see Quiz 17)

1 Anfield. **2** Carlsberg. **3** Emile Heskey. **4** The Czech Republic. **5** Gerard Houllier. **6** Michael Owen. **7** Kenny Dalglish. **8** Ian Rush. **9** Bob Paisley. **10** Emlyn Hughes. **11** Jamie Redknapp. **12** "You'll Never Walk Alone". **13** Holland. **14** John Barnes. **15** Everton. **16** Paul Ince. **17** Kevin Keegan. **18** Alaves. **19** Robbie Fowler. **20** Titi.

Quiz 20 **FA Cup Finals**

LEVEL 1

Answers – see page 334

1 Who won the FA Cup in 2000?

2 Who lost the 2000 FA Cup Final?

3 Which club have won the most FA Cups?

4 How many times have they won it?

5 Who won the FA Cup in 1998?

6 Who were the losing finalists in both 1998 and 1999?

7 Who scored the winning goal in the 1996 Final?

8 Who scored the quickest goal ever in an FA Cup Final?

9 Which was the last old Second Division (new First Division) club to appear in the FA Cup Final?

10 Who was the only player to be sent off in a 20th century FA Cup Final?

11 In which year were Marc Overmars and Nicolas Anelka Final goalscorers?

12 Who beat Manchester United in the 1995 Final?

13 Which was the last FA Cup Final decided on a replay?

14 What was the biggest victory in a Final during the nineties?

15 In which year was the biggest FA Cup Final win of the 1990s?

16 When was the first FA Cup final played at Wembley?

17 Which two teams contested the first FA Cup Final staged at Wembley?

18 When was the last FA Cup final at the "old" Wembley?

19 When was the first FA Cup final?

20 In which year was the first Wembley FA Cup final that went to a replay?

Answers

European Cup (see Quiz 18)

1 Real Madrid. **2** Valencia. **3** Barcelona. **4** Manchester United. **5** False. **6** Barcelona. **7** 1956. **8** Real Madrid. **9** Liverpool. **10** Four times. **11** 1968. **12** Benfica. **13** Wembley. **14** Real Madrid. **15** Eight times. **16** Juventus. **17** Turin. **18** Ajax Amsterdam. **19** 1995. **20** Red Star Belgrade.

Quiz 21 **Scottish Football**

LEVEL 1

Answers – see page 339

1 Which team plays home games at Ibrox Stadium?
2 What are the names of the two Edinburgh Premier League clubs?
3 What colour shirts do Aberdeen play in?
4 Which Henrik is Celtic's Swedish international striker?
5 Which Glasgow team is a Thistle?
6 Where are Scottish FA Cup finals traditionally played?
7 What is the name of Celtic's stadium?
8 Which Scottish city has two teams with grounds only 100 yards apart?
9 Which team won nine championships in a row in the 60s and 70s?
10 Which *A Question of Sport* captain is Rangers' record scorer?
11 Which Scottish manager led Aberdeen to glory before taking over at Manchester United?
12 Liam Brady, Kenny Dalglish and John Barnes have all been managers of which Scottish club?
13 Which Scottish team won nine championships in a row in the 70s and 80s?
14 What colour shirts do Hearts wear?
15 Which Scottish team are known as "the Hi-Bs"?
16 Which Scottish club plays at Pittodrie?
17 Which name groups Celtic and Rangers?
18 What sets Berwick Rangers apart from all other Scottish league teams?
19 Which English striker did Celtic buy from Chelsea before the 2000–01 season?
20 Which former Rangers and Scotland centre-forward went to Newcastle and Everton?

Answers

Midlands Clubs (see Quiz 23)

1 West Bromwich Albion. **2** Molineux. **3** Aston Villa. **4** West Bromwich Albion and Aston Villa, 10 times. **5** Birmingham City. **6** Wolves. **7** Division One. **8** David Jones. **9** Birmingham City. **10** The Hawthorns. **11** Birmingham. **12** Three: Birmingham, West Brom and Wolves. **13** Stoke. **14** Billy Wright. **15** Wolves. **16** Four: Aston Villa, Stoke, West Brom and Wolves. **17** Port Vale and Walsall. **18** Division Two. **19** Britannia Stadium. **20** Coventry City.

Quiz 22 England's World Cups

LEVEL 1

Answers – see page 340

1 Which round did England get to in the 1990 World Cup?

2 Who scored in the first minute against France in the 1982 World Cup?

3 Whose two goals put England out of the 1986 World Cup?

4 Who won the Golden Boot for most goals in the 1986 World Cup?

5 Which England keeper was known as Shilts?

6 Which influential player did Sir Alf Ramsey substitute when England were winning 2–0 against West Germany in Mexico 70?

7 Which African nation did England beat to reach the semi-finals in 1990?

8 Who scored England's penalty against Argentina in the 1998 World Cup?

9 Which Premier League team boss was manager of England during the 1986 and 1990 World Cups?

10 From which World Cup did England exit after penalty misses by Stuart Pearce and Chris Waddle?

11 Who was accused of stealing a bracelet prior to Mexico 70?

12 Where did England play Argentina in France 98: St Etienne or Lens?

13 Who cried after being booked against Germany in 1990?

14 Who scored the disallowed "golden goal" against Argentina in France 98?

15 Which South American nation did England defeat in the 1998 World Cup?

16 Which England goalkeeper made "the save of the century" against Brazil in Mexico 70?

17 Which then-Chelsea player scored the winning goal for Romania against England in 1998?

18 Who scored with a last-minute volley against Belgium in 1990?

19 In which year did England play France, Czechoslovakia, Kuwait, West Germany and Spain?

20 Which England goal in the 1966 Final was confirmed by a linesman?

Answers

Memorable Matches 2 (see Quiz 24)

1 Geli (of Alaves, an own goal). **2** The European Championships. **3** Kenny Dalglish. **4** Dave Beasant. **5** Munich 1860. **6** Internazionale Milan. **7** 4–1. **8** West Germany. **9** 2–1 to Holland. **10** Germany. **11** Holland. **12** Juventus. **13** England. **14** Manchester United. **15** Peter Shilton. **16** 2–2. **17** West Germany. **18** Spain. **19** Charlie George. **20** Gillingham.

Quiz 23 **Midlands Clubs**

LEVEL 1

Answers – see page 337

1 Which club is known as "The Baggies"?

2 Where do Wolves play?

3 Which Midlands club appeared in the 2000 FA Cup final?

4 Which Midlands clubs have appeared in the most FA Cup finals?

5 Who plays at St Andrews?

6 Which Midlands club won the FA Cup in 1960?

7 In which division did Walsall play in 2001–02?

8 Who was the manager of Wolves in at the start of the 2001–02 season?

9 Which Midlands club finished highest in the Nationwide League in 1999–2000?

10 What is the name of West Brom's home ground?

11 In which city do Aston Villa play their home games?

12 How many Midlands clubs were there in Division One in the 2000–01 season?

13 In which city do Port Vale play their home games?

14 Which legendary Midlands player skippered England 70 times?

15 Which club did he play for?

16 How many Midlands clubs were original members of the Football League?

17 Which two Midlands Nationwide League clubs were relegated in 2000?

18 In which division did Stoke City play in 2001–02?

19 What is the name of their ground?

20 Which was the last Midlands club to win the FA Cup?

Answers

Scottish Football (see Quiz 21)

1 Rangers. **2** Hibernian (Hibs) and Heart of Midlothian (Hearts). **3** Red. **4** Larsson. **5** Partick Thistle. **6** Hampden Park. **7** Celtic Park. **8** Dundee. **9** Celtic. **10** Ally McCoist. **11** Alex Ferguson. **12** Celtic. **13** Rangers. **14** Maroon. **15** Hibernian. **16** Aberdeen. **17** The Old Firm. **18** Their ground is in England. **19** Chris Sutton. **20** Duncan Ferguson.

Quiz 24 **Memorable Matches 2**

LEVEL 1

Answers – see page 338

1 Who scored the winner in the 2001 UEFA Cup Final?

2 In which tournament did France beat Portugal in a semi-final in 1984?

3 Who scored the winner for Liverpool in the 1978 European Cup final?

4 Who saved a penalty to help Wimbledon win the FA Cup final in 1988?

5 Who did Leeds beat to qualify for the Champions League proper in August 2000?

6 Celtic beat which Italian giants to win the European Cup in 1967?

7 What was the score when Manchester United beat Benfica in the 1968 European Cup final?

8 Who did Holland play in the European Championship semi-final in 1988?

9 What was the score in that match?

10 Who beat England in the 1990 World Cup semi-final?

11 Who did England beat 4–1 in the Euro 96 group stage?

12 Who did Manchester United defeat in the 1999 Champions League semi-final?

13 Who lost 3–2 to Romania in the group stages of Euro 2000?

14 Who beat Liverpool with a last-minute goal in the FA Cup fourth round in 1999?

15 Who kept goal for England in the "Hand of God" World Cup match?

16 What was the score when Chelsea met Leeds in the 1970 FA Cup final at Wembley?

17 Who knocked England out of the 1970 World Cup?

18 Who did England beat in a penalty shoot-out in the quarter-finals of Euro 96?

19 Whose goal against Liverpool in 1971 won Arsenal the FA Cup?

20 Manchester City beat who in the 1998–99 First Division play-off final?

Answers

England's World Cups (see Quiz 22)

1 Semi-finals. **2** Bryan Robson. **3** Diego Maradona. **4** Gary Lineker. **5** Peter Shilton. **6** Bobby Charlton. **7** Cameroon. **8** Alan Shearer. **9** Bobby Robson. **10** 1990. **11** Bobby Moore. **12** St Etienne. **13** Paul Gascoigne. **14** Sol Campbell. **15** Colombia. **16** Gordon Banks. **17** Dan Petrescu. **18** David Platt. **19** 1982. **20** The third.

Quiz 25 **Grounds**

LEVEL 1

Answers – see page 343

1 Who does battle at Stamford Bridge?

2 Ibrox Stadium is home to which great champions?

3 Which country plays internationals at Windsor Park?

4 Who moved into the Stadium of Light in 1997?

5 Everton play their home games at which ground?

6 The Arsenal Stadium is commonly referred to as... ?

7 Who plays at Highfield Road?

8 In which city is Wales' Millennium Stadium?

9 Crystal Palace and Wimbledon both play at which Park?

10 Down which lane would you find Tottenham Hotspur?

11 Which Reds play at Anfield?

12 Where is Manchester United's theatre of dreams?

13 Who moved home from Ayresome Park to The Riverside?

14 Which country plays internationals at Hampden Park?

15 Which stadium was famous for its twin towers?

16 Who played at The Dell from 1898 to 2001?

17 Leeds United strut their stuff at which ground?

18 Hillsborough is home to which Yorkshire team?

19 Which national team in green plays at Landsdowne Road?

20 Who plays at the Nou Camp: Barcelona, Real Madrid or AC Milan?

Answers

The 80s (see Quiz 27)

1 David Platt. **2** Ray Wilkins. **3** Glenn Hoddle. **4** Mark Hughes. **5** Vinny Jones. **6** Newcastle Utd **7** Gary Lineker. **8** Ian Rush. **9** Gary Mabbutt. **10** Belgium. **11** Celtic. **12** Diego Maradona **13** Manchester United. **14** Liverpool. **15** Marco Van Basten. **16** Bryan Robson. **17** Graeme Souness **18** Everton. **19** Brighton. **20** Scored for both sides.

Quiz 26 **Newcastle United**

LEVEL 1

Answers – see page 344

1 At which stadium do Newcastle United play?

2 What is Newcastle's nickname?

3 Which England captain was Newcastle's leading scorer in 1999–2000?

4 Who is Newcastle United's manager?

5 Who was their dreadlocked Dutch manager?

6 Who beat Newcastle in the 1999 Cup final?

7 Which now former England manager helped to take Newcastle into the top flight as player and later as manager?

8 Which former Manchester Utd striker was once Newcastle's leading goalscorer?

9 What colour shirts do Newcastle play in?

10 Which Kieron did Newcastle United sign from Ipswich in 1999?

11 Which Les left Newcastle for Tottenham in 1997?

12 Which England under–21 striker did Newcastle United sign from Wimbledon for £7m?

13 Which Duncan partnered Alan Shearer in the Newcastle United attack?

14 What was the real name of "Wor Jackie" who scored 179 League goals for Newcastle United?

15 What is the unofficial Newcastle supporters anthem?

16 Which classy England international striker returned to Newcastle as the on-field inspiration of the Keegan era?

17 Who are Newcastle's arch-rivals?

18 Who beat Newcastle in the 1998 FA Cup Final?

19 Which Newcastle United Robert is an England international and is nicknamed "Lurker"?

20 Which Sir John developed the Durham Metro Centre and Newcastle as a Premier League outfit?

Answers

David Beckham (see Quiz 28)

1 London. **2** Seven. **3** Colombia. **4** Spice Girls. **5** He shot from his own half. **6** Argentina. **7** Brooklyn. **8** Nursing his sick son. **9** Got sent off. **10** Third. **11** Second. **12** 1997. **13** Brylcreem. **14** George Best. **15** Preston. **16** Gary Neville. **17** Sarong. **18** An Angel. **19** His hair was cropped. **20** Ferraris.

Quiz 27 **The 80s**

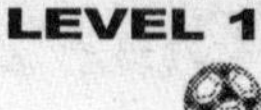

Answers – see page 341

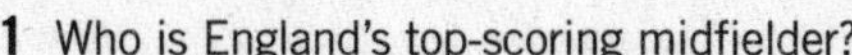

1 Who is England's top-scoring midfielder?

2 Which Manchester Utd and AC Milan midfielder was sent off for throwing the ball at the referee in an England World Cup game in 1986?

3 Of which Tottenham and England midfielder did Jasper Carrott say "I hear he's found God, that must have been one hell of a pass"?

4 Which "Sparky" was at Manchester United and Barcelona in the 80s?

5 Which hod carrier turned footballer turned film star made his name at Wimbledon in the 80s?

6 Which team had Waddle, Keegan and Beardsley in their 80s line-up?

7 Which forward scored a hat-trick against Poland in the World Cup in 1986?

8 Who was Liverpool's ace striker throughout the 80s, apart from one season he spent at Juventus?

9 Who was the Tottenham captain who lifted the UEFA Cup in 1984?

10 In which country was the 1985 European Cup Final between Liverpool and Juventus in which 39 people were killed?

11 Scotland's Paul McStay stayed with which club throughout the 80s?

12 Which Argentinian destroyed England in the 1986 World Cup?

13 Who had McGrath, Strachan and Whiteside in their line-up in the 80s?

14 Lawrenson and Hansen were at the heart of which defence in the 80s?

15 Which Dutch Marco was European Footballer of the Year in 88 and 89?

16 Which Premier League manager was then Manchester United's captain?

17 Who was Liverpool and Sampdoria's midfield hardman?

18 Neville Southall played for which FA Cup and championship-winning side?

19 Which south coast team reached the FA Cup final in 1983?

20 Gary Mabbutt and Tommy Hutchison managed what unusual feat in 80s FA Cup Finals?

Answers

Grounds (see Quiz 25)

1 Chelsea. **2** Rangers. **3** Northern Ireland. **4** Sunderland. **5** Goodison Park. **6** Highbury. **7** Coventry City. **8** Cardiff. **9** Selhurst. **10** White Hart. **11** Liverpool. **12** Old Trafford. **13** Middlesbrough. **14** Scotland. **15** Wembley. **16** Southampton. **17** Elland Road. **18** Sheffield Wednesday. **19** Republic of Ireland. **20** Barcelona.

Quiz 28 **David Beckham**

LEVEL 1

Answers – see page 342

1 David Beckham was born in which city?

2 In what number shirt does he play at Manchester United?

3 Against which team did he score from a free-kick in the 1998 World Cup: Colombia, Argentina or France?

4 Which pop group was David Beckham's wife a member of?

5 What was special about his goal against Wimbledon in 1996?

6 Against which country was Beckham sent off in the 1998 World Cup?

7 What is the name of David Beckham's son?

8 What excuse did David give for missing Manchester Utd training in 1999?

9 What did David do in the 2000 World Club Championship against Necaxa?

10 Where did David finish in *The Sun*'s 1999 poll of hunkiest men?

11 Where did David finish in the voting for FIFA World Player of the Year in 1999 and 2001?

12 In which year was Beckham voted Young Player of the Year?

13 Which 1950s hair product did David officially endorse in 1997?

14 Who said "Beckham's passing isn't great, his heading is negligible and he doesn't score enough goals – apart from that, he's not too bad!"?

15 In March 1995 Beckham went on loan to which club: Preston, Manchester City or West Ham?

16 Who was Beckham's best man? Gary Neville, Phil Neville or Diego Simeone?

17 What item of "women's" clothing was Beckham pictured wearing during the 1998 World Cup?

18 What tattoo does Beckham sport: a Red Devil or an Angel?

19 What changed about David's appearance during the 1999–2000 season?

20 Becks prefers which: Porsches, Ferraris or Volkswagen Beetles?

Answers

Newcastle United (see Quiz 26)

1 St James' Park. **2** The Magpies. **3** Alan Shearer. **4** Bobby Robson. **5** Ruud Gullit. **6** Manchester United. **7** Kevin Keegan. **8** Andy Cole. **9** Black and white stripes. **10** Kieron Dyer. **11** Les Ferdinand. **12** Carl Cort. **13** Duncan Ferguson. **14** Jackie Milburn. **15** "Blaydon Races". **16** Peter Beardsley. **17** Sunderland. **18** Arsenal. **19** Robert Lee. **20** Sir John Hall.

Quiz 29 **Pop and Football**

LEVEL 1

Answers – see page 347

1 Scottish side Clydebank are sponsored by which soggy pop group?
2 Which pop star, confused about his weight, put his record label on Brighton and Hove Albion's shirts?
3 Led Zeppelin's Robert Plant follows which Wanderers?
4 He wears funny glasses but he takes his football seriously. Who?
5 Rod Stewart would cross stormy waters to see which Scottish team?
6 John Barnes did the "Anfield Rap" for which club in 1988?
7 Madness singer Suggs wrote "Blue Day" for which London club?
8 "We Have A Dream" was which country's World Cup anthem in 1982?
9 Why does pop violinist Nigel Kennedy wear claret and blue underpants?
10 "I'm Forever Blowing Bubbles" was the Cockney Rejects' paen to which team?
11 Pop group Oasis's Gallagher brothers follow which Premier League 2000 newcomers?
12 "World in Motion" was New Order's hit intended to inspire which team?
13 Robbie Williams likes his football at the Vale – who's he supporting?
14 "Nice One… "? Who was the focus of the Spurs fans song in 1973?
15 Mick Hucknall is simply red, but which red-shirted team?
16 Which Argentinian's knees had gone "all trembly" in a Chas and Dave hit?
17 "Back Home" was a hit record for which England World Cup squad: 1970, 1974 or 1986?
18 Who were the Glenn and Chris who recorded "Diamond Lights" in 1987?
19 What "is the colour" in a 1972 hit football record?
20 Which North London singing duet – known by their first names – wrote and sang on "Ozzie's Going to Wembley"?

Answers

Arsenal (see Quiz 31)

1 Liverpool. **2** N5. **3** George Graham. **4** 1997–98. **5** 1970–71. **6** Kenny Sansom. **7** David O'Leary. **8** Ian Wright. **9** Middlesbrough. **10** Manchester United. **11** Alan Sunderland. **12** Seven times. **13** Parma. **14** Alan Smith. **15** Zaragoza. **16** Internazionale. **17** Nigel Winterburn. **18** 1993. **19** Sheffield Wednesday. **20** 1886.

Quiz 30 **TV and Football**

LEVEL 1

Answers – see page 348

1 *Football Focus* is which channel's football magazine programme?
2 Which England player and Republic of Ireland manager has presented TV programmes on fishing?
3 What is the name of Sky TV's football-based soap opera?
4 What was unique about television coverage of the 1985–86 season from August to December?
5 How many million viewers watched ITV's coverage of the 1998 World Cup match between England and Argentina? 18m, 22m or 26m?
6 An episode of which classic 70s comedy series showed our heroes desperately avoiding hearing the result of an England match?
7 Supposed Premier League foreigner Julio Geordio appeared on which show?
8 *Boys From The Blackstuff* featured footballers from which club?
9 Which TV fun quiz takes its name from Kenneth Wolstenholme's commentary in the 1966 World Cup?
10 Which ex-Tottenham player has presented TV sports and current affairs?
11 Which daughter of a Leeds United and Wales player presented ITV's Premier League highlights programme on Saturday night in 2001?
12 Who entered *Celebrity Stars in their Eyes* in 1999 as Sacha Distel?
13 ITV football presenter Bob Wilson played for which club?
14 Which imaginary local team do the characters in *EastEnders* support?
15 Which team did comedy cockney bigot Alf Garnett support?
16 Which ex-Wimbledon striker presented *Gladiators*?
17 Frank Skinner and David Baddiel presented which football-related show?
18 Which ex-England manager co-created the BBC TV series *Hazell*?
19 Which former footballer presented *Friday Night's All Wright*?
20 TV drama *My Summer With Des* referred to which football presenter?

Answers

Goals Galore 2 (see Quiz 32)

1 Alan Shearer. **2** Eric Cantona. **3** Patrick Kluivert. **4** Kevin Phillips. **5** Chris Sutton. **6** Kevin Campbell. **7** Thierry Henry. **8** Gianfranco Zola. **9** Ole Gunnar Solskjaer. **10** Ricky Villa. **11** Mario Stanic. **12** Delvecchio. **13** Rivaldo. **14** Bury 6 Derby County 0, 1903. **15** Steve McManaman. **16** Gordon Durie. **17** Real Madrid. **18** Eintracht Frankfurt. **19** 7–3. **20** Ole Gunnar Solskjaer.

Quiz 31 **Arsenal**

LEVEL 1

Answers – see page 345

1 Who did Arsenal beat in their opening home game of the 2000–01 season?
2 In which London postal district do Arsenal play?
3 Who was Arsenal manager from 1986 to 1995?
4 When did Arsenal last win the double?
5 When did Arsenal first win the double?
6 Who is Arsenal's most capped player?
7 Who has made most league appearances?
8 Who is Arsenal's post-World War 2 record goalscorer?
9 Who did Arsenal beat 6–1 away in April 1999?
10 Who did Arsenal beat with a last-minute goal in the 1979 FA Cup final?
11 Who scored the winning goal in that match?
12 How many times have Arsenal won the FA Cup?
13 Who did Arsenal beat in the 1994 European Cup Winners' Cup final?
14 Who scored Arsenal's match winner the last time they won a European competition?
15 Who beat Arsenal the last time they played in the European Cup-winners Cup Final?
16 From whom did Arsenal sign Dennis Bergkamp?
17 Which Arsenal full-back joined West Ham in summer 2000?
18 In which year did Arsenal win both the FA Cup and the Coca-Cola Cup?
19 They played the same team in both finals. Which team?
20 In which year were Arsenal formed?

Answers

Pop and Football (see Quiz 29)

1 Wet, Wet, Wet. **2** Fatboy Slim. **3** Wolverhampton. **4** Elton John. **5** Celtic. **6** Liverpool. **7** Chelsea. **8** Scotland. **9** He supports Aston Villa. **10** West Ham. **11** Manchester City. **12** England. **13** Port Vale. **14** Cyril (Knowles). **15** Manchester United. **16** Ossie (Ardiles). **17** 1970. **18** Hoddle and Waddle. **19** Blue. **20** Chas & Dave.

Quiz 32 **Goals Galore 2**

LEVEL 1

Answers – see page 346?

1 Who scored twice for Newcastle in the 1999 FA Cup semi-final?

2 Who scored two penalties for Manchester Utd in the 1994 FA Cup final?

3 Who scored four goals for Holland in the Euro 2000 quarter-final against Yugoslavia?

4 Who scored 30 goals for Sunderland in season 1999–2000?

5 Who scored on his debut for Celtic after his £7m transfer from Chelsea in summer 2000?

6 Whose goals kept Everton in the Premier League in 1998–99?

7 Which Frenchman scored 26 goals for Arsenal in 1999–2000?

8 Who scored Chelsea's winner in the 1998 Cup Winners' Cup final?

9 Who scored Manchester Utd's winner in the 1999 Champions League final?

10 Who scored the winning goal in the 100th FA Cup final, in 1981?

11 Who scored twice for Chelsea on his debut against West Ham in August 2000?

12 Whose goal put Italy one up against France in the Euro 2000 final?

13 Who scored twice for Barcelona against Manchester United in November 1998?

14 What is the record victory in an FA Cup final?

15 Who scored twice for Liverpool in the 1995 League Cup final against Bolton?

16 Who scored a hat-trick for Rangers in a 5–1 thrashing of Hearts in the 1996 Scottish FA Cup final?

17 Who won the European Cup in 1960 in Glasgow?

18 Who were their opponents in the final?

19 What was the score in that match?

20 Who scored four goals as Manchester United beat Everton in December 1999?

Answers

TV and Football (see Quiz 30)

1 BBC 1. **2** Jack Charlton. **3** *Dream Team.* **4** There was none. **5** 26 million. **6** *Whatever Happened To The Likely Lads.* **7** *The Fast Show.* **8** Liverpool. **9** *They Think It's All Over.* **10** Garth Crooks. **11** Gaby Logan (Yorath). **12** David Ginola. **13** Arsenal. **14** Walford. **15** West Ham. **16** John Fashanu. **17** *Fantasy Football League.* **18** Terry Venables. **19** Ian Wright. **20** Des Lynam.

Quiz 33 **Who Did What? 3**

LEVEL 1

Answers – see page 351

1 Which team lost both the Scottish FA Cup and League Cup finals in 2000?

2 Who took over as manager of Celtic in summer 2000?

3 Who retired from International football after Euro 2000, having scored 30 goals for England?

4 Who scored with his first touch as an England substitute in an October 2001 World Cup qualifying match?

5 Who returned to Holland after managing Chelsea and Newcastle United?

6 Who were relegated to Division One in 2000 after 14 years in the top division?

7 Who were knocked out of Euro 2000 semi finals by a Golden Goal penalty?

8 Who scored England's second goal in the 1966 World Cup Final?

9 Who kept goal for Manchester United and was Denmark's captain?

10 Who moved back to The Valley after seven years of sharing a ground with Crystal Palace?

11 Who shocked the world by beating Italy in the World Cup in 1994?

12 Who held the FA Cup aloft with one hand and his baby with the other?

13 Who played for Turkey in Euro 2000 despite being born in London?

14 Who joined Everton from Monaco in 1998?

15 Who had his floppy locks shaved off during Manchester United's 1999–2000 campaign?

16 Who won 5–0 in Turkey but still were eliminated from the 1999–2000 Champions League?

17 Who received a ban for spitting in the 1999–2000 season?

18 When Eric Cantona assaulted a fan at Selhurst Park, were Manchester United playing Wimbledon or Crystal Palace?

19 Which two countries played in the last international at Wembley stadium?

20 Who was knighted after his team completed a famous treble?

Answers

South America (see Quiz 35)

1 Diego Maradona. **2** Yellow with green trimmings. **3** Ardiles. **4** Light blue and white stripes. **5** Argentina. **6** Pele. **7** Manchester United. **8** His corkscew hair-do. **9** Middlesbrough. **10** Barcelona. **11** Mexico. **12** Ronaldo. **13** Chile. **14** Arsenal. **15** Colombia. **16** Newcastle United. **17** Batistuta. **18** Socrates. **19** Winning it three times. **20** Gustavo Poyet.

Quiz 34 England in Europe

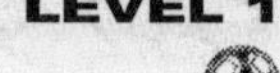

Answers – see page 352

1 Who were England's first opponents in the Euro 2000 finals?

2 What was the score in that match?

3 Who were the only team beaten by England in those finals?

4 Who scored England's winning goal in that match?

5 Who beat England in the semi-final of Euro 96?

6 Who were England's first opponents in the Euro 96 finals?

7 What was the score in that match?

8 Who scored England's second goal against Scotland at Wembley in Euro 96?

9 Who saved a penalty for England in that same match?

10 Who scored England's first goal in the Euro 2000 finals?

11 Who was England's manager during Euro 96?

12 Who did England play in the quarter-finals of Euro 96?

13 The quarter-finals of Euro 96 were played at Wembley, Villa Park, Anfield and which other ground?

14 England's Euro 96 group featured Scotland, Switzerland and which other country?

15 Who beat England in the final group match of Euro 2000?

16 Who gave away a penalty in that same match?

17 Which was the only team to beat England in Euro 92?

18 What was the score in that match?

19 Who scored the winning goal?

20 Which rule was introduced in the quarter-finals of Euro 96?

Answers

Anything But Football (see Quiz 36)

1 Harry Kewell. **2** *Escape to Victory.* **3** Eric Cantona. **4** David Ginola. **5** They are cartoon characters. **6** Margaret Thatcher. **7** David Beckham. **8** Alan Shearer. **9** Vinny Jones. **10** George Best. **11** A fish. **12** Modelling. **13** Diana Ross. **14** Gary Lineker. **15** *Gregory's Girl.* **16** Pizza. **17** *Fever Pitch.* **18** Louise. **19** Gerry and the Pacemakers. **20** Gordon Ramsey.

Quiz 35 **South America**

LEVEL 1

Answers – see page 349

1 Which Argentinian scored the "Hand of God" goal against England in the 1986 World Cup?

2 In what colour shirts do Brazil play?

3 The Argentinian who played for and managed Spurs is called Ossie...

4 In which colour shirts do Argentina play?

5 Claudio Lopez, Diego Simone and Juan Veron play for which country?

6 Perhaps the world's greatest ever player, Edson Arantes do Nascimento has a more commonly used four-letter name. What is it?

7 Which English team played in the first World Club Championship?

8 What feature distinguished Carlos Valderrama from his teammates?

9 South Americans Emerson, Juninho and Ricard have all played for which club in the North East?

10 Brazilian Rivaldo plays for which Spanish giants?

11 Which Central American country hosted the 1970 and 1986 World Cup?

12 Which Brazilian forward cost Inter Milan £18 million in 1997?

13 Lazio's Marcelo Salas hails from which South American country?

14 Brazilian Silvinho plays for which Premier League team?

15 Andres Escobar was murdered after scoring an own-goal when playing for which South American country in the 1994 World Cup?

16 South Americans Mirandinha, Asprilla and Solano have all played for which club in the North East?

17 Which Argentinian arch-marksman Gabriel earned Fiorentina £22 million from Roma?

18 Who was one of Brazil's great players: Plato, Socrates or Descartes?

19 Why did Brazil get to keep the Jules Rimet Trophy?

20 Which Uruguayan moved from Chelsea to Tottenham in 2001?

Answers

Who Did What? 3 (see Quiz 33)

1 Aberdeen. **2** Martin O'Neill. **3** Alan Shearer. **4** Teddy Sheringham. **5** Ruud Gullit. **6** Wimbledon. **7** Portugal. **8** Martin Peters. **9** Peter Schmeichel. **10** Charlton Athletic. **11** Republic of Ireland. **12** Dennis Wise. **13** Muzzy Izzet. **14** John Collins. **15** David Beckham. **16** Chelsea. **17** Patrick Vieira. **18** Crystal Palace **19** England and Germany. **20** Sir Alex Ferguson.

Quiz 36 **Anything But Football**

LEVEL 1

Answers – see page 350

1 Which Leeds star was engaged to *Emmerdale* barmaid Sheree Murphy?
2 Which film starred Sylvester Stallone and featured a football team escaping from a World War II POW camp?
3 Which footballer had a role in the feature film *Elizabeth*?
4 Which French player works for the UN campaign to ban land mines?
5 What does Roy Race have in common with Dennis the Menace?
6 Which Prime Minister tried to introduce ID cards for football supporters?
7 Which footballer is married to a former Spice Girl?
8 Which former England captain appeared in television advertisements for an American hamburger chain?
9 Which footballer had roles in the feature films *Lock, Stock and Two Smoking Barrels* and *Snatch*?
10 Which great 60s Northern Ireland footballer vowed to give up alcohol after being admitted to hospital in 2000?
11 Billy plays in goal in a *Viz* comic strip. What kind of animal is he?
12 Middlesbrough player Christian Karembeu's wife Adriana is associated with which profession?
13 Which American singer began 1994 World Cup by missing a penalty?
14 *An Evening with...* which presenter was a hit West End theatre show?
15 Which 1980 Scottish film featured a boy's infatuation with the female star of his school football team?
16 What kind of food did Pearce, Waddle and Southgate advertise?
17 Which Nick Hornby book and film featured his relationship with Arsenal?
18 Which former Eternal pop star has been linked with Jamie Redknapp?
19 "You'll Never Walk Alone" was a 60s number one for which pop group?
20 Which renowned chef is was on the books of Glasgow Rangers before turning to his new profession?

Answers

England in Europe (see Quiz 34)

1 Portugal. **2** 3–2 to Portugal. **3** Germany. **4** Alan Shearer. **5** Germany. **6** Switzerland. **7** 1–1. **8** Paul Gascoigne. **9** David Seaman. **10** Paul Scholes. **11** Terry Venables. **12** Spain. **13** Old Trafford. **14** Holland. **15** Romania. **16** Phil Neville. **17** Sweden. **18** 2–1 to Sweden. **19** Tomas Brolin. **20** The Golden Goal.

Quiz 37 **Premier League 2**

LEVEL 1

Answers – see page 355

1 Who were the first winners of the Premier League?

2 What was the first televised match from the Premier League?

3 Who were the Premier League runners up that season?

4 Who won the Premier League in 1994–95?

5 Who were relegated from the Premier League in 1996–97, having had three points deducted for failing to fulfil a fixture?

6 Which team has only ever finished first or second in the Premiership?

7 Who led the Premier League after only one game of the 2000–01 season?

8 Who were relegated from the Premier League in 1995–96 and returned in 1999–2000?

9 Which is the biggest ground in the Premier League?

10 What is the highest points total for a Premier League season?

11 In which year was that points total achieved?

12 How many matches did champions Manchester United lose during the 1999–2000 season?

13 Which player was sent off in his first two matches of the 2000–01 season?

14 Who failed to win an away match in the Premier League for 16 months covering part of 1999 and 2000?

15 Which team scored the fewest league goals in a Premier League season?

16 Which team scored the most goals in a Premier League season?

17 Which is the only team to concede 100 goals in a Premier League season?

18 What is the smallest points total for a Premier League season?

19 Which team achieved this distinction?

20 Which Premier League team bought Mark Viduka from Celtic in summer 2000?

Answers

Managers (see Quiz 39)

1 Bobby Robson. **2** Terry Venables. **3** Sir Alf Ramsey. **4** Arsene Wenger. **5** Franz Beckenbauer. **6** Don Revie. **7** Aberdeen. **8** Tottenham Hotspur & Arsenal. **9** Leicester City. **10** Sir Matt Busby. **11** Gordon Strachan. **12** Glenn Hoddle. **13** Brian Clough. **14** Harry Redknapp. **15** Terry Venables. **16** Dutch. **17** Republic of Ireland. **18** Wales. **19** Bill Shankly. **20** Trevor Francis.

Quiz 38 **England Heroes**

LEVEL 1

Answers – see page 356

1. Who was England's hat-trick hero in the 1966 World Cup final?
2. Who is England's all-time top scorer?
3. Who scored 48 international goals before becoming a TV presenter?
4. Which former England hero Kevin became the manager?
5. Who played the first of his 84 matches for England in 1934?
6. Who played his 106th and last international against West Germany in 1970?
7. Which England player was known as "Captain Marvel"?
8. Which England player was leading scorer in the Euro 96 tournament?
9. Which England hero of the 1950s was married to a Beverley Sister?
10. Who scored England's equaliser in the 1990 World Cup semi-final against West Germany?
11. Who is England's youngest-ever goalscorer?
12. Who was regarded as England's best player during Euro 2000?
13. Who was England's goalkeeping hero against Scotland in Euro 96?
14. What made him a hero in that game?
15. Who scored all three goals against Poland in the last group match of the 1986 World Cup finals?
16. Who scored for England against Belgium in the second-round match in Italia 90?
17. Which London player scored 44 goals in 57 appearances for England during the 1960s?
18. Which England hero played his last international against Italy at Wembley in November 1973?
19. Who retired from international football after defeat by Romania in Euro 2000?
20. Who scored England's second goal against Portugal in the opening game of Euro 2000?

Answers

The World Cup (see Quiz 40)

1 1930. **2** Uruguay. **3** Uruguay. **4** Italy. **5** Six. **6** West Germany. **7** England v Uruguay. **8** Japan and Korea. **9** Brazil, four times. **10** Los Angeles. **11** Pickles. **12** Brazil and Italy. **13** Mexico. **14** Holland. **15** Robbie Earle. **16** France. **17** France and Brazil. **18** Didier Deschamps. **19** Once. **20** The Jules Rimet Trophy.

Quiz 39 **Managers**

Answers – see page 353

LEVEL 1

1 Which manager's clubs have included Ipswich Town, England, Barcelona and Newcastle?

2 Who was the England manager on home soil during Euro 96?

3 Who was the manager of the World Cup winning side in 1966?

4 Who is Arsenal's French manager?

5 Which German became the first man to play in and coach a World Cup-winning team?

6 Who was Leeds' manager during their glory years of the 60s and 70s?

7 Which Scottish club did Alex Ferguson manage before Manchester Utd?

8 Which London Premier League teams had George Graham managed?

9 Celtic manager Martin O'Neill moved from which English team in 2000?

10 Which legendary Manchester United manager was celebrated for his young team of the late 50s?

11 Which manager sold Gary McAllister to Liverpool?

12 Who was dismissed as England manager in 1999 after making?

13 Which manager took Nottingham Forest to European Cup finals in the 1979 and 80?

14 Which happy Harry used to be West Ham's manager?

15 Who did Middlesbrough bring in to assist Bryan Robson in 2000–01?

16 What nationality is former Rangers boss Dick Advocaat?

17 Which national team enjoyed their greatest times under Jack Charlton?

18 John Toshack, Bobby Gould, and Mark Hughes have all managed which national team?

19 "If Everton were playing at the bottom of my garden I'd draw the curtains." Which Liverpool manager said that?

20 Which clever Trevor used to be Birmingham City's manager?

Answers

Premier League 2 (see Quiz 37)

1 Manchester United. **2** Nottingham Forest v Liverpool. **3** Aston Villa. **4** Blackburn Rovers. **5** Middlesbrough. **6** Manchester United. **7** Charlton. **8** Manchester City. **9** Old Trafford. **10** 92. **11** 1993–94. **12** Three. **13** Patrick Vieira. **14** Coventry City. **15** Leeds with 28 in 1996–97. **16** Manchester United with 97 in 1999–2000. **17** Swindon in 1993–94. **18** 24. **19** Watford. **20** Leeds United.

Quiz 40 **The World Cup**

LEVEL 1

Answers – see page 354

1 When was the first World Cup held?

2 Where did it take place?

3 Who won the competition?

4 Who won the competition in both 1934 and 1938?

5 How many host countries have won the World Cup?

6 Where was the 1974 tournament held?

7 What was the first match of the 1966 tournament?

8 Where will the 2002 tournament be held?

9 Which country has won the World Cup the most times?

10 In which city was the 1994 final played?

11 What was the name of the dog that found the stolen World Cup trophy in 1966?

12 Which two teams contested the 1970 World Cup final?

13 Where was that tournament played?

14 Who did Argentina beat in the final to win the 1978 trophy?

15 Who scored Jamaica's first goal in World Cup finals in 1998?

16 Where was the 1998 tournament held?

17 Which two teams contested the final?

18 Which player lifted the trophy at the end of the game?

19 How many times have England won the World Cup?

20 What was the original World Cup trophy called?

Answers

England Heroes (see Quiz 38)

1 Geoff Hurst. **2** Bobby Charlton. **3** Gary Lineker. **4** Kevin Keegan. **5** Stanley Matthews. **6** Bobby Charlton. **7** Bryan Robson. **8** Alan Shearer. **9** Billy Wright. **10** Gary Lineker. **11** Michael Owen. **12** David Beckham. **13** David Seaman. **14** He saved a penalty. **15** Gary Lineker. **16** David Platt. **17** Jimmy Greaves. **18** Bobby Moore. **19** Alan Shearer. **20** Steve McManaman.

Quiz 41 **The North West**

LEVEL 1

Answers – see page 359

1 Stanley Matthews played in tangerine for which Lancashire resort side?

2 Dixie Dean is a hero at which Merseyside club?

3 Graeme Souness is in charge at which Premier League Rovers?

4 Are Nationwide League Stockport a United, an Athletic or a County?

5 Shaun "The Goat" Goater is part of which team's strikeforce?

6 Which North West claret and blue team play at Turf Moor?

7 Wesley Brown and Quinton Fortune play for which team?

8 Which Premier League team from the North West have a French manager?

9 In which position does Everton's Kevin Campbell play?

10 Are Tranmere a Town, a Rovers or a Wanderers?

11 Who was Manchester City's young English goalkeeper in 2000?

12 Which team is not in the Football League: Altrincham, Macclesfield Town or Wigan Athletic?

13 Which former Manchester United striker is the Premier League's all-time leading goalscorer?

14 Which team were featured in a TV advert for milk in the 1980s?

15 England legend Tom Finney played for which North End "Lillywhites" in Lancashire?

16 Nat Lofthouse played for these Wanderers, but never at their Reebok Stadium. Who are they?

17 True or false: Bury have won the FA Cup on two occasions?

18 Which Liverpool and Scotland hero managed Blackburn Rovers in their Championship-winning season?

19 Which Lancashire club led Division One at Christmas 2001?

20 Which club in the region has the name Alexandra?

Answers

Nicknames (see Quiz 43)

1 United. **2** Boro. **3** The Owls. **4** The Hammers. **5** The Foxes. **6** The Toffees. **7** The Villains. **8** The Eagles. **9** Pompey. **10** The Hornets. **11** The Dons. **12** The Magpies. **13** The Cottagers. **14** The Saints. **15** Spurs. **16** The Sky Blues. **17** The Red Devils. **18** The Pool or The Reds. **19** The Blues or The Citizens. **20** The Rams.

Quiz 42 **Memorable Matches 3**

LEVEL 1

Answers – see page 360

1 Who conceded four goals in their first game on their return to the Premiership in 2000–01?

2 Who beat Barcelona 3–1 in Europe in 2000?

3 Which keeper thwarted England during a Wembley 1974 World Cup qualifier?

4 Who was he playing for?

5 Which Second Division team beat Manchester United to win the 1976 FA Cup final?

6 Who beat Peru 6–0 to qualify for the final of the 1978 World Cup?

7 Who did Liverpool beat in the final of the European Cup in 1981?

8 Who scored a sensational goal for England against Brazil in 1984?

9 When Liverpool won the title in 1985–86, who scored the winning goal in the final match of the season, at Stamford Bridge?

10 In which match did Schumacher commit his infamous "foul" on Battiston?

11 In which World Cup match did it all go wrong for Chris Waddle and Stuart Pearce?

12 Which World Cup did the Republic of Ireland start with a victory over Italy?

13 Who sensationally beat Germany in the Euro 92 final?

14 Who equalised for France against Brazil in the 1986 World Cup?

15 Who scored the winning penalty in that same quarter-final?

16 Which player had a goal disallowed when England played Argentina in the 1998 World Cup?

17 Who scored a superb goal for Germany against Russia in Euro 96?

18 Which two London teams contested the 1967 FA Cup final?

19 Who missed the deciding penalty in England's World Cup 98 match against Argentina?

20 Who did Chelsea beat in the 1998 Worthington Cup semi-final?

Answers

Chelsea (see Quiz 44)

1 Stamford Bridge. **2** Aston Villa. **3** Ken Bates. **4** Bobby Tambling. **5** Dennis Wise. **6** David Webb. **7** Fifth. **8** Ray and Graham Wilkins. **9** Barcelona. **10** Manchester United. **11** The Blues. **12** "Carefree". **13** Jimmy Floyd Hasselbaink. **14** Gianfranco Zola. **15** Gianluca Vialli. **16** Ron Harris. **17** Ruud Gullit. **18** Lord Attenborough. **19** Real Madrid. **20** Glenn Hoddle.

Quiz 43 **Nicknames**

LEVEL 1

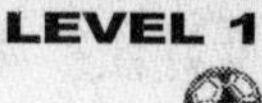

Answers – see page 357

1 Leeds United?
2 Middlesbrough?
3 Sheffield Wednesday?
4 West Ham United?
5 Leicester City?
6 Everton?
7 Aston Villa?
8 Crystal Palace?
9 Portsmouth?
10 Watford?
11 Wimbledon?
12 Newcastle United?
13 Fulham?
14 Southampton?
15 Tottenham Hotspur?
16 Coventry City?
17 Manchester United?
18 Liverpool?
19 Manchester City?
20 Derby County?

Answers

The North West (see Quiz 41)

1 Blackpool. **2** Everton. **3** Blackburn Rovers. **4** County. **5** Manchester City. **6** Burnley. **7** Manchester United. **8** Liverpool. **9** Striker. **10** Rovers. **11** Nicky Weaver. **12** Altrincham. **13** Andy Cole. **14** Accrington Stanley. **15** Preston North End. **16** Bolton Wanderers. **17** True (1900 and 1903). **18** Kenny Dalglish. **19** Burnley. **20** Crewe Alexandra.

Quiz 44 **Chelsea**

LEVEL 1

Answers – see page 358

1 What is the name of Chelsea's ground?
2 Who did Chelsea beat in the 2000 FA Cup Final?
3 Who has been the Chelsea chairman since 1982?
4 Who is Chelsea's current record goalscorer?
5 Which Chelsea player played for England in Euro 2000?
6 Who scored Chelsea's winner in the 1970 FA Cup Final Replay?
7 Where did Chelsea finish in the Premiership in the 1999–2000 season?
8 Which brothers starred for Chelsea during the 1970s?
9 Who knocked Chelsea out of the Champions League in 2000?
10 Who did Chelsea beat 5–0 in the Premiership on 3 October 1999?
11 What is Chelsea's nickname?
12 What is the Chelsea fans' anthem?
13 Who was Chelsea's record signing in 2000?
14 Who was the Footballer of the Year in 1997?
15 Which Italian managed Chelsea in 1998–00?
16 Which player has played in more games for Chelsea than any other?
17 Which Dutch superstar joined Chelsea in 1995?
18 Who is Chelsea's life vice-president?
19 Who did Chelsea beat in the 1971 European Cup Winners' Cup Final?
20 In 1993 who became the Chelsea's third manager in 12 months?

Answers

Memorable Matches 3 (see Quiz 42)

1 Manchester City. **2** Chelsea. **3** Jan Tomaszewski. **4** Poland. **5** Southampton. **6** Argentina. **7** Real Madrid. **8** John Barnes. **9** Kenny Dalglish. **10** 1982 World Cup semi-final. **11** 1990 World Cup semi-final. **12** 1994. **13** Denmark. **14** Michel Platini. **15** Luis Fernandez. **16** Sol Campbell. **17** Jürgen Klinsmann. **18** Chelsea and Spurs. **19** David Batty. **20** Arsenal.

Quiz 45 **Pot Luck**

LEVEL 1

Answers – see page 363

1. How many teams are there in the Premiership?
2. What is the most common score in a professional football match?
3. Who will host Euro 2004?
4. How many substitutes can be named for a Champions League game?
5. Who plays at Priestfield Stadium?
6. Which "Bald Eagle" was a Premier League manager in August 2001?
7. Which Scottish team is nicknamed "The Bankies"?
8. Who won the UEFA Cup in 1999?
9. Who won the Women's FA Cup in 2000?
10. Who won the Division 1 Championship in both 1957–58 and 1958–59?
11. In which year did Sir Matt Busby die?
12. In what year did *Match of the Day* start?
13. Who resigned as manager of Holland after Euro 2000?
14. Who is the manager of Aston Villa?
15. Which Ukrainian striker plays for AC Milan?
16. Who won the Spanish championship in 1999–2000?
17. Who is the author of *Football Against the Enemy*?
18. Which Dutchman Edgar plays for Juventus?
19. Which player lifted the Premier League trophy in May 2000?
20. Which keeper signed for Spurs in the summer of 2000?

Answers

England's World Cups 2 (see Quiz 47)

1 1950. **2** USA. **3** 1–0. **4** Brazil. **5** Uruguay. **6** Uruguay. **7** Portugal. **8** 2–1 to England. **9** 1–0 to Brazil. **10** Three. **11** Paraguay. **12** Fourth. **13** Belgium. **14** 1–0 after extra time. **15** Tunisia **16** Paul Scholes. **17** Romania. **18** Dan Petrescu. **19** Alan Shearer (pen). **20** St Etienne.

Quiz 46 **Centre-Forwards**

LEVEL 1

Answers – see page 364

1. What number does a centre-forward traditionally wear on his shirt?
2. Who played centre-forward for Manchester United in 1999–2000?
3. Who wore the No. 9 shirt for England in Euro 2000?
4. Which centre-forward scored 68 goals in 62 internationals for West Germany?
5. Which Liverpool centre-forward scored five goals in three FA Cup final-winning appearances?
6. Who was Holland's centre-forward when they won the 1988 European Championships?
7. Who played centre-forward for England in the 1966 World Cup final?
8. Which centre-forward did Chelsea sign in summer 2000?
9. Who is Wolves highest-scoring centre-forward ever?
10. Which centre-forward did Manchester City buy from West Ham in summer 2000?
11. Which Everton centre-forward holds the record for most goals in a season in the top division?
12. Which Bournemouth No. 9 holds the record for the most goals in any FA Cup match?
13. How many goals did he score in that match?
14. Which German centre-forward did Spurs sign in 1994?
15. Who captained Manchester United to European Cup success in 1968?
16. Which centre-forward was transferred from Newcastle to Everton in summer 2000?
17. Who was Glasgow Rangers' Dutch centre-forward in 2000?
18. Which ex-Arsenal centre-forward ended his career in 2000 at Burnley?
19. Who was Sunderland's centre-forward in 2000?
20. Who did West Ham sign from Arsenal for free in summer 2000?

Answers

Penalties (see Quiz 48)

1 Gary Lineker. **2** Stuart Pearce. **3** Dennis Bergkamp. **4** Alan Shearer. **5** Brazil. **6** Matt Le Tissier. **7** David Batty. **8** Wimbledon. **9** Tottenham Hotspur. **10** Kanu. **11** Five. **12** Gary McAllister. **13** Dwight Yorke. **14** Charlton. **15** 12 yards. **16** David Seaman. **17** Liverpool. **18** Zidane. **19** Galatasary. **20** Gareth Southgate.

Quiz 47 **England's World Cups 2**

LEVEL 1

Answers – see page 361

1 When did England first take part in the World Cup finals?

2 England suffered an embarrassing defeat in that tournament. Who beat them?

3 What was the score?

4 Where was that tournament held?

5 England lost in the quarter-finals of the 1954 tournament. Who beat them?

6 Who were England's first opponents in the 1966 finals?

7 Who did England beat in the semi-final?

8 What was the score?

9 England played Brazil in the group stages of the 1970 competition. What was the score?

10 How many wins did England have in the group stages of the 1982 tournament?

11 England played a second-round match in 1982 against which South American team?

12 Where did England finish in Italia 90?

13 Who did they beat to reach the quarter-finals of that tournament?

14 What was the score?

15 Who did England play in their opening game in the 1998 finals?

16 Who scored England's second goal in that game?

17 Who did England lose to in the group stages of the 1998 World Cup finals?

18 Who scored the winning goal in that game?

19 Who scored England's first goal in the eighth-final against Argentina?

20 In which city was that match played?

Answers

Pot Luck (see Quiz 45)

1 20. **2** 2–1. **3** Portugal. **4** Seven. **5** Gillingham. **6** Jim Smith. **7** Clydebank. **8** Parma. **9** Arsenal. **10** Wolves. **11** 1994. **12** 1964. **13** Frank Rijkaard. **14** John Gregory. **15** Andrei Shevchenko. **16** Deportivo la Coruna. **17** Simon Kuper. **18** Edgar Davids. **19** Roy Keane. **20** Neil Sullivan.

Quiz 48 **Penalties**

LEVEL 1

Answers – see page 362

1 Who would have equalled Bobby Charlton as England's greatest goalscorer if he hadn't missed a penalty against Brazil?
2 Which "psycho" missed a penalty against Germany in the 1990 World Cup?
3 Which Arsenal player missed a penalty that could have knocked Manchester United out of the FA Cup in 1999?
4 Who scored a penalty for England against Portugal in Euro 2000?
5 Who beat Italy on a penalty shoot-out to win the 1994 World Cup?
6 Who is Southampton's penalty king?
7 Whose missed penalty eliminated England from the 1998 World Cup?
8 Which team won the FA Cup after Dave Beasant saved a penalty?
9 Which team won the FA Cup in 1991 despite missing a penalty?
10 Which Arsenal player missed a penalty awarded to Nigeria in the shoot-out of the 2000 African Cup of Nations final?
11 How many penalties do teams take before the sudden death rule applies?
12 Who missed a penalty for Scotland against England in Euro 96?
13 Who usually takes Manchester United's penalties?
14 In 1998 the First Division play-off between Charlton and Sunderland was decided by a penalty shoot-out. Who won?
15 How far from the goal line is the penalty spot: 8, 10 or 12 yards?
16 Who saved a penalty for England in the Euro 96 quarter-final shoot-out against Spain at Wembley?
17 For which team did Bruce Grobbelar go wobbly-legged in a shoot-out for the 1984 European Cup?
18 Who scored the penalty for France to reach the Euro 2000 final?
19 Who beat Arsenal in the penalty-shoot out for the 2000 UEFA Cup final?
20 Whose miss lost England the shoot-out against Germany in Euro 96?

Answers

Centre-Forwards (see Quiz 46)

1 No. 9. **2** Andy Cole. **3** Alan Shearer. **4** Gerd Müller. **5** Ian Rush. **6** Marco Van Basten. **7** Geoff Hurst. **8** Jimmy Floyd Hasselbaink. **9** Steve Bull. **10** Paulo Wanchope. **11** Dixie Dean, 60 in 1927–28. **12** Ted MacDougall. **13** 9. **14** Jürgen Klinsmann. **15** Bobby Charlton. **16** Duncan Ferguson. **17** Michael Mols. **18** Ian Wright. **19** Kevin Phillips. **20** Davor Suker.

Quiz 49 **Who Did What? 4**

LEVEL 1

Answers – see page 367

1 Who beat Poland to allow England to qualify for the Euro 2000 play-offs: Luxembourg, Bosnia or Sweden?

2 Who declined to take part in the 1999–2000 FA Cup competition?

3 Who reputedly signed a £50,000-a-week contract with Manchester Utd in 1999?

4 Who became the first English club ever to field a team of foreigners?

5 Who gave up alcohol and supposedly took up poetry and playing piano?

6 Who was fined after an alleged cocaine-sniffing goal celebration?

7 Who imitated a famous cocktail guzzling incident after scoring in Euro 96?

8 Who temporarily replaced their manager after he was charged with alleged offences against children?

9 Who did Kevin Keegan leave out of his Euro 2000 squad: Kevin Phillips, Emile Heskey or Andy Cole?

10 Who grabbed Gazza by the unmentionables to earn notoriety?

11 Who agreed to replay their FA Cup tie against Sheffield United after winning with an "unsporting" goal in 1999?

12 Who signed Dion Dublin from Coventry City in 1998?

13 Who had four local MPs demanding they should sack their manager?

14 Who broke his jaw in the 2000 Scottish FA Cup final?

15 Who sold Robbie Keane to Coventry City?

16 Who earned £1m from his testimonial at Old Trafford in 1999?

17 Who appeared in three League Cup finals between 1997 and 2000?

18 Who was threatened with expulsion from Euro 2000 due to their fans?

19 Who broke a leg playing for West Ham while being touted as the best emerging English youngster?

20 Who named Dave Beasant as their player of the year for 1999–2000?

Answers

Goals Galore 3 (see Quiz 51)

1 Gary Lineker. **2** David Beckham. **3** Diego Maradona. **4** Ryan Giggs. **5** Leicester City's. **6** Roberto Di Matteo **7** Alan Shearer. **8** Nicolas Anelka. **9** Les Ferdinand. **10** Ole Gunnar Solksjaer. **11** Fowler. **12** Niall Quinn. **13** Thierry Henry. **14** Pele. **15** Geoff Hurst. **16** Steve McManaman. **17** Ian Wright. **18** Paul Scholes. **19** Arsenal. **20** European Championship.

Quiz 50 **Old Football**

LEVEL 1

Answers – see page 368

1 Which Yorkshire club won the League three times running in the 1920s?

2 Which great Stoke City, Blackpool and England winger had the 1953 FA Cup Final unofficially named after him?

3 Greaves, Mullery and Jennings were stars of which team in the 60s?

4 Which great Scottish striker played for both Manchester City and Manchester United in the 60s?

5 Which Nat was Bolton Wanderers and England's 50s goalscoring hero?

6 For which team did Bonetti, Cooke and Osgood play in the 60s?

7 World Cup heroes Peters, Hurst and Moore played for which London club?

8 In which decade was a live match commentary first broadcast on the radio?

9 Which country shocked the world by beating England in 1950 (and did it again in 1993)?

10 For which country did goal-scoring hero Billy Meredith play?

11 Which 17-year-old helped win the 1958 World Cup for Brazil?

12 Which Billy became the first man to win 100 caps for England, in 1959?

13 What was unique about Queen's Park reaching the English FA Cup Final twice in the 1880s?

14 What do Accrington Stanley, Bradford Park Avenue and Southport have in common?

15 Which Premier League giants began life as Newton Heath?

16 Which club take their name from the armoury at Woolwich in London?

17 Which club are called the Irons after their origins at Thames Ironworks?

18 Who in 1927 became the only club to take the FA Cup out of England?

19 The FA Cup in 1923 is remembered for an appearance by which animal?

20 What was unique about Sir Walter Winterbottom's appointment as manager of England in 1946?

Answers

England Managers (see Quiz 52)

1 Sir Alf Ramsey. **2** Leeds United. **3** Manchester City. **4** Kevin Keegan. **5** Howard Wilkinson. **6** Ipswich Town. **7** Turnip. **8** Terry Venables. **9** Glenn Hoddle. **10** Newcastle United. **11** Bobby Robson. **12** Don Revie. **13** Watford. **14** Barcelona. **15** Disabled people. **16** Paul Gascoigne. **17** "Do I not like that!" **18** 1982 **19** Peter Taylor. **20** Graham Taylor.

Quiz 51 **Goals Galore 3**

LEVEL 1

Answers – see page 365

1 Which *Match of the Day* presenter scored 48 goals for England?

2 Which Manchester United player lobbed Wimbledon keeper Neil Sullivan from near the half-way line?

3 Which Argentinian scored the "Hand of God" goal against England in the 1986 World Cup?

4 Which Welshman scored a fabulous goal for Manchester United against Arsenal in the 1998–99 FA Cup?

5 Tony Cottee was which team's leading scorer in 1999–2000?

6 Which player scored after only 43 seconds in the 1997 FA Cup Final?

7 Which former England captain led the Newcastle attack in 2001?

8 Which French goalscorer left Arsenal for Real Madrid in 1999?

9 Which marksman do Tottenham fans refer to as "Sir Les"?

10 Which Norwegian is Manchester United's "baby-faced assassin"?

11 Which Robbie was a Liverpool goal ace before joining another Robbie in 2001?

12 Who is the Republic of Ireland and Sunderland's towering targetman?

13 Which Arsenal player was the top scorer in Euro 2000?

14 Which player is Brazil's leading goalscorer?

15 Who scored a hat-trick for England in the 1966 World Cup Final?

16 Which Englishman scored in the 2000 European Cup final?

17 Which player revealed a t-shirt proclaiming "Just done it" when he became Arsenal's all-time record goalscorer?

18 Which Manchester United player scored twice for England at Hampden in the Euro 2000 qualifying play-offs?

19 Michael Thomas's last-minute goal at Anfield won the League for which club in 1989?

20 David Trezeguet's last-minute goal won which trophy for France in 2000?

Answers

Who Did What? 4 (see Quiz 49)

1 Sweden. **2** Manchester United. **3** Roy Keane. **4** Chelsea. **5** Tony Adams. **6** Robbie Fowler. **7** Paul Gascoigne. **8** Southampton. **9** Andy Cole. **10** Vinny Jones. **11** Arsenal. **12** Aston Villa. **13** Sheffield Wednesday. **14** Jim Leighton. **15** Wolves. **16** Alex Ferguson. **17** Leicester City. **18** England. **19** Joe Cole. **20** Nottingham Forest.

Quiz 52 **England Managers**

LEVEL 1

Answers – see page 366

1 Whose "wingless wonders" won the World Cup in 1966?

2 Which club did Don Revie take to 60s and 70s glory?

3 Joe Mercer took which club to the League championship?

4 Which England manager played for Scunthorpe, Liverpool, Hamburg, Southampton and Newcastle?

5 Who was England's caretaker manager after both Glenn Hoddle and Kevin Keegan left the job?

6 Bobby Robson was made England manager after success with which team?

7 *The Sun* newspaper portrayed Graham Taylor as which vegetable?

8 Which manager was in charge of England when they hosted Euro 96?

9 Who was appointed after taking charge of Swindon and Chelsea?

10 England manager Bobby Robson was in charge of which team in 2000?

11 Which manager took England to the World Cup semi-finals in 1990?

12 Which England manager resigned to take up a post in the United Arab Emirates in 1977?

13 Graham Taylor has had most success with which club?

14 Terry Venables took which club to the European Cup final in 1986?

15 Alleged remarks about which section of the community resulted in Glenn Hoddle's dismissal as England manager in 1999?

16 Which England player did Bobby Robson claim was "as daft as a brush"?

17 What became ex-England manager Graham Taylor's unwanted catch-phrase after his appearance on a television documentary?

18 Ron Greenwood was England's manager during which World Cup finals: 1974, 1978 or 1982?

19 Which former international was England caretaker coach in 2000–01?

20 Which one out of Bobby Robson, Graham Taylor and Glenn Hoddle never played for England?

Answers

Old Football (see Quiz 50)

1 Huddersfield. **2** Stanley Matthews. **3** Tottenham. **4** Denis Law. **5** Nat Lofthouse. **6** Chelsea. **7** West Ham United. **8** The 1920s. **9** USA. **10** Wales. **11** Pele. **12** Billy Wright. **13** They were Scottish. **14** All were former Football League teams. **15** Manchester United. **16** Arsenal. **17** West Ham. **18** Cardiff City. **19** A white horse. **20** He was the first England manager.

Quiz 53 **Scotland**

LEVEL 1

Answers – see page 371

1 In which stadium do Scotland usually play their home games?

2 Who was the manager of Scotland in 2000?

3 Who was their previous manager?

4 Who knocked Scotland out of Euro 2000?

5 When Scotland beat the Faeroes in Aberdeen in October 1998, what was the score?

6 Who scored Scotland's goals that day?

7 Who scored Scotland's goal against Brazil in the 1998 World Cup?

8 What was the score in the group match against Norway in the same competition?

9 Where was that match played?

10 Who did Scotland play in the last group match of that tournament?

11 What colour shirts do Scotland usually play in?

12 Who did Scotland beat in the group stage of Italia 90?

13 What was the score?

14 What was the score in Scotland's opening match of that tournament against Costa Rica?

15 Who scored Scotland's winner against Switzerland in Euro 96?

16 Who was in goal for Scotland that day?

17 Where was that match played?

18 Scotland were involved in the first international match ever played. Who did they play?

19 When was that match played?

20 What was the score?

Answers

Champions League (see Quiz 55)

1 UEFA Cup. **2** Galatasary. **3** Real Madrid. **4** Once. **5** Wembley. **6** Germany. **7** False. **8** Arsenal. **9** Scotland (Hampden Park). **10** Two. **11** Ajax. **12** Barcelona. **13** Valencia. **14** Norway. **15** AC Milan. **16** Bayern Munich **17** Two. **18** Teddy Sheringham. **19** Spain. **20** Twice.

Quiz 54 **The 90s**

Answers – see page 372

1 In which season did the Premier League begin?

2 Who won the Division 1 title in 2000?

3 Who won the first Premiership title?

4 Who won the Premier League in 1994–95?

5 Who was the leading scorer that season?

6 Which team appeared in five FA Cup finals in the 1990s?

7 How many of those did they win?

8 How many World Cup tournaments were there during the 1990s?

9 When was the first Worthington Cup played?

10 What was the tournament called before that?

11 What was the same tournament called in 1991 and 1992?

12 Which team appeared in six Scottish Cup finals during the 1990s?

13 How many of those did they win?

14 Which two London clubs contested the Charity Shield in 1991?

15 How many Charity Shields did Manchester United win during the 1990s?

16 Which two teams contested the FA Cup Final in 1997 and the Coca-Cola Cup final in 1998?

17 How many English clubs contested the UEFA Cup final during the 1990s?

18 Which was the last English club to appear in the European Cup Winners Cup final?

19 In what year was that match?

20 When did Manchester United last win the European Cup?

Answers

Midfielders (see Quiz 56)

1 Georgi Kinkladze. **2** George Boateng. **3** Mario Stanic. **4** Carlton Palmer. **5** Republic of Ireland 6 Arsenal. **7** Paul Gascoigne. **8** Manchester United and Leeds. **9** Leicester City. **10** Tottenham. **11** Right. **12** Nigel Clough. **13** Roy Keane. **14** Patrick Vieira. **15** Nolberto Solano. **16** Southampton. **17** Argentina. **18** Frank Lampard **19** Vladimir Smicer. **20** Lothar Matthaus.

Quiz 55 **Champions League**

LEVEL 1

Answers – see page 369

1 Teams knocked out of the last qualifying round and finishing third in the first group stage enter which cup in the same season?
2 Which team did Chelsea travel to Turkey to beat 5–0 in 1999?
3 Which team eliminated Manchester United from the 1999–2000 competition?
4 How many times have Manchester United won the Champions League?
5 Where did Arsenal play their home games in 1999–2000?
6 Bayer Leverkusen and Borussia Dortmund have been among which country's Champions League representatives?
7 True or False: Tottenham played in the 1998–99 Champions League?
8 A goal by Gabriel Batistuta for Fiorentina effectively knocked which English club out of the 1999–2000 Champions League?
9 In which country was the 2002 Champions League final played?
10 How many English teams automatically enter the first group stage?
11 Which Dutch team have won the Champions League on two occasions?
12 In which city did Manchester United win the Champions League?
13 Which was the last club to lose consecutive Champions League finals?
14 Rosenborg have been regular representatives of which country?
15 Which Milan team won the competition in 1995?
16 Who did Manchester United beat in the 1999 final: Valencia, Bayern Munich or Barcelona?
17 How many Scottish clubs entered the Champions League in 2001–02?
18 Which Manchester United sub scored the equaliser in the 1999 final?
19 Raul and Morientes both scored in the 2000 final. For what national team do they play?
20 How many times have Real Madrid won the title since 1995?

Answers

Scotland (see Quiz 53)

1 Hampden Park. **2** Craig Brown. **3** Andy Roxburgh. **4** England. **5** 2–1 to Scotland. **6** Burley and Dodds. **7** Collins (pen). **8** 1–1. **9** Bordeaux. **10** Morocco. **11** Dark blue. **12** Sweden. **13** 2–1. **14** 1–0 to Costa Rica. **15** Ally McCoist. **16** Andy Goram. **17** Villa Park. **18** England. **19** 1872. **20** 0–0.

Quiz 56 **Midfielders**

LEVEL 1

Answers – see page 370

1 Who is Derby County's magic Georgian Georgi?
2 Which Ghanaian George patrols Aston Villa's midfield?
3 Which Mario is Chelsea's Croatian midfielder?
4 Which leggy former England international did Coventry sign from Nottingham Forest?
5 For which country does Leeds United's Stephen McPhail play?
6 Everton's Stephen Hughes was signed from which London club?
7 Which midfielder damaged knee ligaments in a Tottenham Cup final and broke a leg in a Lazio training session?
8 Name one of the former clubs of Bradford City's Lee Sharpe?
9 Izzet, Lennon and Savage were which club's midfield teammates?
10 Tim Sherwood won a Championship medal at Blackburn – who did he join after leaving?
11 Where does David Beckham usually play in midfield: left, right or central?
12 Which Nigel played in England midfield and was the son of a great manager?
13 Which Manchester United midfielder was sent off in the 2000 Charity Shield?
14 Who is Arsenal and France's volatile midfield lynchpin?
15 Which Nolberto is Newcastle's sweet-footed South American?
16 For which club does Hassan Kachloul play?
17 Middlesbrough's young midfielder Carlos Marinelli is from which South American country?
18 Which Frank is Chelsea's England Under 21 captain?
19 Which Liverpool Vlad scored for the Czech Republic in Euro 2000?
20 Which Lothar was Germany's ageing midfield ace in Euro 2000?

Answers

The 90s (see Quiz 54)

1 1992–93. **2** Leeds United. **3** Manchester United. **4** Blackburn Rovers. **5** Alan Shearer. **6** Manchester United. **7** Four. **8** Three. **9** 1999. **10** The Coca-Cola Cup. **11** The Rumbelows League Cup. **12** Rangers. **13** Four. **14** Spurs and Arsenal. **15** Four. **16** Chelsea and Middlesbrough. **17** None. **18** Chelsea **19** 1998. **20** 1999.

Quiz 57 **Grounds 2**

Answers – see page 375

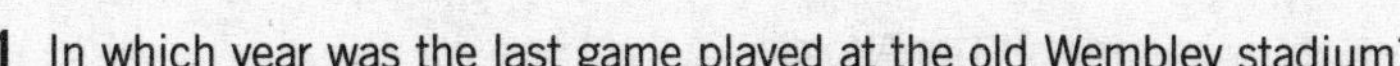

1 In which year was the last game played at the old Wembley stadium?
2 Which team calls Upton Park home?
3 St James' Park is the ground of which North East team?
4 Take the Maine Road to which Premier League team?
5 The San Siro, the Olympico Stadio and the Delle Alpi stadio are in which country?
6 Which team has a cottage down by the Thames?
7 The Foxes turn out at Filbert Street to see which Premier League team?
8 What is the name of Ipswich Town's ground?
9 Who are the pride of Pride Park?
10 Who play their football down in The Valley?
11 Is Maracana Stadium in Brazil or Argentina?
12 Which Rovers come home to Ewood Park?
13 What is the name of the Wolverhampton Wanderers stadium?
14 Tynecastle is the home ground of which Edinburgh club?
15 Which London stadium used to have a popular Shed End?
16 Which Bristol team have played home matches at Twerton Park, Bath?
17 Queens Park Rangers share their Loftus Road ground with which buzzing rugby club?
18 Villa Park is the imaginative name of which Premier League team's ground?
19 Ayresome Park in Middlesbrough, Sunderland's Roker Park and the Baseball Ground in Derby have what in common?
20 Which Premier League club has a popular Stretford End?

Answers

Centre-Halves (see Quiz 59)

1 Jaap Stam. **2** Jackie Charlton. **3** Mickey Droy. **4** Franz Beckenbauer. **5** Tony Adams. **6** Lucas Radebe. **7** Matt Elliott **8** No. 5. **9** Laurent Blanc. **10** Frank Leboeuf. **11** Terry Butcher. **12** Alan Hansen and Mark Lawrenson. **13** Steve Bruce. **14** Dave Watson. **15** Andy Linighan. **16** Colin Hendry. **17** Ugo Ehiogu. **18** Sami Hyypia. **19** Brian Labone. **20** Artur Numan.

Quiz 58 **London Teams**

Answers – see page 376

1 Which London team is known as "The Addicks"?

2 Which team plays its home games at Upton Park?

3 Which two teams share Selhurst Park?

4 Who two clubs play in SW6?

5 Which was the last London team to win the Premier League?

6 Which London club has an Egyptian chairman?

7 Which Nationwide League team is nicknamed "The Bees".

8 Which was the last London team to win the FA Cup?

9 Who plays in E10?

10 Whose stadium is in Bermondsey?

11 Who used to play at the White City?

12 Which Greater London team was twice managed by Graham Taylor?

13 Which London team plays in white shirts with navy blue shorts and socks?

14 Which was the last London team to win the League Cup?

15 Which London team was relegated from the Premier League in 1999-2000?

16 Which London team is known as "The Hammers"?

17 Is Wembley stadium in London?

18 Which London club is managed by Ian Holloway?

19 Who plays in SE16?

20 Which London Premier League clubs have a French manager?

Answers

The North (see Quiz 60)

1 Fish. **2** Scunthorpe United. **3** Huddersfield Town. **4** Sheffield United **5** Chris Waddle. **6** Dean. **7** Hull City. **8** Hillsborough. **9** Leeds United. **10** United. **11** Sheffield Wednesday. **12** Harry. **13** Most spectators were in army uniform. **14** Grimsby Town. **15** Bradford City. **16** Leicester City and Aston Villa. **17** Rugby League. **18** Strongbow. **19** Brass band. **20** Barnsley.

Quiz 59 **Centre-Halves**

LEVEL 1

Answers – see page 373

1 Which Dutchman controversially left Manchester United in August 2001?
2 Who played centre-half for England in the 1966 World Cup final?
3 Which 6 foot, 4 inch bearded stopper dominated the Chelsea defence during the 1970s?
4 Which German centre-half was known as "The Kaiser"?
5 Which Arsenal centre-half was unfairly nicknamed "Donkey"?
6 Which South African plays centre-half for Leeds United?
7 Who is Leicester City's goal-scoring centre-half?
8 What number does the centre-half traditionally wear?
9 Which French centre-half missed the 1998 World Cup final because of suspension?
10 Who took his place?
11 Which England centre-half left Ipswich to join Glasgow Rangers in 1987?
12 Which centre-back pairing now star as BBC-TV football pundits?
13 Which ex-Manchester Utd centre-half now manages Birmingham City?
14 Which Everton centre-half was succeeded by one with the same surname?
15 Which Arsenal centre-half scored the winner in the 1993 FA Cup final replay?
16 Which Blackburn player was Scotland's centre-half during Euro 96?
17 In Middlesbrough's defence Gareth Southgate is paired with which other centre-half?
18 Which Finnish centre-half joined Liverpool in summer 1999?
19 Which centre-half captained Everton for most of the 1960s?
20 Which Dutchman plays No. 5 for Glasgow Rangers?

Answers

Grounds 2 (see Quiz 57)

1 2000. **2** West Ham United. **3** Newcastle United. **4** Manchester City. **5** Italy. **6** Fulham (Craven Cottage). **7** Leicester City. **8** Portman Road. **9** Derby County. **10** Charlton Athletic. **11** Brazil. **12** Blackburn. **13** Molineux. **14** Hearts. **15** Stamford Bridge. **16** Bristol Rovers. **17** Wasps. **18** Aston Villa. **19** All have been demolished in recent years. **20** Manchester United.

Quiz 60 **The North**

LEVEL 1

Answers – see page 374

1 Grimsby Town supporters cheered up the football world with their inflatable what?

2 Which of the following clubs played in the Nationwide League in 2000: Scunthorpe United, Scarborough or Frickley Colliery?

3 Which Yorkshire Terriers play in the McAlpine Stadium?

4 Which Sheffield team play in red and white?

5 Which England penalty-shoot out "villain" helped Sheffield Wednesday to Wembley in 1993?

6 Bradford City's 2000–01 teammates Windass and Saunders share which first name?

7 What is the name of the Football League team: Hull City, Hull Kingston Rovers or Hull FC?

8 At which ground do Sheffield Wednesday play?

9 Martyn, Bakke and Bridges play at which Premier League club?

10 Do Rotherham play under the name of City, United or Academical?

11 Which Sheffield team were relegated in 1999–2000?

12 What nickname was given to former Barnsley manager Dave Bassett?

13 Why was Sheffield United's 1915 FA Cup Final victory known as "The Khaki Cup"?

14 Which Town play in black and white only minutes from the North Sea?

15 The tragic fire at a match in Yorkshire took place at which team's ground?

16 Hull City manager Brian Little previously managed which Premier League Foxes and Villains?

17 Huddersfield Town share their stadium with a team playing which sport?

18 What is emblazoned on the chest of Leeds United shirts?

19 Which group of supporters began what at Sheffield Wednesday matches?

20 Which Yorkshire Tykes never played in the Premiership until 1997–98?

Answers

London Teams (see Quiz 58)

1 Charlton Athletic. **2** West Ham. **3** Crystal Palace and Wimbledon. **4** Chelsea and Fulham. **5** Arsenal. **6** Fulham. **7** Brentford. **8** Chelsea. **9** Leyton Orient. **10** Millwall's. **11** Queens Park Rangers. **12** Watford. **13** Tottenham Hotspur. **14** Tottenham Hotspur. **15** Wimbledon. **16** West Ham. **17** No. **18** Queens Park Rangers. **19** Millwall. **20** Arsenal and Fulham.

Quiz 61 **Shirt Colours**

LEVEL 1

Answers – see page 379

1 Which Owls play in blue and white striped shirts?

2 Which south coast Premiership team play in red and white stripes?

3 What colour are Wolves shirts?

4 West Ham and Aston Villa both play in the same colours. What are they?

5 Which Eagles have red and blue vertical stripes?

6 Are QPR shirts striped or hooped?

7 Which Glasgow team play in green and white hoops?

8 Who are The Reds on Merseyside?

9 Which Pilgrims play in green and white shirts?

10 What colour shirts do Burnley play in?

11 Why are Chelsea called The Blues?

12 What colour shirts do Bradford City play in?

13 Which Baggies play in navy blue and white striped shirts?

14 Which is the blue half of Manchester?

15 What colour shirts do Norwich City play in?

16 What kind of blue do Coventry play in?

17 Which is the blue half of Bristol?

18 Which Tyneside team play in black and white stripes?

19 What colour shirts do Pompey play in?

20 Who are The Lilywhites?

Answers

Tottenham Hotspur (see Quiz 63)

1 George Graham. **2** White shirts, blue shorts. **3** Ukraine. **4** Bill Nicholson. **5** White Hart Lane. **6** David Pleat. **7** Teddy Sheringham. **8** Vega. **9** Jimmy Greaves. **10** Ricardo Villa. **11** Gary Lineker. **12** Sol Campbell. **13** David Ginola. **14** Steve Perryman. **15** Republic of Ireland. **16** Darren Anderton. **17** Alan Sugar. **18** Neil Sullivan. **19** Erik Thorsvedt. **20** Norway.

Quiz 62 **Managers**

LEVEL 1

Answers – see page 380

1 Paul Jewell helped to keep which Yorkshire team in the Premier League in 1999–2000?

2 Joe Royle managed which Premier League club in 2000–01?

3 Ex Swansea manager John Hollins was a cup-winner for which London club?

4 Which former Denmark and Liverpool star is in charge of Kidderminster Harriers?

5 Colin Harvey, Joe Royle and Howard Kendall have managed which Blues?

6 Craig Brown managed which national team from 1993 to 2001?

7 John Gregory is in charge at which Midlands club?

8 Which Italian replaced Graham Taylor as Watford's manager?

9 Sunderland's hot-seat is occupied by which former Everton and Manchester City midfielder?

10 Where did Glenn Hoddle take over from George Graham as manager?

11 Dino Zoff resigned as manager of which national team after Euro 2000?

12 Bertie Mee managed which London side that did the double in 1971?

13 Brian Little, Martin O'Neill and Peter Taylor have all managed which Midlands team?

14 Mick McCarthy is manager of which national team?

15 Which team did Ruud Gullitt manage after Chelsea?

16 Name the Everton boss who had won five championships at Rangers?

17 Bill Nicholson took which London club to glory in 1961?

18 Which London club is managed by French 80s hero Jean Tigana?

19 Tommy Docherty, Ron Atkinson and Matt Busby all managed which club?

20 He has managed Crystal Palace, QPR, Tottenham, Barcelona and Portsmouth. Who is he?

Answers

Pot Luck 2 (see Quiz 64)

1 Ole Gunnar Solskjaer. **2** Udinese. **3** Jean Tigana. **4** 1923. **5** Carling. **6** Ibrox. **7** Nwankwu. **8** Gordon Strachan. **9** Carrow Road. **10** Leeds United. **11** Italy. **12** Utrecht **13** Valencia. **14** Sweden. **15** Lisbon. **16** Pierluigi Collina. **17** Mark Hughes. **18** Crewe Alexandra. **19** Brazil. **20** AC Milan and Internazionale.

Quiz 63 **Tottenham Hotspur**

LEVEL 1

Answers – see page 377

1 Who was Tottenham Hotspur's manager in 2000?

2 What colour shirts and shorts do Tottenham play in at home?

3 Which country does striker Sergei Rebrov come from?

4 Who was the manager of Spurs' double-winning side?

5 What is Tottenham's stadium called?

6 Which former Spurs manager was Director of Football in 2001?

7 Which Spurs forward joined Manchester United and won the treble in 1999?

8 Which Ramon was in Spurs' 2000–01 squad?

9 Which 60s Spurs' striker scored 44 goals for England?

10 Which Argentinian scored for Spurs in the 1981 FA Cup final replay?

11 Which Spurs and England star went on to play for Barcelona and Nagoya Grampus 8?

12 Who was the club captain at the start of the 2000–01 season?

13 Which exiled Frenchman joined Tottenham from Newcastle and left them to play for Aston Villa?

14 Which Spurs' captain lifted the 1980 and 81 FA Cup?

15 Tottenham full-back Stephen Carr plays for which national team?

16 Who is Spurs and England's injury-prone midfielder?

17 Who was Tottenham's high-profile chairman for most of the 1990s?

18 What is the name of Spurs' Scottish international goalkeeper?

19 Which goalkeeper did Tottenham supporters call Erik the Viking?

20 Spurs striker Steffen Iversen has played for which country?

Answers

Shirt Colours (see Quiz 61)

1 Sheffield Wednesday. **2** Southampton. **3** Old Gold. **4** Claret and blue. **5** Crystal Palace. **6** Hooped. **7** Celtic. **8** Liverpool. **9** Plymouth Argyle. **10** Claret and blue. **11** Because of their blue shirts. **12** Claret and amber. **13** West Brom. **14** Manchester City. **15** Yellow. **16** Sky blue. **17** Bristol Rovers. **18** Newcastle United. **19** Blue. **20** Preston North End.

Quiz 64 **Pot Luck 2**

LEVEL 1

Answers – see page 378

1 Who is nicknamed "the baby-faced assassin"?

2 Which team plays in Udine, Italy?

3 Who was the new manager of Fulham in 2000?

4 When was the first Wembley FA Cup final?

5 Who were the first sponsors of the Premier League?

6 What is the name of Glasgow Rangers ground?

7 What is the first name of Arsenal's Kanu?

8 Who managed of Coventry City from November 1996 to October 2001?

9 Where do Norwich City play?

10 Which team sold Eric Cantona to Manchester United?

11 For which country does Paolo Maldini play?

12 From which club did Michael Mols join Glasgow Rangers?

13 Who plays at Mestalla?

14 From which country does Celtic's Henrik Larsson come?

15 In which city do Benfica play?

16 Which famous bald referee took charge of the 1999 Champions League final?

17 Who became Welsh national team manager in 1999?

18 Who plays at Gresty Road?

19 In which country was the FIFA World Club Championship held in 2000?

20 Which two teams share the San Siro stadium in Italy?

Answers

Managers (see Quiz 62)

1 Bradford City. **2** Manchester City. **3** Chelsea **4** Jan Molby. **5** Everton. **6** Scotland. **7** Aston Villa. **8** Gianluca Vialli. **9** Peter Reid. **10** Tottenham Hotspur. **11** Italy. **12** Arsenal. **13** Leicester City. **14** Republic of Ireland. **15** Newcastle United. **16** Walter Smith. **17** Tottenham Hotspur. **18** Fulham. **19** Manchester United. **20** Terry Venables.

Quiz 65 **Premiership Stars 2**

LEVEL 1

Answers – see page 383

1 Which Dutch Dennis has enriched the Premiership with his goals for the Gunners?

2 Who is Blackburn Rovers' "Goal King Cole"?

3 Which tiny Brazilian starred for Middlesbrough during the 1990s?

4 Which tall Norwegian striker led the Chelsea line until joining Rangers?

5 Which Wimbledon striker was transferred to Newcastle during summer 2000?

6 Which French favourite left Spurs for Aston Villa in summer 2000?

7 Which young Malcolm is Derby County's striking sensation?

8 Which Liverpool midfielder's father used to manage West Ham?

9 Which Nicky crossed Stanley Park in summer 2000?

10 Which Dutch superstar was player/manager at Chelsea during the 1990s?

11 Which Glasgow Rangers striker joined Charlton during summer 2000?

12 Which striker left Chelsea for Celtic during summer 2000?

13 Who cost Spurs £5m during summer 2000?

14 Which Premiership star is married to an ex-Spice Girl?

15 Which German star provided dead-ball accuracy for Middlesbrough during 1999–2000?

16 Which American has appeared regularly in the Everton team?

17 Which Moroccan moved from Coventry City to Aston Villa in July 2001?

18 Which Moroccan moved from Southampton to Aston Villa in July 2001?

19 Which Liverpool youngster scored against Argentina in the 1998 World Cup?

20 Whose volley was the Premier League's Goal of the Season in 2000?

Answers

Ireland (see Quiz 67)

1 David O'Leary. **2** Roy Keane. **3** Leeds United. **4** Robbie Keane. **5** Mark Kennedy. **6** Green. **7** Packie Bonner. **8** Italy. **9** Paul McGrath. **10** John Aldridge. **11** Stephen Carr. **12** Niall Quinn. **13** Frank Stapleton. **14** Jason McAteer. **15** Turkey. **16** Dennis Irwin. **17** Steve Staunton. **18** Jack Charlton. **19** Tony Cascarino. **20** Arsenal.

Quiz 66 **Euro 2000**

LEVEL 1

Answers – see page 384

1 What was the opening game of the tournament?

2 What was the score in that match?

3 Who did France play in their opening game?

4 Who finished higher in Group B, Italy or Turkey?

5 Who were co-hosts of the tournament with Belgium?

6 Who did Holland play in their first match?

7 Who scored the quickest goal in the tournament?

8 What was the score between Yugoslavia and Slovenia?

9 Where was England's match against Germany played?

10 France played Holland in the last match of the group stage. What was the score?

11 Holland played Yugoslavia in the quarter-finals. What was the final score?

12 Who scored twice for Portugal against Turkey in their quarter-final match?

13 France, Portugal and Holland were semi-finalists with which other team?

14 Which two teams won through to the final?

15 What was the score in the final?

16 How many goals were scored during the Euro 2000 finals?

17 How many matches were played during the tournament?

18 Which two players top-scored during the tournament?

19 Who scored the fewest goals of any team in the tournament?

20 Which two teams scored the most goals?

Answers

Who Did What? 5 (see Quiz 68)

1 Andy Cole. **2** Aberdeen. **3** Bosman. **4** English clubs. **5** Fulham. **6** Robbie Folwer. **7** Portugal. **8** Yugoslavia. **9** Everton. **10** Eric Cantona. **11** Roger Milla. **12** Michael Laudrup. **13** Brian Kidd. **14** Viv Richards. **15** Pele. **16** Nigeria. **17** Terry Venables. **18** Linesmen. **19** Nayim. **20** Went on strike.

Quiz 67 **Ireland**

LEVEL 1

Answers – see page 381

1 Which Premier League manager scored the Republic of Ireland's most important penalty ever, in the 1990 World Cup?
2 Which Republic of Ireland player captains Manchester United?
3 The Republic of Ireland's Gary Kelly plays at which Premier League club?
4 Which Republic of Ireland striker moved from Coventry to Milan in 2000?
5 Which Republic of Ireland winger plays for Manchester City?
6 In what colour shirts do the Republic of Ireland play?
7 Which Packie was the Republic's goalkeeper throughout the 80s?
8 Which nation knocked the Republic of Ireland out of the 1990 World Cup?
9 Which former Manchester United and Aston Villa defender used to hold the record for most caps won for the Republic of Ireland?
10 Which former Liverpool striker scored 19 goals for the Republic of Ireland?
11 Who is Tottenham's Republic of Ireland full-back?
12 Which Sunderland centre-forward is the leading goalscorer?
13 Which former Arsenal and Manchester Utd forward was the Republic's leading goalscorer?
14 Which Jason plays on the wing for Blackburn Rovers and the Republic?
15 Which country knocked the Republic out of the Euro 2000 play-offs?
16 Which Manchester Utd full-back has played over 50 times for the Republic of Ireland?
17 Who was the first player to win 90 caps for the Republic?
18 Who is the Republic of Ireland's most successful manager?
19 Which Irish forward played his club football for Marseille and Nancy?
20 Liam Brady made his name as a player at which London club?

Answers

Premiership Stars 2 (see Quiz 65)

1 Dennis Bergkamp. **2** Andy Cole. **3** Juninho. **4** Tore Andre Flo. **5** Carl Cort. **6** David Ginola. **7** Malcolm Christie. **8** Jamie Redknapp. **9** Nicky Barmby moved from Everton to Liverpool. **10** Ruud Gullit. **11** Jonatan Johansson. **12** Chris Sutton. **13** Ben Thatcher. **14** David Beckham. **15** Christian Ziege. **16** Joe Max-Moore. **17** Mustapha Hadji. **18** Hassan Kachloul. **19** Michael Owen. **20** Paolo Di Canio.

Quiz 68 **Who Did What? 5**

LEVEL 1

Answers – see page 382

1 Who signed for Manchester United from Newcastle in 1995 for a then British record £7m?

2 Which club won the Scottish FA and League cups as well as the Cup-Winners' Cup in 1983?

3 Who had a ruling named after him after he went to the European Court of Justice over transfer fees for players out of contract?

4 Who were banned indefinitely from European competitions in 1985?

5 Which team played West Ham in the all-London FA Cup final in 1975?

6 Who left Liverpool for Leeds in December 2001?

7 Who did Nuno Gomes score four goals for in Euro 2000?

8 Who did Savo Milosevic score five goals for in Euro 2000?

9 Who won the FA Cup final in 1985 with a Paul Rideout goal?

10 Who won the League Championship four times in his first five seasons in England before retiring to follow an acting career?

11 Who played for Cameroon in the 1994 World Cup at the age of 42?

12 Who played alongside his brother Brian in the Danish national side?

13 Who was the assistant manager of Manchester United who left to manage Blackburn Rovers?

14 Which West Indies batsman played soccer for Antigua & Barbuda in the 1980s?

15 Which famous player played for Santos and New York Cosmos?

16 Which became the first African country to win Olympic gold in 1996?

17 Who utilised a "Christmas tree" formation when England manager?

18 Who became "assistant referees" from the 1996–97 season?

19 Who sunk Arsenal with a goal from the halfway line in the 1995 Cup-Winners Cup final?

20 What did Pierre van Hooijdonk do to leave Nottingham Forest?

Answers

Euro 2000 (see Quiz 66)

1 Belgium v Sweden. **2** 2–1 to Belgium. **3** Denmark. **4** Italy. **5** Holland. **6** Czech Republic. **7** Paul Scholes. **8** 3–3. **9** Charleroi. **10** France 2 Holland 3. **11** Holland 6 Yugoslavia 1. **12** Gomes. **13** Italy. **14** France and Italy. **15** France 2 Italy 1. **16** 85. **17** 31. **18** Patrick Kluivert and Savo Milosevic. **19** Denmark. **20** France and Holland.

Quiz 69 **Nationwide League**

LEVEL 1

Answers – see page 387

1 Of which Nationwide League team was Dave Bassett manager in 2000?

2 Who finished sixth in the table in both 1998–99 and 1999–2000?

3 What is the core business of Football League and FA sponsors Nationwide?

4 Which was striker Clyde Wijnhard's first Nationwide League club?

5 Who lost in the Second Division play-off final in 1999 but won promotion by the same route in 2000?

6 Who did Ade Akinbiyi leave to sign for Leicester City?

7 Who was the new manager of West Bromwich Albion in 2000?

8 Who missed the play-offs by one place in 1999–2000?

9 Which Nationwide League team knocked two Premiership sides out of the FA Cup during the 1999–2000 season?

10 Who was the manager of Nottingham Forest in 2000?

11 Which Lee leads the Pompey attack?

12 Which Nationwide League Division One team plays in Lincolnshire?

13 Who plays at Carrow Road?

14 Which former Manchester United youngster now plays at Huddersfield?

15 In 2000–01 how many Division One teams began with B?

16 Which Nationwide League clubs play on opposite sides of the river Trent?

17 Which Nationwide League team is nicknamed "The Tykes"?

18 Who became the manager of Birmingham City in December 2001?

19 Which Nationwide League won two successive promotions (the first through the playoffs) followed by relegation in 2001?

20 Who plays at the JJB Stadium?

Answers

Wales (see Quiz 71)

1 Red. **2** Cardiff. **3** Neville Southall. **4** Ryan Giggs. **5** Ian Rush. **6** Reached World Cup finals. **7** John Charles. **8** John Toshack. **9** Vinny. **10** Speed. **11** Mark Hughes. **12** Saunders. **13** Ninian Park. **14** Wrexham. **15** Dragon **16** Vetch Field **17** Cardiff City. **18** 90s. **19** Leicester City. **20** John Hartson.

Quiz 70 **Leeds United**

LEVEL 1

Answers – see page 388

1 Which former Leeds manager took charge at Spurs?

2 Which fiery Frenchman left Elland Road in 1993 after winning the championship with Leeds?

3 From which Scottish club did Leeds sign Mark Viduka?

4 Which Irish international did Leeds sign from Milan in 2000–01?

5 Which Leeds midfielder missed in the penalty shoot-out against Argentina in the 1998 World Cup?

6 From which country are Galatasaray, Leeds' opponents in the UEFA Cup 2000 semi final?

7 Who is Leeds' England International goalkeeper?

8 Which Leeds Erik comes from Norway?

9 Who was Leeds United's manager in 2000?

10 Olivier Dacourt previously played for which North West team?

11 Which defender did Leeds sign from West Ham in November 2000?

12 Which legendary Leeds skipper captained Scotland in the 1974 World Cup?

13 Which Darren did Leeds sign from Coventry City?

14 Which manager took Leeds to League, Cup and European glory in the 60s and 70s?

15 Who was Leeds' England and Republic of Ireland World Cup hero?

16 What colours have Leeds played in since the 1960s?

17 Who was the Leeds manager when they won the league in 1991–92?

18 In which position does Leeds' Michael Bridges play?

19 Which Leeds player was the 2000 Young Player of the Year?

20 Which Leeds star of the 60s and 70s reputedly had the hardest shot in football?

Answers

Cup Winners (see Quiz 72)

1 USA. **2** Egypt. **3** S. Africa. **4** Lucas Radebe. **5** Ferencvaros. **6** London Select XI. **7** Marcel Desailly. **8** Marseille & AC Milan. **9** Belgrade. **10** True. **11** South Africa. **12** Laurent Blanc. **13** Inter-Toto. **14** Oliver Bierhoff (Euro 96). **15** False (Rangers won in 1972, Aberdeen in 1985). **16** Jürgen Klinsmann. **17** Two. **18** Manchester Utd. **19** Galatasaray. **20** Copenhagen.

Quiz 71 **Wales**

LEVEL 1

Answers – see page 385

1 What colour shirts do Wales play in?

2 In what city is Wales' National Stadium?

3 Which former Everton goalkeeper is Wales' most capped player?

4 Which English-born Manchester United winger chose to play for Wales?

5 Which former Liverpool star is Wales' leading goalscorer?

6 What did Wales do in 1958 that they haven't done since?

7 Which Welsh legend played for Leeds United and Juventus?

8 Which former Welsh team manager played alongside Kevin Keegan at Liverpool?

9 Which Jones the film star was sent off playing for Wales in 1995?

10 Which Leeds, Everton and Newcastle Gary has won over 50 caps for Wales?

11 Which "Sparky" became Wales' player-manager?

12 Which Bradford City Dean has scored over 20 goals for Wales?

13 Where do Cardiff City play?

14 Which Welsh team famously knocked League Champions Arsenal out of the FA Cup in 1992?

15 Which creature appears on the Wales team's badge?

16 Where do Swansea City play?

17 Who are the only Welsh club to win the FA Cup?

18 In which decade was the League of Wales founded: 50s, 70s or 90s?

19 Robbie Savage plays for Wales and which Premier League club?

20 Which ginger-haired Arsenal, West Ham and Wimbledon striker first played for Wales in 1995?

Answers

Nationwide League (see Quiz 69)

1 Barnsley. **2** Bolton Wanderers. **3** A building society and soccer sponsor. **4** Huddersfield Town. **5** Gillingham. **6** Wolves. **7** Gary Megson. **8** Wolves. **9** Tranmere Rovers. **10** David Platt. **11** Lee Bradbury. **12** Grimsby Town. **13** Norwich City. **14** Ben Thornley. **15** Five. **16** Notts County and Nottingham Forest. **17** Barnsley. **18** Steve Bruce. **19** Manchester City **20** Wigan Athletic.

Quiz 72 **Cup Winners**

LEVEL 1

Answers – see page 386

1 Which country won the women's World Cup in 1996?
2 Who won the African Cup of Nations in 1998?
3 Who lost in the final?
4 Which Leeds player captained the losing side?
5 Which Hungarian side won the Fairs Cup in 1965?
6 Which English club contested the first Fairs Cup in 1958: London Unfair XI, London Select XI or Wimbledon?
7 Which French player won the European Cup in 1993 and 94?
8 Which teams did he play for?
9 Which Red Star won the European Cup in 1991?
10 The game was settled on penalties: True or false?
11 Which country are Kaiser Chiefs from?
12 Which French player was banned from the 1998 World Cup final?
13 Which cup did West Ham win in 1999?
14 Who scored the first golden goal to win a major tournament?
15 A Scottish club has never won the Cup Winners Cup: True or false?
16 Who captained the Germany side that won Euro 96?
17 How many times has Trevor Brooking received an FA Cup winners medal: Ten, two or none?
18 Which team set a record by winning a domestic double and the European Cup in the same season?
19 Which is the only Turkish side to win a major European competition?
20 Where did they play the game that won them the cup?

Answers

Leeds United (see Quiz 70)

1 George Graham. **2** Eric Cantona. **3** Celtic. **4** Robbie Keane. **5** David Batty. **6** Turkey. **7** Nigel Martyn. **8** Erik Bakke. **9** David O'Leary. **10** Everton. **11** Rio Ferdinand. **12** Billy Bremner. **13** Darren Huckerby. **14** Don Revie. **15** Jack Charlton. **16** All White. **17** Howard Wilkinson. **18** Forward. **19** Harry Kewell. **20** Peter Lorimer.

Quiz 73 **Paul Gascoigne**

LEVEL 1

Answers – see page 391

1 What is Paul Gascoigne's nickname?

2 With which club did he make his league debut?

3 Who was pictured holding Gascoigne by his privates?

4 For whom was Gascoigne playing in the infamous 1991 FA Cup final?

5 What was the original reason for Gascoigne crying in the semi-final against Germany in the 1990 World Cup?

6 For which Italian club did Gascoigne play?

7 Which ginger-haired ex-Radio One DJ is Gascoigne's long-time friend?

8 Which item of comedy clothing did Gascoigne wear on his return from the World Cup in 1990?

9 What is the name of Gascoigne's rotund friend and sometime minder?

10 Which Scottish club did Gascoigne play for?

11 In Scotland, what was the consequence of Gascoigne "booking" the referee when returning a dropped yellow card?

12 Which Gascoigne "musical" goal celebration was judged to be inappropriately sectarian?

13 Against which team did Gascoigne score from a free-kick in a Wembley FA Cup semi-final?

14 What did Gascoigne do in a training session for his Italian club that would make him miss many games?

15 Bryan Robson brought Gascoigne from Scotland to play for which club?

16 In what year did Gascoigne make his England debut?

17 For which Premier League club did Gascoigne sign in 2000?

18 In 1996 Gascoigne was voted Footballer of the Year in which country?

19 Against which country did Gascoigne score at Wembley in Euro 96?

20 What did Paul Gascoigne break in November 2000: his nose, his arm or his leg?

Answers

European Football (see Quiz 75)

1 Roma and Lazio. **2** Raul of Real Madrid. **3** Sporting Lisbon. **4** The Stadium of Light. **5** Copa del Rey. **6** Hamburg. **7** PSV. **8** Eindhoven. **9** Paris Saint Germain. **10** Valencia. **11** Naples. **12** Amsterdam. **13** Rotterdam. **14** Real Madrid. **15** Monaco. **16** Serie A. **17** Real Madrid. **18** Marseille. **19** Juventus. **20** The San Siro.

Quiz 74 **Everton**

Answers – see page 392

LEVEL 1

1 Where do Everton play?

2 Who was the manager of Everton as the 2000–01 season began?

3 When was the last time Everton won the FA Cup?

4 Which player holds the league appearance record for the club?

5 Which player is the club's record goalscorer?

6 Who did Everton beat to win the 1966 FA Cup final?

7 When were Everton last league champions?

8 Who was Everton's leading scorer in 1999–2000?

9 Who is the current owner of Everton?

10 Who scored twice in his first match after rejoining the club in summer 2000?

11 Who did Everton beat in the 1985 European Cup Winners' Cup final?

12 Who played for Everton in the 1970 title-winning season and managed them to the same trophy in 1984–85?

13 Which striker left Everton for Barcelona in 1986?

14 Which Everton player won a World Cup winner's medal in 1966?

15 What is the nationality of midfielder Idan Tal?

16 Who managed Everton for 305 days in 1994?

17 Who took over from him?

18 Who did Everton play in the 1987 Charity Shield?

19 Who was "The Golden Vision"?

20 Which centre-forward scored 135 goals for Everton in the 1970s?

Answers

England Captains (see Quiz 76)

1 Bobby Moore. **2** Billy Wright. **3** Paul Ince. **4** Alan Shearer. **5** Johnny Haynes. **6** Eddie Hapgood. **7** David Platt. **8** Bryan Robson. **9** Peter Shilton. **10** Frank Swift. **11** Kevin Keegan. **12** Emlyn Hughes. **13** Jimmy Armfield. **14** Bryan Robson. **15** Ray Wilkins. **16** Mick Mills. **17** Gerry Francis. **18** Martin Peters. **19** Three times. **20** Ron Flowers.

Quiz 75 **European Football**

LEVEL 1

Answers – see page 389

1 Which two clubs share the Olympic Stadium in Rome?

2 Who was reputedly the world's highest-paid player in 2000?

3 Who won the Portuguese championship in 1999–2000?

4 What is the name of Benfica's ground?

5 What is the Spanish Cup called?

6 Who did Tony Yeboah play for in 2000?

7 Who were the Dutch champions in 2000?

8 In which city do they play their football?

9 Which French club bought Nicolas Anelka during summer 2000?

10 Which Spanish club does Gaizka Mendieta play for?

11 Where is the San Paolo Stadium?

12 In which city do Ajax play?

13 In which city do Feyenoord play their football?

14 Who won the European Cup in 2000?

15 Which French club did Glenn Hoddle play for?

16 What is the Italian equivalent of the Premier League?

17 Who play at the Bernabeu?

18 Which French club won the European Cup in 1993 but were subsequently stripped of the title?

19 Which Italian club did Ian Rush play for?

20 In which stadium would you watch the Milan Derby?

Answers

Paul Gascoigne (see Quiz 73)

1 Gazza. **2** Newcastle United. **3** Vinny Jones. **4** Tottenham. **5** He was booked. **6** Lazio. **7** Chris Evans. **8** Fake breasts. **9** "Jimmy Five-bellies" Gardiner. **10** Rangers. **11** He was booked. **12** Pretend flute playing. **13** Arsenal. **14** Broke a leg. **15** Middlesbrough. **16** 1988. **17** Everton. **18** Scotland. **19** Scotland. **20** His arm.

Quiz 76 **England Captains**

LEVEL 1

Answers – see page 390

1 Who is the only England captain to hold up the World Cup trophy?
2 Which Wolves centre-half skippered England in 70 of his 105 appearances?
3 Who was the first black player to captain England?
4 Who led England during Euro 2000?
5 Who captained England to six successive victories between Oct 1960 and May 1961?
6 Which Arsenal player led England during the "Battle of Highbury" against Italy in 1934?
7 Who did Terry Venables name as his England captain for Euro 96?
8 Who captained England in the 1986 World Cup campaign in Mexico?
9 Who took over as captain for the infamous match against Argentina in the same tournament?
10 Which goalkeeper led England during some wartime internationals and two after the war?
11 Which England captain later became the team manager?
12 Which "Crazy Horse" captained England during the 1970s?
13 Who led England before Bobby Moore took over in 1963?
14 Who scored twice when he led England against Israel in February 1986?
15 Which Chelsea brother went on to captain England during the 1980s?
16 Which Ipswich full-back led England during the early 80s?
17 Which QPR midfielder led England eight times in the 1970s?
18 Who took over from his injured team-mate Moore to captain England during 1973–74?
19 How many times did Bobby Charlton skipper England?
20 Which Wolves player captained England in their 10–0 win over the USA in 1964?

Answers

Everton (see Quiz 74)

1 Goodison Park. **2** Walter Smith. **3** 1995. **4** Neville Southall. **5** Dixie Dean. **6** Sheffield Wednesday. **7** 1986–87. **8** Kevin Campbell. **9** Bill Kenwright. **10** Duncan Ferguson. **11** Rapid Vienna. **12** Howard Kendall. **13** Gary Lineker. **14** Ray Wilson. **15** Israeli. **16** Mike Walker. **17** Joe Royle. **18** Coventry City. **19** Alex Young. **20** Bob Latchford.

Quiz 77 **Have Boots, Will Travel**

LEVEL 1

Answers – see page 395

1. Which Man Utd midfielder has played for Forest and Cobh Rangers?
2. Which two strikers joined Arsenal from Inter Milan – separately – having also played for Ajax in Holland?
3. Which Everton player has played for Newcastle, Tottenham, Lazio, Rangers and Middlesbrough?
4. Which England international played at Leeds, went to Blackburn and Newcastle, then returned to Leeds?
5. Which England international returned to Chelsea from Blackburn Rovers?
6. Which Tottenham forward began at QPR, then signed for Newcastle?
7. Which manager had played at Tottenham, Monaco and Chelsea?
8. Which Manchester City forward had played for Derby and West Ham?
9. Which Southampton and England player came from Guernsey and stayed?
10. Which Leicester midfielder played for the blues of Wimbledon and Chelsea?
11. Which Villa forward played for Cambridge, Manchester Utd and Coventry?
12. Which Chelsea midfielder won the World Cup and did the English double both in 1998?
13. Which Scotland and Coventry defender won championships at Blackburn and Rangers?
14. Which Newcastle and England forward hit the net at Southampton and Blackburn Rovers?
15. Which Derby player came from Georgia to play for Man City, then Ajax?
16. Which veteran West Ham defender has spent 13 years at Highbury?
17. Which Premier League manager played for Aberdeen, Manchester United, Leeds United and Coventry City?
18. Which striker's travels have taken him from Norwich to Chelsea to Celtic?
19. Who played for West Bromwich and Manchester United and captained England before becoming a Premiership manager?
20. Which keeper began at Watford before moving to Liverpool, then Villa?

Answers

All Around the World (see Quiz 79)

1 USA. **2** South Korea and Japan. **3** Nigeria. **4** Brazil (4), Argentina (2). **5** South Africa. **6** Gary Lineker. **7** Harry Kewell. **8** Cameroon. **9** 1–0. **10** Nolberto Solano. **11** Australia. **12** Jamaica. **13** George Weah. **14** Jari Litmanen. **15** Colombia. **16** Iran 2–1. **17** China. **18** Cameroon. **19** Iran. **20** Argentina.

Quiz 78 **Alan Shearer**

Answers – see page 396

1 In which city was Alan Shearer born?

2 Which Saints were Shearer's first club?

3 How old was Shearer when he scored his first Football League hat-trick: 17, 18 or 19?

4 Which club paid a record £3.3m to buy him in 1992?

5 Which Celtic player formed the SAS partnership with Shearer that helped win the Championship in 1995?

6 How many goals did he score in the 4–1 victory over Holland in Euro 96?

7 In which year was Shearer voted the PFA and the Writers Footballer of the Year: 1994, 1995 or 1996?

8 Which Newcastle manager signed him in 1996 for £15m?

9 In which European championship was Alan Shearer the top scorer?

10 Has Shearer ever missed a penalty in England's penalty shoot-outs?

11 In Euro 96 who was the only team Shearer didn't score against: Scotland, Spain or Switzerland?

12 In which year did Shearer make his debut for England: 1992, 93 or 94?

13 Which English club tried to sign to Shearer in 1996?

14 Who did Shearer score against on his England debut: Scotland, France or Germany?

15 How did Shearer score against Germany in Euro 96 and Euro 2000?

16 Which of the five penalties has Shearer always taken for England in penalty shoot-outs?

17 Which tournament did Shearer miss because of a knee injury?

18 Against which country did Shearer score a penalty in Euro 2000?

19 Against which country did Shearer score England's winner in Euro 2000?

20 In which year did Shearer retire from international football?

Answers

Tony Adams (see Quiz 80)

1 Essex. **2** None. **3** Centre-back. **4** Tottenham. **5** 1986. **6** It was broken. **7** 1988. **8** False. **9** Euro 96. **10** Cup Winners Cup. **11** Drink driving. **12** Van Basten. **13** *Addicted.* **14** George Graham. **15** Caprice. **16** A donkey. **17** Alan Shearer. **18** Turkey. **19** Adams' first game after leaving prison. **20** *Henry V.*

Quiz 79 **All Around The World**

LEVEL 1

Answers – see page 393

1 Joe Max-Moore and Kasey Keller are from which country?

2 Which two Far East countries are to host the 2002 World Cup finals?

3 Kanu and Celestine Babayaro are from which country?

4 Who has won more World Cups: Argentina or Brazil?

5 Leeds' Lucas Radebe and Bolton's Mark Fish play for which country?

6 Which England international left Spurs to join Grampus Eight in Japan?

7 Which Australian won England's 2000 Young Player of the Year award?

8 Which African country were the first to reach the World Cup quarter finals, losing to England in 1990?

9 What was the score of Argentina's game against Japan in the 1998 World Cup?

10 Which Newcastle United player hails from Peru?

11 Goalkeepers Mark Bosnich and Mark Schwarzer play for which nation?

12 Wimbledon's Robbie Earle scored which country's first-ever World Cup finals goal?

13 Which former World Footballer of the Year hails from Liberia and has played for AC Milan, Chelsea and Manchester City?

14 Who is Liverpool's Finnish forward?

15 Rene Higuita shocked Wembley with his "scorpion kick" save in 1995. For which South American country was he playing?

16 Who won the match between the USA and Iran in the 1998 World Cup?

17 Dundee's for Crystal Palace defender Fan Zhiyi came from which country?

18 Arsenal's Lauren and Middlesbrough's Joseph-Desire Job are from which African country?

19 Which Middle Eastern country did Charlton's Karim Bagheri come from?

20 River Plate and Boca Juniors are teams from which country?

Answers

Have Boots, Will Travel (see Quiz 77)

1 Roy Keane. **2** Dennis Bergkamp and Nwankwu Kanu. **3** Paul Gascoigne. **4** David Batty. **5** Graeme Le Saux. **6** Les Ferdinand **7** Glenn Hoddle. **8** Paulo Wanchope. **9** Matt Le Tissier **10** Dennis Wise. **11** Dion Dublin. **12** Emmanuel Petir. **13** Colin Hendry. **14** Alan Shearer. **15** Georgi Kinkladze. **16** Nigel Winterburn. **17** Gordon Strachan. **18** Chris Sutton. **19** Bryan Robson. **20** David James.

Quiz 80 **Tony Adams**

LEVEL 1

Answers – see page 394

1 In which county was Adams born?

2 Besides Arsenal, which other clubs has Adams played for?

3 In which position does Adams play?

4 Against which team did Adams score the winning goal in the 1993 FA Cup semi-final?

5 In which year was Adams voted Young Player of the Year: 1986, 1987 or 1988?

6 What happened to Stephen Morrow's arm when celebrating winning the League Cup with Tony Adams in 1993?

7 In which year did Adams make his debut for England?

8 True or false: Adams has never scored for England?

9 In which tournament did Adams captain England?

10 Which trophy did Adams lift in 1994?

11 For what offence did Adams receive a custodial sentence?

12 Which Dutch striker so embarrassed Adams in the 1988 European Championship that it took him two years to regain his England place?

13 What is the name of Tony Adams' autobiography?

14 Which manager made Adams Arsenal's youngest-ever captain?

15 With which model was Adams linked in 1999?

16 Which animal did opposing supporters imitate to jibe the young Adams?

17 From which player did Adams take over the England captaincy in 2000?

18 For his display against which country in 1993 did Adams earn the tag "The Lion of Izmir"?

19 Why did 7,000 fans turn out to see an Arsenal reserves game in 1991?

20 Which of Shakespeare's plays did Adams take to read for inspiration in Euro 2000?

Answers

Alan Shearer (see Quiz 78)

1 Newcastle. **2** Southampton. **3** 17. **4** Blackburn Rovers. **5** Chris Sutton. **6** Two. **7** 1996. **8** Kevin Keegan. **9** Euro 96. **10** No. **11** Spain. **12** 1992. **13** Manchester United. **14** France. **15** Header. **16** The first. **17** Euro 92. **18** Romania. **19** Germany. **20** 2000.

Quiz 81 **Commentators**

LEVEL 1

Answers – see page 399

1 Who famously said, "Some people are on the pitch. They think it's all over... it is now!'

2 Which commentator is famous for his sheepskin coat?

3 Who left BBC for ITV in 1999?

4 Who presented ITV's *World of Sport*?

5 Who provided commentary for *Match of the Seventies*?

6 Which ex-player leads Sky Sports' football coverage?

7 Whose was the voice behind *The Big Match*?

8 Who presented *Match of the Day* after Des Lynam's departure?

9 Who ususally presents ITV's highlights programme?

10 Who is the anchorman for *Football Focus*?

11 Who is Channel 4's resident football expert?

12 Who is ITV's current main commentator?

13 Who is his usual expert summariser?

14 Which domestic competition did the BBC show live in 2001–02?

15 Whose *Football Night* dominated Radio 5's football coverage in 2000?

16 Who presents *Football Italia*?

17 Which Dutch ex-player joined the BBC team for Euro 2000?

18 Which 1984 FA Cup-winning striker is Sky Sports' top pundit?

19 Which female presenter moved from Sky Sports to front ITV's Premiership coverage?

20 Which former Scottish international defender regularly appears on *Match of the Day*?

Answers

Eurostars (see Quiz 83)

1 Rivaldo. **2** Luis Figo. **3** Marseille. **4** Mancheter United. **5** Oliver Kahn. **6** Galatasaray. **7** Bert Konterman. **8** Ajax. **9** Barcelona. **10** Roma. **11** Zinedine Zidane. **12** Juventus. **13** Ruud Gullit. **14** Lothar Matthaus. **15** Eusebio. **16** Dennis Bergkamp. **17** Eric Cantona. **18** Sylvain Wiltord. **19** Munich 1860. **20** Abel Xavier.

Quiz 82 **Old Football 2**

LEVEL 1

Answers – see page 400

1 Which club did Danny Blanchflower captain to the double in 1961?
2 Which club suffered the tragedy of the 1958 Munich air crash?
3 Who or what was Accrington Stanley?
4 Which country humiliated England 6–3 at Wembley in 1953?
5 Jock Stein managed the first British team to win the European Cup. Who?
6 Which Tom played for Preston North End and England after World War II and was arguably the best winger England ever had?
7 Bremner, Giles and Gray played for which team in the 60s?
8 Which Portuguese team did Manchester United beat to win the European Cup in 1968?
9 Which was the first World Cup England took part in?
10 Which 1950s and 60s Manchester United manager was famous for his "babes"?
11 In which year was *Match of the Day* first broadcast?
12 Which team were elected to the top division in 1919 and have never left it?
13 In which decade were the first floodlit league games played?
14 Which team used to play at Anfield before leaving in 1892?
15 Pickles the dog discovered which stolen trophy in England in 1966?
16 In 1965–66 what were English League clubs first allowed to do to injured players?
17 Bill Shankly began to mould which team in the 1960s?
18 Which Spanish club won the European Cup five times in succession from 1956?
19 For which country did the great Eusebio play?
20 Which British nation beat world champions England in 1967?

Answers

Pot Luck 3 (see Quiz 84)

1 Atletico Madrid. **2** Sunderland. **3** West Ham. **4** France. **5** Fulham. **6** Arsenal. **7** Chelsea. **8** Worthington (League) Cup. **9** Hearts. **10** Chile. **11** Nationwide Conference. **12** Six. **13** Germany. **14** Wigan. **15** Installed artificial surfaces. **16** Bruce Grobelaar. **17** Alan Shearer. **18** Sulzeer. **19** Manchester United. **20** Derby County.

Quiz 83 **Eurostars**

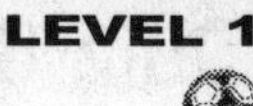

Answers – see page 397

1 Who is Barcelona's biggest Brazilian star?

2 Which Real Madrid player scored for Portugal against England in Euro 2000?

3 Which French club sold Robert Pires to Arsenal in summer 2000?

4 Who does Argentinian midfielder Juan Sebastian Veron play his club football for?

5 Whio saved the decisive penalty of the 2001 Champions League Final?

6 Which European club does Brazilian striker Mario Jardel play for?

7 Which Feyenoord defender joined Glasgow Rangers in summer 2000?

8 Who did Dutch "genius" Johan Cruyff play for in his home country?

9 Which club does Patrick Kluivert play for?

10 Japanese star Nakata plays for which Italian club?

11 Who was the European and World Footballer of the Year in 1999?

12 Where does he play his club football?

13 Which Dutch superstar joined Chelsea in 1995?

14 Who holds the most international caps for Germany?

15 Which Portuguese legend of the 1960s was nicknamed "The Black Panther"?

16 Which Dutch striker joined Arsenal from Inter in 1995?

17 Which Frenchman joined Manchester United from Leeds in 1992?

18 Who scored France's equaliser in the Euro 2000 final against Italy?

19 Which German club signed Norwegian Erik Mykland in summer 2000?

20 Which Portuguese blond bombshell joined Liverpool in 2002?

Answers

Commentators (see Quiz 81)

1 Kenneth Wolstenholme. **2** John Motson. **3** Desmond Lynam. **4** Dickie Davies. **5** Dennis Waterman. **6** Andy Gray. **7** Brian Moore. **8** Gary Lineker. **9** Bob Wilson. **10** Ray Stubbs. **11** Paul Elliott. **12** Clive Tyldesley. **13** Ron Atkinson. **14** AXA-sponsored FA Cup. **15** Trevor Brooking. **16** James Richardson. **17** Johan Cruyff. **18** Andy Gray **19** Gabby Logan (Yorath). **20** Alan Hansen.

Quiz 84 **Pot Luck 3**

LEVEL 1

Answers – see page 398

1 Which team won the Spanish double in 1996?

2 Scottish international Don Hutchison joined which team from Everton?

3 Joe Cole and Michael Carrick are which team's young hopefuls?

4 Zinedine Zidane plays for which country?

5 Harrods owner Mohamed Al Fayed is chairman at which London club?

6 Goals from Overmars and Anelka won the 1998 FA Cup final for who?

7 For whom did Roberto Di Matteo score against Middlesbrough to win the FA Cup Final?

8 Tottenham Hotspur beat Leicester City in what Final in 1999?

9 Which Edinburgh team won the 1998 Scottish Cup Final?

10 For which South American national team does Lazio's Marcelo Salas play?

11 Which league's champions can be promoted to League Division Three?

12 Since season 2000–01 for how many seconds is a goalkeeper allowed to keep hold of the ball?

13 In 2000, England, South Africa and Germany all bid to host the World Cup – who was successful?

14 Which team share the JJB stadium with the town's Rugby League side?

15 Luton Town, Oldham Athletic, QPR and Preston all did what to their pitches in the 80s?

16 Which former Liverpool and Zimbabwe goalkeeper was cleared of match-fixing in the high court?

17 Whose goal against Germany gave England their only victory in Euro 2000?

18 What is the Sol in Sol Campbell short for?

19 Which English side competed in the inaugural FIFA World Club Championship in Brazil in January 2000?

20 Which Premier League team play in white shirts and black shorts?

Answers

Old Football 2 (see Quiz 82)

1 Tottenham Hotspur. **2** Manchester United. **3** An old Football League club (1921–62). **4** Hungary. **5** Celtic. **6** Tom Finney. **7** Leeds United. **8** Benfica. **9** 1950. **10** Matt Busby. **11** 1964. **12** Arsenal. **13** 1950s. **14** Everton. **15** The World Cup. **16** Substitute them. **17** Liverpool. **18** Real Madrid. **19** Portugal. **20** Scotland.

Quiz 85 **The North West 2**

LEVEL 1

Answers – see page 403

1 "Football isn't a matter of life and death. It's more important than that," said which Liverpool legend?

2 Tony Book, Joe Mercer and Malcolm Allison were managers of which club?

3 Which Wanderers reached the 2000 FA Cup semi-final?

4 Which of the Lancashire clubs has spent the most seasons in the top flight?

5 Which team is based in Birkenhead?

6 Which North West Athletic play at the JJB stadium?

7 Who are Preston North End's nearest neighbours and fiercest rivals?

8 Pop group Dario G are named after Crewe Alexandra's long-serving manager. What is his surname?

9 Which North West club shares the name of its ground with a cricket ground?

10 Which North West reds have won more League titles than any other club?

11 Which are the only County playing League football in the North West?

12 Manchester City striker Paulo Wanchope hails from which country?

13 Gallagher, Gillespie and McAteer were in which team's 2000–01 squad?

14 Which Turf Moor Clarets had to win their last game of the season in 1987 to stay in the Football League?

15 Which former Newcastle, Fulham and England manager became Manchester City boss in 2001?

16 Bergsson, Fish and Holdsworth play for which of the region's Wanderers?

17 French defender Laurent Blanc kissed which part of Manchester United's Fabien Barthez's anatomy before each international match?

18 Blackpool's Steve McMahon played for which clubs in the North West?

19 Which team is older, Liverpool or Everton?

20 Which Potteries team, managed by Gudjon Thordarson, have a distinctly Icelandic feel to their squad?

Answers

Midlands Clubs 2 (see Quiz 87)

1 Leicester City and Stoke City. **2** Walsall. **3** Walsall v Port Vale. **4** Birmingham City. **5** Coventry City. **6** Lee Hughes. **7** West Brom. **8** Aston Villa. **9** Coventry City. **10** Walsall. **11** Terry Butcher. **12** Stoke City. **13** Aston Villa. **14** Wolves. **15** Internazionale. **16** Stoke City's. **17** Peter Taylor. **18** Kidderminster Harriers. **19** Leicester City. **20** Coventry City.

Quiz 86 **London Teams 2**

Answers – see page 404

1 Who used to play at Cold Blow Lane?

2 Jimmy Greaves played for three London teams: Spurs, Chelsea and who else?

3 Which club plays in Zampa Road?

4 Which ground featured the Shelf?

5 Who play in SW6?

6 Which London club did Kevin Keegan manage in 1998–99?

7 Who was manager of Arsenal before Arsène Wenger?

8 Which two London rivals contested a 1991 FA Cup semi-final at Wembley?

9 Which London club won the European Cup Winners Cup in 1965?

10 Who plays at Loftus Road?

11 Which London team is the most "athletic"?

12 Which London team finished highest in the 1999–2000 Premier League?

13 Who is the chairman of Watford?

14 Which former West Ham player managed Millwall in 1997–98?

15 Which London team play in white shirts with a red V?

16 Whose last four managers have been an Englishman, a Dutchman and two Italians?

17 Which London club has a Middlesex post code?

18 Which London club began life as Dial Square FC?

19 Whose headquarters are known as 748 High Road?

20 Who plays in E13?

Answers

Premier Stars 3 (see Quiz 88)

1 Made a rude home video. **2** Everton's. **3** The referee. **4** Left. **5** Croatia. **6** Arsenal. **7** Aston Villa. **8** Charlton Athletic. **9** Chelsea. **10** Jody Morris. **11** Middlesbrough. **12** Coventry City. **13** Derby County. **14** Everton. **15** Matt Holland. **16** Ipswich Town. **17** All broke legs. **18** Ade Akimbiyi. **19** Alf-Inge Haaland **20** Jordi Cruyff.

Quiz 87 **Midlands Clubs 2**

LEVEL 1

Answers – see page 401

1 Which Midlands clubs did legendary goalkeeper Gordon Banks play for?
2 Who plays at the Bescot Stadium?
3 If you saw the Saddlers playing the Valiants, who would you be watching?
4 Karren Brady is managing director of which Midlands club?
5 Who plays at Highfield Road?
6 Which West Bromwich striker signed for Coventry City in summer 2001?
7 Leeds United midfielder Johnny Giles had two spells as manager of which Midlands club?
8 For which club does Lee Hendrie play?
9 For which club does Steve Ogrizovic hold the appearances record?
10 Who used to play at Fellows Park?
11 Which ex-Ipswich and Glasgow Rangers defender managed Coventry between 1990 and 1992?
12 Who used to play at the Victoria Ground?
13 From which club did Manchester United buy Dwight Yorke in 1998?
14 Robbie Keane moved from which club to Coventry in 1999?
15 Where did he go after that?
16 Whose stadium will you find in Stanley Matthews Way?
17 Who became manager at Filbert Street in 2000?
18 Which Midlands team were promoted to the Third Division in 1999–2000?
19 For which club did Stan Collymore sign for from Aston Villa?
20 Manager John Sillett led which club to FA Cup glory in 1987?

Answers

The North West 2 (see Quiz 85)

1 Bill Shankly. **2** Manchester City. **3** Bolton. **4** Everton. **5** Tranmere Rovers. **6** Wigan. **7** Blackpool. **8** Gradi. **9** Old Trafford. **10** Liverpool. **11** Stockport. **12** Costa Rica. **13** Blackburn Rovers. **14** Burnley. **15** Kevin Keegan. **16** Bolton. **17** His (bald) head. **18** Liverpool and Everton. **19** Everton. **20** Stoke City.

Quiz 88 **Premier Stars 3**

LEVEL 1

Answers – see page 402

1 What did Rio Ferdinand, Frank Lampard and Kieron Dyer do on their holidays in Ayia Napa?
2 Dave Watson and Richard Gough were which team's ageing club and team captains in 2000?
3 Who got in trouble for punching the air after a Patrik Berger goal for Liverpool?
4 Are Ryan Giggs, Davor Suker and Patrik Berger all right- or left-footed?
5 Former Arsenal and West Ham man Davor Suker played for which European nation?
6 Lauren Bisan-Etame Mayer left Real Mallorca for which Premier League team in 2000?
7 The defender Alpay plays at which Midlands Premier League club?
8 Jonatan Johansson is which London red-shirted team's striker?
9 Eidur Gudjohnsen replaced Chris Sutton at which London club?
10 Which Jody is a rare Englishman at Stamford Bridge?
11 Croatian Alen Boksic has taken up arms at which Riverside club?
12 Which club does Belgian striker Cedric Roussel play for?
13 Which club first fielded Estonian goalkeeper Mart Poom in the Premier League?
14 Stephen and Mark Hughes are unrelated but were together at which club?
15 Which Holland player was captain of Ipswich Town in 2000?
16 Derby County's Craig Burley has an uncle in charge of which top team?
17 What injury has befallen Stuart Pearce (twice), Ian Pearce, Shaka Hislop and Joe Cole at West Ham?
18 Which Ade moved from Wolves to Leicester City?
19 Which Alf-Inge is Norway and Manchester City's midfielder?
20 Which Jordi, a son of a great Dutchman, played a bit-part at Manchester United?

Answers

London Teams 2 (see Quiz 86)

1 Millwall. **2** West Ham. **3** Millwall. **4** White Hart Lane. **5** Chelsea and Fulham. **6** Fulham. **7** Bruce Rioch. **8** Spurs and Arsenal. **9** West Ham. **10** QPR. **11** Charlton Athletic. **12** Arsenal. **13** Sir Elton John. **14** Billy Bonds. **15** Leyton Orient. **16** Chelsea. **17** Brentford. **18** Arsenal. **19** Spurs. **20** West Ham.

Quiz 89 **The 70s 2**

LEVEL 1

Answers – see page 407

1. Which part of your anatomy did a banner claim Norman Hunter would bite?
2. Which England star, now a pundit, played for West Ham in the 70s?
3. Which former QPR manager scored twice in a 5–1 victory over Scotland in 1975?
4. Which multple Premiership-winning team were relegated in 1974?
5. Which London team featured Venables, Marsh and Bowles?
6. Who were the only British team in the 1974 and 1978 World Cup finals?
7. In which postion did Mike Channon play for Southampton and England?
8. Vogts, Beckenbauer and Hoeness played for which World Cup-winning nation in 1974?
9. Which controversial Derby County and Nottingham Forest manager spent 44 days in charge of Leeds United in 1974?
10. Bob Wilson, George Graham and Charlie George played for which team in the 70s?
11. What current European club competition replaced the Inter-Cities Fairs Cup in 1972?
12. Which London club entered the Football League in 1977, made the top flight by 1988 and were relegated in 2000?
13. Cruyff, Neeskens and Rensenbrink played for which country in the 70s?
14. In which position did Peter Bonetti play for Chelsea and England?
15. What fate befell Kevin Keegan and Billy Bremner in the 1974 Charity Shield?
16. Which Doc took Manchester Utd to the 1977 Cup Final?
17. Which 70s Liverpool player was twice European Footballer of the Year?
18. Which team did Ray Clemence help win European Cups in the 70s?
19. Which Scottish "reds" did Alex Ferguson manage in the late 70s?
20. For which club did Kenny Dalglish score over 100 goals before joining Liverpool?

Answers

Who Are They? (see Quiz 91)

1 Everton. **2** Leicester City. **3** Coventry City. **4** France. **5** Watford. **6** Southampton. **7** Chelsea. **8** Aston Villa. **9** Italy. **10** Leeds United. **11** Manchester City. **12** Tottenham Hotspur. **13** Manchester United. **14** Brighton and Hove Albion. **15** Wimbledon. **16** Arsenal. **17** Liverpool. **18** Newcastle United. **19** QPR. **20** West Ham.

Quiz 90 **The 80s 2**

Answers – see page 408

1 Which 80s cup-winning side featured Beasant, Wise and Fashanu?

2 How many times did Spurs win the league championship in the 80s?

3 Which cup did Liverpool win four times in succession in the early 80s?

4 Which Dons were the last non-Glasgow team to win the Scottish Premier Division (in 1985)

5 How many points did a football league team get for a win in 1980–81?

6 What great goalscorer missed Liverpool's penalty in the 1988 FA Cup final?

7 Which manager took Watford to second place in the League in 1982–83?

8 In 1981 which London club became the first to have an artifical pitch?

9 Which former England manager went to manage Barcelona in the 80s?

10 Who was the darling of Newcastle and Tottenham before joining Marseille in 1989?

11 Which 20-year-old Manchester United and Northern Ireland striker scored the winning goal in the 1985 FA Cup final?

12 The occasion of the Hillsborough tragedy of 1989 was an FA Cup semi-final between Nottingham forest and who?

13 Which Ally is Rangers greatest goalscorer and *A Question of Sport* captain?

14 The 80s football TV show *Saint and Greavsie* was presented by which former players?

15 Who did Tottenham sign from Newcastle for £2m in 1988?

16 Which unfairly nicknamed "Quasimodo" won a championship with Liverpool before helping rejuvenate Keegan's Newcastle?

17 Which 80s championship-winning team included Southall, Reid and Gray?

18 Which international 80s team included Tigana, Platini and Giresse?

19 Which "Champagne Charlie" did Arsenal sign from Celtic in the 80s?

20 Which England cricketing hero played for Scunthorpe United in the 80s?

Answers

Who Did What? 6 (see Quiz 92)

1 Emmanuel Petit. **2** Leicester City. **3** Manchester City. **4** Charlton. **5** West Ham. **6** Bradford City. **7** Leeds United. **8** Gary Mabbutt. **9** Peter Taylor. **10** Swindon Town. **11** Arsenal. **12** Peter Beagrie. **13** Henrik Larsson. **14** Alan Shearer. **15** Ian Wright. **16** Tony Yeboah. **17** Paul Gascoigne. **18** Sir Alex Feguson. **19** Bobby Moore. **20** Brian Clough.

Quiz 91 **Who Are They**

LEVEL 1

Answers – see page 405

1 Can the School of Science pupils get back to the top?

2 These Foxes were Premier League strugglers in 2001–02.

3 These Sky Blues had an explosive manager and a Moroccan touch.

4 This team won a successive World Cup and European Championship.

5 Taylor, Blissett and Barnes helped these Hornets to good times in the 80s.

6 Channon, Keegan and Le Tissier have been their stars.

7 Blue is the colour for these continental Kings Road strollers.

8 They might have Merson, Wright and Joachim but they are still the Villains.

9 These Azzurri reached the Euro 2000 final.

10 Revie, Wilkinson... Can O'Leary win the championship for them as well?

11 Maine Road has seen many glory days from this team. But not for years.

12 Bill Nicholson, Keith Burkinshaw and Terry Venables are among this club's successful managers.

13 The biggest club in the world, according to stock market values?

14 Since this south coast outfit reached the FA Cup final in 1984 they have been down, down, down?

15 This small club Crazy Gang made the top flight, and won the FA Cup to boot.

16 Arsene's French polished outfit.

17 "You'll Never Walk Alone" sang this team's Kop as they won everything in sight in the 70s and 80s.

18 Kevin Keegan's Magpies who blew a massive lead in the 1995–96 championship.

19 These Superhoops play at Loftus Road.

20 Ron Greenwood turned this London club into a "Football Academy".

Answers

The 70s 2 (see Quiz 89)

1 "Yer Legs". **2** Trevor Brooking. **3** Trevor Francis. **4** Manchester United. **5** QPR. **6** Scotland. **7** Striker. **8** West Germany. **9** Brian Clough. **10** Arsenal. **11** UEFA Cup. **12** Wimbledon. **13** Holland. **14** Goalkeeper. **15** They were sent off for fighting. **16** Tommy Docherty. **17** Kevin Keegan. **18** Liverpool. **19** Aberdeen. **20** Celtic.

Quiz 92 **Who Did What? 6**

LEVEL 1

Answers – see page 406

1 Who left Arsenal with Marc Overmars for Barcelona in 2000?

2 Who won the Worthington Cup in 2000 with a goal by Matt Elliott?

3 Who were relegated from the Premier League when manager Alan Ball mistakenly told them to play the game out for a draw?

4 Who won the Division One play-off in 1998: Sunderland or Charlton?

5 Which club was ordered to replay a 1999 Worthington Cup game?

6 Who just avoided relegation in 2000, then entered the Inter-Toto Cup?

7 Who were involved in a near disaster at Stanstead airport after a match at West Ham in 1998?

8 Who won the PFA Merit Award in 2000 after a career playing for Tottenham and England despite suffering from diabetes?

9 Who won promotion at Gillingham before moving to Leicester?

10 Who won promotion to Division One under Ossie Ardiles in 1990 only to be found guilty of "financial irregularities" and immediately demoted?

11 Who won the League Cup and FA Cup double in 1993?

12 Who has celebrated his goals for Bradford City by somersaulting?

13 Who broke a leg in a EUFA Cup match playing for Celtic against Lyon?

14 In 1996 who was Blackburn Rovers" leading scorer?

15 Who called the referee "a muppet" at Highbury in 1996?

16 Which Ghanaian won two consecuive Match of the Day goals of the month in 1995 with explosive shots for Leeds United?

17 In 1991 who scored from a free-kick for Spurs in the first FA Cup semi-final at Wembley?

18 Who won the Manager of the Year award on five occasions in the 1990s?

19 Which former England captain died in 1993?

20 Who retired in 1993 after 17 years in charge of Nottingham Forest?

Answers

The 80s 2 (see Quiz 90)

1 Wimbledon. **2** None. **3** The League (Milk) Cup. **4** Aberdeen. **5** Two. **6** John Aldridge **7** Graham Taylor. **8** QPR. **9** Terry Venables. **10** Chris Waddle. **11** Norman Whiteside. **12** Liverpool. **13** Ally McCoist. **14** Ian StJohn and Jimmy Greaves. **15** Paul Gascoigne. **16** Peter Beardsley. **17** Everton. **18** France. **19** Charlie Nicholas. **20** Ian Botham.

Quiz 93 **Pot Luck 4**

LEVEL 1

Answers – see page 411

---

1. Patrick Kluivert plays for which country?
2. Which Harriers were Football League new boys in 2000?
3. Which two London clubs share Selhurst Park?
4. Which ex-Arsenal player's autobiography is called *Mr Wright*?
5. Which Sky pundit former player wagered his hair against Bradford City avoiding relegation in 2000 – and lost?
6. Which club had the original Kop end?
7. Euro 2000 star Luis Figo plays for which country?
8. How many League games do Premiership teams play in a season?
9. Who won a World Cup as a player with England and went to two as the Republic of Ireland's manager?
10. Three times European Footballer of the Year Michel Platini played for which country?
11. Businessman Sam Hammam was associated with which club in the 1980s and 90s?
12. Which Manchester United brothers played for England in Euro 2000?
13. Which country lost the Euro 2000 final in extra time?
14. Upson and Taylor are among which London club's young stars?
15. Which Manchester United midfielder scored a hat-trick for England against Poland in 1999?
16. Ken Bates is the chairman of which Premier League club?
17. Which of these clubs has Alan Shearer not played for: Newcastle United, Blackburn Rovers or Leeds United?
18. In 2000 Chelsea spent £15m on who: Hasselbaink, Stanic or Panucci?
19. Who scored the goal in the "They think it's all over" commentary?
20. Which Middlesbrough and England player never puts his shirt on until he is on the pitch?

Answers

United (see Quiz 95)

1 Newcastle United. **2** False. **3** Davor Suker. **4** Lucas Radebe. **5** Everton. **6** Leeds. **7** Torquay. **8** West Ham. **9** Hartlepool. **10** Dundee. **11** Manchester. **12** Sheffield. **13** Carlisle. **14** Dwight Yorke. **15** Rotherham. **16** Cambridge United. **17** Nigel Martyn. **18** Upton Park. **19** United Arab Emirates. **20** True.

Quiz 94 City

Answers – see page 412

LEVEL 1

1 Which City plays at Vetch Field?
2 Joe Royle has been manager at which City?
3 Which City plays in the Potteries?
4 St James Park is home to which City?
5 Who was the last City to win the FA Cup?
6 Which City is managed by Bruce Rioch?
7 Which City play at Bootham Crescent?
8 How many Citys were there in the Premier League in 2000–01?
9 When City play Rovers in a local derby in Division Two in 2000–01, where is the match being played?
10 Which City play in amber and black striped shirts?
11 Which City is found on Moss Side?
12 Which City escaped relegation from the Premier League in 1999–2000?
13 Which City is nicknamed "The Bluebirds"?
14 Which City won the European Cup Winners' Cup in 1970?
15 Which City won the Worthington Cup in 2000?
16 Which City became United in 1919?
17 Which City would play a local derby against Villa?
18 Which City did Martin O'Neill leave to join Celtic in summer 2000?
19 Which City is nicknamed "The Bantams"?
20 If your team were playing away against the Minstermen, where would the match be played?

Answers

Complete the Name (see Quiz 96)

1 Argyle. **2** North End. **3** Wanderers. **4** Rovers. **5** Villa. **6** Orient. **7** and Hove Albion. **8** Athletic. **9** Town. **10** County. **11** Wanderers. **12** Palace. **13** Albion. **14** Thistle. **15** Rovers. **16** Forest. **17** Rovers. **18** Alexandra. **19** County. **20** Vale.

Quiz 95 **United**

LEVEL 1

Answers – see page 409

1 Which United reached the FA Cup final in 1998 and 1999?

2 True or false: West Ham United are nicknamed the Cockneys?

3 Which former United man plays for Croatia and won the Golden Boot at France 98?

4 Which United captain and centre-half is also captain of South Africa?

5 Newcastle United bought Duncan Ferguson from and sold him back to which club?

6 Which United play at Elland Road?

7 Torquay or Exeter – which one is United?

8 Which United play in claret and blue?

9 Which United have never played at Wembley: Peterborough or Hartlepool?

10 Which Scottish United reached the 1987 UEFA Cup final: Dundee or Ayr?

11 Which United won the "treble" in 1999?

12 Which United are Wednesday's local rivals?

13 Which United is the most northerly in the Nationwide League?

14 Which United striker played World Cup qualifiers for Trinidad and Tobago?

15 Rotherham or Darlington – which one is United?

16 Which team plays in the football league – Cambridge City or Cambridge United?

17 Which United goalkeeper played for England in Euro 2000?

18 Where do West Ham United play?

19 Apart from the United States which other United is a member of FIFA?

20 True or false: Ian Botham played football for Scunthorpe United?

Answers

Pot Luck 4 (see Quiz 93)

1 The Netherlands. **2** Kidderminster. **3** Wimbledon and Crystal Palace. **4** Ian Wright. **5** Rodney Marsh. **6** Liverpool. **7** Portugal. **8** 38. **9** Jack Charlton. **10** France. **11** Wimbledon **11** Gary and Phillip Neville. **13** Italy. **14** Arsenal's **15** Paul Scholes. **16** Chelsea. **17** Leeds United. **18** Hasselbaink. **19** Geoff Hurst. **20** Paul Ince.

Quiz 96 **Complete The Name**

LEVEL 1

Answers – see page 410

1 Plymouth...
2 Preston...
3 Wolverhampton...
4 Tranmere...
5 Aston...
6 Leyton...
7 Brighton...
8 Charlton...
9 Huddersfield...
10 Notts...
11 Bolton...
12 Crystal...
13 West Bromwich...
14 Partick...
15 Blackburn...
16 Nottingham...
17 Raith...
18 Crewe...
19 Derby...
20 Port...

Answers

City (see Quiz 94)

1 Swansea City. **2** Manchester City. **3** Stoke City. **4** Exeter City. **5** Coventry City in 1987. **6** Norwich City. **7** York City. **8** Three. **9** Bristol. **10** Hull City. **11** Manchester City. **12** Bradford City. **13** Cardiff City. **14** Manchester City. **15** Leicester City. **16** Leeds. **17** Birmingham City. **18** Leicester City. **19** Bradford City. **20** York.

Quiz 97 **Pot Luck 5**

LEVEL 1

Answers – see page 415

1 Steven Gerrard and Jamie Carragher are young guns at which club?

2 Which of these teams does not play at home in a red shirt: Arsenal, Newcastle United or Liverpool?

3 Which football club owner is also the owner of top people's store Harrods?

4 Which club's ground has the Stretford End stand behind one goal?

5 Graeme Souness, Kenny Dalglish and Brian Kidd have all managed which club?

6 Croydon met Doncaster Belles in which Cup final in May 2000?

7 Fulham's John Collins played for which national team?

8 Who is found near the benches at football matches?

9 How many games did Kevin Phillips play for England in Euro 2000: One, two or none?

10 How many goals did Thierry Henry score in Euro 2000: Three, two or one?

11 Which Frenchman appeared in a shampoo advert?

12 Which country do Sampdoria come from?

13 Which Premier League manager's autobiography is called *Managing My Life*?

14 True or False: George Best never played in the World Cup Finals?

15 What shirt number did Bobby Moore usually play in for club and country?

16 Alan Curbishley was manager at which London club in 2000?

17 Which Aston Villa and England midfielder admitted to drink, gambling and drug problems while at Arsenal?

18 Which Tottenham Hotspur German player initiated the "diving" goal celebration?

19 Which Football League team have the name Argyle?

20 Which England striker had a soccer school on television in 2000?

Answers

Name That Team (see Quiz 98)

1 Rangers. **2** Manchester City. **3** Sunderland. **4** Tottenham Hotspur. **5** West Ham. **6** Newcastle **7** Southampton. **8** Everton. **9** Liverpool. **10** Ipswich. **11** Aston Villa. **12** Fulham. **13** Blackburn Rovers. **14** Leicester City. **15** Middlesbrough. **16** Bolton Wanderers. **17** Celtic. **18** Arsenal. **19** Chelsea. **20** Manchester United.

Quiz 98 **Name That Team**

LEVEL 1

Answers – see page 413

1 Mols, De Boer, Klos.

2 Weaver, Goater, Wright-Phillips.

3 Gray, Quinn, Phillips.

4 Sullivan, Sheringham, Sherwood.

5 Potts, Cole, Kanoute.

6 Dabizas, Solano, Shearer.

7 Dodd, Kachloul, Pahars.

8 Campbell, Gascoigne, Unsworth.

9 Hyppia, Hamman, Henchoz.

10 George, Holland, Stewart.

11 Barry, Dublin, James.

12 Saha, Marlet, Hayles.

13 Cole, Hughes, Duff.

14 Flowers, Izzet, Eadie.

15 Boksic, Southgate, Ehiogu.

16 Jaskeleinen, Bergsson, Ricketts.

17 Douglas, Larsson, Sutton.

18 Keown, Parlour, Bergkamp.

19 Zola, Le Saux, Hasselbaink.

20 Scholes, Butt, Blanc.

Answers

Pot Luck 6 (see Quiz 99)

1 Highbury. **2** Gascoigne's arm. **3** Wimbledon. **4** Andy Cole. **5** Stanley Matthews. **6** Failed fitness test. **7** 1966 World Cup winners. **8** Nine. **9** Ten **10** Brazil. **11** Dino Zoff. **12** Newcastle. **13** Both also managed Arsenal. **14** Broken leg. **15** England's. **16** Gianfranco Zola. **17** Tottenham. **18** Bristol Rovers. **19** Don Hutchison. **20** Hampden Park.

Quiz 99 **Pot Luck 6**

Answers – see page 414

LEVEL 1

1 Which ground has the Clock End behind one goal?

2 What broke when Paul Gascoigne elbowed George Boateng?

3 Sam Hammam sold his remaining shares in which club in 2000?

4 Who scored his 100th goal for Manchester United at Wimbledon in February 2000?

5 100,000 people attended the funeral of which footballer in 2000?

6 Why didn't Ruud van Nistelrooy sign for Manchester United in June 2000?: He failed a fitness test; they wouldn't give him and his wife a Mercedes; he didn't like English food.

7 Hunt, Stiles, Wilson and Cohen were part of what famous team?

8 Which shirt number does Alan Shearer play in?

9 What shirt number did Pele, Cruyff and Maradona all play in?

10 Which country do Pele's club Santos come from?

11 Which former Italian goalkeeper resigned as manager after Euro 2000?

12 Who have a popular Gallowgate End at their stadium?

13 What do Spurs managers George Graham and Terry Neill have in common?

14 What injury has befallen Stuart Pearce (twice), Shaka Hislop and Joe Cole – all at West Ham?

15 Howard Wilkinson is whose technical director?

16 Which Chelsea forward signed from Italian club Parma in 1996?

17 What was Steve Perryman's only club?

18 Which club have played at Eastville, Bath City's Twerton Park and the Memorial Ground since 1986?

19 Which former Sunderland Don is a self-confessed Newcastle United fan?

20 Which ground was reopened in time for the Scottish FA Cup Final in 1999?

Answers

Pot Luck 5 (see Quiz 97)

1 Liverpool. **2** Newcastle United. **3** Fulham. **4** Manchester United. **5** Blackburn Rovers. **6** The Women's FA Cup Final. **7** Scotland. **8** The fourth official. **9** None. **10** Three. **11** David Ginola. **12** Italy. **13** Alex Ferguson. **14** True. **15** Six. **16** Charlton Athletic. **17** Paul Merson. **18** Jürgen Klinsmann. **19** Plymouth. **20** Michael Owen.

Quiz 1 **Who Did What?**

Answers – see page 419

LEVEL 2

1 Who did Kevin Keegan pick as England captain following Alan Shearer's retirement from international football?
2 Who rejoined Southampton from Blackburn in 1999 having been away for only a year?
3 Which team opted out of the 2000 FA Cup?
4 Who did England international Kieron Dyer play for before his move to Newcastle?
5 In what year did Sir Alf Ramsey die?
6 Which team beat Glasgow Rangers at Ibrox in August 2000?
7 Which English team plays at the Stadium of Light?
8 Who scored the winner in the 2000 FA Cup final?
9 Which referee controversially sent off three players in an Arsenal v Liverpool match in August 2000?
10 Who currently manages Wales and plays for Blackburn?
11 Who won his 50th Scotland Cap in the opening game of World Cup '98?
12 Who became manager of Glasgow Celtic in 2000?
13 Who scored for England in Euro 2000 while playing his club football in Spain?
14 Which former Arsenal player has his own TV chat show?
15 Which leggy Costa Rican led the Manchester City attack in 2000?
16 Who scored twice for Vasco Da Gama in a FIFA Club World Championship match against Manchester United in January 2000?
17 Who was manager of Southampton at the start of the 2000 season?
18 Who won the League Cup in 1996?
19 Who was sent off during the 2000 Charity Shield?
20 Who scored for Leeds in the second leg of the Champions League qualifying round against Munich 1860 in August 2000?

Answers

Who Plays At...? (see Quiz 3)

1 St Johnstone. **2** Motherwell. **3** Rangers. **4** Hearts. **5** Dunfermline. **6** Dundee. **7** Dundee United. **8** Aberdeen. **9** Hibernian. **10** Raith Rovers. **11** Stenhousemuir. **12** St Mirren. **13** Kilmarnock. **14** Ayr United. **15** Celtic. **16** Queen's Park (and Scotland). **17** Falkirk. **18** Dumbarton. **19** Morton. **20** Stranraer.

Quiz 2 **Goals Galore**

LEVEL 2

Answers – see page 420

1 Who scored on his debut for Celtic after moving from Chelsea in summer 2000?

2 Who scored four goals for Man Utd against Newcastle in August 1999?

3 Who scored twice for Germany in the Euro 96 final?

4 Who scored a hat-trick for Chelsea in the FA Cup third round against Hull in January 2000?

5 Who was the last player to score more than one goal in an FA Cup final?

6 Who scored a hat-trick for Everton in a league game against West Ham in February 2000?

7 What is the record score in a World Cup qualifying match?

8 Who scored for Bayern Munich in the 1999 European Cup final?

9 Who scored Manchester United's equaliser in that same match?

10 Who scored a hat-trick for Portugal against Germany in Euro 2000?

11 Who was the last player to score more than once in a League Cup final?

12 Who scored a stunning hat-trick for Arsenal in a league game against Leicester in Feburary 1999?

13 Who scored two own goals in a match between Liverpool and Manchester United in September 1999?

14 Who lost 7–2 to Spurs in a league game in 1999–2000?

15 Who scored a hat-trick on his home debut for Man City in August 2000?

16 Which American scored 8 goals in 18 games for Everton in 1999–2000?

17 Who scored a hat-trick for Charlton in a league game against Southampton in 1999–2000?

18 Which Derby and ex-Middlesbrough striker was known as "The White Feather"?

19 Who lost 5–0 to Everton in the league on Boxing Day 1999?

20 Which Icelandic striker left Bolton for Chelsea in summer 2000?

Answers

The Premier League (see Quiz 4)

1 Charlton. **2** Dave Watson. **3** Doug Ellis. **4** Bradford City. **5** Graham Rix. **6** Lee Bowyer. **7** Wimbledon. **8** Three. **9** Derby County. **10** Ipswich. **11** Manchester City. **12** Mike Reed. **13** Leicester City. **14** Peterborough United. **15** Pierlugi Casiraghi. **16** False (sixth in 1995–96). **17** Southampton. **18** France. **19** Phil Thompson. **20** Lee Dixon.

Quiz 3 **Who Plays At...?**

Answers – see page 417

LEVEL 2

1 McDiarmid Park?

2 Fir Park?

3 Ibrox?

4 Tynecastle?

5 East End Park?

6 Dens Park?

7 Tannadice?

8 Pittodrie?

9 Easter Road?

10 Stark's Park?

11 Ochilview Park?

12 Love Street?

13 Rugby Park?

14 Somerset Park?

15 Parkhead?

16 Hampden Park?

17 Brockville Park?

18 Boghead Park?

19 Cappielow Park?

20 Stair Park?

Answers

Who Did What (see Quiz 1)

1 Tony Adams. **2** Kevin Davies. **3** Manchester United. **4** Ipswich Town. **5** 1999. **6** Celtic. **7** Sunderland. **8** Roberto Di Matteo. **9** Graham Poll. **10** Mark Hughes. **11** John Collins. **12** Martin O'Neill. **13** Steve McManaman. **14** Ian Wright. **15** Paulo Wanchope. **16** Romario. **17** Glenn Hoddle. **18** Aston Villa. **19** Roy Keane. **20** Alan Smith.

Quiz 4 The Premier League

Answers – see page 418

LEVEL 2

1 Which club received their record fee for Danny Mills?

2 Which member of Everton's 2000 squad was the only Premiership player to have managed the club he played for?

3 Who is Aston Villa's "deadly" chairman?

4 Nolan and Atherton joined which team in the 2000 close season?

5 Who was player-manager Vialli's right-hand man at Chelsea?

6 Who was the first Premiership player to collect 14 yellow cards in 1999–2000: Lee Bowyer, Patrick Vieira or Paolo Di Canio?

7 Which relegated side were the only club Manchester United did not beat in their 1999–2000 Premiership-winning season?

8 How many games did Manchester United lose in 1999–2000?

9 Rory Delap was which Premier League club's top scorer in 1999–2000?

10 Brewers Greene King sponsor which Premier League club?

11 *King of the Kippax* is a fanzine of which Premier League club??

12 Which Premier League referee punched the air after a Patrik Berger goal for Liverpool: Graham Poll, Uriah Rennie or Mike Reed?

13 Gerry Taggart was the Player of the Year for which team in 1999–2000?

14 Tottenham's Etherington and Davies were signed from which club?

15 Who did Chelsea cash in their insurance policy on in 2000?

16 True or False, up to and including the 1999–2000 season Everton had never finished in the top half of the Premier League?

17 Which team other than Coventry City had two Moroccans in their squad in 2000–01?

18 Newcastle United's former players Didi and Goma were from which country?

19 Who is Gerard Houllier's right-hand man at Liverpool?

20 Who is the oldest, Tony Adams, Lee Dixon or Martin Keown?

Answers

Goals Galore (see Quiz 2)

1 Chris Sutton. **2** Andy Cole. **3** Oliver Bierhoff. **4** Gustavo Poyet. **5** Eric Cantona scored two penalties in 1994. **6** Nick Barmby. **7** Australia 31 American Samoa 0. **8** Mario Basler. **9** Teddy Sheringham. **10** Sergio Conceicao. **11** Steve McManaman scored twice in 1995. **12** Nicolas Anelka. **13** Jamie Carragher. **14** Southampton. **15** Paulo Wanchope. **16** Joe-Max Moore. **17** Clive Mendonca. **18** Fabrizio Ravanelli. **19** Sunderland. **20** Eidur Gudjohnsen.

Quiz 5 **Football Italia**

LEVEL 2

Answers – see page 423

1 Which team missed their chance of the 1999–2000 Italian championship on the last day of the season?

2 Which Second Division Italian team did Luigi Riva join and take to the top in the 60s?

3 Which Italian team featured Van Basten, Gullit and Rijkaard?

4 What is the name commonly given to the Italian championship?

5 Which Italian team featured Rummenigge, Matthaus and Klinsmann?

6 Inzaghi, Milhajlovic and Simeone starred together at which club?

7 What is the name of the stadium shared by the Rome teams?

8 In which city is the Sampdoria club based?

9 What is the Italian word for football?

10 Gabriel Batistuta moved from Fiorentina to which club in May 2000?

11 Which Italian team play in an all white kit?

12 Which former England captain had a short and unsuccessful stint as manager of Sampdoria?

13 Why is an Italian club awarded a gold star above their badge?

14 What is the Italian word given to the defensive tactical system perfected in the 60s?

15 How much did Inter Milan pay Coventry City for Robbie Keane: £7m, £10m or £13m?

16 Which Chilean helped Lazio to their first European triumph in 1999?

17 Shevchenko, Bierhoff and Maldini play at which Italian club?

18 Which team share the Delle Alpi stadium with Juventus?

19 Giovanni Trapattoni managed which Italian club to six Serie A trophies in ten years?

20 For which Italian team does Brazilian star Ronaldo play?

Answers

Manchester United (see Quiz 7)

1 Ole Gunnar Solskjaer. **2** Ryan Giggs after 15 seconds v Southampton in 1995. **3** Chelsea. **4** George Best. **5** Andy Cole. **6** 7–0 to United. **7** Aston Villa. **8** Maine Road. **9** Brian Kidd. **10** George Best. **11** Newcastle United. **12** Twice, 1993–94 and 1995–96. **13** Eric Cantona. **14** Tommy Docherty. **15** Wes Brown. **16** Duncan Edwards. **17** Karel Poborsky. **18** Bryan Robson. **19** FC Porto. **20** Norman Whiteside.

Quiz 6 **Goalkeepers**

Answers – see page 424

LEVEL 2

1. Who made his League debut for Manchester United aged 37 in April 2001?
2. What is Laurent Blanc's superstition involving Fabian Barthez?
3. What nationality is Middlesbrough's keeper Mark Schwarzer?
4. Which Everton goalkeeper famously refused to leave his posts at half-time as a protest?
5. Which keeper has the record number of Spanish international caps?
6. Which keeper replaced the sick Gordon Banks for England against West Germany in Mexico 1970?
7. Name a former club of West Ham's Shaka Hislop.
8. Which French goalkeeper did Liverpool sign on a free transfer from Leicester City in 2000?
9. Who was Arsenal's Austrian understudy to David Seaman?
10. Which goalkeeper scored for Manchester United in a UEFA Cup tie in 1995–96?
11. Which British goalkeeper was selected for an international squad at the same time as his father was national coach of another country and this goalkeeper was not born in either country?
12. Which keeper scored an own goal on his England debut in June 2000 against Malta?
13. Which keeper holds the record number of caps for Northern Ireland?
14. Which veteran keeper broke his jaw in a Scottish FA Cup final?
15. Which keeper won championship medals with Leeds and Arsenal?
16. Why were keepers Segers and Grobbelaar in the news in 1994?
17. What 42-year-old keeper played for Coventry in 1999–2000?
18. For what country did Toldo keep goal during Euro 2000?
19. Jose Luis Chilavert, free-kick and penalty-taking expert as well as goalkeeper, plays for which country?
20. Which goalkeeper did Manchester United sign from Venezia in August 1999?

Answers

Memorable Matches (see Quiz 8)

1 Arsenal. **2** Ray Houghton. **3** Bulgaria. **4** Cameroon. **5** Inverness Caledonian Thistle. **6** Manchester United. **7** Holland (three in the shoot-out). **8** Romania. **9** Don Hutchison. **10** Chelsea. **11** 7–0. **12** Manchester United. **13** Liverpool. **14** Leeds United. **15** 3–3. **16** 4–3. **17** Manchester City. **18** David Pleat. **19** Manchester United and Arsenal. **20** 6–2.

Quiz 7 **Manchester United**

LEVEL 2

Answers – see page 421

1 Who went on as a sub and scored four goals in a league game against Nottingham Forest in February 1999?
2 Who scored United's quickest-ever goal?
3 Who did United play in Bobby Charlton's last league game for the club?
4 Who is "The Belfast Boy"?
5 Who scored United's winner in the Champions League semi-final against Juventus in 1999?
6 What was the score when United met Barnsley in the league in October 1997?
7 Who did United play in the last league match of the 1999–2000 season?
8 Where did United play their home games in World War II?
9 Who left United in September 1998 to manage Blackburn Rovers?
10 Who scored six goals for United in an 8–2 FA Cup victory over Northampton Town in 1970?
11 Who did United beat in the 1999 FA Cup final?
12 How many times did United win the double in the 1990s?
13 Who scored the winner in the 1996 FA Cup final v Liverpool?
14 Who was United's manager between 1972 and 1977?
15 Who made his international debut for England in April 1999, less than a year after making his first-team debut for United?
16 Which United legend once had the nickname "Boom Boom"?
17 Which Czech joined United in 1996 but left two years later?
18 Who is the longest-serving captain in United's history?
19 Which club did Peter Schmeichel join after United?
20 Which United player became the youngest ever to appear in a World Cup, in 1982?

Answers

Football Italia (see Quiz 5)

1 Juventus. **2** Cagliari. **3** AC Milan. **4** Scudetto (Shield). **5** Inter Milan. **6** Lazio. **7** Olimpico Stadio. **8** Genoa. **9** Calcio. **10** Roma. **11** Parma. **12** David Platt. **13** For ten championship victories **14** Catenaccio. **15** £13m. **16** Marcelo Salas. **17** AC Milan. **18** Torino. **19** Juventus. **20** Inter Milan.

Quiz 8 **Memorable Matches**

LEVEL 2

Answers – see page 422

1 Who won the league championship at Anfield in 1989?
2 Who scored the Republic of Ireland's goal in their memorable 1–0 win over Italy in the 1994 World Cup?
3 Who memorably knocked Germany out of the 1994 World Cup?
4 Who beat Argentina in their 1990 World Cup group match?
5 Whose victory led to the headline "Super Cally Go Ballistic, Celtic Are Atrocious!"?
6 Who beat Nottingham Forest 8–1 in the Premiership in 1998–99?
7 Which country missed five penalties in a close match in Euro 2000?
8 Who did the Republic of Ireland beat on penalties to reach the World Cup quarter finals in 1990?
9 Who scored Scotland's goal in their 1999 1–0 victory over England?
10 Who beat Manchester United 5–0 in the 1999–2000 season?
11 What was the result of Leeds' 1972 humiliation of Southampton?
12 Who inflicted Arsenal's worst defeat for 70 years, in 1990?
13 Who destroyed Nottingham Forest 5–0 in 1988?
14 Who did Colchester memorably knock out of the FA Cup in 1971?
15 What was the result of the second leg of Manchester United's 1999 Champions League semi-final against Barcelona at the Nou Camp?
16 What unusual score appeared in 1996 and 1997 in the games at Anfield between Liverpool and Newcastle United?
17 Who came back from being 1–0 down against Blackburn Rovers to win 4–1 and gain promotion to the Premier League in 2000?
18 Which Luton Town manager famously jigged across the pitch at Maine Road after his side had avoided relegation in 1983?
19 Who had points deducted for an on-pitch brawl in the 1990–91 season?
20 By what score did Rangers get thumped at Celtic Park in the first Old Firm match of the 2000–01 season?

Answers

Goalkeepers (see Quiz 6)

1 Andy Goram. **2** Kissed his bald pate. **3** Australian. **4** Neville Southall. **5** Andoni Zubizarreta. **6** Peter Bonetti. **7** Reading or Newcastle. **8** Peggy Arphexad. **9** Alex Manninger. **10** Peter Schmeichel. **11** Jonathan Gould (Scotland, son of Wales coach Bobby). **12** Richard Wright. **13** Pat Jennings. **14** Jim Leighton. **15** John Lukic. **16** Charged with match-fixing. **17** Steve Ogrizovic. **18** Italy. **19** Paraguay. **20** Massimo Taibi.

Quiz 9 **The Nationwide League**

LEVEL 2

Answers – see page 427

1 Which team lost the Division One play-off semi-finals in three consecutive years before finally winning the Wembley decider?

2 Former Chelsea player and manager John Hollins took which side to Division Two in 1999–2000?

3 Which is the only Nationwide League club in Buckinghamshire?

4 Which side is managed by Jan Molby and plays at Aggborough?

5 O'Neill, Gregory and Sanchez have managed which club?

6 Who is Peterborough United's high-profile manager-owner?

7 Balti Boy Lee Hughes was which Division 1 team's leading scorer in 2000?

8 Which club were relegated from Division Three in 1999 after gaining League status in 1987?

9 Ketsbaia, Bazeley and Emblen featured in which team's line-ups?

10 Which club did Sam Allardyce leave in October 1999?

11 Ricky Hill was with which now Division 3 club when he won three England caps?

12 Which Nationwide League team has ex-Wimbledon benefactor Sam Hamann invested in?

13 Which team are temporarily at home at the Withdean Stadium?

14 Dunn, Duff and Jansen helped which team win promotion from Division 1 in 2001?

15 Who is Brentford's owner-chairman and former manager?

16 Who has won the Division One championship the most times since League re-organisation in 1993?

17 Which Nationwide team reached the FA Cup semi-finals in 2000?

18 Marco Gabbiadini and Jamie Forrester form the strike force at which bunch of cobblers?

19 Which Nationwide League player won his 60th Nothern Ireland cap in October 1995?

20 For which club did Indian international Baichung Bhutia first sign?

Answers

Foreigners in Britain (see Quiz 11)

1 Middlesbrough. **2** Fulham. **3** French. **4** Gianluca Vialli. **5** Belgian. **6** Bayern Munich. **7** Norway. **8** Wolves. **9** Benfica. **10** Liberia. **11** Liverpool. **12** Norway. **13** Cameroon. **14** Abel Xavier. **15** Dutch. **16** West Ham. **17** Everton. **18** Sheffield Wednesday. **19** Bradford City. **20** Lazio.

Quiz 10 **Pot Luck**

Answers – see page 428

LEVEL 2

1 If you watched The Canaries v The Swans, which teams would you see?
2 Who does keeper Dave Beasant play for?
3 Louis Van Gaal manages which national team?
4 Former Arsenal striker Luis Boa Morte now plays for which other London club?
5 Who plays at Home Park?
6 Which country does Sunderland sensation Stanislav Varga come from?
7 Who is the captain of Charlton Athletic?
8 Who replaced Paul Jewell as manager of Bradford City in summer 2000?
9 Who were Manchester United's new sponsors in 2000?
10 Who are reputedly always lucky "when the year ends in the figure one"?
11 For whom does Danish keeper Thomas Sorensen play his club football?
12 Which two teams contest the "Old Firm" derby?
13 Which player was the subject of a "tug-of war" between Middlesbrough and Liverpool in summer 2000?
14 Who plays at Bramall Lane?
15 For which club does Latvian Marian Pahars play?
16 What nationality is Leeds United's Harry Kewell?
17 Who is Middlesbrough's "Ginger Warrior"?
18 Who is the German national coach?
19 Which Italian club have a strike force of Christian Vieri and Ronaldo?
20 For which club did Welsh international striker John Hartson start the 2000–01 season?

Answers

The Nationwide League (see Quiz 12)

1 George Best. **2** Arsenal. **3** Paper Lace. **4** Showaddywaddy. **5** Hibernian. **6** Rod Stewart. **7** Kevin Keegan. **8** David Byrne. **9** "Anfield Rap". **10** The Lightning Seeds. **11** "Nessun Dorma". **12** Nottingham Forest. **13** Gazza. **14** The Three Tenors. **15** Tottenham. **16** St Etienne. **17** Chelsea. **18** Stuart Pearce. **19** 1982. **20** "Three Lions".

Quiz 11 **Foreigners in Britain**

LEVEL 2

Answers – see page 425

1 Which club did French international Christian Karembeu join in summer 2000?
2 Which club does Jean Tigana manage?
3 What nationality is he?
4 Who started the 2000 campaign as the Premier League's only Italian manager?
5 Derby striker Branco Strupar is what nationality?
6 Markus Babbel joined Liverpool in summer 2000 from which German club?
7 Ex-Wimbledon manager Egil Olsen was from which country?
8 For which First Division team does French defender Ludovik Pollet play?
9 Southampton's Moroccan Tahar El Khalej joined them from which club?
10 Manchester City's George Weah comes from which African country?
11 Two Premiership clubs have French managers. One is Arsenal, which is the other?
12 Leeds' Eiric Bakke plays for which country?
13 Arsenal signed Laureano Mayer from Real Mallorca during summer 2000. For whom does he play his international football?
14 Which Portuguese star did Everton sign before Euro 2000?
15 What nationality is Watford's Nordin Wooter?
16 Eyal Berkovic joined Celtic from which London club?
17 Italian Alessandro Pistone left Newcastle in summer 2000 for which club?
18 Petter Rudi plays for which Yorkshire side?
19 Romanian Dan Petrescu left Chelsea for which Yorkshire club in summer 2000?
20 Alen Boksic joined Middlesbrough from which Italian team?

Answers

The Nationwide League (see Quiz 9)

1 Ipswich Town. **2** Swansea City. **3** Wycombe Wanderers. **4** Kidderminster Harriers. **5** Wycombe Wanderers. **6** Barry Fry. **7** WBA. **8** Scarborough. **9** Wolves. **10** Notts County. **11** Luton Town. **12** Cardiff City. **13** Brighton and Hove Albion. **14** Blackburn Rovers. **15** Ron Noades. **16** Sunderland, twice. **17** Bolton Wanderers. **18** Northampton. **19** Nigel Worthington. **20** Bury.

Quiz 12 **Music and Football**

LEVEL 2

Answers – see page 426

1 Pop group The Wedding Present named an album after which footballer?

2 Tottenham's defeat of which team inspired Chas and Dave's "banned" single "The Victory Song"?

3 Which 70s band recorded "Billy Don't Be a Hero" and helped Nottingham Forest with "We've Got the Whole World in our Hands"?

4 The guitarist of which glam 70s rock 'n' roll revivalists is the father of Leicester City's Stefan Oakes?

5 Fish, Jim Diamond and The Proclaimers all support which team?

6 Which international recording star helped Scotland out in 1978 with "Ole Ola (Mulher Brasiliera)"?

7 Which player was "Head over Heels in Love" according to his 1979 hit?

8 Which member of the band Talking Heads is a Dumbarton supporter?

9 Which number one hit included a rap by John Barnes?

10 Which group accompanied Skinner & Baddiel on their "Three Lions" record?

11 Which opera anthem was the 1990 official World Cup song?

12 Who enters the pitch accompanied by "Robin Hood and His Merry Men"?

13 Whose rap song "Geordie Boys" gently hit the charts in 1990?

14 Jose Carreras, Placido Domingo and Luciano Pavarotti performed together before all the 90s World Cups under which name?

15 Three-chord hit-makers Status Quo are supporters of which team?

16 "He's on the Phone" was a hit for which band named after a successful 70s French team?

17 Blur's Damon Albarn follows which London club?

18 Which England full-back introduced the Sex Pistols on stage in 1998?

19 "This Time (We'll Get It Right)" was the World Cup song in which year?

20 Which song were Germany asked to sing at their triumphant Euro 96 homecoming?

Answers

Pot Luck (see Quiz 10)

1 Norwich and Swansea. **2** Nottingham Forest. **3** Holland. **4** Fulham. **5** Plymouth Argyle. **6** Czech Republic. **7** Mark Kinsella. **8** Chris Hutchings. **9** Vodafone. **10** Spurs. **11** Sunderland. **12** Celtic and Rangers. **13** Christian Ziege. **14** Sheffield United. **15** Southampton. **16** Australian. **17** Andy Campbell. **18** Rudi Völler. **19** Internazionale. **20** Wimbledon.

Quiz 13 **Beards and Moustaches**

LEVEL 2

Answers – see page 431

1 Which Liverpool defender and *Match of the Day* expert has maintained a well-groomed moustache?
2 Who was Brazil's bearded captain in the 82 and 86 World Cup finals?
3 Which England goalkeeper has a much-admired moustache?
4 Which Liverpool goalscorer had a "Yosser"-type moustache?
5 Which 60s icon played with a full beard and moustache ensemble?
6 Which player and broadcaster hides his extensive chin with a beard?
7 Who was Ipswich's, Liverpool's and Scotland's moustachioed midfielder?
8 Which side did Paul Mortimer captain in the 80s with full facial hair?
9 Which Portuguese and Everton defender entertained Euro 2000 with his dyed beard?
10 Which Liverpool, Rangers and Sampdoria player's moustache emphasised his hardman image?
11 Which sometime wispish bearded forward played at Spurs and Barcelona?
12 Which Birmingham City, Everton and England 70s marksman carried a full beard?
13 Which 80s bearded England striker scored in Aston Villa's European Cup triumph?
14 Which Northern Irish Wolves striker sported a ranchero-type moustache?
15 Which former Premiership manager favoured a fashionable goatee?
16 For which then non-league giantkillers did hirsute Dickie Guy keep goal?
17 Who was Chelsea's beard-and-moustache combination 70s centre-back?
18 Which chairman's facial hair emphasises his caricature as a farmer?
19 Who played and managed West Ham with a neat beard and moustache?
20 Which scruffily-bearded player scored a memorable FA Cup final goal?

Answers

Leeds United (see Quiz 15)

1 Howard Wilkinson. **2** David Batty. **3** Harte and Kelly (nephew and Uncle). **4** John Charles. **5** Eddie Gray. **6** Bayern Munich. **7** Galatasaray. **8** Jason Wilcox. **9** Brian Clough. **10** Jimmy Floyd Hasselbaink. **11** Allan Clarke. **12** Tony Yeboah. **14** 1995–96. **15** Arsenal. **16** Peter Lorimer. **17** Joe Jordan. **18** Eric Cantona. **19** Johnny Giles. **20** Alan Smith.

Quiz 14 **Shirt Numbers**

Answers – see page 432

LEVEL 2

1 Whose is the most famous of all number 10 shirts?

2 Which great Frenchman wore the number 10 shirt when his country won the 1984 European Championships?

3 Who wore his Manchester United number 7 shirt with the collar up?

4 Which number 6 headed the winner for Chelsea v Leeds in the 1970 FA Cup final replay?

5 Who famously wore the number 6 shirt for West Ham and captained England to World Cup glory in 1966?

6 Who scored 68 goals in 62 matches for Germany often wearing number 13?

7 Who wore number 5 for Spurs and scored to win the 100th FA Cup?

8 Which number 9 scored the winner for Villa in the 1992 European Cup final?

9 Which number 16 led Manchester United to the treble in 1998–99?

10 According to Leeds United fans, who is "England's number 1"?

11 Who is Liverpool's number 10?

12 Which number 7 holds the Premier League record for the furthest successful shot at goal?

13 Who took the Chelsea number 9 shirt from Chris Sutton in summer 2000?

14 Who was England's number 1 when they won the World Cup?

15 Who famous number 6 for Liverpool now appears regularly on BBC's *Match of the Day*?

16 Which diminutive Italian plays in the number 25 shirt for Chelsea?

17 Which England number 9 opened the scoring in the Euro 96 semi-final against Germany?

18 Which number 9 holds the goalscoring record for Glasgow Rangers?

19 Which former number 1 managed his country to the final of Euro 2000?

20 Which number 19 scored six goals as Italy won the 82 World Cup?

Answers

Euro 96 (see Quiz 16)

1 0–0. **2** 1–1. **3** Jürgen Klinsmann. **4** Hristo Stoichkov. **5** 4–1. **6** Ally McCoist. **7** Germany. **8** Czech Republic. **9** Karel Poborsky's. **10** Stuart Pearce. **11** Spain. **12** Alan Shearer. **13** France. **14** Sammer. **15** 1–1. **16** Teddy Sheringham. **17** Jamie Redknapp. **18** Gareth Southgate. **19** Turkey. **20** David Platt.

Quiz 15 **Leeds United**

LEVEL 2

Answers – see page 429

---

1 Who was Leeds United's manager when they won the League in 1992?

2 Which England international returned to the club from Newcastle in 1998?

3 Which two current Leeds United players are related?

4 Who did Leeds United sell to Juventus in 1957?

5 Which Leeds United winger became their manager in 1982?

6 Who defeated Leeds United in the 1975 European Cup final?

7 Which team defeated Leeds United in the 2000 UEFA Cup semi-final?

8 Which wide-midfielder did Leeds sign from Blackburn Rovers in 1999?

9 Which 70s Leeds United manager lasted just 44 days before being sacked?

10 Who did Leeds sell to Atletico Madrid for £12m in 1999?

11 Which "Sniffer" was Leeds" profilic 1970s goalscorer?

12 Which Leeds striker's stunning shots won the BBC Goal of the Month award in August and September 1995?

13 Which manager permanently changed Leeds United's kit to all-white?

14 In which season did Harry Kewell make his debut for Leeds United?

15 Who did Leeds beat to win the 1972 FA Cup?

16 Leeds' leading goalscorer played his first game for them in 1962 and his last in 1985. Who is he?

17 Which Leeds and Scotland centre-forward left Leeds United for Manchester United in 1978?

18 Which forward joined Manchester United from Leeds in 1992 after scoring 14 goals in 25 games?

19 Who was Leeds' Republic of Ireland 60s and 70s midfield genius?

20 Which Leeds striker was called up to the full England squad in August 2000?

Answers

Beards and Moustaches (see Quiz 13)

1 Mark Lawrenson. **2** Socrates. **3** David Seaman. **4** Ian Rush. **5** George Best. **6** Jimmy Hill. **7** John Wark. **8** Aston Villa. **9** Abel Xavier. **10** Graeme Souness. **11** Steve Archibald. **12** Bob Latchford. **13** Peter Withe. **14** Derek Dougan. **15** Gianlucca Vialli. **16** Wimbledon. **17** Mickey Droy. **18** Ken Bates. **19** Billy Bonds. **20** Ricky Villa.

Quiz 16 **Euro 96**

LEVEL 2 

Answers – see page 430

1 What was the result of Scotland's opening match, against Holland?

2 What was the result of England's opening match, against Switzerland?

3 Who scored one of the best goals of the tournament for Germany against Russia?

4 Who scored in each of Bulgaria's matches in the tournament?

5 By what score did England beat Holland in the group stage?

6 Who scored Scotland's only goal in the tournament?

7 A 0–0 draw with which country in their last group game put Italy out of the tournament?

8 Who drew 3–3 with Russia at Anfield to qualify for the knock-out stage?

9 Whose chip won the Czech Republic's quarter-final with Portugal?

10 Who scored in the penalty shoot-out against Spain, having missed his previous England penalty?

11 Whose late goal at Elland Road put them into the quarter-finals?

12 Who scored England's goal after only three minutes of the semi-final?

13 Who did the Czech Republic beat on penalties in their semi-final?

14 Which German was suspended for the semi-final: Reuter, Möller or Sammer?

15 What was the score in the final after 90 minutes?

16 Who was England's only other scorer in the tournament besides Shearer and Gascoigne?

17 Which England half-time substitute was himself substituted in the Scotland match?

18 Whose penalty miss cost England a place in the final?

19 Which country failed to score in the tournament?

20 The semi-final against Germany proved to be whose last ever match for England?

Answers

Shirt Numbers (see Quiz 14)

1 Pele's. **2** Michel Platini. **3** Eric Cantona. **4** David Webb. **5** Bobby Moore. **6** Gerd Müller. **7** Ricardo Villa. **8** Peter Withe. **9** Roy Keane. **10** Nigel Martyn. **11** Michael Owen. **12** David Beckham. **13** Jimmy Floyd Hasselbaink. **14** Gordon Banks. **15** Alan Hansen. **16** Gianfranco Zola. **17** Alan Shearer. **18** Ally McCoist. **19** Dino Zoff. **20** Paolo Rossi.

Quiz 17 **Liverpool**

LEVEL 2

Answers – see page 435

1 How many times have Liverpool won the FA Cup?

2 Who was manager immediately before Gérard Houllier?

3 Who is the most capped Liverpool player?

4 Which former Liverpool great is currently the assistant manager at Anfield?

5 Which fabulous Finn joined the Reds in summer 1999?

6 Whose free-kick gave Liverpool the lead in the league game against Manchester United in March 2000?

7 Whose goals won Liverpool the FA Cup in 1992?

8 When did Liverpool last win the League Cup?

9 For whom does Vladimir Smicer play his international football?

10 What nationality is Stephane Henchoz?

11 Where is Liverpool's Academy based?

12 Who did Liverpool beat to win the FA Cup in 1989?

13 Who was the Liverpool manager that day?

14 Who was Liverpool's captain in 1999–2000?

15 Who holds the Liverpool appearances record?

16 Which former Liverpool legend is the most successful manager ever in British football?

17 Which Liverpool player scored the first goal ever shown on *Match of the Day*?

18 Which Liverpool striker was a scoring substitute against Albania in September 2001?

19 From which club did Liverpool sign Sander Westerveld?

20 Who is the latest of the few to play for both Liverpool and Everton?

Answers

Scotland Internationals (see Quiz 19)

1 Kenny Dalglish. **2** Billy Bremner. **3** Ally MacLeod. **4** Brazil. **5** Archie Gemmill. **6** England. **7** Costa Rica. **8** Jim Baxter. **9** Gary McAllister. **10** Paul McStay. **11** Andy Goram. **12** 0–0. **13** Morocco. **14** John Collins. **15** Jim Leighton. **16** Willie Ormond. **17** Denis Law. **18** Alex McLeish. **19** Zaire. **20** 5–1.

Quiz 18 **Nicknames**

LEVEL 2

Answers – see page 436

1 Oldham Athletic?

2 Swansea City?

3 Millwall?

4 Huddersfield Town?

5 Port Vale?

6 Sheffield United?

7 Exeter City?

8 Colchester United?

9 Bury?

10 Mansfield Town?

11 Stoke City?

12 Wycombe Wanderers?

13 Grimsby Town?

14 Brentford?

15 Northampton Town?

16 Rochdale?

17 Gillingham?

18 Luton Town?

19 Peterborough United?

20 Hartlepool United?

Answers

Pot Luck 2 (see Quiz 20)

1 Wimbledon. **2** Hristo Stoichkov. **3** They re-entered as "Lucky Losers". **4** Leicester City. **5** Attilio Lombardo **6** Kanu. **7** Robbie Fowler. **8** Steve Bould. **9** Howard Wilkinson. **10** Swansea. **11** John Hartson. **12** Brighton and Hove Albion. **13** AC Milan. **14** Vasco de Gama. **15** Faith healer. **16** Lauren. **17** Barry Ferguson. **18** Alan Curbishley. **19** Bobby Robson. **20** The Football Association.

Quiz 19 **Scotland Internationals**

LEVEL 2

Answers – see page 433

1 Who is Scotland's most capped player?
2 Which Scotland captain was banned "for life" along with four other players after a night club incident in Copenhagen?
3 Which manager led Scotland to the World Cup in Argentina in 1978?
4 Who did Scotland play in the opening game of the '98 World Cup?
5 Whose brilliant dribble and goal against Holland gave Scotland a chance of qualification for the knockout stage of the '78 World Cup?
6 Which country conceded a goal to Holland that denied Scotland qualification to the knockout stage of Euro 96?
7 Which Central American country beat Scotland in the 1990 World Cup?
8 Which player will forever be remembered for sitting on the ball during Scotland's 1967 victory over World Champions England?
9 Which Scottish midfielder retired from international football in 1998?
10 Which Celtic midfielder won 76 caps for Scotland from 1984 to 1997?
11 Which Scotland goalkeeper has also represented his country at cricket?
12 What was the result when Scotland met Brazil in the 1974 World Cup?
13 Who beat Scotland 3–0 in St Etienne in the 1998 World Cup?
14 Which former Celtic and Everton midfielder retired from international football on joining Fulham in 2000?
15 Which goalkeeper played 91 times for Scotland from 1983 to 1999?
16 Which manager took Scotland to the 1974 World Cup?
17 Who debuted for Scotland aged 18 and became equal leading goalscorer?
18 Who hasn't managed Scotland: Sir Matt Busby, Sir Alex Ferguson or Alex McLeish?
19 Which African team did Scotland beat 2–0 in the 1974 World Cup?
20 What was the score when Scotland's "Wembley Wizards" famously beat England in 1928?

Answers

Liverpool (see Quiz 17)

1 Five times. **2** Roy Evans. **3** Ian Rush. **4** Phil Thompson. **5** Sami Hyypia. **6** Patrik Berger. **7** Michael Thomas and Ian Rush. **8** 2001. **9** Czech Republic. **10** Swiss. **11** Kirkby. **12** Everton. **13** Kenny Dalglish. **14** Jamie Redknapp. **15** Ian Callaghan. **16** Bob Paisley. **17** Roger Hunt. **18** Robbie Fowler. **19** Vitesse Arnhem in Holland. **20** Avel Xavier.

Quiz 20 **Pot Luck 2**

LEVEL 2

Answers – see page 434

1. Dave Bassett, Joe Kinnear and Egil Olsen have all managed which club?
2. Which Bulgarian hero went to play in the Japanese J-League?
3. In which way were Darlington lucky in the 2000 FA Cup competition?
4. Which team's players and officials were charged over their ticket distribution in the 1999 Worthington Cup Final?
5. Which bald Italian briefly managed Crystal Palace?
6. In 1999, who apologised to the opposition for his first goal for Arsenal?
7. Who was fined for making an unsavoury gesture at Graeme Le Saux?
8. In 1999, who left Highbury for Sunderland after 11 years at Arsenal?
9. Who took charge of the England squad in between Hoddle and Keegan?
10. Cyril the Swan is which team's mascot?
11. Who kicked Eyal Berkovic in the head in a West Ham training session?
12. Which near bankrupt team wear the logo "Skint" on their shirts?
13. Silvio Berlusconi is the owner of which Italian club?
14. Which Brazilian team beat Manchester United 3–1 in the 2000 World Club Championship?
15. What role did Eileen Drewery play in England's 1998 World Cup campaign?
16. Which 2000 Premier League newcomer's surname is Bisan-Etame Mayer?
17. Which Rangers player was the Scottish Footballer of the Year in 2000?
18. At the start of the 2000–2001 season who was easily the Premier League's longest serving manager?
19. Which English manager "discovered" Ronaldo?
20. Who moved from their home at Lancaster Gate in 2000?

Answers

Nicknames (see Quiz 18)

1 The Latics. **2** The Swans. **3** The Lions. **4** The Terriers. **5** The Valiants. **6** The Blades. **7** The Grecians. **8** The U's. **9** The Shakers. **10** The Stags. **11** The Potters. **12** The Chairboys. **13** The Mariners. **14** The Bees. **15** The Cobblers. **16** The Dale. **17** The Gills. **18** The Hatters. **19** The Posh. **20** The Pool.

Quiz 21 The North East

LEVEL 2

Answers – see page 439

1 What was the last year Newcastle won the FA Cup?

2 Who was manager of Sunderland in 1993?

3 Who is Middlesbrough's most-capped player?

4 Who did Bryan Robson take over from as manager of Middlesbrough?

5 How much did Atletico Madrid pay for Juninho in July 1997?

6 What was the name of Middlesbrough's former ground?

7 If you were watching a match at Victoria Park, in which town would you be?

8 Sunderland's record league victory was 9–1, away, in 1908. Who were the opposition?

9 Who holds the appearances record at Sunderland?

10 What honour did Middlesbrough win in 1976?

11 Where did Sunderland finish in the Premier League in 1999–2000?

12 At which club did Kevin Phillips used to play?

13 Who scored Sunderland's winner in the 1973 FA Cup final?

14 Which Vauxhall Conference team did Newcastle defeat on the way to the FA Cup final in 1998?

15 Who did Newcastle play in 1999 FA Cup semi-final?

16 Which Newcastle player went without a squad number during Ruud Gullit's reign?

17 What is the name of Middlesbrough's training facility?

18 Who plays at the Feethams Ground?

19 In which Division do they play?

20 Noel Whelan joined Middlesbrough from which club in summer 2000?

Answers

Spanish Soccer (see Quiz 23)

1 Deportiva La Coruña. **2** Athletic Bilbao. **3** Valencia. **4** Barcelona. **5** Madrid. **6** Michael Robinson. **7** Espanyol. **8** Atletico Madrid. **9** Real Zaragoza. **10** Seville. **11** John Toshack. **12** Sunderland. **13** Louis Van Gaal. **14** Three. **15** Redondo. **16** White shirts, black shorts. **17** Barcelona. **18** Johan Cruyff. **19** Nicolas Anelka. **20** Barcleona.

Quiz 22 **South American Soccer**

LEVEL 2

Answers – see page 440

1 In which country are the club Flamengo based?

2 Brazilian Mirandinha played for which English team in 1987–88?

3 Argentinian Alberto Tarantini joined which English club in 1978?

4 What is the difference between the Copa America and the Copa Libertadores?

5 In which country are the club Peñarol based?

6 Who won the 2001 Copa America?

7 With which Brazilian club is Pele associated?

8 In which country are the club Boca Juniors based?

9 With which club did Mexican Hugo Sanchez win the European Golden Boot?

10 In which country do Cruz Azul, America and Necaxa play?

11 Which player's clubs include Boca Juniors (twice), Barcelona, Napoli, Sevilla and Newell's Old Boys?

12 Who was the only Uruguayan playing in the Premier League in 2000?

13 Who won the inaugural World Club Championship in Brazil in 2000?

14 Who did Real Betis sign from Sao Paulo for £21m in 1997?

15 Which Brazilian was the first player to win the World Footballer of the Year award in successive seasons?

16 Gabriel Batistuta, Mario Kempes and Marcelo Salas all played for which famous Buenos Aires team?

17 Which Colombian celebrated his goals at Newcastle with a somersault?

18 Who is Sunderland's Honduran?

19 Which Colombian was South American Player of the Year in 1987 and 1994?

20 Which Argentinian played for Real Madrid and Spain and was twice European Footballer of the Year?

Answers

The 70s (see Quiz 24)

1 Leeds United. **2** None. **3** Spurs and Wolves. **4** Bobby Moore. **5** Ipswich Town. **6** Leighton James. **7** Celtic. **8** Asa Hartford. **9** Viv Anderson. **10** Sammy Nelson. **11** Hereford. **12** Ricky George. **13** Chelsea. **14** Trevor Francis. **15** Kenny Dalglish. **16** Don Revie. **17** Billy Bremner and Kevin Keegan. **18** Argentina. **19** Derby County. **20** Brian Clough.

Quiz 23 **Spanish Soccer**

LEVEL 2

Answers – see page 437

1 Which team won the Spanish league in 1999–2000?
2 Which club admits only players of Basque ethnic origin?
3 Which Spanish team lost in the 2000 Champions League final?
4 Which Spanish club bought Petit and Overmars from Arsenal?
5 In which city is the Bernabéu stadium?
6 Which former Liverpool player is a football presenter on Spanish TV?
7 Who are the smaller Spanish League team in Barcelona?
8 Jimmy Floyd Hasselbaink was the Spanish league's top scorer in 1999–2000 despite playing for which struggling team?
9 For which team did Nayim win the Cup Winners Cup in 1995 with a goal from the halfway line?
10 In which city are Real Betis based?
11 Which Welshman has managed Real Madrid (twice), Real Sociedad and Deportiva La Coruña?
12 Which English team did Athletic Bilbao model their strip on?
13 Who was sacked as Barcelona's coach in 2000 and soon took up a position as coach of Holland?
14 How many Spanish teams were in the 2000 Champions League semi-finals?
15 Which Argentinian is captain of Real Madrid?
16 In what colours do Valencia play?
17 Which Spanish team did Bobby Robson coach?
18 Which manager guided Barcelona to four successive Liga championships as well as European Cup and Cup Winners Cup glory?
19 Which "malcontent" scored for Real Madrid in both legs of the 2000 Champions League semi-final?
20 Which club beat Leeds United 4–0 in the Champions League in 2000?

Answers

The North East (see Quiz 21)

1 1955. **2** Terry Butcher. **3** Wilf Mannion. **4** Lennie Lawrence. **5** £12m. **6** Ayresome Park. **7** Hartlepool. **8** Newcastle United. **9** Jim Montgomery. **10** The Anglo-Scottish Cup. **11** Seventh. **12** Watford. **13** Ian Porterfield. **14** Stevenage. **15** Spurs. **16** Rob Lee. **17** Rockliffe. **18** Darlington. **19** Third Division. **20** Coventry City.

Quiz 24 **The 70s**

LEVEL 2

Answers – see page 438

1 Colchester United beat a mighty First Division team in one of the greatest giant killing acts in English football in 1971. Who did they beat?
2 How many 70s Scottish FA Cup finals featured neither Celtic or Rangers?
3 The 1972 UEFA Cup final was the only one contested by two English teams. Who were they?
4 Which English legend played his 1,000th league game in May 1977 before retiring from football?
5 Which East Anglian team won the FA Cup in 1978?
6 Which winger scored Wales' winning goal against England in 1977?
7 Who won their ninth consecutive league title in Scotland in 1974?
8 Whose proposed transfer from West Brom to Leeds was cancelled when it was revealed the player had a "hole in the heart"?
9 Who became the first black player to represent England, in 1978?
10 Which Arsenal player was suspended for dropping his shorts in April 1979?
11 Which Southern League team beat Newcastle in the 1972 FA Cup third round?
12 Who scored the winning goal?
13 Who did Stoke beat in the 1972 League Cup final?
14 Who became Britain's first million pound footballer, in 1979?
15 Who did Liverpool sign from Celtic in August 1977?
16 Who resigned as England manager in July 1977?
17 Which two players were sent off during the 1974 Charity Shield?
18 Where was the 1978 World Cup played?
19 Who won their second First Division in four years, in 1974–75?
20 Who was in charge at Elland Road for 43 days in 1974?

Answers

South American Soccer (see Quiz 22)

1 Brazil. **2** Newcastle United. **3** Birmingham City. **4** America is for nations, Libertadores for clubs. **5** Uruguay. **6** Colombia. **7** Santos. **8** Argentina. **9** Real Madrid. **10** Mexico. **11** Diego Maradona. **12** Gustavo Poyet of Chelsea. **13** Corinthians. **14** Denilson. **15** Ronaldo. **16** River Plate. **17** Faustino Asprilla. **18** Milton Nunez. **19** Carlos Valderrama. **20** Alfredo Di Stefano.

Quiz 25 The League Cup

Answers – see page 443

LEVEL 2

1 When was the first League Cup competition?
2 Who were the first winners?
3 When did the League Cup become the Coca-Cola Cup?
4 When did the League Cup Final move to Wembley?
5 Which club has won the competition the most times?
6 Which Scottish player scored both Arsenal goals in the 1987 Final against Liverpool?
7 For which team did Andy Gray score a League Cup winning goal?
8 Who lost in both the 1997 and 1998 Finals?
9 Who won the competition in both 1989 and 1990?
10 Which Italian player scored in the 1997 Final?
11 Who contests the League Cup?
12 What is the League Cup currently called?
13 When Liverpool and Everton played each other in the 1984 Final who won?
14 When Sheffield Wednesday won the competition in 1991, who did they beat in the Final?
15 Who won the tournament in 2000?
16 Which was the last London team to win the League Cup?
17 Who won the League Cup four times in a row in the early 1980s?
18 What was the tournament called in 1991 and 1992?
19 Which Scottish TV pundit scored for Liverpool in the 1981 League Cup Final replay?
20 Who beat QPR 3–0 to win the 1986 Final?

Answers

Managers (see Quiz 27)

1 Peter Taylor. **2** Gillingham. **3** John Gregory. **4** Danny Wilson. **5** Colin Lee. **6** Sam Allardyce. **7** Lou Macari. **8** Christian Gross. **9** Graham Taylor. **10** Arsenal. **11** Howard Kendall. **12** Steve Coppell. **13** West Ham with eight. **14** Brian Clough. **15** Franz Beckenbauer. **16** Two. **17** Peter Reid. **18** Ron Atkinson. **19** Alan Ball. **20** George Graham.

Quiz 26 **French Football**

LEVEL 2

Answers – see page 444

1 Who were the French League champions in 1999–2000?

2 Which Channel ferry port part-timers made the 2000 French cup final?

3 Who became the only French club to win the European Cup in 1993, but were later stripped of the title?

4 What is the name of the major club in Paris?

5 In what colour shirts do St Etienne play?

6 Which French international returned to play in France after spells at Arsenal and Real Madrid, only to return to England in 2001–02?

7 Which former Monaco coach is now boss of a Premier League team?

8 Who left Lens to join Leeds United in 2000?

9 French heroes Henry and Trezeguet played together at which club?

10 Which Republic of Ireland striker left Marseilles for Nancy?

11 Which French stadium was opened for the 1998 World Cup?

12 Which England star joined Monaco in 1987?

13 Who captained France to victory in the finals of the World Cup and European Championship?

14 At the home of which club did England lose to Argentina in 1998?

15 Who was voted French Player of the Year in 1994, but was never picked again for the French national team?

16 Who left Marseilles to join Arsenal in 2000?

17 Who played for Auxerre, Marseilles, Bordeaux, Montpellier and Nimes before leaving for England?

18 Which Premier League manager was formerly manager of the French national team?

19 Who scored France's equalising goal in the Euro 2000 final?

20 Chris Waddle and Trevor Steven both played for which French club?

Answers

Rangers (see Quiz 28)

1 Mo Johnston. **2** Borussia Dortmund. **3** Ally McCoist. **4** Marco Negri. **5** The Treble. **6** Colin Hendry. **7** Barry Ferguson. **8** Fiorentina. **9** Nine. **10** David Murray. **11** True. **12** Dick Avocaat. **13** USA. **14** Arthur Numan. **15** 1971. **16** Gordon Durie. **17** Jorg Alberz. **18** Lorenzo Amoruso. **19** Leeds United. **20** Chris Woods.

Quiz 27 **Managers**

LEVEL 2

Answers – see page 441

1 Who became manager of Leicester City in summer 2000?

2 Where was he previously?

3 Who led Aston Villa out for the 2000 FA Cup final?

4 Who was sacked by Sheffield Wednesday and took over at Bristol City during 2000?

5 Which ex-Spurs and Chelsea striker is now in charge at Molineux?

6 Who managed Bolton as they reached the 2000 FA Cup semi-final?

7 Which former Manchester United player now pulls the strings at Huddersfield?

8 Who was surprisingly offered the job of head coach at Spurs in 1997?

9 Who gave up the managership at Watford in 1987 and took the job again ten years later?

10 Who did Leeds manager David O'Leary play most of his club football for?

11 Which ex-player managed Everton three times during the 1980s and 1990s?

12 Who has been manager at Crystal Palace four times?

13 Which Premier League team has had fewest managers in its history?

14 Which manager has had the longest post-war career?

15 Who captained West German to World Cup victory in 1974 and then managed them to victory in the same competition in 1990?

16 After how many matches of the 1998 season did Ruud Gullit replace Kenny Dalglish as manager at Newcastle?

17 Who managed Sunderland when they returned to the Premiership in 1999?

18 Who managed Manchester United between 1981 and 1986?

19 Which World Cup winner was manager at Maine Road in 1985–86?

20 Who did David O'Leary succeed as manager of Leeds United?

Answers

The League Cup (see Quiz 25)

1 1961. **2** Aston Villa. **3** 1982. **4** 1967. **5** Liverpool (six). **6** Charlie Nicholas. **7** Wolves. **8** Middlesbrough. **9** Nottingham Forest. **10** Fabrizio Ravanelli. **11** All teams in the Football League and Premier League. **12** The Worthington Cup. **13** Liverpool. **14** Manchester United. **15** Leicester City. **16** Spurs in 1999. **17** Liverpool. **18** The Rumbelows League Cup. **19** Alan Hansen. **20** Oxford United.

Quiz 28 **Rangers**

Answers – see page 442

LEVEL 2

1 Which Rangers striker joined Leeds United in 1980

2 Which German side knocked Rangers out of the 2000 EUFA Cup?

3 Who is Rangers' all-time leading goalscorer?

4 Which Italian striker makes a habit of falling out with Rangers' management?

5 What did Rangers achieve in 1998–99 for only the second time in 20 years?

6 Which Scotland captain returned from Rangers to England in 2000?

7 Which Rangers midfielder scored his first goal for Scotland against the Republic of Ireland in May 2000?

8 From which Italian club did Rangers sign Andrei Kanchelskis?

9 How many championships did Rangers win consecutively from 1989?

10 Who is Rangers' steel magnate chairman?

11 True or False: Rangers have won more championships than any other club in the world?

12 Who was Rangers' Dutch manager until late in 2001?

13 Former Rangers midfielder Claudio Reyna is an international with which country?

14 Which Rangers defender played twice for Holland in Euro 2000?

15 When was the Ibrox disaster, in which 66 people were killed?

16 Who scored for Rangers in three FA Cup finals in the 70s?

17 Which German former "Ger" is nicknamed "The Hammer" because of his spectacular goals?

18 Which Italian was made Rangers' club captain in the 1998–99 season?

19 Which English team did Rangers beat in the European Cup in 1992?

20 Which Rangers goalkeeper went a record 1196 minutes without conceding a goal in 1986–87?

Answers

French Football (see Quiz 26)

1 Derek Parlane. **2** Calais. **3** Marseilles. **4** Paris St Germain (PSG). **5** Green. **6** Anelka. **7** Arsene Wenger. **8** Olivier Dacourt. **9** AS Monaco. **10** Tony Cascarino. **11** Stade de France. **12** Glenn Hoddle 13 Didier Deschamps. **14** St. Etienne. **15** David Ginola. **16** Derek Johnstone. **17** Eric Cantona. **18** Gerard Houllier. **19** Sylvain Wiltord. **20** Marseilles.

Quiz 29 **Who Plays At...? 2**

LEVEL 2

Answers – see page 447

1 Deepdale?
2 The County Ground?
3 Pride Park?
4 Brunton Park?
5 The City Ground?
6 Meadow Lane?
7 Fratton Park?
8 Blundell Park?
9 The Valley?
10 Brisbane Road?
11 Dean Court?
12 Plainmoor?
13 The New Den?
14 Roots Hall?
15 Spotland?
16 Boundary Park?
17 Gay Meadow?
18 Layer Road?
19 Hillsborough?
20 Kenilworth Road?

Answers

Old Football (see Quiz 31)

1 Manchester City or Liverpool. **2** Celtic. **3** Newcastle United. **4** Bobby Charlton. **5** Italy. **6** Stan Cullis. **7** John White. **8** Alfredo Di Stefano. **9** Eusebio. **10** Tottenham Hotspur. **11** West Ham United. **12** Jimmy Hill. **13** Pat Jennings. **14** Wales and Northern Ireland. **15** Ipswich Town. **16** Manchester City. **17** Sir Stanley Rous. **18** Russia. **19** First £1000 transfer. **20** The 50s.

Quiz 30 **Africa**

LEVEL 2

Answers – see page 448

1. Which Cameroon international became a favourite during the 1990 World Cup?
2. Which Nigerian striker played on Merseyside between 1994 and 1996?
3. Who is the only African player in the Manchester Utd first team squad?
4. Where does he come from?
5. Which Liberian striker joined Manchester City in summer 2000 after a year at Chelsea?
6. For which African country did Bruce Grobbelaar play?
7. Chelsea's Celestine Babayaro plays his international football for which country?
8. Which African nation celebrated reaching the World Cup finals for the first time in the summer of 2001?
9. Moroccan Tahar El Khalej joined Southampton from which Portuguese team?
10. Who won the 1998 African Nations Cup?
11. How often is the African Nations Cup held?
12. Which was the last African team to play England?
13. For which country did Ibrahim Sunday play?
14. Which African country was in the running to stage the 2006 World Cup?
15. Which country topped England's group in the 1986 World Cup?
16. Who did England beat in the quarter-finals of the 1990 tournament?
17. Which Nigerian striker joined Arsenal in January 1999 from Internazionale?
18. Who contested the final of the 2000 African Nations Cup?
19. Who won the tournament?
20. In which African country was French star Just Fontaine born?

Answers

Pot Luck 3 (see Quiz 32)

1 Charlton Athletic. **2** Holsten. **3** Four. **4** Five: Crewe Alexandra, Oxford United, Wrexham, Halifax Town and Exeter City. **5** Leyton Orient. **6** Stuart Pearce. **7** Mikael Silvestre. **8** Ntl. **9** David Ginola. **10** John Beresford. **11** Newcastle United. **12** Edgar Davids. **13** Crystal Palace. **14** £2m. **15** Bryan Hamilton. **16** Dave Challinor. **17** Ray Clemence. **18** Ron Atkinson. **19** Halifax Town. **20** Chelsea.

Quiz 31 **Old Football**

Answers – see page 445

LEVEL 2

1 Name one of the teams Sir Matt Busby played for in the 1930s?
2 Which 1967 European Cup winners were dubbed the "Lisbon Lions"?
3 Which team won the FA Cup three times during the 1950s?
4 Which England player was European Footballer of the Year in 1966?
5 "The Battle of Highbury" in 1934 was a friendly between England and which other country?
6 Which manager masterminded Wolves' treble in the 1950s?
7 Which Tottenham and Scotland player was killed when struck by lightning in 1964?
8 Which Argentinian was the architect of Real Madrid's 50s European Cup domination?
9 Who was top scorer in the 1966 World Cup?
10 Which team won the FA Cup three times during the 1960s?
11 Which team did Ron Greenwood manage to Cup success in the 1960s?
12 Which former *Match of the Day* presenter is credited with getting the maximum wage abolished in 1961?
13 Which goalkeeper scored in the 1967 Charity Shield between Tottenham and Manchester United?
14 Which two teams from the British Isles reached the quarter-finals of the 1958 World Cup?
15 Sir Alf Ramsey managed which 60s championship-winning side?
16 The "Revie Plan" took which side to the 1955 and 1956 FA Cup finals?
17 Which famous English referee became president of FIFA in 1961?
18 Who did West Germany defeat in the 1966 World Cup semi-final?
19 Which record was set when Alf Common was transferred from Sunderland to Middlesbrough in 1910?
20 In what decade did the white ball come into official use?

Answers

Who Plays At...? 2 (see Quiz 29)

1 Preston North End. **2** Swindon Town. **3** Derby County. **4** Carlisle United. **5** Nottingham Forest. **6** Notts County. **7** Portsmouth. **8** Grimsby Town. **9** Charlton Athletic. **10** Leyton Orient. **11** Bournemouth. **12** Torquay United. **13** Millwall. **14** Southend United. **15** Rochdale. **16** Oldham Athletic. **17** Shrewsbury Town. **18** Colchester United. **19** Sheffield Wednesday. **20** Luton Town.

Quiz 32 **Pot Luck 3**

LEVEL 2

Answers – see page 446

1 Which Premiership outfit had Hunt, Robinson and Pringle in its 2000–01 squad?

2 Which beer company sponsors Spurs?

3 How many Uniteds are there in the 2000–01 Premier League?

4 How many Football League teams have the letter x in their name?

5 Who plays at the Matchroom Stadium?

6 Which West Ham veteran broke a leg twice during the 1999–2000 season?

7 Which Frenchman partnered Jaap Stam in the Manchester United defence during 1999–2000?

8 Which communications company holds a 9 per cent stake in Everton?

9 Which French football star advertises L'Oreal "because he's worth it"?

10 Which former Newcastle defender now plies his trade at The Dell?

11 With which English club did Philippe Albert make his name?

12 Which Dutchman plays football in glasses?

13 Which London club does Clinton Morrison play for?

14 How much did Fulham pay for Louis Saha in summer 2000?

15 Who was the manager of Norwich City at the beginning of the 2000–01 season?

16 Which Stockport and ex-Tranmere player has the longest throw-in in British football?

17 Tottenham's Stephen Clemence is the son of which famous English goalkeeper?

18 Who managed Sheffield Wednesday between 1989 and 1991 and again between 1997 and 1998?

19 Who plays at The Shay?

20 Which Premier League side fielded a team in the 1998–99 season in which every player was born outside the mainland of England?

Answers

Africa (see Quiz 30)

1 Roger Milla. **2** Daniel Amokachi. **3** Quinton Fortune. **4** South Africa. **5** George Weah. **6** Zimbabwe. **7** Nigeria. **8** Senegal. **9** Benfica. **10** Egypt. **11** Every two years. **12** Tunisia, in the 1998 World Cup. **13** Ghana. **14** South Africa. **15** Morocco. **16** Cameroon. **17** Nwankwo Kanu. **18** Nigeria and Cameroon. **19** Cameroon. **20** Morocco.

Quiz 33 **The FA Cup**

LEVEL 2

Answers – see page 451

1 How many FA Cup finals were played at the old Wembley?

2 Which Man City keeper broke his neck in the 1956 FA Cup final?

3 The FA Cup has once been won by a team not based in England. Which team was it?

4 What is the name of the Cup Final hymn?

5 Who is the only player to be sent off in an FA Cup final?

6 Whose spectacular diving header brought the scores level in the 1987 final between Coventry and Tottenham?

7 Who was manager at Wimbledon when they won the cup in 1988?

8 Who scored twice for Crystal Palace to force a replay against Manchester United in the 1990 final?

9 Whose short appearance in the 1991 final was his last for Spurs?

10 In which year was the FA Cup first sponsored by Littlewoods?

11 Which London team was banned from the competition during the 1994–95 season, but later reinstated?

12 In which year was "The Matthews Final"?

13 Only two clubs won the FA Cup two years running during the 20th century: Spurs and which other club?

14 Who scored the quickest Cup final goal?

15 Who scored the opening goal for Manchester United in the 1999 final?

16 Which final was known as "The Dustbin Final"?

17 Which legendary keeper was in goal for Leicester when they played Spurs in the 1961 final?

18 Who scored both West Ham's goals in the 1975 final against Fulham?

19 In which year was the FA Cup final first televised in full?

20 Which was the first year in which the losers went up to collect their medals before the winners?

Answers

Old Players (see Quiz 35)

1 Martin Peters. **2** Leicester City. **3** Italy. **4** Real Madrid. **5** Mannion. **6** Fulham and QPR. **7** Jack Milburn. **8** Duncan Edwards. **8** 1968. **9** Ian Storey-Moore. **10** Johnny Haynes. **11** Carter. **12** Manchester United **13** Peters, Moore and Hurst. **14** AC Milan. **15** France. **16** Moore, Collins, Charlton. **17** Garrincha. **18** Tottenham Hotspur. **19** Shackleton. **20** Swift.

Quiz 34 **European Cup**

Answers – see page 452

LEVEL 2

1 Which club have won the European Cup the most times?
2 Which English club have won the European Cup the most times?
3 Which English club won the trophy in 1979 and 1980?
4 Which Eastern European side beat Barcelona in the 1986 Final?
5 Which English manager took Barcelona to the Final in 1986?
6 Which Spanish team reached the 1983 European Cup Final?
7 Who beat Sampdoria to win the 1992 final played at Wembley stadium?
8 Where was Real Madrid's 7–3 Cup Final victory in 1960 played?
9 Waddle, Papin and Pele played in which team's final defeat in 1991?
10 Who beat Leeds United to win the European Cup in 1975?
11 In which year were English teams except Liverpool allowed to re-enter the tournament after the Heysel ban?
12 How many Portuguese clubs have won the European Cup?
13 How many Dutch clubs have won the European Cup?
14 Which ex-player managed Barcelona in their European Cup triumph?
15 Which two Dutchmen both scored two goals in AC Milan's 1989 Cup Final victory?
16 Which Englishman played against Nottingham Forest in the 1980 European Cup Final?
17 Which Frenchman scored the winning goal in the tragic 1985 Final?
18 Prosinecki, Pancev and Savicevic were in which 1991 winning side?
19 Which British club reached the European Cup semi-finals three times between 1970 and 1974?
20 Which England defender scored in two of Liverpool's European Cup victories?

Answers

British Players Abroad (see Quiz 36)

1 John Charles. **2** Ian Rush. **3** Gary Lineker. **4** Steve McManaman. **5** Terry Venables. **6** Kevin Keegan. **7** Luther Blissett. **8** Bobby Robson. **9** Marseille. **10** £5.5m. **11** Paul Gascoigne. **12** Denis Law. **13** Mark Hughes. **14** John Collins. **15** Kevin Campbell. **16** Laurie Cunningham. **17** Liam Brady. **18** Graeme Souness. **19** Ray Wilkins. **20** Jimmy Greaves.

Quiz 35 **Old Players**

LEVEL 2

Answers – see page 449

1 Who left West Ham in an exchange deal involving Jimmy Greaves during the 1969–70 season?

2 For which club did Gordon Banks play when he won the World Cup?

3 "Gigi" Riva starred for which country in the 1960s and 70s?

4 Which club did the great Ferenc Puskas join in 1956?

5 Which Wilf was a post-war Middlesbrough and England forward?

6 For which London teams did Rodney Marsh play in the 1960s?

7 Who was Bobby and Jack Charlton's Newcastle United and England goalscoring uncle?

8 In which year was George Best voted European Footballer of the Year?

9 Which double-barrelled named forward played for Nottingham Forest and Manchester United in the1960s?

10 Which Craven Cottage hero was England's first £100-a-week player?

11 Which Raich was Sunderland, Derby County and England's famous inside forward?

12 Paddy Crerand was a midfielder for which English club in the 1960s?

13 Which three West Ham players were England World Cup winners?

14 Nordahl, Gren and Liedholm were which club's Swedish trio?

15 Just Fontaine won the 1958 Golden Boot playing for which country?

16 Which three Bobbys won the Footballer of the Year award in consecutive years in the 1960s?

17 Who was the Brazilian star winger of the 1958 and 1962 World Cups?

18 Alan Gilzean joined which English club in the 1960s?

19 Which Newcastle and England Len was dubbed "the clown prince of football" in the 1950s?

20 Which Frank was Manchester City and England's post-war goalkeeper?

Answers

The FA Cup (see Quiz 33)

1 72, plus five replays. **2** Bert Trautmann. **3** Cardiff City. **4** "Abide With Me". **5** Kevin Moran of Manchester United. **6** Keith Houchen. **7** Bobby Gould. **8** Ian Wright. **9** Paul Gascoigne. **10** 1995. **11** Spurs. **12** 1953. **13** Newcastle in 1951 and 1952. **14** Roberto Di Matteo after 43 seconds in 1997. **15** Teddy Sheringham. **16** The 1960 final between Wolves and Blackburn. **17** Gordon Banks. **18** Alan Taylor. **19** 1938. **20** 1992.

Quiz 36 **British Players Abroad**

LEVEL 2

Answers – see page 450

1 Who was the first major British player to play abroad after World War II?

2 Who noted that Italy "was like a foreign country" on his arrival to play for Juventus in 1987?

3 Which English striker won the UEFA Cup in 1989 playing for Barcelona?

4 Which ex-Liverpool playmaker featured for Real Madrid in 1999–2000?

5 Who was nicknamed "El Tel" during his time as Barcelona manager?

6 Which English player was Euro Footballer of the Year in 1978 and 79?

7 Who was allegedly transferred "by mistake" from Watford to AC Milan for £1m in 1983?

8 Which English manager had success at Barcelona, PSV Eindhoven and Porto?

9 Which French club did Chris Waddle move to from Spurs in 1989?

10 David Platt became the most expensive player in British history when he left Aston Villa for Bari in 1991. How much did he cost?

11 Who moved from Spurs to Lazio in 1992?

12 Who left Man City for Torino in 1961 but returned to United a year later?

13 Which Welsh player played for Barcelona, Bayern Munich and Manchester United between 1986 and 1988?

14 Which current Fulham midfielder also played for AS Monaco?

15 Which current Everton striker had a spell in Turkey with Trabzonspor?

16 Which winger was killed in a car crash while with Real Madrid?

17 Which Irish genius had success in Italy during the 1980s?

18 Who left Sampdoria in 1985 to take over at Glasgow Rangers?

19 Which ex-Chelsea player had three years with AC Milan between 1984 and 1987?

20 Which striker left Chelsea for Milan in 1961 only to return to Spurs a year later?

Answers

European Cup (see Quiz 34)

1 Real Madrid. **2** Liverpool. **3** Nottingham Forest. **4** Steaua Bucharest. **5** Terry Venables. **6** Real Sociedad. **7** Barcelona. **8** Hampden Park. **9** Marseilles. **10** Bayern Munich. **11** 1990. **12** Two (Benfica and Porto). **13** Three (Ajax, Feyenoord and PSV). **14** Johann Cruyff. **15** Van Basten and Gullit. **16** Kevin Keegan. **17** Michel Platini. **18** Red Star Belgrade. **19** Celtic. **20** Phil Neal.

Quiz 37 **Gingers**

LEVEL 2

Answers – see page 455

---

1 Who is Arsenal and England's red-haired wide midfielder?

2 Who was Leeds and Scotland's fiery ginger genius?

3 Which redheaded Coventry City and Wolves favourite gained fame with his part in the "donkey-kick" free-kick in the 70s?

4 Which Manchester United carrot-top has scored a hat-trick for England?

5 Which strawberry blond defender has given great service to Liverpool, Aston Villa and the Republic of Ireland?

6 Which ginger striker has played for Yugoslavia and Croatia?

7 Who was Leicester City's peroxided red-headed dynamo who followed his boss to Celtic?

8 Who was Liverpool's flame-haired "supersub" in the 70s?

9 Which Scottish ginger-topped centre-half crossed North London from Spurs to Arsenal in 1977?

10 Which fiery character left Leeds United for Bradford City in 2000?

11 Who was Celtic and Scotland's ginger-haired impish winger in the 70s?

12 Which Welshman nearly took his red locks to Tottenham but eventually stayed with Wimbledon in 2000?

13 Which of England's 1966 World Cup heroes sported ginger locks?

14 Which Premier League manager has kept his red hair and enthusiasm?

15 Which Premier League captain and Northern Irish international is easily identifiable from his ginger hair?

16 Which brightly-topped Scottish midfielder played at Everton, Rangers and Bradford City?

17 Villa's red-haired Tommy Johnson joined which Scottish club in 2000?

18 Ginger bonce Perry Groves played for which London team in the 90s?

19 For which country was wild redhead Alexei Lalas a star?

20 Which redhead became the first player from the former East Germany to be voted European Footballer of the Year, in 1996?

Answers

Wales (see Quiz 39)

1 Leighton James. **2** Bryan Flynn. **3** Brazil. **4** Mike England was Wales' manager. **5** Cliff Jones and Terry Medwin. **6** Ian Rush. **7** Ryan Giggs. **8** Robbie Savage. **9** Noel Blake. **10** Fulham. **11** Craig Bellamy. **12** John Charles. **13** Gary Sprake. **14** Joe Jordan. **15** Mark Pembridge. **16** Bobby Gould. **17** John Toshack. **18** Germany. **19** Dean Saunders. **20** No (9).

Quiz 38 **Arsenal**

LEVEL 2

Answers – see page 456

1 When did Arsenal last win the FA Cup?

2 Which legendary full-back left Arsenal for West Ham in summer 2000?

3 Which keeper played 472 league games for Spurs and then 237 for Arsenal?

4 Who did Arsenal beat to clinch the league title in 1971?

5 Who did Arsenal beat to win the FA Cup that season and so win the double?

6 Who was manager of Arsenal when they were beaten by Walsall in a Milk Cup-tie in 1983?

7 Who top-scored for Arsenal when they won the league title in 1991?

8 How many games did Arsenal lose that season?

9 Who did Arsenal beat in both the League Cup and FA Cup finals in 1993?

10 Martin Keown joined Arsenal from which other club?

11 In what year was Arsenal founded?

12 Which Danish midfielder's transfer was at the centre of allegations of financial wrong-doings that ended with George Graham's sacking in 1995?

13 How many times have Arsenal appeared in the League Cup final?

14 How many times have they won it?

15 Which Arsenal player was voted Footballer of the Year in 1971?

16 Keeper John Lukic has played for Arsenal and which other club throughout his career?

17 How many times have Arsenal won the league title?

18 When was the last time?

19 What is the official name of the Arsenal ground?

20 For which country does full back Silviniho play his international football?

Answers

Pot Luck 4 (see Quiz 40)

1 Bramble. **2** John Aldridge. **3** Most World Cup games (21). **4** Peter Reid. **5** Justice Taylor Report. **6** Bobby Charlton. **7** Emerson Thome. **8** The Rokermen changed grounds. **9** Norwich. **10** Feyenoord (1970). **11** Australia. **12** Busby Babes. **13** Marseilles. **14** Crystal Palace. **15** Coventry. **16** Jimmy Greaves. **17** Carlos Alberto. **18** Coventry, Leicester, Liverpool, Oxford. **19** Ukraine. **20** Dundee.

Quiz 39 **Wales**

LEVEL 2 

Answers – see page 453

1 Which Welsh short-sighted 70s winger made his name at Burnley?
2 Which diminutive Burnley and Leeds midfielder won 66 caps between 1975 and 1984?
3 Who eliminated Wales from the quarter finals of the 1958 World Cup?
4 In which way did England lead Wales in the late 70s and early 80s?
5 Which Welsh wingers were part of the Tottenham double-winning side?
6 Which Welshman was part of Liverpool's double-winning team?
7 Which Welshman has twice helped Manchester United to the double?
8 Which Welsh midfielder was originally dropped from the game against Italy for being disrespectful to Paolo Maldini's shirt?
9 Which Blackburn Rovers goal ace is eligible to play for Wales because of his parents' commonwealth status?
10 Wales defenders Melville and Coleman play for which League team?
11 Which Wales star joined Coventry City from Norwich City in 2000?
12 Which Welsh player was voted Juventus's best ever foreign player?
13 Who was the Welsh keeper in Don Revie's powerful Leeds United team?
14 A "Hand of God" goal by which former Leeds and Manchester United striker put Scotland rather than Wales into the 1978 World Cup?
15 Which Everton midfielder has won over 35 caps for Wales?
16 Which former Wimbledon boss took over as manager of Wales in 1995?
17 Which successful club manager played 40 times for Wales and managed them for 47 days?
18 Wales shocked the football world by earning a 1–1 draw in which country in the European Championship qualifying rounds in 1995?
19 Who scored Wales' goal in the 1–0 victory over Brazil in Cardiff in 1991?
20 Did Vinny Jones win more than 10 caps for Wales?

Answers

Gingers (see Quiz 37)

1 Ray Parlour. **2** Billy Bremner. **3** Willie Carr. **4** Paul Scholes. **5** Steve Staunton. **6** Robert Prosinecki. **7** Neil Lennon. **8** David Fairclough. **9** Willie Young. **10** David Hopkin **11** Jimmy Johnstone. **12** John Hartson. **13** Alan Ball. **14** Gordon Strachan. **15** Steve Lomas. **16** Stuart McCall. **17** Celtic. **18** Arsenal. **19** USA. **20** Matthias Sammer.

Quiz 40 **Pot Luck 4**

LEVEL 2

Answers – see page 454

1 Which Titus is Ipswich's promising young defender?

2 Who was the first person to miss a penalty in a Wembley FA Cup final?

3 What record does Maradona share with Matthaus?

4 Whose managerial performance was the subject of the BBC's *Premier Passions*?

5 What was the name of the report that gave rise to the all-seater stadiums?

6 Which England player's portrait hangs in the National Portrait Gallery?

7 Who is Sunderland's Brazilian defender?

8 Why did Sunderland have to change their nickname?

9 Craig Bellamy and Darren Eadie left which club for Premiership pastures?

10 Who was the first Dutch club to win the European cup?

11 Middlesbrough's Paul Okon hails from which country?

12 What was the nickname given to the team that featured Duncan Edwards, Roger Byrne and Eddie Colman?

13 Which French team was relegated from the First Division in 1993 after being found guilty of match-fixing?

14 Which Terry Venables side was given the tag "team of the 80s"?

15 Which team ended a 16-month run without an away win with a victory at Southampton in August 2000?

16 Which Englishman scored on his debut for AC Milan in 1961?

17 Who was the last skipper to collect the Jules Rimet trophy?

18 Which four League club cities are mentioned on the *Monopoly* board?

19 Shakhtar Donetsk were which country's surprise qualifiers in the 2000–01 Champions League?

20 Ivano Bonetti was manager of which Scottish Premier League club?

Answers

Arsenal (see Quiz 38)

1 1998. **2** Nigel Winterburn. **3** Pat Jennings. **4** Spurs. **5** Liverpool. **6** Terry Neill. **7** Alan Smith. **8** One. **9** Sheffield Wednesday. **10** Everton. **11** 1886. **12** John Jensen. **13** Five times. **14** Twice. **15** Frank McLintock. **16** Leeds United. **17** Eleven times. **18** 1997–98. **19** The Arsenal Stadium. **20** Brazil.

Quiz 41 **Bobby Charlton**

Answers – see page 459

LEVEL 2

1 How many appearances did Charlton make for United?
2 In which year did Charlton make his England debut?
3 How many goals did he score in the 1968 European Cup final against Benfica?
4 How many goals did he score for England during his career?
5 In what year was Bobby Charlton born?
6 How many times did Manchester United win the league title with Charlton in the side?
7 Bobby Charlton won his 100th England cap in 1970. Who were the opposition that day?
8 In which year was Charlton voted both the Football Writers and European Footballer of the Year?
9 Which was Bobby Charlton's first World Cup?
10 How many times was Bobby Charlton booked in his career?
11 How many goals did Charlton score in his career at United?
12 How many goals did he score in the 1966 World Cup Finals?
13 In which year did Charlton retire from playing?
14 What did he do next?
15 With which other two clubs was he associated before returning to United as a director?
16 How many England caps did Charlton win?
17 When did Charlton become Sir Bobby?
18 Bobby Charlton won only one FA Cup winner's medal with United; who were their opponents at Wembley that day?
19 In which year was it?
20 How many times did Charlton captain his country?

Answers

Chelsea (see Quiz 43)

1 John Dempsey. **2** Athens, Greece. **3** Peter Houseman. **4** Maidstone, Kent. **5** John Spencer. **6** 150. **7** CSKA Moscow. **8** Tony Hateley. **9** Liverpool. **10** Bobby Tambling. **11** Dan Petrescu. **12** David Speedie. **13** Everton. **14** Hibs. **15** Glenn Hoddle. **16** The Chelsea FC Chronicle. **17** Stoke City. **18** "Blue is the Colour". **19** Nine months. **20** Tottenham Hotspur.

Quiz 42 **Scottish Domestic**

LEVEL 2

Answers – see page 460

1 Scotland internationals Ally McCoist and Ian Durrant left Rangers to play at which club?
2 What colour shirts do Dundee wear?
3 David Narey and Maurice Malpas were heroes of which club?
4 Which team play at McDiarmid Park?
5 In which year did Celtic break Rangers run as Scottish champions?
6 Apart from Aberdeen who is the only non-Glasgow team to be crowned Scottish champions?
7 Who did Rangers beat 7–0 in the semi-final of the 2000 FA Cup?
8 Which Fife team beat Celtic in a penalty shootout in the 1995 League Cup to win a place in Europe?
9 Which Accies beat Rangers at Ibrox in 1995?
10 Jim Jeffries was manager of which Premier League team before joining Bradford City?
11 Hansen, Rough and Johnston are famous old boys of which club?
12 Which club signed Eyal Berkovic from West Ham in 1999?
13 In which colour shirts do Heart of Midlothian play?
14 Which club play at Firhill Park?
15 Lovell, Paatelainen and Lehmann appeared in which team's line-up?
16 Miller, Cooper and McGhee were which team's Cup-Winners Cup winners?
17 Which Scottish team were formerly known as Ferranti Thistle?
18 Which club arose out of the amalgamation of Inverness teams in 1994?
19 How many of the starting Scotland eleven that beat England in the Euro 2000 play-offs in 1999 were playing in the Scottish League?
20 Which "County" played in the Highland League until joining the Scottish League in 1995?

Answers

Local Derbies (see Quiz 44)

1 Glasgow. **2** Arsenal. **3** Milan and Internazionale. **4** Juventus and Torino. **5** 1984. **6** Seven: London, Manchester, Liverpool, Nottingham, Sheffield, Birmingham and Bristol. **7** 1996. **8** Spurs won 3–1. **9** Rome. **10** Newcastle and Sunderland. **11** Fulham. **12** 1984. **13** Hibs and Hearts. **14** Goodison Park. **15** Nick Barmby. **16** Stanley Park. **17** Sandy Brown. **18** United won 2–0. **19** Celtic won 6–2. **20** Notts County v Forest in 1892.

Quiz 43 **Chelsea**

Answers – see page 457

LEVEL 2

1 Who scored Chelsea's equaliser against Real Madrid in the European Cup Winners' Cup final replay in 1971?
2 Where was that match played?
3 Which former Chelsea winger died tragically in a car crash in 1977?
4 Where was Andy Townsend born?
5 Who signed for Chelsea from Glasgow Rangers in August 1992?
6 In all, how many goals did Peter Osgood score for Chelsea?
7 From which team was Dmitri Kharine signed in 1982?
8 Who was Chelsea's first £100,000 signing?
9 Against which team did Paul Elliott receive his career-ending injury in 1992?
10 Who scored five goals for Chelsea in a 6–2 league win at Villa Park in 1966?
11 Who is Chelsea's most capped player?
12 Who was Kerry Dixon's usual striking partner?
13 Who did Pat Nevin join on leaving Chelsea in 1988?
14 From which team did Gordon Durie join Chelsea in 1986?
15 Which England manager had been player-manager for Chelsea?
16 What was the Chelsea matchday programme originally called?
17 Who beat Chelsea in the League Cup Final in 1972?
18 What was the name of Chelsea's hit single released that same year?
19 For how long was Danny Blanchflower manager of Chelsea?
20 Against which club did George Weah score his first goal for Chelsea?

Answers

Bobby Charlton (see Quiz 41)

1 754. **2** 1958. **3** Two. **4** 49. **5** 1937. **6** Three times. **7** Northern Ireland. **8** 1966. **9** 1962 in Chile. **10** Once, but it was later recinded by the FA. **11** 247. **12** Three. **13** 1973. **14** He became manager of Preston North End. **15** Waterford and Wigan. **16** 106. **17** 1974. **18** Leicester City. **19** 1963. **20** Twice.

Quiz 44 **Local Derbies**

Answers – see page 458

LEVEL 2

1 In which city does the "Old Firm" derby take place?

2 Who are Tottenham's local derbies played against?

3 Which two teams contest the Milan derby?

4 If you were in Turin, which two teams would you watch in the local derby?

5 In which year was the League Cup final a local derby?

6 In how many English cities can you find a derby?

7 In which year was the last Manchester derby of the 20th century?

8 Who won the local derby FA Cup semi-final between Spurs and Arsenal in 1991?

9 In which city do Lazio play their derby games?

10 Who contests England's North-East derby?

11 Which team is regarded as Chelsea's local rival?

12 Prior to 2001–02, when was the last time these two teams met in the the league?

13 Which two teams play in the Edinburgh derby?

14 The Merseyside derby is played at Anfield and which other ground?

15 Which England player moved from one Merseyside rival to the other in summer 2000?

16 What is the name of the park that sits between the Liverpool and Everton grounds?

17 Which Evertonian's name became synonymous with an "own goal" when he scored one in a derby in 1969?

18 Manchester United played City in Denis Irwin's testimonial before the start of the 2000–01 season. Who won the match?

19 Who won the first Glasgow derby of the 2000–01 season?

20 Which was the first ever official English local league derby?

Answers

Scottish Domestic (see Quiz 42)

1 Kilmarnock. **2** Dark Blue. **3** Dundee United. **4** St. Johnstone. **5** 1998. **6** Dundee United. **7** Ayr United. **8** Raith Rovers. **9** Hamilton Academical. **10** Hearts. **11** Partick Thistle **12** Celtic. **13** Maroon. **14** Partick Thistle. **15** Hibernian. **16** Aberdeen's. **17** Meadowbank Thistle. **18** Inverness Caledonian Thistle. **19** Five. **20** Ross County.

Quiz 45 **Hairstyles**

LEVEL 2

Answers – see page 463

1 Which Colombian had a head full of curly locks?

2 Which legendary Brighton centre-back played in a headband?

3 Which former Manchester United Czech forward sported an alice band?

4 Which club sold dreadlock caps in celebration of their manager's hair?

5 Which French World Cup winner wears his hair in a ponytail?

6 Which Newcastle and Tottenham player was best known for the footballer's mullet hairstyle?

7 Which entire 1998 World Cup team (except one) dyed their hair peroxide blonde after qualifying for the second stage of the tournament?

8 Which player's hair style led him to be teased with the chant: "He's got a pineapple on his head."

9 What colour does Taribo West dye his hair when playing for Nigeria?

10 Which country left Redondo out of their squad because he wouldn't get his hair cut?

11 What did Bobby Charlton and Ralph Coates both do with their hair?

12 Which long-haired striker sunk Liverpool in the 1971 FA Cup final?

13 Which goalkeeper is usually seen sporting a ponytail?

14 Which Arsenal player has a dyed red streak?

15 What colour did Robbie Fowler, Neil Lennon and Gazza all dye their hair?

16 Which West Ham defender possibly didn't make the England squad because of his skinhead crop?

17 Who appeared on a shampoo advert with expertly coiffeured hair?

18 What was Kevin Keegan's 70s contribution to football hair fashion?

19 Which entire Premier League squad began the 1995–96 season with a number one crop?

20 Who is Manchester United's dome-headed keeper?

Answers

Bad Boys (see Quiz 47)

1 Peter Storey. **2** Cathay Pacific. **3** Charlie Nicholas. **4** Roy Keane. **5** Jody Morris. **6** Frank Lampard. **7** Tony Adams. **8** Rangers. **9** Arsenal. **10** Dennis Wise. **11** Paul Merson. **12** Stanley Bowles. **13** Kenny Sansom. **14** Duncan Ferguson. **15** Chris Armstrong. **16** Graham Rix. **17** Mark Bosnich. **18** Jimmy Johnstone. **19** Diego Maradona. **20** Teddy Sheringham.

Quiz 46 **Celebrity Fans**

Answers – see page 464

LEVEL 2

1 Cricket umpire Dicky Bird and Michael Parkinson support which home town team?
2 Commentator John Motson can't get to see his favourites too often?
3 Johnny Briggs (Mike Baldwin) closes the factory to see which Lancashire team?
4 Eddie Large and Bernard Manning would be glad to see their side back with the big boys?
5 Does Jeremy Paxman ask tough questions of his northern heroes?
6 Sean Bean's allegiances are tatooed on his arm?
7 Julian Lloyd Webber hears some sweet music in the East?
8 Frank Skinner's boys haven't given him much to laugh about?
9 Michael Palin would travel the world to see which team?
10 Chancellor of the Exchequer Gordon Brown has a taxing time at which Scottish team?
11 Luciano Pavarotti supports a giant of European football?
12 Formula One's Johnny Herbert races to which Premiership team?
13 Which Spanish team do Placido Domingo and Julio Iglesias sing their hearts out for?
14 Finlay Quayle and Irvine Welsh share a love of which big city side?
15 Uri Geller's team could certainly do with some magic?
16 Which team does comedian Jim Davidson hope will "nick, nick" a goal?
17 Funny man Vic Reeves favours an unfashionable north-eastern outfit?
18 Does TV's Nick Hancock think it's all over for his team?
19 Tory MP Kenneth Clarke has a lot of time for the reds?
20 After a Big Breakfast Johnny Vaughan will be off to see who?

Answers

Eastern Europe (see Quiz 48)

1 Red Star Belgrade. **2** Marseilles. **3** 1953. **4** Alen Boksic. **5** Quarter-finals. **6** 6–1 to Holland. **7** Romanian. **8** Partizan. **9** Split. **10** Ukrainian. **11** Red Star Belgrade. **12** CSKA Sofia. **13** 1994. **14** Bulgaria. **15** Zbigniew Boniek. **16** Dynamo Kiev in 1986. **17** Savo Milosevic. **18** Four: Yugoslavia, Romania, Czech Republic and Slovenia. **19** Yugoslavia, letting in 13 goals in four games. **20** Lev Yashin.

Quiz 47 **Bad Boys**

LEVEL 2

Answers – see page 461

1 Which Arsenal defender was found guilty of importing pornography?

2 Which airline's plane were England players accused of damaging in 1996?

3 Which Arsenal star stole a chip then allegedly hit a woman in Ibiza?

4 Which Man Utd captain allegedly assaulted two women in a night club?

5 Which Chelsea player allegedly assaulted someone in a supermarket?

6 Which England midfielder was dropped by Sven Göran Eriksson after an incident in a Heathrow hotel bar?

7 Which international served a prison sentence for drink driving in 1990?

8 Who were England stars Butcher, Roberts and Woods playing for when charged with "conduct likely to provoke a breach of the peace" in 1987?

9 For which team was David Hillier playing when allegedly involved in a bag-stealing operation at an airport?

10 Who had an altercation with a taxi driver outside Scribes club?

11 Which former Arsenal and England forward confessed to a gambling and cocaine addiction?

12 Which 70s QPR star reputedly blew £500,000 on gambling?

13 Which 80s Arsenal and England full-back was reputedly given a transfer in order to clear his gambling debts?

14 Which international has earned the nickname "Duncan Disorderly"?

15 Which Tottenham forward was found guilty of smoking cannabis?

16 Which assistant manager was imprisoned for underage sex in 1999?

17 Which Man. Utd goalkeeper was arrested on his stag night?

18 Which legendary Scottish winger and boozer was found drunk and stranded in the Irish Sea in a rowing boat?

19 Who got a second 15-month worldwide ban after failing a drug test at USA 94?

20 Which Manchester United striker was forced to publicly apologise for going to a night club shortly before the 98 World Cup?

Answers

Hairstyles (see Quiz 45)

1 Carlos Valderrama. **2** Steve Foster. **3** Karel Poborsky. **4** Chelsea. **5** Emmanuel Petit. **6** Chris Waddle. **7** Romania. **8** Jason Lee. **9** Green. **10** Argentina. **11** Flick a long strand across their bald patch. **12** Charlie George. **13** David Seaman. **14** Freddie Ljungberg. **15** Peroxide blond. **16** Julian Dicks. **17** David Ginola. **18** The curly perm. **19** Wimbledon. **20** Fabien Barthez.

Quiz 48 **Eastern Europe**

Answers – see page 462

LEVEL 2

1. Who won the European Cup in 1991?
2. Which French team did they beat in the final?
3. In which year did the Mighty Magyars famously crush England 6–3 at Wembley?
4. Which Croatian joined Middlesbrough in summer 2000?
5. In which round were Yugoslavia beaten in Euro 2000?
6. Who did they lose to?
7. What nationality is the great Gheorghe Hagi?
8. There are two major teams in Belgrade: Red Star and which other?
9. Hajduk are based in which Yugoslavian city?
10. What nationality is Andrei Kanchelskis?
11. Which club is known at home as Crvena Zvezda?
12. With which Eastern European club did Hristo Stoichkov make his name?
13. In which year did he win the European Footballer of the Year award?
14. For whom did he play his international football?
15. Which great Polish player had success in Italy with Juventus and Roma in the 1980s?
16. Which was the last Eastern European team to win the European Cup Winners Cup?
17. Which Eastern European player was equal top scorer in Euro 2000?
18. How many Eastern European teams qualified for Euro 2000?
19. Of those teams, who had the worst defensive record?
20. Who was the first Soviet player to be European Footballer of the Year?

Answers

Celebrity Fans (see Quiz 46)

1 Barnsley. **2** Boston United. **3** Burnley. **4** Manchester City. **5** Leeds. **6** Sheffield United. **7** Orient. **8** West Bromwich Albion. **9** Sheffield Wednesday. **10** Raith Rovers. **11** Juventus. **12** West Ham. **13** Real Madrid. **14** Hibernian. **15** Reading. **16** Charlton Athletic. **17** Darlington **18** Stoke City. **19** Nottingham Forest. **20** Chelsea.

Quiz 49 **The UEFA Cup**

LEVEL 2

Answers – see page 467

1 What was the UEFA Cup originally called?

2 In which year did the first tournament take place?

3 Who were England's representatives in that first final?

4 When was the tournament first called the UEFA Cup?

5 Which country provided both teams for the 1998 final?

6 For most of its life the UEFA Cup final was played over two legs. When did this change?

7 Which was the last Scottish team to appear in the final?

8 Which was the last English team to win the trophy?

9 Who did they beat in the final?

10 Liverpool won a memorable final against which German team in 1973?

11 Which north-eastern team won the Fairs Cup against Ujpest Dozsa in 1969?

12 Who won the competition in 2000?

13 In which city do they play their football?

14 Who did they beat in the final?

15 Where was the 1999 final between Parma and Marseille played?

16 Which English city provided finalists in both 1960 and 1961?

17 Which Argentinian scored for Napoli when they beat Stuttgart to win the 1989 tournament?

18 Which East Anglian club won the tournament in 1981?

19 In which year did the only all-English final take place?

20 When did Leeds last appear in the UEFA Cup final?

Answers

World Cup 98 (see Quiz 51)

1 USA. **2** Zero. **3** Spain. **4** Marcelo Salas. **5** Christian Vieri. **6** Scored an own goal. **7** Mexico's. **8** Laurent Blanc. **9** Diego Simone. **10** Gabriel Batistuta. **11** Zinadine Zidane. **12** Croatia won 3–0. **13** Denmark. **14** Croatia. **15** Ronald De Boer. **16** Frank Leboeuf. **17** Davor Suker. **18** Two. **19** Ronaldo. **20** Marcel Desailly.

Quiz 50 **West Ham United**

LEVEL 2

Answers – see page 468

1 What was West Ham's original name?

2 Who did West Ham play in the 1923 "White Horse" FA Cup final?

3 In what year did West Ham first win the FA Cup?

4 Who took over from Ron Greenwood as manager in 1974?

5 Which former West Ham great played for Fulham against the Hammers in the 1974 FA Cup final?

6 Which Hammer scored a rare header to win the 1980 FA Cup final against Arsenal?

7 What is the official name of West Ham's home ground?

8 Which player holds the club's league appearances record?

9 Who is West Ham's most capped player?

10 Who was the assistant manager during the 2000–01 season?

11 What are West Ham's away colours?

12 How many times have West Ham won the FA Cup?

13 In what year did West Ham win the European Cup Winners' Cup?

14 Who did they beat in the final?

15 Who scored twice in that match?

16 How many times have West Ham reached the League Cup final?

17 Which Croatian striker did the Hammers sign for free from Arsenal in summer 2000?

18 Which defender left West Ham for Palace during summer 2000?

19 Who beat West Ham 6–0 in the 1990 Littlewoods Cup semi-final?

20 Where did West Ham finish in the Premier League in 1999–2000?

Answers

Non-League Football (see Quiz 52)

1 Stevenage. **2** Chester City. **3** Yeovil. **4** Kidderminster, Macclesfield or Stevenage. **5** Rushden and Diamonds. **6** Brighton. **7** Coventry City. **8** Chris Waddle. **9** Newcastle United. **10** Wimbledon. **11** Blyth. **12** Barnet. **13** Borough. **14** Town. **15** Victoria. **16** Returned to Football League after relegation. **17** Malcolm Christie. **18** Nigel Clough. **19** Ron Atkinson. **20** Two (Colchester United and Wycombe Wanderers, both in Division Two).

Quiz 51 **World Cup 98**

LEVEL 2

Answers – see page 465

1 Which team completed Group F in the finals along with Germany, Yugoslavia and Iran?
2 How many points did Japan get in their first round group?
3 In the best game of the first round Nigeria came back to beat which team 3–2?
4 Who scored two goals for Chile in their 2–2 first round draw with Italy?
5 Which Italian striker scored four times in the first round group stage?
6 Why will Tommy Boyd remember Scotland's opening game with Brazil?
7 Luis Hernandez was which country's blond World Cup star?
8 Who scored the first Golden Goal in World Cup history to eliminate Paraguay from the tournament?
9 Who did David Beckham kick out at to be sent off in the second round match against Argentina?
10 Who scored Argentina's penalty after five minutes of the match against England?
11 Which French star was suspended for their second-round game?
12 What was the score in Germany's quarter-final with Croatia?
13 Who shocked Brazil by scoring after two minutes in their quarter-final, but eventually lost 2–3?
14 Who did France meet in the semi-final?
15 Which Dutch player missed the deciding penalty in their semi-final?
16 Who replaced the suspended Laurent Blanc in the French final team?
17 Who won the Golden Boot with a goal in the third place play-off match?
18 How many of France's goals did Zidane score in the final?
19 Which Brazilian was passed fit only 45 minutes before the final?
20 Which Frenchman was sent off in the final?

Answers

The UEFA Cup (see Quiz 49)

1 The Inter-Cities Fairs Cup. **2** 1958. **3** London. **4** 1972. **5** Italy. **6** 1998: it became a one-off match. **7** Dundee United in 1987. **8** Spurs in 1984. **9** Anderlecht. **10** Moenchengladbach. **11** Newcastle United. **12** Galatasaray. **13** Istanbul. **14** Arsenal. **15** Moscow. **16** Birmingham. **17** Diego Maradona. **18** Ipswich Town. **19** 1972. **20** 1971.

Quiz 52 **Non-League Football**

LEVEL 2

Answers – see page 466

1 Which non-League club had a dispute with Newcastle United when they chose to play at their own ground in the FA Cup in 1998?
2 Which League team were relegated to the Conference in 2000?
3 Which non-League team were once notorious for their sloping pitch?
4 Name one of the three Conference champions who were denied promotion to the Football League because their ground was inadequate.
5 Brian Talbot managed which Non-League team to the Conference title in 2001?
6 Which South Coast team were beaten on penalties by Sudbury Town in the 1997 FA Cup?
7 Which First Division team were beaten by Sutton in the FA Cup only two years after they had won it?
8 Which future England player was discovered playing for Tow Law Town?
9 Hereford United, then in the Southern League, earned a famous victory over which team helped by a Goal of the Season from Ronnie Radford?
10 Who won the FA Cup only 11 years after joining the Football League?
11 Which Spartans are a famous North East non-league club?
12 Which club did manager Barry Fry take into the Football League in 1991?
13 Nuneaton and Stevenage have which club name in common?
14 Complete the non-league team name: Hednesford ...?
15 Complete the non-league team name: Northwich ...?
16 What feat did Halifax Town and Lincoln City achieve?
17 Which current Derby County forward came from non-League football?
18 Which famous manager's son is in charge at Burton Albion?
19 Which retired flamboyant manager spent his playing days skippering Oxford United from the Southern League to the Second Division?
20 In 2001–02, how many former Conference clubs were playing in a division higher than Division 3?

Answers

West Ham United (see Quiz 50)

1 Thames Ironworks FC. **2** Bolton Wanderers. **3** 1964. **4** John Lyall. **5** Bobby Moore. **6** Trevor Brooking. **7** Boleyn Ground. **8** Billy Bonds. **9** Bobby Moore. **10** Frank Lampard. **11** All white. **12** Three times. **13** 1965. **14** Munich 1860. **15** Alan Sealey. **16** Twice. **17** Davor Suker. **18** Neil Ruddock. **19** Oldham Athletic. **20** Ninth.

Quiz 53 **The 80s**

LEVEL 2

Answers – see page 471

1 Which English club won the European Cup in 1980?

2 For how long were English clubs banned from European competitions after the Heysel tragedy?

3 Who won the World Cup in 1986?

4 Which camera company sponsored the football league during the 1980s?

5 Who won the European Championship in 1988?

6 Who scored five goals for Ipswich as they beat Southampton 5–3 in a league match in 1982?

7 In which country was the 1982 World Cup played?

8 Which three brothers all appeared for Southampton in a league game in 1988?

9 Which 80s manager claimed referees were "intimidated" at Anfield?

10 Which manager grabbed, punched and kissed some fans in 1989?

11 Who did Arsenal beat with an injury time-goal to win the league championship in 1989?

12 Which Spurs keeper became a hero when his two penalty saves won them the UEFA Cup in 1984?

13 When were the last Home Internationals held?

14 Who scored a memorable goal as England beat Brazil in Rio in 1984?

15 Who became England manager in June 1982?

16 When did Barclays Bank start sponsoring the Football League?

17 Who won the League Cup in 1989?

18 Who beat Arsenal in 1988 to win the League Cup for the first time in their 98-year history?

19 Who won the league and FA Cup double in 1986?

20 Who banned away fans from their Kenilworth Road ground in 1985?

Answers

Overseas Grounds (see Quiz 55)

1 Maracana. **2** AS Monaco. **3** Stadium of Light. **4** The Rose Bowl, Pasadena. **5** Nou Camp, Barcelona. **6** Bayern Munich. **7** Bernabeu. **8** San Siro. **9** Moscow. **10** Poland. **11** Sampdoria and Genoa. **12** England 0 USA 1 **13** Santiago. **14** Heysel. **15** Estonia. **16** Chile. **17** Charleroi. **18** Copenhagen. **19** Ajax. **20** Stade de France.

Quiz 54 **German Football**

LEVEL 2

Answers – see page 472

1 What is the name of the German league?

2 Who did Bayern beat in the 1974 European Cup final?

3 How many times in a row did Bayern win the European Cup during the 1970s?

4 Which former Leeds striker later played for Hamburg?

5 Which German team did French international Yourri Djorkaeff join?

6 Which Norwegian star joined Munich 1860 in summer 2000?

7 What is Andy Moller's nickname?

8 Whose penalty helped West Germany beat England in the quarter-finals of the 1972 European Championships?

9 Who scored a penalty before West Germany had even touched the ball in the 1974 World Cup final?

10 Who defeated West Germany in the 1982 World Cup final?

11 Who scored West Germany's two goals in the 1986 World Cup final?

12 Who scored Germany's winner from the penalty spot in Italia 90?

13 How many Argentinian players were sent off in that final?

14 Who memorably defeated Germany in the quarter-finals of the 1994 World Cup?

15 Who scored against them that day?

16 Prior to 2001, which was the last German club to win the European Cup?

17 Who scored twice in the final that year and then went on to play for Liverpool and Fulham?

18 Which German club did Chelsea beat in the 1998 European Cup Winners Cup final?

19 Which other teams were in Germany's Euro 2000 group?

20 Who took over as team manager after that tournament?

Answers

Hat-Tricks (see Quiz 56)

1 Henrik Larsson. **2** Paul Scholes. **3** Luxembourg. **4** Manchester City. **5** Luther Blissett. **6** Real Madrid's. **7** Matt Le Tissier. **8** Poland. **9** Marco Van Basten. **10** Alan Shearer. **11** Stan Collymore. **12** Patrick Kluivert. **13** Robbie Fowler. **14** One. **15** Michael Bridges. **16** Charlton Athletic. **17** Paul Gascoigne's. **18** Nwankwo Kanu. **19** Eric Cantona. **20** Rangers.

Quiz 55 **Overseas Grounds**

LEVEL 2

Answers – see page 469

1 In which ground do Brazil host most international matches?

2 Which French team play at the Louis II stadium?

3 Which Lisbon ground shares its name with a Premier League stadium?

4 Which stadium hosted the 1994 World Cup final in USA?

5 Where did Manchester United win the 1999 European Cup Final?

6 Which German team play at the country's national stadium?

7 What is the name of Real Madrid's famous stadium?

8 Which ground is home to Milan and Internazionale?

9 The Luzhniki Stadium, originally Spartak's ground but now home to Torpedo, is in which city?

10 Which country play most their home matches at the Stadion Slaski in Katowice?

11 Which two clubs share the Luigi Ferraris stadium in Italy?

12 What famous match took place at Belo Horizonte in 1950?

13 The match between Chile and Italy in 1962, which was dogged by foul play and serious violent conduct, became known as the Battle of..?

14 Which stadium was rebuilt after a tragedy and renamed the Stade de Roi Baudouin?

15 Who were Scotland meant to be playing in the Kadriorg Stadium in 1996 when they kicked off with no opposition?

16 Which South American country used their National Stadium as a prison and execution centre after a right-wing coup in 1973?

17 Which city's Euro 2000 ground was deemed by many experts to be unsafe because of its steep temporary terracing?

18 In which city did Arsenal play the 2000 UEFA Cup final?

19 Which Dutch team moved to the country's national stadium in 1996?

20 Which ground was built for the 1998 World Cup?

Answers

The 80s (see Quiz 53)

1 Nottingham Forest. **2** Five years, 1985–90. **3** Argentina. **4** Canon. **5** Holland. **6** Alan Brazil. **7** Spain. **8** Danny, Rodney and Ray Wallace. **9** Alex Ferguson. **10** Brian Clough. **11** Liverpool. **12** Tony Parks. **13** 1984. **14** John Barnes. **15** Bobby Robson. **16** 1987. **17** Nottingham Forest. **18** Luton Town. **19** Liverpool. **20** Luton Town.

Quiz 56 **Hat-Tricks**

LEVEL 2

Answers – see page 470

1 Who scored a hat-trick for Celtic against Rangers in August 2000?
2 Who scored a hat-trick for England against Poland in 1999?
3 Who did Alan Shearer score a hat-trick against at Wembley in 1999?
4 Tony Adcock, Paul Stewart and David White all scored hat-tricks in whose 10–1 defeat of Huddersfield Town in 1987?
5 Which Watford player scored a hat-trick on his England debut in 1982?
6 Puskas and Di Stefano both scored hat-tricks in whose 7–3 European Cup final victory over Eintracht Frankfurt?
7 Who scored a hat-trick for Southampton in 86 when only eighteen?
8 Who did Gary Lineker score a hat-trick against in the 86 World Cup?
9 Who scored a hat-trick against England in Euro 88?
10 Who scored a hat-trick for Southampton in 88 when only seventeen?
11 Who scored a hat-trick in 1999 after being "rescued" by Leicester City?
12 Who scored a hat-trick for Holland against Yugoslavia in Euro 2000?
13 Who scored a hat-trick in five minutes against Arsenal in 1994?
14 How many of Geoff Hurst's World Cup hat-trick came in the 90 minutes?
15 Which Leeds signing scored a hat-trick in his second game in 1999?
16 Clive Mendonca scored a play-off hat-trick at Wembley in 1998 to send which team to the Premier League?
17 Whose hat-trick for Tottenham included two free-kicks floated past Derby keeper Peter Shilton in 1990?
18 Whose sensational hat-trick in the last 20 minutes enabled Arsenal to come back from 0–2 to beat Chelsea in 1999?
19 Who scored a hat-trick for Leeds United against Liverpool in the 1992 Charity Shield?
20 Gordon Durie scored a hat-trick for whom in a 1996 Scottish Cup final?

Answers

German Football (see Quiz 54)

1 The Bundesliga. **2** Atletico Madrid. **3** Three times, 1974, 75 and 76. **4** Tony Yeboah. **5** Kaiserslautern. **6** Erik Mykland. **7** "Cry Baby". **8** Gunter Netzer. **9** Johan Neeskens for Holland. **10** Italy. **11** Rummenigge and Völler. **12** Andreas Brehme. **13** Two. **14** Bulgaria. **15** Stoichkov and Letchkov. **16** Borussia Dortmund in 1997. **17** Karlheinz Reidle **18** Stuttgart. **19** England, Portugal and Romania. **20** Rudi Völler.

Quiz 57 **Everton**

LEVEL 2

Answers – see page 475

1 What was Everton's original name?

2 What is Everton's motto?

3 What is Everton's training ground called?

4 Who is the most successful captain in Everton's history?

5 From whom did Everton sign Peter Reid in 1982?

6 Who is the club's top post-war goalscorer?

7 Who scored the famous winning goal for Everton in the Merseyside derby in October 1978?

8 Which Everton keeper was known as "Handbag" by Liverpool fans?

9 Who scored twice for the Toffees in the 1966 FA Cup final?

10 Who famously played in white boots for Everton in the late 1960s?

11 Which dazzling striker signed for Everton from Anderlecht in 1976 but left for Chelsea two years later?

12 Who won £10,000 from the *Daily Express* for scoring 30 goals during the 1977–78 season?

13 Which Republic of Ireland player crossed Stanley Park from Liverpool to Everton in 1982?

14 Which striker scored a hat-trick on his league debut, against Newcastle in 1988?

15 Who scored 20 goals in his first season for Everton, in 1990–91?

16 In which year did Everton win a European trophy?

17 What was the main colour of Everton's away shirts in season 2000–01?

18 To whom did Everton sell John Spencer in 1998?

19 Have Everton ever won the League Cup?

20 Where did Everton finish in the Premier League in 1999–2000?

Answers

Transfers (see Quiz 59)

1 Mo Johnston. **2** Pierre Van Hooijdonk. **3** Duncan Ferguson. **4** Coventry City. **5** Alan Ball. **6** Nothing. **7** Paul Gascoigne. **8** 1996 (Alan Shearer's move from Blackburn to Newcastle for £15 million). **9** Paul Ince. **10** Edu. **11** Tony Cascarino. **12** Christian Vieri. **13** Chris Sutton. **14** Thierry Henry. **15** Jaap Stam. **16** John Hartson. **17** Barcelona. **18** Winterburn and Suker. **19** Robbie Keane. **20** Duncan Ferguson.

Quiz 58 **Celtic**

Answers – see page 476

LEVEL 2

1 Which French club knocked Celtic out of the 2000 UEFA Cup?

2 What is Celtic's nickname?

3 What did Fergus McCann do at Celtic in 1994?

4 In what year did Celtic hero Kenny Dalglish join Liverpool?

5 Which striker did Celtic sign from Chelsea in 2000?

6 Which manager was sacked after their Cup humiliation against Inverness in January 2000?

7 Who took over as manager temporarily until Martin O'Neill's appointment?

8 From which English Premier League club did Celtic sign Bobby Petta?

9 How many championships did Celtic win consecutively from 1966?

10 Which 90s Celtic hero joined Sheffield Wednesday and then West Ham?

11 Who did Celtic beat to win the European Cup final in 1967?

12 Which Celtic forward went on as Scotland's substitute in both Euro 2000 play-off games with England?

13 Which year did Celtic win the championship and prevent Rangers winning "ten in a row"?

14 Where did Celtic play in 1994–95 while Celtic Park was being rebuilt?

15 Which Scottish international midfielder won 76 caps for Scotland between 1984 and 1997?

16 Which "Champagne Charlie" rejoined Celtic in 1990?

17 Which member of Celtic's 1953–54 double-winning team engineered their revival in 1965?

18 Which English team did Celtic beat in the European Cup in 1970?

19 Celtic's leading scorer in 1999–2000 left the club at the end of the season. Who?

20 Which Channel Four Italian football expert played for Celtic?

Answers

Hard Men (see Quiz 60)

1 Tommy Smith. **2** Norman Hunter. **3** Ron Harris. **4** Vinnie Jones. **5** Graeme Souness. **6** Harald Schumacher. **7** John Fashanu. **8** John Hartson. **9** David Cross. **10** Dean Saunders. **11** Patrick Vieira. **12** Nicky Butt. **13** Manchester United. **14** Leeds United. **15** Vinnie Jones. **16** Leeds and Spurs. **17** Terry Butcher. **18** Celtic v Rangers. **19** Ron Harris. **20** Roy Keane.

Quiz 59 **Transfers**

Answers – see page 473

LEVEL 2

1 Whose transfer from Watford to Rangers in 1989 caused uproar?

2 Who joined Vitesse Arnhem in June 1999 after refusing to play for Nottingham Forest ever again?

3 Who rejoined Everton from Newcastle in August 2000?

4 Who spent £1m on Arsenal youth player Jay Bothroyd in 2000?

5 Who did Arsenal break the existing British transfer record for in 1971?

6 How much did German international Markus Babbel cost Liverpool?

7 Whose price was reduced by £3.5m after he was injured in 1991?

8 When were two English clubs last involved a world record transfer deal?

9 Which West Ham player angered fans by appearing in a Manchester United shirt before signing for them in 1989?

10 Which Brazilian was set to join Arsenal in the summer of 2000, but arrived with an invalid passport?

11 Which Republic of Ireland striker reputedly cost Gillingham a set of tracksuits?

12 Which Italian forward went to and returned from Spain in deals amounting to over £50m?

13 Who did Chelsea sell for £6m in 2000 – a year after paying out £10m for him?

14 Who did Arsenal buy from Juventus for £10.5m in 1999?

15 Who was Manchester United's most expensive signing out of Andrew Cole, Fabien Barthez and Jaap Stam?

16 Which Wimbledon player did Tottenham back out of buying at the last minute in 2000?

17 Who sold Ronaldo for £18m in 1997?

18 Which players went on free transfers from Arsenal to West Ham in 2000?

19 Who replaced Lee Bowyer as Britain's most expensive teenager in 1999?

20 Who moved to Rangers in 1994 for a record Scottish fee?

Answers

Everton (see Quiz 57)

1 St Domingo FC. **2** Nil Satis Nisi Optimum ('Nothing but the best is good enough'). **3** Bellefield. **4** Kevin Ratcliffe. **5** Bolton Wanderers. **6** Graeme Sharpe. **7** Andy King. **8** Gordon West. **9** Mike Trebilcock. **10** Alan Ball. **11** Duncan McKenzie. **12** Bob Latchford. **13** Kevin Sheedy. **14** Tony Cottee. **15** Peter Beardsley. **16** 1985. **17** White. **18** Motherwell. **19** No. **20** 13th.

Quiz 60 **Hard Men**

Answers – see page 474

LEVEL 2

1 Which Liverpool player wrote a book entitled *The Hard Way*?

2 Which Leeds player was said to "bite yer legs"?

3 Which Chelsea defender "dealt with" Eddie Gray in the 1970 FA Cup final?

4 Who, allegedly, deliberately hurt Steve McMahon with an early tackle in the 1988 FA Cup final?

5 Who was sent off in his first match as player-manager of Rangers in 1986?

6 Which German keeper committed an horrendous foul on France's Patrick Battiston in the 1982 World Cup semi-final?

7 Which Wimbledon player's elbow broke Gary Mabbutt's cheekbone?

8 Who kicked Eyal Berkovic in the head during a West Ham training session?

9 Which West Ham striker was known as "Psycho"?

10 Whose tackle ended Chelsea defender Paul Elliott's professional career?

11 Which Arsenal player was sent off in both the first and second games of the 2000–01 season?

12 Which Manchester United player was sent off twice in September 1998?

13 Which club was criticised for intimidating referees during 1999–2000?

14 Which club had players arrested and charged with GBH during 1999–2000?

15 Which player was fined for his part in the release of a video called *Soccer's Hard Men* in 1992?

16 Which two teams were fined for a brawl during a league game in the 1999–2000 season?

17 Which Rangers player was fined £500 for kicking a door after a match against Aberdeen in 1988?

18 Which match featured 3 sendings off and 8 other bookings in May 1999?

19 Which Chelsea defender earned the nickname "Chopper" for his combative performances?

20 Who was sent off during the 2000 Charity Shield match?

Answers

Celtic (see Quiz 58)

1 Lyon. **2** The Bhoys. **3** Bought 51 per cent of the club. **4** 1977. **5** Chris Sutton. **6** John Barnes. **7** Kenny Dalglish. **8** Ipswich Town. **9** Nine. **10** Paulo Di Canio. **11** Inter Milan. **12** Mark Burchill. **13** 1998. **14** Hampden Park. **15** Paul McStay. **16** Charlie Nicholas. **17** Jock Stein. **18** Leeds United. **19** Mark Viduka. **20** Paul Elliott.

Quiz 61 **The North**

LEVEL 2

Answers – see page 479

1 Geoffrey Richmond was Scarborough Chairman before joining which Yorkshire club?
2 In which colour shirts do Grimsby Town play?
3 Which Yorkshire team reached the FA and League Cup finals in 1993?
4 Which Yorkshire team became the first to be promoted automatically from the Conference in 1987?
5 Which Yorkshire side used to play at Leeds Road?
6 Which manager exchanged Sheffield Wednesday for Leeds in 1988?
7 Which Yorkshire club was voted out of the Football League in 1970?
8 Which Yorkshire team was the only visiting side to win at Old Trafford in season 1995–96, when a 3–0 victory knocked Manchester United out of the Coca-Cola Cup?
9 Which mecurial Italian joined Bradford City from Aston Villa in 2000?
10 In which colour shirts do Sheffield United play?
11 Which Yorkshire team play at Boothferry Park?
12 David Pleat, Ron Atkinson and Trevor Francis have all managed which team?
13 Jimmy Adamson, Jimmy Armfield and George Graham have all managed which northern team?
14 Which team regained their league status in 1998 after five years in the Conference?
15 Scunthorpe, Scarborough or Doncaster – which was the League team in 2001?
16 Which Party's MPs put Sheffield Wednesday under pressure to sack manager Danny Wilson in 2000?
17 Which hot midfielder joined Leeds from Sheffield United in 1976?
18 For which Yorkshire team did Belgian international Gilles de Bilde first sign?
19 Allan Clarke returned to Leeds after managing which Yorkshire side?
20 Which Yorkshire city's teams took part in an FA Cup semi-final at Wembley?

Answers

World Cup 94 (see Quiz 63)

1 He was murdered. **2** Sweden. **3** Saudi Arabia. **4** Greece. **5** Ray Houghton. **6** New York. **7** Hristo Stoichkov. **8** Five. **9** USA. **10** Holland. **11** Gianfranco Zola. **12** Bebeto. **13** Diego Maradona. **14** Jurgen Klinsmann. **15** Roberto Baggio's. **16** Bulgaria. **17** Sweden. **18** Franco Baresi. **19** Roberto Baggio. **20** Romario.

Quiz 62 **Italia 90**

Answers – see page 480

LEVEL 2

1 Who won the tournament?

2 Which Italian striker hit the headlines with his goals?

3 Who sensationally beat Scotland in their opening game?

4 On which island did the English fans camp during the first phase of the tournament?

5 Who did England play in their opening game?

6 Who did the Republic of Ireland beat in the second phase?

7 Who famously scored their winning penalty in that match?

8 Who put Brazil out of the tournament with a 1–0 win in the second phase?

9 Where was England's second phase match against Belgium played?

10 Who scored England's winner in that match?

11 Who did England play in the quarter-finals?

12 What was unique about their opponents in that match?

13 Whose singing dominated Italia 90?

14 What was unique about the semi-finals?

15 Who did England play in their semi-final?

16 Which England player wept when he was booked in the semi-final?

17 Who missed England's penalties in the semi-final shoot out?

18 In which city was the Argentina v Italy semi-final played?

19 How was the final decided?

20 Who was captain of the losing team in the Final?

Answers

Nationwide 2 (see Quiz 64)

1 Torquay United. **2** Lionel Louch (1914). **3** 1954. **4** 3. **5** 1922. **6** False. **7** Wigan Athletic. **8** 1970s. **9** Division 3. **10** Plymouth Argyle. **11** 2. **12** Fulham. **13** Lincoln City. **14** Dave Bassett. **15** Wimbledon. **16** AFC Bournemouth. **17** False. **18** Bristol City and Stoke City. **19** Stoke City. **20** Rotherham United.

Quiz 63 **World Cup 94**

LEVEL 2

Answers – see page 477

1 What was the ultimate consequence of Andreas Escobar's own goal against the USA?

2 Which team had Thomas Ravelli in goal during the tournament?

3 Which Middle-Eastern team beat Belgium in round one?

4 Which European team scored none and conceded ten in three games?

5 Whose goal for the Republic of Ireland defeated Italy in the opening Group E game?

6 In which city did Ireland play Italy?

7 Which Golden Boot winner scored in every round up to the semi-final?

8 How many goals did Oleg Salenko score in Russia's 6–1 victory over Cameroon in the first round group match?

9 Which team's line-up included Wynalda, Dooley and Lalas?

10 Which country beat the Irish 2–0 to send them home?

11 Which future Chelsea player was sent off when Italy met Nigeria in the second round?

12 Which Brazilian initiated a cradle-rocking goal celebration after his goals in the tournament?

13 Which legendary player was thrown out of the tournament after failing a drugs test in the competition?

14 Which striker scored five goals for Germany in the tournament?

15 Which Italian's last-minute goal eliminated Nigeria?

16 Who knocked Germany out of the competition in the quarter-finals?

17 Which country lost to Brazil in the semi-final?

18 Who was Italy's captain in the final and missed their first penalty?

19 Who missed Italy's fifth penalty and lost them the final?

20 Which striker scored five goals for Brazil and converted his penalty in the final shoot-out?

Answers

The North (see Quiz 61)

1 Bradford City. **2** Black and White. **3** Sheffield Wednesday. **4** Scarborough. **5** Huddersfield. **6** Howard Wilkinson. **7** Bradford Park Avenue. **8** York City. **9** Benito Carbone. **10** Red and White. **11** Hull City. **12** Sheffield Wednesday. **13** Leeds United. **14** Halifax Town. **15** Scunthorpe. **16** Labour. **17** Tony Currie. **18** Sheffield Wednesday. **19** Barnsley. **20** Sheffield United and Wednesday.

Quiz 64 **Nationwide 2**

Answers – see page 478

LEVEL 2

1 Which club used to play at Teignmouth Road?

2 Who was Southend United's first international?

3 In which year did Port Vale reach the FA Cup semi-final?

4 What was Norwich City's highest finish in the Premier League?

5 In what year were York City formed?

6 Manchester United have played in the Nationwide League. True or False?

7 Which club did Bruce Rioch take over as manager of in June 2000?

8 In which year did Cambridge United play their first Football League game – 1900s, 1940s or 1970s?

9 Which Division did Notts County win in 1997–98?

10 Which club did Peter Shilton manage between 1992 and 1995?

11 How many times did Sunderland win the Division 1 championship in the 1990s?

12 Which Nationwide League team gave their manager to the country in 1999?

13 Which Nationwide team are known as the Red Imps?

14 Who took over from Graham Taylor at Watford in 1984?

15 Which club were formed in 1889 but did not turn professional until 1964?

16 What is Bournemouth's full name?

17 Non-League clubs are allowed to enter the League Cup – true or false?

18 Which teams contested the Auto Windscreens Shield Final in 2000?

19 Who won?

20 Which team won the Division 3 Championship in 1981?

Answers

Italia 90 (see Quiz 62)

1 West Germany. **2** "Toto" Schillaci. **3** Costa Rica. **4** Sardinia. **5** Republic of Ireland. **6** Romania. **7** David O'Leary. **8** Argentina. **9** Bologna. **10** David Platt. **11** Cameroon. **12** They were the first African country ever to reach the World Cup quarter-finals. **13** Luciano Pavarotti. **14** They were both decided on penalties. **15** West Germany. **16** Paul Gascoigne. **17** Pearce and Waddle. **18** Naples. **19** A penalty. **20** Diego Maradona.

Quiz 65 **Champions League**

LEVEL 2

Answers – see page 483

1 When was the "Champions League" proper introduced?

2 How was the new competition different from the old?

3 Who won the competition in 1992?

4 Where was the final played that year?

5 Which current Chelsea star scored for AC Milan in the 1994 final?

6 Which team appeared in the 1993, 1994 and 1995 finals?

7 Which Italian team appeared in the 1996, 1997 and 1998 finals?

8 How many of those three finals did they win?

9 Which current Arsenal star played for Ajax in the 1996 final?

10 Who beat Manchester United in the quarter-finals of the 1997 competition?

11 How did the competition change in 1998?

12 Who won the competition that year?

13 Who did they beat in the final?

14 Who did Manchester United play in the first match of the 1998–99 competition?

15 Which country do they come from?

16 Who else were in Manchester United's group?

17 What was the result of United's quarter-final first leg against Inter?

18 Who scored United's semi-final winner?

19 Who did United defeat in the final?

20 How did the competition change in 1999?

Answers

The 90s (see Quiz 67)

1 Liam Brady. **2** Jack Walker. **3** Grey. **4** Ryan Giggs. **5** Littlewoods and Worthington. **6** England played at home outside of Wembley. **7** Barry Hearn. **8** Brian Little. **9** Ally McCoist. **10** Alan Shearer. **11** Gary Nelson. **12** Newcastle. **13** Oldham. **14** George Weah. **15** Brian Clough. **16** Dean Saunders. **17** David Platt. **18** Hristo Stoichkov. **19** Eric Cantona **20** John Aldridge.

Quiz 66 **Name That Team**

Answers – see page 484

1 Armstrong, Bramble, Clapham?

2 Arca, Haas, Schwartz?

3 Delap, Dodd, Davies?

4 Boa Morte, Collins, Saha?

5 Weaver, Wanchope, Wright-Phillips?

6 Helguson, Hughes, Hyde?

7 Haslam, Hendon, Hinchcliffe?

8 Savage, Scowcroft, Sinclair?

9 Forssell, Gallas, Hasselbaink?

10 Duff, Dunn, Short?

11 Wallace, Warhurst, Whitlow?

12 Ray, Robinson, Roussel?

13 Ball, Branch, Briscoe?

14 Barthez, Blanc, Brown?

15 Barmby, Berger, Biscan?

16 Kanoute, Lomas, Moncur?

17 Richards, Sullivan, Taricco?

18 Parlour, Pennant, Pires?

19 Holdsworth, Horsfield, Hughes?

20 Barton, Bassedas, Bellamy?

Answers

Goals Galore 2 (see Quiz 68)

1 Paulo Wanchope. **2** Yugoslavia. **3** Niall Quinn. **4** Leeds United. **5** Ipswich Town. **6** Yugoslavia. **7** Newcastle United. **8** Newcastle United. **9** Norwich City. **10** Alan Mullery. **11** Burnley. **12** Two. **13** Cedric Roussel. **14** Clive Allen. **15** Spain. **16** Michael Owen. **17** Carsten Jancker. **18** Dion Dublin. **19** Matt Elliott. **20** Ian Rush.

Quiz 67 **The 90s**

LEVEL 2

Answers – see page 481

1 Who had spells in charge of Brighton and Celtic in the 90s?

2 Which Blackburn chairman's millions bought them success in the 90s?

3 In which colour shirts did Manchester United play for one half in 1996?

4 Who made his club and international debut in 1991 at the age of 17?

5 Which two other names did the Coca-Cola Cup go under in the 90s?

6 What occurred at Leeds in 1995 that hadn't happened since 1966?

7 Which boxing promoter took over Leyton Orient in 1995?

8 Who left Leicester City to take over at Aston Villa in 1995?

9 Who scored Scotland's only goal in Euro 96?

10 Who won the PFA Footballer of the Year award twice in the 90s?

11 *Left Foot Forward* and *Left Foot in the Grave* are whose soccer memories?

12 Who finished Premier League runners-up despite holding a 12-point lead in January?

13 Which club reached a League Cup final and two FA Cup semi-finals in the decade before being relegated in 1994?

14 Who is the only African to win the World Footballer of the Year award?

15 Which 90s manager was allegedly involved in brown-paper-bag bungs?

16 Which international played for Derby County, Liverpool, Aston Villa, Galatasary and Nottingham Forest in the 90s?

17 Which England international spent four years in the early 90s playing for three Italian teams?

18 Which Bulgarian won four Spanish Championships, a European Cup and helped his country to a World Cup semi-final in the 90s?

19 In the 90s, who became the first player to win back-to-back championships with different clubs?

20 Which Scouser played in two 90s World Cup finals while in his 30s?

Answers

Champions League (see Quiz 65)

1 1992. **2** It was no longer exclusively a knockout competition. **3** Barcelona. **4** Wembley. **5** Marcel Desailly. **6** AC Milan. **7** Juventus. **8** One. **9** Kanu. **10** Monaco. **11** Runners-up were allowed in as well as champions. **12** Real Madrid. **13** Juventus. **14** LKS Lodz. **15** Poland. **16** Barcelona and Bayern Munich. **17** 2–0 to United. **18** Andy Cole. **19** Bayern Munich. **20** More teams and a second group stage were added.

Quiz 68 **Goals Galore 2**

Answers – see page 482

LEVEL 2

1. Who scored a hat-trick on his home debut for Man City in 2000?
2. Which team scored three late goals to draw with Slovenia in Euro 2000?
3. Who equalled Frank Stapleton's Republic of Ireland scoring record with a goal against South Africa in 2000?
4. Who signed Celtic's top scorer in the 2000 close season?
5. David Johnson was which team's leading goalscorer in 1999–2000?
6. Who did Holland knock six goals past in Euro 2000?
7. Who beat Tottenham 6–1 in an FA Cup replay in 1999?
8. For which club did Andy Cole score 41 goals in 1993–94?
9. Iwan Roberts was which club's leading goalscorer in 1999–2000?
10. Which England veteran won the BBC Goal of the Season with a cracking volley for Fulham in 1974?
11. Andy Payton was the Division Two leading scorer in 1999–2000, with 27 goals for which club?
12. How many goals did Chris Sutton score in his season at Chelsea?
13. In 1999–2000 which Belgian striker joined Coventry City on loan and played for Wolves in 2001–02?
14. Who scored 50 goals for Tottenham Hotspur in 1986–87?
15. Who beat Yugoslavia 4–3 in Euro 2000 to knock Norway out of the tournament?
16. Who scored England's goal against France in 2000 in Paris?
17. Who scored Germany's goal against England in Munich in September 2001?
18. Who scored eight goals in his first eight games for Coventry City in 1994?
19. Which centre-half won the 2000 Worthington Cup for Leicester City with two headed goals?
20. Which Liverpool player has scored the most goals in FA Cup Finals?

Answers

Name That Team (see Quiz 66)

1 Ipswich Town. **2** Sunderland. **3** Southampton. **4** Fulham. **5** Manchester City. **6** Watford. **7** Sheffield Wednesday. **8** Leicester City. **9** Chelsea. **10** Blackburn Rovers. **11** Bolton Wanderers. **12** Wolverhampton Wanderers. **13** Burnley. **14** Manchester United. **15** Liverpool. **16** West Ham United. **17** Tottenham Hotspur. **18** Arsenal. **19** Birmingham City. **20** Newcastle United.

Quiz 69 **Euro 2000**

LEVEL 2

Answers – see page 487

1 Which city hosted the opening game of the finals?

2 Which team in the quarter-finals qualified for Euro 2000 through the play-offs?

3 Who were the only team to win all of their qualifying matches?

4 Sergio Conceicao scored a hat-trick against Germany. For which team?

5 Nils Johan Semb's team went out after the first stage. Who are they?

6 Who scored England's second goal against Portugal?

7 Who was awarded a penalty in the eighty-ninth minute and so won their first match?

8 In which town did England play Portugal?

9 What was the result when Holland met France in Group D?

10 Who scored two goals in Holland's 6–1 demolition of Turkey?

11 Who was sent off in the quarter-final between Romania and Italy?

12 From whose cross did Alan Shearer head England's winning goal against Germany?

13 Who won their semi-final after being awarded a penalty in extra-time?

14 Who missed a last-minute penalty and gave France a 2–1 quarter-final victory over Spain?

15 Members of which team received long international suspensions for their ugly protests at a refereeing decision?

16 Which Italian forward missed two gilt-edged chances in the final?

17 Who scored France's winning goal in the final?

18 Frank de Boer missed one of Holland's penalties in normal time of the semi-final – who missed the other?

19 Which player conceded a late penalty to Romania, which ended England's participation in the tournament?

20 Which two teams scored 13 goals in the finals?

Answers

Holland and Belgium (see Quiz 71)

1 Anderlecht. **2** Brussels. **3** Charleroi. **4** Rotterdam. **5** Philips. **6** Bobby Robson. **7** Ajax. **8** Anderlecht. **9** Franz Thijssen and Arnold Muhren. **10** Club Brugge. **11** Ajax and Mechelen. **12** Ajax. **13** Johan Cruyff. **14** PSV Eindhoven. **15** Two. **16** Semi-finals. **17** PSV Eindhoven. **18** Barcelona. **19** Aaron Winter. **20** Amsterdam.

Quiz 70 **Euro Championship Pre–1992**

LEVEL 2

Answers – see page 488

1 What was the original name of this tournament?

2 What is the actual name of the trophy?

3 In which year was the trophy first contested?

4 Who won that first tournament?

5 How often is the tournament held?

6 When did England first join the competition?

7 How was the 1968 semi-final between Italy and USSR decided?

8 Who won the 1972 tournament?

9 Where was the 1984 competition held?

10 Who did France beat in the final that year?

11 What is the furthest England have gone in the competition?

12 How many points did England get in the group stage of the 1988 tournament?

13 Where was the tournament held that year?

14 Who won that tournament?

15 Who did they beat in the semi-final?

16 Who did they play in the final?

17 In which city was the final held?

18 Where was the 1976 tournament held?

19 Who won that tournament?

20 Which is the only final ever to have gone to a replay?

Answers

African Football (see Quiz 72)

1 The Ivory Coast. **2** Morocco. **3** Nigeria. **4** Ghana. **5** Cameroon. **6** Algeria. **7** Cameroon. **8** Morocco. **9** Top. **10** England. **11** Italy. **12** South Africa. **13** Green. **14** Zambia. **15** None (eliminated after three draws). **16** Zaire. **17** Egypt. **18** South Africa. **19** Ghana and Egypt. **20** Morocco.

Quiz 71 **Holland and Belgium**

Answers – see page 489

LEVEL 2

1 Who won the Belgian league in 1999–2000?

2 In which city are they based?

3 At which Belgian club's ground did England play two matches in Euro 2000?

4 In which city do Feyenoord play?

5 With which electrical company are PSV Eindhoven associated?

6 Which Englishman managed PSV between 1990 and 1992?

7 Which Dutch team won the European Cup in 1995?

8 Which Belgian team appeared in both the 1983 and 1984 UEFA Cup finals?

9 Which two Dutchmen played for Ipswich against AZ 67 in the 1981 UEFA Cup final?

10 Which Belgian team did Liverpool defeat to win the 1975 UEFA Cup?

11 The 1988 European Cup Winners Cup final was contested by a team from Holland and a team from Belgium. Who were they?

12 Who won the European Cup three years running at the beginning of the 1970s?

13 Who scored both goals for Ajax in the 1972 final against Inter?

14 Who won the Dutch league in 1999–2000?

15 How many goals did Belgium score in Euro 2000?

16 In which round were Holland eliminated from Euro 2000?

17 From which club did Aston Villa sign Belgian Luc Nilis in summer 2000?

18 Dutch star Winston Bogarde joined Chelsea from which club in August 2000?

19 Who holds the appearances record for Holland?

20 In which city do Ajax play?

Answers

Euro 2000 (see Quiz 69)

1 Brussels. **2** Turkey. **3** Czech Republic. **4** Portugal. **5** Norway. **6** Steve McManaman. **7** Holland. **8** Eindhoven. **9** Holland 3 France 2. **10** Marc Overmars. **11** Georghe Hagi. **12** David Beckham. **13** France **14** Raul. **15** Portugal. **16** Alessandro Del Piero. **17** David Trezeguet. **18** Patrick Kluivert. **19** Phillip Neville. **20** Holland and France.

Quiz 72 **African Football**

Answers – see page 486

LEVEL 2

1 Which African country are called "The Elephants" and have never played in a World Cup?
2 Who became the first African side to qualify for the World Cup, in 1970?
3 Which African country won the Olympic gold in 1996?
4 Which African team are known as "the Black Stars"?
5 Which country won the 2000 African Cup of Nations?
6 Which African country beat West Germany in the 1982 World Cup?
7 Which country's team are called "the Indomitable Lions"?
8 Who won their 1986 World Cup group ahead of England, Poland and Portugal?
9 Where did Nigeria finish in both their 1994 and 1998 World Cup final groups?
10 Which country knocked Cameroon out of the 1990 World Cup?
11 Which country knocked Nigeria out of the 1994 World Cup with a last-gasp goal?
12 Which country's team are nicknamed "Bafana Bafana" (The Boys)?
13 In which colour shirts do Nigeria play?
14 Which country had most their team killed in a plane crash in 1993?
15 How many games did Cameroon lose in the 1982 World Cup?
16 Which African country did Scotland beat 2–0 in the 1974 World Cup?
17 Which African country did England beat 1–0 in the 1990 World Cup?
18 Who hosted and won the 1996 African Cup of Nations?
19 Including the 2000 competition, which two teams have both won the African Cup of Nations four times?
20 Which African country beat Scotland 3–0 in the 1998 World Cup?

Answers

Euro Championship Pre–1992 (see Quiz 70)

1 European Nations Cup. **2** The Henri Delaunay Cup. **3** 1960. **4** USSR. **5** Every four years. **6** 1964. **7** Toss of a coin. **8** West Germany. **9** France. **10** Spain. **11** Semi-finals. **12** 0. **13** West Germany. **14** Holland. **15** West Germany. **16** USSR **17** Munich. **18** Yugoslavia. **19** Czechoslovakia. **20** 1968, Italy v Yugoslavia.

Quiz 73 **Rest of the World**

LEVEL 2

Answers – see page 491

1. Who won the Turkish League in 1999–2000?
2. In which city do Boca Juniors play?
3. If you watched the Rio derby, which two teams would you see?
4. What is the nickname of the Australian national team?
5. Which Brazilian club did Manchester United defeat to win the Toyota Inter-Continental Cup in 1999?
6. Who were the champions of Brazil in 1999?
7. What is the nationality of the footballing Flo brothers?
8. Which is the longest-running international football competition?
9. In which city do River Plate play?
10. For whom did Pele play his club football?
11. Who won the Greek league in 1999–2000?
12. What is the North American football league called?
13. In which year did New Zealand make its only appearance in the World Cup finals?
14. What is the Copa Libertadores?
15. In which year was the World Cup last held outside Europe?
16. In which city do Vasco Da Gama play?
17. Liverpool's Brad Friedel is what nationality?
18. Brazilian Mario Jardel left Portuguese club Porto for which other club in summer 2000?
19. Who won the Libertadores Cup in 2000?
20. In which country do Rayos Del Nacaxa play?

Answers

London (see Quiz 75)

1 Millwall. **2** QPR. **3** (Woolwich) Arsenal. **4** Wimbledon. **5** Inter Milan. **6** Yes (1962–63). **7** Irish. **8** Brentford. **9** Gerry Francis. **10** Brentford. **11** West Ham United. **12** British. **13** Republic of Ireland. **14** QPR. **15** Sergei Rebrov (with Dynamo Kiev in Ukraine). **16** Thierry Henry. **17** France. **18** Steed Malbranque. **19** Crystal Palace. **20** Fulham.

Quiz 74 The Midlands

LEVEL 2

Answers – see page 492

1 Which club demolished their Trinity Road stand in the summer of 2000?
2 Which team's late-70s brown away kit is widely accepted as the ugliest in history?
3 Which Zimbabwean forward left Coventry City for Birmingham City?
4 Which manager was dismissed as England Under–21 boss in 1999 and a Midlands Premier League club in 2001?
5 Which "troublesome" Leicester City forward was fined for fire extinguisher japes in Spain shortly after being signed in 2000?
6 David Jones is in the hot seat at which Midlands club?
7 At which club did Karren Brady become the first female managing director?
8 Former Liverpool midfielder Mike Marsh was an important part of which team's rise into the Nationwide League?
9 Which English team play at Gay Meadow and have won the Welsh Cup six times?
10 Which club did Barry Fry successfully take to the play-offs in 2000?
11 Who was John Sillet's FA Cup winning managing-director partner?
12 Which Wolves forward joined Leicester City in 2000?
13 Which Midlands club gets called the Throstles or the Baggies?
14 Which team missed doing "the double" in 1959–60 by one point?
15 Spink, Cowans and Morley helped win which club's greatest prize?
16 In which colour shirts do Notts County play?
17 Who is Leicester City's Scottish international centre-half?
18 Which Midlands club sold both their top two 1999–2000 scorers at the end of the season?
19 In how many of England's 1990 World Cup games did Wolves' Steve Bull play?
20 In what year did Trevor Francis take over as Birmingham City manager?

Answers

Manchester City (see Quiz 76)

1 Ardwick FC. **2** "The Citizens". **3** Moss Side. **4** Alan Oakes. **5** Blackburn Rovers. **6** Colin Bell. **7** Lee Bradbury. **8** Joe Mercer. **9** Malcolm Allison. **10** Manchester United. **11** Tony Book. **12** Neil Young. **13** The European Cup Winners Cup. **14** West Bromwich Albion. **15** Francis Lee. **16** Denis Law. **17** Wolves. **18** Rodney Marsh. **19** Dennis Tueart. **20** Steve Daley.

Quiz 75 **London**

Answers – see page 489

LEVEL 2

1 Which London club has had its ground closed by the Football Association more than any other in the League?

2 Which London club had an artificial pitch in the 1980s?

3 Which London club dropped their first name when they moved grounds in 1913?

4 Cunningham, Ardley and Leaburn have played in which London team?

5 Arsenal signed Kanu and Bergkamp from which Italian team?

6 Have Leyton Orient ever played in the top flight?

7 What nationality is Charlton skipper Mark Kinsella?

8 Which London club play in red and white stripes?

9 Which former England captain twice became manager of QPR?

10 Apart from QPR, for which other London club did Stan Bowles appear?

11 Which London club played a cup-tied player in a Worthington Cup quarter-final, causing the game to be replayed?

12 Which was the largest nationality group in the 2000–01 Chelsea squad?

13 Charlton keeper Dean Kiely has represented which country?

14 Morrow, Wardley and Kiwomya have played for which London team?

15 Which current member of the Spurs team has won the championship every year from 1993–2000?

16 Which Arsenal player scored on his last seven Premiership appearances in the 1999–2000 season?

17 West Ham's Frederic Kanoute comes from which country?

18 Which Fulham player shares his first name with the hero of *The Avengers*?

19 Malcolm Allison, Terry Venables and Steve Coppell have all managed which London side?

20 Which club did Kevin Keegan manage before taking charge of England?

Answers

Rest of the World (see Quiz 73)

1 Galatasaray. **2** Buenos Aires, Argentina. **3** Flamengo and Fluminense. **4** The Socceroos. **5** SE Palmeiras. **6** Corinthians. **7** Norwegian. **8** The Copa America. **9** Buenos Aires. **10** Santos. **11** Olympiakos. **12** Major League Soccer. **13** 1982. **14** The South American Club Cup. **15** 1994, in the USA. **16** Rio. **17** American. **18** Galatasaray. **19** Boca Juniors. **20** Mexico.

Quiz 76 **Manchester City**

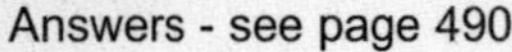
Answers - see page 490

1 What was Manchester City's original name?

2 Apart from "The Blues" what is Manchester City's other nickname??

3 In which part of Manchester is Maine Road situated?

4 Who holds the appearances record for the club?

5 Who did Manchester City beat in April 2000 to clinch promotion to the Premiership?

6 Who is Manchester City's most capped player?

7 Who did Manchester City sign from Portsmouth for £3m in July 1997?

8 Who took over as manager of the club in 1965?

9 Who joined him as his assistant soon after?

10 Who did City pip for the First Division Championship in 1967–68?

11 Who led City up the steps at Wembley to receive the FA Cup in 1969?

12 Who scored the only goal of that game?

13 In 1970 they won a double; the League Cup and which other trophy?

14 Who did City beat to win the League Cup that year?

15 Which City player was the First Division's top scorer in season 1971–72?

16 Which former United favourite scored for City to relegate his former club in 1974?

17 City lost the League Cup final that year. Who did they lose to?

18 Which City player refused to collect his loser's tankard after that match?

19 City won the League Cup again in 1976. Who scored a spectacular winner that day?

20 City shattered the British transfer record in 1979 when they signed which player from Wolves?

Answers

The Midlands (see Quiz 74)

1 Aston Villa. **2** Coventry City. **3** Peter Ndlovu. **4** Peter Taylor. **5** Stan Collymore. **6** Wolves. **7** Birmingham City. **8** Kidderminster Harriers. **9** Shrewsbury Town. **10** Peterborough. **11** George Curtis. **12** Ade Akinbiyi. **13** West Bromwich Albion. **14** Wolves. **15** Aston Villa. **16** Black and White. **17** Matt Elliott. **18** Coventry City. **19** Four. **20** 1996.

Quiz 77 The North West

LEVEL 2

Answers – see page 495

1 Which is the most north-westerly team in the Nationwide League?

2 What is the name of Carlisle's ground?

3 Who was named manager of Rochdale in late 2001?

4 In which division do Macclesfield Town currently play?

5 From which Nationwide League ground can Blackpool Tower be seen?

6 Who is Blackpool's most famous player?

7 Which two Cumbrian towns had teams in the football league, but no longer do so?

8 Which centre-half did Blackpool sell to QPR in 2000?

9 Which Merseyside team used to play home matches on Friday nights?

10 Which North West club's stadium is named after a shoe manufacturer?

11 In the main stand at Deepdale, whose face is picked out by white-coloured seats?

12 When did Blackpool last play in the top two divisions of English football?

13 Which was the last Lancashire club to lose its Football League status?

14 What is the name of Blackburn's ground?

15 Who left Manchester United to take over as manager at Blackburn in December 1998?

16 To whom did Workington lose their place in 1977?

17 Who were the losers in the 1953 FA Cup Final?

18 In which year did Barrow lose their place in the Football League?

19 Which former international coach was Blackburn Rovers' manager for 16 months?

20 What is the name of Burnley's ground?

Answers

Sent Off! (see Quiz 79)

1 David Beckham. **2** Willie Johnston **3** Antonio Rattin. **4** Peter Shilton. **5** Laurent Blanc. **6** Bruno Ribeiro. **7** 1968. **8** Tony Gale. **9** Crystal Palace. **10** Georghe Hagi. **11** Vinnie Jones. **12** They started fighting **13** Tim Flowers. **14** Paul Scholes. **15** For Rangers against Celtic **16** Patrick Vieira. **17** Roy Keane. **18** Yugoslavia **19** Sir Alex Ferguson. **20** Kevin Moran.

Quiz 78 **Who Did What? 2**

LEVEL 2

Answers – see page 496

1 Who changed sponsors from JVC to Dreamcast?

2 Who scored for Chelsea in the 1997 and 2000 FA Cup finals?

3 Who promised that Rangers would sign Catholics in 1985?

4 Whose reign as Wales manager ended when they failed to qualify for the 1994 World Cup?

5 Who wrote an autobiography called *The Good, the Bad and the Bubbly*?

6 Dave Bassett managed which club for three days in 1984?

7 Who was fined £45,000 for spitting at Neil Ruddock?

8 Which European trophy did Newcastle win in 1969?

9 Who counted himself out of England's Euro 2000 squad in an attempt to get fit to play for Tottenham?

10 Which Wolves striker played for England while in the Third Division?

11 Who was the first black player to captain England?

12 Who scored a UEFA Cup semi-final hat-trick for Arsenal against Werder Bremen in 2000?

13 Who came from Malaysia to score 13 goals for Leicester in 1999–2000?

14 Which former England striker joined Burnley from Celtic in 1999 and retired a year later?

15 Which team-mate scrapped with David Batty during a Blackburn Rovers European tie in 1995?

16 Who wrote in *Inside Mr Enderby*: "Five days shalt thou labor, as the Bible says. The seventh day is the Lord thy God's. The sixth day is for football"?

17 Who won the Charity Shield for four consecutive years in the 80s?

18 Which Everton forward scored for England in the under 21's Euro 2000?

19 Which silver-haired Italian joined Middlesbrough in 1996?

20 Who supplied four players when England played France at Wembley in 1999?

Answers

The 60s (see Quiz 80)

1 Match fixing. **2** Manchester City. **3** Pat Jennings. **4** Swindon Town. **5** Geoff Hurst. **6** Celtic. **7** Alf Ramsey. **8** Spurs. **9** John White. **10** Ian St John. **11** Ron Springett. **12** Celtic. **13** Dave Mackay. **14** Two. **15** Everton. **16** Real Madrid. **17** January 1960. **18** 9–3 to England. **19** West Bromwich Albion. **20** Jeff Astle.

Quiz 79 **Sent Off!**

LEVEL 2

Answers – see page 493

1 Which England player was sent off against Argentina in the 98 World Cup?

2 Which disgraced Rangers, WBA and Scotland winger was sent off 21 times in his first-class career?

3 Who was the Argentinian sent off against England in 1966?

4 Who was sent off for the first time in his 671st League game in 1993?

5 Who was sent off in a 1998 World Cup semi-final?

6 Who was sent off in Leeds United's 1999 UEFA Cup defeat at Roma?

7 Alan Mullery became the first England player to be sent off, When?

8 Which West Ham player was sent off in the '93 FA Cup semi-final?

9 Who were Manchester United playing when a dismissed Eric Cantona attacked an abusive supporter?

10 Which great Romanian international was sent off in the 2000 UEFA Cup final against Arsenal?

11 Who was sent off playing for Wales against Georgia in 1995, and 10 other times in domestic competition?

12 What happened after Francis Lee and Norman Hunter's dismissal in 1974?

13 Which Blackburn Rovers goalkeeper was sent off after only 72 seconds against Leeds United in 1995?

14 Who was sent off playing for England in a Euro 2000 qualifier against Sweden?

15 For and against whom were Mark Walters, Terry Hurlock and Mark Hateley sent off in one match in 1991?

16 Who was sent off twice within three days of the 2000–01 season?

17 Who was sent off in the 2000 Charity Shield?

18 Who had a player sent off in each of their Euro 2000 Group C matches?

19 Who was sent off along with David Beckham when Manchester United met Necaxa in the 2000 World Club Championship in Brazil?

20 Who was sent off in the 1985 FA Cup Final?

Answers

The North West (see Quiz 77)

1 Carlisle United. **2** Brunton Park. **3** John Hollins. **4** Third Division. **5** Bloomfield Road. **6** Stanley Matthews. **7** Barrow and Workington. **8** Clarke Carlisle. **9** Tranmere Rovers. **10** Bolton Wanderers (Reebok Stadium) **11** Tom Finney. **12** 1978. **13** Southport. **14** Ewood Park. **15** Brian Kidd. **16** Wimbledon. **17** Bolton Wanderers. **18** 1972. **19** Roy Hodgson. **20** Turf Moor.

Quiz 80 **The 60s**

LEVEL 2

Answers – see page 494

1 What kind of scandal rocked English football in 1963?

2 Who won the league championship in 1968?

3 Which keeper scored for Spurs against Manchester United in the 1967 Charity Shield?

4 Which Third Division team beat Arsenal in the 1969 League Cup final?

5 Who scored six when West Ham beat Sunderland 8–0 in 1968?

6 Which Scottish club won the European Cup in 1967?

7 Who was the manager of Ipswich Town when they won the First Divsion title in 1962?

8 Who became the first English team to win a European trophy when they beat Atletico Madrid in 1963?

9 Which Spurs player was killed when struck by lightning in 1964?

10 Who scored Liverpool's winner in the 1965 FA Cup final and then went on to be a successful TV pundit?

11 Which England keeper kept goal for Sheffield Wednesday in the 1966 FA Cup final?

12 Who won the Scottish treble in 1969?

13 Which Derby player was joint Footballer of the Year with Tony Book in 1969?

14 How many World Cups were there in the 1960s?

15 Mike Trebilcock scored two goals for which '60s FA Cup-winning side?

16 Who did Manchester United beat to reach the 1968 European Cup final?

17 When was the footballers' maximum wage law abolished?

18 What was the score in the annual England v Scotland fixture at Wembley in April 1961?

19 Which Midlands club won the FA Cup in 1968?

20 Who scored the winning goal?

Answers

Who Did What? 2 (see Quiz 78)

1 Arsenal. **2** Roberto Di Matteo. **3** Graeme Souness. **4** Terry Yorath. **5** George Best. **6** Crystal Palace. **7** Patrick Vieira. **8** Steve McManaman. **9** Darren Anderton. **10** Steve Bull. **11** Paul Ince. **12** Ray Parlour. **13** Tony Cottee. **14** Ian Wright. **15** Graeme Le Saux. **16** Anthony Burgess. **17** Everton. **18** Francis Jeffers. **19** Fabrizio Ravenelli. **20** Arsenal.

Quiz 81 **Teddy Sheringham**

Answers – see page 499

LEVEL 2

1 At which club did Teddy start his league career?

2 Which manager signed him in 1992?

3 Which former Leeds manager was his first boss?

4 With which Republic of Ireland striker did he form a deadly partnership?

5 What was controversial about his transfer to Tottenham in 1993?

6 Which manager signed Teddy for Spurs?

7 Against which country did Teddy score two goals in Euro 96?

8 In what year did Teddy win his first professional trophy?

9 Which overseas striker did Sheringham form a partnership with at Tottenham?

10 Where was Teddy involved in a incident involving a dentist chair and Flaming Lamborghinis?

11 Who was Sheringham bought to replace at Manchester United?

12 Did Sheringham score from a penalty in the Euro 96 semi-final shoot-out against Germany?

13 Against which team did Sheringham score in a FA Cup final?

14 Which number shirt did Teddy hold at Old Trafford?

15 At which of his clubs is Teddy the all-time top goalscorer?

16 Who did Teddy replace in the opening minutes of the 1999 FA Cup final?

17 In which year did Teddy win the Premiership Golden Boot?

18 Did Sheringham score the first or second of Manchester United's 1999 European Cup Final goals?

19 Who did Sheringham replace when brought on as substitute in the 1999 European Cup Final?

20 Which team does Teddy claim to hate with every bone in his body?

Answers

Premiership Stars (see Quiz 83)

1 Wes Brown. **2** Stan Collymore. **3** Ipswich Town. **4** Olivier Dacourt. **5** Mark Kennedy. **6** Liverpool. **7** Luton Town. **8** South Africa. **9** Nigel Winterburn. **10** Chelsea. **11** Michael Ricketts. **12** Fumaca. **13** Derby County. **14** Colombia. **15** Matt Le Tissier. **16** Southampton. **17** Paolo Di Canio. **18** Aston Villa. **19** Gillingham. **20** West Ham United.

Quiz 82 **England**

Answers – see page 500

LEVEL 2

1 Who did England play in their first match after Euro 2000?

2 What was the score in that match?

3 What was the score of the previous meeting between the two sides?

4 Which other teams were in England's World Cup 2002 qualifying group?

5 Where is the World Cup 2002 going to be held?

6 Apart from England, how many other teams have won the World Cup?

7 When did England first lose to European opponents?

8 When did England first lose at Wembley to European opponents?

9 How many people are thought to have watched England's friendly against Argentina before Euro 2000?

10 Who was the last England manager not to have managed in the England's top division?

11 Who did England play in their last ever Home International Championship fixture?

12 Why was the Championship discontinued?

13 Against whom did England lose their first match after winning the World Cup in 1966?

14 Where did England first play their home games?

15 Where was England's abandoned match against the Republic of Ireland in Feburary 1995?

16 When did England last beat France in an international match?

17 Who was England's official goalkeeping coach in Euro 2000?

18 Which keeper gave away two penalties when playing for England against Malta in a warm-up game for Euro 2000?

19 Where did England play their opening fixture of Euro 2000?

20 Who were England's first opponents in the qualifying group for World Cup 2002?

Answers

Pot Luck 5 (see Quiz 84)

1 USA. **2** None. **3** Germany. **4** Two. **5** Rangers and Spurs. **6** Uzbekistan. **7** 1972. **8** Tottenham Hotspur. **9** Barcelona. **10** Arsenal. **11** Opta. **12** None. **13** Colchester United. **14** Southend Utd. **15** Leicester City. **16** Cheltenham Town. **17** False (Dakar). **18** Chelsea. **19** Hapoel Tel Aviv. **20** Kenny Miller.

Quiz 83 **Premiership Stars**

LEVEL 2

Answers – see page 497

1 Which young Manchester United defender missed the whole of the 1999–2000 season through injury?

2 Which controversial Leicester striker broke a leg at Pride Park shortly after signing for the club?

3 For which Premiership team does Titus Bramble play?

4 Who did Leeds sign from Lens for £7.2m during summer 2000?

5 After unhappy spells at Liverpool and Wimbledon, who started the 2000–01 Premiership season with Manchester City?

6 For which Premiership team does Stephane Henchoz play?

7 From whom did Arsenal sign Matthew Upson?

8 Charlton's Shaun Bartlett plays for which international side?

9 Which former Arsenal full-back plays for West Ham?

10 For which Premiership team does Jody Morris play?

11 Which Bolton super-sub scored 10 goals off the bench to help them back into the Premier League?

12 According to Newcastle fans, who is "the only Brazilian on earth who can't play football"?

13 For whom did "Kinky" Kinkladze terrorise defences in 2000–01?

14 Aston Villa striker Juan Pablo Angel has represented which country?

15 Who scored the last goal in senior competitive football at The Dell in May 2001?

16 Defender Jo Tessem plays for which south coast club?

17 Which Premier League player received the FIFA Fair Play Award in December 2001?

18 Where does England left back Gareth Barry play his club football?

19 From which Division One club did Leicester City sign Junior Lewis in 2001?

20 For which Premier League team does Michael Carrick play?

Answers

Teddy Sheringham (see Quiz 81)

1 Millwall. **2** Brian Clough. **3** George Graham. **4** Tony Cascarino. **5** Subject of "bung" allegations. **6** Terry Venables. **7** Holland. **8** 1999. **9** Jürgen Klinsmann. **10** Hong Kong. **11** Eric Cantona. **12** Yes. **13** Newcastle United. **14** Ten. **15** Millwall. **16** Roy Keane. **17** 1992–93. **18** First. **19** Jesper Blomqvist. **20** Arsenal.

Quiz 84 **Pot Luck 5**

LEVEL 2

Answers – see page 498

1 In which county was the NASL?

2 How many times have Scotland reached the second round of an international tournament?

3 In which country did Cha Bum-Kun play most of his club football?

4 How many league rounds were there in the Champions League in 1999–2000?

5 John Hartson failed fitness tests preventing his transfer to which two clubs?

6 Which team won the Asian Cup in 1994?

7 In what year was the first UEFA Cup?

8 Who won it?

9 Who were the first Spanish League champions?

10 Which England club has not been out of the top division since 1919?

11 Who are the official statisticans of the Premier League?

12 Which league club plays home games at the Stade de France in Paris?

13 Which is the only Football/Premier League club to have all six letters of "SOCCER" in its name?

14 Which team plays at Roots Hall?

15 Which club found itself in trouble over tickets for the Worthington Cup final in 1999?

16 Which club had Jamie Victory on their books in 2001–02?

17 Patrik Vieira was born in France – true or false?

18 Which club's first manager was John Tait Robertson?

19 Which Israeli team knocked out both Chelsea and Parma in the 2001–02 UEFA Cup?

20 Who was Scottish Young Player of the Year in 2000?

Answers

England (see Quiz 82)

1 France. **2** 1-1. **3** 2–0 to France. **4** Germany, Finland, Greece and Albania. **5** Japan and South Korea. **6** Six. **7** 1929. **8** 1953. **9** 26 million. **10** Sven Goran Ericksson. **11** Scotland. **12** Financial reasons. **13** Scotland. **14** Kennington Oval. **15** Lansdowne Road, Dublin. **16** 1997. **17** Ray Clemence. **18** Richard Wright. **19** Eindhoven. **20** Germany.

Quiz 85 **Supporters**

LEVEL 2

Answers – see page 503

1 Whose fans "only sing when they're fishing"?

2 Whose fans sing an aria from *Rigoletto*?

3 Where do they sing "The Blaydon Races"?

4 What is Chelsea's theme song?

5 For which team do the "Pompey Chimes" ring out?

6 Which fans allegedly get to eat the nicest pies?

7 Whose fans used to stand in "the jungle"?

8 Which team had more fans arrested than any other during 1999–2000?

9 Where are you most likely to hear the song "Bubbles"?

10 Whose fans sit at the Gwladys Street end?

11 Whose fans greet their team's victories in finals with a chorus of "Ee-ay-addio, we won the Cup"?

12 At which end of Anfield did Liverpool's fans stand?

13 Who sang the unforgettable "Ozzie's going to Wembley"?

14 Whose fans carried out a "pants" protest in the mid–1990s?

15 Whose fans are featured on the Pink Floyd LP *Meddle*?

16 Whose fans are likely to be reading *A Kick Up the Rs*?

17 Who was serenaded by supporters with, "He's French, he's quick, his name's a porno flick"?

18 Whose fans have nicknamed their new player "Ralph" Lauren?

19 Whose fans were voted worst dressed by a men's magazine in 1999–2000?

20 Whose fans are likely to be reading *Heroes and Villains*?

Answers

Substitutes (see Quiz 87)

1 1965. **2** One substitute could replace an injured player. **3** Charlton's Keith Peacock. **4** David Fairclough. **5** Dennis Clarke of West Brom in 1968. **6** Bobby Charlton. **7** Ricky Villa. **8** Clubs couldn't afford a 13th man. **9** Ian Wright. **10** Gary Lineker. **11** Teddy Sheringham. **12** Rudi Völler. **13** Gianluca Vialli. **14** Brian McClair. **15** Teddy Sheringham and Ole Gunnar Solskjaer. **16** Gianfranco Zola. **17** Mateja Kezman of Yugoslavia went on as a sub after 87 minutes against Norway and was sent off 44 seconds later. **18** Ole Gunnar Solskjaer. **19** Up to seven. **20** Five named, three used.

Quiz 86 **Family Connections**

LEVEL 2

Answers – see page 504

1 Which team does the son of England goalkeeper Ray Clemence play for?

2 Graham and Ray Wilkins played together at which club?

3 True or False: Phillip and Gary's father is named Neville Neville?

4 What relation is Ian Harte to his Leeds teammate Gary Kelly?

5 Which brothers played together for Manchester United in the 1977 FA Cup final?

6 Which brothers played together at Leeds but never for Scotland?

7 Which Nottingham Forest manager gave his son his debut?

8 True or False: Robbie and Roy Keane are cousins?

9 Which father and son both played for Nottingham Forest and Scotland?

10 Ian Wright's son Shaun Wright-Williams made his Premiership debut in 2000 for which team?

11 The footballing Milburns are related to which other footballing brothers?

12 Three brothers played for Southampton, two of them for Leeds and one of them for Rangers. Which family?

13 Cyril Knowles' brother Peter left Wolves to become what in 1969?

14 Les, Paul, Clive, Martin and Bradley are from which footballing family?

15 Which Manchester United player chose to have his first name rather than his famous father's surname on his back?

16 Which brothers Rene and Willy played in the 1978 World Cup final?

17 Which brothers signed together for Barcelona in 1999?

18 True or False: Scottish manager Craig Brown and football commentator Jock Brown are brothers?

19 Who is former Norwich and Everton boss Mike Walker's footballing son?

20 Which Fashanus played for Norwich and Wimbledon respectively?

Answers

Northern Ireland (see Quiz 88)

1 Windsor Park, Belfast. **2** Sammy McIlroy. **3** 1986. **4** Knocked out in the group stage. **5** 1984, the last year it was played. **6** 1–0,May 1999. **7** Malta. **8** 1–0 to Northern Ireland. **9** Bulgaria, Czech Republic, Iceland and Denmark. **10** Steve Lomas. **11** Quarter-finals in 1958. **12** Bertie Peacock. **13** Billy Bingham. **14** Terry Neill. **15** Danny Blanchflower. **16** Norman Whiteside. **17** 1–0 to Northern Ireland. **18** Gerry Armstrong. **19** France. **20** 1–0 to Northern Ireland.

Quiz 87 **Substitutes**

LEVEL 2

Answers – see page 501

1. When were substitutes first introduced to English league football?
2. What was the first rule?
3. Who was the first substitute in English football?
4. Which Liverpool player was known as "supersub" during the 1970s?
5. Who was the first substitute to be used in an FA Cup final?
6. Who did Ramsey take off with England 2–1 up against Germany in 1970?
7. Who broke down in tears after being substituted in the 1981 FA Cup final and then scored twice in the replay to win it for Spurs?
8. Why was the Football League's 1982 plan to allow two subs rejected?
9. Who went on as a substitute and scored twice for Crystal Palace in the 1990 FA Cup final?
10. Who was substituted in his last match for England in 1992 and denied the opportunity of equalling Bobby Charlton's England scoring record?
11. Who went on as a substitute for Roy Keane and scored Manchester United's first goal in the 1999 FA Cup final?
12. Who went on as a sub for West Germany and equalised against Argentina in the 1986 World Cup final?
13. Who played two minutes of the 1997 FA Cup final for Chelsea, and went on to win the trophy as manager three seasons later?
14. Which Manchester United sub scored their fourth goal in the 1994 FA Cup final?
15. Which two subs scored for Man Utd to win the 1999 European Cup?
16. Who came off the bench to win the 1998 Cup Winners' Cup?
17. Which player had the shortest time on the field during Euro 2000?
18. Who went on for Man Utd after 72 minutes and scored four in 1999?
19. How many subs can be named for a Champions League game?
20. How many subs can be named and used in the Premiership in 2000–01?

Answers

Supporters (see Quiz 85)

1 Grimsby Town's. **2** West Ham's. **3** Newcastle. **4** "Carefree". **5** Portsmouth. **6** Cambridge United's. **7** Celtic's. **8** Leeds United's. **9** Upton Park. **10** Everton's. **11** Liverpool's. **12** Spion Kop. **13** Spurs' fans. **14** Reading's. **15** Liverpool's. **16** QPR's. **17** Emmanuel Petit. **18** Arsenal's. **19** West Brom's. **20** Aston Villa's.

Quiz 88 **Northern Ireland**

LEVEL 2

Answers – see page 502

1 Where do Northern Ireland traditionally play their home games?

2 Who took over from Lawrie McMenemy as manager of Northern Ireland in 2000?

3 When was the last time Northern Ireland played in the World Cup finals?

4 How far did they get in that tournament?

5 When was the last time Northern Ireland won the Home International Championship?

6 When was the last time Northern Ireland beat the Republic?

7 Who did Northern Ireland play in their opening match of the 2002 World Cup qualifiers?

8 What was the score in that match?

9 Who are the other teams in the group?

10 Who captains the team for the World Cup 2002 campaign?

11 What is the furthest Northern Ireland have ever gone in the World Cup?

12 Which manager gave George Best his first taste of international football?

13 Who took over from that manager?

14 Who scored Northern Ireland's winning goal against England at Wembley in 1972?

15 One of Northern Ireland's greatest results was 2–2 against the "total football" Dutch in 1976. Who was in charge for that match?

16 Which Northern Ireland player became the youngest ever to play in a World Cup match, in Spain in 1982?

17 What was the result of the final group game against Spain that year?

18 Who scored for Northern Ireland?

19 Who did Northern Ireland lose to in the second round?

20 What was the score when World Cup runners-up West Germany visited Belfast in November 1982?

Answers

Family Connections (see Quiz 86)

1 Tottenham. **2** Chelsea. **3** True. **4** His nephew. **5** Brian and Jimmy Greenhoff. **6** Eddie and Frank Gray. **7** Brian Clough. **8** False. **9** Archie and Scot Gemmill. **10** Manchester City. **11** Charltons. **12** Wallace. **13** Jehovah's Witness. **14** Allens. **15** Jordi Cruyff. **16** de Kerkhof. **17** Ronald and Frank de Boer. **18** True. **19** Ian Walker. **20** Justin and John.

Quiz 89 **Republic of Ireland**

LEVEL 2

Answers – see page 507

1 Who is the most capped player for the Republic?

2 Who is the Republic's record goalscorer?

3 What is the Republic's record victory?

4 In 1994 the Republic won their first ever game in the World Cup finals. Who did they beat?

5 Who scored the winner that day?

6 Who scored two goals against Malta in 1989 to send the Republic to the World Cup finals for the first time?

7 In which year did Jack Charlton become the Republic's manager?

8 Who did the Republic beat in the opening game of the 1988 European Championships?

9 Who was the first black player to play for the Republic?

10 Who became the Republic's first player-manager, in 1973?

11 Who was the first Republic of Ireland player sent off in an international?

12 Which player has captained the Republic more than any other?

13 Which other teams were in the Republic's World Cup 2002 qualifying group?

14 Which player captained the Republic in the 2002 qualifying campaign?

15 Which Irish sensation was transferred to Inter in summer 2000?

16 Who took over in 1996 as the Republic's team manager?

17 Who did the Republic play in their opening game of the 2002 World Cup campaign?

18 What was the score in that match?

19 The Republic played a European Championships play-off against which team at Anfield in 1995?

20 What was strange about the Republic not qualifying for the 1992 European Championships?

Answers

England 2 (see Quiz 91)

1 Paul Scholes. **2** Graham Taylor. **3** Alan Smith. **4** Peter Shilton. **5** 1–1. **6** Fastest Goal. **7** Duncan Edwards. **8** Steven Gerrard. **9** Belgium. **10** Fair Play Award. **11** Bobby Robson. **12** 2–2. **13** Luxembourg. **14** Sweden. **15** Platt. **16** Michael Owen. **17** Steve Guppy. **18** Andrew Cole. **19** Mike Channon. **20** Yes (53).

Quiz 90 **Michael Owen**

Answers – see page 508

LEVEL 2

1 In which year was Michael Owen born?

2 Where was he born?

3 Against whom did he make his Liverpool debut?

4 In what year was that?

5 What happened in that match?

6 How many goals did he score in total in his first season?

7 Which award did he win at the end of that season?

8 Against whom did he make his debut for England?

9 Against whom did he score his first goal for England?

10 Later that season Michael scored a wonder goal. What was the occasion?

11 Which award did he win later that year?

12 In September 1998 Michael gave Dave Beasant a big surprise. What was it?

13 How many goals did he score in total that season?

14 In 1999–2000 Michael suffered a serious injury. What went wrong?

15 How many appearances did he make that season for Liverpool?

16 How many goals did he score?

17 How many games did he play at Euro 2000?

18 How many goals did he score?

19 What does Michael list as his hobbies?

20 Against whom did Michael score in England's first match after Euro 2000?

Answers

Who Did What? 3 (see Quiz 92)

1 Neil McCann. **2** Winston Bogarde. **3** Craig Brown. **4** Lillian Thuram. **5** Terry Venables. **6** Bobby Moore. **7** George Best. **8** Tommy Docherty. **9** Pat Jennings. **10** Michael Knighton. **11** Brian Clough. **12** Jock Stein. **13** Kenny Dalglish. **14** Sunderland. **15** Peter Shilton. **16** Graeme Souness. **17** Malcolm Macdonald. **18** Terry Venables. **19** David Pleat. **20** Robbie Keane.

Quiz 91 **England 2**

LEVEL 2

Answers – see page 505

---

1 Who was the first English player to be sent off in a Wembley international?

2 Which England manager gave Carlton Palmer his first cap?

3 Who replaced Gary Lineker in England's 1992 defeat by Sweden?

4 Who was made captain for the 1990 third-place play-off after 124 games for his country?

5 What was the result of the match against Poland at Wembley that England needed win to qualify for the 1974 World Cup?

6 Which World Cup record did Bryan Robson set in 1982 against France?

7 Who in 1955 became the youngest England player of the 20th century?

8 Which Liverpool player won his first cap against Ukraine in 2000?

9 Against which team did a late David Platt goal save England from a penalty shoot-out in the 1990 World Cup?

10 What did England win in the 1990 World Cup?

11 After a 1–1 draw in Saudi Arabia what manager was the target of the newspaper headline "In the Name of Allah Go?"

12 What was the England v Portugal half-time score in Euro 2000?

13 Which was the only country England managed to beat away from home in their Euro 2000 qualifying group?

14 Which team beat England in their Euro 2000 qualifying group?

15 Who scored most goals for England: David Platt or Bryan Robson?

16 Which England player failed to complete a full game in Euro 2000?

17 Which Leicester City player won his only cap in 1999?

18 Who made his England debut in 1995 and won his eighth cap in 2000?

19 Which Southampton and Manchester City striker scored 21 goals for England in the 70s?

20 Did Glenn Hoddle win more than 50 England caps?

Answers

Republic of Ireland (see Quiz 89)

1 Paul McGrath. **2** Frank Stapleton. **3** 8–0 v Malta in 1983. **4** Italy. **5** Ray Houghton. **6** John Aldridge. **7** 1986. **8** England. **9** Chris Hughton. **10** Johnny Giles. **11** John Dempsey. **12** Andy Townsend. **13** Holland, Portugal, Cyprus, Andorra, Estonia. **14** Roy Keane. **15** Robbie Keane. **16** Mick McCarthy. **17** Holland. **18** 2–2. **19** Holland. **20** They did not lose any of their qualifying games.

Quiz 92 **Who Did What? 3**

LEVEL 2

Answers – see page 506

1 Who scored the winner for Scotland against Latvia in a World Cup qualifier in September 2000?

2 Which Dutch defender moved from Barcelona to Chelsea in August 2000?

3 Who managed Scotland during the 1998 World Cup?

4 Which French defender scored twice in the 1998 World Cup semi-final?

5 Who managed Barcelona to the 1986 European Cup final?

6 Who was arrested in Colombia for stealing an emerald bracelet in 1970?

7 Who knocked the ball out of Gordon Banks' hands and scored for Ireland in 1971, although the goal was disallowed?

8 Who was sacked as manager of Manchester United in 1977?

9 Which keeper saved two penalties for Spurs in a game at Anfield in 1973?

10 Who attempted a takeover of Manchester United in 1990?

11 Who made a "V" sign at his team's fans when they booed Arsenal's Charlie Nicholas in a league game in 1987?

12 Which Scotland manager died at pitchside shortly after seeing his team play Wales in 1985?

13 Who resigned as manager of Liverpool in February 1991?

14 Where did Jason McAteer play his club football in February 2002?

15 Which keeper was sent off for the first time in his career in his 971st league game?

16 Who was the first Rangers manager to sign a catholic player?

17 Who became the first paid director in football in 1981?

18 Who was sacked as manager of Spurs in 1993?

19 Who resigned as Spurs manager after allegations of kerb-crawling came to light?

20 Who scored for the Republic of Ireland against Holland in Amsterdam in September 2000?

Answers

Michael Owen (see Quiz 90)

1 1979. **2** Chester. **3** Wimbledon. **4** 1997. **5** He scored in a 1–1 draw. **6** 21. **7** Young Player of the Year. **8** Chile. **9** Morocco. **10** World Cup eighth final v Argentina. **11** BBC Sports Personality of the Year. **12** He scored four in a game against Forest. **13** 23. **14** Hamstring. **15** 30. **16** 12. **17** Three. **18** One. **19** Golf and snooker. **20** France.

Quiz 93 **Short Players**

LEVEL 2

Answers – see page 511

1 Which Brazilian star's name means "Little Man" in Portuguese?
2 Which Tottenham winger is often smaller than the young mascot?
3 Which terrier-like Leeds' skipper took on many men taller than his five feet, four inches?
4 Who is Aston Villa's diminutive full back?
5 Which Stoke City and Everton player was nicknamed "Inchy"?
6 Which tempestuous Italian brought his five feet and six inches to Aston Villa and Bradford City?
7 Which Aston Villa forward is a full six inches shorter than Dion Dublin?
8 Who's the tallest Blue out of Deschamps, Wise, Zola and Morris?
9 Tiny England forward Wilf Mannion was a hero at which League club?
10 Which Leeds and Wales pocket battleship later managed Wrexham?
11 Who is Derby County's smallest and possibly most skilful player?
12 Which small but perfectly formed playmaker managed to outjump Peter Shilton to a high ball in the 1986 World Cup?
13 Which small striker has seen Manchester City through the divisions?
14 Which Liverpool star is the shortest: Danny Murphy, Steven Gerrard, Vladimir Smicer?
15 Which World Cup winning shorty managed Swindon Town, West Bromwich, Newcastle and Tottenham?
16 Who is the tallest Hammer out of Joe Cole, Nigel Winterburn and Steve Potts?
17 Which English League-based Spaniard stands at five feet and six inches?
18 Who is the smallest out of Scholes, Barmby and Owen?
19 For which club did impish winger "Jinky" Johnstone play?
20 Which diminutive German midfielder won a World Cup winners medal in 1990 and a European championship winners medal in 1996?

Answers

Nicknames 2 (see Quiz 95)

1 Hibernian. **2** Torquay. **3** Mansfield Town. **4** Darlington. **5** Forfar Athletic. **6** Clyde. **7** Shrewsbury Town. **8** Macclesfield Town. **9** Morton. **10** Hull City. **11** Lincoln City. **12** Rochdale. **13** Bournemouth. **14** Dunfermline. **15** Stirling Albion. **16** Exeter City. **17** Crystal Palace. **18** Cardiff City. **19** Barnsley. **20** Partick Thistle.

Quiz 94 **Penalty Shootouts**

LEVEL 2

Answers – see page 512

1 How many penalties does each side take before "sudden death"?

2 In which year was the first major cup final settled on penalties?

3 Which tournament was it?

4 What happened in the Final?

5 When was the first World Cup penalty shootout?

6 Spurs won a major European trophy in a penalty shootout in 1984. Who did they beat?

7 That same year Liverpool had the same success in a different competition. What year was that?

8 Which competition did Liverpool win?

9 Terry Venables' Barcelona beat Gothenburg on penalties to qualify for the 1986 European Cup Final, against which opponents?

10 What was the score at the end of the match?

11 Who set a record in the shootout?

12 When did the FA first decide to settle the FA Cup final on penalties?

13 In which World Cup were both semi-finals decided on penalties?

14 Who won them?

15 Who were the first First Division side knocked out of the FA Cup on penalties?

16 How many penalties were there in all in the England 1998 World Cup game against Argentina?

17 Which two England players misssed that night?

18 Antonin Panenka's penalty won the European Championship for which nation?

19 Which was the first World Cup settled on penalties?

20 Which country missed five penalties (in the match and the shootout) to crash out in the semi-finals of Euro 2000?

Answers

Kenny Dalglish (see Quiz 96)

1 1951. **2** Glasgow. **3** Celtic. **4** Jock Stein. **5** 1972. **6** 102. **7** 30. **8** Denis Law. **9** 1977. **10** Kevin Keegan. **11** Bruges. **12** 21. **13** Player/manager. **14** Three. **15** 1989 FA Cup. **16** Stress. **17** Blackburn Rovers. **18** 1995. **19** Newcastle United. **20** 2000.

Quiz 95 **Nicknames 2**

LEVEL 2 

Answers – see page 509

1 The Hibees?

2 The Gulls?

3 The Stags?

4 The Quakers?

5 The Loons?

6 The Bully Wee?

7 The Shrews?

8 The Silkmen?

9 The Ton?

10 The Tigers?

11 The Red Imps?

12 The Dale?

13 The Cherries?

14 The Pars?

15 The Binos?

16 The Grecians?

17 The Eagles?

18 The Bluebirds?

19 The Colliers?

20 The Jags?

Answers

Short Players (see Quiz 93)

1 Juninho. **2** Jose Dominguez. **3** Billy Bremner. **4** Alan Wright. **5** Adrian Heath. **6** Benito Carbone. **7** Julian Joachim. **8** Deschamps. **9** Middlesbrough. **10** Brian Flynn. **11** Georgi Kinkladze. **12** Diego Maradona. **13** Paul Dickov. **14** Danny Murphy (5ft 9in). **15** Osvaldo Ardiles. **16** Nigel Winterburn. **17** Albert Ferrer. **18** Paul Scholes. **19** Celtic. **20** Thomas Hassler.

Quiz 96 **Kenny Dalglish**

LEVEL 2

Answers – see page 510

1 In which year was Kenny Dalglish born?

2 Where was he born?

3 For which club did he sign first?

4 Which manager signed him?

5 In which year did he play his first international?

6 How many caps did he get for Scotland during his career?

7 How many goals did he score in those games?

8 He is top equal top scorer for Scotland with which other player?

9 When did Kenny move to Liverpool?

10 Who did he replace as "King of the Kop"?

11 In 1978 he scored the winner for Liverpool to win the European Cup against which team?

12 How many goals did Kenny score when Liverpool won the league that same season?

13 What role did Kenny play at Liverpool during the double-winning 1985–86 season?

14 How many league titles did Kenny win as Liverpool manager?

15 What was Dalglish's last trophy as Liverpool boss?

16 Why did Dalglish resign as manager?

17 With which club did he get back into football management?

18 In which year did he win the title again?

19 What was his next club?

20 When did Dalglish give up his interest in Celtic?

Answers

Penalty Shootouts (see Quiz 94)

1 Five. **2** 1980. **3** European Cup Winners Cup. **4** Arsenal lost 5–4 to Valencia. **5** 1982, West Germany v France, semi-final. **6** Anderlecht. **7** 1984. **8** European Cup. **9** Steaua Bucharest. **10** 0–0. **11** Helmut Ducadam saved four penalties for Steaua. **12** The 1990 FA Cup final replay. **13** 1990. **14** West Germany and Argentina. **15** Manchester United in 1992. **16** Twelve. **17** Paul Ince and David Batty. **18** Czechoslovakia. **19** Brazil v Italy, 1994. **20** Holland.

Quiz 97 **Dennis Wise**

LEVEL 2

Answers – see page 514

1 In which year was Dennis Wise born?
2 For which club did Dennis Wise originally sign as an apprentice?
3 Who was his first manager?
4 How many league appearances did he make for Wimbledon?
5 When did he move to Chelsea?
6 What was the score on his Leicester City debut?
7 Against whom did he score his first Chelsea goal?
8 Which was the first trophy Dennis Wise lifted as Chelsea captain?
9 By what nickname is he known?
10 Which manager signed him from Chelsea?
11 Which Leicester teammate used to polish Dennis Wise's boots at Chelsea?
12 What was Wise's best goal haul in any one season for Chelsea?
13 When did Dennis Wise make his England debut?
14 How many goals had Dennis Wise scored for England by Euro 2000?
15 How many years did he go between matches against Chelsea?
16 After being left out for some years, Keegan brought Wise back to play for England in 2000. Who was that against?
17 How many appearances did he make for England during Euro 2000?
18 Who did Chelsea play in Dennis Wise's testimonial?
19 How many league appearances did he make for Chelsea in season 1999–2000?
20 How many league goals did he score in the same season?

Answers

Chairmen and the Board (see Quiz 99)

1 Alan Sugar. **2** Rangers. **3** Arsenal. **4** Manchester United. **5** Ken Bates. **6** Harry Redknapp (when at West Ham). **7** Leicester City. **8** Aston Villa. **9** Norwich City. **10** Manchester City (Francis Lee). **11** AC Milan. **12** Leeds United. **13** It was blank. **14** Tottenham. **15** Chairmen-managers. **16** Jimmy Hill. **17** Terry Venables. **18** Newcastle United. **19** Elton John. **20** Chelsea.

Quiz 98 **Players' Nicknames**

LEVEL 2

Answers – see page 515

1 What was Paul Ince's self-proclaimed nickname?

2 Who was known as the Gentle Giant?

3 Who was Manchester United's Sparky?

4 Which Nottingham Forest and England defender was the original "Psycho"?

5 Who at Tottenham is known as "Shaggy" or "Sicknote"?

6 Who was Chelsea's 70s Chopper?

7 Which Tottenham, Liverpool and West Ham defender earned the epithet "Razor"?

8 Which of the "Magnificent Magyars" was nicknamed "The Galloping Major"?

9 Which Everton and Leeds player was "The Little General"?

10 Who was known as "Captain Marvel"?

11 Which Englishman was known as "Mighty Mouse" when he played in Germany?

12 Which long-serving winger was called "The Wizard of Dribble"?

13 Which ex-Manchester United Czech star was nicknamed "the Express Train"?

14 Who was known as the Preston Plumber?

15 Which Russian was the Black Panther?

16 Who was "The Lion of Vienna"?

17 Who was Der Bomber?

18 Which manager was called The Doc?

19 Which player's nickname stemmed from his fondness for chips?

20 Which Italian is known as "the Divine Ponytail"?

Answers

Dennis Wise (see Quiz 97)

1 1966. **2** Southampton. **3** Lawrie McMenemy. **4** 127. **5** July 1990. **6** Leicester 0, Bolton 5. **7** Sunderland. **8** The 1997 FA Cup. **9** "Wisey". **10** Peter Taylor. **11** Muzzy Izzet. **12** 10 goals. **13** 1991 against Turkey. **14** One. **15** 11. **16** Argentina. **17** Three. **18** Bologna. **19** 30. **20** 4.

Quiz 99 **Chairmen and the Board**

LEVEL 2

Answers – see page 513

1 Who was Tottenham's cheap computer salesman chairman?

2 David Murray is chairman at which Scottish club?

3 David Dein is in charge of business at which club?

4 Where did it look like the Sky was the limit for Martin Edwards?

5 Which chairman is a famous farmer at Chelsea?

6 Who threatened resignation when his board sold Andy Impey to Leicester without telling him?

7 Barrie Pierpoint made Martin O'Neill's life interesting at which club?

8 Which is the "Deadly" Doug Ellis club where no manager is safe?

9 With Delia among them which club has the tastiest board meetings?

10 Who "benefitted" from their 70s goalscoring hero taking over in 1994?

11 Which Italian club is run by a former Prime Minister and head of the country's biggest media network?

12 Chairman Peter Ridsdale became high profile when his club had Turkish problems. Which is his club?

13 What was odd about the chapter in Len Shackleton's autobiography entitled "What directors know about football"?

14 Now on the board at Nottingham Forest, Irving Scholar previously had troubled times at which club?

15 What kind of chairman are/were Noades, Knighton and Reames?

16 Which football pundit has been on the board at Fulham and Coventry?

17 Which player, manager and pundit has been on the board at QPR, Tottenham and Portsmouth?

18 Which club's fans saw their chairman resign after comments he made about their centre-forward and the attractiveness of local women?

19 Which rock star chairman cried when his side lost the 84 Cup final?

20 Whose board member Matthew Harding died in a helicopter crash?

Answers

Players' Nicknames (see Quiz 98)

1 The Guv'nor. **2** John Charles. **3** Mark Hughes. **4** Stuart Pearce. **5** Darren Anderton. **6** Ron Harris. **7** Neil Ruddock. **8** Ferenc Puskas. **9** Bobby Collins. **10** Bryan Robson. **11** Kevin Keegan. **12** Stanley Matthews. **13** Karel Poborsky. **14** Tom Finney. **15** Lev Yashin. **16** Nat Lofthouse. **17** Gerd Müller. **18** Tommy Docherty. **19** Liam "Chippy" Brady. **20** Roberto Baggio.

Quiz 1 **Referees**

Answers – see page 519

LEVEL 3

1 Which referee sent off Hamann, McAllister and Vieira when Liverpool played Arsenal in August 2000?
2 Which Scot refereed two Euro 2000 matches?
3 Which Italian refereed the Euro 2000 final?
4 Which referee got in hot water in 1999 for apparently celebrating a Liverpool goal?
5 Who was the first black referee on the Premier League list?
6 Which referee was knocked over by Paolo Di Canio?
7 Which referee is a Harrow schoolmaster?
8 Who was the first woman to referee a professional national-league match?
9 What is the retirement age for referees in the Football and Premier Leagues?
10 Which famous match did Gottfried Dienst referee?
11 Which English referee awarded a penalty in the opening minutes of the 1974 World Cup final?
12 Which Welsh referee was involved in a series of controversial decisions in the 1970s and 1980s?
13 What did referee Rob Harris mistakenly allow Tranmere to do in 1999?
14 Which referee failed to caution Gazza for his 1991 FA Cup Final exploits?
15 Who was the 70s larger-than-life bald smiling referee?
16 What happened to both Uriah Rennie and Paul Alcock in May 2000?
17 What monumental decision did Peter Willis make in 1985?
18 Which referee did Emmanuel Petit push to receive a suspension in 1997?
19 What was significant about Kidderminster Harriers home match with Nuneaton Borough in the 1999 Vauxhall Conference?
20 What did Ian Wright call referee Robbie Hart?

Answers

Bobby Moore (see Quiz 3)

1 1941. **2** Fulham. **3** San Antonio Thunder and Seattle Sounders. **4** 108. **5** FA Cup and European Cup Winners' Cup. **6** No. 6. **7** 1962. **8** Peru. **9** Lima. **10** Two. **11** 1975. **12** Stealing an emerald bracelet. **13** 1973. **14** Italy. **15** Wembley. **16** 1–0 to Italy. **17** Scotland. **18** 5–0 to England. **19** 1993. **20** Cancer.

Quiz 2 **Goalkeepers**

Answers – see page 520

LEVEL 3

1 In addition to Erwin Van der Saar, who else kept goal for Holland in Euro 2000?

2 Which club did Charlton goalkeeper Simon Royce join in summer 2000?

3 In which country was Everton goalkeeper Steve Simonsen born?

4 For which country did Quim play as a substitute goalkeeper in Euro 2000?

5 For which club does Italy's Francesco Toldo play?

6 Which goalkeeper was South American Footballer of the Year in 1996?

7 Which goalkeeper scored with a drop kick for Hibernian in 1988?

8 Which goalkeeper became player-manager at Plymouth in 1992?

9 In 2000 which goalkeeper completed his 23rd season at a Nationwide League club?

10 Which former international goalkeeper was sacked as coach of Fortuna Köln at half-time in their 1999 match with Waldhorf Mannheim?

11 In 1995 which goalkeeper played for Manchester City in the Premier League at the age of 43?

12 Which goalkeeper saved eight of ten penalties he faced in 1977–78?

13 Which goalkeeper was fined for giving a Nazi salute at White Hart Lane?

14 Who is Dundee United's Scotland Under 21 goalkeeper?

15 Who has played in goal for Wigan Athletic and Northern Ireland?

16 Which former Arsenal, Coventry and Wolves striker's goalkeeping son made his international debut in 1999?

17 Which keeper made his international debut in 1999 at the age of 31?

18 Dave Beasant was Player of the Year at which club in 1999–2000?

19 Finnish international goalkeeper Tuevo Moilanen has played at which British club?

20 Which two goalkeepers played in all their team's Premiership games in 1999–2000?

Answers

Football Awards (see Quiz 4)

1 Most goals. **2** Professional Footballers Association. **3** The PFA and the Football Writers' Association Player of the Year. **4** Carling Manager and Player of the Month. **5** FIFA. **6** Roy Keane. **7** 1948. **8** Stanley Matthews. **9** David Ginola. **10** Spurs. **11** Henrik Larsson. **12** Zinedine Zidane. **13** Juventus. **14** Ronaldo. **15** Bobby Charlton. **16** Gianfranco Zola. **17** George Weah. **18** Paul Gascoigne. **19** Jürgen Klinsmann. **20** Ian Rush.

Quiz 3 **Bobby Moore**

Answers – see page 517

LEVEL 3

1 In which year was Bobby Moore born?

2 Apart from West Ham, which was Moore's only other English club?

3 Which two American clubs did he play for?

4 How many England caps did he win?

5 Which two cup winner's medals did he win with West Ham?

6 Which number shirt did he usually wear for West Ham?

7 In which year did he win his first England cap?

8 Who were England playing that day?

9 Where was that match played?

10 How many goals did he score for England?

11 In which year did Moore lead a team out in the FA Cup final against West Ham?

12 For what alleged offence was Moore arrested in Colombia in 1970?

13 In which year did Moore make his last England appearance?

14 Who were England playing that day?

15 Where was that match played?

16 What was the score?

17 Against which opposition did Moore make his 100th appearance for England?

18 What was the score in that match?

19 In which year did he die?

20 What caused his death?

Answers

Referees (see Quiz 1)

1 Graham Poll. **2** Hugh Dallas. **3** Pier-Luigi Collina. **4** Mike Reed. **5** Uriah Rennie. **6** Paul Alcock. **7** David Elleray. **8** Wendy Toms. **9** 43. **10** 1966 World Cup final. **11** Jack Taylor. **12** Clive Thomas. **13** Substitute a dismissed player. **14** Roger Milford. **15** Roger Kirkpatrick. **16** Dropped from Premier list. **17** First FA Cup final sending off **18** Paul Durkin. **19** All officials were women. **20** A Muppet.

Quiz 4 **Football Awards**

Answers – see page 518

LEVEL 3

1. For what is "The Golden Boot" awarded?
2. What do the letters PFA stand for?
3. What are English football's two major seasonal awards?
4. What major monthly awards are made?
5. Which organisation elects the World Footballer of the Year?
6. Which player won both major English awards in 2000?
7. When was the English Football Writers' Footballer of the Year title first awarded?
8. Who was the first player to receive the English Football Writers' Footballer of the Year award?
9. Who was both the PFA and the Football Writers' Player of the Year in 1999?
10. Who was he playing for at the time?
11. Who won both of the Scottish equivalent awards that year?
12. Who was both European and World Footballer of the Year in 1998?
13. Which club was he playing for at the time?
14. Who was FIFA World Footballer of the Year in 1996?
15. Who was European Footballer of the Year in 1966?
16. Who was the English Football Writers' Player of the Year in 1997?
17. Who was FIFA's World Footballer of the Year in 1995?
18. Which Englishman was the Scottish Footballer of the Year in 1996?
19. Which German was the English Football Writers' Player of the Year in 1995?
20. Which Welshman was the European Golden Boot award winner in 1984?

Answers

Goalkeepers (see Quiz 2)

1 Sander Westerveld. **2** Leicester City. **3** England. **4** Portugal. **5** Juventus. **6** José Luis Chilavert. **7** Andy Goram. **8** Peter Shilton. **9** Alan Knight. **10** Harald Schumacher. **11** John Burridge. **12** Paul Cooper. **13** Mark Bosnich. **14** Paul Gallagher. **15** Jim Carroll. **16** Bobby Gould's son, Jonathan. **17** Roger Freestone. **18** Nottingham Forest. **19** Preston North End. **20** Martyn (Leeds) and Walker (Spurs).

Quiz 5 **Wanderers**

Answers – see page 523

LEVEL 3

1 Who scored three goals for Bolton Wanderers in their 2000 play-off semi-finals against Ipswich?

2 Which Wanderers are in the Jewson Eastern Counties League: Ipswich, Lowestoft or Clacton?

3 Which Wanderers were founded under the name "Forest"?

4 Which former England international midfielder plays at Wolves?

5 Which Premier League club manager began his career at Wycombe Wanderers?

6 Which brothers temporarily saved Wolverhampton Wanderers from extintion in 1982?

7 Who is Bolton Wanderers' Icelandic international defender?

8 Which Wanderers won the FA Cup in three successive seasons?

9 Which Wanderers are in the Eircom League Division One: Bray, Monaghan or Cobh?

10 Riodairibord Wanderers are a leading club in which country?

11 In which country have The Wanderers won the League four times?

12 Who is the manager at Wycombe Wanderers?

13 On which condition did the Wanderers hand the FA Cup back in 1878?

14 How much did Wolverhampton Wanderers receive for Robbie Keane in August 1999?

15 Who was Wycombe Wanderers' leading scorer in 1999–2000?

16 Who defeated Bolton Wanderers in the 1999 play-offs?

17 In which year were The Wanderers disbanded?

18 What did Wycombe Wanderers win in 1991 and 1993?

19 Which Wanderers were founded under the name Christ Church FC?

20 How many Wanderers were among the original 12 Football League teams?

Answers

Other Cups (see Quiz 7)

1 Chelsea. **2** Liverpool. **3** Middlesbrough. **4** Newcastle United. **5** Fiorentina. **6** Swindon Town. **7** Genoa. **8** Derby County. **9** Chelsea. **10** Chesterfield. **11** Ten. **12** Wolves. **13** St Mirren. **14** Blackburn Rovers. **15** Leyland Daf. **16** Tranmere Rovers. **17** Auto Windscreens. **18** Reading. **19** Napoli. **20** Millwall.

Quiz 6 **Supporters**

LEVEL 3

Answers – see page 524

1 Which team are associated with the violent Inter-City Firm?

2 What is the name given to groups of club-sponsored fans travelling to Italian games?

3 Which teams supporters were credited with starting taking inflatables to matches in the 90s?

4 Which team is the focus of *The Ugly Inside* fanzine?

5 Which team's fans gained a reputation for taking celery to matches?

6 Left on the Shelf was a pressure group formed by which team's upporters?

7 In the 90s which club's supporters formed a political party and polled 14,838 votes?

8 Which team's supporters left an unlit petrol bomb by chairman David Kohler's home?

9 A demonstration by which team's supporters led to the abandonment of their 1996 match against York City?

10 www.squareball.co.uk is a website dedicated to which team?

11 *One Nil Down... Two One Up* was which club's successful 90s fanzine?

12 Which club's supporters voted their hippo mascot seventh in their best player poll of 1997–98?

13 *The City Gent* fanzine is dedicated to which team?

14 Of which club is the famous half-naked Tango Man a supporter?

15 Which film theme does the band inspire travelling England fans to sing?

16 What is the name given to groups of loyal supporters in Italy?

17 Which supporters' unofficial anthem is "Blue Moon"?

18 Which team were encouraged by their fans sounding of the chimes?

19 Which team's fans took a bull to grounds on their 90s FA Cup run?

20 Which team's fanzine is called *Brian Moore's Head Looks Uncannily Like the London Planetarium*?

Answers

Scandals (see Quiz 8)

1 Eric Cantona. **2** Bruce Grobbelaar. **3** Diego Maradona. **4** Paolo Rossi. **5** Marseille. **6** Bernard Tapie. **7** Torino. **8** George Graham. **9** Brian Clough. **10** Vinnie Jones. **11** Peter Swan and Tony Kay. **12** Brazil. **13** Leeds City. **14** Dennis Wise. **15** Roma. **16** Hungary. **17** Lou Macari. **18** Swindon Town. **19** Terry Venables. **20** Arsenal and Manchester United.

Quiz 7 **Other Cups**

Answers – see page 521

LEVEL 3

1 Who won the Full Members Cup in 1986?

2 Who won the only Screen Sport Super Cup ever played, in 1986?

3 Who won the Anglo-Scottish Cup in 1976?

4 Who won the Texaco Cup in both 1974 and 1975?

5 Who won the Anglo-Italian Cup in 1974?

6 Which West Country club won the Anglo-Italian Cup Winners' Cup in 1969 and the Anglo-Italian Cup in 1970?

7 Who won the Anglo-Italian Cup in 1996?

8 Who won the Watney Cup in 1970?

9 Who won the Zenith Data Systems Cup in 1990?

10 Who won the only Football League Group Cup ever played?

11 How many Anglo-Italian Cup competitons were played?

12 Who won the Texaco Cup in 1971 and the Sherpa Van Trophy in 1988?

13 Which is the only Scottish club to have won the Anglo-Scottish Cup?

14 Who won the Full Members Cup in 1987?

15 Who took over sponsorship of the Sherpa Van Trophy in 1990?

16 Who won the trophy that season?

17 Who currently sponsors that trophy?

18 Who won the Simod Cup in 1988?

19 Who won the Anglo-Italian Cup in 1975?

20 Who won the Football League Trophy in 1983?

Answers

The Wanderers (see Quiz 5)

1 Dean Holdsworth. **2** Ipswich. **3** The Wanderers. **4** Andy Sinton. **5** John Gregory. **6** Bhatti. **7** Gudni Bergsson. **8** The Wanderers. **9** Bray. **10** Zimbabwe. **11** Uruguay. **12** Lawrie Sanchez. **13** No team could ever keep it. **14** £6 million. **15** Sean Devine. **16** Watford. **17** 1881. **18** FA Trophy. **19** Bolton Wanderers. **20** Two.

Quiz 8 **Scandals**

Answers – see page 522

LEVEL 3

1 Who was given 120 hours community service for attacking a fan in 1995?

2 Which goalkeeper was at the centre of a match-fixing scandal in 1994?

3 Who was arrested in Argentina in 1991 on drugs charges?

4 Which Italian striker was banned from playing in 1980 for illegal betting?

5 Who had the European Cup taken away from them in 1993 for bribery?

6 Who was their president jailed for his part in the affair?

7 Which Italian club was accused of procuring prostitutes for match officials in 1994?

8 Who was dismissed by Arsenal in 1995 for receiving "bungs"?

9 Which manager was fined by the FA for striking a fan in 1989?

10 Who was banned after biting a reporter's nose in a Dublin bar in 1994?

11 Which two England players were banned for life for match fixing in 1965?

12 In which country were four club directors and five referees arrested for match fixing in 1994?

13 Who was expelled from the league for making illegal payments to players?

14 Who was sentenced to prison for assaulting a taxi driver in 1995?

15 Which Italian club was banned when its president was arrested for trying to bribe the referee before a European Cup semi-final in 1986?

16 In which country were 40 players and officials arrested for their part in match fixing in 1988?

17 Which Swindon manager was fined £7,500 for betting on his team's FA Cup tie against Newcastle in 1990?

18 Which club was demoted to Division Three after winning a Second Division Play-off in 1990?

19 Who was the first manager involved in "bung" speculation, in 1993?

20 Which two clubs had points deducted in 1990 as a result of a mass brawl between the two sets of players?

Answers

Supporters (see Quiz 6)

1 West Ham United. **2** *Tifosi.* **3** Manchester City. **4** Southampton. **5** Chelsea. **6** Tottenham. **7** Charlton Athletic. **8** Luton Town. **9** Brighton and Hove Albion. **10** Leeds United. **11** Arsenal. **12** Stoke City. **13** Bradford City. **14** Sheffield Wednesday. **15** The Great Escape. **16** *Ultras.* **17** Manchester City. **18** Portsmouth. **19** Hereford United. **20** Gillingham.

Quiz 9 **Continental Coaches**

Answers – see page 527

LEVEL 3

1 Who did Jo Bonfrere coach in the 2000 African Cup of Nations?
2 Which World Cup team did Tele Santana coach in 1982 and 1986?
3 Who became Germany's caretaker manager after Euro 2000?
4 Which Italian was the first foreign manager to win the Bundesliga?
5 Which coach of Bulgaria was also their most-capped player and highest scorer?
6 Who was appointed as Spain's coach in 1992?
7 Which great player took charge of Charleroi in 2000?
8 Who did Fatih Terim manage after taking Turkey to Euro 96?
9 Euro 2000 managers Camacho and Boskov had been player and manager respectively for which championship-winning team?
10 Which Dutch manager is credited with creating "total football"?
11 Which manager filled Barcelona's 2000 team with Dutchmen and won the double?
12 Which two-time Soviet Union manager scored four goals in the 1970 World Cup?
13 Who took over as French coach from Gérard Houllier in 1993?
14 Which manager led West Germany to at least third place in four World Cup finals?
15 Swedish skipper Nils Liedholm later became a coach in which country?
16 Which midfielder coached Hungary after winning 100 caps for them?
17 Which Argentinian World Cup winning captain later became their coach?
18 Which coach of Italy was previously president of Lazio?
19 Jamaica's 1998 World Cup manager Rene Simoes is from which country?
20 Who was Denmark's triumphant Euro 92 coach?

Answers

Record Scores (see Quiz 11)

1 Arbroath 36, Bon Accord 0. **2** England 13, Ireland 0. **3** Preston North End 26, The Hyde 0. **4** Manchester United 9, Ipswich Town 0. **5** 10–0. **6** Australia 31, American Samoa 0. **7** Bury 6, Derby County 0 (1903). **8** 10 (Joe Payne Luton, 1936). **9** William "Dixie" Dean (60 in 1927–28). **10** George Camsell (9, for Middlesbrough, 1926–27). **11** Arthur Birch (5 for Chesterfield, 1923–24). **12** 15–1. **13** 7–3. **14** Manchester United. **15** 97. **16** 1999–2000. **17** Francis Lee, 13 for Manchester City, 1971–72 **18** Five. **19** 13. **20** Spain 12, Malta 1.

Quiz 10 **Pot Luck**

Answers – see page 528

LEVEL 3

1 Which team supplied the most Football Writers' Footballer of the Years in the 1990s?

2 Which Aston Villa full-back was the subject of a rejected compensation claim by Brighton?

3 Which team's goalkeeper scored in the last seconds to keep them in the Football League in 1999?

4 Which Italian club are nicknamed the *Rossoneri*?

5 Which Tottenham player fled from a *This is Your Life* performance?

6 In which year did Italy re-allow foreign players in their league?

7 Who were the first club to win the FA Cup without an Engliand-eligible player?

8 The Thames Valley Royals was a proposed merger of which two teams?

9 In France what is a *Semaine Anglaise*?

10 Which country won the first three FIFA Futsal (indoor football) World Championships?

11 Whose ground's official name is the Stadio Giuseppe Meazza?

12 Which Hughie was Scotland's pre-war goalscoring hero?

13 Who is Spain's most capped player?

14 Since 1980 where has the World Club Cup been played?

15 How does a Japanese team earn two points in a J-League game?

16 Which team has appeared the most times in the Women's FA Challenge Cup final?

17 Which Scottish ground supposedly means "dungheap" in Gaelic?

18 Who was the first player born after 1966 World Cup to play for England?

19 What is English about AC Milan and Athletic Bilbao?

20 Who was the first Nigerian to play in the Premiership?

Answers

Family Connections (see Quiz 12)

1 Steffen Iversen. **2** First siblings on referees list. **3** Steve Gatting. **4**. Fritz and Otmar Walter (1954). **5** David O'Leary. **6** The Nevilles. **7** The Morgans. **8** Two. **9** The Koemans. **10** The Laudrups. **11** Kenny Dalglish. **12** Coventry. **13** Newcastle Utd. **14** Nicky Summerbee. **15** Cyrille Regis. **16** Baresi. **17** Mpenza. **18** Jeff and Jim Whitley. **19** Wrexham. **20** Ron and Allan Harris.

Quiz 11 **Record Scores**

Answers – see page 525

1 What is the record score in British football?
2 What is England's record victory?
3 What is the record score in English football?
4 What is the Premier League's highest score?
5 What is the highest score in a League Cup match?
6 What is the highest score in a World Cup match?
7 What is the record score in an FA Cup final?
8 What is the highest number of goals scored by one player in an English league match?
9 Which player scored the most goals in any one season?
10 Which player scored the most hat-tricks in a season?
11 Which keeper scored the most goals in a season?
12 What is the record score in a Scottish league match?
13 What is the record score in the European Cup final (apart from penalties)?
14 Which team has scored the most goals in a Premiership season?
15 How many goals did they score that season?
16 Which season was that?
17 Which player holds the record for penalties scored in a season?
18 What is the highest number of penalties awarded in any one game?
19 What is the greatest number of goals scored by one player in a Scottish Cup match?
20 What is the record score in a European Championship match?

Answers

Continental Coaches (see Quiz 9)

1 South Africa. **2** Brazil. **3** Rudy Völler. **4** Giovanni Trapattoni. **5** Hristo Bonev. **6** Javier Clemente. **7** Enzo Scifo. **8** Galatasaray. **9** Real Madrid. **10** Rinus Michels. **11** Louis Van Gaal. **12** Anatoly Byshovets. **13** Aimee Jacquet. **14** Helmut Schön. **15** Italy. **16** Jozsef Bozsik. **17** Daniel Passarella. **18** Dino Zoff. **19** Brazil. **20** Richard Møller Nielsen.

Quiz 12 **Family Connections**

Answers – see page 526

LEVEL 3

1 Which of Britain's Scandinavian contingent had an international goalscoring father?

2 How did Graham and David Laws make history in 1996–97?

3 Which brother of an England cricket captain played in the 1983 FA Cup final?

4 Who were the first brothers to play in a World Cup winning team?

5 Which Arsenal defender appeared in the same international team as his brother?

6 Whose sister is an England international netball player?

7 Which brothers were wingers for Tottenham and QPR in the 70s?

8 How many of Liam Brady's brothers played for English or Irish league clubs?

9 Who are the only siblings to have won European championship medals?

10 Which two brothers were in FIFA's 1998 World Cup all-star squad?

11 Which famous player and manager's son plays for Norwich City?

12 Which English club have two of their manager's sons in their squad?

13 Gary and Stephen Caldwell are in which Premier League team's 2000–01 squad?

14 Which son of a Manchester City legend became a Nottingham Forest player in November 2001?

15 Who is Bristol Rovers forward Jason Roberts's former England goalscoring uncle?

16 Which brothers Guiseppe and Franco played against each other in 80s Milan derbies?

17 Name the brothers who played for Belgium in Euro 2000?

18 Which Manchester City brothers are Northern Ireland internationals?

19 For which team does Sir Alex Ferguson's son play?

20 Which brothers played in the 1967 FA Cup final?

Answers

Pot Luck (see Quiz 10)

1 Tottenham. **2** Gareth Barry. **3** Carlisle (Jimmy Glass). **4** AC Milan. **5** Danny Blanchflower. **6** 1980. **7** Liverpool in 1986. **8** Oxford United and Reading. **9** A mid-week match. **10** Brazil. **11** Inter and AC Milan's. **12** Gallacher. **13** Andoni Zubizarretta. **14** Tokyo. **15** A Golden Goal win. **16** Doncaster Belles. **17** Pittodrie. **18** Tony Adams. **19** Both have anglicised names. **20** Efan Ekoku.

Quiz 13 **The Boardroom**

Answers – see page 531

LEVEL 3

1. What did the acronym SUAM stand for in 1999, an organisation opposed to conglomerates taking over football?
2. London ticket agent Stan Flashman was chaiman of which club in the 90s?
3. Manchester United were 385p, Tottenham were 100p – what price were Millwall floated at?
4. Which former Everton owner had a similar role at Tranmere Rovers?
5. At which club is Geoffrey Richmond chairman?
6. What was the name of the media group that took over Leeds United in 1996?
7. What was the name of the family who ran Chelsea from 1905 until the 1970s?
8. "He's fat, he's round, he's never at the ground." To which chairman or owner were Oxford and Derby supporters referring?
9. Who "bought" Crystal Palace in 1998?
10. At which club was Ken Bates chairman before he bought Chelsea?
11. At which club is Freddy Shepherd currently chairman?
12. David Sheepshanks is chairman at which club?
13. At which club did Belotti and Archer manage to unite the whole of football against them?
14. Which club did Rodney Marsh aim to help turn into "the Macclesfield of the South?"
15. Who has the big chair in the Middlesbrough boardroom?
16. The Hill-Wood family have long been connected with which club?
17. Peter Kenyon took over from which high-profile chief executive?
18. Bryan Richardson ruled the roost at which former Premier League club?
19. Steve Archibald bought which club in 2000?
20. From which former QPR chairman did Terry Venables buy a 51% stake of Portsmouth for £1 in 1996?

Answers

Manchester United (see Quiz 15)

1 Parma. **2** Brondby **3** Roy Keane. **4** David Beckham. **5** Ronny Johnsen. **6** Four. **7** Alan Hansen. **8** Borussia Dortmund. **9** £800,000. **10** John Curtis. **11** David May. **12** Brawl on the pitch v Arsenal **13** Possible conflict of interest. **14** Mark Hughes. **15** Andy Cole. **16** George Best. **17** Dennis Irwin. **18** Arthur Albiston. **19** None. **20** Bobby Charlton's.

Quiz 14 **Who Did What?**

Answers – see page 532

LEVEL 3

1 Who scored Scotland's opening goal in the 1998 World Cup in France?

2 Who scored for Internazionale in both the 1997 and 1998 UEFA Cup Finals?

3 Which Brazilian scored 1,281 goals in his career?

4 Who won the Division One championship in 1966–67?

5 Who scored for Leeds in the 1965 FA Cup final against Liverpool?

6 Who was the first £1m player?

7 Which player holds the record for goals scored during the final stages of a single World Cup?

8 Which club provided 11 players for Belgium in an international against Holland in 1964?

9 Who was the FIFA official most responsible for the creation of the World Cup?

10 Who scored a hat-trick for England against Poland in the 1986 World Cup?

11 Who kept goal on more than 100 occasions for Sweden?

12 Who scored twice for Norwich against Bayern Munich in their 1993–94 UEFA Cup tie?

13 Who won the Scottish Premier League title in 1997–98?

14 Who went unbeaten for 42 matches between November 1977 and November 1978?

15 Who was the Premiership's leading scorer in 1994–95 and 1995–96?

16 Which non-league team has beaten more league teams in FA Cup ties than any other?

17 Who scored Wimbledon's winner against Liverpool in the 1988 FA Cup Final?

18 Who currently sponsors the FA Cup competition?

19 Who won the first FA Cup final?

20 Who won the League Cup in 1966?

Answers

Extra Time & Penalties (see Quiz 16)

1 30 minutes. **2** 1934. **3** Royal Engineers v Old Etonians, 1875. **4** 1996. **5** 1991. **6** 1984, Liverpool v Roma. **7** Valencia. **8** Spurs. **9** 1983. **10** Aberdeen. **11** England 2 West Germany 2. **12** Seven. **13** 1877. **14** Three. **15** 1-1. **16** Euro 96. **17** Oliver Bierhoff. **18** David Trezeguet. **19** Five. **20** Brazil beat Italy on penalties.

Quiz 15 **Manchester United**

Answers – see page 529

LEVEL 3

1 From which club did United sign Jesper Blomquist?

2 From which club did United sign Peter Schmeichel?

3 Who was Manchester United's Player of the Year in 2000?

4 Which United midfielder was at Tottenham as a junior?

5 Which United player was signed from Turkish club Besiktas?

6 How many goalkeepers did Manchester United use in 1999–2000?

7 Who "damned" United's 1995–96 season by saying "You don't win anything with kids?"

8 Who knocked United out of the 1997 Champions League?

9 How much did Manchester United lose buying and selling Massimo Taibi?

10 Who did Manchester United sell to Blackburn Rovers in the summer of 2000?

11 Who was the only member of Manchester United's 1999 FA Cup final team without an international cap?

12 For what were Manchester United fined £50,000 in 1990?

13 Who stopped BskyB's takeover of United in 1998?

14 Who scored United's goals in their 1992 Cup Winners Cup final victory?

15 Who did Solksjaer replace in the 1999 European Cup final?

16 Which former player missed United's 1999 European Cup final goals after leaving the stadium early?

17 Who played in both of United's 90's European finals?

18 Who played in United's 1977, 1983 and 1985 FA Cup final victories?

19 How many penalties were given against United at Old Trafford between 1993 and 2000?

20 Which United player's European appearance record did Dennis Irwin break in 1999?

Answers

The Boardroom (see Quiz 13)

1 Supporters United Against Murdoch. **2** Barnet **3** 20p. **4** Peter Johnson. **5** Bradford City. **6** Caspian. **7** Mears. **8** Robert Maxwell. **9** Mark Goldberg. **10** Oldham Athletic. **11** Newcastle United. **12** Brighton and Hove Albion. **13** Ashford Town. **14** Ashford Town. **15** Steve Gibson. **16** Arsenal. **17** Martin Edwards. **18** Coventry. **19** East Fife. **20** Jim Gregory.

Quiz 16 **Extra Time & Penalties**

LEVEL 3

Answers – see page 530

1. How long is a normal period of extra time?
2. In which year did the World Cup Final first go to extra time?
3. Which was the first FA Cup final to go to extra time?
4. When was the "Golden Goals" rule first introduced?
5. When did the FA decide to settle the FA Cup final on penalties after one replay?
6. When was the first European Cup final settled after penalties?
7. Arsenal lost the European Cup Winners' Cup final in 1980 after extra time and penalties. Who beat them?
8. Despite being two-legged, the 1984 EUFA Cup final went to extra time and penalties. Who won it?
9. Which was the last European Cup Winners' Cup final settled after extra time?
10. Which Scottish club won the tournament that year?
11. What was the score after 90 minutes of the 1966 World Cup final?
12. How many matches involving England have gone to extra time?
13. In which year did the first Scottish FA Cup final go to extra time?
14. How many goals did Manchester United score during extra time in the 1968 European Cup final?
15. What was the score after 90 minutes of England's World Cup semi-final against Germany in the 1990 World Cup?
16. What was the first major tournament involving Golden Goals?
17. Which player scored the winner in that final?
18. Who scored the Golden Goal winner for France in the Euro 2000 final?
19. How many goals were scored during extra time in the 1970 World Cup semi-final between Italy and West Germany?
20. How was the 1994 World Cup final settled?

Answers

Who Did What? (see Quiz 14)

1 John Collins. **2** Zamorano. **3** Pele. **4** Manchester United. **5** Billy Bremner. **6** Johan Cruyff. **7** Just Fontaine, 13 goals for France in 1958. **8** Anderlecht. **9** Jules Rimet. **10** Gary Lineker. **11** Thomas Ravelli. **12** Jeremy Goss. **13** Celtic. **14** Nottingham Forest. **15** Alan Shearer. **16** Yeovil Town, with 17 wins. **17** Lawrie Sanchez. **18** AXA. **19** The Wanderers. **20** West Brom.

Quiz 17 **South America**

Answers – see page 535

LEVEL 3

1 Club Deportivo Los Millonarios, Atlético Junior and América de Cali play in which country?

2 In which South American country did Liverpool finish third in the league on three occasions in the early 70s?

3 From which club did Tottenham sign Ossie Ardiles?

4 The Copa CONMEBOL is equivalent to which European competition?

5 Which player did Newcastle United sign from Boca Juniors?

6 1981 Copa Libertadores runners-up Cobreloa are from which country?

7 1997 Copa Libertadores runners-up Sporting Cristal are from which country?

8 In which colours do Santos play?

9 From which club did PSV sign Ronaldo?

10 Danubio, Bella Vista and Defensor Sporting play in which country?

11 In which city are Vasco de Gama based?

12 Which Argentinian team play in the "Chocolate Box"?

13 Which country's clubs have won the Copa Libertadores most often?

14 Who did Barcelona buy from Boca Juniors for £3 million in 1982?

15 Kempes, Batistuta and Ruggeri all played for which South American club?

16 Which South American team won the 2000 World Club Championship?

17 Which veteran Brazilian star scored twice for Vasco de Gama against Manchester United in the 2000 World Club Championship?

18 Which two Urugayan teams play home games at the national stadium?

19 Which club did Juninho and Denilson leave to play in Europe?

20 From which Argentinian team did Lazio buy Marcelo Salas?

Answers

Stranger than Strange (see Quiz 19)

1 Mark Hughes. **2** Four substitutes scored. **3** David Icke. **4** Substitute Di Canio. **5** Ian Wright. **6** The coach, Jupp Heynkes. **7** Ball burst. **8** Dave Beasant. **9** Boris Mikhailov. **10** Jorge Campos. **11** Yugoslavia. **12** Faroe Isles. **13** Richard Gough. **14** Rene Higuita. **15** Jimmy Hill. **16** Gerry Francis. **17** Ken Bailey. **18** He was sent off. **19** Gianni Rivera. **20** He believed the world would soon end.

Quiz 18 **Liverpool**

Answers – see page 536

LEVEL 3

1 What is the fewest number of goals conceded by Liverpool in a league season?

2 What is Liverpool's longest unbeaten league sequence?

3 Against which team did Liverpool play their first match with Bill Shankly as manager?

4 Who were the first team to beat Liverpool at Anfield in the European Cup?

5 How many times have Liverpool been relegated from the top flight?

6 Against which team did Robbie Fowler score his first hat-trick?

7 Which club did Liv erpool defeat in the 2000–01 UEFA Cup semi-final?

8 How many times was Bob Paisley named Manager of the Year?

9 Which former Liverpool player was also a junior volleyball international?

10 Against which team did Michael Owen make his 100th Liverpool appearance?

11 Against which club did Emile Heskey score his first goal for the Reds?

12 Who made the most appearances for Liverpool in the 2000–01 season?

13 Which club has inflicted the worst defeat on Liverpool?

14 Where was Emile Heskey born?

15 Who runs the Liverpool reserve team?

16 Prior to 2000–01, when was Liverpool's last victory against Manchester United?

17 Who scored Liverpool's winner against Chelsea at Anfield in 1999–2000?

18 Whose goal denied Liverpool a place in the 2000–01 Champions League?

19 From which team did Gérard Houllier sign Bernard Diomede?

20 Who is Liverpool's first-team coach?

Answers

John Gregory (see Quiz 20)

1 Northampton Town. **2** Brighton. **3** Terry Venables. **4** Derby County. **5** Assistant manager at Portsmouth. **6** Alan Ball. **7** January 1990. **8** Seven years. **9** Wycombe Wanderers. **10** 1998. **11** Liverpool. **12** Stan Collymore. **13** Mark Bosnich. **14** Seventh. **15** Savo Milosevic. **16** Alan Thompson. **17** 36 hours. **18** Dwight Yorke. **19** Paul Merson. **20** Bolton Wanderers.

Quiz 19 **Stranger than strange**

Answers – see page 533

LEVEL 3

1 Who played for Wales and Bayern Munich on the same day in 1988?

2 What was strange about Barnet's 5–4 win over Torquay in 1993?

3 Which strange Chelsea and Coventry goalkeeper appeared on *Wogan*?

4 What allegedly did the referee ask West Ham to do in their 1999 UEFA Cup tie with Steaua Bucharest?

5 Who announced his football retirement on a US chat show in June 2000?

6 Who did Real Madrid sack eight days after winning the European Cup in 1998?

7 Which unusual event occurred in both the 1946 and 1947 FA Cup finals?

8 Which former Wimbledon and Chelsea player broke a toe when trying to break the fall of a bottle of salad cream with his foot in 1990?

9 Which goalkeeper appeared with a full head of hair at Reading having been bald in the 1994 World Cup?

10 Which international goalkeeper designed his own multi-coloured shirts?

11 Which team's reserve was sent off after two minutes in Euro 2000?

12 Which tiny footballing nation beat Austria 1–0 in 1990?

13 Which Scottish captain was born in Scandinavia?

14 Which scorpion-kicking goalkeeper was jailed for his role in a kidnapping?

15 Which TV analyst ran the line in a 1972 First Division match?

16 Which manager appeared on TV as a teenage pigeon-fancier?

17 Who used to turn up to England matches in a top hat, a Union Jack waistcoat and red hunting jacket?

18 What record did Dean Gibb set in a penalty shootout in an FA Cup match for Bedlington Terriers?

19 Which 1969 European Footballer of the Year became an Italian Member of Parliament?

20 For what reason did Argentinian keeper Carlos Roa turn down a contract at Real Mallorca?

Answers

South America (see Quiz 17)

1 Colombia. **2** Uruguay. **3** Huracan. **4** UEFA Cup. **5** Nolberto Solano. **6** Chile. **7** Peru. **8** White. **9** Cruzeiro. **10** Uruguay. **11** Rio de Janeiro. **12** Boca Juniors. **13** Argentina. **14** Maradona. **15** River Plate. **16** Corinthians. **17** Romario. **18** Peñarol and Nacional. **19** Sao Paulo. **20** River Plate.

Quiz 20 **John Gregory**

LEVEL 3

Answers – see page 534

1 Which club originally signed John Gregory as a player?

2 Which was his next club?

3 Who signed him for QPR?

4 Which was Gregory's last club as a player?

5 What was Gregory's first managerial position?

6 Who was in charge of the club at the time?

7 When was Gregory sacked by Portsmouth?

8 How long was it before Gregory got back into football management?

9 With which club did he make his management comeback?

10 When was he appointed manager at Villa?

11 Who did Villa play in his first match in charge?

12 Who scored twice in that match to bring a smile to Gregory's face and three points for Villa?

13 Who was Villa's keeper when Gregory took over?

14 Where did Villa finish in the table in Gregory's first season in charge?

15 Who was Gregory's first major sale at Villa?

16 Who was his first major purchase?

17 For how long was David Unsworth a Villa player?

18 Who did Gregory sell to Manchester United at the start of the 1998–99 season?

19 Which ex-Arsenal player did Gregory sign from Middlesbrough in September 1998?

20 Who did Villa beat in the FA Cup semi-final in April 2000?

Answers

Liverpool (see Quiz 18)

1 16 in 1978–79. **2** 31 games. **3** Cardiff City. **4** Ferencvaros. **5** Three times. **6** Fulham. **7** Barcelona. **8** Six times. **9** Alan Hansen. **10** Huddersfield Town. **11** Coventry City. **12** Markus Babbel. **13** Birmingham City. **14** Leicester. **15** Joe Corrigan. **16** 1995. **17** David Thompson. **18** Bradford City's David Wetherall. **19** Auxerre. **20** Sammy Lee.

Quiz 21 **The 90s**

Answers – see page 539

LEVEL 3

1 "It's not like it said in the brochure." Part of which manager's threat to quit in 1992?
2 Which Premier club vice-president died in '96 after 57 years with the club?
3 Who shocked Brazil beating them 1–0 in the 1998 CONCACAF Gold Cup?
4 Who lasted 32 days in charge of Manchester City in 1996?
5 Which Tottenham player became the first player to be suspended for feigning an injury, in 1992–93?
6 Who did USA beat on penalties in the 1999 Women's World Cup final?
7 Who was sacked for the eighth time at the same club in 1993?
8 Which team resigned from the Football League in 1992?
9 Which Leicester City player scored ninetieth minute own goals on two occasions in 1998–99?
10 Which Reading player was the League's top scorer in 1993–94?
11 Who inflicted England's first home World Cup defeat in 1997?
12 What was memorable about Oxford United's game against Sunderland in February 1999?
13 Who retired in 1993 after managing the same club for 21 years?
14 In which year was the Republic of Ireland against England match abandoned due to supporter violence?
15 Who beat Vitesse Arnhem and Bayern Munich in the UEFA Cup in '93–94?
16 Who was Liam Brady's assistant manager at Celtic?
17 Who was fined after calling German football officials "brainless" in 1994?
18 Who beat the Maldives 17–0 in a World Cup qualifier in 1997?
19 Which team missed a last-minute penalty that would have won them the 1993–94 Spanish League?
20 Which League experimented with kick-ins rather than throw-ins in 1993–94?

Answers

Nicknames (see Quiz 23)

1 The Shrimpers. **2** The Wasps. **3** The Hatters. **4** The Spiders. **5** The Gable Endies. **6** The Quakers. **7** The Railwaymen. **8** The Wee Rovers. **9** The Bairns. **10** The Warriors. **11** The Silkmen. **12** The U's. **13** The Merry Millers. **14** The Pirates. **15** The Spireites. **16** The Bees. **17** The Honest Men. **18** The Loons. **19** The Binos. **20** The Clarets.

Quiz 22 **Leeds United**

Answers – see page 540

LEVEL 3

1 In which season did Norman Hunter and Billy Bremner depart from Elland Road?

2 In which season did John Charles score 42 goals?

3 At what age did Peter Lorimer make his Leeds United debut?

4 Which Leeds substitute scored a hat-trick in nine minutes against Walsall in the FA Cup in 1995?

5 Who was sent off in Leeds 2000 UEFA Cup semi-final at Elland Road?

6 An on-pitch brawl with which club landed Leeds a hefty fine in 2000?

7 Who made the most appearances for Leeds in the 2000–01 season?

8 Who knocked Leeds out of the 1998–99 UEFA Cup?

9 Whose eight goals in 1996–97 made him Leeds top goalscorer that season?

10 To whom did Leeds offer the manager's job when George Graham left?

11 From which club did Duncan McKenzie sign for Leeds?

12 Whose wild challenge on Stephen Clemence precipitated a mass brawl in 1999–2000?

13 Who hit two hat-tricks in 11 days for Leeds in 1995?

14 Who did Leeds sign from Liverpool in 1996?

15 Which team did Leeds beat on the day they won the championship in 1992?

16 Which club did Jack Charlton leave Leeds for in 1973?

17 How many of Eric Cantona's 17 Leeds goals came in Europe?

18 Who did Leeds beat to win the Fairs Cup in 1971?

19 Who scored the winning goal in Leeds' 1968 League Cup final victory?

20 Who was the only Leeds player to appear in Euro 2000?

Answers

Chelsea (see Quiz 24)

1 John Hollins. **2** Peter Houseman. **3** "The Meat'. **4** Pat Nevin. **5** Frank Sinclair. **6** Erland Johnsen. **7** Peter Bonetti. **8** Ian Hutchinson. **9** Albert Ferrer. **10** Colin Pates. **11** Ted Drake. **12** Clive Walker. **13** Kerry Dixon. **14** Doug Rougvie. **15** Pierluigi Casiraghi. **16** Graham Roberts with 13 in 1988–89. **17** Sampdoria. **18** Australia. **19** 21. **20** Allan Harris.

Quiz 23 **Nicknames**

Answers – see page 537

LEVEL 3

1 Southend United?

2 Alloa Athletic?

3 Stockport County?

4 Queen's Park?

5 Montrose?

6 Darlington?

7 Crewe Alexandra?

8 Albion Rovers?

9 Falkirk?

10 Stenhousemuir?

11 Macclesfield Town?

12 Oxford United?

13 Rotherham United?

14 Bristol Rovers?

15 Chesterfield?

16 Barnet?

17 Ayr United?

18 Forfar Athletic?

19 Stirling Albion?

20 Burnley?

Answers

The 90s (see Quiz 21)

1 Kevin Keegan. **2** Bob Paisley. **3** USA. **4** Steve Coppell. **5** Gordon Durie. **6** China. **7** Barry Fry. **8** Maidstone. **9** Frank Sinclair. **10** Jimmy Quinn. **11** Italy. **12** First pay-per-view match. **13** Jim McLean (Dundee Utd). **14** 1995. **15** Norwich City. **16** Joe Jordan. **17** Franz Beckenbauer. **18** Iran. **19** Deportivo La Coruña. **20** Diadora.

Quiz 24 **Chelsea**

Answers – see page 538

LEVEL 3

1 Who holds the record for most consecutive appearances for Chelsea?

2 Who was Chelsea's "chess expert"?

3 What was manager Bobby Campbell's nickname?

4 Who took "the worst penalty in the world" for Chelsea against Manchester City?

5 Who was Chelsea's first Jamaican international?

6 Which Norwegian defender was signed by Chelsea from Bayern Munich in 1989?

7 Which Chelsea keeper was known as "The Cat"?

8 Whose long throw was such a feature for Chelsea in the late 1960s and early 1970s?

9 Who is the only Spanish-born player ever to have played for Chelsea?

10 Who was Chelsea captain the day they won the Full Members Cup at Wembley in 1986?

11 Who did Tommy Docherty succeed as Chelsea boss in 1962?

12 Who scored Chelsea's winner against Bolton in 1983, a win that saved them from Third Division football?

13 Which Chelsea striker was known as "Mary"?

14 Who gave away a penalty in the closing minutes of a League Cup match drawn 4–4 against Sheffield Wednesday at Hillsbrough in 1985?

15 Who signed from Lazio in June 1988 but played only 15 games before injury ended his career?

16 Who scored the most penalties in one season for Chelsea?

17 From which club did Ruud Gullit join the Blues?

18 In which country was Tony Dorigo born?

19 How many managers have Chelsea had in their history?

20 Which Chelsea player went on to be Terry Venables's assistant manager at Barcelona?

Answers

Leeds United (see Quiz 22)

1 1976–77. **2** 1953–54. **3** 15. **4** Phil Masinga. **5** Harry Kewell. **6** Tottenham Hotspur. **7** Lee Bowyer. **8** Roma. **9** Rod Wallace. **10** Martin O'Neill. **11** Nottingham Forest. **12** Lee Bowyer. **13** Tony Yeboah. **14** Ian Rush. **15** Sheffield United. **16** Middlesbrough. **17** Five. **18** Juventus. **19** Terry Cooper. **20** Eirik Bakke.

Quiz 25 **Everton**

LEVEL 3

Answers – see page 543

1 What is Everton's record league victory?

2 Who was Everton's manager between 1961 and 1973?

3 For how many matches did Everton go undefeated in 1984–85 to set a club record?

4 What were Everton's first colours?

5 What nickname did those colours earn for the team?

6 What is the record number of league goals Everton have scored in one season?

7 What is Everton's record attendance?

8 Who is the youngest player ever to have played for Everton?

9 What is Everton's record league defeat?

10 Who is Everton's leading goalscorer in European competitions?

11 How many managers have Everton had in their history?

12 Who scored on his debut for Everton against Newcastle on the first day of the 1996–97 season?

13 How many league goals did Gary Lineker score in season 1985–86?

14 Who was sent off in the 1980 FA Cup semi-final against West Ham, shortly after scoring a penalty?

15 Whose first goals came in 1995 in a 2–1 win against Liverpool at Anfield?

16 Who did Everton beat 7–1 in the league at Goodison in November 1996?

17 Against which team did Everton need three replays to progress in the FA Cup in 1988?

18 Who did Everton beat 5–0 at Goodison in a league game in December 1999?

19 In which round were Everton knocked out of the FA Cup in 1999–2000?

20 Where did Neville Southall go when he left Everton in 1999?

Answers

Name of Quiz (see Quiz 27)

1 Arsenal. **2** Tottenham. **3** Brentford. **4** Crystal Palace. **5** West Ham United. **6** Leyton Orient. **7** The club was formed by workers at an arms factory. **8** West Ham. **9** Wimbledon. **10** Charlton Athletic. **11** Crystal Palace. **12** Fulham. **13** Leyton Orient. **14** Millwall. **15** Wimbledon. **16** West Ham. **17** Spurs, 5–1 v Atletico Madrid, ECWC, 1963. **18** QPR. **19** Millwall. **20** Charlton Athletic.

Quiz 26 **Gianluca Vialli**

LEVEL 3

Answers – see page 544

1 In which year was Vialli born?

2 In which Italian city was he born?

3 With which club did he win the Serie A title in Italy in 1991?

4 How many international goals did he score?

5 Who said of Vialli, "I used to take him out for a few beers and he just couldn't handle it"?

6 Whose underpants did Vialli sprinkle with pepper before he put them on?

7 How many Italian caps did he win?

8 In 1992 he became the world's most expensive player. With which club?

9 For whom did he make his Italian League debut?

10 What was the last trophy Vialli won as a player in Italy?

11 Which was the first medal he won as a player at Chelsea?

12 When did he take over as manager of Chelsea?

13 When Vialli led Chelsea to European glory in 1998, how many years was it since they had done such a thing?

14 Against which club did Vialli score twice to help Chelsea to a 4–2 victory in the 1996 FA Cup?

15 Against who did he make his Chelsea debut as a player?

16 His first match as Watford manager was against which club?

17 Which European trophies did Vialli win as a player?

18 How many World Cups did Vialli play in?

19 How many trophies did he win as a player and manager at Chelsea?

20 When was he sacked as manager of Chelsea?

Answers

The Midlands (see Quiz 28)

1 Coventry City. **2** Nigel Spink. **3** 1919–1920. **4** Kevin Ratcliffe. **5** Kidderminster Harriers. **6** Red Star Belgrade. **7** Wolves. **8** Birmingham City. **9** Ray Graydon. **10** Aston Villa and Wolves. **11** Crewe Alexandra. **12** George Boateng. **13** Rory Delap. **14** Lee Hendrie. **15** Kevin Kilbane. **16** Notts County. **17** Jermaine Pennant. **18** Mark Delaney. **19** Peter Withe. **20** Wolves.

Quiz 27 **London**

Answers – see page 541

LEVEL 3

1 Which was the first London team to beat Manchester United in the 2000–01 league season?

2 Which London club was managed by Gerry Francis between 1994 and 1997?

3 Whose ground is situated in Braemar Road?

4 Which London club were runners up in the 1990 FA Cup competition?

5 Which London club have had only nine managers?

6 Of which London club is Barry Hearn the chairman?

7 Why are Arsenal known as "The Gunners"?

8 Which London club's overall top scorer is Vic Watson?

9 Which London club is owned by a Norwegian business consortium?

10 Which London club used to play at Siemen's Meadow?

11 Of which London club was Attilio Lombardo player/manager in 1998?

12 At which London club was Chris Coleman when he had a serious car accident?

13 Which London club started life in 1881 as Glyn Cricket and Football Club?

14 Current Republic of Ireland manager Mick McCarthy managed which London club between 1992 and 1996?

15 For which London club does Alan Cork hold the appearances record?

16 Which London club lost 2–8 at home to Blackburn Rovers in a First Division game in 1963?

17 Which London club won the final of a European competition by a four-goal margin?

18 Which London club was managed by Tommy Docherty in 1968 and 1979–80?

19 Of which London club is Theo Paphitis the chairman?

20 For which London club does Sam Bartram hold the most league appearances record?

Answers

Everton (see Quiz 25)

1 9–1, on two occasions. **2** Harry Catterick. **3** 28. **4** Black shirts with a scarlet slash. **5** "The Black Watch'. **6** 121. **7** 78,299. **8** Joe Royle (16 years and 9 months). **9** 4–10 away to Spurs, 1958. **10** Fred Pickering. **11** 19. **12** Gary Speed. **13** 30. **14** Brian Kidd. **15** Andrei Kanchelskis. **16** Southampton. **17** Sheffield Wednesday. **18** Sunderland. **19** Quarter-finals. **20** Stoke City.

Quiz 28 **The Midlands**

Answers – see page 542

LEVEL 3

1 Sky Sports presenter Richard Keys is a supporter of which Midlands team?

2 Who was Aston Villa's goalkeeper in the 1982 European Cup final?

3 In which year did West Bromwich Albion win the League Championship?

4 Which former Welsh international is Shrewsbury's manager?

5 Which is the only Nationwide League club in the county of Worcestershire?

6 Who were Leicester City's first opponents in the 2000–2001 UEFA Cup?

7 Mark McGhee left Leicester City to take over which club as manager?

8 Which club's winger Jon McCarthy broke a leg twice in 1999–2000?

9 Which former Aston Villa hero is manager at Walsall?

10 Which other Midlands clubs has Coventry City's Stephen Frogatt played?

11 Leicester signed both Robbie Savage and Neil Lennon from which club?

12 Which Aston Villa star was born in Ghana?

13 Which Derby player made his debut for the Republic of Ireland in 1998?

14 Which Aston Villa youngster played in the 2000 European Under 21 Championship?

15 Which West Bromwich Albion international joined Sunderland in the 1999–2000 season?

16 Sam Allardyce took which Midlands club to the 1998 Third Division championship?

17 Which Notts County teenager controversially signed for Arsenal in 1999?

18 Which Aston Villa player was sent off in the 2000 Worthington Cup semi-final at Wembley?

19 Which player won the League Championship with Aston Villa and Nottingham Forest?

20 Which Midlands club won the old First, Second, Third and Fourth Division championships?

Answers

Gianluca Vialli (see Quiz 26)

1 1964. **2** Cremona. **3** Sampdoria. **4** 16. **5** Graeme Souness. **6** Graeme Souness's. **7** 59. **8** Juventus. **9** Cremonese. **10** The European Cup with Juventus in 1996. **11** The FA Cup in 1997. **12** February 1998. **13** 27 years. **14** Liverpool. **15** Southampton. **16** Manchester City. **17** All three. **18** Two, 1986 and 1990. **19** Five. **20** September 2000.

Quiz 29 **The North East**

Answers – see page 547

LEVEL 3

1 Who scored Sunderland's winning goal in the 1973 FA Cup Final?

2 Which former Hartlepool player won his first cap for Scotland in 1999?

3 Which future Premier League manager took Darlington back to the Football League in 1990?

4 Which FA Cup giant-killing Geordies beat Preston North End and Scarborough in 1990?

5 Which FA Cup giant-killing Geordies beat Stoke City in 1978?

6 Which former League team from the North East folded in 1973?

7 Next to Shearer who scored the most goals for Newcastle in 1999–2000?

8 In which year was Peter Reid appointed Sunderland manager?

9 Who was Middlesbrough's top scorer in 1999–2000?

10 Which club prevented Newcastle from reaching a third consecutive FA Cup final in 2000?

11 Who scored four goals for Sunderland in 1999–2000 despite only ever appearing as a substitute?

12 Which club bought Brian Clough from Middlesbrough in 1961?

13 How many of Newcastle's 1998 FA Cup Final team played in the 1999 Final?

14 Which former England international scored twice for Hartlepool in 1998–99?

15 Which well-travelled forward left Darlington for Northampton in the summer of 2000?

16 Who left Middlesbrough for WBA in a British record transfer in 1979?

17 Which North East team have scored three goals against Manchester United on three occasions in the Premier League?

18 Which 1999 signing set Sunderland's record transfer fee?

19 From which club did Newcastle sign Nikos Dabizas?

20 Which club has a fanzine called *Fly Me to the Moon*?

Answers

Who Did What? 2 (see Quiz 31)

1 Lee Bowyer. **2** Kilmarnock. **3** Everton. **4** Faustino Asprilla. **5** Oleg Salenko, for Russia v Cameroon, 1994. **6** Davor Suker. **7** Raith Rovers. **8** Mike Channon. **9** Paul McGrath. **10** Terry Venables. **11** Derek Fazackerley. **12** AC Milan. **13** Alfie Conn. **14** Preston North End. **15** Manchester United. **16** Rangers. **17** Craig Brown. **18** Stanley Matthews. **19** Swindon Town. **20** Canon.

Quiz 30 **Republic of Ireland**

Answers – see page 548

LEVEL 3

1 Who is credited with introducing football to Ireland?

2 In which year did Irish football split in a north/south divide?

3 In which year did FIFA accept the Irish Free State as an international team?

4 When and where did they play their first international match?

5 The Irish Free State won their first international against which nation?

6 When was the Irish Free State's first World Cup match?

7 In which year was the Irish Free State team first called Ireland?

8 When was the team first called the Republic of Ireland?

9 In 1956 Ireland beat the World Champions 3–0 in a friendly. Who were their victims?

10 Who were the first League of Ireland team to play in the European Cup?

11 In November 1966 who beat the Republic to deny them a place in the World Cup finals?

12 Who scored four goals for the Republic against Turkey in October 1975?

13 In 1978 the Republic played Northern Ireland for the first time. What was the score?

14 Which club failed to reach the European Cup quarter-final after losing to Celtic in 1979?

15 What is the Republic's record victory?

16 What was the score when the Republic met England in the 1990 World Cup?

17 Against which opponents did Frank Stapleton score in 1990 to set a goalscoring record for the Republic?

18 Who scored the Republic's first ever goal at Windsor Park, in 1993?

19 In which American city did Ireland lose to Holland in the 1994 World Cup finals?

20 What is the name of the projected new stadium in Dublin in which the Republic will play their games from 2002?

Answers

Tottenham Hotspur (see Quiz 32)

1 Espen Baardsen. **2** King and Young. **3** Darren Anderton. **4** 1994–95. **5** Neil Sullivan **6** Les Ferdinand. **7** Bill Nicholson OBE. **8** Gary Docherty. **9** Graham Roberts. **10** "Push and Run'. **11** Allan Neilsen. **12** Justin Edinburgh. **13** Peters and Mullery. **14** Les Ferdinand. **15** Lineker. **16** Southampton. **17** Dumitrescu. **18** Sullivan and Thatcher. **19** £11 million. **20** Hoddle and Taylor.

Quiz 31 **Who Did What? 2**

Answers – see page 545

LEVEL 3

1 Who scored for Leeds Utd in their Champions League home tie with AC Milan in September 2000?

2 Who won the Tennent's Scottish Cup in 1997?

3 Which team has made the highest number of FA Cup semi-final appearances?

4 Who scored a hat-trick for Newcastle in a European Cup match against Barcelona in 1997–98?

5 Who holds the record for most goals in one match in the final stages of the World Cup?

6 Who was the leading goalscorer in the 1998 World Cup?

7 Who won the Scottish League Cup in 1995?

8 Who is Southampton's highest goalscorer?

9 Who is the Republic of Ireland's most capped player?

10 Who took over from Graham Taylor as England manager?

11 Who holds the league appearances record for Blackburn Rovers?

12 Which Italian team won the European Cup in 1989?

13 Which player won a Scottish Cup winner's medal with both Rangers and Celtic?

14 Who won the first Football League title in 1888–89?

15 Which team has appeared in most FA Cup finals?

16 Which club won the European Cup Winners' Cup, in 1972?

17 Who managed Scotland during the 1998 World Cup?

18 Which 42-year-old played for England v Denmark in May 1957?

19 Which Third Division team beat Arsenal to win the League Cup in 1969?

20 Who were the first sponsors of the Football League?

Answers

The North East (see Quiz 29)

1 Ian Porterfield. **2** Don Hutchison. **3** Brian Little. **4** Whitley Bay. **5** Blyth Spartans. **6** Gateshead. **7** Gary Speed. **8** 1995. **9** Hamilton Ricard. **10** Chelsea. **11** Danny Dichio. **12** Sunderland. **13** Five. **14** Peter Beardsley. **15** Marco Gabbiadini. **16** David Mills. **17** Middlesbrough. **18** Stefan Schwarz. **19** Olympiakos Athens. **20** Middlesbrough.

Quiz 32 **Tottenham Hotspur**

Answers – see page 546

LEVEL 3

1 Which Norwegian goalkeeper did Tottenham sell to Watford in 2000?

2 Who two Spurs played in England's under 21 Euro 2000?

3 Which Tottenham midfielder started his career at Portsmouth?

4 In which season were Spurs originally banned from the FA Cup?

5 Who made the most appearances for Tottenham in the 2000–01 season?

6 Before Rebrov, who was Tottenham's record signing?

7 Which popular figure at White Hart Lane is Tottenham's president?

8 Which Tottenham player made his debut for the Republic of Ireland in the 2000 Toulon tournament?

9 Who scored the equalising goal against Anderlect in the 1984 UEFA Cup final at White Hart Lane?

10 For what tactics were Arthur Rowe's 1950s Tottenham team renowned?

11 Who scored Tottenham's goal in the 1999 Worthington Cup final?

12 Which Tottenham player was sent off in the 1999 Worthington Cup final?

13 Which two Tottenham players were in England's 1970 World Cup team against West Germany?

14 Who did Tottenham pay Newcastle £4.2 million for in July 1997?

15 Who scored two goals in Tottenham's 1991 FA Cup semi-final victory over Arsenal?

16 Which team did Spurs beat 7–2 in the 1999–2000 season?

17 Who is missing from the Ossie Ardiles "famous five': Barmby, Klinsmann, Sheringham, Anderton ... ?

18 Which two players did George Graham sign from Wimbledon in 2000?

19 How much did Tottenham pay Dynamo Kiev for Sergei Rebrov?

20 Which two former Spurs were Premier League managers in the 2000–2001 season?

Answers

Republic of Ireland (see Quiz 30)

1 John McAlery. **2** 1921. **3** 1923. **4** 1926, Turin. **5** Belgium. **6** 1934. **7** 1936. **8** 1954. **9** West Germany. **10** Shamrock Rovers. **11** Spain. **12** Don Givens. **13** 0–0. **14** Dundalk. **15** 8–0 v Malta, 1983. **16** 1–1. **17** Malta. **18** Alan McLoughlin. **19** Orlando. **20** The Arena.

Quiz 33 **Spain**

Answers – see page 551

LEVEL 3

1 For which club does Raul play?
2 Which club play at the Vicente Calderon stadium?
3 What colour shirts do Barcelona play in?
4 Which is Spain's oldest club?
5 In which year did Spain win their first major trophy?
6 In which year did Barcelona first win the European Cup?
7 Who won the Spanish League title in 2000?
8 What nationality is Deportivo's Roy Makaay?
9 Who did Valencia sign in 2000 to replace Claudio Lopez?
10 Which club has Jose Manuel Mane as their coach?
11 Who is the *pichichi*?
12 What nationality is Barcelona's Rivaldo?
13 Which Madrid team was relegated from the top flight in 2000?
14 For which team does keeper Iker Casillas play?
15 Which other Spanish team did Real Madrid play in the 2000 Champions League final?
16 Which player opened the scoring in that match?
17 Who took over from Johan Cruyff as manager of Barcelona?
18 For which club does striker Joseba Etxeberria play?
19 From which club did Internazionale buy defender Francisco Farinos in summer 2000?
20 For which club do Russian internationals Karpin and Mostovoi play?

Answers

Italy (see Quiz 35)

1 Atalanta. **2** Lazio. **3** Stadio Ennio Tardini. **4** Florence. **5** Roma. **6** Internazionale. **7** 18. **8** Marco Delvecchio. **9** Roma. **10** Parma. **11** Several players were away at the Olympics. **12** Cagliari. **13** Inter and Lazio. **14** Juventus in 1996. **15** 1982. **16** Three times. **17** Alberto Malesani. **18** Silvio Berlusconi. **19** Juventus and Parma. **20** Helenio Herrera.

Quiz 34 **Pot Luck 2**

Answers – see page 552

LEVEL 3

1 Before Chelsea's win in October 1999 who were the last team to beat Manchester United 5–0?

2 What non-league team did Bulgarian international Bontcho Guentchev play for in 1999?

3 Which Premier League team scored the most headed goals in 1999–2000?

4 From which country does Newcastle United's Lomana Lua Lua hail?

5 Which former England international played for Ross County in 1999?

6 Who scored a hat-trick after betting on his own team to beat Barnsley in 2000?

7 Daniel Amokachi was the first what since Cliff Marshall?

8 Which club's ground is featured in LS Lowry's painting "Going to the Match"?

9 Which player's portrait hangs in the Scottish Portrait Gallery?

10 What was the name of England's 1966 World Cup mascot?

11 Which man played in all four divisions of the Football/Premier League in 2000–01?

12 What role did Archibald Leitch play in British football?

13 Which university runs a course of Football Industries?

14 In which competition did Nicolas Anelka score his first goal for Real Madrid in 2000?

15 Which team were called the Manchester United of Division Three in 1999?

16 Which Premier League player completed the most crosses in 1999–2000?

17 According to *The Times* which West Ham player was the dirtiest in the Premier League in 2000–01?

18 Which are the three clubs in the Football/Premier League not to contain any of the letters of "soccer"?

19 For which country did Nandor Hidegkuti play?

20 Which club had the lowest average Premiership attendance from 1997 to 2000?

Answers

Terry Venables (see Quiz 36)

1 Sir Alf Ramsey. **2** The Nou Camp. **3** Thingummywigs. **4** They Used to Play on Grass. **5** Steve Archibald. **6** Allan Harris. **7** Anthony Newley. **8** Play at all levels. **9** Chief Executive. **10** Iran. **11** 1985. **12** The League Cup (1965). **13** Malcolm Allison. **14** Crystal Palace. **15** Peter Beardsley. **16** Terry Fenwick. **17** Arsenal. **18** Rest of the World. **19** *Panorama*. **20** Nayim.

Quiz 35 **Italy**

Answers – see page 549

LEVEL 3

1 Who plays in the city of Bergamo?

2 Who won the Italian league in 2000?

3 What is the name of Parma's ground?

4 In which Italian city do Fiorentina play?

5 For which club does Brazilian Cafu play?

6 Which club have Ronaldo and Christian Vieri as their strike force?

7 How many clubs are there in Serie A?

8 Who scored Italy's goal in the Euro 2000 final?

9 For which club does he play?

10 For which club does Matias Almeyda play?

11 Why did Serie A not start until 1 October in 2000?

12 Which is the leading Sardinian club?

13 Which two Italian teams contested the 1998 UEFA Cup final?

14 Which was the last Italian club to win the European Cup?

15 When did Italy last win the World Cup?

16 How many times have they won the trophy?

17 Who managed Parma during the 1999–2000 season?

18 Which Italian politician owns AC Milan?

19 Which two Italian teams contested the 1995 UEFA Cup final?

20 Which Italian coach was known as "Il Mago" (the Magician)?

Answers

Spain (see Quiz 33)

1 Real Madrid. **2** Atletico Madrid. **3** Blue and red stripes. **4** Athletic Bilbao. **5** 1964, European Championship. **6** 1992. **7** Deportivo la Coruna. **8** Dutch. **9** John Carew. **10** Alaves. **11** The league's top scorer. **12** Brazilian. **13** Atletico. **14** Real Madrid. **15** Valencia. **16** Gaizka Mendieta. **17** Bobby Robson. **18** Athletic Bilbao. **19** Valencia. **20** Celta Vigo.

Quiz 36 **Terry Venables**

Answers – see page 550

LEVEL 3

1 Venables grew up in the same town as which other England manager?

2 Which ground he would come to know well was the venue for his last appearance in a Chelsea shirt?

3 What were the names of the hats with attached wigs that Venables marketed in the 60s?

4 What was the name of the novel Venables co-wrote in 1971?

5 Who did Venables sign to replace Maradona at Barcelona?

6 Who was his managerial assistant from Crystal Palace to Barcelona?

7 Who did Venables impersonate on TV's Celebrity Stars in their Eyes?

8 Venables was the first to do what as an England player?

9 What was his job title when he and Alan Sugar took over at Tottenham?

10 Who did his Australia team lose to in the 1998 World Cup qualifying play-offs?

11 In which year did Venables become the first Briton to be named World Manager of the Year?

12 In which competition did Venables score a Cup final goal?

13 Who was manager when Venables joined Crystal Palace as coach in 1976?

14 Which is the only English club Venables has managed but has had no financial interest in?

15 Which player did Venables bring back from international wilderness in his first England match?

16 Which defender played under Venables at Palace, QPR and Tottenham?

17 For which club did Venables sign a contract to take over at the beginning of the 1986–87 season?

18 Which team did Venables manage in the Football League Centenary Match?

19 Which TV series first raised allegations about Venables's financial dealings?

20 Which Barcelona player did Venables bring to Tottenham when he took charge?

Answers

Pot Luck 2 (see Quiz 34)

1 Newcastle (1996). **2** Hendon. **3** Newcastle United. **4** Zaire. **5** Mark Hateley. **6** Steve Claridge. **7** Black player at Everton. **8** Bolton Wanderers' Burnden Park. **9** Danny McGrain. **10** World Cup Willie. **11** Tony Cottee. **12** Stadium architect. **13** Liverpool. **14** World Club Championship. **15** Peterborough **16** Nolberto Solano (Newcastle). **17** Paulo Wanchope. **18** Fulham, Gillingham, Millwall. **19** Hungary. **20** Southampton.

Quiz 37 **Germany**

Answers – see page 555

LEVEL 3

1 What is the name given to a derby game in Germany?

2 For which club does German international Oliver Neuville play?

3 Which East German side entered the reunified Bundesliga with Hansa Rostock in in 1990?

4 For which German team did Mark Hughes play?

5 Which German World Cup winner was on the bench for Real Madrid in their 2000 Champions League final?

6 Who were relegated in 1998–99?

7 Sebastian Deisler plays for which German club?

8 Which German club won the 1992 European Cup Winners Cup?

9 Who is Bayern Munich's manager?

10 Which German team won the 1997 UEFA Cup?

11 Who was Bayern Munich's leading scorer in their 1999–2000 Champions League campaign?

12 Who scored Germany's only goal in Euro 2000?

13 Which Scot played for Bayern Munich in the 1990 European Cup semi-finals?

14 What is or who are the DFB Pokal?

15 Which German was European Footballer of the Year in 1980 and 1981?

16 Which German side play in white shirts with red and black flashing?

17 Which player did Liverpool buy from Borussia Mönchengladbach in 1996?

18 Who was Germany's manager in Euro 2000?

19 Who are the only country to have beaten Germany in a penalty shoot-out in a major competition?

20 Which "non-German" club has won the German League?

Answers

Who Did What? 3 (see Quiz 39)

1 Carlisle United. **2** Manchester United. **3** Paul Ince. **4** David Sullivan. **5** Italy. **6** Don Hutchison. **7** Cheltenham. **8** Wilson. **9** Barnsley. **10** Dundee. **11** Crewe Alexandra. **12** Mark Venus. **13** Malcolm Allison. **14** Brian Clough. **15** Allan Simonsen. **16** Ken Bates. **17** Bruce Rioch. **18** Scottish FA Cup final. **19** *Hampden Babylon.* **20** Roy Keane.

Quiz 38 **Literary Football**

Answers – see page 556

LEVEL 3

1 *The Glory Game* was Hunter Davies's classic study of which club?

2 Which Millwall and Republic of Ireland player's diary was *It's Only A Game*?

3 *This One's On Me* was which troubled 50s and 60s star's autobiographical account

4 *Left Foot in the Grave* is Gary Nelson's account of life at which club?

5 *Flat Back Four* is which pundit's guide to tactics?

6 *Manchester United Ruined my Life* is written by a supporter of which team?

7 What collection forms the annual book entitled *The Wrong Kind of Shirts*?

8 *The Greatest Footballer You Never Saw* was about which Reading and Cardiff player?

9 Who is the subject of Dave Hill's *Out of his Skin*?

10 *Strikingly Different* is which England forward's autobiography?

11 *Football is My Passport* is which England captain's account?

12 What is the subject of John Sampson's *Awaydays*?

13 *The Soccer Tribe* was whose anthropological study of football supporters?

14 Who wrote the classic entitled *The Football Man*?

15 What was the subject of Pete Davies's *All Played Out*?

16 *Clown Prince of Soccer* was which England forward's autobiography?

17 Whose *World Cup Diary* upset some of England's players in 1998?

18 Which event is the focus of *The Day Italian Football Died*?

19 Which team is the subject of David Winner's *Brilliant Orange*?

20 What is the title of Chris Hulme's account of a prison football team?

Answers

England (see Quiz 40)

1 Alan Shearer. **2** 1985. **3** David Platt. **4** Jimmy Armfield. **5** 7–1. **6** Ray Wilkins. **7** Cagliari. **8** 2–0. **9** Steve Guppy. **10** Paul Gascoigne. **11** Richard Wright. **12** Clive Allen. **13** 2–2. **14** Paul Ince. **15** Paul Parker. **16** David Batty. **17** Kevin Keegan. **18** Nick Barmby. **19** Don Revie. **20** Des Walker.

Quiz 39 **Who Did What? 3**

LEVEL 3 

Answers – see page 553

1 Who sold Matt Jansen to Crystal Palace in 1997–98?

2 Which club scored a total of 10 goals with none conceded in two games at Valley Parade in 1999 and 2000?

3 Which England player received a three-match international ban in 1999?

4 Who bought Birmingham City in 1993?

5 Who won the Euro 2000 under 21 tournament?

6 Who scored for Scotland against Latvia in their opening World Cup 2002 qualifying match?

7 Neil Grayson is the star of which Nationwide League team?

8 What was Ryan Giggs's surname when he played for England schoolboys?

9 Chris Morgan was which team's Player of the Year in 1999–2000?

10 Who were the only visiting team to win at Ibrox in the 1999–2000 Premier League?

11 Who won the PFA Fair play trophy seven times (1994–2000)?

12 Which Ipswich Town defender previously played for Wolverhampton Wanderers?

13 Which manager became recognisable by his fedora headwear?

14 Which manager was recognisable by an old green sweatshirt?

15 Which former Charlton player was coach of the Faroe Islands in their Euro 2000 qualifiers?

16 Which chairman tried to erect an electric fence at his ground in 1985?

17 Who took over as Wigan Athletic's manager in June 2000?

18 In which 1999–2000 final was Thomas Solberg sent off?

19 What is the name of Stuart Cosgrove's account of sex and scandal in Scottish football?

20 Who was Manchester United's leading goalscorer in their 1999–2000 Champions League campaign?

Answers

Germany (see Quiz 37)

1 Klassiker. **2** Bayer Leverkusen. **3** Dynamo Dresden. **4** Bayern Munich. **5** Bodo Illgner. **6** Borussia Mönchengladbach. **7** Hertha Berlin. **8** Werder Bremen. **9** Ottmar Hitzfeld. **10** Schalke 04. **11** Paulo Sergio. **12** Mehmet Scholl. **13** Alan McInally. **14** The German FA Cup. **15** Karl Heinz-Rumminegge. **16** Hamburg SV. **17** Patrik Berger. **18** Erich Ribbeck. **19** Czechoslovakia. **20** Rapid Vienna (1941).

Quiz 40 **England**

Answers – see page 554

LEVEL 3

1 Who was the only England player booked in their final Euro 2000 match?

2 In what year did Gary Lineker score his first goal for England?

3 Which player was controversially brought down by Ronald Koeman in England's World Cup qualifier in Rotterdam in 1993?

4 Who was appointed as the FA's headhunter when Graham Taylor resigned?

5 What was the score when England played San Marino in November 1993?

6 Who was the most capped player under Ron Greenwood?

7 Where did England play all of their group matches in the 1990 World Cup?

8 What was the half-time score in England's Euro 2000 qualifying play-off at Hampden?

9 Which left-sided player made his debut against Belgium in 1999?

10 Who did Graham Taylor controversially leave out of his first England team?

11 Which Euro 2000 squad member was the only player to be dropped in Kevin Keegan's first post-tournament squad?

12 Which striker made his debut as an England substitute against Brazil in Rio in 1984?

13 What was the half-time score in England's Euro 2000 tie against Portugal?

14 Who earned England's penalty against Romania in Euro 2000?

15 Who deflected Brehme's free-kick to give Germany the lead in the 1990 World Cup semi-final?

16 Who was sent off playing for England in Warsaw in 1999?

17 Who did Bobby Robson controversially leave out of his first England team?

18 Who played his first game for five years against Brazil in 2000?

19 Which manager introduced bingo sessions and carpet bowls to England training camps?

20 Who brought down Marc Overmars to give Holland an equalising penalty at Wembley in 1993?

Answers

Literary Football (see Quiz 38)

1 Tottenham. **2** Eamonn Dunphy. **3** Jimmy Greaves. **4** Torquay United. **5** Andy Gray. **6** Manchester City. **7** Quotations. **8** Robin Friday. **9** John Barnes. **10** Gary Lineker. **11** Billy Wright. **12** England hooliganism. **13** Desmond Morris. **14** Arthur Hopcraft. **15** England 1990. **16** Len Shackleton. **17** Glenn Hoddle. **18** Torino air disaster. **19** Holland. **20** *Manslaughter United.*

Quiz 41 **Scotland**

Answers – see page 559

LEVEL 3

1. Who scored Scotland's winner in their Euro 96 match against Switzerland?
2. Which Scottish player and manager was known as the "chocolate soldier"?
3. When did Scotland join FIFA?
4. Who was known as "wee Bud"?
5. At which stadium did Scotland play Finland in 1998?
6. Who kept goal for Scotland during all three of their 1998 World Cup matches?
7. Who did Craig Brown take over from as Scotland manager?
8. Whose penalty goal against Wales secured Scotland a place in the 1986 World Cup in Mexico?
9. Which Scottish player won the 1964 European Footballer of the Year award?
10. Which Scottish player scored on his debut that day?
11. What was the score when Scotland beat Wales at Anfield in the 1978 World Cup qualifier?
12. Who were Scotland's first opponents in the 1978 World Cup Finals?
13. Who scored for Scotland that day?
14. Who did Scotland beat in their final match to qualify for Italia 90?
15. When did Scotland last qualify for the European Championships?
16. Who were their first opponents in that tournament?
17. Who defeated Scotland in their last match in the 1998 World Cup Finals?
18. How many Scottish caps did Pat Nevin win?
19. Where did the Scotland squad stay during the 1998 World Cup campaign?
20. Who scored Scotland's winner against Argentina at Hampden in 1990?

Answers

All Around the World (see Quiz 43)

1 All white. **2** New England Revolution. **3** China. **4** 1986. **5** Malaysia. **6** Japan. **7** Los Angeles Aztecs. **8** Zico. **9** Canberra. **10** Afghanistan. **11** Bora Milutinovic. **12** Steve Potts. **13** Qatar. **14** Armenia. **15** Hong Kong. **16** Ayatollah Khomeini. **17** Japan. **18** Perth Glory. **19** Saudi Arabia. **20** Al Nassr.

Quiz 42 **Pot Luck 4**

Answers – see page 560

LEVEL 3

1 Who is the "Alexandra" in Crewe Alexandra?
2 Which England opponents substituted all eleven players in June 1990?
3 Who was the first foreign player to be the Scottish Footballer of the Year?
4 Which club was supported by the U-boat crew in the TV series *Das Boot*?
5 Which club were originally known as the Black Arabs?
6 Which is the only Scottish club to have had an artificial pitch?
7 Which English player was the UEFA Cup leading scorer in 1976–77?
8 For which two teams has the Sugar Puffs honey monster played?
9 What was the title of the ITV documentary about Graham Taylor?
10 Who were the only League club not to join a mass protest resignation from the FA in 1965?
11 "You've beaten them once. Now go and do it again." Whose extra time instructions?
12 Who was the last player from outside the top division to win the English writers Footballer of the Year award?
13 Who won championship medals with Blackburn and Everton?
14 Which innovation did FIFA experiment with in the USA and Egypt in the 2000–01 season?
15 Which was the first national newspaper to publish a Fantasy Football League?
16 Which country's supporters won the 1997 FIFA Fair Play Award?
17 Which ground other than Wembley has twin towers?
18 "When you get used to caviar, it's difficult to come back to sausages." Said which Premiership manager?
19 In which season did British Rail stop running football specials?
20 Who said "If Arsenal were playing in my back garden, I'd pull the curtains?'

Answers

Memorable Matches (see Quiz 44)

1 David Beckham. **2** USA. **3** Michael Owen. **4** Wrexham. **5** Manchester City 10, Huddersfield Town 1, 1987 (White Stewart and Adcock). **6** England (3–2 v Italy). **7** Brazil 4, Italy 1. **8** Sunderland. **9** France won 4–3 on penalties. **10** Denmark. **11** 1997. **12** Michel Platini. **13** Frank Leboeuf. **14** 6–1. **15** Germany. **16** Manchester United. **17** Internazionale. **18** Paul Ince and David Batty. **19** Rapid Vienna. **20** Sheffield Wednesday.

Quiz 43 **All Around the World**

LEVEL 3

Answers – see page 557

1 In which colours do the New Zealand team play?
2 For which Massachusetts club did Alexei Lalas play?
3 Which country has the fourth best record in World Cup qualifying games but has never reached the finals?
4 In which year did Canada reach the World Cup finals?
5 For which country has Soh Chin Aun been credited with 250 international appearances?
6 Which non-South American country played in the 1999 Copa America?
7 Which US team did Johan Cruyff join on leaving Barcelona?
8 Which Brazilian played for J-League team Kashima Antlers?
9 In which city is Australia's national football stadium?
10 Where were Pakistani players arrested for playing in shorts in 2000?
11 Which coach has taken four different countries into the World Cup second round?
12 Which West Ham defender in 2000–01 was born in the USA?
13 Al Saad, Al Wakra and Al Rayyan are successful teams in which country?
14 Ararat Yerevan won the Soviet "double" in 1973. In which country do they now play?
15 Apart from Britain and the USA, in which other country did Bobby Moore and George Best play?
16 "Tonight the strong and arrogant opponent felt the bitter taste of defeat." Which leader's official statement?
17 Masami Ihara was which country's World Cup finals captain?
18 What is the full name of Australia's Perth team?
19 Which country qualified for the finals of the Asian Cup of Nations every time it was held from 1984 to 1996?
20 Which United Arab Emirates team competed in the 2000 World Club Championship?

Answers

Scotland (see Quiz 41)

1 Ally McCoist. **2** Graeme Souness. **3** 1873. **4** Willie Johnston. **5** Easter Road. **6** Jim Leighton. **7** Andy Roxburgh. **8** Davie Cooper. **9** Denis Law. **10** Jim McCalliog. **11** 2–0 to Scotland. **12** Peru. **13** Joe Jordan. **14** Norway. **15** 1996. **16** Holland. **17** Morocco. **18** 28. **19** St Remy. **20** Stewart McKimmie.

Quiz 44 **Memorable Matches**

Answers – see page 558

1. Ryan Giggs scored a wonder goal to help Man Utd beat Arsenal in the 1999 FA Cup semi-final replay. Who scored United's other goal?
2. Who did Iran defeat in the group stage of France 98?
3. Who scored England's goal when they lost to Romania in France 98?
4. Which Fourth Division team sensationally beat Arsenal 2–1 in the FA Cup in 1992?
5. Which was the last Football League match to have one team with three players scoring at least three goals each?
6. Who won the "Battle of Highbury" in 1934?
7. What was the score in the 1970 World Cup final in Mexico?
8. Norwich City won the Milk Cup in 1985. Who did they beat in the final?
9. Brazil and France clashed in the 1986 World Cup quarter-final. What happened?
10. Who defeated Germany in the European Championship final in 1992?
11. In which year did Roberto Di Matteo score his 43-second FA Cup final goal?
12. Who scored for Juventus in the match that followed the Heysel tragedy?
13. Who equalised for Chelsea in the last minute in a fourth-round FA Cup tie against Oxford in 1999?
14. Holland beat Yugoslavia in the quarter-finals of Euro 2000, by what score?
15. Who did Croatia beat in the quarter-final of the 1998 World Cup?
16. Which team scored twice in the last two minutes to beat Liverpool in a fourth-round FA Cup-tie in 1999?
17. Who did Celtic beat to win the European Cup final in 1967?
18. Which two England players missed penalties as they lost to Argentina in the 1998 World Cup?
19. Who did Everton beat in the 1985 European Cup Winners' Cup final?
20. Who beat Manchester United to win the Rumbelows Cup in 1991?

Answers

Pot Luck 4 (see Quiz 42)

1 Princess Alexandra. **2** Malta. **3** Brian Laudrup. **4** Schalke 04. **5** Bristol Rovers. **6** Stirling Albion. **7** Stan Bowles. **8** Newcastle and Man. Utd. **9** *An Impossible Job.* **10** Chelsea. **11** Sir Alf Ramsey. **12** Alan Mullery (Fulham 1975). **13** Bobby Mimms. **14** Two referees. **15** *Daily Telegraph.* **16** Republic of Ireland. **17** Feethams (Darlington). **18** Arsène Wenger. **19** 1975–76. **20** Tommy Docherty.

Quiz 45 **France**

Answers – see page 563

LEVEL 3

1 Which French stars retired from international football after the friendly against England in 2000?

2 Who is France's leading goalscorer in international football?

3 Which French club saw better days as European Cup runners-up in 1956 and 1959?

4 Which European Footballer of the Year was Just Fontaine's strike partner in the 1958 World Cup?

5 Which French club did Zidane help to the 1996 UEFA Cup final?

6 How many games did France win in normal time in Euro 2000?

7 Did the French Euro 2000 victors have more players playing in Italy or England?

8 How many games did France win in normal time in the 1998 World Cup?

9 Which ex-Premier League player scored for Marseilles against Chelsea in the 2000 Champions League?

10 Which French defender joined West Ham from Metz?

11 Which Frenchman played in the 2000 Champions League final?

12 Which French coach took them to Euro 2000 glory?

13 From which French club did Arsenal sign Gilles Grimandi?

14 Which French club did George Weah help win a League championship in 1994?

15 Which French champions became known as Matra Racing, then Racing '92?

16 Which city hosted the Brazil versus Holland 1998 World Cup semi-final?

17 Which team play at the Geoffroy-Guichard stadium?

18 Who was the only member of the France Euro 2000 winning team who was playing in France at the beginning of the 2000–01 season?

19 In which country was French international Patrick Vieira born?

20 Who did Liverpool sign from Lens in 1999?

Answers

African Football (see Quiz 47)

1 Mustapha Hadji. **2** Ghana. **3** Algeria. **4** Ivory Coast. **5** Argentina. **6** 2–1 to Eire. **7** Sent off against Argentina (1990). **8** Albert Johanneson. **9** Dele Adebola. **10** Lua Lua Lomana. **11** Nigeria. **12** Tunisia. **13** Mali. **14** Salif Keita. **15** Zaire. **16** Barcelona. **17** Cameroon. **18** Zimbabwe. **19** Victor Ikpeba. **20** Mali.

Quiz 46 **Jack Charlton**

LEVEL 3

Answers – see page 564

1 In which year was Jack Charlton born?

2 How many teams did he manage during his career?

3 How many England caps did he win?

4 In which year did he make his Football League debut?

5 In which year did he win his first England cap?

6 At which club did he take up his first managerial post?

7 What did he achieve in his first year as manager?

8 How many clubs did Jack Charlton play for during his career?

9 For how long was he manager of Newcastle?

10 In which year did he retire from playing?

11 When was he appointed manager of the Republic of Ireland?

12 In 1988 they qualified for the European Championships. Who were their most celebrated victims during that tournament?

13 Who granted Jack Charlton an audience during Italia 90?

14 How far did the Republic get during that tournament?

15 Whose scalp did the Republic famously take during the 1994 World Cup?

16 Which other club did Charlton manage?

17 In which year was Jack Charlton voted Footballer of the Year?

18 In which year was he voted Manager of the Year?

19 For how long was he in charge at Sheffield Wednesday?

20 In which year did he retire from management?

Answers

The 80s (see Quiz 48)

1 Trevor Brooking. **2** Liverpool. **3** Everton. **4** Terry Venables. **5** Gary Mabbutt. **6** Sunderland. **7** Oxford United. **8** Diego Maradona. **9** Luton Town. **10** Chorley. **11** Everton. **12** Joe Miller. **13** 1989. **14** Celtic. **15** Avi Cohen. **16** Aston Villa. **17** West Ham. **18** Bob Paisley. **19** Gordon Smith of Brighton. **20** Liverpool won 3–1.

Quiz 47 **African Football**

Answers – see page 561

1 Which Spanish League player was the 1998 African Footballer of the Year?
2 Hearts of Oak, Asante Kotoko and Obuasi Goldfields play in which country?
3 Which African country beat West Germany in the 1982 World Cup?
4 In which country was the African Cup of Nations all time leading scorer Laurent Pokou born?
5 Which country did Nigeria beat to win the Olympic gold in 1996?
6 What was the result when the Republic of Ireland played South Africa in the 2000 Nike Cup in the USA?
7 What place do Kana Byik and Massing have in Cameroon's World Cup history?
8 Which South African scored a hat-trick for Leeds United in the Fairs Cup in 1966?
9 Who is Birmingham City's Nigerian-born striker?
10 Which Premier League striker comes from Zaire and started his career at Colchester?
11 In which African country did George Weah play after leaving Liberia?
12 Tarak Dhiab, Faouzi Rouissi and Adel Sellimi are footballing legends of which African country?
13 The Eagles is the nickname of which North African country?
14 Which St Etienne player was France Football magazine's first African Footballer of the Year, in 1970?
15 PSV Eindhoven's Kalusha Bwalya came from which African country?
16 For which Spanish side did Nigerian Emmanuel Amunike play?
17 Jean Manga-Onguene was the coach of which 1998 World Cup finalists?
18 Black Aces, Black Rhinos and Wankie play in which country's league?
19 Whose shot was deemed not to have crossed the line in the 2000 African Cup of Nations final penalty shoot-out?
20 Where was the 2002 African Cup of Nations finals tournament staged?

Answers

France (see Quiz 45)

1 Blanc and Deschamps. **2** Michel Platini. **3** Stade de Reims. **4** Raymond Kopa. **5** Bordeaux. **6** Three. **7** Italy. **8** Five. **9** Ibrahim Bakayoko. **10** Sebastian Schemmel. **11** Nicolas Anelka. **12** Roger Lemerre. **13** Monaco. **14** PSG. **15** Racing Club de Paris. **16** Marseilles. **17** Saint Etienne. **18** Sylvain Wiltord. **19** Senegal. **20** Vladimir Smicer.

Quiz 48 **The 80s**

Answers – see page 562

LEVEL 3

1 Who scored a rare header to win the FA Cup final for West Ham in 1980?

2 Who won the Milk Cup in 1984?

3 Which team lost the 1984 Milk Cup final but won the FA Cup the same year?

4 Who was Barcelona's manager when they lost the European Cup in 1986?

5 Who scored an own goal in the 1987 FA Cup final?

6 Who beat Chelsea in the Milk Cup semi-final in 1985 and sparked a riot as a result?

7 Which club won the Milk Cup for the only time in their history in 1986?

8 Who set up Argentina's winning goal in the 1986 World Cup final?

9 Which club were thrown out of the Littlewoods Cup in 1986 for refusing to allow away fans into their ground?

10 Which non-league team beat Wolves 3–0 in the first round of the FA Cup in 1987?

11 Who ended Liverpool's 29-match unbeaten run in March 1988?

12 Who scored Celtic's winner in the Old Firm Scottish Cup final in 1989?

13 In which year did Don Revie die?

14 Which Scottish team scored five goals in one match but were still eliminated from the 1990 European Cup Winners' Cup?

15 Who scored a goal and an own goal on his debut for Liverpool in 1980?

16 Which team used only 14 players during their championship-winning season in 1981?

17 Which team were ordered to play a 1980 Cup Winners' Cup match behind closed doors, following crowd trouble?

18 Who retired as manager of Liverpool after the 1983 Milk Cup final?

19 Who missed when he should have scored in the final minutes of the 1983 FA Cup final?

20 Who won the first all-Merseyside FA Cup final, in 1986?

Answers

Jack Charlton (see Quiz 46)

1 1935. **2** Four. **3** 35. **4** 1953. **5** 1965. **6** Middlesbrough. **7** Promotion to the First Division. **8** One, Leeds United. **9** Fourteen months. **10** 1973. **11** 1986. **12** England. **13** The Pope. **14** Quarter-finals. **15** Italy. **16** Sheffield Wednesday. **17** 1967. **18** 1974. **19** Six years. **20** 1996.

Quiz 49 **Arsenal**

Answers – see page 567

LEVEL 3

1 Which Arsenal signing was voted Player of the Tournament for the 2000 African Nations Cup?

2 Who was Arsenal's fourth-choice goalkeeper in the 2001–02 season?

3 Which former England captain was manager of Arsenal between 1962 and 1966?

4 When did Arsenal move to Highbury?

5 Who did Arsenal beat 6–1 in a league game in April 1999?

6 From whom did Arsenal sign full-back Lee Dixon?

7 Where was David Seaman born?

8 Where did Christopher Wreh go on loan in 1998?

9 Who was manager of Arsenal when they won the double in 1971?

10 Which Arsenal striker was the First Division's joint top-scorer in 1977?

11 Who celebrated a goal against Coventry in 1979 by dropping his shorts in front of the crowd?

12 Who was man of the match for Arsenal in the 1979 FA Cup final?

13 Who scored Arsenal's first goal in the championship decider against Liverpool at Anfield in 1989?

14 Who top scored for Arsenal in the championship-winning 1990–91 season?

15 Entering the 2001–02 season, who was the leading League goalscorer out of Tony Adams, Martin Keown, Lee Dixon, Ray Parlour?

16 Who are Arsenal's current sponsors?

17 What were Arsenal called between 1913 and 1927?

18 What was the score when Arsenal met Manchester United at Highbury in the league in November 2001?

19 What is Arsenal's record league victory?

20 Who is Arsenal's vice-chairman?

Answers

West Ham United (see Quiz 51)

1 Rome. **2** Ron Greenwood. **3** Frank Lampard Snr. **4** 8–0 v Rotherham, 1958. **5** 1904. **6** 8 games in 1985. **7** All white. **8** 101 in 1957–58. **9** Sheffield Wednesday. **10** 1994. **11** Derby County. **12** 1980. **13** Liverpool. **14** 67. **15** Dynamo Tbilisi. **16** To become England manager. **17** West Ham 5 Castilla 1. **18** Six times. **19** Alan Devonshire. **20** Eyal Berkovic, after being kicked in training by John Hartson.

Quiz 50 **Old Football**

Answers – see page 568

LEVEL 3

1 Who did Arsenal break the transfer record for when signing him in 1938?
2 Who was the Italian manager when they won the World Cup in 1938?
3 In which year did the Pools Panel first sit?
4 Who lost the League Championship by 0.686 of a goal in 1964–65?
5 What kind of exhibition was the World Cup stolen from in 1966?
6 Who set a transfer record when he moved from Swansea to Tottenham in 1958?
7 Whose fierce tackling in the FA Cup final brought them jeers from the crowd on their lap on honour in 1960?
8 Which England forward was interned in Germany during the Great War?
9 Who defied Football League and entered the European Cup in 1956?
10 For which country did Josef Masopust, 1962 Footballer of the Year, play?
11 In 1965 who were the first Eastern bloc club to win a European cup?
12 Who was Berwick Rangers goalkeeper and manager when they sensationally knocked Rangers out of the FA Cup in 1967?
13 In 1959 who reached 100 League goals in fewer matches than any previous player?
14 Who scored in an FA Cup final, but watched his team win the match from his hospital bed?
15 How many England internationals died in the 1958 Munich air disaster?
16 Which Yeovil player-manager later took Fulham to Wembley?
17 How many people watched the 1948 FA Cup final on television?
18 Players from which two teams were banned for match-fixing in the 1914–15 season?
19 Which manager took Northern Ireland to the 1958 World Cup finals?
20 Which team lost their League status at the end of the 1969–70 season?

Answers

Nationwide League (see Quiz 52)

1 David Lloyd. **2** Newcastle United. **3** Marco Gabbiadini. **4** Darren Caskey. **5** Andy Clarke. **6** Stoke City. **7** Huddersfield Town. **8** Swindon Town. **9** Sheffield United. **10** Preston N.E. **11** Shrewsbury Town. **12** Lennie Lawrence. **13** Oldham Athletic. **14** Portsmouth. **15** Southend. **16** Neil Warnock. **17** Swindon Town. **18** Millwall. **19** Reading. **20** Bury.

Quiz 51 **West Ham United**

LEVEL 3

Answers – see page 565

1 In which city was Paolo Di Canio born?

2 Who was manager of West Ham from 1961 to 1974?

3 Who was Harry Redknapp's assistant manager?

4 What is West Ham's record league victory?

5 When did West Ham move to the Boleyn Ground?

6 What is West Ham's longest sequence of league wins?

7 What are West Ham's away colours?

8 What is West Ham's record goal tally for a league season?

9 From which club did West Ham sign Paolo Di Canio?

10 In which year did Harry Redknapp take over as manager of the club?

11 Who did West Ham beat 5–1 in a league game in April 1999?

12 When did West Ham last win the FA Cup?

13 From which club did West Ham buy Neil Ruddock?

14 How many England caps did Martin Peters win in his career?

15 Who knocked the Hammers out of the Cup Winners' Cup in 1981?

16 Why did Ron Greenwood leave West Ham?

17 What was the score in the match between West Ham and Castilla of Spain that was played behind closed doors in 1980?

18 How many times have West Ham reached the FA Cup semi-final stage?

19 Who scored West Ham's opening goal in the FA Cup semi-final replay against Everton in 1980?

20 Who said "If my head had been a ball, it would have ended in the top corner of the net"?

Answers

Arsenal (see Quiz 49)

1 Lauren Mayer. **2** Graham Stack. **3** Billy Wright. **4** 1913. **5** Middlesbrough. **6** Stoke City. **7** Rotherham. **8** AEK Athens. **9** The late Bertie Mee. **10** Malcolm Macdonald. **11** Sammy Nelson. **12** Liam Brady. **13** Alan Smith. **14** Alan Smith. **15** Tony Adams (32). **16** Dreamcast. **17** The Arsenal. **18** 3–1 to Arsenal. **19** Arsenal 12 Loughborough 0, 1900. **20** David Dein.

Quiz 52 **Nationwide League**

Answers – see page 566

LEVEL 3

1 Which former British Davis Cup tennis captain bought Hull City in 1997?

2 Who won their first 11 games in the First Division in 1992–93?

3 Which Darlington striker was the top Third Division scorer in 1999–2000?

4 Which Reading midfielder was chosen in the 1999–2000 PFA Divisional Team of the Season?

5 Which former Wimbledon striker scored the winner for Peterborough in the 2000 Third Division play-off final?

6 Which Nationwide club are sponsored by Britannia Building Society?

7 *Hanging on the Telephone* is a fanzine of which Nationwide League club?

8 The Nationwide Building Society sponsor which Nationwide League team where their head office is?

9 Paul Devlin was which Nationwide team's player of the year in 1999–2000?

10 Which Third Division team had the highest average attendance in 1999–2000: Millwall, Stoke City or Preston N.E.?

11 Which Nationwide team play in blue and amber striped shirts?

12 Who did Luton Town dismiss as their boss in 2000?

13 Slumberland sponsor which Nationwide League team?

14 Steve Claridge was player of the year at which Nationwide club in 1999–2000?

15 Who went from the First Division to the Third in consecutive years from 1996–98?

16 Which manager won play-offs with Notts County and Huddersfield Town?

17 From which club did Oxford United sign Joey Beauchamp?

18 Which Second Division team sacked their joint-managers in September 2000?

19 Who played their last game at Elm Park in 1998?

20 Which Lancashire team regularly used to kick off home matches at 3.15pm?

Answers

Old Football (see Quiz 50)

1 Bryn Jones. **2** Vittorio Pozzo. **3** 1963. **4** Leeds United. **5** Stamp. **6** Cliff Jones. **7** Wolves. **8** Steve Bloomer. **9** Manchester United. **10** Czechoslovakia. **11** Ferencvaros. **12** Jock Wallace. **13** Brian Clough. **14** Roy Dwight. **15** Four. **16** Alec Stock. **17** One million. **18** Liverpool and Man. Utd. **19** Peter Doherty. **20** Bradford Park Avenue.

Quiz 53 **Manchester City**

LEVEL 3 

Answers – see page 571

1 What is Manchester City's best ever finishing position in the Premier League??
2 Which former City player was manager at the club between 1974 and 1979?
3 In which city was Paul Dickov born?
4 Who made the most Premier League appearances for Manchester City in 2000–01?
5 Who were the opponents in City's last European match?
6 From whom did City buy defender Spencer Prior in 1999–2000?
7 What is City's record league victory?
8 Who scored City's first goal in the 1976 League Cup final?
9 Who did City beat in their last match of the season to win the league championship in 1968?
10 Who top scored for City that season?
11 How much did Joe Mercer pay for Colin Bell?
12 What is City's longest sequence of league games without a win?
13 At which club did Malcolm Allison first meet Tony Book?
14 How many England caps did Mike Summerbee win?
15 Who did City beat in the final of the European Cup Winners' Cup in 1970?
16 In which city did they play that match?
17 Who is the youngest player ever to play for City?
18 Who took over from Brian Horton as City manager in 1995?
19 Who is the current reserve team manager at City?
20 Who is City's highest league scorer?

Answers

East Anglia & Essex (see Quiz 55)

1 1973. **2** Johnny Gavin. **3** Layer Road. **4** Newmarket Road. **5** David Webb. **6** AZ Alkmaar. **7** 1992. **8** George McKenzie (8, Eire). **9** Mick Mills. **10** Bryan Hamilton. **11** 22nd clean sheet in a season. **12** Third round. **13** Tesfaye, Southend. **14** Ipswich. **15** Third in 1992–93. **16** Allan Hunter. **17** Seven matches in 1990. **18** Internazionale. **19** Ray Crawford. **20** John Lyall.

Quiz 54 **The West Country**

LEVEL 3

Answers – see page 572

1 The *Evening Herald* sponsor which West Country team?

2 Which Ashton Gate team did Bristol City merge with in 1900?

3 Which West Country team released all of their players in the summer of 2000?

4 Bristol Rovers are nicknamed the Pirates but what do their fans call them?

5 Whose love of Scotland inspired Plymouth's name Argyle?

6 Which former Bristol City striker is in Manchester City's 2000–01 squad?

7 Which West Country club replaced Aberdare Athletic in the Football League in 1927?

8 Which West Country club play in red and white striped shirts?

9 Which West Country club sold their two 1999–2000 leading scorers by September 2000?

10 Who won the Anglo-Italian League Cup-winners Cup in 1970 and 1971?

11 Which 2000 England striker had an earlier spell at Ashton Gate?

12 Who was Swindon Town's manager when they won promotion in 1992–93?

13 Who joined Manchester United from Torquay United for £180,000 in 1988?

14 From which West Country side did Tony Book join Manchester City?

15 How many seasons did Bristol City spend in the top flight in the 70s?

16 In what colour shirts do Plymouth play?

17 From which club did Derby County sign Dean Sturridge?

18 Who followed his father into the Bristol Rovers side and later played for England?

19 Who had the highest average attendance in 1999–2000: Plymouth, Exeter or Torquay?

20 Billy Mercer was which West Country club's Player of the Year in 1999–2000?

Answers

Jody Morris (see Quiz 56)

1 Hammersmith. **2** 1978. **3** FA School of Excellence. **4** December 1995. **5** February 1996. **6** Middlesbrough. **7** 5ft 5 ins (165cm). **8** Blackpool. **9** 2000–01. **10** Oldham Athletic. **11** Luxembourg. **12** Manchester United. **13** Galatasaray. **14** Richmond. **15** Five. **16** Southampton. **17** Young Player of the Year. **18** Arthur Bell. **19** 21, 8 as sub. **20** Pending court case.

Quiz 55 **East Anglia & Essex**

LEVEL 3

Answers – see page 569

1 In which year did Ipswich Town win the Texaco Cup?

2 Who is Norwich City's highest goalscorer?

3 What is the name of Colchester United's ground?

4 Where did Norwich City first play?

5 Which FA Cup winner was manager at Southend between 1986 and 1987, and 1988 and 1992?

6 Who did Ipswich Town defeat to win the UEFA Cup in 1981?

7 In which year did Colchester United win the FA Trophy?

8 Who is Southend's most capped player?

9 Who holds the league appearances record for Ipswich Town?

10 Who is the current director of football at Norwich City?

11 What club record did Ipswich set in March 1999?

12 What is the furthest that Southend have ever gone in the League Cup?

13 Who is Titus Bramble's brother and which Nationwide League club does he play for?

14 Where was Ipswich's Titus Bramble born?

15 What is Norwich City's best finishing position in the Premier League?

16 Who is Ipswich Town's most capped player?

17 What is Southend's longest sequence of league wins?

18 Which Italian giants visited Carrow Road in November 1993 for a UEFA Cup tie?

19 Who scored twice in Colchester's legendary FA Cup victory against Leeds in 1971?

20 Who was the Ipswich Town manager between 1990 and 1994?

Answers

Manchester City (see Quiz 53)

1 Ninth (in 1992–93). **2** Tony Book. **3** Glasgow. **4** Steve Howey. **5** Moenchengladbach. **6** Derby County. **7** 10–1 v Huddersfield in 1987. **8** Peter Barnes. **9** Newcastle United. **10** Neil Young. **11** £45,000. **12** 17 matches, between 1979 and 1980. **13** Bath City. **14** Eight. **15** Gornik Zabrze. **16** Vienna. **17** Glyn Pardoe. **18** Alan Ball. **19** Asa Hartford. **20** Tommy Johnson.

Quiz 56 **Jody Morris**

Answers – see page 570

LEVEL 3

1 Where was Jody born?

2 In which year was that?

3 From which famous football school did he graduate?

4 When did he sign for Chelsea?

5 When did make his first team debut?

6 Who were Chelsea playing that day?

7 How tall is Jody?

8 Against which club did Jody score his first goal for Chelsea?

9 In which season did Jody reach the 100 first team appearance mark for Chelsea?

10 Against which club did Jody make his FA Cup debut?

11 Jody was sent off in an England Under 21 game in 1998. Who were the opponents that day?

12 In October 1999 Jody scored in a 5–0 victory. Who were the opposition that day?

13 Against which club did Jody make his full debut in the Champions League?

14 Where did Jody go to school?

15 How many yellow cards did Jody pick up during 2000–01?

16 Jody scored in a Coca-Cola Cup fourth round match in November 1997. Who were the opponents?

17 What Chelsea honour did Jody win in 1996?

18 Who were Jody's kit sponsors during the first few years of this career?

19 How many league appearances – and those as substitute – did Jody make in 2000–01?

20 Why was Jody not considered for the England Under 21 team for the 2000 European Championship?

Answers

The West Country (see Quiz 54)

1 Plymouth Argyle. **2** Bedminster. **3** Exeter City. **4** The Gas. **5** Queen Victoria. **6** Shaun Goater. **7** Torquay United. **8** Exeter City. 9 Bristol Rovers. **10** Swindon Town. **11** Andy Cole. **12** Glenn Hoddle. **13** Lee Sharpe. **14** Bath City. **15** Four. **16** Green and black stripes. **17** Torquay United. **18** Gary Mabbutt. **19** Plymouth. **20** Bristol City.

Quiz 57 **Scottish Football**

LEVEL 3

Answers – see page 575

1 Who is Aberdeen's most capped player?

2 When did Dundee last win the Scottish League Cup?

3 Who is Hibernian's highest goalscorer?

4 What colour shirts do Kilmarnock play in?

5 What is the name of Clyde's stadium?

6 Who is the manager of Morton?

7 Which European competition did Raith Rovers play in during 1995–96?

8 Who is Celtic's most capped player?

9 Which Scottish Premier League team play in maroon shirts?

10 Who won the Scottish Cup in 1991?

11 Who is Dundee's highest goalscorer?

12 Who is Rangers' assistant manager?

13 In which town do Queen of the South play?

14 What is the capacity of East Fife's Bayview Stadium?

15 Which Frenchman opened the scoring for Rangers in the 1999 Coca-Cola Cup Final?

16 What did Stenhousemuir achieve in 1999?

17 Why was the Scottish Cup not awarded in 1909?

18 How many teams play in Falkirk?

19 Up to 2000, how many times had Rangers appeared in the Scottish League Cup final?

20 In which town do Ross County play?

Answers

Bad Boys (see Quiz 59)

1 Gary Croft. **2** Peter Storey. **3** George Graham. **4** Dwight Yorke and Andy Cole. **5** Ray Parlour. **6** Faustino Asprilla. **7** Chesterfield. **8** Ian Wright. **9** Jim Baxter. **10** George Best. **11** Edmundo. **12** Babb and Kennedy. **13** Simon Garner. **14** Sammy Nelson. **15** Paolo Rossi. **16** Jamie Lawrence. **17** Terry Fenwick. **18** Wimbledon. **19** Zvonimir Boban. **20** Eric Cantona.

Quiz 58 **Local Rivals**

Answers – see page 576

LEVEL 3

1 Which team changed their nickname in the 80s to emulate their rivals?

2 Which local rivals shared a ground and were both relegated in 1980–81?

3 Which city hosts the derby game between Piroozi and Esteghlal?

4 In which country does the derby game between Olimpia and Club Guarani take place?

5 Who plays Boca Juniors in the Buenos Aires derby?

6 Who are Ayr United's local rivals?

7 Which side play St Pauli in their derby match?

8 Marler Estates tried to merge which rival clubs in 1987?

9 How many London Underground stations separate the closest to Chelsea and Fulham's grounds?

10 Which local rivals were the Faroe Islands' only opponents from 1930–69?

11 Who are Schalke 04's local rivals?

12 Have there been more Liverpool wins, Everton wins or draws in the history of the Merseyside derby?

13 With which club do Clydebank ground-share?

14 Which local rivals of Linfield left the league in 1949?

15 Which rival side did Graeme Souness infuriate by planting his team's flag in their pitch?

16 Who are Burnley's local rivals?

17 Who are East Fife's neighbouring side?

18 For which rivals do Cambridge United reserve their greatest contempt?

19 In which city are UNAM and America local rivals?

20 Which team are Barcelona's nearest if not fiercest rivals?

Answers

Eastern Europe (see Quiz 60)

1 Hristo Stoichkov. **2** Ujpesti Dozsa. **3** Slovakia. **4** Olympiakos. **5** Slovenia. **6** Gica Popescu. **7** Yugoslavia. **8** Shakhtar Donetsk. **9** Red Star Belgrade. **10** Juventus. **11** Hansa Rostock. **12** Oleg Blokhin. **13** Dejan Savicevic. **14** Kazimierz Deyna. **15** Andrei Shevchenko. **16** Robert Prosinecki. **17** Brother-in-law. **18** Adrian Ilie. **19** Sparta Prague. **20** Dragan Stojkovic.

Quiz 59 **Bad Boys**

Answers – see page 573

LEVEL 3

1 Who was punished for driving while disqualified and trying to pass himself off as the son of snooker star Dennis Taylor?

2 Who received a six-month sentence for running a brothel in 1979?

3 Whose 1998 temporary downfall was attributed to Rune Hauge?

4 According to the *News of the World* which Manchester United players were involved in a "three-in-a-bed love romp" in 1999?

5 Who, in his wild days, was fined after an altercation with a rickshaw driver while on a Far East tour?

6 Which former Premier League star fired a gun in a crowded bar?

7 Darren Brown was chairman of which club, in trouble with the League and FA, in 2001?

8 Who trashed the referee's changing room after getting sent off in 1999?

9 Which Scot was accused of stealing the Scottish FA Cup final ball?

10 Who was arrested for drink driving outside Buckingham Palace?

11 Which Brazilian got himself in trouble for giving beer to chimps?

12 Which Irish players were arrested for damaging a police officer's car?

13 Which Blackburn Rovers goalscorer was sent to prison for disposing of cash held as matrimonial assets?

14 Who was banned for two matches for dropping his shorts to supporters?

15 Who became a hero shortly after serving a ban for match-fixing?

16 Whose criminal record led him to be banned from playing for Jamaica.

17 Which Tottenham and England defender received a four month jail sentence in 1992 for drink-driving offences?

18 Which club were fined when nine of their players dropped their shorts in a testimonial match?

19 Which Croatian international went on the run after being accused of assaulting a Serb policeman?

20 Who was arrested after a row with a 1994 World Cup official?

Answers

Scottish Football (see Quiz 57)

1 Willie Miller. **2** 1974. **3** Gordon Smith. **4** Blue and white vertical stripes. **5** Broadwood. **6** Billy Stark. **7** UEFA Cup **8** Paddy Bonner. **9** Hearts. **10** Motherwell. **11** Alan Gilzean. **12** Bert Van Lingen. **13** Dumfries. **14** 2000. **15** Stephane Guivarc'h. **16** Promotion for the first time in their history. **17** Due to rioting between Old Firm fans. **18** Two, Falkirk and East Stirlingshire. **19** 27 times. **20** Dingwall.

Quiz 60 **Eastern Europe**

Answers – see page 574

LEVEL 3

1 Who was originally banned for life for his part in the Bulgarian Cup Final brawl in 1985?

2 Which club changed their name to Ujpesti Torna Egylet in 1990?

3 Kosice, Spartak Trnava and Tatran Presov play in which country's league?

4 For which 2000 Champions League team did Slovenian Zahovic play?

5 Which country did Maribor Teatanic represent in the 1999–2000 Champions League?

6 Which Romanian defender announced his retirement from international football after Euro 2000?

7 FK Obilic surprisingly won the 1998 league title in which country?

8 Who were the Ukrainian team drawn in Arsenal's 2000–2001 Champions League group?

9 Which East European team play at the Crvena Zvezda stadium?

10 For which West European team did Poland's Zbigniew Boniek play?

11 Who were the last team to win the East German league championship?

12 Which Soviet Union goalscoring legend became manager of Olympiakos and then a Ukrainian MP?

13 Which Yugoslavian international scored in the 1994 European Cup final?

14 Which Polish captain played for Manchester City?

15 Which Dynamo Kiev striker joined AC Milan in 1997?

16 Which legendary player scored for Croatia Zagreb against Manchester United in the 1999–2000 Champions League?

17 What relation is Gica Popescu to Georghe Hagi?

18 Which Romanian played in the 2000 Champions League final?

19 Tomas Rosicky is which team's teenage playmaker?

20 Which veteran Yugoslav captain plays in Japan's J-League?

Answers

Local Rivals (see Quiz 58)

1 Crystal Palace. **2** Bristol City and Rovers. **3** Tehran. **4** Paraguay. **5** River Plate. **6** Kilmarnock. **7** Hamburg SV. **8** Fulham and QPR. **9** Two. **10** Shetland Islands. **11** Borussia Dortmund. **12** Liverpool. **13** Greenock Morton. **14** Belfast Celtic. **15** Fenebahce. **16** Blackburn Rovers. **17** Raith Rovers. **18** Peterborough United. **19** Mexico City. **20** Espanyol.

Quiz 61 **Sol Campbell**

Answers – see page 579

LEVEL 3

1 In which year did Sol make his England debut?
2 What is the name Sol short for?
3 In which city was Campbell born?
4 Which Premier League player played in the same boys' district team as Sol?
5 How many England under 21 caps did Sol earn?
6 Against which team did Sol score two goals to earn a 2–2 draw at White Hart Lane in 1998–99?
7 Which pop star did the *Daily Star* suggest Sol had unsuccessfully asked out?
8 Against which country in World Cup '98 did Sol have a goal disallowed?
9 In which position did Sol play for England against France in September 2000?
10 How many minutes did Sol play for against Scotland in Euro '96?
11 From where did Spurs sign Campbell?
12 Against which team did a Campbell own goal knock Spurs out of the UEFA Cup?
13 Which trophies, if any, has Campbell lifted as Tottenham captain?
14 Which manager brought Sol into the Spurs team?
15 What is Sol's middle name?
16 Which number shirt does Sol wear at Arsenal?
17 When was Sol first given the captaincy of England?
18 In which position did Campbell begin his Spurs career?
19 What injury kept Sol out of the England World Cup qualifiers in October 2000?
20 Against which London club did Sol score a winning header in October 2000?

Answers

The 70s (see Quiz 63)

1 George Best. **2** Gordon Banks. **3** Salonika. **4** Rangers. **5** 1977. **6** Liverpool. **7** Jim Montgomery. **8** Frank Worthington. **9** Celtic. **10** 1971. **11** Liverpool. **12** Bill Nicholson. **13** Two. **14** 1973. **15** Jan Tomaszewski. **16** Terry Paine. **17** Liverpool's Ian Callaghan. **18** Bobby Moore. **19** Chris Nicholl. **20** £400,000.

Quiz 62 **Scandinavia**

Answers – see page 580

LEVEL 3

1 Which Scandinavian team knocked Inter Milan out of the 2000–2001 Champions League qualifying rounds?

2 What nationality is Munich 1860's Erik Mykland?

3 Which club does Bent Skammelsrud play for?

4 How many footballing brothers are there in the Flo family?

5 Which Dane played in Bolton's midfield in the Premier League in 2001–02?

6 Between which months does the Norwegian league season run?

7 In which city do Swedish club AIK play?

8 Which English club did Helsingborgs beat in the 1996 UEFA Cup?

9 For which Danish club did Brian Laudrup first play league football?

10 Which country knocked England out of the 1994 World Cup?

11 Who was the England manager at the time?

12 In which country do Silkeborg – who won their first national cup final in 2001 – play?

13 Which was the last Scandinavian club to reach the European Cup final?

14 From which club did Valencia buy striker John Carew?

15 Which country do Helsingborgs come from?

16 What is the Trippeligaen?

17 What is Helsingborgs stadium called?

18 Against which Norwegian team did Chelsea's Gianluca Vialli hit five goals in two matches in 1998?

19 In which country do Trelleborgs play?

20 Which Tottenham striker was born in Norway?

Answers

Sir Alex Ferguson (see Quiz 64)

1 Arsenal. **2** Inter Milan. **3** David Elleray. **4** May 2005. **5** Queens Park. **6** East Stirlingshire. **7** 1999. **8** 1986. **9** Necaxa. **10** None. **11** Rest of the World. **12** Five. **13** St. Mirren. **14** Two. **15** 1990 FA Cup. **16** *Managing My Life*. **17** Glasgow. **18** Ron Atkinson. **19** 1997–98. **20** David Beckham.

Quiz 63 **The 70s**

LEVEL 3

Answers – see page 577

1 Who scored six goals for Manchester United against Northampton in an FA Cup match in Feburary 1970?

2 Who was voted Footballer of the Year in 1972?

3 Where did Leeds lose to AC Milan in the 1973 ECW Cup final?

4 Who won the Scottish treble in 1976?

5 In which year did Kevin Keegan leave Liverpool for Hamburg?

6 Who won the First Division title with a 3–1 victory at Molineux in May 1976, consigning Wolves to relegation at the same time?

7 Whose double save helped to win Sunderland the FA Cup in 1973?

8 Who was the First Division's top scorer in 1979?

9 Who beat Leeds in the semi-final of the European Cup in 1970?

10 In which year did Jimmy Greaves retire from football?

11 Which club provided six players for England against Switzerland in 1977?

12 Who resigned as Spurs manager in 1974?

13 How many replays did it take to settle the League Cup final of 1977 between Aston Villa and Everton?

14 When was league football first played on Sundays?

15 Of whom did Alf Ramsey say "I have never seen a better performance at Wembley by a visiting goalkeeper"?

16 Which ex-England winger retired in 1977 after 824 league games for Southampton and Hereford?

17 Who was voted Footballer of the Year in 1974?

18 Which deputy keeper saved a penalty for West Ham in a League Cup semi-final against Stoke in 1972?

19 Which Aston Villa defender scored all four goals in a 2–2 draw with Leicester in March 1976?

20 How much did Liverpool pay for Celtic's Kenny Dalglish in 1977?

Answers

Sol Campbell (see Quiz 61)

1 1996. **2**. Sulzeer. **3** London. **4** Muzzy Izzet. **5** 11. **6** Manchester United. **7** Mel C. **8** Argentina. **9** Right-back. **10** Five. **11** The FA School of Excellence. **12** Kaiserslauten. **13** The Worthington Cup. **14** Terry Venables. **15** Jeremiah. **16** 23. **17** May 1998. **18** Midfield. **19** Shoulder. **20** West Ham.

Quiz 64 **Sir Alex Ferguson**

Answers – see page 578

LEVEL 3

1 In 1999 of which team did Alex Ferguson say "the players are belligerent and like a scrap?'

2 What Champions League opponents did Alex expect to be "Scheming, cheating and ref-baiting?'

3 Which referee did Ferguson accuse of trying to rob United of the 1999 championship?

4 Which month and year has Ferguson set for his retirement?

5 At which Scottish club was Ferguson a teenage apprentice?

6 At which club did Ferguson begin his management career?

7 In which year did he become Sir Alex?

8 In which year did Ferguson take over as manager of Scotland?

9 Against which team in January 2000 was Alex Ferguson sent off?

10 How many Scotland caps did Ferguson win?

11 Who did United play in Ferguson's record-breaking 1999 testimonial?

12 How many times did he win the Manager of the Year award in the 90s?

13 Which club did Sir Alex win the Scottish First Division with in 1977?

14 How many times have Alex Ferguson's teams won the European Cup Winners Cup?

15 What was the first trophy Ferguson won with Manchester United?

16 What was the name of Ferguson's 1999 autobiography?

17 In which city was Ferguson born?

18 Who did Ferguson take over from at Manchester United?

19 Which was the only season of the 90s that Ferguson's team failed to pick up a trophy?

20 Who said: "Alex Ferguson is the best manager I've ever had at this level. Well, he's the only manager I've actually had at this level. But he's the best manager I've ever had."?

Answers

Scandinavia (see Quiz 62)

1 Helsingborg. **2** Norwegian. **3** Rosenborg. **4** Five. **5** Per Frandsen. **6** April to October. **7** Stockholm. **8** Aston Villa. **9** Brondby. **10** Holland. **11** Graham Taylor. **12** Denmark. **13** Malmo of Sweden in 1979. **14** Rosenborg. **15** Sweden. **16** The Norwegian Premier League. **17** Räsunda Stadium, Stockholm. **18** Tromso. **19** Sweden. **20** Steffen Iversen.

Quiz 65 **Premiership Stars**

Answers – see page 583

LEVEL 3

1 Which young Aston Villa and England defender was born in Hastings?

2 Which Saint went on as a second half sub and scored twice in a 3–3 draw at Old Trafford in September 1999?

3 Who top scored for Liverpool during 1999–2000?

4 Who scored twice as Chelsea beat Sunderland 4–0 on the opening day of the 1999–2000 season?

5 Which forward did West Ham buy from QPR in 1997?

6 Who made most appearances for Newcastle during 1998–99?

7 As of 1 January 2002, who has played the most Premier League games for Manchester United?

8 Which Manchester United defender missed every game but two through injury in 1999–2000?

9 Who was teh first Scotsman to play in 300 Premier League matches??

10 For which Premiership club does youngster Ashley Cole play?

11 Which player made the most clean tackles and committed the second highest number of fouls in 2000–01 season?

12 Who signed Steven Hughes from Arsenal in 1999–2000?

13 Who signed Marcus Stewart for £2.5m in summer 2000?

14 Of which club is Peter Ridsdale the chairman?

15 For which club does Eidur Gudjohnsen play?

16 Which club might have Dyer, Hughes, Speed and Lee as the midfield?

17 From whom did Tottenham sign Mauricio Taricco?

18 Who has played the most Premier League matches for Arsenal?

19 Who was Middlesbrough's Player of the Season in 1999–2000?

20 Where does Norwegian Jo Tessam play?

Answers

Ful-Back/Wing-Back (see Quiz 67)

1 Sir Alf Ramsey. **2** Gianluca Zambrotta. **3** Sampdoria. **4** Roma. **5** Winston Bogarde. **6** George Burley. **7** Andreas Brehme (1990). **8** Lee Martin. **9** Stuart Pearce. **10** Sparta Prague. **11** Anderlecht. **12** 1991. **13** Tarhar El Khalej. **14** Inter Milan. **15** Paul Breitner. **16** Antonio Cabrini. **17** Cyril Knowles. **18** Roberto Carlos. **19** Tony Dorigo. **20** Keith Newton.

Quiz 66 **Paul Scholes**

LEVEL 3

Answers – see page 584

1 In which year was Paul Scholes born?

2 Where was he born?

3 In which year did he sign trainee forms for Manchester United?

4 Against whom did he make his league debut?

5 How many goals did he score in that game?

6 In which season did he become a first-team regular at Old Trafford?

7 What is his squad number?

8 Who did Paul support as a youngster?

9 Which club award did Paul win in 1993?

10 Against whom did Paul make his full England debut?

11 What was significant about Paul's goal against Inter in March 1999?

12 Why did Paul not go to Brazil in January 1999?

13 What is the name of Paul Scholes's son?

14 Against whom did Paul score a hat-trick for England at Wembley?

15 How tall is Paul?

16 Why did Paul miss the Champions League final in 1999?

17 Paul scored in his first England match at Wembley. Who were the opposition that day?

18 Against whom did Paul score in an FA Cup final?

19 Who were the opposition when Paul was sent off in an England international in June 1999?

20 Who did Paul score against in the opening game of the 1998 World Cup?

Answers

Old Football 2 (see Quiz 68)

1 Alf Common. **2** Lord Alfred Kinnaird, 9. **3** 1938. **4** John Thomson. **5** Arsenal. **6** 1901. **7** Leeds City's. **8** 1930. **9** Spain. **10** Arsenal v Sheffield United, 1927. **11** George V. **12** Pongo Waring. **13** Manchester City. **14** Italy. **15** Hampden Park, Glasgow. **16** Hughie Gallacher. **17** Preston North End. **18** Millwall. **19** Sheffield United and Chelsea. **20** Frank Swift.

Quiz 67 **Full-Back/Wing-Back**

LEVEL 3

Answers – see page 581

1 Who was the last former full-back to manage England?

2 Which Italian full-back was sent off in a Euro 2000 semi-final?

3 With which club side is Yugoslavia's Nenad Sakic a wing-back?

4 Where does French wing back Vincent Candela play his club football?

5 Which Chelsea wing-back was signed from Barcelona?

6 Which former full-back was the Premier League Manager of the Year in 2001?

7 Which Leeds United forward became a full-back in the 1980–81 season?

8 Which Manchester United full-back scored in the 1990 FA Cup final replay?

9 Who was the last full-back to score in an FA Cup final?

10 Against which opposition did Arsenal's Silvinho score a wonder goal in their opening 2000 Champions League match?

11 From which club did Chelsea sign Celestine Babayaro?

12 In which year did Dennis Irwin make his Republic of Ireland debut?

13 What is the name of Southampton's Moroccan full-back?

14 From which club did Manchester United sign Mickael Silvestre?

15 Which full-back scored in the 1974 World Cup final?

16 Which Italian full-back missed a penalty in the 1982 World Cup final?

17 Which former England full-back died in 1991 while manager of Darlington?

18 Which wing-back scored four goals in Real Madrid's triumphant 1999–2000 Champions League campaign?

19 Which Australian-born full-back won a Championship medal with Leeds United in 1992?

20 Which Everton full-back made his last appearance for England against West Germany in the 1970 World Cup?

Answers

Premiership Stars (see Quiz 65)

1 Gareth Barry. **2** Matt Le Tissier. **3** Michael Owen. **4** Gustavo Poyet. **5** Trevor Sinclair. **6** Shay Given **7** Ryan Giggs. **8** Ronny Johnsen. **9** Gary McAllister. **10** Arsenal. **11** Olivier Dacourt. **12** Everton. **13** Ipswich Town. **14** Leeds United. **15** Chelsea. **16** Newcastle. **17** Ipswich Town. **18** Lee Dixon. **19** Paul Ince. **20** Southampton.

Quiz 68 **Old Football 2**

Answers – see page 582

LEVEL 3

1 Who was English football's first £1000 player?

2 Which player holds the record number of appearances in the FA Cup final?

3 In which year were numbered shirts first worn for league games?

4 Which Celtic keeper died after a collision with a Rangers player in 1931?

5 Of which team was Herbert Chapman manager when he died in 1934?

6 In which year did Spurs first win the FA Cup?

7 Whose players were auctioned off when the team was expelled from the league in 1919?

8 In which year did the first World Cup take place?

9 In May 1929 England lost to a foreign team for the first time. Which team?

10 What was the first match broadcast live on radio?

11 Who became the first reigning monarch to attend the Cup final, in 1914?

12 Which Aston Villa player top scored in the First Division in 1932?

13 In 1926 which club became the first to reach the FA Cup final and be relegated from the First Division in the same season?

14 Who won the World Cup in 1934?

15 Which British ground held a world record crowd of 149,547 for an international in 1937?

16 Who scored five goals for Scotland in a 7–3 victory against Ireland in 1929?

17 Who became the first English league and cup double winners, in 1888–89?

18 Who became the first Third Division side to reach the FA Cup semi-final, in 1937?

19 Who contested the "Khaki Cup final" in 1915?

20 Which Manchester City keeper was so overcome at winning the FA Cup in 1934 that he fainted?

Answers

Paul Scholes (see Quiz 66)

1 1974. **2** Salford. **3** 1991. **4** Ipswich Town. **5** Two in a 2–3 defeat. **6** 1994–95. **7** 18. **8** Oldham Athletic. **9** Young Player of the Year. **10** Italy. **11** First United player since Norman Whiteside to score on Italian soil. **12** Hernia operation. **13** Aaron Jake. **14** Poland. **15** 5 ft 7 in (170c m). **16** Suspension. **17** Moldova. **18** Newcastle. **19** Sweden. **20** Tunisia.

Quiz 69 **World Cup 1998**

LEVEL 3

Answers – see page 587

1 Who did Scotland play in their opening game?

2 Who scored an own goal in that game?

3 Who did South African play in their first match?

4 Italy drew 2–2 in their opening match of the tournament – against which other nation?

5 Who did France defeat 4–0 in a group stage match?

6 Despite beating Bulgaria 6–1 in their last group game, who was eliminated from the tournament?

7 Who won the group stage game between Germany and the USA?

8 Who topped England's Group G?

9 Which country scored their first World Cup goal, in a group stage match against Croatia?

10 Who came back from 2–0 down against Holland to get a draw and qualify for the second round?

11 What was the score in the group match between Holland and Belgium?

12 Which Mexican performed the "Bounce" during the tournament?

13 Which African country beat Spain 3–2 in a group stage match?

14 Who did Brazil beat 4–1 in a second round match?

15 Who did Dennis Bergkamp score a sensational winner against in the quarter-finals?

16 Who did the hosts defeat to secure a semi-final place?

17 Where was the Brazil v Holland semi-final played?

18 Who won the third place play-off?

19 Who did they beat to claim their place?

20 Who scored France's third goal in the Final?

Answers

Transfers (see Quiz 71)

1 Gianluigi Lentini. **2** Clive Allen. **3** Steve Simonson. **4** Michael Hughes. **5** Tore Andre Flo (Chelsea to Rangers, £12m, 2000). **6** Rushden & Diamonds. **7** Juan Sebastian Veron (Lazio to Manchester United, £28.1m). **8** Udinese. **9** Allan Clarke. **10** Edu. **11** John Hartson. **12** Highest fee set by tribunal. **13** Crystal Palace. **14** John Jensen. **15** £6m. **16** Christian Vieri. **17** Duncan Ferguson. **18** Steve Bould. **19** Keith Gillespie. **20** Alain Goma.

Quiz 70 **Euro 2000**

Answers – see page 588

LEVEL 3

1 What was the score in the group match between Germany and Romania?

2 Who defeated Spain 1–0 in a group stage match?

3 Who went 3–0 down to Slovenia and got back for a 3–3 draw in their opening match of the tournament?

4 Who scored Italy's winner against Turkey in their group stage match?

5 Who beat Yugoslavia with a 90th-minute penalty in the last game of their group?

6 Who scored twice for the Czech Republic in a group match against Denmark?

7 What was the score in the group match between Holland and France?

8 Who topped England's Group A?

9 How many teams failed to win a single game in the tournament?

10 How many penalties were awarded during the tournament?

11 Which player scored the fastest goal in the competition?

12 Which was the only team beaten by co-hosts Belgium?

13 Who scored for Sweden against Italy in their group stage match?

14 Which country conceded most goals in the tournament?

15 Which Spurs player scored for Norway against Spain in a group stage game?

16 Who did Turkey play in the quarter-finals?

17 Who were the lowest scorers in the tournement?

18 Who scored Spain's goal from the penalty spot in their quarter-final match against France?

19 Who did Italy beat in the semi-final?

20 Who scored France's 90th-minute equaliser in the final?

Answers

Non-League (see Quiz 72)

1 Duane Darby. **2** Dave McEwan. **3** Peterhead. **4** Canvey Island. **5** Dagenham and Redbridge. **6** Farnborough Town. **7** Altrincham. **8** Stevenage Borough. **9** Nuneaton Borough. **10** Emley. **11** Nigel Clough. **12** Barry Hayles. **13** Colwyn Bay. **14** Eintracht Trier. **15** WBA. **16** Ian Wright. **17** Stan Collymore. **18** Surrey. **19** Edgar Street. **20** Andy Townsend.

Quiz 71 **Transfers**

Answers – see page 585

LEVEL 3

1 Whose transfer from Torino to Milan in 1992 set a world record fee that was unbroken for four years?

2 Which £1.25 million signing played only three friendlies for Arsenal before joining Crystal Palace in 1980?

3 Which Tranmere player cost Everton the record fee for a goalkeeper in 1998?

4 Who was the first British player to be transferred under the Bosman ruling?

5 What is the biggest transfer deal involving a player moving from England to Scotland?

6 Which club did Morecambe's Justin Jackson join for £175,000 in 2000, creating a record fee between non-league clubs?

7 Which player was the subject of the largest transfer deal in the Premier League in 2001?

8 Amoroso and Appiah joined Parma from which club in June 1999?

9 Which player was the subject of a record transfer fee in 1968 and 1969?

10 Whose £6 million transfer to Arsenal collapsed after a passport fiasco?

11 Medicals stopped whose moves to Rangers and Tottenham in 2000?

12 Which transfer record does Chris Bart-Williams hold?

13 Which club sold Gareth Southgate and Chris Armstrong in 1994?

14 Which Dane was one of George Graham's "bung" transfer deals?

15 West Ham bought Marc Vivien Foe for £3.5 million in 1999. How much did they receive for him six months later?

16 Who was transferred three times from 1997–2000 for over £60 million?

17 Who is the most expensive Scotsman ever?

18 Which player did not receive a free transfer in 2000: Steve Bould, Peter Atherton or John Scales?

19 Who went to Newcastle as part of Andy Cole's move to Manchester Utd?

20 For which player did Fulham pay Newcastle £4 million in March 2001?

Answers

World Cup 1998 (see Quiz 69)

1 Brazil. **2** Tommy Boyd. **3** France. **4** Chile. **5** Saudi Arabia. **6** Spain. **7** Germany won 2–0. **8** Romania. **9** Jamaica. **10** Mexico. **11** 0–0. **12** Cuauhtemoc Blanco. **13** Nigeria. **14** Chile. **15** Argentina. **16** Italy. **17** Marseille. **18** Croatia. **19** Holland. **20** Emmanuel Petit.

Quiz 72 **Non-League**

LEVEL 3

Answers – see page 586

1 Who was the Nationwide Conference's leading scorer in 2000–01?

2 Who did Tottenham sign from Dulwich Hamlet in 1999?

3 Who won the Scottish Highland League in 1999–2000?

4 Who won the 2001 FA Umbro Challenge Trophy?

5 Who drew 1–1 with Charlton Athletic in the 1999–2000 FA Cup?

6 Which Hampshire team were the 2000–01 Ryman League winners?

7 Which 80s Conference champions were relegated to the Unibond League in 1999–2000?

8 Who are the only Conference winners since 1986 not to have played League football?

9 From which non-league club did Derby County sign Malcolm Christie?

10 Which Yorkshire club took West Ham to a replay in the FA Cup third round in 1999?

11 Who is Burton Albion's manager?

12 Which 2000–2001 Fulham goalscorer played for Stevenage Borough?

13 Which Welsh team play in the Unibond League?

14 Which German non-league team beat Schalke 04 and Borussia Dortmund in the 1996–97 German Cup?

15 Which League team went out of the third round of the FA Cup in 1991 to Woking?

16 Which 90s England international had joined Crystal Palace from Greenwich Borough in 1985?

17 Which 90s England international joined Crystal Palace from Stafford Rangers in 1990?

18 In which county do Corinthian Casuals play home games?

19 What is the name of Hereford's United ground?

20 Which Irish captain started his career at Welling and then Weymouth?

Answers

Euro 2000 (see Quiz 70)

1 1–1. **2** Norway. **3** Yugoslavia. **4** Inzaghi. **5** Spain. **6** Vladimir Smicer. **7** 3–2 to Holland. **8** Portugal. **9** Four. **10** 13 (8 were scored). **11** Paul Scholes. **12** Sweden. **13** Henrik Larsson. **14** Yugoslavia, nine goals. **15** Steffen Iversen. **16** Portugal. **17** Denmark, no goals. **18** Mendieta. **19** Holland. **20** Sylvain Wiltord.

Quiz 73 **Who Did What? 4**

Answers – see page 591

LEVEL 3

1 Who said "I know Tony Adams is playing because he is the only name I know. All these Viallis, Vieiras and Viagras"?

2 Which Portuguese player signed for Spurs from Sporting Lisbon?

3 Which club completed a post-war record of 12 successive home league wins in April 1999?

4 Who is the longest-serving club chaplain?

5 Which club scored seven goals in 25 minutes in an FA Cup match against Southport in 1932?

6 Which Leyton Orient player played for France against England in 1992?

7 Who scored five goals for Gillingham in a league game at Burnley in February 1999?

8 Who was the first English league club to tour South America?

9 Who set a club record of 28 games undefeated in 1984–85?

10 Who won their first match at Villa Park for 63 years in February 1999?

11 Who scored a hat-trick on his debut for Bristol Rovers in 1977?

12 What did Aston Villa do in a match against Celta Vigo in October 1998?

13 Who was the top scorer in Portuguese football from 1997 to 2000?

14 Who scored a hat-trick for Portugal against Germany at Euro 2000?

15 Who left Dortmund for Schalke in summer 2000?

16 Who scored twice for Vasco Da Gama against Manchester United in the FIFA World Club Championship in January 2000?

17 Who won the Portuguese championship for five years in a row between 1995 and 1999?

18 With which club did Brazilian captain Dunga begin his career?

19 Which keeper joined Brescia in summer 2000?

20 Who were Brazilian champions in 1999?

Answers

Dennis Bergkamp (see Quiz 75)

1 1998 World Cup. **2** Tottenham. **3** Two. **4** Jürgen Klinsmann. **5** One. **6** Norwich. **7** £7.5 million. **8** Southampton. **9** Argentina. **10** Three. **11** Cup Winners Cup. **12** A fear of flying. **13** Quarter-finals. **14** Kanu. **15** Denis Law. **16** None. **17** 1998. **18** September 1997. **19** Wim Jonk. **20** 1990.

Quiz 74 **International Legends**

LEVEL 3

Answers – see page 592

1 Who introduced *catenaccio* defending to Italian football during the 1960s?
2 Which Italian defender was known as the "Emperor of Milan"?
3 Which Spanish player was known as "The Vulture"?
4 Who scored the winner for AC Milan in the 1990 European Cup final?
5 Which Romanian midfielder was sent off playing against Arsenal in the 2000 UEFA Cup Final??
6 Complete the great 1970s French midfield line-up: Giresse, Platini and...?
7 Which legendary German team won three European Cups in a row?
8 Which Dutchman scored the winner for Barcelona in the 1992 European Cup final aganst Sampdoria?
9 Of which Argentinian-born player was it said that "He is the greatest player I have ever seen. The things he does in a match will never be equalled"?
10 Whose legendary forward line of the 1950s was known as *La Maquina*?
11 Whose life story was told in a film entitled *Sua Majestade o Rei*?
12 Who captained Bayern Munich to victory in the 1967 ECWC?
13 Which Belgian midfielder holds the record for international appearances for his country?
14 Which Italian legend was known as *Il Bambino D'Oro*?
15 Which Mexican of the 1980s was legendary for somersaulting after he had scored?
16 Apart from Pele, who is the only other player to score in four World Cups?
17 Who inspired Barcelona to a 5–0 victory against rivals Real Madrid in his first season as manager?
18 Which Italian player was voted Man of the Match in the 1982 World Cup final defeat of West Germany?
19 Which two London clubs did the 1998 World Cup Golden Boot winner play for?
20 Who top scored in the 1978 World Cup finals, including two goals in the final for Argentina against Holland?

Answers

Who Did What 5 (see Quiz 76)

1 Daniel Amokachi. **2** Shimizu S-Pulse. **3** Bill Slater, 1951. **4** Blackburn Rovers. **5** Lincoln City. **6** Barnet. **7** Swindown Town. **8** Anderlecht. **9** Red Star Belgrade. **10** Craig Johnston. **11** David Platt. **12** Tony Ford. **13** Lee Clark. **14** Teofilo Cubillas. **15** Jan Tomaszewski. **16** Rushden and Diamonds. **17** Manchester City. **18** Peru. **19** Neville Southall. **20** Michael Owen.

Quiz 75 **Dennis Bergkamp**

Answers – see page 589

LEVEL 3

1 In which competition did Bergkamp become Holland's highest scorer?

2 Which club did Dennis support as a boy?

3 How many goals did Bergkamp score against England at Wembley in 1993?

4 Who did Bergkamp replace at Inter Milan?

5 How many championships did Bergkamp win at Ajax?

6 Which English team did Bergkamp, then at Inter, score against in both UEFA Cup legs in 1993?

7 How much did Bergkamp cost Arsenal?

8 Against whom did Bergkamp score a hat-trick in his first season at Arsenal?

9 A goal against which team earned Bergkamp the 1998 World Cup Goal of the Tournament?

10 For how many years running was Bergkamp the Dutch league's top scorer?

11 Which trophies did Bergkamp win with Inter Milan?

12 What does Bergkamp refuse to do?

13 Apart from the final, what was the only round of the 1999–2000 UEFA Cup in which Bergkamp failed to score?

14 Which substitute replaced Bergkamp in the 1999–2000 UEFA Cup final?

15 Which footballer is Bergkamp named after?

16 How many goals did Dennis score in Euro 2000?

17 In what year was Bergkamp voted the Football Writers and PFA Footballer of the Year?

18 When was Bergkamp given first, second and third places in *Match Of The Day*'s goal of the month competition?

19 Which Ajax team-mate signed with Bergkamp for Inter Milan?

20 In which year did Bergkamp make his international debut?

Answers

Who Did What? 4 (see Quiz 73)

1 Jack Walker. **2** Jose Dominguez. **3** Sunderland. **4** Rev. Michael Chantry at Oxford Utd. **5** Newcastle. **6** Amara Simba. **7** Robert Taylor. **8** Exeter City in 1914. **9** Everton. **10** Coventry City. **11** Bobby Gould. **12** Fielded a whole team of players born in England. **13** Mario Jardel. **14** Sergio Conceicao. **15** Andy Moller. **16** Romario. **17** Porto. **18** Internacional of Porto Alegre. **19** Pavel Srnicek. **20** Corinthians.

Quiz 76 **Who Did What? 5**

Answers – see page 590

LEVEL 3

1 Who was Nigeria's top scorer in the 1994 World Cup?

2 Which Japanese team did Ossie Ardiles manage in 1996?

3 Who was the last amateur to play in an FA Cup Final?

4 Which Nationwide team had two players in England's 2000 European Under-21 championship squad?

5 Who were the first team to be automatically relegated from the league?

6 Men's magazine *Loaded* sponsored which now former Nationwide League team?

7 *The 69er* is a fanzine of which Nationwide League club?

8 Who beat West Ham in the 1976 Cup Winners Cup final?

9 Darko Pancev's penalty won the European Cup for which team?

10 Which former Liverpool player helped develop the "Predator" football boot?

11 Which England international was sold four times in the 90s for fees amounting to over £21 million?

12 Which Rochdale player received the PFA merit award in 1999?

13 Which Sunderland player was transfer-listed after wearing a "sad Mackem b******s" t-shirt to Wembley?

14 Which Peruvian international played for Fort Lauderdale Strikers?

15 Who was Poland's goalkeeper in their 1973 match against England at Wembley?

16 Who were runners-up to Kidderminster Harriers in the 1999–2000 Vauxhall Conference?

17 Which club used to play at Pink Bank Lane and Reddish Lane?

18 Who were ranked higher by FIFA in January 2000, Nigeria or Peru?

19 Who made a return to the Premiership for Bradford City against Leeds in March 2000?

20 Who made his England debut in a 2–0 defeat by Chile at Wembley in 1998?

Answers

International Legends (see Quiz 74)

1 Helenio Herrera. **2** Franco Baresi. **3** Emilio Butragueno. **4** Frank Rijkaard. **5** Gheorghe Hagi. **6** Tigana. **7** Bayern Munich. **8** Ronald Koeman. **9** Alfredo Di Stefano. **10** River Plate's. **11** Eusebio. **12** Franz Beckenbauer. **13** Jan Ceulemans. **14** Gianni Rivera. **15** Hugo Sanchez. **16** Uwe Seeler. **17** Johan Cruyff. **18** Marco Tardelli. **19** Arsenal and West Ham (Davor Suker). **20** Mario Kempes.

Quiz 77 **Glenn Hoddle**

LEVEL 3

Answers – see page 595

1 Which Tottenham legend has been credited with "discovering" Hoddle?

2 Which England keeper did Hoddle beat for his first League goal?

3 Which trophy did Hoddle help win in 1975?

4 Against which team did Hoddle score the 1980 *Match of the Day* Goal of the Season?

5 Which Arsenal player was Hoddle's England roommate?

6 Which player was preferred to Hoddle in most of England's 1982 World Cup games?

7 A defeat against which country in 1988 marked the end of Hoddle's international career?

8 Which Cups did Hoddle win with Tottenham?

9 Which manager took Hoddle to Monaco?

10 Who did Hoddle replace as manager of Swindon Town?

10 Which team did Hoddle's Swindon Town beat in the 1993 play-offs?

11 In which season did Hoddle join Chelsea as player manager?

12 Which club defeated Hoddle's Chelsea in the Cup-winners Cup semi-final?

13 Who did Hoddle appoint as England's assistant manager?

14 Which player did Hoddle sign from his previous club in autumn 2001?

15 What was the name of Hoddle's controversial faith healer?

16 How old was Hoddle when he was appointed England manager?

17 Which creative player was given one last chance for England by Hoddle?

18 Which striker did Hoddle sign for Chelsea for £1.25 million?

19 Who were England's last opposition under Hoddle's management?

20 Who did Hoddle sell to Everton a month after taking over at Southampton?

Answers

Penalty! (see Quiz 79)

1 Mark Crossley. **2** Ioan Ganea. **3** David Platt. **4** Turkey. **5** Georghe Hagi. **6** Deportivo La Coruña. **7** Rudi Voller. **8** Jose Luis Chilavert. **9** Antonin Panenka. **10** Mike Newell **11** Patrik Berger. **12** Darren Barnard. **13** Eric Cantona. **14** Emmanuel Kunde. **15** Ally McCoist. **16** Lee Dixon. **17** Francis Lee. **18** Dwight Yorke. **19** Erland Johnsen **20** Frank de Boer.

Quiz 78 **True or False?**

LEVEL 3

Answers – see page 596

1 Reigning champions Leeds United failed to win an away match in 1992–93.

2 "Dixie" Dean's real name was Albert.

3 Ferenc Puskas scored hat-tricks in two European Cup finals.

4 Preston North End have the biggest pitch in the Football League.

5 Bobby Robson was sacked by PSV after taking them to the 1993 UEFA Cup Final.

6 Gheorghe Hagi played for Barcelona and Real Madrid.

7 Pierre van Hooijdonk left Nottingham Forest on a free transfer.

8 Alan Hansen captained Scotland in the 1986 World Cup.

9 Chelsea signed Gabriele Ambrosetti from Vicenza.

10 George Cohen and Ray Wilson are the only 1966 England World Cup heroes not to have been decorated.

11 Jeff Winter was on the 2000–01 FIFA refereeing list.

12 Spartak, Dynamo and Lokomotiv Moscow all took part in the 2000–01 Champions League.

13 Opel have sponsored AC Milan, Bayern Munich, Paris St Germain and the Republic of Ireland.

14 Steve Stone scored twice on his first two full appearances for England.

15 Relegated Blackpool had three players in the PFA Divisional Team of the Season in 1999–2000.

16 Arsenal paid less to bring Thierry Henry to Highbury than Juventus paid Monaco for him in 1999.

17 Fabien Barthez moved to Manchester United for a world record fee for goalkeeper.

18 Clydebank and Greenock Morton shared grounds in 1999–2000.

19 Roy Keane was sent off twice in Ireland's 2000 Nike Cup in the USA.

20 Davor Suker and Patrick Vieira both missed in the penalty shoot-out in the 2000 UEFA Cup final.

Answers

Team Colours (see Quiz 80)

1 Light and dark blue quarters. **2** Blue. **3** Sheffield United. **4** Red and white. **5** Liberia **6** Green. **7** Barcelona. **8** South Africa. **9** Yellow. **10** Red. **11** Claret and sky blue. **12** The Dell. **13** White. **14** All white. **15** Dark Blue. **16** Indigo blue (grey). **17** Jimmy Hill. **18** Greece. **19** Atletico Madrid. **20** Inter Milan.

Quiz 79 **Penalty!**

LEVEL 3

Answers – see page 593

1 Who saved Gary Lineker's penalty in the 1991 FA Cup final?
2 Who scored Romania's last-minute penalty against England in Euro 2000?
3 Which England star missed a penalty in his first match in the Italian league?
4 A converted penalty by Tayfur in the play-offs helped which team to Euro 2000?
5 Who scored a penalty against Leeds United at Elland Road in the 2000 UEFA Cup semi-final?
6 Miroslav Djukic's 1994 missed penalty cost who a championship?
7 A foul on which player earned a penalty for West Germany in the 1990 World Cup final?
8 Which keeper scored a hat-trick of penalties in Argentina in 1999?
9 Whose penalty won Czechoslovakia the 1976 European Championship?
10 Who scored a penalty in the play-offs to send Blackburn to the Premiership in 1992?
11 Who scored a penalty in the Euro '96 final?
12 Which Barnsley player missed a penalty in the 2000 play-offs?
13 Who was the only person in the 20th century to score two penalties in an FA Cup final?
14 Who scored Cameroon's penalty against England in the 1990 World Cup?
15 Which Kilmarnock player's only goal in 1999–2000 came from a penalty?
16 Whose converted penalty set off a mass brawl at Highbury in 1990?
17 Who has scored the most penalties in a English league season?
18 Whose cheeky penalty knocked Sheffield United out of the 1996 FA Cup?
19 Who earned a controversial penalty for Chelsea against Leicester City in the FA Cup in 1997?
20 Who scored Holland's penalty against the Czech Republic in Euro 2000?

Answers

Glenn Hoddle (see Quiz 77)

1 Martin Chivers. **2** Peter Shilton. **3** World Youth Cup. **4** Nottingham Forest. **5** Graham Rix. **6** Graham Rix. **7** USSR. **8** FA and League. **9** Arsène Wenger. **10** Osvaldo Ardiles. **11** Leicester City. **11** 1993–94. **12** Real Zaragoza. **13** John Gorman. **14** Dean Richards. **15** Eileen Drewery. **16** 38. **17** Matthew Le Tissier. **18** Gavin Peacock. **19** Czech Republic **20** Mark Hughes.

Quiz 80 **Team Colours**

Answers – see page 594

LEVEL 3

1 What colour are Wycombe Wanderers shirts?

2 What colour shirts did Manchester United wear in the 1968 European Cup final?

3 Which Division One club's 2000–2001 away kit was gold and lilac?

4 What colours do Kidderminster Harriers play in?

5 Which country's entire squad wore red boots in the 1996 African Cup of Nations?

6 Which colour shirts do Slovenia wear?

7 Which major European club refuse to have a sponsorship name on their shirts?

8 Which African team play in gold and black shirts?

9 What colour were Celtic's 2000–2001 away shirts?

10 What is the colour of the sash on River Plate's shirts?

11 What colours did Crystal Palace play in before Malcolm Allison changed them?

12 At which ground did Manchester United wear grey shirts for the first half before changing them for the second half because they were "bad luck"?

13 In what colour shirts do Russia play?

14 What is the least successful FA Cup final colour combination?

15 What colour were Tottenham Hotspur's 2000–2001 away shirts?

16 In which colour shirts did England play Germany in the Euro '96 semi-final?

17 Which Coventry manager changed their colours to Sky Blue?

18 Lazio's colours are based on which country's flag?

19 Which Spanish club's nickname *Los Colchomeros* (mattress makers) derives from their shirt colours?

20 Which Italian club's nickname *Negrazzurri* derives from their shirt colours?

Answers

True or False? (see Quiz 78)

1 True. **2** False. **3** True. **4** False. **5** False. **6** True. **7** False. **8** False. **9** True. **10** False. **11** False. **12** False. **13** True. **14** True. **15** False. **16** True. **17** False. **18** True. **19** False. **20** True.

Quiz 81 **Strikers**

Answers – see page 599

LEVEL 3

1 Who scored twice for Liverpool against Wimbledon in April 2000?

2 Who top scored for Charlton as they won promotion from the First Division in 1999–2000?

3 Who scored a sensational goal for Rangers in Monaco in a 2001 Champions League group match?

4 Which Southampton player scored 10 goals in 10 Premier League matches in November and December 2000?

5 Against whom did Sergei Rebrov score his first goals for Spurs?

6 From which club did Southampton sign Marian Pahars?

7 Who scored a spectacular 20-yarder for Fiorentina against Manchester United in the Champions League in November 1999?

8 Who scored for England in a friendly match in Paris in September 2000?

9 Who scored 30 goals for Sunderland in his first season of Premier League football, 1999–2000?

10 How many goals did Flo and Zola get between them for Chelsea in 1999–2000?

11 How many goals did Mark Viduka score for Celtic in his 37-game Scottish League career?

12 At which club did the much travelled striker Lee Bradbury finiish the 2000–01 season?

13 Which Villa striker broke his neck in a freak accident in 1999?

14 Who scored twice for Newcastle against Man United in February 2000?

15 Which Everton striker was sent off in the Merseyside derby in September 1999?

16 Who top scored for Charlton Athletic in 2000–01?

17 Who scored Ipswich Town's winner against Internazionale in the 2001–02 UEFA Cup third round, first leg, at Portman Road?

18 Who was the 1999–2000 Scottish Golden Boot winner?

19 For which team did Cameroonian stiker Patrick Suffo sign in summer 2000?

20 Which former Manchester United apprentice scored 25 goals for Preston during 1999–2000?

Answers

Novices (see Quiz 83)

1 Steve Moran. **2** Gareth Barry. **3** Lee Bowyer. **4** Ashley Cole. **5** Roque Santa Cruz. **6** David Nish. **7** Jimmy Greaves. **8** Seventeen. **9** Eighteen. **10** Twenty-one. **11** Francis Jeffers. **12** Three. **13** Shaun Wright-Phillips. **14** Titus Bramble. **15** Fowler and Giggs. **16** Jermaine Defoe. **17** Andy Gray. **18** Kenny Miller. **19** Seth Johnson. **20** Lee Sharpe.

Quiz 82 **Politics**

Answers – see page 600

LEVEL 3

1 Which manager reacted with disgust when compared with Margaret Thatcher?
2 Who was West Germany's 1970s Marxist defender?
3 Which Arsenal star appeared at an 80s Conservative party rally at Wembley?
4 Which manager sent a congratulations message to John Major from his sick bed in 1992?
5 Which of Sunderland's 1973 FA Cup winning team later went into politics?
6 Which country's referees went on strike in 1997?
7 Which political issue contributed to England's lowest home crowd, against Chile in 1989?
8 Politicians Michael Foot and David Owen support which club?
9 Which former Premier League manager insisted he was a communist?
10 Which Scottish team is supported by two 2000 cabinet ministers?
11 Who was the 80s Minister of Sport who tried to introduce identity cards?
12 Who links the Green Party to Coventry City?
13 Which apartheid apologist MP was a chairman at Luton Town?
14 Which politician was behind the dubious success of Marseilles in the early 1990s?
15 Why was Barcelona able to revert to its Catalan name in 1975?
16 Who wore a slogan under his West Ham shirt supporting striking Essex firemen in 1998?
17 Which club were forced to add Ambrosiana to their name to dilute their Leninist connotations?
18 Which football figure started the Forza Italia political party?
19 Which country withdrew from 1996 African Cup of Nations for political reasons?
20 Who dedicated his World and European Footballer of the Year awards to Nelson Mandela?

Answers

Veterans (see Quiz 84)

1 Mark Walters. **2** Dragan Stojkovic. **3** David Watson. **4** David Seaman. **5** Swansea City. **6** Blackpool. **7** Tony Parks. **8** Barry Horne. **9** Peter Davenport. **10** Bobby Mimms. **11** Chris Fairclough. **12** Peter Schmeichel. **13** McCall and Saunders. **14** Tony Cottee. **15** Gascoigne. **16** Stuart Pearce. **17** 47. **18** John Burridge. **19** Pat Bonner. **20** Lothar Matthäus.

Quiz 83 **Novices**

Answers – see page 597

LEVEL 3

1 Which Southampton forward, a PFA Young Player of the Year, never won an international cap?

2 Who was the youngest member of England's Euro 2000 squad?

3 Who left Charlton in a then record British fee for a teenager?

4 Which 19-year-old scored his first goal for Arsenal in September 2000?

5 Which Bayern Munich signing was the world record fee for a 17-year-old?

6 Who is the youngest FA Cup final captain?

7 Who is the youngest player to score 100 League goals?

8 How old was Pele when he played in the 1958 World Cup finals?

9 How old was Michael Owen when he scored his first England goal?

10 How old was Duncan Edwards when he died in the Munich air disaster?

11 Who is the youngest: Alan Smith, Michael Owen or Francis Jeffers?

12 How many players in Leeds United's 2000 semi-final matches against Galatasaray were under 21?

13 Which 17-year-old made his Manchester City debut in 1999–2000?

14 Which 19-year-old Ipswich Town defender scored his first Premier League goal in 2000–01?

15 Which two players have won the PFA Young Player of the Year award on two occasions?

16 Which 17-year-old scored his first goal for West Ham in September 2000?

17 Who won the PFA Player and Young Player of the Year awards in the same season?

18 Who was the Scotland's 2000 Young Player of the Year?

19 Which Derby County player was booked in England's opening two fixtures of the under 21 Euro 2000?

20 Which 2000–2001 Premier League player won all eight of his England caps before he was 24?

Answers

Strikers (see Quiz 81)

1 Emile Heskey. **2** Andy Hunt. **3** Giovanni van Bronckhorst. **4** James Beattie. **5** Everton. **6** Skonto Riga **7** Batistuta. **8** Michael Owen. **9** Kevin Phillips. **10** 14. **11** 30. **12** Portsmouth. **13** Dion Dublin. **14** Alan Shearer. **15** Francis Jeffers. **16** Jonatan Joahnsson. **17** Alun Armstrong. **18** Celtic's Mark Viduka. **19** Sheffield Wednesday. **20** Jon Macken.

Quiz 84 **Veterans**

Answers – see page 598

LEVEL 3

1 Which former Rangers, Liverpool and England player was at Bristol Rovers in 2000–01?

2 Which Euro 2000 captain played in Euro 84?

3 Who was the eldest defender in Everton's 2000–01 squad?

4 Which member of England's Euro 2000 squad was born before the 1966 World Cup victory?

5 For which team is Nick Cusack a veteran midfielder?

6 For which team were over 35s Paul Beesley and Mike Newell playing in 2000–01?

7 Which 2000 Halifax player won a UEFA Cup winners medal?

8 Which former Everton FA Cup winner joined League newcomers Kidderminster Harriers?

9 Which Macclesfield Town player won his only England cap in 1985?

10 Which Mansfield Town player has two League Championship medals?

11 Which 37-year-old 2000–01 York City defender has a League champions medal?

12 Which goalkeeper played in both a 1985 and a 2000 League Championship winning side, in different countries?

13 Who were Bradford City's 2000–01 two over 35-year-old internationals?

14 Who last played for England in 1989, but scored 13 goals in the Premier League in 1999–2000?

15 Which is the oldest player: Paul Gascoigne, Paul Ince or Brian Deane?

16 Which 2000 England player was first capped in 1987?

17 How old was Peter Shilton when he made his last League appearance?

18 Who is the oldest player to have played in the Premier League?

19 Who spent 19 seasons at Celtic between 1978 and 1997?

20 Who played in the 1987 and 1999 European Cup finals?

Answers

Politics (see Quiz 82)

1 Alex Ferguson. **2** Paul Breitner. **3** Charlie Nicholas. **4** Graeme Souness. **5** Vic Halom. **6** Spain. **7** Underground strike. **8** Plymouth Argyle. **9** Egil Olsen. **10** Raith Rovers. **11** Colin Moynihan. **12** David Icke. **13** David Evans. **14** Bernard Tapie. **15** Franco died. **16** Ian Wright. **17** Inter Milan. **18** Silvio Berlusconi. **19** Nigeria. **20** Ruud Gullit.

Quiz 85 **Who Played For?**

LEVEL 3

Answers – see page 603

1 Liverpool, Wrexham, Chelsea, Huddersfield Town and Wales?

2 Arsenal, Manchester United, Ajax, Derby, Le Havre, Blackburn Rovers and Republic of Ireland?

3 Spurs, Watford, Real Mallorca, WBA and Northern Ireland?

4 Newcastle, Nottingham Forest, Reading, Manchester City and Northern Ireland?

5 CSKA Sofia, Barcelona, Parma, NY-NJ MetroStars and Bulgaria?

6 Tonnerre Yaounde, St Denis, Monaco, Bastia, Montpellier and Cameroon?

7 Montpellier, Everton, Marseille and Nigeria?

8 Orient, WBA, Wimbledon, Real Madrid and England?

9 Sampdoria, Juventus, Chelsea and Italy?

10 Manchester United, Newcastle, Blackburn Rovers and Northern Ireland?

11 Cambridge Utd, Manchester United, Coventry City, Aston Villa and England?

12 Southampton, Blackburn Rovers, Leicester City, Stockport County and England?

13 Auxerre, Newcastle, Rangers, Guingamp and France?

14 Borussia Monchengladbach, Inter Milan and Germany?

15 Feyenoord, PSV, AC Milan, Sampdoria, Chelsea and Holland?

16 Borussia Monchengladbach, Barcelona, Charlton and Denmark?

17 Crystal Palace, Arsenal, Luton Town, Aberdeen, Chelsea and Wales?

18 Crystal Palace, Leeds United, Bradford City and Scotland?

19 Flamengo, Deportivo La Coruna, Botafogo, Cruzeiro, Vitoria and Brazil?

20 West Ham, Spurs, Norwich City, Sheffield United and England?

Answers

Rovers & Rangers (see Quiz 87)

1 Tranmere. **2** Blackburn. **3** QPR. **4** Glasgow. **5** Bristol. **6** Blackburn. **7** QPR. **8** Bristol. **9** Raith. **10** Berwick. **11** QPR. **12** Tranmere. **13** QPR. **14** Bristol. **15** QPR. **16** Blackburn. **17** Doncaster. **18** Bristol. **19** Glasgow. **20** Tranmere.

Quiz 86 **Managers**

Answers – see page 604

LEVEL 3 

1 Which former Coventry City player took over as manager of Solihull Borough in January 2000?

2 Which Ajax coach gave a debut to Marco Van Basten?

3 Which former England goalscorer managed Leeds United in their 1955–56 promotion season?

4 At which League club did Ian Atkins take over as manager in June 2000?

5 Who was the Internazionale Milan's coach in December 2001?

6 In 1995 who was the last non-Celtic or Rangers Scottish Manager of the Year?

7 Which Italian club has Graeme Souness managed?

8 Which Irish club did Geoff Hurst manage after leaving WBA?

9 Which manager had his autumn 2001 resignation rejected by the club chairman?

10 Who was Belgium's Euro 2000 manager?

11 Which manager was fined by the FA after indiscretions at the 2000 Worthington Cup Final?

12 Bela Guttmann steered which club to European success in the 60s?

13 Which former Arsenal and England striker led Chelsea to their 1954–55 League title?

14 Which club did Malcolm Crosby manage for 27 days in 1998?

15 At which club was Craig Brown assistant manager from 1972–77?

16 Who was Cameroon's coach in the 2000 African Cup of Nations?

17 Which former England striker was sacked by Doncaster Rovers 12 days into the 1997–8 season?

18 For how many games did John Toshack manage Wales in 1994?

19 How much compensation did Tottenham pay Leeds United for George Graham?

20 Which two relegated clubs did Billy McNeill manage in 1986–87?

Answers

Men of Many Clubs (see Quiz 88)

1 10. **2** Burnley. **3** Eric Nixon in 1986–87. **4** Seven. **5** Gordon Cowans. **6** Marco Branca. **7** Dean Saunders. **8** Benito Carbone. **9** 12. **10** Chester, Liverpool, Juventus, Leeds, Newcastle, Sheffield Utd and Wrexham. **11** Three. **12** Eight. **13** Brian Laudrup. **14** Eric Cantona. **15** Paolo Di Canio. **16** Bontcho Guentchev. **17** Paul Ince. **18** Mark Hateley. **19** Nine. **20** Peter Davenport.

Quiz 87 **Rovers & Rangers**

Answers – see page 601

LEVEL 3

1 Which Rovers play in Birkenhead?
2 For which Rovers does Derek Fazackerley hold the appearances record?
3 For which Rangers does Chris Kiwomya lead the line?
4 Of which Rangers is Dick Advocaat the manager?
5 Which Rovers play at the Memorial Stadium?
6 Which Rovers are managed by Graeme Souness?
7 For which Rangers is Alan McDonald the most capped player?
8 Malcolm Allison managed which Rovers between 1992 and 1993?
9 Which Rovers play at Stark's Park?
10 Which Rangers beat Rangers in a Scottish Cup match in 1966–67?
11 That year another Rangers won the League Cup in England. Which one?
12 Which Rovers won the Leyland Daf trophy in 1990?
13 Which Rangers were originally called St Jude's?
14 Which Rovers used to play at Eastville?
15 Which Rangers beat Partizan Belgrade 6–2 in the 1984–85 UEFA Cup?
16 Which Rovers played West Ham in the League War Cup final in 1940?
17 Which Rovers lost their place in the football league in 1998?
18 Which Rovers finished bottom of Division One in 1992–93?
19 Which Rangers lost twice to Ajax in the 1996–97 European Cup competition?
20 Which Rovers were originally called Belmont AFC?

Answers

Who Played For? (see Quiz 85)

1 Joey Jones. **2** Frank Stapleton. **3** Gerry Armstrong. **4** Tommy Wright. **5** Hristo Stoichkov. **6** Roger Milla. **7** Ibrahim Bakbayoko. **8** Laurie Cunningham. **9** Gianluca Vialli. **10** Keith Gillespie. **11** Dion Dublin. **12** Tim Flowers. **13** Stephane Guivarc'h. **14** Lothar Matthäus. **15** Ruud Gullit. **16** Allan Simonsen. **17** Peter Nicholas. **18** David Hopkin. **19** Bebeto. **20** Martin Peters.

Quiz 88 **Men of Many Clubs**

LEVEL 3

Answers – see page 602

1 For how many clubs has striker Steve Claridge played?
2 Where did Arsenal's Lee Dixon begin his career?
3 Which keeper played for five clubs in four divisions in one season?
4 For how many clubs did David Platt play for during his career?
5 Which player had three spells at Aston Villa?
6 Which forward played for eight Italian clubs before joining Middlesbrough?
7 Which Welsh striker started his career in Wales, played in England, Turkey and Portugal, then returned to play for Bradford City?
8 Who played for Torino, Napoli and Inter before joining Sheff Wed?
9 For how many clubs did keeper Les Sealey play?
10 Name Ian Rush's seven clubs.
11 For how many countries did Ladislao Kubala play?
12 Striker Marco Gabbiadini has played for how many clubs?
13 Which great Danish striker played only seven games for Chelsea before leaving for FC Copenhagen in 1998?
14 Who won championship medals with different clubs in two seasons at the beginning of the 1990s?
15 Who went from Juventus to AC Milan, Celtic, Sheff Wed, and West Ham?
16 Which 1994 World Cup semi-finalist played for Etur in his native Bulgaria, Sporting Lisbon, Ipswich Town, Luton Town, CSKA Sofia and Hendon before 2000?
17 Who started his career at West Ham, moved to Man Utd, then to Inter, then to Liverpool and then to Middlesbrough?
18 Which striker started his career at Coventry, then played in Italy, France and Scotland before finishing at Hull City?
19 For how many teams has defender Noel Blake played?
20 Which striker played for Forest, Man Utd, Middlesbrough, Sunderland, Airdrie, St Johnstone, Stockport and Macclesfield?

Answers

Managers (see Quiz 86)

1 David Busst. **2** Johan Cruyff. **3** Raich Carter. **4** Carlisle United. **5** Hector Cuper. **6** Jimmy Nicholl. **7** Torino. **8** Cork City. **9** Steve Bruce. **10** Robert Waseige. **11** John Aldridge. **12** Benfica. **13** Ted Drake. **14** Oxford United. **15** Motherwell. **16** Pierre Lechantre. **17** Kerry Dixon. **18** One. **19** £3 million. **20** Manchester City and Aston Villa.

Quiz 89 **Glasgow Rangers**

Answers – see page 607

LEVEL 3

1 In which year did Rangers win their only European trophy?

2 Who did Dick Advocaat take over from as manager at Ibrox?

3 Who holds the league appearances record for Rangers?

4 How many times have Rangers won the Scottish League?

5 Who beat Rangers in the European Cup Winners' Cup final in 1967?

6 Who scored a hat-trick for Rangers in the 1996 Scottish Cup final?

7 In which year did the nine-in-a-row series of league championships for Rangers begin?

8 In which year was the Rangers centenary?

9 Where was the 1972 European Cup Winners' Cup final played?

10 Which Rangers player was voted Footballer of the Year in 1975?

11 How many times have Rangers won the treble?

12 How many replays were needed before Rangers won the Scottish FA Cup against Hibernian in 1979?

13 Who joined Rangers as player/manager from Sampdoria in 1985?

14 Who did Rangers play in their first match under Graeme Souness?

15 Who is the club's all-time top scorer?

16 Which Englishman scored twice for the Gers in the 1996 League Cup final?

17 In which year did winger Davie Cooper win his first Scottish Cup winner's medal with Rangers?

18 Who is the chairman of Rangers?

19 Who top scored for Rangers during 1998–99?

20 Who was the first black player to play for the Gers?

Answers

Town & County (see Quiz 91)

1 Ipswich. **2** Mansfield. **3** Ross County. **4** Huddersfield. **5** Halifax. **6** Stockport. **7** Derby. **8** Swindon. **9** Northampton. **10** Stockport. **11** Shrewsbury. **12** Cheltenham. **13** Derby. **14** Luton. **15** Grimsby. **16** Swindon. **17** Macclesfield. **18** Cheltenham. **19** Grimsby. **20** Derby.

Quiz 90 **David Seaman**

LEVEL 3 

Answers – see page 608

1 In which county was David Seaman born?
2 Which club released him before he had played a first-team match?
3 With which club was he playing when he won England under–21 honours?
4 In which year did Seaman make his first full England appearance?
5 In which year did he make his second full England appearance?
6 Who did he replace as Arsenal goalkeeper?
7 The song by rock group Lush "And Seaman will be disappointed with that..." refers to which match?
8 How many clean sheets did Seaman keep during Arsenal's triumphant 1994 Cup Winners' Cup run?
9 Whose penalty did he save to put England in the semi-finals of Euro '96?
10 How many penalties did Seaman save in the 1995 Cup Winners Cup semi-final shootout against Sampdoria?
11 What change did David Seaman make to his appearance at the start of the 2000–2001 season?
12 Which of England's Euro 2000 games did Seaman miss?
13 How much did Arsenal pay QPR for him?
14 What injury kept Seaman out of the Arsenal team in the first 12 matches of the 1999–2000 season?
15 How many clean sheets did Seaman keep in the league in 1999–2000?
16 Which team-mate helped pull Seaman from a car crash in April 2000?
17 What is Seaman's short and enigmatic nickname?
18 Which Italian international's penalty did Seaman save to win the 1995 Cup Winners' Cup semi-final shootout against Sampdoria?
19 Which TV presenter was Seaman's best man at his wedding?
20 On which joint did David Seaman have major surgery in late 2001?

Answers

Who's the Slaphead? (see Quiz 92)

1 Steve Bould. **2** Alan Wright. **3** Zinadine Zidane. **4** Terry Mancini. **5** Ray Wilkins. **6** Lato. **7** Alan Gilzean. **8** Ray Graydon. **9** Mills and Armstrong. **10** Danny Mills. **11** Yordan Letchkov. **12** Mark Draper. **13** Ralph Coates. **14** Boris Mikhailov. **15** Archie Gemmill. **16** Carsten Janker. **17** Pierluigi Collina. **18** Terry Hennessey. **19** Frank Leboeuf. **20** Clive Walker.

Quiz 91 **Town & County**

Answers – see page 605

LEVEL 3

1 Which Town play in Suffolk?

2 Which Town are nicknamed The Stags?

3 Which County joined the Scottish League in 1994?

4 Which Town used to play at Leeds Road?

5 Which Town did Jim McCalliog manage in 1990 and 1991?

6 Which County play at Edgeley Park?

7 Which is the only County to have played in the Premier League?

8 Which Town won the Anglo-Italian Cup in 1970?

9 Which Town play in claret with white shirts?

10 For which County did Tony Dinning play?

11 Which Town play at Gay Meadow?

12 Which Town play in the county of Gloucester?

13 For which County did Mart Poom keep goal?

14 For which Town did Joe Payne hit 10 goals in one game in 1936?

15 Which Town only "sing when they're fishing"?

16 Which Town won the League Cup in 1969?

17 Which Town play at the Moss Rose Ground?

18 For which Town does striker Martin Devaney score goals?

19 Which Town play in Cleethorpes?

20 Which County did Burnley beat in the 2000 FA Cup?

Answers

Rangers (see Quiz 89)

1 1972. **2** Graeme Souness. **3** John Grieg. **4** 49 times. **5** Bayern Munich. **6** Gordon Durie. **7** 1988. **8** 1973. **9** Barcelona. **10** Sandy Jardine. **11** Five times. **12** Two. **13** Graeme Souness. **14** Hibs. **15** Ally McCoist. **16** Paul Gascoigne. **17** 1978. **18** David Murray. **19** Danny Wallace. **20** Mark Walters.

Quiz 92 **Who's the Slaphead?**

Answers – see page 606

LEVEL 3

1 Steve who balded gracefully in the Sunderland defence after doing the double in 1998?

2 The smallest and baldest full-back in the Premier League?

3 Z–Z (thinning on) Top?

4 "Henry" showed some cheek as a Gunner?

5 There's nothing butch about this domehead?

6 Poland's follically-challenged 1974 World Cup Golden Boot?

7 Dundee and Tottenham striker who used his shining pate to great effect?

8 Former Walsall manager – sacked in January 2002 – who thinned in his Villa days?

9 Middlesbrough's late 70s "lighthouse brothers"?

10 Danny is an England under 21 moonhead?

11 Bulgarian as a coot, he destroyed Germany's 1990 World Cup?

12 Southampton's 2000 signing is a former Leicester and Villa baldie?

13 Burnley and Tottenham star who copied Sir Bobby's hairstyle?

14 Reading's toupee-wearing Bulgarian keeper?

15 Derby midfielder who gave Scotland a goal to remember?

16 Bayern and Germany's shaven-headed striker?

17 Top Italian shinehead referee?

18 Birmingham, Forest, Derby and Wales 60s bald and solid defender?

19 Beefy former Chelsea World Cup winner?

20 Chelsea's flash 70s winger?

Answers

David Seaman (see Quiz 90)

1 Yorkshire. **2** Leeds United. **3** Peterborough United. **4** 1988. **5** 1991. **6** John Lukic. **7** 1991 FA Cup semi-final. 8 Six. **9** Nadal. **10** Three. **11** A ponytail. **12** Against Romania. **13** £1.3 million. **14** Calf. **15** Five. **16** Lee Dixon. **17** "H". **18** Attilo Lombardo. **19** Bob Wilson. **20** Shoulder.

Quiz 93 **Goals Galore 2**

Answers – see page 611

LEVEL 3

1 How many goals did Australia score in their four World Cup qualifying group games in 2001?

2 Who scored seven goals in the first seven games of the 2000–01 Premiership season?

3 Who top scored for champions Manchester United in the 1999–2000 season?

4 Who is Newcastle United's all-time top league scorer?

5 Who is regarded as the all-time top scorer in world football?

6 Who is the top scorer in a single World Cup match?

7 Who holds the record for most international goals in a career?

8 Who holds the record for most goals in FA Cup finals?

9 Who scored the only FA Cup final hat-trick at Wembley?

10 What is the record number of goals scored by one player in a Premier League season?

11 What is the record number of goals scored by one player in a League Cup final?

12 Who were joint top scorers in the First Division in 1984–85?

13 How many goals did England score v Yugoslavia in a European Championship qualifier in Belgrade in 1988?

14 What was the score in the 1990 FA Cup semi-final between Liverpool and Crystal Palace?

15 Which player top scored in the first Premier League season?

16 Who is Liverpool's all-time leading league goalscorer?

17 What was the score in the league game that marked John Aldridge's last appearance for Liverpool?

18 What league record was set in that match?

19 Who is Leeds United's all-time leading league goalscorer?

20 Who did Arsenal beat 7–0 in the 1993–94 European Cup Winners' Cup?

Answers

Losers (see Quiz 95)

1 Chelsea. **2** Sheffield Wednesday. **3** Arsenal. **4** West Ham. **5** 20. **6** Holland. **7** Sunderland in 1992. **8** Arsenal in the 1980 European Cup Winners' Cup. **9** Hamburg. **10** 7–0. **11** Seven games. **12** Arsenal. **13** QPR. **14** Hearts. **15** Manchester City. **16** Leeds United. **17** Ayr United. **18** England. **19** Germany. **20** Germany.

Quiz 94 **Hard Men**

Answers – see page 612

LEVEL 3

1 Who left George McCluskey needing nine stitches in a knee in 1986?

2 Who was banned five times between 1964 and 1967?

3 Who, in 1994, became the first player to accumlate 61 points since the disciplinary system began in 1972–73?

4 What is the nickname of Spanish hard man Andoni Goicoechea?

5 Which Spurs' hard man spat out two teeth during the 1981 FA Cup Final?

6 How many England caps did Tommy Smith win?

7 Who stamped on Gareth Southgate in the 1994 FA Cup semi-final?

8 Which Sunderland player received 14 bookings in 1998–99?

9 Who broke Southampton's Glen Cockerill's jaw in 1988?

10 Who was sent off for the 13th time, against Chelsea, in January 2000?

11 Which defender was booked for the 64th time in ten seasons in 1987?

12 Who was booked within five seconds of a league match in '91 and '92?

13 Which former West Ham hard man played for Canvey Island in their 2001–02 FA Cup run?

14 Which Scottish international was sent off 21 times in his career?

15 For how many matches was Andoni Goicoechea banned after breaking Maradona's ankle?

16 How many times had Dennis Wise been sent off by the end of the 2000–01 season?

17 Which hard man scored for Brighton against his old team in their 1983 FA Cup run?

18 Which country finished a World Cup Final with only nine men on the pitch?

19 Which Italian marked and kicked Maradona out of a 1982 World Cup tie?

20 Which hard man's tackle on French star Jacky Simon led to the FA demanding his omission from the England team?

Answers

True or False? 2 (see Quiz 96)

1 True. **2** True, at Bramall Lane, the Oval and in Birmingham. **3** False, it was after 3 seconds. **4** True. **5** False, it was Watford. **6** False, it was in 1996. **7** True. **8** True. **9** True. **10** False, it was Torquay. **11** True. **12** True. **13** False, it was Scarborough. **14** False, he scored their second goal of three. **15** False, it was 674. **16** True, they won 2–0. **17** True. **18** False, it was three. **19** False, Italy beat them in the final. **20** True.

Quiz 95 **Losers**

LEVEL 3 

Answers – see page 609

1. Who lost on penalties in the 1997 Charity Shield?
2. Who lost to Arsenal in both FA Cup and League Cup finals in 1993?
3. Who lost to AC Milan in the 1994 European Super Cup?
4. Who lost 4–2 and 7–1 to Manchester United in the 1999–2000 league season?
5. How many league teams have lost FA Cup ties to non-league Yeovil Town?
6. Who lost in the 1978 World Cup Final?
7. Who were the first FA Cup final losers to go up the Wembley steps first to collect their medals?
8. Who were the first team to lose a major European final on penalties?
9. Who did Nottingham Forest beat to retain the European Cup in 1980?
10. What was the score in Manchester United's worst league defeat?
11. What is Chelsea's longest sequence of league defeats?
12. Who finished second in the Premier League in 1999–2000?
13. Who did Spurs beat in a replay to win the FA Cup in 1982?
14. Who lost 5–1 in the 1996 Scottish Cup final?
15. Who lost 5–2 to Leeds in the FA Cup fourth round in 2000?
16. Who lost to Coventry in the 1987 FA Cup semi-final?
17. Who lost 7–0 to Rangers in the Tennent's Scottish Cup semi-final in 2000?
18. Who did Brazil beat in the final match of Le Tournoi in Paris in 1997?
19. Who lost to Denmark in the European Championship final in 1992?
20. Who did England beat, for the first time in 34 years, in Charleroi in Euro 2000?

Answers

Goals Galore 2 (see Quiz 93)

1 66. **2** Michael Owen. **3** Dwight Yorke. **4** Jackie Milburn. **5** Artur Friedenreich, Brazil (1329). **6** Archie Thompson, Australia, 15 v American Samoa in 2001. **7** Puskas, 83. **8** Ian Rush, 5. **9** Stan Mortensen, 1953. **10** 34. **11** Two. **12** Kerry Dixon and Gary Lineker. **13** They won 4–1. **14** 4–3 to Palace. **15** Teddy Sheringham. **16** Roger Hunt. **17** Liverpool 9 Crystal Palace 0. **18** Liverpool had eight scorers. **19** Peter Lorimer. **20** Standard Liege.

Quiz 96 **True or False? 2**

LEVEL 3

Answers – see page 610

1 Liverpool's Titi Camara was the first player from Guinea to play in the Premiership?

2 The first floodlit matches took place in 1878?

3 Chelsea's Vinnie Jones was booked after four seconds of a match against Sheffield United in 1992?

4 Celtic's Jimmy McGrory scored 410 goals in 408 matches before the war?

5 Bristol City won the Second Division championship in 1997–98?

6 Eric Cantona scored the winning goal in the FA Cup final in 1995?

7 Ali Fakih, a Lebanese goalkeeper, did not concede a goal for 1516 minutes?

8 Steve Bull scored 100 goals in two seasons for Wolves between 1987 and 1989?

9 Germany did not win a single game during the Euro 2000 finals?

10 Blackpool became the first team to win promotion on penalties, in 1991?

11 Chris Waddle was voted Player of the Season in 1993?

12 The first football pools coupons were issued in 1920?

13 Kidderminster Harriers became the first team automatically promoted to the football league in 1987?

14 Keith Houchen scored the winner for Coventry against Spurs in the 1987 FA Cup final?

15 The greatest number of clubs that have contested the FA Cup is 676?

16 Bournemouth knocked Manchester United out of the FA Cup in 1984?

17 Bobby Moore saved a penalty for West Ham in the 1972 League Cup semi-final against Stoke?

18 Ladislao Kubala played in internationals for four different countries just after the war?

19 Czechoslovakia won the World Cup in 1934?

20 The Jules Rimet trophy was stolen in Brazil and was never recovered?

Answers

Hard Men (see Quiz 94)

1 Graeme Souness. **2** Billy Bremner. **3** Terry Hurlock. **4** The Butcher of Bilbao. **5** Graham Roberts. **6** One. **7** Roy Keane. **8** Kevin Ball. **9** Paul Davis. **10** Steve Walsh. **11** Mark Dennis. **12** Vinnie Jones. **13** Julian Dicks. **14** Willie Johnston. **15** 21. **16** 11. **17** Jimmy Case. **18** Argentina (1990). **19** Claudio Gentile. **20** Nobby Stiles.

Quiz 97 **Sackings**

Answers – see page 615

LEVEL 3

1 Who was sacked as manager of Chelsea in September 2000?

2 Who was sacked in October 2000 as manager of Brazil?

3 Who was sacked by Newcastle in 1992 to make way for Kevin Keegan?

4 Whose contract as England manager was terminated in February 1999 following his controversial comments on disabled people?

5 Who was sacked as manager of Newcastle after just two matches of the 1998–99 season?

6 Who was sacked as manager of Port Vale in 1999 after 15 years in charge?

7 Which England manager was sacked in 1974 after 11 years in charge?

8 Who was sacked as manager of Manchester United for breaking the 'moral code"?

9 Who was dismissed as manager of Arsenal for illegal transfer payments?

10 Which legendary player was sacked by Spanish club Seville in 1993 for his disappointing performances?

11 Who was sacked by Everton in November 1994 after 305 days in charge?

12 Who was sacked as manager of Manchester United in November 1986?

13 Who was sacked by Spurs in May 1993 but managed to get himself reinstated by means of a court order?

14 Which World Cup winner was sacked as manager of Chelsea in April 1981?

15 Who was sacked as Wolves manager in 1995, after 18 months, for failing to bring Premiership football to Molineux?

16 Who was sacked as Nottingham Forest boss in January 1999?

17 By which two clubs was Ruud Gullit sacked as manager?

18 Who was sacked as Manchester City boss in 1980 after two spells with them?

19 Who was sacked as manager of Everton in 1990 only to return as assistant manager six days later?

20 Who was sacked as manager of Leeds United in 1997?

Answers

Wales (see Quiz 99)

1 Ian Rush. **2** Mark Hughes. **3** 1–0 to Argentina. **4** 1988. **5** Wales 4 England 1. **6** M Thomas, Walsh, L James and an o.g. **7** Gary Speed. **8** Scotland. **9** 1936–37. **10** John Hartson. **11** Paul Jones. **12** Wales lost 4–6. **13** Two, Barry Town and Cwmbran. **14** Italy, Denmark, Switzerland and Belarus. **15** Fourth. **16** Anfield, Liverpool. **17** Neville Southall. **18** John Toshack. **19** Newcastle United. **20** Northern Ireland.

Quiz 98 **Memorable Matches 2**

Answers – see page 616

1 Who did Leeds beat to win the Centenary FA Cup final in 1972?
2 What happened in the Division Two match at Maine Road between Manchester City and Huddersfield in November 1987?
3 By how many goals did Rangers beat Aberdeen to win the Tennent's Scottish Cup final in May 2000?
4 What was the score in the World Cup qualifier between Italy and England in Rome in October 1997?
5 In which year did Roger Osborne score the winning goal for Ipswich in the FA Cup final?
6 Liverpool played Celtic in which competition in 1997–98?
7 Which team scored nine goals in two local derbies against Fulham in 1983–84?
8 Which two teams drew 4–4 in the Division 1 play-off final at Wembley in 1998, before the match was decided on penalties?
9 Which was the first Wembley FA Cup final to go to a replay?
10 Who beat Rangers 1–0 in the 1994 Scottish Cup final?
11 What was the score in the first FA Cup final, in 1872?
12 What did the Republic of Ireland do to Northern Ireland in Belfast in 1994?
13 What was significant about the 1983 European Cup final?
14 Where was the 1983 FA Cup final replay played?
15 Which English team were knocked out of the UEFA Cup by Atletico Madrid in 1997–98?
16 Who won the 1982 World Cup match between England and France?
17 Who scored England's second goal against Scotland in Euro 96?
18 Which non-league team beat Coventry City in the FA Cup in 1989?
19 What happened at the UEFA cup match between Moscow Spartak and Haarlem in Moscow in 1992?
20 Who won the all-Merseyside FA Cup final of 1989?

Answers

Kevin Keegan (see Quiz 100)

1 Arthur Cox in 1984. **2** Southampton. **3** 49. **4** Scunthorpe. **5** John Toshack. **6** Newcastle United. **7** 321. **8** Hamburg. **9** Lawrie McMenemy. **10** Two years. **11** 63. **12** 1982. **13** 1992. **14** 1951. **15** QRR **16** Terry McDermott. **17** Fulham. **18** 'Mighty Mouse'. **19** 1999. **20** Four.

Quiz 99 **Wales**

Answers – see page 613

LEVEL 3

1 Who has scored most goals as a Welsh international?

2 Who took over from Bobby Gould as manager of Wales?

3 Wales played Argentina in Tokyo in 1992. What was the score?

4 In which year was Wales' only victory against Italy?

5 What was the score of the Wales v England match at Wrexham in 1980?

6 Who scored the Welsh goals that day?

7 Who scored Wales' winner against Moldova in Cardiff in September 1995?

8 Who were Wales' first international opponents?

9 When did Wales last win the Home International Championship outright?

10 Who scored Wales' winner against Scotland in May 1997?

11 Who kept goal for Wales against Jamaica in March 1998?

12 What was the score when Wales played Turkey in Istanbul in 1997?

13 How many Welsh clubs have contested the European Cup?

14 Who were in Wales' qualifying group for Euro 2000?

15 Where did Wales finish in the group?

16 Where did Wales play their home match against Denmark in that competition?

17 Who is Wales's most capped player?

18 Who acted as Wales's manager for one match in 1994?

19 Where does Welsh international Craig Bellamy play his club football?

20 Against whom did keeper Neville Southall make his debut for Wales in 1982?

Answers

Sackings (see Quiz 97)

1 Gianluca Vialli. **2** Wanderlay Luxemburgo. **3** Ossie Ardiles. **4** Glenn Hoddle. **5** Kenny Dalglish. **6** John Rudge. **7** Sir Alf Ramsey. **8** Tommy Docherty. **9** George Graham. **10** Maradona. **11** Mike Walker. **12** Ron Atkinson. **13** Terry Venables. **14** Geoff Hurst. **15** Graham Taylor. **16** Dave Bassett. **17** Chelsea and Newcastle. **18** Malcolm Allison. **19** Colin Harvey. **20** Howard Wilkinson.

Quiz 100 **Kevin Keegan**

LEVEL 3

Answers – see page 614

1. Who said of Wor Kev 'No other player in the world could have had such a dramatic effect on the club and its supporters"?
2. From which club did Newcastle sign Kevin Keegan in 1984?
3. How many goals did Keegan score during his playing days with the Magpies?
4. For which club did Keegan make his league debut?
5. Who was Keegan's main strike partner at Liverpool?
6. Who did Keegan and Liverpool beat in the 1974 FA Cup final?
7. How many appearances did Keegan notch up for the Reds?
8. Who did Keegan join when he left Liverpool in 1977?
9. Who was manager at Southampton when he returned to England in 1980?
10. How long did Keegan stay on the south coast?
11. How many England caps did he win?
12. In which year did Keegan win his OBE?
13. When did Keegan become manager of Newcastle?
14. In which year was Keegan born?
15. Against whom did Keegan make his playing debut for Newcastle?
16. Who was Keegan's assistant manager at Newcastle?
17. Where did Keegan go after his term as manager of Newcastle?
18. What was Keegan's nickname at Liverpool?
19. When did Keegan take over as England manager?
20. How many matches did England lose under Keegan's leadership?

Answers

Memorable Matches 2 (see Quiz 98)

1 Arsenal. **2** Manchester City won 10–1. **3** 4–0. **4** 0–0. **5** 1978. **6** UEFA Cup. **7** Chelsea. **8** Charlton and Sunderland. **9** Chelsea v Leeds, 1970. **10** Dundee United. **11** Wanderers 1 Royal Engineers 0. **12** Beat them 4–0. **13** First time for seven years without an English club. **14** Wembley. **15** Aston Villa. **16** England won 3–1. **17** Paul Gascoigne. **18** Sutton United. **19** 340 crushed to death on stairway. **20** Liverpool.

Quiz 101 **Midfielders**

LEVEL 3

Answers – see page 619

1 Who captained Charlton when they returned to the Premier League in 2000?

2 Who left Man City in 1989 for West Ham, then returned to City in 1998?

3 Which Barnsley midfielder was voted Division One Player of the Year in 1999–2000 and was then sold to Blackburn?

4 Which French midfield great of the 1980s is now manager of Fulham?

5 Which legendary hard man leads the midfield for both Manchester United and the Republic of Ireland?

6 Who made his Anfield debut for Liverpool v Sunderland in September 2000?

7 Which midfielder arrived at Highbury from Marseille during summer 2000?

8 Which former Manchester United and Rangers midfielder was born in Kirograd in the Ukraine?

9 Which former Arsenal midfielder went on to coach at Stamford Bridge?

10 Which midfielder had success with Aberdeen, Manchester United and Leeds before going into management with Coventry City?

11 Who scored the winner for Man City in the 1981 FA Cup semi-final v Ipswich?

12 Which former Burnley and Everton midfielder appeared in the FA Cup final in 1984, 1985 and 1986?

13 Which midfielder played for Peter Taylor at Dover, Gillingham, Leicester and Brighton?

14 Which midfielder scored for England in a September 2001 World Cup qualifieri?

15 Which midfielder became player-manager at Gillingham in 2000?

16 Which midfielder, born in Maidstone, played for Southampton, Norwich, Chelsea, Aston Villa and Middlesbrough during his career?

17 In 2000–01, whose midfield occasionally read: Powell, Burley, Johnson, Kinkladze?

18 Which Leeds and England midfielder missed a vital international penalty in 1998 and did not start a game in 2000?

19 For whom does young Michael Carrick patrol the midfield?

20 Who is the inspirational midfielder and skipper of Preston North End?

Answers

Injuries (see Quiz 103)

1 Robbie Keane. **2** Ruud van Nistelrooy. **3** Jimmy Greaves. **4** Stomach illness. **5** Terry Butcher. **6** Tony Adams. **7** Steve Foster. **8** Alessandro Nesta. **9** Alan Wright. **10** Ten (every season). **11** Thierry Henry. **12** Jamie Redknapp. **13** Paul Gerrard (Everton). **14** David Batty. **15** Hamstrings. **16** Screaming at team-mates. **17** Brooking and Keegan. **18** Charlie George. **19** Ankle. **20** Wlodzimierez Lubanski.

Quiz 102 **FA Cup**

Answers – see page 620

LEVEL 3

1 Chris Kelly became which non-league team's 'Lip" on their 1975 FA Cup run?

2 What do West Brom, West Ham, Southampton and Sunderland have in common?

3 Who were the 'lucky losers" in 2000?

4 What have the Wanderers, Blackburn, Newcastle and Tottenham (twice) achieved?

5 In 2000–01, 572 teams entered the FA Cup. how many ties were scheduled??

6 What do Mark Hughes, John Barnes and Roy Keane have in common?

7 Who were the last team to win the FA Cup with an all-English side?

8 Which team did Arsenal beat 2–1 twice in the 1999 FA Cup?

9 Who since 1900 has won the most FA Cup winner's medals?

10 Who since 1900 has been the winning FA Cup captain on three occasions?

11 What FA Cup fact ties Tom Finney, Johnny Haynes and George Best?

12 Who were the last team to win the FA Cup without an international player?

13 Who knocked champions Arsenal out of the FA Cup in 1992?

14 What was the last year that both semi-finals were local derbies?

15 Who won the first FA Cup tie to be decided on a penalty shoot-out?

16 What 'double" did West Bromwich Albion win in 1931?

17 In the 70s who became the first substitute to score in an FA Cup final?

18 In which way did Manchester United win the FA Cup against the odds in 1990?

19 Which Hertfordshire team's cup run ended in an acrimonious match against Newcastle in 1998?

20 Manchester City, Leicester, Brighton and Middlesbrough all were what?

Answers

Last-gasp Goals (see Quiz 104)

1 Spain. **2** Gary Stevens. **3** David Hopkin. **4** Gillingham. **5** Dani. **6** Dwight Yorke. **7** Poland. **8** Stuart Pearce. **9** Paul Gascoigne. **10** 117th. **11** Roberto Baggio. **12** Andy Linighan. **13** Motherwell. **14** Julius Aghahowa of Nigeria. **15** Luis Hernandez. **16** Alan Smith. **17** France. **18** Paul Scholes **19** Republic of Ireland. **20** Martin Keown.

Quiz 103 **Injuries**

Answers – see page 617

LEVEL 3

1 Which Republic of Ireland striker ruptured a knee cartilage in 1998 by stretching to pick up his TV remote control?

2 Whose knee gave out a few days after failing a medical in 2000?

3 Which injured player did Geoff Hurst replace in England's 1966 team?

4 What kept Gordon Banks out of England's 1970 tie with West Germany?

5 Which player had ten facial stitches during half-time of England's 1990 World Cup qualifier in Sweden?

6 Who missed the rest of the tournament after an injury in England's first Euro 2000 game?

7 Which captain missed the 1983 Wembley Cup Final due to injury?

8 Which international broke Gazza's leg in a training session in 1994?

9 Which Premier League full-back needed treatment for a knee strain caused by stretching to reach the accelerator in his new Ferrari?

10 How may times since the Premier League began has David Seaman missed at least three League matches for Arsenal?

11 Which Arsenal player needed treatment after hitting himself in the face with the corner flag in a goal celebration?

12 Which substitute was injured in England's Euro '96 tie with Scotland?

13 Which goalkeeper was injured in the incident which led to Paolo di Canio handling the ball so he could get treatment?

14 Which star's injury was put back when he was run over by a tricycle?

15 Which injury kept Michael Owen out of much of the 1999–2000 season?

16 How did Man United keeper Alex Stepney break his jaw in 1975?

17 Which two injured players went on in a double substitution in England's last 1982 World Cup match?

18 Which Arsenal legend never fully recovered from cutting off a big toe with a lawnmower?

19 Injuries to what part of his body ended Marco Van Basten's career?

20 Which Polish hero missed the 1974 World Cup because of injury?

Answers

Midfielders (see Quiz 101)

1 Mark Kinsella. **2** Ian Bishop. **3** Craig Hignett. **4** Jean Tigana. **5** Roy Keane. **6** Bernard Diomede. **7** Robert Pires. **8** Andrei Kanchelskis. **9** Graham Rix. **10** Gordon Strachan. **11** Paul Power. **12** Trevor Steven. **13** Junior Lewis. **14** Steven Gerrard. **15** Andy Hessenthaler. **16** Andy Townsend. **17** Derby County's. **18** David Batty. **19** West Ham. **20** Sean Gregan.

Quiz 104 **Last-gasp Goals**

Answers – see page 618

LEVEL 3

1 Who scored two goals in the last minute to win a crucial Euro 2000 tie?
2 Who scored Brighton's 87th-minute equaliser in the 1984 FA Cup final?
3 Whose 1997 last-minute goal won the play-offs for Crystal Palace?
4 Headers from Steve Butler and Andy Thomson in the last six minutes of extra time won the 2000 play-offs for which side?
5 Whose goal seven minutes from time against Chelsea rescued his team in the 2000 Champions League quarter-final?
6 Who scored an 81st-minute goal to salvage a point in Manchetser United's World Club championship tie with Necaxa in 2000?
7 Against whom did Ian Wright score his first England goal, in the 84th minute?
8 Whose last-minute free-kick goal was disallowed in England's 1990 World Cup match with Holland?
9 Whose first England goal came in the 88th minute against Albania in '89?
10 In which minute did Zidane score to win the Euro 2000 tie with Portugal?
11 Who hit Italy's last-gasp equaliser in the '94 World Cup tie with Nigeria?
12 Who headed Arsenal's last-minute goal in the 1993 FA Cup final?
13 Who won the Scottish FA Cup in 1991 with a last-minute goal by Kirk?
14 Who scored three goals in as many games as a very late substitute in the 2000 African Cup of Nations?
15 Who scored Mexico's stoppage-time goal against Holland in World Cup '98?
16 Who passed to Michael Thomas for his 1989 title-winning last-gasp goal?
17 Bellone scored a last-minute winner for which Euro '84 team?
18 Whose last-gasp goal against Inter Milan took Manchester United through to the Champions League semi-finals in 1999?
19 A late goal by Stavrevski put paid to whose Euro 2000 group qualification?
20 Who scored Arsenal's last-gasp winner in their 2000 Champions League match against Shakhtar Donetsk?

Answers

FA Cup (see Quiz 102)

1 Leatherhead. **2** Won the Cup when in Division Two. **3** Darlington. **4** Won the Cup in successive years. **5** 571 (every team, except Liverpool, lost one tie). **6** They are the last three of nine men to have played in five finals. **7** West Ham. **8** Sheffield Utd. **9** Mark Hughes, four. **10** Bryan Robson. **11** They never won the Cup. **12** Sunderland. **13** Wrexham. **14** 1993. **15** Aston Villa. **16** Won the Cup and promotion. **17** Eddie Kelly. **18** Every game was away. **19** Stevenage Borough. **20** Relegated Cup finalists.

How to Set Up Your Own Pub Quiz

It isn't easy, get that right from the start. This isn't going to be easy. Think instead of words like; "difficult", "taxing" and "infuriating". A bit like a Wednesday night cup-tie against Yeovil. Consider yourself with damp palms and a dry throat and then, when you have concentrated on that, put it out of your mind and think of the recognition you will receive at your local. Imagine all the regulars lifting you high upon their shoulders, dancing and weaving their way around the pub. Just like they did in '66. It won't help but it's good to dream every once in a while.

What you will need:

- A good selection of biros (never be tempted to give your own pen up, not even to family members)
- A copy of *The Biggest Football Pub Quiz Book Ever!*
- A set of answer sheets photocopied from the back of the book
- A good speaking voice and possibly a microphone and an amp
- A pub or bar with enough tables and chairs for all the participants
- Something to keep your throat lubricated
- At least one replacement throat-lubricator close by
- At least one assistant to supply throat-lubricators as well as collecting and checking answer sheets
- A scoreboard so everyone can see how they're doing

Answer Sheet

Player/Team ....

Round ....

1	**11**
2	**12**
3	**13**
4	**14**
5	**15**
6	**16**
7	**17**
8	**18**
9	**19**
10	**20**

Answer Sheet

Player/Team ....

Round ....

1 ____________________	**11** ____________________
2 ____________________	**12** ____________________
3 ____________________	**13** ____________________
4 ____________________	**14** ____________________
5 ____________________	**15** ____________________
6 ____________________	**16** ____________________
7 ____________________	**17** ____________________
8 ____________________	**18** ____________________
9 ____________________	**19** ____________________
10 ____________________	**20** ____________________

ALSO AVAILABLE

THE BEST PUB QUIZ BOOK EVER!

Containing over 10,000 questions and answers, this book is divided into over 300 quizzes on all of your favourite and maybe not so favourite subjects. A must for every Pub Quiz fanatic.

ISBN 1 85868 182 0
£6.99
Available from all good bookshops

THE BEST POP PUB QUIZ BOOK EVER!

Containing 6,000 questions and answers, this book is divided into over 100 individual quizzes on all of your favourite pop music subjects. Essential reading for Pub Quiz fanatics.

ISBN 1 85868 258 4
£6.99
Available from all good bookshops